Search through the complete book in PDF!

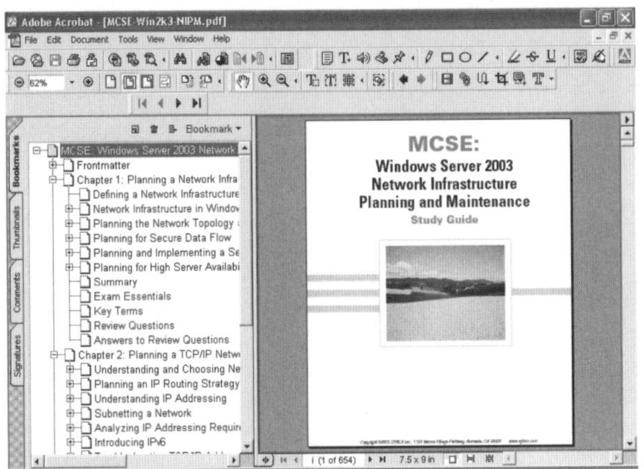

- Access the entire *MCSE: Windows Server 2003 Network Infrastructure Planning and Maintenance Study Guide*, complete with figures and tables, in electronic format.
- Search the *MCSE: Windows Server 2003 Network Infrastructure Planning and Maintenance Study Guide* chapters to find information on any topic in seconds.
- Look up any Key Term, along with other general terms, in the Glossary.

Use the Electronic Flashcards for PCs, Pocket PCs, or Palm devices to jog your memory and prep last-minute for the exam!

- Reinforce your understanding of key concepts with these hardcore flashcard-style questions.
- Download the Flashcards to your Palm device, and go on the road. Now you can study anywhere, any time.

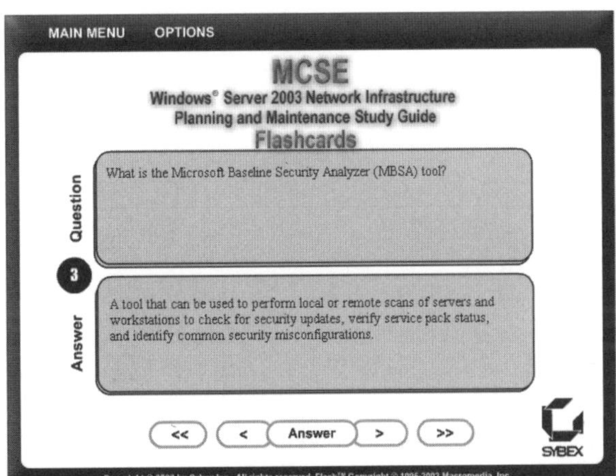

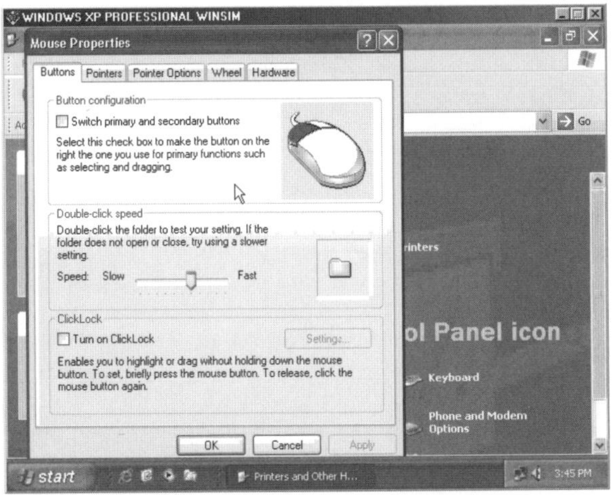

Prepare for Microsoft's tough simulation questions with the WinSim program!

- Use the simulators to guide you through real-world tasks step-by-step, or watch the movies to see the "invisible hand" perform the tasks for you.

MCSE: Windows Server 2003 Network Infrastructure Planning and Maintenance Study Guide

Exam 70-293

OBJECTIVE	CHAPTER
Planning and Implementing Server Roles and Server Security	
Configure security for servers that are assigned specific roles.	7
Plan a secure baseline installation.	7
Plan a strategy to enforce system default security settings on new systems.	
Identify client operating system default security settings.	
Identify all server operating system default security settings.	
Plan security for servers that are assigned specific roles. Roles might include domain controllers, Web servers, database servers, and mail servers.	7
Deploy the security configuration for servers that are assigned specific roles.	
Create custom security templates based on server roles.	
Evaluate and select the operating system to install on computers in an enterprise.	7
Identify the minimum configuration to satisfy security requirements.	
Planning, Implementing, and Maintaining a Network Infrastructure	
Plan a TCP/IP network infrastructure strategy.	2
Analyze IP addressing requirements.	
Plan an IP routing solution.	
Create an IP subnet scheme.	
Plan and modify a network topology.	2, 3
Plan the physical placement of network resources.	
Identify network protocols to be used.	
Plan an Internet connectivity strategy.	3
Plan network traffic monitoring. Tools might include Network Monitor and System Monitor.	10
Troubleshoot connectivity to the Internet.	3
Diagnose and resolve issues related to Network Address Translation (NAT).	
Diagnose and resolve issues related to name resolution cache information.	
Diagnose and resolve issues related to client configuration.	
Troubleshoot TCP/IP addressing.	2
Diagnose and resolve issues related to client computer configuration.	
Diagnose and resolve issues related to DHCP server address assignment.	
Plan a host name resolution strategy.	4
Plan a DNS namespace design.	
Plan zone replication requirements.	
Plan a forwarding configuration.	
Plan for DNS security.	
Examine the interoperability of DNS with third-party DNS solutions.	
Plan a NetBIOS name resolution strategy.	5
Plan a WINS replication strategy.	
Plan NetBIOS name resolution by using the Lmhosts file.	
Troubleshoot host name resolution.	5
Diagnose and resolve issues related to DNS services.	
Diagnose and resolve issues related to client computer configuration.	
Planning, Implementing, and Maintaining Routing and Remote Access	
Plan a routing strategy.	3
Identify routing protocols to use in a specified environment.	
Plan routing for IP multicast traffic.	3

OBJECTIVE	CHAPTER
Planning, Implementing, and Maintaining Routing and Remote Access *(continued)*	

Plan security for remote access users.
  Plan remote access policies.
  Analyze protocol security requirements.
  Plan authentication methods for remote access clients.
	6

Implement secure access between private networks. Create and implement an IPSec policy.	6
Troubleshoot TCP/IP routing. Tools might include the route, tracert, ping, pathping, and netsh commands and Network Monitor.	3
Planning, Implementing, and Maintaining Server Availability	

Plan services for high availability.
  Plan a high availability solution that uses clustering services.
  Plan a high availability solution that uses Network Load Balancing.
	9

Identify system bottlenecks, including memory, processor, disk, and network related bottlenecks. Identify system bottlenecks by using System Monitor.	10
Implement a cluster server.	9
Monitor Network Load Balancing. Tools might include the Network Load Balancing Monitor Microsoft Management Console (MMC) snap-in and the WLBS cluster control utility.	9
Monitor servers that provide network services. Tools include System Monitor, Event Viewer, and service logs.	10

Plan a backup and recovery strategy.
  Identify appropriate backup types. Methods include full, incremental, and differential.
  Plan a backup strategy that uses volume shadow copy.
  Plan system recovery that uses Automated System Recovery (ASR).
	10

Recover from cluster node failure.	9
Planning and Maintaining Network Security	

Configure network protocol security.
  Configure protocol security in a heterogeneous client computer environment.
  Configure protocol security by using IPSec policies.
	6

Configure security for data transmission. Configure IPSec policy settings.	6

Plan for network protocol security.
  Specify the required ports and protocols for specified services.
  Plan an IPSec policy for secure network communications.
	6

Plan secure network administration methods.
  Create a plan to offer Remote Assistance to client computers.
  Plan for remote administration by using Terminal Services.
	10

Plan security for wireless networks.	8

Plan security for data transmission.
  Secure data transmission between client computers to meet security requirements.
  Secure data transmission by using IPSec.
	6

Troubleshoot security for data transmission. Tools might include the IP Security Monitor MMC snap-in and the Resultant Set of Policy (RSoP) MMC snap-in.	6
Planning, Implementing, and Maintaining Security Infrastructure	
Configure Active Directory directory service for certificate publication.	8

Plan a public key infrastructure (PKI) that uses Certificate Services.
  Identify the appropriate type of certificate authority to support certificate issuance requirements.
  Plan the enrollment and distribution of certificates.
  Plan for the use of smart cards for authentication.
	8

Plan a framework for planning and implementing security.
  Plan for security monitoring.
  Plan a change and configuration management framework for security.
	7

Plan a security update infrastructure. Tools might include Microsoft Baseline Security Analyzer and Microsoft Software Update Services.	7

Exam objectives are subject to change at any time without prior notice and at Microsoft's sole discretion. Please visit Microsoft's Web site (`www.microsoft.com/traincert`) for the most current listing of exam objectives.

MCSE:
Windows® Server 2003 Network Infrastructure Planning and Maintenance
Study Guide

Suzan Sage London

with James Chellis

San Francisco • London

Associate Publisher: Neil Edde
Acquisitions Editor: Jeff Kellum
Developmental Editor: Jeff Kellum
Production Editor: Liz Burke
Technical Editors: Donald Fuller, James Kelly
Copyeditor: Kathy Grider-Carlyle
Compositor: International Composition Corporation
Graphic Illustrator: International Composition Corporation
CD Coordinator: Dan Mummert
CD Technician: Kevin Ly
Proofreaders: Nancy Riddiough, Emily Hsuan, Laurie O'Connell
Indexer: Ted Laux
Book Designer: Bill Gibson
Cover Designer: Archer Design
Cover Photographer: Colin Peterson, PhotoDisc

Library of Congress Card Number: 2003106719

ISBN: 0-7821-4262-1

Manufactured in the United States of America

10 9 8 7 6 5 4 3 2 1

To Our Valued Readers:

Thank you for looking to Sybex for your Microsoft Windows 2003 certification exam prep needs. We at Sybex are proud of the reputation we've established for providing certification candidates with the practical knowledge and skills needed to succeed in the highly competitive IT marketplace. Sybex is proud to have helped thousands of Microsoft certification candidates prepare for their exams over the years, and we are excited about the opportunity to continue to provide computer and networking professionals with the skills they'll need to succeed in the highly competitive IT industry.

With its release of Windows Server 2003, and the revised MCSA and MCSE tracks, Microsoft has raised the bar for IT certifications yet again. The new programs better reflect the skill set demanded of IT administrators in today's marketplace and offers candidates a clearer structure for acquiring the skills necessary to advance their careers.

The authors and editors have worked hard to ensure that the Study Guide you hold in your hand is comprehensive, in-depth, and pedagogically sound. We're confident that this book will exceed the demanding standards of the certification marketplace and help you, the Microsoft certification candidate, succeed in your endeavors.

As always, your feedback is important to us. Please send comments, questions, or suggestions to support@sybex.com. At Sybex we're continually striving to meet the needs of individuals preparing for IT certification exams.

Good luck in pursuit of your Microsoft certification!

Neil Edde
Associate Publisher—Certification
Sybex, Inc.

Software License Agreement: Terms and Conditions

The media and/or any online materials accompanying this book that are available now or in the future contain programs and/or text files (the "Software") to be used in connection with the book. SYBEX hereby grants to you a license to use the Software, subject to the terms that follow. Your purchase, acceptance, or use of the Software will constitute your acceptance of such terms.

The Software compilation is the property of SYBEX unless otherwise indicated and is protected by copyright to SYBEX or other copyright owner(s) as indicated in the media files (the "Owner(s)"). You are hereby granted a single-user license to use the Software for your personal, noncommercial use only. You may not reproduce, sell, distribute, publish, circulate, or commercially exploit the Software, or any portion thereof, without the written consent of SYBEX and the specific copyright owner(s) of any component software included on this media.

In the event that the Software or components include specific license requirements or end-user agreements, statements of condition, disclaimers, limitations or warranties ("End-User License"), those End-User Licenses supersede the terms and conditions herein as to that particular Software component. Your purchase, acceptance, or use of the Software will constitute your acceptance of such End-User Licenses.

By purchase, use or acceptance of the Software you further agree to comply with all export laws and regulations of the United States as such laws and regulations may exist from time to time.

Reusable Code in This Book

The author(s) created reusable code in this publication expressly for reuse by readers. Sybex grants readers limited permission to reuse the code found in this publication, its accompanying CD-ROM or available for download from our website so long as the author(s) are attributed in any application containing the reusable code and the code itself is never distributed, posted online by electronic transmission, sold, or commercially exploited as a stand-alone product.

Software Support

Components of the supplemental Software and any offers associated with them may be supported by the specific Owner(s) of that material, but they are not supported by SYBEX. Information regarding any available support may be obtained from the Owner(s) using the information provided in the appropriate read.me files or listed elsewhere on the media.

Should the manufacturer(s) or other Owner(s) cease to offer support or decline to honor any offer, SYBEX bears no responsibility. This notice concerning support for the Software is provided for your information only. SYBEX is not the agent or principal of the Owner(s), and SYBEX is in no way responsible for providing any support for the Software, nor is it liable or responsible for any support provided, or not provided, by the Owner(s).

Warranty

SYBEX warrants the enclosed media to be free of physical defects for a period of ninety (90) days after purchase. The Software is not available from SYBEX in any other form or media than that enclosed herein or posted to www.sybex.com. If you discover a defect in the media during this warranty period, you may obtain a replacement of identical format at no charge by sending the defective media, postage prepaid, with proof of purchase to:

SYBEX Inc.
Product Support Department
1151 Marina Village Parkway
Alameda, CA 94501
Web: `http://www.sybex.com`

After the 90-day period, you can obtain replacement media of identical format by sending us the defective disk, proof of purchase, and a check or money order for $10, payable to SYBEX.

Disclaimer

SYBEX makes no warranty or representation, either expressed or implied, with respect to the Software or its contents, quality, performance, merchantability, or fitness for a particular purpose. In no event will SYBEX, its distributors, or dealers be liable to you or any other party for direct, indirect, special, incidental, consequential, or other damages arising out of the use of or inability to use the Software or its contents even if advised of the possibility of such damage. In the event that the Software includes an online update feature, SYBEX further disclaims any obligation to provide this feature for any specific duration other than the initial posting.

The exclusion of implied warranties is not permitted by some states. Therefore, the above exclusion may not apply to you. This warranty provides you with specific legal rights; there may be other rights that you may have that vary from state to state. The pricing of the book with the Software by SYBEX reflects the allocation of risk and limitations on liability contained in this agreement of Terms and Conditions.

Shareware Distribution

This Software may contain various programs that are distributed as shareware. Copyright laws apply to both shareware and ordinary commercial software, and the copyright Owner(s) retains all rights. If you try a shareware program and continue using it, you are expected to register it. Individual programs differ on details of trial periods, registration, and payment. Please observe the requirements stated in appropriate files.

Copy Protection

The Software in whole or in part may or may not be copy-protected or encrypted. However, in all cases, reselling or redistributing these files without authorization is expressly forbidden except as specifically provided for by the Owner(s) therein.

To the Orchid, for believing, and to Rafael, for healing.

Acknowledgments

A book of this scope is the result of not just one, but many pairs of unseen hands. Special thanks are due to the following individuals whose invisible touch has helped to shape this book into the final form, which you now hold in your hands.

To James Chellis, thank you for your vision and guidance. I am honored to count you as a friend and mentor.

To Jeff Kellum, thank you for guiding and shaping the book since the earliest stages. Your attention to style and content helped to ensure that our book added significant value to the series. And thank you for making my initial project with Sybex an overwhelmingly pleasant experience!

To Liz Burke, thank you for keeping the workflow flowing so that we could meet our publication date. You orchestrated an array of specialists and a bevy of deadlines with the finesse of a maestro.

To Donald Fuller, thank you for contributing your expertise. Your natural curiosity and quest for technical perfection helped us to anticipate and answer the reader's questions.

To Kathy Grider-Carlyle, thank you for your sharp eye for detail and for being grammatically correct.

To the rest of the production and editorial team, thank you for spotting and correcting my flaws and for your assistance in bringing the electronic pages to life.

Contents at a Glance

Introduction *xvii*

Assessment Test *xxxiii*

Chapter 1	Planning a Network Infrastructure: A Technology Primer	1
Chapter 2	Planning a TCP/IP Network Infrastructure	25
Chapter 3	Planning a Network Connectivity Strategy	89
Chapter 4	Planning a DNS Strategy	175
Chapter 5	Planning a WINS Strategy	237
Chapter 6	Planning Secure Network Access	299
Chapter 7	Planning Server-Level Security	385
Chapter 8	Planning Certificate Services	461
Chapter 9	Planning High Availability Services	531
Chapter 10	Planning Network Monitoring, Remote Administration, and Recovery	575

Glossary 659

Index *693*

Contents

Introduction *xvii*

Assessment Test *xxxiii*

Chapter 1 Planning a Network Infrastructure: A Technology Primer 1

Defining a Network Infrastructure 2
Network Infrastructure in Windows Server 2003 3
- Network Configuration and Connectivity Improvements 4
- Data Security Improvements 4
- Security Infrastructure Improvements 6
- High Availability Improvements 6

Planning the Network Topology and Name Resolution Strategies 7
- Planning TCP/IP and the Network Topology Strategy 7
- Planning a Routing Strategy 9
- Planning an Internet Connectivity Strategy 9
- Planning a Name Resolution Strategy 9

Planning for Secure Data Flow 10
- Planning a Remote Access Strategy 11
- Planning Protocol Security 12

Planning and Implementing a Security Infrastructure 13
- Planning Policy-Based Security for Server Roles 14
- Planning a Security Update Infrastructure 14
- Enhancing Authentication through Certificate Services 15

Planning for High Server Availability 15
- Planning Clustering and Network Load Balancing 16
- Planning Secure Methods for Remote Administration 16
- Monitoring Network Performance 17
- Planning a Disaster Recovery Strategy 17

Summary 18
Exam Essentials 19
Key Terms 19
Review Questions 20
Answers to Review Questions 23

Chapter 2 Planning a TCP/IP Network Infrastructure 25

Understanding and Choosing Network Protocols 27
- How Network Protocols Work 28
- Network Packets 28
- Protocols and Binding 29

Connectionless versus Connection-Oriented Protocols 29
Network Protocols and Windows Server 2003 30
Planning an IP Routing Strategy 32
Hardware versus Software Routing 32
Static versus Dynamic Routing 33
Understanding IP Addressing 35
The Hierarchical IP Addressing Scheme 36
Network Address Classes 37
Subnetting a Network 38
Subnetting Concepts 39
Subnetting Examples 48
Analyzing IP Addressing Requirements 55
Choosing an Address Assignment Model 56
Choosing a System for the IP Subnet Structure 59
Choosing Public or Private Addresses 60
Planning for Automatic IP Configuration 62
Introducing IPv6 63
Benefits of IPv6 64
The IPv6 Address Space 65
Automatic Configuration in IPv6 67
Troubleshooting TCP/IP Addressing 68
Identifying the TCP/IP Configuration 69
Testing IP Communications 71
Troubleshooting DHCP 76
Summary 77
Exam Essentials 78
Key Terms 79
Review Questions 81
Answers to Review Questions 86

Chapter 3 Planning a Network Connectivity Strategy 89

Understanding IP Routing 91
How Routing Works 91
Types of Routing 94
Routing in Windows Server 2003 102
Managing IP Routing 103
Creating and Managing Interfaces 103
Setting IP Routing Properties 120
Managing Routing Protocols 122
Defining Static Routes 129
Filtering TCP/IP Packets 132
Creating Packet Filters 133
Creating VPN Packet Filters 135
Troubleshooting IP Routing 137

Understanding Network Connectivity 141
Understanding Private Addressing 142
NAT in Windows Server 2003 142
The Fate of the Outbound Packet 143
The Fate of the Inbound Packet 144
NAT Editors 145
ICS versus NAT 145
Installing ICS 145
Planning NAT 148
Installing NAT 148
Adding and Removing NAT Interfaces 151
Configuring NAT Properties 157
Summary 161
Exam Essentials 162
Key Terms 163
Review Questions 165
Answers to Review Questions 171

Chapter 4 Planning a DNS Strategy 175

Understanding DNS 176
What DNS Does 177
DNS and Windows Server 2003 179
DNS Terminology 180
How DNS Works 181
Planning a DNS Namespace 192
Understanding Domain Names 193
DNS Namespace Options 194
Planning DNS Zones 196
Selecting the Appropriate Zone Type 196
Selecting the Zone Data Location 197
Securing Zones 199
Integrating DNS and WINS 202
Planning DNS Zone Replication and Delegation 205
Creating Secondary Zones 205
Zone Transfers and Replication 205
Securing Zone Transfers 207
Delegating Zones 208
Determining DNS Caching and Forwarding 209
Caching-Only Servers 209
Stub Zones 210
Conditional Forwarders 211
Forward-Only Servers 212
Planning DNS Server Resources 212
Planning General DNS Server Requirements 213

Planning for Server Capacity 213
Securing DNS 214
Troubleshooting Host Name Resolution 216
Monitoring DNS 217
Troubleshooting DNS 218
Summary 224
Exam Essentials 224
Key Terms 225
Review Questions 227
Answers to Review Questions 234

Chapter 5 Planning a WINS Strategy 237

Understanding NetBIOS Name Resolution 238
How Name Resolution Works 239
WINS in Windows Server 2003 240
The WINS Process 241
The WINS Database 243
Supporting Non-WINS Clients 243
Using LMHOSTS as an Alternative to WINS 246
Introducing WINS Replication 249
Designing a WINS Strategy 251
Determining How Many WINS Servers to Install 252
Planning for Availability and Fault Tolerance 253
Securing the WINS Infrastructure 253
Monitoring WINS Client Traffic 254
Planning Replication Partnerships 255
Comparing WINS Deployment Scenarios 261
Implementing WINS 264
Using the WINS Snap-In 265
Controlling WINS Replication 270
Monitoring WINS 278
Using WINS Statistics 278
Viewing WINS Records 279
Compacting the WINS Database 281
Deleting and Tombstoning WINS Records 281
Configuring Inter-Forest WINS Replication 282
Troubleshooting WINS 283
General Considerations 283
Using the *Nbtstat* Command 284
Summary 286
Exam Essentials 286
Key Terms 287
Review Questions 289
Answers to Review Questions 296

Chapter 6 Planning Secure Network Access 299

Evaluating Remote Access Security 300
- Remote Access Services 301
- Remote Access Security 305

Planning Remote Access Policies 313
- Modifying the Default Remote Access Policies 313
- Creating a Remote Access Policy 320

Evaluating IP Security 324
- IPSec Fundamentals 326
- IPSec in Practice 338
- Planning an IPSec Deployment 339

Implementing IPSec 341
- Using the IP Security Policy Management Console 341
- Managing Policies 344
- Configuring IPSec Policies 351
- Configuring IPSec for Tunnel Mode 362

Troubleshooting Security for Data Transmission 368
- Verifying Effective Results of IPSec Policies with Resultant Set of Policy (RSoP) 370
- Monitoring IPSec Status with the IP Security Monitor 371
- Viewing IPSec-Related Events in the Event Log 372
- Best Practices for Troubleshooting IPSec 374

Summary 375

Exam Essentials 376

Key Terms 377

Review Questions 378

Answers to Review Questions 383

Chapter 7 Planning Server-Level Security 385

Introducing Server Roles 386
- Using the Configure Your Server Wizard 391
- Using the Manage Your Server Tool 393

Evaluating the Windows Server 2003 Editions 395

Managing Server Configurations with Security Policy 401
- Understanding Group Policy and Active Directory 402
- Configuring Security Settings Options 414
- Configuring System Options 429

Analyzing Security Configurations with the Security Configuration and Analysis Tool 433
- Specifying a Security Database 434
- Importing a Security Template 434
- Performing a Security Analysis 437
- Reviewing the Security Analysis and Resolving Discrepancies 437

Deploying Security Policies 441

Planning a Security Update Infrastructure 443
Using Microsoft Software Update Services 444
Using Microsoft Baseline Security Analyzer 447
Summary 449
Exam Essentials 450
Key Terms 451
Review Questions 452
Answers to Review Questions 458

Chapter 8 Planning Certificate Services 461

Understanding the Public Key Infrastructure 463
Key PKI Concepts 464
Elements of a PKI 467
PKI Terminology 473
Planning and Managing the Certificate Server 478
Installing Microsoft Certificate Server 478
Controlling the CA Service 484
Configuring the CA 488
Configuring Revocation and Trust 497
Managing Certificates 505
Introducing the Certificates Snap-In 505
Viewing and Changing Certificate Properties 506
Requesting New Certificates 510
Rekeying an Existing Certificate 514
Renewing a Certificate 514
Importing, Exporting, and Locating Certificates 515
Summary 519
Exam Essentials 520
Key Terms 522
Review Questions 523
Answers to Review Questions 528

Chapter 9 Planning High Availability Services 531

Evaluating Availability and Scalability Solutions 532
Identifying Threats to High Availability 534
Evaluating Scalability Methods 535
Evaluating Clustering Technologies 535
Planning Server Clusters 536
Understanding the Terminology 537
Analyzing Business and Application Requirements 538
Evaluating Application Deployment Considerations 539
Determining the Cluster Model 547
Planning Multisite Clusters 550
Networking the Cluster 552

Planning Network Load Balancing 554
Monitoring NLB 556
Administering NLB Remotely 560
Recovering from Cluster Node Failure 560
Backing Up Cluster Data 560
Recovering from Cluster Failure 561
Summary 563
Exam Essentials 564
Key Terms 565
Review Questions 566
Answers to Review Questions 573

Chapter 10 Planning Network Monitoring, Remote Administration, and Recovery 575

Monitoring Network Traffic 577
Installing the Network Monitor Driver and Application 578
Using Network Monitor 581
Monitoring and Optimizing System Performance 589
Understanding System Monitor 590
Monitoring Server Performance with System Monitor 595
Using Additional Tools to Monitor Performance 612
Planning Secure Remote Administration Methods 620
Planning to Remotely Administer Computers with Remote Desktop for Administration 621
Planning to Offer Remote Assistance to Client Computers 628
Planning a Backup and Recovery Strategy 634
Using Windows Backup 634
Using Volume Shadow Copy 645
Using Automated System Recovery 647
Summary 650
Exam Essentials 650
Key Terms 651
Review Questions 652
Answers to Review Questions 657

Glossary 659

Index 693

Table of Exercises

Exercise	**3.1**	Creating a Demand-Dial Interface	108
Exercise	**3.2**	Installing the RIP and OSPF Protocols	123
Exercise	**3.3**	Adding and Removing Static Routes	131
Exercise	**3.4**	Creating PPTP Packet Filters	135
Exercise	**3.5**	Monitoring Routing Status	138
Exercise	**3.6**	Installing NAT on an RRAS Server	149
Exercise	**4.1**	Simple DNS Testing	218
Exercise	**4.2**	Using the Nslookup Command	222
Exercise	**5.1**	Installing the WINS Service	265
Exercise	**5.2**	Configuring WINS Replication	274
Exercise	**5.3**	Manually Compacting the WINS Database with the Jetpack Utility	281
Exercise	**5.4**	Using the *Nbtstat* Command	285
Exercise	**6.1**	Configuring Security Options in the RRAS Server's Properties	309
Exercise	**6.2**	Managing Remote Access Policies and Profiles	316
Exercise	**6.3**	Network Protocol Security and Enabling IPSec on the Local Computer	342
Exercise	**6.4**	Enabling IPSec for an Entire Domain	347
Exercise	**6.5**	Customizing and Configuring the Local Computer IPSec Policy and Rules for Transport Mode	361
Exercise	**6.6**	Configuring a Policy for IPSec Tunnel Mode	364
Exercise	**6.7**	Monitoring IPSec Logon Activity	373
Exercise	**7.1**	Using the Configure Your Server Wizard	392
Exercise	**7.2**	Using the Manage Your Server Tool	394
Exercise	**7.3**	Creating a Custom MMC Console to Manage Security Policy for a New GPO	411
Exercise	**7.4**	Setting Password Policies	416
Exercise	**7.5**	Setting Account Lockout Policies	418
Exercise	**7.6**	Setting Audit Policies	422
Exercise	**7.7**	Setting Local User Rights	426
Exercise	**7.8**	Defining Security Options	428
Exercise	**7.9**	Using the Security Configuration and Analysis Tool	438
Exercise	**8.1**	Assigning Permissions to Templates	493
Exercise	**8.2**	Enabling Automatic Enrollment	495

Exercise 8.3 Creating a New CTL . . . 499
Exercise 8.4 Revoking a Certificate . . . 501
Exercise 8.5 Requesting a Certificate . . . 510
Exercise 8.6 Issuing Certificates . . . 513
Exercise 8.7 Using the Certificate Export Wizard . . . 515
Exercise 8.8 Using the Certificate Import Wizard . . . 517
Exercise 10.1 Installing the Network Monitor Driver and Application . . . 578
Exercise 10.2 Capturing Data with Network Monitor . . . 583
Exercise 10.3 Creating a Capture Filter with Network Monitor . . . 586
Exercise 10.4 Creating a Baseline Report . . . 596
Exercise 10.5 Monitoring System Memory . . . 600
Exercise 10.6 Monitoring the System Processor . . . 602
Exercise 10.7 Configuring Multiple Processors . . . 603
Exercise 10.8 Monitoring the Disk Subsystem . . . 605
Exercise 10.9 Monitoring the Network Subsystem . . . 606
Exercise 10.10 Monitoring Network Services . . . 610
Exercise 10.11 Establishing a Remote Desktop Connection . . . 628
Exercise 10.12 Using the Backup Wizard . . . 638
Exercise 10.13 Using the Restore Wizard . . . 640
Exercise 10.14 Backing Up System State Data . . . 643
Exercise 10.15 Performing ASR Backups and Restores with the Automated System Recovery Wizard . . . 647

Introduction

Microsoft's Microsoft Certified Systems Administrator (MCSA) and Microsoft Certified Systems Engineer (MCSE) tracks for Windows Server 2003 are the premier certifications for computer industry professionals. Covering the core technologies around which Microsoft's future will be built, this program provides powerful credentials for career advancement.

This book has been developed to give you the critical skills and knowledge you need to prepare for one of the core requirements of both the MCSA and MCSE certifications in the new Windows Server 2003 track: Planning and Maintaining a Microsoft Windows Server 2003 Network Infrastructure (Exam 70-293).

The Microsoft Certified Professional Program

Since the inception of its certification program, Microsoft has certified almost 1.5 million people. As the computer network industry increases in both size and complexity, this number is sure to grow—and the need for *proven* ability will also increase. Companies rely on certifications to verify the skills of prospective employees and contractors.

Microsoft has developed its Microsoft Certified Professional (MCP) program to give you credentials that verify your ability to work with Microsoft products effectively and professionally. Obtaining your MCP certification requires that you pass any one Microsoft certification exam. Several levels of certification are available based on specific suites of exams. Depending on your areas of interest or experience, you can obtain any of the following MCP credentials:

Microsoft Certified Systems Administrator (MCSA) on Windows Server 2003 The MCSA certification is the latest certification track from Microsoft. This certification targets systems and network administrators with roughly 6 to 12 months of desktop and network administration experience. The MCSA can be considered the entry-level certification. You must take and pass a total of four exams to obtain your MCSA. Or, if you are an MCSA on Windows 2000, you can take one Upgrade exam to obtain your MCSA on Windows Server 2003.

Microsoft Certified Systems Engineer (MCSE) on Windows Server 2003 This certification track is designed for network and systems administrators, network and systems analysts, and technical consultants who work with Microsoft Windows XP and Server 2003 software. You must take and pass seven exams to obtain your MCSE. Or, if you are an MCSE on Windows 2000, you can take two Upgrade exams to obtain your MCSE on Windows Server 2003.

MCSE versus MCSA

In an effort to provide those just starting off in the IT world a chance to prove their skills, Microsoft introduced its Microsoft Certified Systems Administrator (MCSA) program.

Targeted at those with less than a year's experience, the MCSA program focuses primarily on the administration portion of an IT professional's duties. Therefore, there are certain Windows exams that satisfy both MCSA and MCSE requirements, namely exams 70-270, 70-290, and 70-291.

Of course, the goal of any MCSA should be to eventually obtain his or her MCSE. However, don't assume that, because the MCSA has to take two exams that also satisfy an MCSE requirement, the two programs are similar. An MCSE must also know how to design a network. Beyond these two exams, the remaining MCSE required exams require the candidate to have much more hands-on experience.

Microsoft Certified Application Developer (MCAD) This track is designed for application developers and technical consultants who primarily use Microsoft development tools. Currently, you can take exams on Visual Basic .NET or Visual C# .NET. You must take and pass three exams to obtain your MCAD.

Microsoft Certified Solution Developer (MCSD) This track is designed for software engineers and developers and technical consultants who primarily use Microsoft development tools. As of this printing, you can get your MCSD in either Visual Studio 6 or Visual Studio .NET. In Visual Studio 6, you need to take and pass three exams to obtain your MCSD. In Visual Studio .NET, you must take and pass five exams.

Microsoft Certified Database Administrator (MCDBA) This track is designed for database administrators, developers, and analysts who work with Microsoft SQL Server. As of this printing, you can take exams on either SQL Server 7 or SQL Server 2000. You must take and pass four exams to achieve MCDBA status.

Microsoft Certified Trainer (MCT) The MCT track is designed for any IT professional who develops and teaches Microsoft-approved courses. To become an MCT, you must first obtain your MCSE, MCSD, or MCDBA, and then you must take a class at one of the Certified Technical Training Centers. You will also be required to prove your instructional ability. You can do this in various ways: by taking a skills-building or train-the-trainer class, by achieving certification as a trainer from any of several vendors, or by becoming a Certified Technical Trainer through CompTIA. Last of all, you will need to complete an MCT application.

Microsoft recently announced two new certification tracks for Windows 2000: MCSA: Security and MCSE: Security. In addition to the core operating system requirements, candidates must take two security specialization core exams, one of which can be CompTIA's Security+ exam. MCSE: Security candidates must also take a security specialization design exam. As of this printing, no announcement had been made on the track for Windows Server 2003. Check out Microsoft's Web site at `www.microsoft.com/traincert.com` for more information.

How Do You Become Certified on Windows Server 2003?

Attaining an MCSA or MCSE certification has always been a challenge. In the past, students have been able to acquire detailed exam information—even most of the exam questions—from online "brain dumps" and third-party "cram" books or software products. For the new exams, this is simply not the case.

Microsoft has taken strong steps to protect the security and integrity of its certification tracks. Now prospective candidates must complete a course of study that develops detailed knowledge about a wide range of topics. It supplies them with the true skills needed, derived from working with Windows XP, Server 2003, and related software products.

The Windows Server 2003 certification programs are heavily weighted toward hands-on skills and experience. Microsoft has stated that "nearly half of the core required exams' content demands that the candidate have troubleshooting skills acquired through hands-on experience and working knowledge."

- Fortunately, if you are willing to dedicate the time and effort to learn Windows XP and Server 2003, you can prepare yourself well for the exams by using the proper tools. By working through this book, you can successfully meet the exam requirements to pass the Planning and Maintaining a Microsoft Windows Server 2003 Network Infrastructure (70-293) exam.

This book is part of a complete series of MCSA and MCSE Study Guides, published by Sybex Inc., that together cover the core MCSA and MCSE operating system requirements, as well as the Design requirements needed to complete your MCSE track. Please visit the Sybex Web site at `www.sybex.com` for complete program and product details.

MCSA Exam Requirements

Candidates for MCSA certification on Windows Server 2003 must pass four exams.

For a more detailed description of the Microsoft certification programs, including a list of all the exams, visit Microsoft's Training and Certification Web site at `www.microsoft.com/traincert`.

You must take one of the following client operating system exams:

- Installing, Configuring, and Administering Microsoft Windows 2000 Professional (70-210)
- Installing, Configuring, and Administering Microsoft Windows XP Professional (70-270)

plus the following networking operating system exams:

- Managing and Maintaining a Microsoft Windows Server 2003 Environment (70-290)
- Implementing, Managing, and Maintaining a Microsoft Windows Server 2003 Network Infrastructure (70-291)

plus one of a number of electives, including:

- Implementing and Supporting Microsoft Systems Management Server 2 (70-086)
- Installing, Configuring, and Administering Microsoft Internet Security and Acceleration (ISA) Server 2000, Enterprise Edition (70-227)
- Installing, Configuring, and Administering Microsoft SQL Server 2000 Enterprise Edition (70-228)
- CompTIA's A+ and Network+ exams
- CompTIA's A+ and Server+ exams

Also, if you are an MCSA on Windows 2000, you can take one Upgrade exam: Managing and Maintaining a Microsoft Windows Server 2003 Environment for an MCSA Certified on Windows 2000 (70-292).

MCSE Exam Requirements

Candidates for MCSE certification on Windows Server 2003 must pass seven exams, including one client operating system exam, three networking operating system exams, one design exam, and two electives.

For a more detailed description of the Microsoft certification programs, visit Microsoft's Training and Certification Web site at `www.microsoft.com/traincert`.

You must take one of the following client operating system exams:

- Installing, Configuring, and Administering Microsoft Windows 2000 Professional (70-210)
- Installing, Configuring, and Administering Microsoft Windows XP Professional (70-270)

plus the following networking operating system exams:

- Managing and Maintaining a Microsoft Windows Server 2003 Environment (70-290)
- Implementing, Managing, and Maintaining a Microsoft Windows Server 2003 Network Infrastructure (70-291)
- Planning and Maintaining a Microsoft Windows Server 2003 Network Infrastructure (70-293)
- Planning, Implementing, and Maintaining a Microsoft Windows Server 2003 Active Directory Infrastructure (70-294)

plus one of the following Design exams:

- Designing a Microsoft Windows Server 2003 Active Directory and Network Infrastructure (70-297)
- Designing Security for a Microsoft Windows Server 2003 Network 2000 Server Technologies (70-298)

plus one of a number of electives, including:

- Implementing and Supporting Microsoft Systems Management Server 2.0 (70-086)
- Installing, Configuring, and Administering Microsoft Internet Security and Acceleration (ISA) Server 2000, Enterprise Edition (70-227)
- Installing, Configuring, and Administering Microsoft SQL Server 2000 Enterprise Edition (70-228)
- Designing and Implementing Databases with Microsoft SQL Server 2000 Enterprise Edition (70-229)
- The Design exam not taken as a requirement

Also, if you are an MCSE on Windows 2000, you can take two Upgrade exams: Managing and Maintaining a Microsoft Windows Server 2003 Environment for an MCSA Certified on

Windows 2000 and Planning, Implementing, and Maintaining a Microsoft Windows Server 2003 Environment for an MCSE Certified on Windows 2000. In addition, if you are an MCSE in Windows NT, you do not have to take the client requirement, but you do have to take the networking operating system, design, and an elective.

Windows 2000 Server and Windows Server 2003 Certification

Microsoft recently announced that they will distinguish between Windows 2000 and Windows Server 2003 certifications. Those who have their MCSA or MCSE certification in Windows 2000 will be referred to as "certified on Windows 2000." Those who obtained their MCSA or MCSE in the Windows Server 2003 will be referred to as "certified on Windows Server 2003."

If you are certified in Windows 2000, you can take either one Upgrade exam (for MCSA) or two Upgrade exams (for MCSE) to obtain your certification on Windows Server 2003.

Microsoft also introduced a clearer distinction between the MCSA and MCSE certifications, by more sharply focusing each certification. In the new Windows Server 2003 track, the objectives covered by the MCSA exams relate primarily to administrative tasks. The exams that relate specifically to the MCSE, however, deal mostly with design-level concepts. So, MCSA job tasks are considered to be more hands-on, while the MCSE job tasks involve more strategic concerns of design and planning.

The Planning and Maintaining a Microsoft Windows Server 2003 Network Infrastructure Exam

The Planning and Maintaining a Microsoft Windows Server 2003 Network Infrastructure exam covers concepts and skills related to planning and maintaining a Windows Server 2003 network infrastructure. It emphasizes the following elements of server management:

- Planning and Implementing Server Roles and Server Security
- Planning, Implementing, and Maintaining a Network Infrastructure
- Planning, Implementing, and Maintaining Routing and Remote Access
- Planning, Implementing, and Maintaining Server Availability
- Planning and Maintaining Network Security

This exam requires you to pay close attention to business objectives. You will be building on previous "how-to" knowledge (for instance, how to configure a DNS zone), and you will be challenged to understand *why* a particular solution is best in a given scenario (for instance, why you would choose a particular zone type and configuration to solve the needs of two companies that are merging).

If you want to prepare fully for the exam, you must do more than simply read each chapter this book. Hands-on, real-world experience is the critical ingredient that will mark the difference between pass and fail. You'll also want to practice with the end-of-chapter review questions and the Bonus Exam questions on the CD.

Microsoft provides exam objectives to give you a general overview of possible areas of coverage on the Microsoft exams. Keep in mind, however, that exam objectives are subject to change at any time without prior notice and at Microsoft's sole discretion. Please visit Microsoft's Training and Certification Web site (`www.microsoft.com/traincert`) for the most current listing of exam objectives.

Types of Exam Questions

In an effort to both refine the testing process and protect the quality of its certifications, Microsoft has focused its Windows XP and Server 2003 exams on real experience and hands-on proficiency. There is a greater emphasis on your past working environments and responsibilities, and less emphasis on how well you can memorize. In fact, Microsoft says a certification candidate should have at least six months of hands-on experience.

Microsoft will accomplish its goal of protecting the exams' integrity by regularly adding and removing exam questions, limiting the number of questions that any individual sees in a beta exam, and adding new exam elements.

Exam questions may be in a variety of formats. Depending on which exam you take, you'll see multiple-choice questions, as well as select-and-place and prioritize-a-list questions. Simulations and case study–based formats are included as well. Let's take a look at the types of exam questions and examine the adaptive testing technique, so you'll be prepared for all of the possibilities.

With the release of Windows 2000, Microsoft stopped providing a detailed score breakdown. This was mostly because of the various and complex question formats. Previously, each question focused on one objective. The Windows Server 2003 exams, however, contain questions that may be tied to one or more objectives from one or more objective sets. Therefore, grading by objective is almost impossible. Also, Microsoft no longer offers a score. Now you will only be told if you pass or fail.

For more information on the various exam question types, go to `www.microsoft.com/traincert/mcpexams/policies/innovations.asp`.

MULTIPLE-CHOICE QUESTIONS

Multiple-choice questions come in two main forms. One is a straightforward question followed by several possible answers, of which one or more is correct. The other type of multiple-choice question is more complex and based on a specific scenario. The scenario may focus on several areas or objectives.

SELECT-AND-PLACE QUESTIONS

Select-and-place exam questions involve graphical elements that you must manipulate to successfully answer the question. For example, you might see a diagram of a computer network, as shown in the following graphic taken from the select-and-place demo downloaded from Microsoft's Web site.

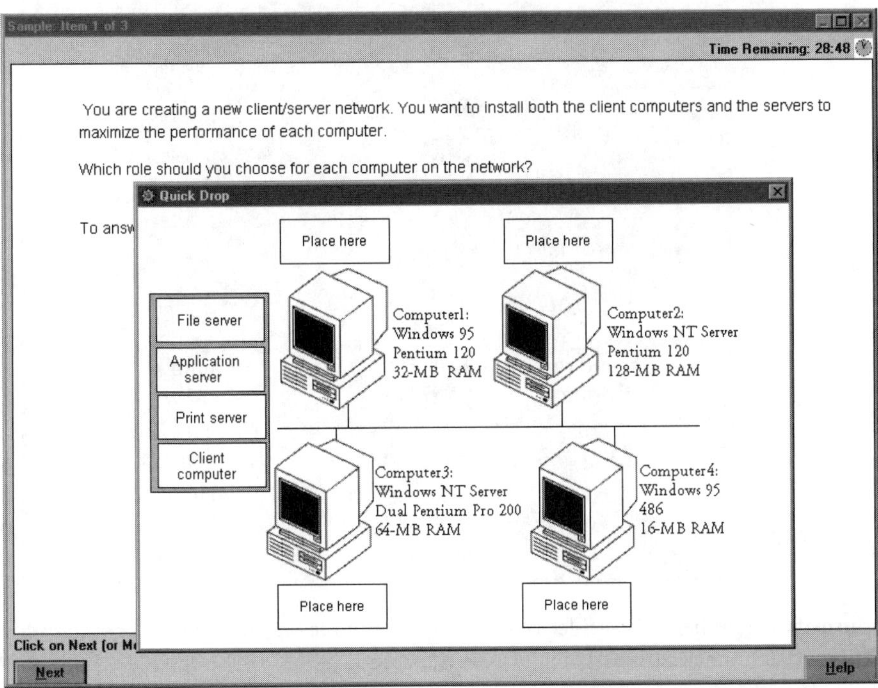

A typical diagram will show computers and other components next to boxes that contain the text "Place here." The labels for the boxes represent various computer roles on a network, such as a print server and a file server. Based on information given for each computer, you are asked to select each label and place it in the correct box. You need to place *all* of the labels correctly. No credit is given for the question if you correctly label only some of the boxes.

In another select-and-place problem you might be asked to put a series of steps in order, by dragging items from boxes on the left to boxes on the right, and placing them in the correct order.

One other type of select-and-place question might require you to build a list, or place steps in proper order.

SIMULATIONS

Simulations are the kinds of questions that most closely represent actual situations and test the skills you use while working with Microsoft software interfaces. These exam questions include a mock interface on which you are asked to perform certain actions according to a given scenario. The simulated interfaces look nearly identical to what you see in the actual product, as shown in this example:

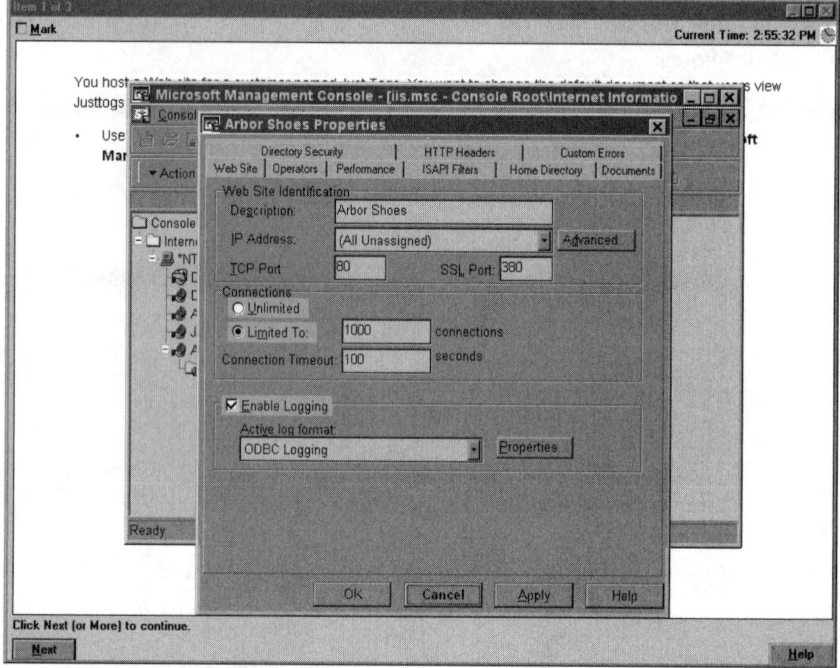

Because of the number of possible errors that can be made on simulations, be sure to consider the following recommendations from Microsoft:

- Do not change any simulation settings that don't pertain to the solution directly.
- When related information has not been provided, assume that the default settings are used.
- Make sure that your entries are spelled correctly.
- Close all the simulation application windows after completing the set of tasks in the simulation.

The best way to prepare for simulation questions is to spend time working with the graphical interface of the product on which you will be tested.

We recommend that you study with the WinSim 2003 product, which is included on the CD that accompanies this Study Guide. By completing the exercises in this Study Guide and working with the WinSim 2003 software, you will greatly improve your level of preparation for simulation questions.

CASE STUDY–BASED QUESTIONS

Case study–based questions first appeared in the MCSD program. These questions present a scenario with a range of requirements. Based on the information provided, you answer a series of multiple-choice and select-and-place questions. The interface for case study–based questions has a number of tabs, each of which contains information about the scenario.

At present, this type of question appears only in most of the Design exams.

Microsoft will regularly add and remove questions from the exams. This is called *item seeding*. It is part of the effort to make it more difficult for individuals to merely memorize exam questions that were passed along by previous test-takers.

Exam Question Development

Microsoft follows an exam-development process consisting of eight mandatory phases. The process takes an average of seven months and involves more than 150 specific steps. The MCP exam development consists of the following phases:

Phase 1: Job Analysis Phase 1 is an analysis of all the tasks that make up a specific job function, based on tasks performed by people who are currently performing that job function. This phase also identifies the knowledge, skills, and abilities that relate specifically to the performance area being certified.

Phase 2: Objective Domain Definition The results of the job analysis phase provide the framework used to develop objectives. Development of objectives involves translating the job-function tasks into a comprehensive package of specific and measurable knowledge, skills, and abilities. The resulting list of objectives—the *objective domain*—is the basis for the development of both the certification exams and the training materials.

Phase 3: Blueprint Survey The final objective domain is transformed into a blueprint survey in which contributors are asked to rate each objective. These contributors may be MCP candidates, appropriately skilled exam-development volunteers, or Microsoft employees. Based on the contributors' input, the objectives are prioritized and weighted. The actual exam items are written according to the prioritized objectives. Contributors are queried about how they spend their time on the job. If a contributor doesn't spend an adequate amount of time actually performing the specified job function, his or her data are eliminated from the analysis. The blueprint survey phase helps determine which objectives to measure, as well as the appropriate number and types of items to include on the exam.

Phase 4: Item Development A pool of items is developed to measure the blueprinted objective domain. The number and types of items to be written are based on the results of the blueprint survey.

Phase 5: Alpha Review and Item Revision During this phase, a panel of technical and job-function experts reviews each item for technical accuracy. The panel then answers each item and reaches a consensus on all technical issues. Once the items have been verified as being technically accurate, they are edited to ensure that they are expressed in the clearest language possible.

Phase 6: Beta Exam The reviewed and edited items are collected into beta exams. Based on the responses of all beta participants, Microsoft performs a statistical analysis to verify the validity of the exam items and to determine which items will be used in the certification exam. Once the analysis has been completed, the items are distributed into multiple parallel forms, or *versions*, of the final certification exam.

Phase 7: Item Selection and Cut-Score Setting The results of the beta exams are analyzed to determine which items will be included in the certification exam. This determination is based on many factors, including item difficulty and relevance. During this phase, a panel of job-function experts determines the *cut score* (minimum passing score) for the exams. The cut score differs from exam to exam because it is based on an item-by-item determination of the percentage of candidates who answered the item correctly and who would be expected to answer the item correctly.

Phase 8: Live Exam In the final phase, the exams are given to candidates. MCP exams are administered by Prometric and Virtual University Enterprises (VUE).

Tips for Taking the Planning and Maintaining a Microsoft Windows Server 2003 Network Infrastructure Exam

Here are some general tips for achieving success on your certification exam:

- Arrive early at the exam center so that you can relax and review your study materials. During this final review, you can look over tables and lists of exam-related information.
- Read the questions carefully. Don't be tempted to jump to an early conclusion. Make sure you know *exactly* what the question is asking.
- On simulations, do not change settings that are not directly related to the question. Also, assume default settings if the question does not specify or imply which settings are used.
- For questions you're not sure about, use a process of elimination to get rid of the obviously incorrect answers first. This improves your odds of selecting the correct answer when you need to make an educated guess.

Exam Registration

You may take the Microsoft exams at any of more than 1,000 Authorized Prometric Testing Centers (APTCs) and VUE Testing Centers around the world. For the location of a testing center near you, call Prometric at 800-755-EXAM (755-3926), or call VUE at 888-837-8616. Outside the United States and Canada, contact your local Prometric or VUE registration center.

Find out the number of the exam you want to take, and then register with the Prometric or VUE registration center nearest to you. At this point, you will be asked for advance payment for the exam. The exams are $125 each, and you must take them within one year of payment. You can schedule exams up to six weeks in advance or as late as one working day prior to the date of the exam. You can cancel or reschedule your exam if you contact the center at least two working days prior to the exam. Same-day registration is available in some locations, subject to space availability. Where same-day registration is available, you must register a minimum of two hours before test time.

You may also register for your exams online at `www.prometric.com` or `www.vue.com`.

When you schedule the exam, you will be provided with instructions regarding appointment and cancellation procedures, ID requirements, and information about the testing center location. In addition, you will receive a registration and payment confirmation letter from Prometric or VUE.

Microsoft requires certification candidates to accept the terms of a Non-Disclosure Agreement before taking certification exams.

Is This Book for You?

If you want to acquire a solid foundation in planning and maintaining a Server 2003 network infrastructure, and your goal is to prepare for the exam by learning how to use and manage the new operating system, this book is for you. You'll find clear explanations of the fundamental concepts you need to grasp, and plenty of help to achieve the high level of professional competency you need to succeed in your chosen field.

If you want to become certified as an MCSE, this book is definitely for you. However, if you just want to attempt to pass the exam without really understanding how to plan and maintain a Windows Server 2003 network infrastructure, this Study Guide is *not* for you. It is written for people who want to acquire hands-on skills and in-depth knowledge of in planning and maintaining a Server 2003 network infrastructure.

What's in the Book?

What makes a Sybex Study Guide the book of choice for over 100,000 MCPs? We took into account not only what you need to know to pass the exam, but what you need to know to take what you've learned and apply it in the real world. Each book contains the following:

Objective-by-Objective Coverage of the Topics You Need to Know Each chapter lists the objectives covered in that chapter.

The topics covered in this Study Guide map directly to Microsoft's official exam objectives. Each exam objective is covered completely.

Assessment Test Directly following this introduction is an Assessment Test that you should take. It is designed to help you determine how much you already know about planning and maintaining a Server 2003 network infrastructure. Each question is tied to a topic discussed in the book. Using the results of the Assessment Test, you can figure out the areas where you need to focus your study. Of course, we do recommend you read the entire book.

Exam Essentials To highlight what you learn, you'll find a list of Exam Essentials at the end of each chapter. The Exam Essentials section briefly highlights the topics that need your particular attention as you prepare for the exam.

Key Terms and Glossary Throughout each chapter, you will be introduced to important terms and concepts that you will need to know for the exam. These terms appear in italic within the chapters, and a list of the Key Terms appears just after the Exam Essentials. At the end of the book, a detailed Glossary gives definitions for these terms, as well as other general terms you should know.

Review Questions, Complete with Detailed Explanations Each chapter is followed by a set of Review Questions that test what you learned in the chapter. The questions are written with the exam in mind, meaning that they are designed to have the same look and feel as what you'll see on the exam. Question types are just like the exam, including multiple choice, exhibits, and select-and-place.

Hands-On Exercises In each chapter, you'll find exercises designed to give you the important hands-on experience that is critical for your exam preparation. The exercises support the topics of the chapter, and they walk you through the steps necessary to perform a particular function.

Real World Scenarios Because reading a book isn't enough for you to learn how to apply these topics in your everyday duties, we have provided Real World Scenarios in special sidebars. These explain when and why a particular solution would make sense, in a working environment you'd actually encounter.

Interactive CD Every Sybex Study Guide comes with a CD complete with additional questions, flashcards for use with an interactive device, a Windows simulation program, and the book in electronic format. Details are in the following section.

What's on the CD?

With this new member of our best-selling Microsoft certification Study Guide series, we are including quite an array of training resources. The CD offers numerous simulations, bonus exams, and flashcards to help you study for the exam. We have also included the complete contents of the Study Guide in electronic form. The CD's resources are described here:

The Sybex E-book for *MCSE: Windows Server 2003 Network Infrastructure Planning and Maintenance Study Guide* Many people like the convenience of being able to carry their whole Study Guide on a CD. They also like being able to search the text via computer to find specific information quickly and easily. For these reasons, the entire contents of this Study Guide are supplied on the CD, in PDF. We've also included Adobe Acrobat Reader, which provides the interface for the PDF contents as well as the search capabilities.

WinSim 2003 We developed the WinSim 2003 product to allow you to experience the multimedia and interactive operation of working with Windows Server 2003. WinSim 2003 provides both audio/video files and hands-on experience with key features of Windows Server 2003. Built around the Study Guide's exercises, WinSim 2003 will help you attain the knowledge and hands-on skills you must have in order to understand Windows Server 2003 (and pass

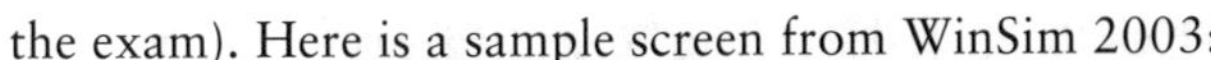

the exam). Here is a sample screen from WinSim 2003:

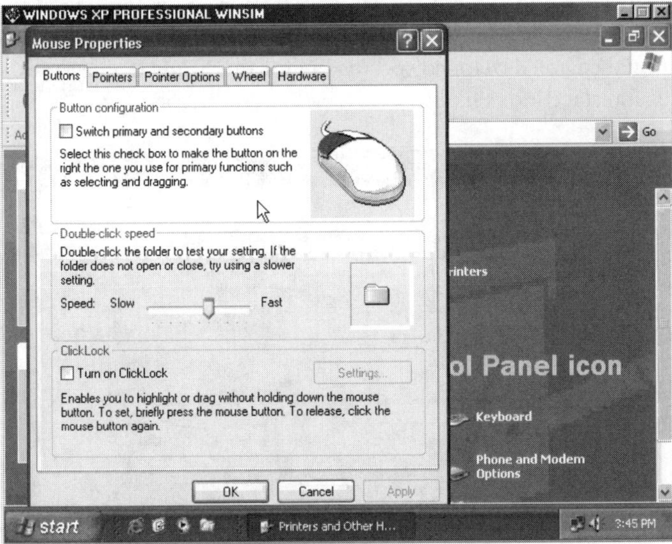

The Sybex Test Engine This is a collection of multiple-choice questions that will help you prepare for your exam. There are four sets of questions:

- Two bonus exams designed to simulate the actual live exam.
- All the questions from the Study Guide, presented in a test engine for your review. You can review questions by chapter or by objective, or you can take a random test.
- The Assessment Test.

Here is a sample screen from the Sybex Test Engine:

Assessment Test

Mark Time Left: 1 hr 19 min(s) Question: 2 of 30

You are troubleshooting DHCP address assignments and want to find out whether a client is using an APIPA address. Which command should you use?

A. ipconfig /renew

B. ipconfig /refresh

C. ipconfig /displaydns

D. ipconfig /all

E. ipconfig

Your Answer:

< > Show Answer Finish ?

Sybex MCSE Flashcards for PCs and Handheld Devices The "flashcard" style of question offers an effective way to quickly and efficiently test your understanding of the fundamental concepts covered in the exam. The Sybex Flashcards set consists of more than 100 questions presented in a special engine developed specifically for this Study Guide series. Here's what the Sybex Flashcards interface looks like:

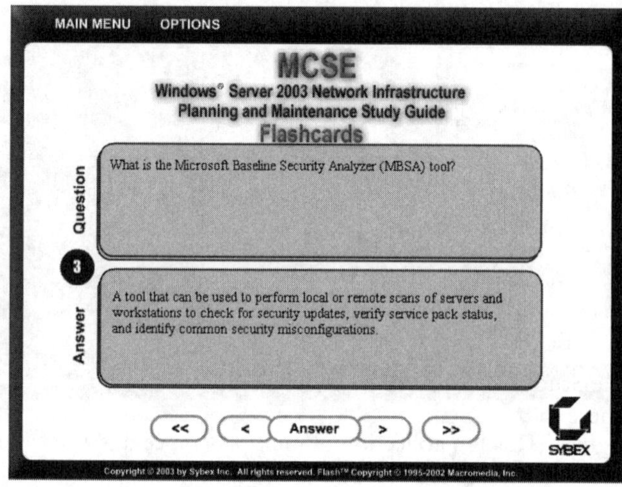

Because of the high demand for a product that will run on handheld devices, we have also developed a version of the flashcard questions that you can take with you on your Palm OS PDA (including the PalmPilot and Handspring's Visor).

In addition, if you bought this book as part of the *MCSE: Windows 2003 MCSE: Windows 2003 Certification Kit* box set, you will find two bonus CDs—one including an 180-day evaluation version of Windows Server 2003 and another including two additional practice exams per book. Further information can be found in the `readme` files on the CDs.

How Do You Use This Book?

This book provides a solid foundation for the serious effort of preparing for the exam. To best benefit from this book, you may want to use the following study method:

1. Take the Assessment Test to identify your weak areas.
2. Study each chapter carefully. Do your best to fully understand the information.
3. Complete all the hands-on exercises in the chapter, referring back to the text as necessary so that you understand each step you take. If you don't have access to a lab environment in which you can complete the exercises, install and work with the exercises available in the WinSim 2003 software included with this Study Guide.

To do the exercises in this book, your hardware should meet the minimum hardware requirements for Windows Server 2003. The following section contains a list of recommended hardware and software we think you should have in your home lab.

4. Read over the Real World Scenarios to improve your understanding of how to use what you learn in the book.
5. Study the Exam Essentials and Key Terms to make sure you are familiar with the areas upon which you need to focus.
6. Answer the review questions at the end of each chapter. If you prefer to answer the questions in a timed and graded format, install the Sybex Test Engine from the book's CD and answer the chapter questions there instead of in the book.
7. Take note of the questions you did not understand, and study the corresponding sections of the book again.
8. Go back over the Exam Essentials and Key Terms.
9. Go through the Study Guide's other training resources, which are included on the book's CD. These include WinSim 2003, electronic flashcards, the electronic version of the chapter review questions (try taking them by objective), and the two bonus exams.

To learn all the material covered in this book, you will need to study regularly and with discipline. Try to set aside the same time every day to study, and select a comfortable and quiet place in which to do it. If you work hard, you will be surprised at how quickly you learn this material. Good luck!

Hardware and Software Requirements

You should verify that your computer meets the minimum requirements for installing Windows Server 2003. We suggest that your computer meet or exceed the recommended requirements for a more enjoyable experience.

The exercises in this book assume that you have two computers, a Windows Server 2003 domain controller and a Windows XP Professional computer that is part of the domain.

Contacts and Resources

To find out more about Microsoft Education and Certification materials and programs, to register with Prometric or VUE, or to obtain other useful certification information and additional study resources, check the following resources:

Microsoft Training and Certification Home Page

`www.microsoft.com/traincert`

This Web site provides information about the MCP program and exams. You can also order the latest Microsoft Roadmap to Education and Certification.

Microsoft TechNet Technical Information Network

www.microsoft.com/technet

800-344-2121

Use this Web site or phone number to contact support professionals and system administrators. Outside the United States and Canada, contact your local Microsoft subsidiary for information.

Prometric

www.prometric.com

800-755-3936

Contact Prometric to register to take an MCP exam at any of more than 800 Prometric Testing Centers around the world.

Virtual University Enterprises (VUE)

www.vue.com

888-837-8616

Contact the VUE registration center to register to take an MCP exam at one of the VUE Testing Centers.

MCP Magazine Online

www.mcpmag.com

Microsoft Certified Professional Magazine is a well-respected publication that focuses on Windows certification. This site hosts chats and discussion forums, and it tracks news related to the MCSE program. Some of the services cost a fee, but they are well worth it.

Windows & .NET Magazine

www.windows2000mag.com

You can subscribe to this magazine or read free articles at the Web site. The study resource provides general information on Windows Server 2003, Windows XP, and Windows 2000 Server.

Cramsession on Brainbuzz.com

cramsession.brainbuzz.com

Cramsession is an online community focusing on all IT certification programs. In addition to discussion boards and job locators, you can download one of several free cram sessions, which are nice supplements to any study approach you take.

Assessment Test

1. Which of the following options describe advantages of the RIPv2 routing protocol? Choose all that apply.

   A. Supports VLSM

   B. No limit on hop counts

   C. Ability to hierarchically structure the router area into subdivisions

   D. Authentication support

   E. Multicast announcing

2. You are troubleshooting DHCP address assignments and want to find out whether a client is using an APIPA address. Which command should you use?

   A. `ipconfig /renew`

   B. `ipconfig /refresh`

   C. `ipconfig /displaydns`

   D. `ipconfig /all`

   E. `ipconfig`

3. Which of the following backup types sets the archive bit for each file that is backed up? Choose two.

   A. Normal

   B. Copy

   C. Differential

   D. Incremental

   E. Daily

4. What is the purpose of IGMP proxy mode?

   A. Listens for IGMP membership report packets and tracks group membership

   B. Forwards IGMP membership report packets to an IGMP router

   C. Uses an IP-in-IP interface to encapsulate packets in order to send multicast traffic across non–multicast-compatible routers

   D. Receives the list of multicast hosts from the Internet multicast backbone (MBone) so that the hosts can send multicast packets

5. Which of the following options describes the behavior of WINS replication in Windows Server 2003?

   A. Configuring a trust relationship between two domains is not necessary in order to set up WINS replication between WINS servers in either of the two domains.

   B. Disabling File and Printer Sharing For Microsoft Networks on all computers that will not be used to share resources increases replication traffic.

   C. A full-mesh design, in which push/pull partnerships are configured between all WINS servers, results in the highest possible availability and consistency.

   D. Automatic partnership configuration information requires a persistent connection.

6. Your network has seven VPN servers that are using PPTP. You want to configure the VPN servers so that you keep out non-VPN traffic. Which of the following actions should you take? Choose two.

   A. Configure a filter to allow traffic for protocol ID 47 to the destination address of the PPTP interface.

   B. Configure a filter to allow traffic bound for the destination TCP port 1723.

   C. Configure a filter to allow traffic for protocol ID 500 to the destination address of the PPTP interface.

   D. Configure a filter to allow traffic for protocol ID 47 to the destination TCP port 1723.

7. Which of the following options describes the main difference between RIP and OSPF?

   A. OSPF immediately propagates changes to its neighbors; RIP sends periodic broadcasts.

   B. RIP uses manually configured routing tables; OSPF uses dynamic routing.

   C. OSPF can be configured on any number of interfaces; RIP can only be configured in one direction on a single interface.

   D. Both maintain link state, but RIP has a practical limitation of 14 hops.

8. Which of the following options describes the Start of Authority (SOA) record?

   A. The SOA defines the general parameters for the DNS zone, including who the authoritative server is for the zone.

   B. The SOA uses the `in-addr.arpa` domain to reverse-resolve DNS queries.

   C. The SOA follows the format: `ldap.tcp.chellis.net SRV 10 100 389 hsv.chellis.net`

   D. The SOA follows the format: `servername IN A 192.168.0.204`

9. You are planning the DNS strategy for your company. You need to provide DNS services to a remote office with a limited bandwidth connection to corporate headquarters. Which type of DNS server should you implement at the remote office?

   A. Configure stub zones on the server

   B. Configure a conditional forwarder

   C. Configure a forward-only server

   D. Configure a caching-only server

   E. Configure a primary zone server

   F. Configure a secondary zone server

10. Which of the following options describes the behavior of a stub zone?

    A. A DNS server hosting a stub zone in one network will reply to queries for names in the other network with only a list of all the authoritative DNS servers for that zone.

    B. A DNS server hosting a stub zone in one network will respond with the specific DNS servers that are designed to handle the name resolution traffic for that zone.

    C. A DNS server hosting a stub zone in one network will forward DNS queries for external DNS names to DNS servers outside of its own network.

    D. A DNS server hosting a stub zone in one network will send recursive queries to root hints servers on the Internet.

    E. A DNS server hosting a stub zone in one network will neither build up a cache, nor perform recursion if the query fails.

11. Which of the following command-line options will enable you to check the status of the local NetBIOS name cache and verify the MAC address of the local computer?

    A. Enter **nbtstat -c *name***, where ***name*** is the NetBIOS name of your computer.

    B. Enter **ipconfig -all /netstat**.

    C. Enter **ipconfig /nbtstat *name***, where ***name*** is the NetBIOS name of your computer.

    D. Enter **nbtstat -a *name***, where ***name*** is the NetBIOS name of your computer.

12. What is the purpose of the built-in group DnsUpdateProxyGroup?

    A. Grants the secure rights required so that your DHCP servers will perform updates by proxy for any DHCP clients

    B. Grants the secure rights required so that your DHCP servers will perform updates by proxy for only those DHCP clients configured to use secure dynamic updates

    C. Grants the secure rights required so that your DHCP servers will perform updates by proxy for NT-based DHCP clients

    D. Enables secure dynamic updates on all DHCP client computers

13. You are integrating non-WINS clients into your Windows Server 2003 WINS infrastructure. Which of the following actions must you take?

    A. Configure the WINS proxy agent on the WINS server computer for the local subnet.

    B. Configure the WINS proxy agent on a WINS client computer on the local subnet.

    C. Configure the WINSProxy option on the DHCP Relay Agent.

    D. Configure the WINS proxy agent on the WINS server computer for the local scope.

    E. Configure the WINS proxy agent on a WINS client computer on each subnet where the non-WINS clients are located.

14. Which of the following commands can you use to publish certificates and CRLs?
    A. `certpublish -dsutil`
    B. `dsutil -certpublish`
    C. `dspublish -certutil`
    D. `certutil -dspublish`

15. You want to configure IPSec for additional security on your Windows Server 2003 network using the least amount of administrative effort. All clients are Windows XP. How should you apply the IPSec policies?
    A. Apply the Server (Request Security) policy to all servers on the network. Apply the Client (Require Security) policy to all clients on the network.
    B. Apply the Server (Require Security) policy to all servers on the network. Apply the Client (Request Security) policy to all clients on the network.
    C. Apply the Server (Require Security) policy to all servers on the network. Apply the Client (Respond Only) policy to all clients on the network.
    D. Apply the Server (Request Security) policy to all servers on the network. Apply the Client (Allow Security) policy to all clients on the network.
    E. Apply a custom policy requiring IPSec for client-server traffic to all servers on the network. Apply the Client (Respond Only) policy to all clients on the network.

16. Which of the following options describe L2TP tunneling in Windows Server 2003?
    A. L2TP provides stronger encryption than PPTP.
    B. The authorization process is a function of the VPN stack.
    C. L2TP establishes an unencrypted, unauthenticated tunnel.
    D. L2TP was designed exclusively for VPN use as a tunneling protocol.

17. Which of the following options are configured in the default remote access policy? Choose two.
    A. Authentication-Type
    B. Day-and-Time-Restrictions
    C. Windows-Groups
    D. Tunnel-Type
    E. MS-RAS-Vendor
    F. Deny remote access permission
    G. Allow remote access permission

18. You are planning for automatic IP configuration through DHCP on your Windows Server 2003 network. Which of the following options are characteristics of automatic IP configuration in Windows Server 2003? Choose all that apply.

    A. BootP and DHCP hosts can be mixed on the same network.

    B. Network-attached printers should be dynamically assigned IP addresses from the same subnet as the clients they service.

    C. Network servers should be dynamically assigned IP addresses from the same subnet as the clients they service.

    D. A DHCP Relay Agent must be configured on subnets without a DHCP server.

19. You are configuring security policies to establish server-level security. Which of the following describes the behavior of Group Policy options?

    A. Use the Block Inheritance option when you want only the GPO you had set for your container to be applied.

    B. Use the Block Inheritance option when you want to set corporate-wide policies without allowing administrators of lower-level containers to override your settings

    C. Use the Disabled option when you want to block the application of a GPO to a container

    D. Use the No Override option to prevent higher-level GPOs from overriding a lower-level GPO on any containers for which the lower-level GPO is applied

20. You are using RRAS servers with a nonpersistent demand-dial connection in a multiple subnet environment. You want to prevent routing updates for these connections from being broadcast to the entire network, but you want the changes to propagate to the other RRAS servers. Which solution should you choose?

    A. Area border routers (ABRs)

    B. OSPF

    C. RIPv1

    D. RIPv2

21. Which of the following options describes the behavior of SUS?

    A. SUS clients can include Windows 2003, 2000, XP, NT and 9*x*.

    B. SUS offers server-to-server synchronization.

    C. SUS enables you to manage operating system patches, security updates, and configurations.

    D. SUS clients can download updates only from approved SUS servers.

22. You are planning a security update infrastructure for Windows Server 2003. You have existing scripts that call `hfnetchk.exe`. Which of the following command lines should you run in the scripts to use the most current version of MBSA?

   A. `hfnetchk.exe /mbsa -nosum`

   B. `hfnetchk.exe /mbsa -nosum`

   C. `mbsa.exe /hfnetchk`

   D. `mbsacli.exe /hf`

   E. `mbsacli.exe /hfnetchk`

23. What happens when you renew a certificate?

   A. The key pair always changes.

   B. You may elect to keep the existing key pair or request a new key pair.

   C. The certificate attributes will not change.

   D. This action will reestablish security in the event that the private key has been compromised.

24. You need to plan a strategy for high availability. Which of the following options describes the standby server configuration?

   A. Standby servers are good for larger applications that require a lot of resources such as processing power, memory, and input/output (I/O) bandwidth.

   B. In the event of a failure on one node, the processing load for all applications in the cluster will be equally distributed across the remaining nodes.

   C. In the event of a failure on one node, the processing load for the failed application in the cluster will be equally distributed across the remaining nodes.

   D. Standby servers eliminate the possibility of a single point of failure.

25. Which of the following options are used to secure Remote Assistance?

   A. Configure the firewall to allow or prohibit traffic through port 3998.

   B. Configure the firewall to allow or prohibit traffic through port 3389.

   C. Configure the firewall to allow or prohibit traffic through port 4090.

   D. Configure the firewall to allow or prohibit traffic through port 1433.

26. Which of the following options describes the affinity behavior of clustered applications in Windows Server 2003?

   A. With strong affinity, groups will always be located together on the same node.

   B. With strong anti-affinity, groups will always be kept apart.

   C. With group affinity, applications are always targeted to specific nodes as configured by the administrator.

   D. With group affinity, dependencies are established between groups that determine the relative location of groups within a cluster.

   E. Exchange virtual servers are an example of groups that use weak affinity.

27. You are planning a high availability strategy for a multisite Windows Server 2003 network. Which of the following cluster models should you choose?

A. Local quorum

B. Single quorum device

C. Multiple quorum device

D. Majority node set

28. You are planning an IP addressing strategy for intranet servers on your Windows Server 2003 network. You want to ensure that these servers cannot be directly accessed from the Internet in order to maintain security. Which address range can you use to meet this objective?

A. `172.32.0.1` through `172.168.255.254`

B. `10.255.255.0` through `10.255.255.255`

C. `192.168.0.0` through `192.168.18.254`

D. `192.162.0.1` through `192.168.0.0`

29. You want to quickly determine the average load on a DNS server. Which of the following performance counters should you monitor?

A. DNS Server > Bytes Total/Sec

B. DNS > Total Query Received/Sec

C. DNS Server > Total Query Received/sec

D. DNS Server > Total Number of Registrations/Sec

30. You want to implement the strongest possible security for your root CA. What should you do?

A. Configure the root CA as a standalone CA.

B. Configure the root CA as an enterprise CA.

C. Disconnect the root CA from the network.

D. Configure the root CA to only publish CRLs manually.

Answers to Assessment Test

1. A, D, E. RIPv2 is a distance vector routing protocol that supports VLSM, authentication, and multicast announcing. Although more complex and therefore more resource-intensive, OSPF is a link state routing protocol that offers advantages over RIPv2, including no limit on hop counts and the ability to hierarchically structure the routers into subdivisions (areas). See Chapter 2 for more information.

2. D. The `ipconfig /all` command will display the full IP configuration information for all network adapters on a host. If the address is in the range `168.254.x.y`, then APIPA is active. See Chapter 2 for more information.

3. A, D. The Normal and Incremental backup types set the archive bit for each file that is backed up. See Chapter 10 for more information.

4. B. IGMP proxy mode essentially acts like a multicast host, except that it forwards IGMP membership report packets to an IGMP router. This provides a list of multicast-enabled hosts to an upstream router that normally would not be aware of the hosts. Typically, IGMP proxy is used on single-router networks connected to the Internet. The IGMP proxy sends the list of multicast hosts to the multicast-capable portion of the Internet known as the Internet multicast backbone, or MBone, so that the hosts can receive multicast packets. IGMP router mode listens for IGMP membership report packets and tracks group membership.

   An IP-in-IP interface is created when you want to encapsulate packets from a multicast router so that they can be sent across any router, including a non-multicast router. See Chapter 3 for more information.

5. A. In Windows Server 2003, having a trust relationship between two domains is not necessary in order to set up WINS replication between WINS servers in either of the two domains. See Chapter 5 for more information.

6. A, B. You need at least two filters to adequately screen out non-PPTP traffic. The first filter allows traffic with a protocol ID of 47, the Generic Routing Encapsulation protocol (GRE), to pass to the destination address of the PPTP interface. The second filter allows inbound traffic bound for TCP port 1723 (the PPTP port) to come into the PPTP interface. See Chapter 3 for more information.

7. A. The main difference between the RIP and OSPF routing protocols is that RIP sends periodic broadcasts to announce changes to the routing topology, while OSPF immediately propagates changes to its neighbors. Both protocols use dynamic routing and can be configured on any available interfaces. RIP is a distance vector protocol with a practical limitation of 15 router-to-router hops. OSPF is a link state routing protocol. See Chapter 3 for more information.

8. A. The Start of Authority (SOA) record defines the general parameters for the DNS zone, including who the authoritative server is for the zone. The pointer (PTR) records are used to perform reverse lookups. The service records (SRV) follow the format: `ldap.tcp.chellis.net SRV 10 100 389 hsv.chellis.net`. The host records (A) follow the format: `hostname IN A 192.168.0.204`. See Chapter 4 for more information.

9. D. Use caching-only servers when you have a remote office with a limited bandwidth connection to corporate headquarters. See Chapter 4 for more information.

10. A. The purpose of a stub zone is to keep a DNS server that hosts a parent zone aware of the authoritative DNS servers for its child zone. A DNS server hosting a stub zone in one network will reply to queries for names in the other network with only a list of all the authoritative DNS servers for that zone. It will not respond with the specific DNS servers that are designed to handle the name resolution traffic for that zone. See Chapter 4 for more information.

11. D. The `nbtstat -a` ***name*** command will enable you to check the status of the local NetBIOS name cache and verify the MAC address of the local computer. See Chapter 5 for more information.

12. A. The built-in group DnsUpdateProxyGroup grants the secure rights required so that your DHCP servers will perform updates by proxy for any DHCP clients. It is used to enable the DHCP servers to perform updates by proxy for those clients that cannot perform DNS updates on their own behalf, such as Windows NT-based DHCP clients. Secure dynamic updates are a feature of Active Directory–Integrated DNS and can be enabled for Windows 2000 and higher clients. See Chapter 4 for more information.

13. B. The WINS proxy agent listens for NetBIOS broadcast queries and attempts to register and resolve names on behalf of b-node network clients. This enables non-WINS clients to use WINS indirectly to register and resolve NetBIOS names. Because NetBIOS broadcast queries are nonroutable, the WINS proxy agent must be configured on the same subnet as the non-WINS clients. The WINS proxy agent can run only on a WINS client computer. See Chapter 5 for more information.

14. D. Certificates are published to Active Directory by default. You can use the `certutil -dspublish` command to publish certificates and CRLs. See Chapter 6 for more information.

15. C. The three default IPSec policies are: Client (Respond Only), Server (Request Security), and Server (Require Security). In this scenario, you would apply the Server (Require Security) policy to all servers on the network. Then you would apply the Client (Respond Only) policy to all clients on the network. See Chapter 6 for more information.

16. C. L2TP is a tunneling protocol that establishes an unencrypted, unauthenticated tunnel and is used in conjunction with IPSec to provide secure VPN communications. L2TP provides no inherent security. The authorization process is a function of the remote access server, not the VPN stack. L2TP was designed to be a general-purpose tunneling protocol, not limited to VPN use. See Chapter 6 for more information.

17. B, F. The default remote access policy defines the Day-and-Time-Restrictions attribute to permit all times on all days and sets the permission to Deny Remote Access Permission. See Chapter 6 for more information.

18. A, D. BootP and DHCP hosts can be mixed on the same Windows Server 2003 network. All subnets that will be serviced by DHCP must have a means of servicing local DHCP traffic. Because DHCP works through local, nonroutable broadcasts, either a DHCP server or a DHCP Relay Agent is required on all subnets. Network servers and network-attached printers should have static IP addresses configured with reservations in DHCP for those IP addresses. The convention is to assign these addresses at the low end of a scope of addresses for a group of clients served by the servers and devices. See Chapter 2 for more information.

19. A. The Block Inheritance option is used to allow the child container to block GPO inheritance from parent containers. You would use this option if you did not want child containers to inherit GPO settings from parent containers and only wanted the GPO you had set for your container to be applied. The No Override option is used to specify that child containers can't override the policy settings of higher-level GPOs. Use this option when you want to set corporate-wide policies without allowing administrators of lower-level containers to override your settings. The Disabled option is used to specify that the GPO is not applied to this container. You would use the Disabled option if you wanted to define a policy on a higher-level container to be applied to all down-level containers, without actually applying the policy to the parent container itself. See Chapter 7 for more information.

20. D. In this scenario, you need RIPv2. RIPv1 would not work because it broadcasts changes to the entire network. OSPF would not work because the connection is a nonpersistent demand-dial interface. Area border routers are simply special versions of OSPF routers. See Chapter 3 for more information.

21. B. Microsoft Software Update Services (SUS) is based on Windows Update technology and allows you to automatically deploy operating system patches to Windows 2003, 2000, and XP clients. SUS offers server-to-server synchronization, so that one authoritative server downloads the updates, and other servers point to it instead of Windows Update for the latest patches. SUS can be configured so that approved updates are automatically downloaded from an SUS server or so that updates are automatically downloaded from the Microsoft Web site. See Chapter 7 for more information.

22. D. The command-line interface `mbsacli.exe` has a new flag (`/hf`) to indicate an HFNetChk-style scan. This means that if you already have scripts that call `hfnetchk.exe`, you can just replace it with a call to `mbsacli.exe /hf` followed by any valid HFNetChk v3.81 flag(s). See Chapter 7 for more information.

23. B. When you renew a certificate, you may elect to keep the existing key pair or request a new key pair. Some of the certificate attributes will change. If the private key has been compromised, you must revoke the old certificate in order to reestablish security. See Chapter 8 for more information.

24. A. Standby servers are a variation of the N+I configuration in which idle nodes are prepared to take on the work of one or more active nodes. They are good for larger applications that require a lot of resources such as processing power, memory, and input/output (I/O) bandwidth. In the event of a failure on one node, all applications are still hosted on separate servers. See Chapter 9 for more information.

25. B. To control whether a person within the organization can request help outside of the organization using Remote Assistance, you must configure the firewall to permit inbound and outbound traffic through port 3389. See Chapter 10 for more information.

26. D. Group affinity is used to establish dependencies between groups that determine the relative location of groups within a cluster. With strong affinity, they will be placed together on the same node, if possible. They can also be set up to have strong or weak anti-affinity. With strong anti-affinity, groups will be kept apart if at all possible. Because running more than one instance of Exchange on the same node is not recommended, Exchange virtual servers are an example of groups that use anti-affinity. See Chapter 9 for more information.

27. D. The majority node set quorum model is intended for sophisticated, end-to-end clustering solutions. Each node maintains its own copy of the cluster configuration data. The quorum resource ensures that the cluster configuration data is kept consistent across the nodes. For this reason, majority node set quorums are typically found in geographically dispersed clusters. See Chapter 9 for more information.

28. C. In this scenario, you would use a private IP addressing strategy for increased security. Private IP address ranges include the `10.0.0.0/8` network (`10.0.0.1` to `10.255.255.254`), the `172.16.0.0/12` network (`172.16.0.1` to `172.31.255.254`), and the `192.168.0.0/16` network (`192.168.0.1` to `192.168.255.254`). See Chapter 2 for more information.

29. B. The DNS > Total Query Received/Sec performance counter measures the average number of queries received by a DNS server every second and is the best measure of average load on a DNS server. See Chapter 10 for more information.

30. C. The strongest possible security for your root CA involves disconnecting it from the network so that no security compromise is possible via network access. You still must ensure physical security for the computer that acts as the root CA. See Chapter 8 for more information.

Planning a Network Infrastructure: A Technology Primer

The effective planning and maintenance of the network infrastructure is fundamental to all other network tasks and objectives. Whatever role you play in the design, implementation, and maintenance of a Windows network, you'll gain a critical edge when you can visualize the integration of the individual components in your Windows network architecture.

We designed this initial chapter to empower you with a high-level overview of the subject of planning a network infrastructure. By the end of this chapter, you'll understand the big picture of network planning. Armed with this foundation, you will find it much easier to fill in the details with the chapters to follow.

In this chapter, you'll get a sneak preview of Windows Server 2003's security enhancements and new tools for building a secure and highly available network. We'll start by defining network infrastructure, next we'll preview what's new in this version, and then we'll tackle four key objectives in your mission to plan and maintain a network infrastructure:

- Planning the network topology and name resolution strategies
- Planning for the secure flow of data
- Planning a security infrastructure
- Planning to ensure high server availability across the network

Throughout the chapter, we'll identify best practices in planning that will be an invaluable aid—both on the exam *and* in the real world.

We'll cover advanced networking topics in this guide, so you'll get the most benefit out of it if you have acquired a level of knowledge and experience commensurate with passing Microsoft Exam 70-291: "Implementing, Managing, and Maintaining a Microsoft Windows Server 2003 Network Infrastructure." You can best prepare for Exam 70-291 by complementing your real-world experience with *MCSA/MCSE: Windows Server 2003 Network Infrastructure Implementation, Management, and Maintenance Study Guide* by Michael Chacon, James Chellis, and Matt Sheltz.

Defining a Network Infrastructure

In its broadest sense, a *network infrastructure* can be viewed as all of the hardware and software components that together support the flow and processing of digital information.

The physical hardware is used to interconnect computers and users. The physical infrastructure includes things like transmission media. This media includes POTS (Plain Old Telephone Service) telephone lines, cable lines, satellites and antennas, as well as the more familiar routers, aggregators, repeaters, and other devices that control transmission paths. Infrastructure is sometimes defined to also include the software used to send, receive, and manage the signals that are transmitted. Microsoft follows this definition and, we will use the same definition in this book.

Infrastructure is the set of fundamental backend technologies, or "pieces" of a network, that enable secure access to network resources, allow secure communications to take place across that network, and facilitate secure Internet connectivity.

The networking and communications infrastructure is the most fundamental aspect of a network operating system. This layer defines a network operating system's ability to provide connectivity and interoperability with client systems and other server-based operating systems. Infrastructure includes the following components and services:

- Physical devices and media used for communication
- Transmission Control Protocol/Internet Protocol (TCP/IP) networking services
- IP management and addressing services
- Name resolution services
- Remote access and virtual private networking (VPN) services
- Routing and wide area network (WAN) connectivity
- Internet and extranet connectivity
- Authentication and security services
- High availability services

Network Infrastructure in Windows Server 2003

Since Windows Server 2003 is based on progressive improvements to the NT 4 kernel, you can think of the progression from NT 4 to Windows 2000 Server to Windows Server 2003 as evolutionary steps rather than radical departures. Each new incarnation touts better performance and a number of new features to better assist you in your role as caretaker of the servers. The most revolutionary change that was introduced in Windows 2000 was *Active Directory*, which fused the directory service concept of Exchange Server 5.5 into the way the operating system holds and references objects such as users, sites, and domains.

Take note of an important trend. In case you're new to Windows, or you simply haven't noticed, security is becoming increasingly native to all other network and server functionality. Security in its broadest sense can include such diverse goals as providing protection against hackers, enabling support personnel—and only support personnel—to administer desktops remotely, restricting network access at a granular protocol level, and even providing the ability to quickly recover lost data. Windows Server 2003 takes this approach to a new level for Microsoft, infusing security throughout all other functions. Nowhere is this more apparent than in the new tools for building a secure network infrastructure.

In the following sections, you'll be introduced to these new features in Windows Server 2003.

Network Configuration and Connectivity Improvements

The Windows Server 2003 network infrastructure features improvements in network and Internet connectivity and provides more granular control of the network configuration settings. These improvements include:

Group Policy Improvements to Network Configuration You can now control most network configuration settings at a granular level with the new Group Policy improvements in Windows Server 2003. DNS client settings overrode server settings, which caused the hassle of tracking down conflicting settings and possibly having to physically visit a DNS client computer if it was incorrectly configured. In Windows Server 2003, you can configure some of the DNS client settings on computers running Windows Server 2003 within Group Policy. In addition, you can use Group Policy to allow or restrict a user's ability to configure the network user interface.

Group Policy is introduced in *MCSA/MCSE: Windows Server 2003 Environment Management and Maintenance Study Guide* by Lisa Donald with Suzan London and James Chellis (Sybex, 2003), and it is covered in detail in *MCSE: Windows Server 2003 Active Directory Planning, Implementation, and Maintenance Study Guide* by Anil Desai with James Chellis (Sybex, 2003).

Network Bridging Network bridging allows administrators to interconnect network segments in a multi-segment network, using multihomed Windows Server 2003 computers. You can bridge the multiple adapters so that devices on each of the network segments can communicate with each other through the bridge. You can also use network bridging to enable computers on the interconnected network segments to connect to the Internet using Internet Connection Sharing (ICS).

Point-to-Point Protocol over Ethernet (PPPoE) Windows Server 2003 now includes a native PPPoE driver for making broadband connections to certain ISPs. Windows 2000 Server required additional software to make such connections. Small businesses or satellite offices may also utilize PPPoE's demand-dial capabilities to integrate with the Routing and Remote Access Service and Network Address Translation (NAT).

Data Security Improvements

Windows Server 2003 security is greatly improved with the implementation of the IPv6 protocol and improvements to the IP Security Protocol (IPSec), which include a highly effective new tool for managing IPSec protocol security policies and greater flexibility with IPSec-based VPNs and IPSec-protected applications across a NAT. The data security improvements include:

IPv6 IPv6 is the next generation protocol of the Internet layer protocols of the TCP/IP protocol suite. IPv6 solves the current problems of IPv4 with respect to address depletion, security, autoconfiguration, and extensibility.

IPSec and Resultant Set of Policy (RSoP) IPSec, the IP Security protocol, now has a potent tool to assist in its implementation: the Resultant Set of Policy (RSoP) tool, which will enable the administrator to predict the effective outcome of IPSec policies before putting them into effect. The RSoP tool is an extremely powerful tool for planning and troubleshooting Group Policy. RSoP enables the administrator to forecast how Group Policy changes would affect a targeted user or computer, thereby preventing expensive mistakes. Administrators can also use RSoP to verify the policies currently in effect on a remote target computer.

L2TP/IPSec and IPSec/NAT Windows administrators who harangued over the difficulties inherent in using IPSec-based VPNs or IPSec-protected applications across a NAT will find relief in Windows Server 2003. You can now use Layer Two Tunneling Protocol over IPSec (L2TP/IPSec), which enables you to implement an IPSec-based VPN, or you can allow an IPSec connection to pass through a NAT, which benefits you if you want to use IPSec-protected applications across a NAT interface.

Real World Scenario

Internetworking Businesses Securely Using IPSec

As the network administrator of a B2B financial services company with a suite of Web-enabled financial management products, you want to ensure the highest possible security for remote access to partner applications and e-mail. Many of the users in the Business Development division work from home offices on Fridays and require access to e-mail. They frequently work on proposals that contain highly sensitive financial data from prospective clients. Ensuring that e-mail access can occur only over a secured connection is imperative. In addition, the Engineering department requires access from an application server on a perimeter network in the organization to a business partner's application server in order to test new functionality in one of the proprietary applications they developed.

To ensure secure remote mail access, you decide to implement an IPSec-based VPN using L2TP/IPSec. This will enable you to create a secured tunnel for communication over the Internet and exert a granular level of control over the security of the data transmission using IPSec policies. This method will ensure that Exchange Server traffic from a perimeter network to the internal network remains highly secure.

You recognize that the act of connecting a perimeter network application server to a business partner's application server over the Internet presents its own security challenges. In Windows Server 2003, you can accomplish your objective by implementing IPSec over NAT, which will eliminate the need for a VPN server.

In Windows Server 2003, the new flexibility with IPSec offers many potential applications for secure businesses networking.

Security Infrastructure Improvements

Improvements to the security infrastructure in Windows Server 2003 make it easier to secure wireless connections and to manage X.509 certificates for secure user authentication. The security infrastructure improvements include:

Improved Security for Wireless Connections Windows Server 2003 secures wireless (IEEE 802.1X) LANs that support public certificates deployed using autoenrollment or smart cards.

Certificate Autoenrollment and Autorenewal Windows Server 2003 makes it possible to automatically enroll and deploy X.509 certificates to users. As certificates expire, they can be automatically renewed. Certificate autoenrollment and autorenewal make it easier and faster to deploy smart cards. By automatically expiring and renewing certificates, these features also improve the security of wireless connections.

High Availability Improvements

Microsoft gave us several new tools to improve system availability and recoverability. Support for newer versions of protocols such as IPv6 and RDP v 5.1 increases the flexibility of these tools. The system availability improvements include:

Network Load Balancing and IPSec Network Load Balancing (NLB) provides scalability and high availability of TCP/IP-based applications and services, by combining multiple servers into a single, load balancing cluster. The most common use for NLB is to distribute incoming Web requests among its cluster of Internet server applications (such as Internet Information Services applications). In Windows Server 2003, NLB now supports IPSec traffic. We'll cover exactly what IPSec does and why it's so critical in a moment.

Understanding IPSec is very important to network infrastructure planning, both for the exam and in real-world network administration.

Network Load Balancing Manager Windows Server 2003 offers a new Network Load Balancing Manager, which provides a single point of configuration and management for load balancing of NLB clusters. This makes it so much easier than rooting around in a number of miscellaneous consoles.

Remote Desktop for Administration Terminal Services' remote administration mode (as it was known in Windows 2000) has received a major facelift and a new name—Remote Desktop for Administration. Under the new version of the Remote Desktop Protocol (RDP v5.1), it now supports an extended feature set. Unlike its predecessor, RDP v5.1 also has the ability to remote the actual console session of the server.

Volume Shadow Copy Volume shadow copy is a very slick feature that enables users to view and restore previous versions of files that have been modified, overwritten, or deleted. If you enable the feature on the server or network share, a user simply needs to right-click the file in Windows Explorer and select Properties in order to find previous versions of their files. Volume shadow copy also has a restore feature that enables Windows-based client computers to view and recover previous versions of their files without IT intervention. This means fewer support calls for you or your staff.

Automated System Recovery (ASR) Automated System Recovery (ASR) limits downtime in disaster recovery situations by enabling one-step restore of the operating system, system state, and network hardware configuration. This feature is completely new to Windows Server 2003, and it ensures consistent data recovery of servers if a serious failure occurs. You can now configure the Backup application included with Windows to use ASR for system restores. In fact, you can even combine it with Remote Installation Services to automate system restores across the network without user intervention.

This section introduced you to new features of Windows Server 2003 as they relate to your mission to plan and implement a network infrastructure. The next section is an overview of your key objectives in said mission: planning the network topology and name resolution strategies, planning for the secure flow of data, planning and implementing a security infrastructure, and planning for high server availability across the network.

Planning the Network Topology and Name Resolution Strategies

The *network topology* describes the physical and logical structure of your network. Investing in a little study and planning now to implement best practices in network design will pay huge dividends in the future in terms of reduced support costs and effort once the network design is in place.

The first step in planning a network infrastructure is to plan the topology in light of resource requirements, company size, growth projections, and other technical and business criteria. Where will you locate your servers? What are the bandwidth constraints and resource requirements that you must take into account when planning the physical design of the network? What tradeoffs between performance, security, and ease of administration are you willing to make? You must consider server locations, protocols to use, bandwidth requirements, and routing strategy. Most companies require Internet connectivity, so you must determine whether and how your users will have access to the Internet. Finally, it is critical to plan your strategy for name resolution and implement the appropriate services.

The following section provides an overview of the things you must plan in order to accomplish this objective.

Planning TCP/IP and the Network Topology Strategy

No doubt you're already intimately familiar with Transmission Control Protocol/Internet Protocol (TCP/IP), the industry standard protocol suite that hails back to the earliest days of the Internet. Due to its versatility, it is the network protocol of choice in almost every networking scenario you will encounter.

You should recall that TCP/IP actually encompasses a suite of protocols. The main protocols are IP and TCP. IP manages routing and addressing, while TCP manages delivery, flow control, and sequencing.

To pass Microsoft Exam 70-293, you must have an intimate familiarity with TCP/IP because it is the foundation for most other tasks related to planning and implementing a network infrastructure. The following sections discuss these tasks and how they fit into the bigger picture.

Designing the Network Topology

As mentioned previously, the network topology describes the physical and logical structure of your network. Planning your network infrastructure begins with the creation of diagrams that depict the physical and logical structures of your network, both as it currently exists and for the new design. In order to create your diagrams, you must have an inventory of your network, its servers, client computers, and hardware.

The network diagrams provide you with a blueprint for architecting your network. The logical diagrams also provide you a visual overview of your IP addressing and subnetting strategy.

Designing an IP Addressing Scheme

Designing an appropriate IP addressing scheme is a foundational task upon which all other network services and functions build. A good IP addressing scheme will take into account factors related to security and ease of administration.

An important part of this process is implementing DHCP, a task with which you should already be familiar. You will need to determine which computers will function as DHCP servers, and whether those servers will run other network services.

DHCP is covered in detail in *MCSA/MCSE: Windows Server 2003 Network Infrastructure Implementation, Management, and Maintenance Study Guide* by Michael Chacon with James Chellis (Sybex, 2003).

Determining an IP Subnetting Strategy

Once you have determined the physical layout of your network and the resource requirements, you can determine a strategy for IP subnets. Planning a strategy that optimizes the flow of network traffic over physical and departmental geographies is important.

Subnetting is the process of subdividing a single logical network address space into multiple smaller networks called *subnets*. Subnetting results in reduced network traffic, faster performance, simplified management, and simplified troubleshooting. It's important to design an IP addressing and subnetting strategy that implements best practices, so that you can reduce administrative overhead and enhance scalability for your organization.

We'll delve into the specific details about TCP/IP addressing and subnetting in detail in Chapter 2, "Planning a TCP/IP Network Infrastructure."

Planning a Routing Strategy

Like a Redundant Array of Independent Disks (RAID), which can be controlled through hardware or software, *routing* can also be accomplished either through hardware or a software solution. In a real-world network, the critical function of routing will most likely be performed through hardware. It's a faster, cheaper, more powerful means of getting your digital bits and bytes from Node A to Node Z. In Windows Server 2003, the routing function is handled through software and managed through the Routing and Remote Access Services administrative tool, which you'll recall from Windows 2000 Server.

The subject of routing is important enough to deserve its own book. In fact, many books have been written about individual routing protocols. Companies like Cisco and Nortel Networks service an entire industry sector based on the routing of network data.

Exam coverage is limited to the software implementation of routing through Routing and Remote Access Services (RRAS) in Windows Server 2003. We'll discuss it in detail in Chapter 3, "Planning a Network Connectivity Strategy."

Planning an Internet Connectivity Strategy

Internet connectivity is a critical consideration for today's networks. In this book, you will learn how to plan methods for connecting to the Internet. In addition, you will learn how to troubleshoot problems with NAT, name resolution, and client configurations.

Name resolution is a critical element of your network infrastructure, so we'll discuss the use of DNS and WINS in Windows Server 2003 in the next section.

Chapter 3 covers all aspects of Internet connectivity in Windows Server 2003.

Planning a Name Resolution Strategy

Name resolution services resolve host names to IP addresses. For Windows Server 2003, you will need to know how to implement the *Domain Name Service (DNS)*, which resolves host names to IP addresses. Many networks use a Unix-based DNS, but Microsoft has its own DNS service, which is now easier to integrate with Unix-based DNS services. The *Windows Internet Name Service (WINS)* resolves Network Basic Input Output Service (NetBIOS) computer names to IP addresses. Usually the NetBIOS computer name is the same as the host name, but this is not always the case. If you're fortunate enough to be running an all-Windows 200*x* environment, and you aren't running any NetBIOS-aware applications, then you can finally stop using WINS. If you aren't so fortunate, you'll still need it for backward compatibility with earlier Windows versions and NetBIOS-aware applications, such as Microsoft Exchange Server.

The core functionality of these services has not changed. You should already have a strong understanding of how to implement and configure both DNS and WINS from previous studies and experience. Later in this book, you will learn how to plan and troubleshoot an infrastructure for name resolution.

Chapter 4, "Planning a DNS Strategy," and Chapter 5, "Planning a WINS Strategy," address planning and troubleshooting considerations for DNS and WINS, respectively.

Domain Name Service (DNS)

DNS is a network name resolution service that resolves a fully qualified domain name (FQDN) such as host.redmond.microsoft.com to an IP address such as 172.16.0.12. It consists of a distributed database of host names that uses a hierarchical naming system in a logical tree structure called the domain name space.

DNS is the primary method for name resolution in Windows Server 2003. It is required before you can deploy Active Directory; but conversely, you can deploy DNS without Active Directory. Integrating DNS with Active Directory is the best way to enhance the security and performance of the DNS service. Active Directory is a type of directory service available in Windows Server 2000 and higher. It stores information about objects such as users and computers in a central database.

Planning and designing your DNS infrastructure requires multiple considerations, including planning the DNS namespace, planning DNS server placement, planning DNS zones, and controlling the DNS client configuration.

Although you should already have a good grasp of how to install and configure DNS, Chapter 4 will walk you through the concepts of planning a logical namespace, planning zones, and planning interoperability with other domain name services. You'll find the troubleshooting section toward the end of the chapter especially helpful as you begin to implement DNS in your network.

Windows Internet Naming Service (WINS)

WINS is used to resolve NetBIOS computer names to IP addresses, and it is gradually being phased out of modern Windows networks. Networks that consist entirely of Windows 2000, XP, or Windows Server 2003 computers and that do not run any NetBIOS-aware applications can employ DNS as the exclusive means of name resolution. If you are running any earlier server or client versions of Windows on the network, such as NT Server 4 or Windows 9*x*, you must implement WINS. If you are running any NetBIOS-aware applications, such as Microsoft Exchange Server, on your network, you must implement WINS.

Using the `LMHOSTS` file for NetBIOS name-to-IP address resolution is still possible and sometimes preferable.

In Chapter 5, you'll find a troubleshooting section that will be helpful should your operating system (OS) versions require you to implement WINS or should you run into any snags using the LMHOSTS file as an alternative.

Planning for Secure Data Flow

Today's networks face a number of security threats. A critical part of your role involves planning to ensure the secure flow of data. There are a couple of ways to accomplish this end. You can ensure that all remote access connections are secured against outside attack through the use of Remote Access Policies and secure protocol choices for VPN communications. You can also implement protocol security through IPSec policies. The new RSoP tool is a policy analyzer that enables you to forecast the effective result of multiple policies.

In the following sections, we will look at the enhancements to secure communications in Windows Server 2003.

Planning a Remote Access Strategy

Remote Access services are secured in three different ways:

- By securing the RRAS server through permissions and the Remote Access Policies tool
- By securing the traffic between the RRAS server and its clients using protocol security and data encryption
- By using secure authentication methods

Planning an RRAS infrastructure—complete with Remote Access policies, protocol security, data encryption, and secure authentication—is a complex objective. Chapter 6, "Planning Secure Network Access," will cover the complexities of this objective and present examples of the numerous potential applications and configurations.

Using a Remote Access Policy

A Remote Access policy is an ordered set of rules that define whether connections are authorized or rejected. Each rule contains one or more conditions, a set of profile settings, and a remote access permission setting.

Remote Access policies validate a number of connection settings before authorizing the connection. Upon authorization, the remote access policy profile specifies a set of connection restrictions for that profile.

If you choose to implement Remote Authentication Dial-In User Service (RADIUS) to manage authentication centrally, you can also manage Remote Access policies from a central location. (RADIUS is discussed later in the "Using Secure Authentication" section.)

Using Protocol Security and Data Encryption

Windows Server 2003 supports L2TP/IPSec for the highest possible protocol security. Clients that support 128-bit encryption keys can use L2TP/IPSec. You should set a standard for your remote users to encrypt data with the highest level of data encryption possible. Windows XP and the Windows Server 2003 family support 128-bit encryption keys. Older clients (such as Windows 98 with the latest service pack) can also handle L2TP/IPSec.

Using Secure Authentication

Choosing the most secure authentication protocols supported by the client is obviously your best alternative. Secure authentication protocols include Microsoft Challenge Handshake Authentication Protocol (MS-CHAPv2) and Extensible Authentication Protocol (EAP).

You also need to consider whether or not to use Windows Authentication or RADIUS as the authentication provider. Windows authentication can be used only if all of the RRAS servers are Windows-based. With two or more RRAS servers, you should consider using RADIUS to centralize the authentication of remote access connections. RADIUS offers a means of centrally managing remote client authentication. RADIUS is an industry standard method of managing mutual hardware (machine to machine) authentication. RADIUS itself is vendor-neutral. The Internet Authentication Services (IAS) is Microsoft's implementation of RADIUS. A benefit of using RADIUS is that you can more easily manage your Remote Access policies. RADIUS traffic should be encrypted with IPSec.

Planning Protocol Security

IP Security (IPSec) is a framework of open standards for ensuring private, secure communications over IP networks through the use of cryptographic security services. Like TCP/IP, IPSec is vendor-neutral. Microsoft considers IPSec to be the long-term direction for secure networking.

Your knowledge of IPSec will be tested thoroughly on the exam.

IPSec has two goals:

- To protect IP packets
- To defend against network attacks

IPSec accomplishes its goals through a combination of cryptography-based protection services, security protocols, and dynamic key management. It can even be used to block receipt or transmission of specific traffic types.

IPSec is based on an end-to-end security model. This means that only the sending and receiving computers need to know anything about the traffic being secured. They assume that the data is being transmitted over a non-secure medium, and each computer handles security at its own end. Intermediary devices that only route the data don't even have to support IPSec; they just have to forward the traffic.

Enterprise scenarios in which IPSec can be deployed include:

- Client/server and peer-to-peer LANs
- Router-to-router, gateway-to-gateway across a WAN
- Dial-up and VPN remote access

When considering whether and how to implement IPSec, keep in mind that careful advance planning can ensure that your network is safe from intruders.

IPSec is a highly detailed topic and will be discussed in detail in Chapter 6.

Implementing IPSec is accomplished by creating IPSec policies and managing those policies through the use of the IP Security Monitor and IP Security Policy Management snap-ins. These snap-ins are available through the Microsoft Management Console (MMC).

Managing IPSec through Policies

Protocol security is implemented through policies. IPSec policies are configured using the IP Security Policy Management MMC snap-in and monitored using the IP Security Monitor MMC snap-in. IPSecmon is no longer used to manage IP security.

To use IPSec in your network, you create IPSec policies, which are then applied to Active Directory objects such as computers, domains, sites, and Organizational Units (OUs). You create policies to apply through a combination of rules, actions, and filters.

Rules govern how and when an IPSec policy applies to communication. You can use rules to secure communications based on the source, destination, and type of IP traffic (IP packet filtering). Planning this process carefully is important because the rules can get very complicated and difficult to troubleshoot. If you implemented IPSec policies in Windows 2000 Server, it's likely that you spent a significant amount of time troubleshooting some policies gone awry. Fortunately, Windows Server 2003 has a slick new tool that will prevent a lot of future headaches by pinpointing potential trouble with IPSec policies before they are effectively applied.

Analyzing IPSec Policies Using the RSoP Tool

The Resultant Set of Policy tool (also known as RSoP) will be your salvation if you work with IPSec policies. RSoP is to IPSec policies what the Security Configuration and Analysis tool is to security policies. RSoP is a feature of Group Policy, and it enables you to accomplish two very important tasks:

- You can view the results of a set of policies before you actually apply them.
- You can view the current policy set in effect on a remote computer.

This functionality will enable you to quickly and effectively implement policies that ensure secure data transmission without preventing communication from occurring. By implementing protocol security through IPSec policy with the help of the RSoP tool, you can exert a granular level of control over the security of all IP-based communications in your network.

Planning and Implementing a Security Infrastructure

We began this chapter with a definition of network infrastructure. But what is a security infrastructure, and what is the difference between the two? Microsoft has used the term *security infrastructure* to loosely describe the combination of services and tools that provide a framework for security in the network. In this section, we will first discuss how role-based security can be implemented for servers using a security policy. We will then introduce tools for planning a security update infrastructure. Finally, we will examine how to increase security through certificate-based authentication services.

Planning Policy-Based Security for Server Roles

A server that is installed to provide a specific service on the network is said to be functioning in a server role. A server role describes the functional purpose of a network server. There are roles for application servers, such as mail, Web, database, and media servers. There are also roles for servers that host network resources, such as file and print servers. There are roles for servers that provide network infrastructure services such as name resolution and connectivity. The Configure Your Server Wizard provides an easy-to-use interface for adding server roles, and the Manage Your Server tool provides a portal to management consoles, utilities, and help information organized by server role.

In Windows Server 2003, you can create a policy-based strategy for managing customized security configurations targeted to the role in which a server will function. First, you will plan a baseline for security for servers that are assigned specific roles. You'll then create custom security templates based on server roles. You can analyze existing security configurations against the standardized configuration templates you've created. The Security And Analysis Configuration utility is used to analyze your security configuration and create custom security templates. You can compare existing security configurations to default or custom templates that represent varying levels of security for different types of servers, such as general Windows servers and domain controller servers.

Once created, these standardized configurations can be effectively deployed throughout the organization using Group Policy Objects (GPOs).

Server roles are covered in Chapter 7, "Planning Server-Level Security".

Planning a Security Update Infrastructure

Networks are constantly evolving, and a network administrator must keep abreast of new security challenges and fixes. Windows Server 2003 provides two tools that assist you in planning a security update infrastructure:

Microsoft Baseline Security Analyzer The Microsoft Baseline Security Analyzer is a tool that enables you to scan and evaluate the security of your system. This tool provides you with a streamlined method of identifying common security misconfigurations. MBSA v1.2 will include support for Windows Server 2003.

Microsoft Software Update Services You will want to configure Automatic Updates so that you are automatically notified when new security fixes become available. You can configure Automatic Updates to automatically download updates and install them without manual intervention. Microsoft Software Update Services (SUS) is a solution for automatic updates that gives an administrator more control over updates and makes it easier to deploy patches. Microsoft SUS is a simplified solution targeted for medium-sized enterprises as a means to manage and distribute critical Windows patches. You can think of SUS as an intranet-hosted version of the Windows Update service. An advantage of SUS is that it provides more efficient administration of critical updates. In the past, an administrator needed to check the Windows Update website or the Microsoft Security website to see what was new. Then she had to manually download and deploy the patches to each affected node. SUS solves these problems by automatically downloading updates to an SUS server for testing and automatically distributing updates once they are approved. SUS is particularly powerful in combination with Active Directory, although Active Directory is not a requirement.

Planning a security update infrastructure is covered in Chapter 7.

Enhancing Authentication through Certificate Services

Windows 2000 introduced you to certificate authentication through new features such as IPSec, Kerberos authentication, and public keys. Certificate authentication can be used to secure e-mail clients and Internet communication, to support smart cards, and to secure communication on wireless LANs. A public key infrastructure (PKI) is a comprehensive system of authentication tools and technologies that integrates digital certificates, public key cryptography, and certificate authorities into an enterprise network security architecture. A PKI uses digital certificates and certification authorities to verify and authenticate the validity of each party that is involved in an electronic transaction through the use of public key cryptography.

In Windows Server 2003, all of the functions of certificate authentication can be coordinated through Microsoft *Certificate Services*. You may alternately choose to employ a third-party certificate service, which would most likely be a Unix-based certificate service that you already use in-house. A Windows 2003 Certificate Server can integrate to any third-party Certificate Server as long as that server supports the X.509 standard. Microsoft Certificate Services is fully integrated with Active Directory to provide secure client authentication and communications.

There is a wealth of considerations for implementing a certificate authentication service, and we cover them in depth throughout Chapter 8, "Planning Certificate Services."

Planning for High Server Availability

Network administrators strive to achieve near-100% network uptime. Given the need for periodic maintenance, and the probability of encountering eventual hardware failure or operating system glitches, you'll occasionally need to take a server down. However, if you've planned well and have implemented a stable, reliable network infrastructure with an eye toward best practices, then the downing of a server will not affect the availability of network resources. Windows Server 2003 offers some new tools to help you maintain a high degree of server availability. We will look at these in the following sections.

Planning Clustering and Network Load Balancing

A cluster is a group of two or more computers that work together to provide higher availability, reliability, and scalability than could be obtained by using a single independent system. This is known as *clustering*. Application software and data are available on several servers linked together in a cluster configuration.

When a server within a cluster experiences failure, resources are dynamically redirected and a process called *failover* automatically shifts the workload of the failed server to another server in the cluster. The failover process ensures continuous availability of critical applications and data. The end user usually experiences a limited failure; however, once he or she refreshes the browser or reconnects to the application, he or she is able to work again.

Although clusters are built to recover from failure, they do not actually provide fault tolerance with regard to user data. The task of recovering a user's work or a user's session state is handled by the application software.

Cluster technologies guard against three specific types of failure:

- Application or service failure
- System or hardware failure
- Site failure (for instance, power or connectivity outages)

Microsoft uses a three-part clustering strategy in Windows 2003 Server:

- Server clusters maintain data integrity and provide failover support for back-end applications and services, especially those provided by database servers.
- Network Load Balancing provides failover support for IP-based applications and services, especially IIS or other Web application services, and addresses bottlenecks caused by front-end Web services.
- Component Load Balancing addresses the unique scalability and availability needs of middle-tier applications.

As you read earlier in the chapter, *Network Load Balancing (NLB)* is a special type of clustering used most commonly to distribute incoming Web requests among a cluster of Internet server applications (IIS applications, for instance).

As you consider implementing a clustering solution, it's important to carefully consider the cluster organization you plan to use. Your goal is to organize servers according to their function, which means that Web servers, application servers, and database servers will all be organized differently.

Chapter 9, "Planning High Availability Services," will teach you how to plan a clustering strategy for your network.

Planning Secure Methods for Remote Administration

Although the choice to implement a clustering strategy will bring you peace of mind from knowing your servers will be able to dynamically recover from failure, you'll still want to keep an eye on them from afar. Windows Server 2003 enables you to do just that through Remote Desktop for Administration, which was formerly known as Terminal Services in Remote Administration mode. This tool will enable you, among other things, to easily connect to any server to capture and analyze performance-monitoring data.

You'll learn all about implementing secure remote administration methods in Chapter 10, "Planning Network Monitoring, Remote Administration, and Recovery."

Monitoring Network Performance

As the keeper of the network, you must strive to become invisible. When no one pays you heed, it's usually a good sign that your network is running smoothly. In order to ensure optimal network performance, you need a tool to monitor both server performance and network traffic.

You've probably used System Monitor in the past to monitor and optimize your server at the local machine level; there are a myriad of performance counters and objects which also enable you to monitor performance at the network level and capture network traffic for analysis.

For example, because abnormal network counter values frequently indicate problems with a server's memory, processor, or disks, the best approach is to monitor network counters in conjunction with the server counters `Processor>% Processor Time`, `PhysicalDisk>% Disk Time`, and `Memory>Pages/sec` on the target server computer.

In addition to monitoring network and server objects, you must understand how to monitor the event logs and service logs (for example, the DNS log) for network-related conditions. Combined, these resources provide you with a starting point for troubleshooting a multitude of network errors and conditions.

In Chapter 10, you'll learn how to implement a comprehensive strategy to monitor and optimize network performance using the tools provided in Windows Server 2003.

Planning a Disaster Recovery Strategy

A *disaster recovery* plan (DRP), also known as a business continuity plan (BCP) or business process contingency plan (BPCP)—details how an organization will avoid and recover from potential disasters, such as power outages and server failures. Planning how to recover from disaster is an important consideration for even the smallest networks. As an organization grows in size and complexity, however, the complexity of the network services required to support the organization grows as well. Knowing where network configuration data is stored and how to recover it when necessary is an extremely important, though frequently overlooked, component in an organization's network infrastructure strategy.

You may have a flawless plan for recovering user data and bringing servers back online quickly, but if you haven't included a plan for restoring the network configuration data, your other efforts could be in vain in the event of a crisis. As an adjunct to your existing backup and recovery strategy, you need to address the special considerations for network configuration data and services.

Fortunately, Windows Server 2003 makes it even easier to restore network servers and network configuration data, without the need to memorize esoteric file names and paths. If you administer a large network, you will likely choose to implement the new Automated System Recovery feature combined with Remote Installation Services to automate complete system restores across the network without user intervention.

In Chapter 10, you'll learn how to ensure that you can restore network servers, services, and configuration data in a variety of disaster recovery scenarios.

Summary

In this chapter, you learned:

- What is meant by network infrastructure. Network infrastructure can be viewed as all of the hardware and software components that together support the flow and processing of digital information.
- Key considerations in planning your network topology and name resolution services. Considerations for the network topology include the physical layout of the network, IP addressing, routing, subnetting, and Internet connectivity. Name resolution services include DNS and WINS. DNS is used for host name-to-IP address resolution. WINS is used for NetBIOS name-to-IP address resolution. WINS must be used for backward-compatibility in networks that do not have all Windows 2000 and higher computers.
- Tools and methods for securing the flow of data transmissions. Remote access is secured through the Routing and Remote Access console. Protocol security is implemented using IPSec policies. Secure remote administration is established using Terminal Services.
- Key considerations in planning a secure network infrastructure. Certificate Services interacts with Active Directory to provide secure authentication services. The Baseline Security Analyzer tool enables you to scan and evaluate the security of your system. Software Update Services enables an administrator to approve an update and to automatically download and install updates and patches to client machines and servers.
- Tools and methods for ensuring high availability of all servers on your network. Services that ensure high availability include Clustering and Network Load Balancing. Network performance is monitored using specific counter objects in System Monitor. Disaster recovery tools include volume shadow copy and Automated System Recovery.

Exam Essentials

Understand the new features related to network infrastructure in Windows Server 2003. These features include heightened protocol security with IPSec6 and smoother interoperability with heterogeneous networks.

Know the key considerations in planning a network topology and implementing TCP/IP. Key considerations include the physical layout of the network, IP addressing, routing, subnetting, and Internet connectivity.

Understand the difference between DNS and WINS. DNS is used for computer name-to-IP address resolution. WINS is used for NetBIOS name-to-IP address resolution. WINS is used for backward-compatibility in networks that run Windows versions earlier than Windows 200*x* and/or NetBIOS-aware applications such as Microsoft Exchange Server.

Know what tools and services are available to secure data transmissions. Remote access is secured through the Routing and Remote Access console. Protocol security is implemented using IPSec policies. IPSec policies are configured using the IP Security Policy Management MMC snap-in, and they are monitored using the IP Security Monitor MMC snap-in. The Resultant Set of Policy (RSoP) tool is a new policy analyzer that enables the administrator to forecast the effective result of multiple policies before deploying them throughout the network. Secure remote administration is established using Remote Desktop Administration.

Know what tools and services are available to implement a security infrastructure. Know the purpose of Certificate Services and how it interacts with Active Directory to provide secure authentication services.

Know what tools and services are available to ensure high availability of all the servers on your network. Services that ensure high availability include clustering and Network Load Balancing. Network performance is monitored using specific counter objects in System Monitor. Disaster recovery tools include volume shadow copy and Automated System Recovery.

Key Terms

Before you take the exam, be certain you are familiar with the following terms:

Active Directory
Certificate Services
clustering
disaster recovery
Domain Name Service (DNS)
IP Security (IPSec)
name resolution
network infrastructure
Network Load Balancing (NLB)
network topology
routing
security infrastructure
subnetting
Windows Internet Naming Service (WINS)

Review Questions

1. Each of the following combinations lists server and client operating systems in a hypothetical network. In which of the networks must you have a WINS server? (Choose all that apply.)
   - **A.** Network W: All Windows-based servers and clients
   - **B.** Network X: Windows 2000 and higher servers, and Windows XP clients
   - **C.** Network Y: Windows 2003 domain controllers, Windows NT 4 member servers, and Windows 2000 Professional and higher clients
   - **D.** Network Z: Windows 2003 servers and Windows XP clients
   - **E.** There is insufficient information provided.
2. DNS is used for what type of name resolution?
   - **A.** Forward lookup
   - **B.** Reverse lookup
   - **C.** Host name-to-IP-address
   - **D.** Domain name-to-NetBIOS-name
3. The Public Key Infrastructure functions with which of the following to ensure secure client authentication?
   - **A.** IPSec
   - **B.** NLB
   - **C.** Certificate Services
   - **D.** RSoP
4. Which of the following options are new in Windows Server 2003?
   - **A.** NLB
   - **B.** Clustering
   - **C.** IPSec
   - **D.** RSoP
5. Which of the following describes the capabilities of PPPoE? (Choose all that apply.)
   - **A.** It enables you to establish broadband connections to certain ISPs without requiring additional software.
   - **B.** It enables you to establish broadband connections to certain ISPs in conjunction with additional software.
   - **C.** Its demand-dial capabilities integrate with RRAS, but not with NAT.
   - **D.** Its demand-dial capabilities integrate with RRAS and NAT.

6. Which of the following options describe the benefits of autoenrollment and autorenewal of X.509 certificates? (Choose all that apply.)

   A. Enables secure authentication for wireless LANs

   B. Makes it easier and faster to deploy smart cards

   C. Enables PPPoE

   D. Enables L2TP/IPSec

7. Which of the following options is true regarding Network Load Balancing?

   A. NLB provides failover support for IP-based applications only.

   B. NLB is frequently used with backend database and mail servers.

   C. NLB is more fault-tolerant than server clusters.

   D. NLB is new to Windows Server 2003.

8. Which of the following tools are used to plan a security update infrastructure? (Choose all that apply.)

   A. Certificate Services

   B. PKI

   C. Microsoft Baseline Security Analyzer

   D. Microsoft Software Update Services

9. Which of the following options can work together with RADIUS to provide highly secure centralized authentication for remote access clients?

   A. Windows Authentication

   B. L2TP/IPSec

   C. ICS

   D. IPSec

10. In Windows Server 2003, what are the two main functions of the IPSec protocol?

    A. To protect IP packets and defend against attacks

    B. To facilitate L2TP traffic and to facilitate NAT traffic

    C. To provide secure VPN communications and secure remote administration

    D. To provide secure client authentication and data encryption

11. In Windows Server 2003, routing is accomplished through which of the following native methods?

    A. Hardware routing only

    B. Software and hardware routing

    C. Static routing tables only

    D. Dynamic routing tables only

12. Which of the following statements regarding clustering technology is not true?
    A. Server clusters provide no fault tolerance for user data.
    B. In the event of a server failure, the failover process will ensure that the end user does not experience any type of error or interruption in service.
    C. Cluster technologies guard against power outages.
    D. Network Load Balancing is most commonly used with Web application services.

13. Which of the following tools is used to monitor IPSec policies?
    A. IP Security Monitor
    B. IPSecmon
    C. RSoP
    D. IPv6

14. Which of the following statements about IPSec is NOT true?
    A. IPSec uses a combination of cryptography-based protection services, security protocols, and dynamic key management.
    B. IPSec can provide secure router-to-router communications across a WAN.
    C. IPSec is based on an end-to-end security model in which the transmission medium is assumed to be secure.
    D. IPSec is based on an end-to-end security model in which the transmission medium is assumed to be nonsecure.

15. Windows Server 2003 can act as a client to a third-party DNS implementation, such as domain name services on Unix.
    A. True
    B. False

Answers to Review Questions

1. E. The correct answer is E because not enough information is provided. WINS servers are used to provide name resolution services in networks running versions of Windows earlier than Windows 2000 Server and clients earlier than Windows 2000 Professional. Options B and D are, therefore, conditionally false, because a WINS server is not required *unless* NetBIOS-aware applications such as Microsoft Exchange Server are in use. Option A does not indicate the Windows versions and, therefore, it cannot be determined whether option A is true or false.

2. C. Forward and reverse lookups are types of DNS queries that attempt to resolve names. DNS resolves host names to IP addresses. There is no such thing as domain name-to-NetBIOS-name resolution.

3. C. PKI works with Certificate Services to ensure secure client authentication. The IP Security Protocol (IPSec) ensures protocol security. NLB is a service that ensures high availability of servers. The Resultant Set of Policy (RSoP) tool is a new policy analyzer that is used with Group Policy to forecast the effective result of multiple policies before deploying them within an organization.

4. D. NLB, clustering, and IPSec have been available since Windows 2000 Server. Resultant Set of Policy is a new tool that is used to display effective Group Policy settings on a client machine. RSoP was introduced in XP Professional, but it is now a snap-in in Windows 2003 Server.

5. A, D. Windows Server 2003 includes a native PPPoE driver that enables you to establish broadband connections to certain ISPs without requiring additional software. You can also use its demand-dial capabilities integrated with RRAS and NAT.

6. A, B. Autoenrollment and autorenewal are new features of X.509 certificate management in Windows Server 2003. They both enable secure authentication for wireless LANs and make it easier and faster to deploy smart cards. PPPoE and L2TP/IPSec describe communications protocols, and they are not benefits of securing user authentication through X.509 certificates.

7. A, B. NLB uses server clusters to provide failover support for IP-based applications—especially Web application servers—and was introduced in Windows 2000 Server.

8. C, D. Microsoft Baseline Security Analyzer and Microsoft Software Update Services are tools used to plan a security update infrastructure. Certificate Services and PKI are used for secure client authentication.

9. D. RADIUS can be implemented to use IPSec to provide highly secure centralized authentication for remote access clients.

10. A. IPSec's main role is to keep data secure. With this in mind, the two main functions are to protect packets and defend against attacks. You can run L2TP/IPSec or IPSec over NAT can facilitate secure network traffic, but this is a secondary benefit. IPSec does not provide client authentication or data encryption. Therefore it is necessary to pair it with an encryption protocol such as L2TP so that it is not possible to read the data with a packet sniffer.

11. C. Although all of the options describe valid methods of routing that can be implemented in Windows Server 2003 networks, the only method that is native to the OS is through the use of static routing tables. A multihomed Windows Server 2003 computer can function as a router using RRAS (Routing and Remote Access Service), which is a software implementation of routing. A hardware implementation of routing simply describes the use of a physical routing device. Software and hardware routers can be combined in the same network. Windows Server 2003 RRAS fully supports dynamic routing tables via both RIP and OSPF routing protocols. Static routing tables are also supported.

12. B. Although the failover process will ensure the continuous availability of applications and services in the event that a node in the cluster fails, the end user will probably experience a limited failure that will require him to refresh the browser or reconnect to the application to resume working.

13. A. IPSec policies are configured using the IP Security Policies MMC snap-in, and they are monitored using the IP Security Monitor MMC snap-in. As of Windows Server 2003, IPSecmon is no longer used to manage IP security. The Resultant Set of Policy (RSoP) tool is a new policy analyzer that enables the administrator to forecast the effective result of multiple policies before deploying them throughout the network. IPv6 is the newest version of the IP protocol.

14. C. IPSec is based on an end-to-end security model in which the transmission medium is assumed to be nonsecure.

15. A. Windows Server 2003 can use domain name services from a third party such as a Unix DNS provider.

Planning a TCP/IP Network Infrastructure

MICROSOFT EXAM OBJECTIVES COVERED IN THIS CHAPTER:

✓ **Plan and modify a network topology.**

- Plan the physical placement of network resources.
- Identify network protocols to be used.

✓ **Plan a TCP/IP network infrastructure strategy.**

- Analyze IP addressing requirements.
- Plan an IP routing solution.
- Create an IP subnet scheme.

✓ **Troubleshoot TCP/IP addressing.**

- Diagnose and resolve issues related to client computer configuration.
- Diagnose and resolve issues related to DHCP server address assignment.

Network architects consider many factors when they make design decisions about the network infrastructure. They strive to create a network that exhibits the best combination of objectives such as availability, security, manageability, and performance.

The role of good planning in designing a TCP/IP network is as critical as it is transparent to the end-user. Whether you design a new network from scratch or enhance an existing TCP/IP infrastructure, you can be certain that utilizing best practices and engaging in careful planning now will save you countless hours and headaches when administering the network in the future.

A Windows network consists of a physical network and a logical network. The logical network describes the TCP/IP address structure discussed in this chapter and maps somewhat to the physical network, which consists of the cabling, routers, and other network devices that establish physical connectivity. Although for most organizations, you'll be modifying an existing TCP/IP network rather than designing a new one from scratch, a conceptual understanding of good design principles will benefit you both in troubleshooting and when the time comes to make changes to your network.

Designing a physical network encompasses many topics that are beyond the scope of this book. Routing and Internet connectivity will be discussed in detail in Chapter 3, "Planning a Network Connectivity Strategy."

In an existing network, impending business events and advancing technology often trigger the need to change or upgrade the internetwork. An impending business event, such as a company merger or acquisition, might necessitate that you change your addressing scheme. As technology advances and your organization grows, you'll want to add new features and scale the internetwork to meet the needs of your company. This may involve improving your security implementation, such as migrating from IPv4 to IPv6 protocol security, or devising new strategies for routing.

After reading this chapter, you'll be equipped to design a logical TCP/IP network infrastructure, plan its implementation, and scale to meet future needs. We'll begin with a discussion of the structure and purpose of network protocols. Next, we'll review the fundamentals of IP addressing and subnetting. This chapter introduces IPv6, the newest version of IP, with an eye toward interoperability with the existing version, IPv4. We'll then dive into the steps needed to plan a TCP/IP infrastructure, covering everything from designing an IP addressing strategy to subnetting and supernetting. The chapter finishes with an intensely practical coverage of troubleshooting TCP/IP address allocation and IP-level connectivity. You'll learn how to troubleshoot DHCP, which is sure to come in handy in your day-to-day administration and support tasks.

Understanding and Choosing Network Protocols

Protocols are nothing more than a mutually agreed-upon set of rules defining the way in which two parties (people, computers, network devices, etc.) can exchange information. Protocols that work together to provide a layer or layers of the Open Systems Interconnect (OSI) model provide that level's functionality and are known as a *protocol stack* or *protocol suite*.

Protocols actually work at different levels of the OSI model, but they fall neatly into three distinct groups, as seen in the following list and in Figure 2.1:

Application Protocols These provide for application-to-application interaction and data exchange.

Transport Protocols These establish communication sessions between computers.

Network Protocols These handle issues such as routing and addressing information, error checking, and retransmission requests.

FIGURE 2.1 The seven layers of the OSI model map to three categories of protocols.

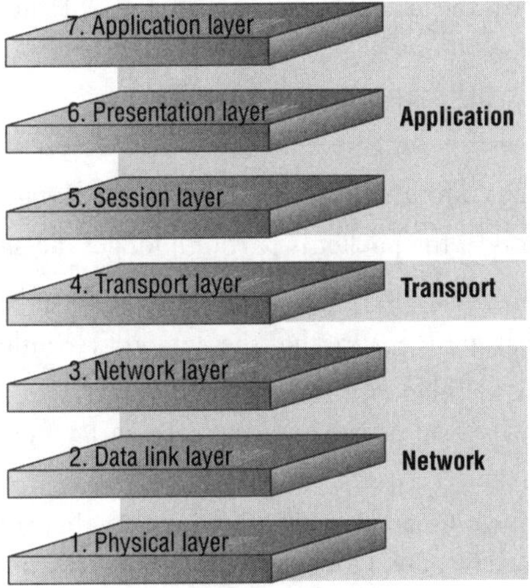

In the following sections, we'll introduce you to how network protocols work, how packets are assembled in order to transmit data, how protocols are bound to network adapters, the difference between connection-oriented and connectionless protocols, and how to choose from the network protocols that are available in Windows Server 2003.

How Network Protocols Work

A network protocol defines a set of basic steps that computers must perform to transmit and receive data across a network. For instance, in order for one computer to send a message to another computer, the first computer must perform the following steps:

1. Break the data into small sections called *packets.*
2. Add addressing information to the packets, identifying the destination computer.
3. Deliver the data to the network card for transmission over the network.

The receiving computer must reverse those three steps:

1. Accept the data from the network adapter card.
2. Remove the transmitting information that was added by the transmitting computer.
3. Reassemble the packets of data into the original message.

Each computer needs to perform the same steps, in the same way and in the correct order, so that the data will arrive and be reassembled correctly. If one computer uses a protocol with different steps or even the same steps with different parameters (such as different sequencing, timing, or error correction), the two computers won't be able to communicate with each other.

Network Packets

Networks primarily send and receive small chunks of data called *packets.* Network protocols at various levels of the OSI model construct, modify, and disassemble packets as they move data down the sending stack, across the network, and back up the OSI stack of the receiving computer. Packets have the following components:

- A source address specifying the sending computer
- A destination address specifying where the packet is being sent
- Instructions that tell the computer how to pass the data along
- Reassembly information (if the packet is part of a longer message)
- The data to be transmitted to the remote computer (often called the *packet payload*)
- Error-checking information to ensure that the data arrives intact

These components are assembled into slightly larger chunks; each packet contains three distinct parts (listed here and seen in Figure 2.2), and each part contains some of the components listed above:

Header A typical header includes an alert signal to indicate that the data is being transmitted, source and destination addresses, and clock information to synchronize the transmission.

Data This is the actual data being sent. It can vary (depending on the network type) from 48 bytes to 4 kilobytes.

Trailer The contents of the trailer (or even the existence of a trailer) vary among network types, but it typically includes a cyclical redundancy check (CRC). The CRC helps the network determine whether or not a packet has been damaged in transmission.

FIGURE 2.2 The structure of a packet

Protocols and Binding

Many different protocol stacks can perform network functions, and many different types of network interface cards can be installed in a computer. A computer may have more than one card, and a computer may use more than one protocol stack at the same time.

Protocol binding is what links the protocol stack to the network device driver for the network interface adapter. Several protocols can be bound to the same card; for instance, both TCP/IP and NWLink can be bound to the same Ethernet adapter. In addition, one computer with several interface adapters—for instance, a server that must be able to communicate with both a local area network (LAN) and a network backbone—can have the same protocol bound to two or more network cards.

The binding process can be used throughout the OSI layers to link one protocol stack to another. The device driver (which implements the data link layer) is bound to the network interface card (which implements the physical layer). TCP/IP can be bound to the device driver, and the NetBIOS session layer can be bound to TCP/IP.

Bindings are particularly important to Windows Server 2003, because you'll often want to change the bindings so that protocols you don't need on a particular network aren't bound to some network adapters. For example, it's very common to unbind the NetBIOS protocol from the network card connected to a web server's Internet connection.

Connectionless versus Connection-Oriented Protocols

Communication between computers can be arranged in one of two ways: connectionless and connection-oriented. Understanding the differences between them is important because different Windows Server 2003 services use both types. We will look at them separately in the following sections.

Connectionless Protocols

Talking about a connectionless protocol for a network might seem like an oxymoron, but you use at least two connectionless protocols just about every day: radio and television. *Connectionless protocols* optimistically assume that all data will get through, so the protocol doesn't guarantee delivery or correct packet ordering. Think of shouting a message out of your window to someone walking by outside—there's no guarantee that they'll hear you, but it's quick and easy. These optimistic assumptions mean that no protocol overhead is spent on these activities, so connectionless protocols tend to be fast. The Internet Protocol (IP), part of the TCP/IP protocol standard, is an example of a connectionless Internet transport protocol. IP provides logical addressing and provides a best-effort delivery of packets (datagrams). IP's role in transmitting datagrams is analogous to writing an address on an envelope and dropping it in a mailbox, with faith that the postal service will do the rest. The User Datagram Protocol (UDP), part of the TCP/IP protocol standard, is another example of a connectionless Internet transport protocol.

Connectionless systems normally work well on lightly loaded networks such as most local area networks. Unfortunately, they break down quickly in large or heavily loaded networks where packets can be dropped due to line noise or router congestion.

All is not lost for connectionless transports, however, because higher-level protocols will know what data has not reached its destination after some time and request a retransmission. However, connectionless systems don't necessarily return data in sequential order, so the higher-level protocol must sort out the data packets.

Connection-Oriented Protocols

Connection-oriented systems work more closely to the way your telephone does—you have to dial a number and establish a connection to the other end before you can send a message. *Connection-oriented protocols* pessimistically assume that some data will be lost or disordered in most transmissions. They guarantee that transmitted data will reach its destination in the proper sequence and that all data will get through. To accomplish this, connection-oriented protocols retain the transmitted data and negotiate for a retransmission when needed. Once all the needed data has arrived at the remote end, it can be reassembled into its proper sequence and passed to the higher-level protocols. This means that any application can depend on a connection-oriented transport to reliably deliver data exactly as it was transmitted. Transmission Control Protocol (TCP) is an example of a connection-oriented Internet protocol. Layering TCP on top of the IP protocol is analogous to adding registered mail service to all of your outgoing mail. Like registered mail, TCP is an additional service that adds overhead to a packet (the "envelope") but guarantees delivery of the message to the recipient.

For local area systems where data isn't likely to be dropped, it makes sense to push serialization and guaranteed delivery up to higher-level protocols that are less efficient because they won't be used often anyway. But in wide area networks (WANs) like the Internet, it would simply take too much time for higher-level protocols to sort out what data had been sent and what was missing, so the transport protocol takes measures to guarantee that all the data gets through in order.

Network Protocols and Windows Server 2003

Network protocols exist to enable clients and servers to communicate across a network. TCP/IP is the most common network protocol in use in modern networks. TCP/IP is required to use Active Directory and is the default protocol for Windows Server 2003. However, Windows Server 2003 includes the AppleTalk network protocol for compatibility with Macintosh computers and NWLink for compatibility with NetWare file servers and networks. NetBEUI is finally being phased out, and it is no longer included in Windows Server 2003. Network protocols are installed by adding a network protocol, by adding a client service, or by downloading and/or installing the protocol if it is not included with Windows Server 2003. A brief discussion of NetBEUI, NWLink, and TCP/IP follows.

NetBEUI

Since the days of peer-to-peer networking, Windows-based computers have referred to each other by using NetBIOS names. *Network Basic Input/Output System (NetBIOS)* provided a method by which Windows-based computers could find each other and locate resources on the network. NetBIOS Extended User Interface (NetBEUI) is a nonroutable protocol that was developed to handle NetBIOS traffic. IBM developed NetBEUI in the mid-1980s to support small LAN workgroups of 2 to 200 user computers under OS/2 and LAN Manager. Modern networks need a more robust solution, and WINS was developed for that purpose. A WINS server can resolve NetBIOS names to IP addresses on behalf of clients, and the WINS server uses TCP/IP to communicate, so NetBEUI has become obsolete.

Microsoft no longer supports NetBEUI, but you can still install the protocol if needed. Just manually copy the necessary files from the Windows Server 2003 CD to the server's hard drive.

NetBIOS name resolution through WINS is covered in detail in Chapter 5, "Planning a WINS Strategy."

AppleTalk

The *AppleTalk* protocol is included for compatibility with Macintosh computers. AppleTalk is installed as a network protocol through the Properties tab of a given network connection.

NWLink

NWLink is Microsoft's implementation of Novell's IPX/SPX protocol stack, which is used in Novell NetWare. Think of NWLink as IPX for Windows, where NWLink is the networking component that implements the network protocol IPX.

IPX is included with Windows Server 2003 primarily to allow Windows Server 2003 to interconnect with "legacy" Novell NetWare servers and networks.

Microsoft's intent remains to make it easy to "enhance" existing NetWare installations with Windows clients and servers, conveniently easing the eventual assimilation of Novell networks.

NWLink is bundled as a component of the Client Service for Netware client service and is automatically installed when you install that client.

TCP/IP

TCP/IP is by far the most widely used protocol for interconnecting computers across networks and the Internet. It is routable and supports multiple platforms, and it features centralized numbering and name assignment, which enables support for advanced name and address resolution services including DNS and the Dynamic Host Control Protocol (DHCP). TCP/IP is actually a suite of protocols that serve a variety of functions in addition to the routing and addressing functions of the protocols TCP and IP.

Most networks, whether they are Windows-based or Unix-based, use *IP version 4 (IPv4)*. IPv6 is the newest version of the protocol suite and in the coming years will replace IPv4. For now, it is backward-compatible with IPv4 so that network engineers can plan a gradual migration to the new version.

In network communications, TCP handles connection-oriented matters such as flow control and error control, while IP handles addressing and routing functions.

For the remainder of this chapter, only TCP/IP will be discussed. For further discussion on implementing NetBIOS for backward compatibility with legacy networks—that is, networks that aren't composed of all Windows 200*x*/XP or higher computers—see Chapter 5.

Planning an IP Routing Strategy

With the physical and logical structure of the network taking shape, we can design a strategy for routing IP traffic across the network.

Routing simply describes the process of moving data across network dividing lines. We'll discuss IP's functions in detail later in this chapter, but for now it is enough to know that it handles individual node and network addresses, as well as subnet masking. Specialized routing protocols function to determine the best path available from Point A to Point Z based on the network identity provided by IP.

In the following sections, you'll learn how to decide between hardware versus software routing, static routing versus dynamic routing protocols, and distance vector versus link state routing protocols.

Hardware versus Software Routing

Dedicated hardware routers handle heavier routing demands better than software-based routing. However, Windows Server 2003 includes routing capabilities; therefore, you can use a Windows Server 2003 computer as a cost-effective way to handle light routing loads.

Routers work at Layer 3 of the OSI model, the Network Layer. Interconnecting devices such as bridges and switches function at OSI Layer 2, the Data Link Layer. Because a router has greater overhead demands, it will have relatively higher latency than less intelligent interconnecting devices.

However, enterprise internetworks that are subdivided into numerous segments will require a variety of hardware routers with different functionality at various locations on the internetwork.

You can choose to mix the two, so that you have a combination of hardware and software routing.

Windows Server 2003 offers a software-based routing solution, the Routing and Remote Access Service (RRAS), which you may choose to implement in a small, segmented network where there is relatively light traffic between subnets. This can save the cost of a dedicated hardware router, and it can add up to a more cost-effective implementation of routing in small or medium networks.

Static versus Dynamic Routing

Routers use either static or dynamic routing to obtain route information. Static routing allows a systems engineer to manually enter route information and manage local routing tables on a given server. Static routes must be used on a dial-on demand interface.

Dynamic routing is an IP-based routing protocol that gets the route information dynamically and uses it to build the routing table on a given router, share information with other routers, and calculate the best path to the destination on the fly.

You can even choose to implement dynamic routing for the most part but use static routing on some paths (for example, to force traffic over a given path that is longer but includes a high-bandwidth link). You can also add a static route as a redundant backup. We will look at both static and dynamic routing a bit more in-depth in the following sections.

Routing is covered in detail in Chapter 3.

Static Routing

In *static routing*, a systems engineer uses the `route add` command to manually enter the following route information on a given server:

- The IP address of the destination network
- The IP address of an adjacent router (referred to as the *next hop*)
- The metric for the given path, based on the number of router hops. This will be used to calculate the best path.
- The number of the router port interface from which the packets will travel to their destination

Static routing doesn't scale well. As a manual process, it is prone to simple human errors which can lead to huge problems on the network. Even worse, it cannot adapt to topology changes. Therefore, when you add or remove routers, you must visit every routing device to make the change to the local routing table.

The differences between static and dynamic routing are comparable to the differences between administering domain name resolution manually via the local `HOSTS` file and dynamically via DNS.

Dynamic Routing

In *dynamic routing*, routable data protocols (such as the TCP/IP or IPX network protocol suites) carry traffic from a sending computer to a destination computer. IP-based routing protocols work with routable data protocols but they are different in that they are specialized protocols used by routers to communicate reachability details to one another, as well as determine the best path to a destination network.

The routing protocol establishes a metric based on the number of hops to a destination network. The router then uses this metric to compare potential paths and select the best path to the destination network. Routing tables map destination network IDs to the IP address of the next hop.

Routing protocols also enable routers to share routing information with each other. Dynamic IP routers update their routing tables automatically.

The types of dynamic routing protocols include distance vector and link-state routing protocols.

Distance Vector Protocols

A *distance vector routing protocol* broadcasts 2 pieces of information: the distance and the vector. The *distance* is the number of hop counts to a network destination, and the *vector* is the direction in which a network destination can be reached. This information is calculated using the distance vector or the Bellman-Ford algorithm.

A router sends updates to its immediate neighbors at regularly scheduled intervals, at which each neighbor then adds its own distance value to the table and forwards it on to its immediate neighbors. This eventually results in a cumulative table with the distances to each network destination.

While they improve upon static routing, distance vector protocols can take several minutes to detect and correct for topology changes.

However, they're simple, and simple can be good—especially when it relates to easy configuration and administration. Therefore, if you have a smaller network and can live with lower performance, distance vector is your routing protocol.

Most of the distance vector protocols calculate routing metrics by using a *hop count*. The hop count is the number of routers that a datagram must cross through to get to its destination. The *routing metric* is a number used to weight a given route so that the router can pick the best path out of several potential routes.

Routing Information Protocol (RIP) is the most widely used of the distance vector protocols. RIP version 1 (RIP v1) was the first routing protocol used with TCP/IP. RIP version 2 (RIP v2) provides new features including authentication support, multicast announcing, and better support for classless networks.

With RIP, the maximum hop count from the first router to the destination is 15, meaning that you can't have more than 15 routers in a group, and any destination over 15 hops away is deemed unreachable. But if you're smart about it, and you use a hierarchical structure, 15 hops can cover you for an awful lot of destinations. The Windows Server 2003 version of RIP v1 supports 14 hops. Windows Server 2003 also supports RIP v2.

Link State Protocols

Link state routing protocols offer faster convergence and are more scalable, more reliable, and require less bandwidth than distance vector protocols. They have a downside though: they're also more complex and resource-intensive, so memory or processor speed may become an issue.

Unlike the chatty distance vector protocols that broadcast updates to every router in the group at regular intervals, link state protocols only send updates when a network link changes state—hence the name. A change in the state of a network link triggers a link-state advertisement, which is then broadcast as a notification to the other routers.

The *Open Shortest Path First (OSPF)* protocol is the most popular link-state routing protocol. OSPF compiles a complete topological database of the internetwork. RIP calculates the cost of each path strictly by hop count. OSPF uses a different algorithm, the shortest path first (SPF), or Djikstra algorithm, to calculate the least-cost path, enabling it to base its decision on a calculation of several metrics such as link speed and reliability in addition to hop count. This obviously makes it even more reliable and faster than RIP.

Other advantages of OSPF over RIP include no limit on hop counts, reduced processor demand in LAN environments due to multicast frames, and the ability to hierarchically structure the router area into subdivisions, thereby reducing memory and CPU overhead on a router. It also supports variable-length subnet masks and noncontiguous subnets, which we'll cover later in this chapter in the section on "Analyzing IP Addressing Requirements".

When considering which type of routing protocol to use in your network, you should use a simpler distance vector routing protocol (such as RIP) only if you have a small and simple network and you do not anticipate future growth. If you have a large, complex network, use a newer, more sophisticated link-state routing protocol such as OSPF.

RIP v1 is still widely in use in private networks, but it does not support VLSM and is not recommended for use in enterprise environments. Use RIPv2 or OSPF if you need to support variable length subnet masks (VLSM), which are covered later in this chapter.

Understanding IP Addressing

Understanding IP addressing is critical to understanding how TCP/IP works and, therefore, knowing how to successfully implement it in your internetwork environment. We'll take a step back to review the key concepts in IP addressing and subnetting because the rest of the chapter assumes a high level of familiarity with these concepts. You should also be familiar with binary notation and binary-to-decimal conversion.

The fastest way to accomplish binary-to-decimal and decimal-to-binary conversion, as well as hexadecimal conversion, is to use the Calculator. In the menu bar, choose View ➤ Scientific. Use either the radio buttons or the appropriate function keys to toggle between Hex (F5), Dec (F6), or Bin (F8) formats.

Pay special attention to the problems and solutions presented in this book, because the design process brings everything together. In the following sections, we'll review the hierarchical IP addressing scheme and the network address classes in preparation for the subnetting discussion to follow.

The Hierarchical IP Addressing Scheme

An IP address is a numeric identifier assigned to each machine on a TCP/IP network. It designates the location of the device it is assigned to on the network. This is the software address, so don't confuse it with the hardware address (referred to as the MAC address), which is hard-coded in the device or network interface card.

An IP address is made up of 32 bits of information. These bits are divided into four sections (sometimes called *octets* or *quads*) containing one byte (8 bits) each. There are three methods for specifying an IP address:

- Dotted-decimal, as in `130.57.30.56`
- Binary, as in `10000010.00111001.00011110.00111000`
- Hexadecimal, as in `82 39 1E 38`

All of these examples represent the same IP address.

The 32-bit IP address is a structured or hierarchical address, as opposed to a flat or nonhierarchical one. A good example of a flat addressing scheme is a driver's license number. In some states, the range of legal numbers on a driver's license isn't broken up in any meaningful way (say, by county of residence or date of issuance). There's no partitioning to the sequence of numbers. If this method had been used for IP addressing, every machine on the Internet would have needed a totally unique address, just as each driver's license number is unique. The good news about flat addressing is that it can handle a large number of addresses, namely 4.3 billion (a 32-bit address space with two possible values for each position—either zero or one—giving you 2^{32}, which equals approximately 4.3 billion). However, if every address were totally unique, every router on the Internet would need to store the address of each and every *other* machine on the Internet. Efficient routing would not be possible, even if only a fraction of the possible addresses were used.

This is why the IP-addressing scheme uses a hierarchical addressing scheme, which breaks the address space up into ordered chunks. Telephone numbers are a great example of this type of addressing. The first section of a telephone number, the area code, designates a very large area; the area code is followed by the prefix, which narrows the scope to a local calling area. The final segment, the customer number, zooms in on the specific connection. At a glance, you can quickly determine that the number 415-626-*xxxx* is located in the San Francisco Bay Area (area code 415) in the metropolitan San Francisco area (the 626 exchange).

IP addresses work the same way as phone numbers. Instead of treating the entire 32 bits as a unique identifier, one part of the IP address is designated as the network address, and the other part as a node address, giving it a layered, hierarchical structure. The network address uniquely identifies each network. Every machine on the same network shares that network address as part of its IP address. In the IP address `130.57.30.56`, for example, the `130.57` is the network address.

The node address (or host address) is assigned to, and uniquely identifies, each machine in a network. This part of the address must be unique because it identifies a particular machine—an individual, as opposed to a network that is a group. This number can also be referred to as a host address. In the sample IP address `130.57.30.56`, the `.30.56` is the node address.

Network Address Classes

The designers of the Internet decided to create classes of networks based on network size. Table 2.1 provides a summary of the three classes of networks, which will be described in more detail in the following sections.

TABLE 2.1 Network Address Classes

Class	Format	Leading Bit Pattern in Binary Notation	Decimal Range of First Byte of Network Address	Maximum Number of Networks	Maximum Nodes per Network
A	Node	0	1 to 126	126 ($2^7 - 2$)	16,777,214 ($2^{24} - 2$)
B	Node	10	128 to 191	16,384 (2^{14})	65,534 ($2^{16} - 2$)
C	Node	110	192 to 223	2,097,152 (2^{21})	254 ($2^8 - 2$)

Class A format is `Network.Node.Node.Node`.

Class B format is `Network.Network.Node.Node`.

Class C format is `Network.Network.Network.Node`.

To ensure efficient routing, the Internet's designers defined a mandate for the leading-bits section of the address for each different network class. For example, because a router knows that a Class A network address always starts with a zero in binary notation, the router might be able to speed a packet on its way after reading only the first bit of its address. The chart illustrates how the leading bits of a network address are defined.

The maximum number of networks is 2 raised to the power of the number of bits available for manipulation in the network address. The maximum nodes per network is 2 raised to the power of the number of bits in the host address *minus* 2—you can't count the "all zeros" or the "all ones" addresses. Also note that Class A loses two of its potential maximum number of networks due to the fact that the "all zeros" (0.0.0.0) and 127 network addresses are reserved.

Some IP addresses are reserved for special purposes and shouldn't be assigned to nodes. Table 2.2 lists the members of this exclusive club, along with the reason for their exclusion.

TABLE 2.2 Special Network Addresses

Address	Function
Network portion of the address set to all zeros	Refers to "this network" (that is, the network or subnet to which a node belongs).

TABLE 2.2 Special Network Addresses *(continued)*

Address	Function
Network portion of the address set to all 1s	This network and all related subnets.
Network address 127	Reserved for loopback tests. Designates the local node and allows that node to send a test packet to itself without generating network traffic.
Node address of all zeros	Used when referencing a network without referring to any specific nodes on that network. Usually used in routing tables.
Node address of all 1s	Broadcast address for all nodes on the specified network (for example, 128.2.255.255 means all nodes on network 128.2, a Class B address).
Entire IP address set to all zeros	Used by the RIP protocol to designate the default route.
Entire IP address set to all 1s (same as 255.255.255.255)	Broadcast to all nodes on the current network. Sometimes called an "all ones broadcast."

Class D networks, used for multicasting only, use the address range 224.0.0.0 to 239.255.255.255. Class E networks (reserved for experimental and future use) cover 240.0.0.0 through 255.255.255.255.

Subnetting a Network

If an organization is large and has lots of computers, or if its computers are geographically dispersed, it makes good sense to divide its large physical and logical network into smaller ones connected together by routers. These smaller nets are called *subnets*. The benefits to using subnets include the following:

Reduced Network Traffic Without routers, packet traffic could choke the entire network. With routers, most traffic will stay on the local network—only packets destined for remote networks will pass through the router and over to another subnet. This traffic reduction also improves overall performance.

Simplified Management In a medium to large organization, it is easier to identify and isolate network problems in an interconnected group of smaller networks than it is within a single, all-encompassing enterprise network.

The original designers of the IP protocol envisioned a small Internet with just tens of networks and hundreds of hosts. Their addressing scheme used a network address for each physical network. As you can imagine, this scheme and the unforeseen growth of the Internet have created a few problems.

Due to the exponential growth rate of the Internet and inherent difficulties in obtaining accurate host counts, no one actually *knows* exactly how many computers are on the Internet today. The Internet Software Consortium reports a host count of 171,638,297 as of January, 2003 (Source: Internet Software Consortium (http://www.isc.org/) "Internet Domain Survey, Jan 2003"). RFC1296 discusses the potential problems with obtaining an accurate count of hosts on the Internet.

To name one problem with the address scheme, a single network address can be used to refer to multiple physical networks. However, an organization can request individual network addresses for each one of its physical networks. If these requests were granted, there wouldn't be enough addresses to go around. Another problem relates to routers—if each router on the Internet needed to know about every physical network, routing tables would be impossibly huge. There would be an overwhelming amount of administrative overhead to maintain those tables, and the resulting physical overhead on the routers (in terms of CPU cycles, memory, disk space, and so on) would be massive. Because routers exchange routing information with each other, an additional, related consequence would be that a terrific overabundance of network traffic would result.

Although there's more than one way to approach this dilemma, the principal solution is the one that will be covered in this book—subnetting. As you might guess, *subnetting* is the process of carving a single IP network into smaller logical subnetworks. This trick is achieved by subdividing the host portion of an IP address to create something called a *subnet address*. The actual subdivision is accomplished through the use of a *subnet mask*.

In the following sections, we'll cover the fundamental concepts of subnetting and give you powerful shortcuts that will enable you to easily and rapidly calculate subnets. You'll then get to practice by example.

Subnetting Concepts

Before you can implement subnetting, you need to determine your current requirements and plan how best to implement your subnet scheme. Follow these guidelines:

- Determine the number of required network IDs: one for each subnet and one for each WAN connection.
- Determine the number of required host IDs per subnet: one for each TCP/IP device, including computers, network printers, and router interfaces (simply, any device that contains a NIC card).

Based on these two data points, you need to create:

- One subnet mask for your entire network
- A unique subnet ID for each physical segment
- A range of host IDs for each unique subnet

An organization with a single network address can have a subnet address for each individual physical network, in the same way that children are given distinct first names but inherit the family surname to distinguish that they actually belong to the same family. Unique first names are like subnet addresses for people. It's important to remember that each subnet is still part of the shared network address, but it also has an additional identifier denoting its individual subnetwork number. This identifier is called a *subnet address.*

Subnetting solves several addressing problems. First, if an organization has several physical networks but only one IP network address, it can handle the situation by creating subnets. Next, because subnetting allows many physical networks to be grouped together, fewer entries in a routing table are required, notably reducing network overhead. Finally, these things combine to collectively yield greatly enhanced network efficiency.

The following sections discuss how subnetting is used to hide information from public exposure, how to subnet a network, and how to calculate the number of subnets to be yielded by a given subnet mask.

Many new laptops come with a built-in wireless network interface. Remember to count this interface when determining the total number of IP addresses needed. Otherwise you could run out of IP addresses, as did a client of ours when they bought 20 new laptops and exceeded the allowable number of IPs on the subnet.

Information Hiding

Subnetting is often used to hide information from public scrutiny. Let's use the classic Widget, Inc. in an example. Suppose that the routers on the Internet are configured to refer to a single network address, `130.57`. Widget's systems engineers can implement subnetting to hide the corporate intranet from public view. To do this, they would use one IP addressing scheme for externally visible resources and a different IP addressing scheme for internal resources so that these resources cannot be accessed directly from the outside world. The routers on the Internet see only one external address for the Widget network. The internal Widget routers use the subnet addresses to route the packets to the correct internal subnet when packets come into Widget's corporate network. Therefore, the complexity of Widget, Inc.'s network can be hidden from the rest of the Internet. This is called *information hiding.*

Information hiding also benefits the routers inside the Widget network. Without subnets, each Widget router would need to know the address of each machine on the entire Widget network—causing additional overhead and poor routing performance. The subnet scheme eliminates the need for each router to know about every machine on the entire Widget network. Their routers need only the following two types of information:

- The addresses of the subnets to which they are attached
- The other subnet addresses

How to Subnet a TCP/IP Network

Subnetting is implemented by assigning a subnet address to each machine on a given physical network. For example, in Figure 2.3, each machine on Subnet 1 has the subnet address 1.

Next, you'll see how a subnet address is incorporated into the rest of the IP address.

The network portion of an IP address can't be altered. Every machine on a particular network must share the same network address. In Figure 2.3, you can see that all of Widget, Inc.'s machines have the network address `130.57`. That principle is constant. In subnetting, the host address is the one that's manipulated; the network address doesn't change. The subnet address scheme takes a part of the host address and recycles it as a subnet address. Bit positions are "borrowed" from the host address to be used for the subnet identifier. Figure 2.4 shows how an IP address can be given a subnet address.

FIGURE 2.3 The Widget, Inc. network and subnets

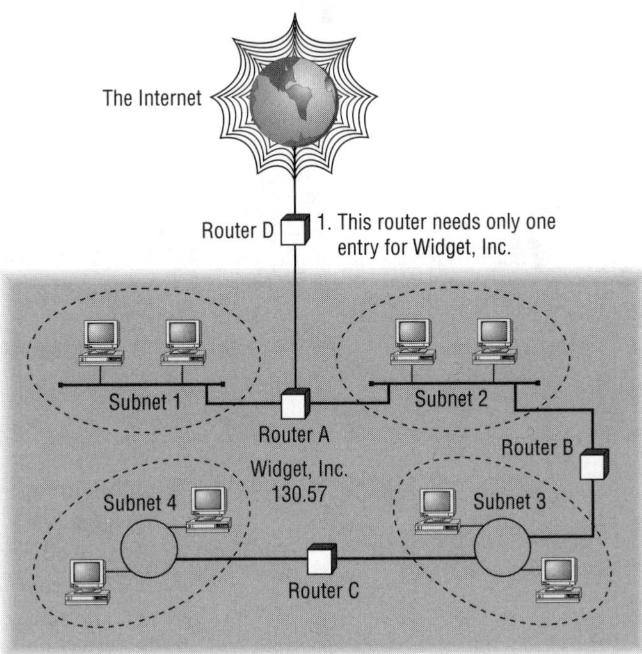

FIGURE 2.4 Network versus host addresses

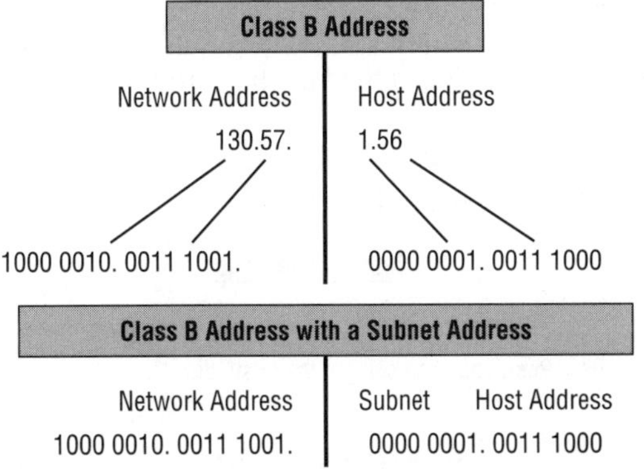

Because the Widget, Inc. network is a Class B network, the first 2 bytes specify the network address and are shared by all machines on the network—regardless of their particular subnet. Here, every machine's address on the subnet must have its third byte read 0000 0001. The fourth byte, the host address, is the unique number that identifies the actual host within that subnet. Figure 2.5 illustrates how a network address and a subnet address can be used together.

FIGURE 2.5 A subnet in the Widget, Inc. network

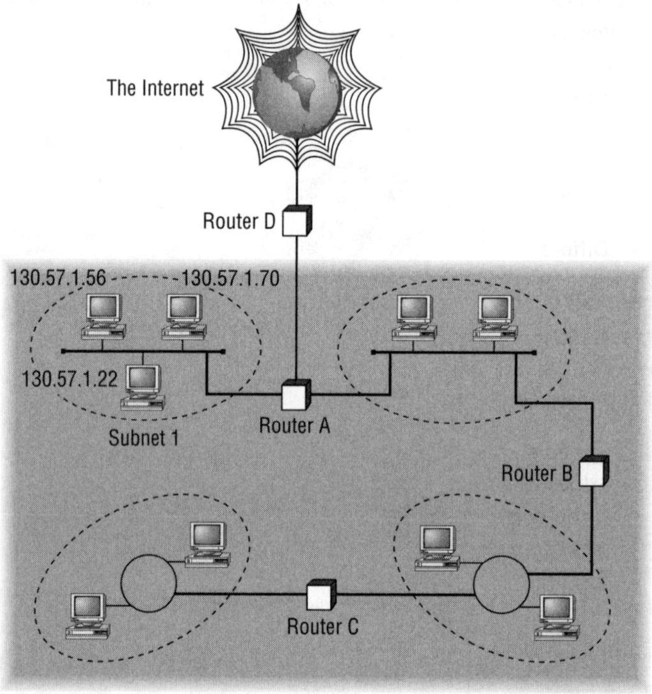

For the subnet address scheme to work, every machine on the network must know which part of the host address will be used as the subnet address. This is accomplished by assigning each machine a subnet mask.

The systems engineer creates a 32-bit subnet mask comprised of ones and zeros. The ones in the subnet mask represent the positions that refer to the network or subnet addresses. The zeros represent the positions that refer to the host part of the address. This combination is illustrated in Figure 2.6.

FIGURE 2.6 The subnet mask revealed

Subnet Mask Code

1s = Positions representing network or subnet addresses

0s = Positions representing the host address

Subnet Mask for Widget, Inc.

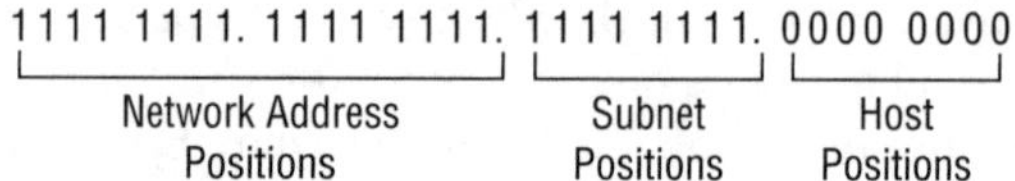

In our Widget, Inc. example, the first 2 bytes of the subnet mask are ones because Widget's network address is a Class B address, formatted as `Network.Network.Node.Node`. The third byte, normally assigned as part of the host address, is now used to represent the subnet address. Hence, those bit positions are represented with ones in the subnet mask. The fourth byte is the only part in our example that represents the unique host address.

The subnet mask can also be expressed using the decimal equivalents of the binary patterns. The binary pattern of 1111 1111 is the same as decimal 255. Consequently, the subnet mask in our example can be denoted in two ways, as shown in Figure 2.7.

FIGURE 2.7 Different ways to represent the same mask

Subnet Mask in Binary: 1111 1111. 1111 1111. 1111 1111. 0000 0000

Subnet Mask in Decimal: 255 . 255 . 255 . 0

(The spaces in the above example are only for illustrative purposes.
The subnet mask in decimal would actually appear as 255.255.255.0.)

Not all networks need to have subnets. Therefore, not all networks need to use subnet masks. If a network does not specify a subnet mask, it uses the default subnet mask. (This is the same as saying the network doesn't have a subnet address.) The default subnet masks for the different classes of networks are shown in Table 2.3. (Now you know the origin of the familiar `255.255.255.0`!)

TABLE 2.3 Special Network Addresses

Class	Format	Default Subnet Mask
A	`Network.Node.Node.Node`	`255.0.0.0`
B	`Network.Network.Node.Node`	`255.255.0.0`
C	`Network.Network.Network.Node`	`255.255.255.0`

Once the systems engineer has created the subnet mask and assigned it to each machine, the IP software applies the subnet mask to the IP address to determine its subnet address. The word "mask" carries the implied meaning of "lens" in this case—the IP software looks at its IP address through the lens of its subnet mask to see its subnet address. An illustration of an IP address being viewed through a subnet mask is shown in Figure 2.8.

In this example, the IP software learns through the subnet mask that, instead of being part of the host address, the third byte of its IP address is now going to be used as a subnet address. The IP software then looks at the bit positions in its IP address that correspond to the mask, which are 0000 0001.

The final step is for the subnet bit values to be matched up with the binary numbering convention and converted to decimal. In the Widget, Inc. example, the binary-to-decimal conversion is simple, as illustrated in Figure 2.9.

FIGURE 2.8 Applying the subnet mask

Subnet Mask Code

1s = Positions representing network or subnet addresses
0s = Positions representing the host address

Positions relating to the subnet address.

Subnet Mask:	1111 1111. 1111 1111. 1111 1111. 0000 0000
IP address of a machine on subnet 1:	1000 0010. 0011 1001. 0000 0001. 0011 1000
(Decimal: 130.57.1.56)	

Bits relating to the subnet address.

FIGURE 2.9 Converting the subnet mask to decimal

Binary Numbering Convention

Position/Value: ←— (continued)	128 64 32 16 8 4 2 1
Widget third byte:	0 0 0 0 0 0 0 1
Decimal Equivalent:	0 + 1 = 1
Subnet Address:	1

By using the entire third byte of a Class B address as the subnet address, it is easy to set and determine the subnet address. For example, if Widget, Inc. wants to have a Subnet 6, the third byte of all machines on that subnet will be 0000 0110 (decimal 6 in binary).

Using the entire third byte of a Class B network address for the subnet allows for a fair number of available subnet addresses. One byte dedicated to the subnet provides eight bit positions. Each position can be either a one or a zero, so the calculation is 2^8, or 256. Because you cannot use the two patterns of all zeros and all ones, you must subtract two for a total of 254. Thus our Widget, Inc. can have up to 254 total subnetworks, each with up to 254 hosts.

Although the official IP specification limits the use of zero as a subnet address, some products actually permit this usage. Microsoft's TCP/IP stack allows it, as does the software in most routers (provided you enable this feature). This gives you one additional subnet. However, you should not use a subnet of zero (all zeros) unless all of the software on your network recognizes this convention.

Using Subnet Masks to Determine Network and Host Portions of IP Addresses

Computers use Boolean calculations to determine which portion of the IP address is allocated to the network identification and which is allocated to the host address. The calculation process is called *ANDing.* In the ANDing operation, binary ones and zeros are added together. All operations (0 + 0, 0 + 1, 1 + 0) result in 0, except 1 + 1 (which results in 1).

In the process of ANDing, the computer compares a subnet mask to an IP address, for example:

Subnet mask	255.255.255.0	11111111.11111111.11111111.00000000
IP address	192.168.7.5	11000000.10101000.00000111.00000101
Result =	192.168.7.0	11000000.10101000.00000111.00000000

In this example, the network portion of the address is identified as 192.168.7.0. To compute the host portion of the address, the subnet mask is inverted and the operation becomes:

Inverted subnet mask	255.255.255.0	00000000.00000000.00000000.11111111
IP address	192.168.7.5	11000000.10101000.00000111.00000101
Result =	0.0.0.5	00000000.00000000.00000000.00000101

Thus, the host portion of the address is identified as 0.0.0.5.

All of these binary calculations become tedious, so you'll be relieved to know that there are shortcuts you can use. These shortcuts are discussed in the sidebar "Subnetting Shortcuts" later in this chapter.

Calculating the Number of Subnets

The formulas for calculating the maximum number of subnets and the maximum number of hosts per subnet are listed here:

- 2^x number of masked bits in subnet mask – 2 = maximum number of subnets
- 2^x number of unmasked bits in subnet mask – 2 = maximum number of hosts per subnet

Technically speaking, the number of subnets is actually the difference between the lowest significant bit in the subnet mask and the lowest significant bit in the default subnet mask. You'll probably find it much easier to think of it this way.

In the formulas, *masked bits* refers to bit positions of 1, and *unmasked bits* refers to positions of 0. The downside to using an entire byte of a node address as your subnet address is that you reduce the possible number of node addresses on each subnet. As explained earlier, a Class B address without subnetting has 65,534 unique combinations of ones and zeros that can be used for node addresses.

If you use an entire byte of the node address for subnetting, you then have only one byte remaining for the host addresses, leaving only 254 possible host addresses. If any of your subnets will be populated with more than 254 machines, you have a problem. To solve it, you would then need to shorten the subnet mask, thereby lengthening the number of bits available for the host address; this gives you more available host addresses on each subnet. A side effect of this solution is that it shrinks the number of available subnets.

Figure 2.10 shows an example of using a smaller subnet address. A company called Acme, Inc. expects to need a maximum of 14 subnets. In this case, Acme does not need to take an entire byte from the host address for the subnet address. To get its 14 different subnet addresses, it only needs to snatch 4 bits from the host address ($2^4 - 2 = 14$). The host portion of the address has 12 usable bits remaining ($2^{12} - 2 = 4{,}094$). Each of Acme's 14 subnets could then potentially have a total of 4,094 host addresses; 4,094 machines on each subnet should be plenty.

FIGURE 2.10 An example of a smaller subnet address

Acme, Inc.

Network Address: 132.8 (Class B; net.net.host.host)
Example IP Address: 1000 0100. 0000 1000. 0001 0010. 0011 1100
Decimal: 132 . 8 . 18 . 60

Subnet Mask Code

1s = Positions representing network or subnet addresses
0s = Positions representing the host address

Subnet Mask:
Binary: 1111 1111. 1111 1111. 1111 0000. 0000 0000
Decimal: 255 . 255 . 240 . 0
(The decimal '240' is equal to the binary '1111 0000.')

Positions relating to the subnet address.

Subnet Mask: 1111 1111. 1111 1111. 1111 0000. 0000 0000
IP address of a Acme machine: 1000 0100. 0000 1000. 0001 0010. 0011 1100
(Decimal: 132.8.18.60)

Bits relating to the subnet address.

Binary to Decimal Conversion for Subnet Address

Subnet Mask Positions:	1	1	1	1	0	0	0	0
	↓	↓	↓	↓				
Position/Value: ← (continue)	128	64	32	16	8	4	2	1
Third Byte of IP address:	0	0	0	1	0	0	1	0
Decimal Equivalent:						0 + 16 = 16		
Subnet Address for this IP address:								16

Calculating subnets is easy once you have the right tools. Memorize the values in the sidebar titled "Subnetting Shortcuts." They will give you the power to rapidly calculate subnets on the fly, and thus assist you tremendously on the exam and in real life.

Subnetting Shortcuts

IP addresses are 32-bit values that consist of four octets, or four sets of 8 bits each. They can be expressed in binary format, such as 10101100.00010000.00000111.00000101, or in decimal format, as in 172.16.7.5. Each bit place in binary represents a decimal value. Decimal values of the bit places, from left to right, are as follows:

128	64	32	16	8	4	2	1

In binary, each bit place can represent a value of either 1 (on) or 0 (off). Binary-to-decimal conversion is accomplished by adding the bit sums of the positions that are "on"—or in other words, the values of the ones places. Thus, 10101100 becomes 128 + 32 + 8 + 4, or 172.

Subnetting involves "borrowing" bits from the host portion of the address and adding them to the network portion of the address. These borrowed bits are known as "high bits." The "high-bit" sums, or sums of the bit names as added from left to right, are as follows:

10000000 = 128

11000000 = 192

11100000 = 224

11110000 = 240

11111000 = 248

11111100 = 252

11111110 = 254

11111111 = 255

For some, it's easier to understand this by viewing the high-bit sums as they increase in order horizontally:

128	192	224	240	248	252	254	255
1	1	1	1	1	1	1	1

The "high-bit" sum replaces the right-most octet with a zero value in the default subnet mask for a given address class. For example, 255.255.**0**.0, or 11111111.11111111.**000**00000.00000000 becomes 255.255.**224**.0, or 11111111.11111111.**111**00000.00000000 when you borrow 3 bits from the host address. By subtracting the "high-bit" sum (which represents the decimal value of the extra bits borrowed from the host address to add to the network address) from 256 (which represents the number of possible decimal values for the octet, as possible values within the range 0–255 equal 256 because you count the zero), you can determine the base number from which you can calculate the actual network addresses resulting from a subnet mask.

Memorizing the "high-bit" sums will enable you to rapidly calculate the base for the subnets, and thereby determine the actual network addresses. This will become clear through the examples in this book.

In binary, each bit place can represent a value of either 1 or 0. This means each bit place has two possible values. Therefore, to determine the total number of possible values for a portion of a 32-bit IP address, you would raise 2 to the number of bits being used for that portion of the address. By memorizing the powers of 2, you'll be able to rapidly calculate the number of networks available based on the number of bits being used for the network portion of the IP address, and the number of hosts available based on the number of bits being used for the host portion of the IP address. Powers of 2 are as follows:

$2^1 = 2$

$2^2 = 4$

$2^3 = 8$

$2^4 = 16$

$2^5 = 32$

$2^6 = 64$

$2^7 = 128$

$2^8 = 256$

$2^9 = 512$

$2^{10} = 1{,}024$

$2^{11} = 2{,}048$

$2^{12} = 4{,}096$

$2^{13} = 8{,}192$

$2^{14} = 16{,}384$

Once you've memorized these values, you'll be amazed at the intuitive speed with which you can calculate subnets.

Subnetting Examples

Understanding how to apply subnetting is extremely important—both for the exam and in the real world. Now is your opportunity to get some practice applying subnetting. We will begin with Class C because it uses only 8 bits for the node address, so it's the easiest to calculate, not to mention that the vast majority of networks are Class C rather than Class A or Class B.

Because the Class C networks are also running out, there are many networks that now use Classless Inter-Domain Routing (CIDR). We'll discuss classless routing later in the chapter.

Subnetting the Class C Network

As you know, a Class C network uses the first 3 bytes (24 bits) to define the network address. This leaves you 1 byte (8 bits) with which to address hosts. So, if you want to create subnets (out of the last byte), your options are limited because of the small number of bits left available.

If you break down your subnets into chunks smaller than the default Class C, then figuring out the subnet mask, network number, broadcast address, and router address can be kind of confusing. Table 2.4 summarizes how you can break a Class C network down into one, two, four, or eight smaller subnets, with the subnet masks, network numbers, broadcast addresses, and router addresses. The first 3 bytes have simply been designated `x.y.z`. (Note that the table assumes you can use the all-zero subnet, too.)

TABLE 2.4 Class C Subnets

Number of Desired Subnets	Subnet Mask	Network Number	Router Address	Broadcast Address	Remaining Number of IP Addresses
1	255.255.255.0	x.y.z.0	x.y.z.1	x.y.z.255	253
2	255.255.255.128	x.y.z.0	x.y.z.1	x.y.z.127	125
	255.255.255.128	x.y.z.128	x.y.z.129	x.y.z.255	125
4	255.255.255.192	x.y.z.0	x.y.z.1	x.y.z.63	61
	255.255.255.192	x.y.z.64	x.y.z.65	x.y.z.127	61
	255.255.255.192	x.y.z.128	x.y.z.129	x.y.z.191	61
	255.255.255.192	x.y.z.192	x.y.z.193	x.y.z.255	61
8	255.255.255.224	x.y.z.0	x.y.z.1	x.y.z.31	29
	255.255.255.224	x.y.z.32	x.y.z.33	x.y.z.63	29
	255.255.255.224	x.y.z.64	x.y.z.65	x.y.z.95	29
	255.255.255.224	x.y.z.96	x.y.z.97	x.y.z.127	29

TABLE 2.4 Class C Subnets *(continued)*

Number of Desired Subnets	Subnet Mask	Network Number	Router Address	Broadcast Address	Remaining Number of IP Addresses
8 *(cont.)*	255.255.255.224	x.y.z.128	x.y.z.129	x.y.z.159	29
	255.255.255.224	x.y.z.160	x.y.z.161	x.y.z.191	29
	255.255.255.224	x.y.z.192	x.y.z.193	x.y.z.223	29
	255.255.255.224	x.y.z.224	x.y.z.225	x.y.z.255	29

For example, suppose you want to divide a Class C network, `200.211.192.x`, into two subnets. As you can see in the table, you'd use a subnet mask of `255.255.255.128` for each subnet. The first subnet would have network number `200.211.192.0`, router address `200.211.192.1`, and broadcast address `200.211.192.127`. You could assign IP addresses `200.211.192.2` through `200.211.192.126`—that's 125 different IP addresses. (Notice that heavily subnetting a network results in the loss of a progressively greater percentage of addresses to the network number, broadcast address, and router address.) The second subnet would have network number `200.211.192.128`, router address `200.211.192.129`, and broadcast address `200.211.192.255`.

You may ask yourself, How can you subnet a Class C network as in the table above? If you use the $2^x - 2$ calculation, the subnet 128 in the table doesn't make sense! It turns out that there's a legitimate reason to do it this way:

1. Remember that using subnet zero is discouraged—according to the RFCs—but by using it you can subnet your Class C network with a subnet mask of 128. This uses only 1 bit, and according to your trusty calculator, $2^1 - 2 = 0$, giving you zero subnets.
2. By using a router that supports subnet zero, you can assign 1 through 127 for hosts and 129 through 254 as stated in the table. This saves a bunch of addresses! If you were to stick to the method defined by RFC standards, the best you could gain is a subnet mask of 192 (2 bits), which allows you only two subnets ($2^2 - 2 = 2$).

To determine the first subnet number, subtract the subnet mask from 256. Our example yields the following equation: 256 – 192 = 64. Therefore, 64 is your first subnet. The subtraction must occur in the subnetted section of the mask. If you divide that number into 256, it will tell you the number of subnets—in this case, 4 (and then subtract 2 to determine validity).

To determine a second subnet number, add the first subnet number to itself. To determine a third subnet number, add the first subnet number to the second subnet number. To determine a fourth subnet number, add the first subnet number to the third subnet number. Keep adding the first subnet number in this fashion until you reach the actual subnet number. For example, 64 plus 64 equals 128, so your second subnet is 128. 128 plus 64 is 192. Because 192 is the subnet mask, you cannot use it as an actual subnet. This means your valid subnets are 64 and 128.

The numbers between the subnets are your valid hosts. For example, the valid hosts in a Class C network with a subnet mask of 192 are as follows:

- Subnet 64: 65 through 126, which gives you 62 hosts per subnet (using 127 as a host would mean your host bits would be all ones). That's not allowed because the all-ones format is reserved as the broadcast address for that subnet.
- Subnet 128: 129 through 190. What happened to 191 through 254? The subnet mask is 192, which you cannot use, and 191 would be all ones and used as the broadcast address for this subnet. Anything above 192 is also invalid for this subnet because these are automatically lost through the subnetting process.

As you can see, this solution wastes a lot of precious addresses: 130 to be exact! In a Class C network, this would certainly be hard to justify—the 128 subnet is a much better solution if you only need two subnets.

Okay, so what happens if you need four subnets in your Class C network?

By using the calculation of $2x - 2$ (where x is the number of masked bits), you would need 3 bits to get six subnets ($2^3 - 2 = 6$). What are the valid subnets and what are the valid hosts of each subnet? Let's figure it out.

11100000 is 224 in binary and would be our subnet mask. This must be the same on all workstations.

You're likely to see test questions that ask you to identify the problem with a given configuration. If a workstation has the wrong subnet mask, the router could assume that the workstation is on a different subnet than it actually is. When that happens, the misguided router won't forward packets to the workstation in question. Similarly, if the mask is incorrectly specified in the workstation's configuration, that workstation will observe the mask and send packets to the default gateway when it shouldn't.

To figure out the valid subnets, subtract the subnet mask from 256. 256 – 224 = 32, so 32 is your first subnet. The other subnets would be 64 (32 + 32), 96 (64 + 32), 128 (96 + 32), 160 (128 + 32), and 192 (160 + 32). The valid hosts are the numbers between the subnet numbers except the numbers that equal all ones. The all-ones numbers would be 63, 95, 127, 159, and 191. Remember that using all ones is reserved for the broadcast address of each subnet. Your valid hosts are shown in the following list:

Subnet	Hosts
32	33 to 62
64	65 to 94
96	97 to 126
128	129 to 158
160	161 to 190
192	193 to 222

You can add one more bit to the subnet mask. You were using 3 bits, which gave you 224. By adding the next bit, the mask now becomes 240 (11110000).

By using 4 bits for the subnet mask you get 14 subnets because $2^4 - 2 = 14$. This subnet mask also gives you only 4 bits for the host addresses or 14 hosts per subnet. As you can see, the amount of hosts per subnet gets reduced rather quickly when subnetting a Class C network.

The first valid subnet for subnet 240 is 16 (256 – 240 = 16). Your subnets are then 16, 32, 48, 64, 80, 96, 112, 128, 144, 160, 176, 192, 208, and 224. Remember that you cannot use the actual subnet number as a valid subnet, so 240 is invalid as a subnet number. The valid hosts are the numbers between the subnets, except for the numbers that are all ones—the broadcast address for the subnet.

Therefore, your valid subnets and hosts are as follows:

Subnet	Hosts
16	17 to 30
32	33 to 46
48	49 to 62
64	65 to 78
80	81 to 94
96	97 to 110
112	113 to 126
128	129 to 142
144	145 to 158
160	161 to 174
176	177 to 190
192	193 to 206
208	209 to 222
224	225 to 238

Subnetting the Class B Network

Because a Class B network has 16 bits for host addresses, you have plenty of available bits to play with when figuring out a subnet mask. Remember that you have to start with the leftmost bit and work toward the right. For example, a Class B network would look like X.Y.0.0, with the default mask of 255.255.0.0. Using the default mask would give you one network with 65,534 hosts.

The default mask in binary is 11111111.11111111.00000000.00000000. The ones represent the network, and the zeros represent the hosts. So when creating a subnet mask, the leftmost bit(s) will be borrowed from the host bits (the zeros, not the ones) to become the subnet mask. You use the remaining bits available for hosts.

If you use only one bit, you have a mask of 255.255.128.0. This mask will be somewhat harder to subnet than the Class C 128 subnet mask. With 16 bits, you typically don't need to worry about a shortage of host IDs, so using 128 just isn't worth the trouble. The first mask you should use is 255.255.192.0, or 11111111.11111111.11000000.00000000.

You now have the three parts of the IP address: the network address, the subnet address, and the host address. A 192 mask is figured out the same way as a Class C 192 address, but this time you'll end up with a lot more hosts.

There are two subnets because $2^2 - 2 = 2$. The valid subnets are 64 and 128 (256 – 192 = 64, and 64 + 64 = 128). However, there are 14 bits (zeros) left over for host addressing. This gives you 16,382 hosts per subnet ($2^{14} - 2 = 16{,}382$). Here's a list of the range of IP addresses available for hosts in each subnet:

Subnet	Hosts
64	X.Y.64.1 through X.Y.127.254
128	X.Y.128.1 through X.Y.191.254

If you add another bit to our subnet mask, you would make it 11111111.11111111.11100000.00000000 or 255.255.224.0. Now, there are six subnets ($2^3 - 2 = 6$). The valid subnets are 32, 64, 96, 128, 160, and 192 (256 – 224 = 32). The valid hosts are listed below:

Subnet	Hosts
32	X.Y.32.1 through 63.254
64	X.Y.64.1 through 95.254
96	X.Y.96.1 through 127.254
128	X.Y.128.1 through 159.254
160	X.Y.160.1 through 191.254
192	X.Y.192.1 through 223.254

So, if you use a 255.255.224.0 subnet mask, you can create six subnets, each with 8,190 ($2^{13} - 2 = 8{,}190$) hosts per subnet.

You can add a few more bits to the subnet mask to see what happens. If you use 9 bits for the mask, it gives you 510 subnets ($2^9 - 2 = 510$). With only 7 bits for hosts, you still have 126 hosts per subnet ($2^7 - 2 = 126$). The mask looks like this:

11111111.11111111.11111111.10000000 or 255.255.255.128

You could add even more bits to see what you get. If you use 14 bits for the subnet mask, you get 16,382 subnets ($2^{14} - 2 = 16{,}382$), but this gives us only two hosts per subnet ($2^2 - 2 = 2$). The subnet mask would look like this:

11111111.11111111.11111111.11111100 or 255.255.255.252

Why would you ever use a 14-bit subnet mask with a Class B address? Actually, this approach is very common. Think about having a Class B network and using a subnet mask of

255.255.255.0. You'd have 254 subnets and 254 hosts per subnet, right? Imagine also that you have a network with many WAN links. Typically, you'd have a direct connection between each site. Each of these links must be on its own subnet or network. There will be two hosts on these subnets—one address for each router port. If you used the mask as described above (255.255.255.0), you would waste 252 host addresses per subnet. By using the 255.255.255.252 subnet mask, you have many, many subnets available—each with only two hosts. This situation is perfect for a point-to-point WAN link.

You can use this approach only if you are running a routing algorithm like EIGRP or OSPF (which we will talk about later in this book). These routing protocols allow what is called *variable length subnet masks (VLSM)*. VLSM allows you to run the 255.255.255.252 subnet mask on your interface to the WANs and run 255.255.255.0 on your router interfaces in your LAN. It works because routing protocols like EIGRP and OSPF transmit the subnet mask information in the update packets that it sends to the other routers. RIP doesn't transmit the subnet mask and, therefore, cannot use VLSM.

Real World Scenario

Subnetting and the WAN Link

You are the systems engineer of a large enterprise internetwork for a multinational financial corporation with a Class B network address. This network has many WAN links.

There is a direct connection between each physical site. Each of these links must be on its own subnet or network. There will be a total of two hosts on each of these subnets—one address for each router port. Using a subnet mask of 255.255.255.0 results in 254 subnets and 254 hosts per subnet. However, because you only need two host addresses per subnet, this results in 252 wasted host addresses per subnet. How can you design a more efficient subnetting strategy for the WAN links?

You may choose instead to use 14 additional bits for the subnet mask. If you use 14 additional bits for the subnet mask you get 16,382 subnets ($2^{14} - 2 = 16{,}382$), but this gives us only two hosts per subnet ($2^2 - 2 = 2$). The subnet mask would look like this:

11111111.11111111.11111111.11111100 or 255.255.255.252

By using the 255.255.255.252 subnet mask, you have many, many subnets available—each with only two hosts. This approach is a very common solution to the problem of subnetting WAN links.

In this case, you must use a link-state routing protocol such as OSPF (which we discussed earlier in this chapter in the section on routing). OSPF supports what is called *variable length subnet masks (VLSM)*. VLSM allows you to run the 255.255.255.252 subnet mask on your interface to the WANs, and run the 255.255.255.0 subnet mask on the router interfaces in your LAN. This works because routing protocols like OSPF transmit the subnet mask information in the update packets that they send to the other routers. RIP doesn't transmit the subnet mask, and this is the reason it does not support VLSM.

Subnetting the Class A Network

Class A networks have a large number of host bits available. A default Class A network subnet mask is only 8 bits or `255.0.0.0`, giving you a whopping 24 bits for hosts to play with.

If you use a mask of `11111111.1111111.00000000.00000000`, or `255.255.0.0`, you'll have 8 bits for subnets or 254 subnets ($2^8 - 2 = 254$). This leaves 16 bits for hosts, or 65,534 hosts per subnet ($2^{16} - 2 = 65{,}534$). Instead, you could split the 24 bits evenly between subnets and hosts, giving each one 12 bits. The mask would look like this: `11111111.11111111.11110000.00000000` or `255.255.240.0`. This mask has 4,094 valid subnets, each with 4,094 valid hosts ($2^{12} - 2 = 4{,}094$) available. Knowing which hosts and subnets are valid is a lot more complicated than it was for either Class B or C networks.

The second octet will be somewhere between 1 and 254. However, the third octet you will need to figure out. Because the third octet has a 240 mask, you'll get 16 (256 – 240 = 16) as your base subnet number. The third octet must start with 16 and will be the first subnet, the second subnet will be 32, and so on. This means that your valid subnets are as follows:

`X.1-254.16.1` through `X.1-254.31.254`

`X.1-254.32.1` through `X.1-254.47.254`

`X.1-254.48.1` through `X.1-254.63.254`

And so on for the remaining bits.

Microsoft exams have started using a different nomenclature to depict subnetted addressing schemes. This method is known as *CIDR notation*, and it identifies the number of bits used to refer to the network address. For example, an address of `131.107.2.0` with a subnet mask of `255.255.255.0` is listed as `131.107.2.0/24` because the subnet mask contains 24 ones. This address is referred to as a "slash 24 network." An address listed as `141.10.32.0/19` would have a subnet mask of `255.255.224.0`, or 19 ones (default subnet mask for a Class B plus 3 bits), and it would be referred to as a "slash 19 network." CIDR and CIDR notation will be discussed later in this chapter.

Analyzing IP Addressing Requirements

So far, you've learned how to plan a routing strategy, as well as how to implement IP addressing and subnetting. Armed with this knowledge, you are prepared to delve into the process of planning a strategy for TCP/IP implementation.

In the following pages, we'll cover how to design a structured address assignment model, which includes choosing between classful or classless IP addressing, between classful or classless routing, and between flat routing or route summarization. It also includes planning for noncontiguous subnets, planning VLSMs, and planning supernetting and CIDR.

Next, you'll choose a method for address allocation. You'll determine whether to assign IP addresses randomly, by organizational chart, by region, or by topology. You'll choose a public and/or private addressing scheme. You will then choose an IP configuration method (i.e., DHCP).

We begin with the considerations in choosing an address assignment model.

Choosing an Address Assignment Model

A structured address assignment model makes it easier to administer enterprise internetworks. It helps you understand network maps, quickly locate specific devices, and easily employ systematic troubleshooting procedures.

Best practices include assigning address blocks on the basis of the physical network instead of a departmental basis, so that you ensure scalability. This also adds stability to the network's addressing structure and eases administration, for instance when user workstations are moved to a new location.

Routers and servers should be assigned static addresses, while workstations get addresses assigned by the DHCP server. It is best to use meaningful numbers for static addresses, such as reserving addresses at one end of a range for routers or servers.

To design a structured model for assigning addresses, you take the following steps:

- Choose classful or classless IP addressing.
- Choose classful or classless routing.
- Choose flat routing or route summarization.
- Plan noncontiguous subnets.
- Plan variable length subnet masks (VLSM).
- Plan supernetting and Classless Inter-Domain Routing (CIDR).

We'll discuss each of these topics in turn.

Choosing Classful or Classless IP Addressing

The distinction between classful and classless IP addressing basically involves whether or not you will implement subnetting.

Classful IP addressing includes only the standard Class A, B, and C addresses and does not allow for subdividing the networks. *Classless IP addressing* allows you to use subnet addressing to better use the address space. Recall that this lets you "borrow" extra bits from the host portion of the address to divide the network into subnets.

There's a shorthand way to indicate your subnets, which is by using network prefix length notation, also known as *Classless Inter-Domain Routing (CIDR)* notation. This is displayed as `<IP address>/<# of bits>`, where # of bits indicates the network/subnet part and the remaining bits represent the host part of the IP address. Here's an example:

```
129.54.12.35/24
```

The 24 refers to the number of bits used in the network address. This is the same as the number of ones in a subnet mask shown in binary notation.

What if you need only 32 subnets instead of 256? In this instance, on each of the 32 subnets you could have up to $2^{11} - 2$, or 2,046 hosts. In CIDR notation, the IP address is `129.54.12.35/21`. The subnet mask in both decimal and binary formats looks like this:

```
255.255.248.0

11111111 11111111 11111000 00000000
```

Choosing Classful or Classless Routing Protocols

Routing protocols can either use the standard address classes or they can recognize subnetted network addresses. *Classful routing protocols* can only recognize IP addresses that are based on the standard Class A, B, or C IP addresses. When classful routing protocols, such as RIP v1, are used, IP hosts and routers are unable to recognize subnets.

Classless routing protocols were created to enable subnet masking. They transmit the variable prefixes of the subnetted network ID. The advantage of prefix flexibility is that you can combine several networks as one routing table entry and, thereby, greatly reduce routing overhead. Examples of classless routing protocols are RIP v2, OSPF, and Border Gateway Routing Protocol (BGP).

You may need to upgrade from classful to classless routing in the event that you will implement supernetting with CIDR or subnets of differing sizes with VLSM. VLSM and CIDR will be described a little later in this chapter.

Choosing Route Summarization or Flat Routing

In a hierarchical routing infrastructure, *route summarization* (or aggregation) describes one route in a routing table that represents many routes. Therefore, a routing table entry for the highest level in the hierarchy, the entire network, is also the route used for subnets and sub-subnets. This means that packets designated for a subnet of a network will be sent to the subnetwork by way of a router with the main network's address. For instance, packets intended for the `130.57.40` network, a subnet of the `130.57` network would be sent through a router in the `130.57` network.

In a *flat routing* infrastructure, each network segment gets its own entry in every router's routing table. The network IDs have no network/subnet structure and, therefore, can't be summarized.

RIP-based IPX internetworks use flat network addressing and have a flat routing infrastructure.

The benefit of route summarization is that you can contain topology changes from one area of the network within only that area. It will require more planning in advance, but the payoff comes in simplified route tables and less information to be exchanged. You need to use classless routing protocols, and all IP addresses used need to have identical high-order bits. The actual prefix length can be any number up to 32 bits.

We'll talk a little more about route summarization in conjunction with VLSMs and CIDR in the following section.

Planning for Noncontiguous Subnets

When subnets of a class-based network ID do not share a neighboring router, they are known as *noncontiguous subnets.*

There is a caution if you use classful routing, in which all summarization is automatic. Classful routing protocols can't recognize subnets because they don't transmit subnet and prefix length information. This means that using classful protocols together with noncontiguous subnets can impede communication because each subnet can have the same network ID.

Planning Variable Length Subnet Masks (VLSMs)

Now that we have classless routing protocols, subnetting isn't limited to equal-sized subnets anymore. With *variable length subnet masks (VLSMs)*, you can have different-sized subnets in the same network. You can create subnets of different sizes by applying different masks to the address space.

When using VLSMs, make sure you do not accidentally overlap blocks of addresses. If possible, start with equal-size subnets and then subdivide them.

Frequently, VLSMs are used where there is a point-to-point WAN link between a serial port on each of two routers. Remember In the Real World Scenario earlier in the chapter when we discussed how such a WAN link requires the creation of a small subnet, consisting of only two addresses? Without VLSM, you might divide a Class C network ID into an equal number of two-device subnets. If only one WAN link is in use, then all the subnets but one serve no purpose and 252 host addresses are wasted per subnet.

With VLSM, you can divide the Class C network into sixteen workgroup subnets of 14 nodes each. To do this, you use a prefix of 28 bits, which results in a subnet mask of `255.255.255.240`. Then you sub-subnet by using a prefix of 30 bits (a subnet mask of `255.255.255.252`), splitting one of the 16 into eight smaller subnets of two nodes each.

If you have numerous WAN links, it is strongly recommended that you use route summarization to reduce the administrative and performance overhead. Otherwise, each subnet requires an additional entry in the routing table.

Planning Supernetting and Classless Inter-Domain Routing (CIDR)

Due to the growth of the Internet, Class B network IDs are facing rapid depletion. To solve this problem, organizations can now be assigned a range of Class C network IDs and fuse them into a larger network, a process known as *supernetting*. Supernetting works in the opposite direction from subnetting in that it allows you to fuse contiguous subnets into larger supernets by "borrowing" bits from the network part of the address. Supernetting is not limited to Class C addresses, but because it is frequently used with Class C network numbers, our examples will follow this format.

For example, rather than allocating a Class B network ID to an organization that has 2,000 hosts, IANA might allocate a range of eight Class C network IDs. Each Class C network ID only accommodates 254 hosts by itself, but together they provide a total of 2,032 host IDs. The organization can use these Class C network numbers with a Class B subnet mask (`255.255.0.0`) to fuse the entire group of subnets together.

This is a great way to conserve Class B network IDs, but it creates a new problem of its own. Internet routers face being overwhelmed with routes because they need to have all of the supernetted network IDs in their routing tables just to route IP packets to that company. Enter *Classless Inter-Domain Routing (CIDR)*, which is route summarization for the Internet. CIDR collapses multiple network ID entries into a single one that relates to all of the company's Class C network IDs. Recall from the section "Choosing Route Summarization or Flat Routing" that a hierarchical routing infrastructure can be used to aggregate multiple routes into a single entry in a routing table.

A supernetted subnet mask has the starting network ID and the number of network IDs allocated. The following demonstrates how eight Class C network IDs are allocated. This indicates the contiguous allocation of eight Class C network IDs, starting with network ID `220.78.168.0`. Note that the first 21 bits are the same in both rows. The last 3 bits of the third octet, which are borrowed from the network ID, range from 000 to 111. In decimal, the range is 0 to 7, or 8 total contiguous subnets, which are combined into one supernet:

Starting Network ID	`220.78.168.0`	11011100 01001110 10101000 00000000
Ending Network ID	`220.78.175.0`	11011100 01001110 10101111 00000000

If you use CIDR, a block of supernetted addresses, such as those above, is known as a CIDR block. Below you see the single CIDR entry that appears in the routing table:

Network ID	Subnet Mask	Subnet Mask (Binary)
`220.78.168.0`	`255.255.248.0`	11111111 11111111 11111000 0000000

This entry represents all eight Class C network IDs allocated to the example organization. To determine whether a packet should be forwarded to the destination network, the router compares only the bits above the ones in the subnet mask. If they match, the router forwards the packet to that network. If they don't match, the router does not forward the packet to that network.

In network prefix notation, the CIDR entry is `220.78.168.0/21`.

RIPv2, OSPF, and BGPv4 all support CIDR. Windows Server 2003 supports RIPv2 and OSPF in addition to RIPv1.

Choosing a System for the IP Subnet Structure

When determining how to actually create subnets and group clients within those subnets in your network, you need to choose a system based on your organization's business and technical structure. All methods are not equal as far as the end result. You'll want to create subnets in such a way that route summarization can take place, so that data is routed in the most efficient way possible. The best method will result in a stable, highly scalable internetwork. The least desirable method results in instability and an unscalable TCP/IP infrastructure. There are four ways you can choose to allocate addresses:

Randomly Assigning Addresses Random address allocation is both the most common address allocation method and the least desirable. If you only have a small network and expect no significant growth, then this might be an appropriate approach. However, if the network grows, this method can result in instability due to the difficulty in summarizing a bunch of arbitrary routes.

Assigning Addresses by Organization Chart You can choose to create subnets based on a pool of addresses preassigned to a department or team. For example, Sales may be designated as 10.2.0.0/16. The address 10.2.1.0/24 might be the subnet for the sales team at one site and 10.2.2.0/24 might be the subnet for the sales team at another site. Limited possibilities for summarization might exist to the extent that contiguous subnets remain unassigned, but, as a rule, this kind of addressing scheme does not scale well.

Assigning Addresses by Geographical Region You can choose to create subnets based on the geographical location of office sites throughout your organization. A greater degree of summarization is possible when you use an address structure based on location. However, as the internetwork of a geographically diverse organization scales and continues to grow, fewer routes will be available for summarization.

Assigning Addresses by Network Topology The network topology describes the physical layout of a network. Addressing by topology creates a router-centric addressing structure. This is the best way to ensure that summarization takes place and that the internetwork will be the most scalable and stable.

Choosing Public or Private Addresses

If you use a direct (that is, routed) connection to the Internet, you must use public addresses. If you use an indirect connection, such as a proxy server or network address translator (NAT), you should use private addresses. Even an organization not connected to the Internet should use private addresses and not unauthorized addresses to allow for greater flexibility in the future should that organization need to connect to the Internet.

Public, private, and unauthorized addresses are described in the following sections. We will also look at how to translate network and port addresses.

Public Addresses

Public addresses are assigned by an Internet name register such as the Internet Assigned Numbers Authority (IANA) and guaranteed to be globally unique to the Internet. When public addresses are assigned, the routers of the Internet have those routes programmed in so that the public addresses will be reachable on the Internet.

Private Addresses

A *private address* is a predefined set of IP addresses for workstations and servers within a company that do not need to be directly connected to the Internet. These private address blocks are defined in RFC 1918:

10.0.0.0/8 This is a Class A network ID that allows the following range of valid IP addresses: 10.0.0.1 to 10.255.255.254. It has 24 host bits that can be used for any subnetting scheme within the private organization.

172.16.0.0/12 This network can be used either as a block of 16 Class B network IDs or as a 20-bit assignable address space (20 host bits) that can be used for any subnetting scheme within the private organization. The 172.16.0.0/12 private network allows the following range of valid IP addresses: 172.16.0.1 to 172.31.255.254.

192.168.0.0/16 This network can be used either as a block of 256 Class C network IDs (the subnet mask would be 255.255.255.0) or as a 16-bit assignable address space (16 host bits) that can be used for any subnetting scheme within the private organization. The 192.168.0.0/16 private network allows the following range of valid IP addresses: 192.168.0.1 to 192.168.255.254.

Because IP addresses in the private address space will never be assigned by IANA as public addresses, routes for private addresses will never exist in the Internet routers. The private address space can be used over and over again by any number of organizations, which helps to prevent the depletion of public addresses.

Private addresses are not reachable from the Internet. Therefore, Internet traffic from a host with a private address must go out in one of two ways:

- Requests go through a gateway (an example is a proxy server), which has a valid public address.
- Its private address is translated into a valid public address by a NAT device (such as a router or a Windows PC running ICS) before it goes forth on the Internet.

Real World Scenario

Using Private Addressing in Your Network

As the systems engineer of a biotechnology company in the heart of Silicon Valley, you are vigilant to implement best practices in security for every aspect of your network. You want to achieve the best balance between giving your users the Internet connectivity they need and protecting them from malicious attack from the outside world.

One of the many strategies you adopt is the use of private addressing on your intranet. Every user has a private address that cannot be reached from the outside world. You have implemented Network Address Translation and firewall services on the network. You have also used different private addressing schemes to distinguish the main users on the private intranet 192.168.0.0 from the machines on the highly secure Storage Area Network (SAN) 10.0.0 where highly confidential lab data is stored on a separate network that is not accessible to the main users. The SAN runs on a fast Gigabit Ethernet (GigE) backbone for nimble access to data to benefit the highly complex data modeling operations that take place on specialized application servers.

In this way, you can shield data and users from unwelcome prying eyes. You also isolate traffic to gain optimal throughput for those users and services with the most need for speed.

Unauthorized Addresses

If you are administering a private network with no plans to ever connect to the Internet, you can choose any network addresses, even public addresses that are already assigned to other organizations. These addresses are known as unauthorized (or illegal) addresses. You cannot connect to the Internet using *unauthorized addresses*. Down the road if you decide to connect directly to the Internet, you'll have to change your current addressing scheme, which can be an administrative nightmare. You will have to then change all of the IP addresses on every node in the network.

For this reason, it's best not to use an unauthorized addressing scheme if there is a remote chance of someday wanting to make a connection between your network and the Internet.

Network and Port Address Translation

A *Network Address Translator (NAT)*, which is specified in RFC 3022, is an IP router that can translate IP addresses from private or unauthorized public network addresses used internally within a company to public addresses used externally, for instance on the Internet. NAT is most often used to protect internal systems on the private network from outsider attack.

This can be a good security solution for a small business that would normally obtain a public IP address from an Internet Service Provider (ISP) for each computer on its network. With NAT, the business can hide its internal users behind a "fake" public address allocated by the ISP.

Another variation of NAT is the Port Address Translator (PAT). PAT maps private IP addresses to a specific TCP or UDP port running on top of a public IP address. This is used, for instance, in Windows Internet Connection Sharing, where many computers can share one Internet connection.

Network Address Translation is covered in detail in Chapter 3.

Planning for Automatic IP Configuration

Before the advent of DHCP, an administrator had to manually assign and configure IP addresses on each network node. In a small workgroup, it was relatively easy to manage address assignments. However, this method is error-prone and not scalable. Most organizations choose to use DHCP for automatic assignment and configuration of IP addresses. After the initial installation and configuration efforts are completed, DHCP is very low-maintenance.

DHCP is based on the older Bootstrap Protocol (BootP) standard.

BootP and DHCP hosts can be mixed on the same network.

DHCP simplifies IP address management because the DHCP server automatically allocates IP addresses and related TCP/IP configuration settings to DHCP-enabled clients on the network. This is especially useful in networks where there are many mobile users, whose network configurations are frequently changing.

The DHCP server dynamically assigns specific addresses from a manually designated range of addresses called a *scope*. Clients can get assignments no matter where they are located or how frequently they move. If you use DHCP, you must also use a name resolution service such as DNS or WINS or both.

Prior to deploying DHCP, you must reserve addresses for network servers and devices such as printers, which should have a static IP address so that they can be consistently located on the network.

Either a DHCP server or a DHCP Relay Agent must be configured for each subnet. DHCP works through local, non-routable broadcasts. For subnets without a DHCP server, the *DHCP relay agent* can be configured to listen for DHCP traffic, intercept requests, and forward them to a DHCP server on a remote subnet.

You can learn how to implement DHCP in MCSA/MCSE: Windows Server 2003 Network Infrastructure Implementation, Management, and Maintenance Study Guide by Michael Chacon and Matt Sheltz with James Chellis (Sybex, 2003).

Introducing IPv6

The current version of IP, known as version 4, or IPv4, has not changed much since IP was first introduced in 1981 in RFC 791. This is a strong tribute to the design of the protocol, as it has succeeded the test of scalability to the demands of today's Internet. However, the designers could not anticipate over two decades ago, before the advent of the PC, that the Internet would explode at an exponential rate and, as a result, threaten to exhaust the almost 4.3 billion available addresses in the IPv4 address space. NAT and CIDR have provided a temporary solution to the problem of address space depletion, but the time has come for a more scalable solution.

In addition, the continual advance of technology introduces new challenges for security and performance. IPv4 lacks built-in security, and as a result, protocol security is available only to specialized protocols within the TCP/IP suite, such as SSL, PPTP, and S-HTTP. IPv4 is a relatively high-overhead protocol, which introduces problems with real-time applications like videoconferencing that demand rapid transmission of data packets. IPv4 also has limitations when it comes to routing. The current method of IPv4 address allocation has resulted in over 70,000 routes in the routing tables of the Internet's backbone routers. The larger route tables become, the longer it takes to route packets to their destinations.

IPv4 configuration can be cumbersome. The need for subnets, subnet masks, and supernets increase the overhead of packets by adding information. This results in a performance penalty and increases the size of routing table entries as well as the time it takes for a packet to reach its final destination. Host configuration is less complicated than it was before the days of DHCP, but imagine if the protocol could configure itself and render DHCP obsolete.

Enter *IP version 6 (IPv6)*. Version 6 of the IP protocol (IPv6) was designed to resolve the problems of addressing, scalability, security, and performance inherent in IPv4. IPv6, previously known as IPng for Next Generation, is a new suite of protocols and standards that features a radically more scalable 128-bit address space, built-in security, a streamlined packet, and self-configuration intelligence. IPv6 is a rapidly evolving standard that is supported on only the newest operating systems, including Windows Server 2003, Windows XP, Linux kernel version 2.4.18, and Mac OS 10.2. Fortunately, IPv6 promises to coexist peacefully with IPv4, so network engineers can plan a gradual migration to the new standard.

Adventuresome early adopters of IPv6 can look to `www.6bone.net`, the worldwide test site and IPv6 backbone. The site is available for testing interoperability and connectivity.

IPv6 is installed as a protocol in Windows Server 2003. As of the time of this writing, an unsupported prerelease version is available on XP. It is installed and uninstalled using the `ipv6 install` and `ipv6 uninstall` commands. The same services that you recognize from IPv4 are available in version 6. Services such as DHCP are named DHCPv6. The names of TCP/IP troubleshooting utilities are appended with a 6, as in `ping6`. The exception is `ipconfig`, which is replaced with the `ipv6 if` command.

In the following sections, we'll uncover the benefits of IPv6, the structure of the IPv6 addressing scheme, and IPv6 addressing automation.

If you want more details about IPv6 after reading this primer, start with RFC's 2273, 1974, and 2460. IPv6 is a rapidly evolving standard, so the RFC's may be obsolete by the time you read this book.

Benefits of IPv6

IPv6 introduces many new features that offer solutions to IPv4's limitations in scalability, security, and performance. In the following sections, we'll explore the benefits of IPv6 and discover the advantages it offers for low overhead, a more scalable address space, mobile user support, built-in security, and real-time application performance, to name just a few benefits.

Scalability

The 128-bit address space introduced in IPv6 solves the problem of address space depletion. With the advent of wired appliances and the explosive growth of the Internet, no one can predict how many more nodes are joining on a daily basis because the increase is so exponential. The larger address space also eliminates the need for subnets, subnet masks, and supernets, all of which are implemented on the assumption that an address class is either too large or too small.

IP address configuration is further simplified and automated in IPv6 through a combination of stateless and stateful configuration, autodiscovery, autoconfiguration, and autoregistration. Automatic configuration at the protocol level is especially beneficial to roving mobile users.

Security

IPv6 features built-in security so that security features are available for all protocols in the stack instead of only specialized protocols such as SSL, PPTP, and S-HTTP. IPv6 offers the following built-in security features:

- *Packet authentication*, which verifies that a packet is actually from the sender
- *Packet integrity*, which verifies that a data packet was not altered in transit
- *Packet confidentiality*, which verifies that the payload of a data packet cannot be read by hackers

These features protect against two security challenges:

- IP spoofing
- Sniffing

IP spoofing involves the impersonation of a computer using a stolen IP address in order to obtain passwords and other data or to conceal the true identity of a computer being used for a *Denial of Service (DoS)* attack. Formerly it was necessary to use a combination of a firewall and router solution to guard against IP spoofing. Now the authentication headers are built into the packet, providing both authentication and integrity.

Sniffing involves a device or application that monitors and analyzes network traffic. Sniffers are not intended to be used maliciously. They are intended to optimize network throughput, but they can be used maliciously to intercept and read data packets on a network. Formerly, sniffer detection tools were necessary to guard against unauthorized sniffing. The solution may have involved a complicated set of hardware and/or software tools. Now the extension header specifies that the payload is encrypted. End-to-end encryption ensures that malicious parties are unable to read the contents of intercepted data packets.

IPSec is implemented as a component of IPv6 that adds another layer of security by creating a secure, TCP/IP-level, point-to-point connection between two nodes. This feature lends security to applications that lack or have minimal built-in security.

Performance

The IPv6 address is now stored in hexadecimal format, which is significantly more compact than binary. Combined with the fact that additional configuration of subnets, subnet masks, and supernets is no longer needed, the amount of space required to actually store the IP address is greatly reduced. The result is smaller, more efficient datagrams and routing tables.

Smaller packets mean faster, smoother multimedia and real-time applications. Streaming audio and video are smoother. Videoconferencing no longer has to be out of sync. The speaker's lips will move in concert with his voice instead of looking like a badly dubbed kung fu movie from 1970. How? Because IPv6 introduces the concept of a "flow" of packets. With this concept, a set of packets receives special handling so that data is streamed in the most efficient way possible.

Now that you've been introduced to the benefits of IPv6, you are probably wondering how IPv6 manages to bring together all of these great improvements. We'll look at the address space next.

The IPv6 Address Space

IPv6 is based on a 128-bit address space consisting of 8 sets of 16 bits each, expressed as 4 hexadecimal digits. In contrast to the binary (base-2) and decimal (base-10) systems, hexadecimal is a base-16 system that uses numerals 0–9 and the characters A-F to represent the values 10–15 for a total of 16 possible values. You'll recognize hex format from hardware values such as I/O addresses and MAC addresses. Hex is a superior system in that it is more compact and thus consumes less space to store addresses.

An IPv6 address uses colons to demarcate each 16-bit block. This notation is known as *colon-hexadecimal format.* An IPv6 address looks like this:

```
21DA:00D3:0000:2F3B:02AA:00FF:FE28:9C5A
```

The same address in binary format looks like this:

```
0010000111011010    0000000011010011    0000000000000000
00101111001110110000001010101010    0000000011111111    1111111000101000
1001110001011010
```

You can see how much more efficient the hexadecimal format is. Addresses can be further simplified through the use of shorthand notation. Leading zeros can be removed, so that our example becomes the second address below:

`21DA:00D3:0000:2F3B:02AA:00FF:FE28:9C5A`

(Notice the leading zeros in bold print.)

`21DA:D3:0:2F3B:2AA:FF:FE28:9C5A`

Another means of shorthand notation is the use of the double colon (`::`) to replace a sequence of zeros. The double colon can be used only one time in an address. Following is a *before* and *after* example of an IPv6 address using the double colon (notice the two leading zeros and the sequence of zeros in bold print):

`0AC4:`0000:0000:0000:0000:0000:0000:0600

`AC4::600`

The same 128 bits in binary format can be stored with a mere 6 bits in hex! You can clearly see how useful this is in making packet headers and routing tables more efficient.

N.B.: In IPv6, the term "host" is no longer used interchangeably with the term "node" to describe IP devices and computers.

The address range for the entire IPv6 address space goes from `0000:0000:0000:0000:0000:0000:0000:0000` to `FFFF:FFFF:FFFF:FFFF:FFFF:FFFF:FFFF:FFFF`.

I promised you interoperability with IPv4, so here's how IPv4 and IPv6 can coexist: IPv4 addresses are implemented as a subset of the IPv6 address space. Therefore, routers can be configured to recognize both IPv4 and IPv6 traffic and they can also translate between versions. This enables a network engineer to design subnets based on IPv6 and integrate them within an existing IPv4 environment. Clients can remain on IPv4 until all servers and routers are upgraded and client operating systems have all been upgraded to one of the OS versions supporting IPv6 mentioned earlier.

Converting an IPv4 address to IPv6 is simple: just insert leading zeros to create an IPv4-compatible IPv6 address as follows:

The IPv4 address `209.64.12.10` in decimal becomes

`0000:0000:0000:0000:0000:0000:`**209.64.12.10**

or

:: **209.64.12.10** in shorthand.

This IPv6 address carries the IPv4 address in the familiar dotted-decimal notation embedded in the low-order 32 bits. These addresses allow IPv6 packets to be dynamically tunneled over IPv4 routing infrastructure.

Addresses for IPv4-only nodes that do not support IPv6 are called IPv4-mapped IPv6 addresses, and they are represented as follows:

0000:0000:0000:0000:0000:0000:FFFF:209.64.12.10

or

::FFFF:209.64.12.10

Because of its vastly larger address space, IPv6 has rendered subnetting irrelevant for years. Supernetting is likewise obsolete. Remember, subnets, subnet masks, and supernets are all implemented on the assumption that an address class is either too large or too small.

Like IPv4, IPv6 defines special addresses. The *unspecified address* consists of all zeros and is used to send a broadcast or DHCP client request from a computer that does not yet have a configured address. The loopback address is `::1`. The *site-local address* represents the local site and uses `FEC0:` as the leading block. This is similar to the leading bits used to represent address classes in IPv4. The *link-local address*, which leads with `FE80:`, is used for a single, nonrouted network segment and can autoconfigure an IP based on the MAC address. It's similar to the `169.254` network address in Automatic Private IP Addressing (APIPA). The *multicast address* leads with `FF` and is used to identify a group of computers that will receive a broadcast to this address. Finally, the *anycast address* is used in the same way as the multicast address, but the packet only goes to the nearest member in the group and is used to locate the closest server for a resource such as DHCP.

Automatic Configuration in IPv6

Because IPv6 has more configuration intelligence than its predecessor, DHCP might in time be rendered as obsolete as supernetting. Configuration in IPv6 is of two types:

- Stateless configuration
- Stateful configuration

Stateless configuration is used in the absence of a DHCP server. The computer builds its own address starting with the *on-link prefix* (the network part of the address) and appending its own MAC address. This process uses Duplicate Address Detection (DAD) to check for duplicate addresses on the network.

Stateful configuration is used with a DHCPv6 server, which handles IP address allocation and configuration.

Both types of configuration assign a limited lifetime and automatic renumbering to ensure that addresses expire and are refreshed.

IPv6 has three types of automatic configuration:

Autodiscovery Also known as Neighbor Discovery, *autodiscovery* is a means for nodes to discover information about the local network and available routers. Autodiscovery uses the link-local address along with the Neighbor Discovery Protocol (NDP) to send ICMPv6 discovery messages. Routers use Router Advertisement (RA) multicast packets to advertise their existence, announce the on-link prefix, and signal stateless or stateful configuration.

Autoconfiguration *Autoconfiguration* is used in stateless configuration. A node transmits a Neighbor Solicitation (NS) query to its desired address. If it receives a Neighbor Advertisement (NA) response from another node, then the address is already in use. Individual nodes listen to all NA confirmations and other traffic to keep tabs on who's still alive at particular IP addresses. This information is cached and periodically verified by individual nodes by transmitting NS queries. In the absence of a response, the query is deleted from the local cache. NS, NA, and DAD replace the ARP protocol.

Autoregistration IPv6 features automatic registration in DNS for servers. This is known as *autoregistration.*

Although IPv6 offers many advantageous new features, it is a rapidly evolving standard which is still very new and, therefore, it will be years before it is readily implemented in modern production environments. The rest of this chapter focuses on troubleshooting TCP/IP version 4. In subsequent chapters, the discussion will assume the use of IPv4, and special notes will be used to call out features of IPv6 in relation to DNS, IPSec, and other topics.

Troubleshooting TCP/IP Addressing

Regardless of how well you plan your implementation of TCP/IP, you're bound to run into difficulties that require you to be able to troubleshoot TCP/IP addressing. This section shows you what to do when you run into trouble with TCP/IP. We start with a review of troubleshooting tools—`ipconfig`, `ping`, `tracert` and `pathping`—and then proceed into the particulars on how to troubleshoot specific client configuration issues using these tools.

Troubleshooting with `ipconfig` is covered in greater detail in Chapter 4, "Planning a DNS Strategy." Troubleshooting with the `tracert` and `pathping` utilities is covered in greater detail in Chapter 3.

When something doesn't work, the initial reaction is to start looking for the appropriate tool to fix the problem. It's inevitably faster to start by asking a couple of very simple questions:

- What should work?
- What does work?
- What doesn't work?
- What changed since the last time it worked?

There isn't a fixed sequence of steps to troubleshoot all TCP/IP-related problems on your network. Your approach will depend on the particular scenario. There are, however, some basic guidelines that fit most situations you'll encounter.

The first thing to do is to verify the physical connection. Next, test the local host's configuration parameters. If all is well, check the routing configuration, and if it checks out, then see if you have an issue with name resolution.

Troubleshooting routing and name resolution are complex subjects that we'll cover in detail in later chapters. For help in troubleshooting routing, see Chapter 3. For assistance with name resolution issues, see Chapter 4 and Chapter 5.

Identifying the TCP/IP Configuration

The most basic troubleshooting step you should take is to verify the TCP/IP configuration. You want to verify that all settings have been assigned correctly by the DHCP server (or entered correctly for manual configurations).

You can accomplish this and more with the *ipconfig* command line utility. `Ipconfig` lists the IP address, subnet mask, and default gateway. You can also see more advanced TCP/IP parameters, such as WINS server and primary DNS suffix when you employ the `/all` switch.

The syntax for the `ipconfig` utility is listed below:

```
ipconfig [/? | /all | /renew [adapter] | /release [adapter] | /flushdns |
   /displaydns | /registerdns | /showclassid adapter | /setclassid
   adapter [classid] ]
```

Table 2.5 lists of all of the available command-line options (available by typing **`ipconfig /?`**):

TABLE 2.5 `Ipconfig` Command-Line Options

Option	Description
`/all`	Display full configuration information.
`/renew [`***adapter***`]`	Renew the IP address for the specified adapter.
`/release [`***adapter***`]`	Release the IP address for the specified adapter.
`/flushdns`	Purges the DNS Resolver cache.
`/displaydns`	Display the contents of the DNS Resolver Cache.
`/registerdns`	Refreshes all DHCP leases and re-registers DNS names.
`/show`***classid adapter***	Displays all the dhcp class IDs allowed for adapter.
`/set`***classid adapter***	Modifies the dhcp class id.

The `ipconfig /all` command will provide a detailed report for the current TCP/IP configuration on all adapters. Here's an example of the output from `ipconfig /all`:

```
F:\Documents and Settings\Administrator>ipconfig /all

Windows IP Configuration

   Host Name . . . . . . . . . . . . : delta
   Primary Dns Suffix  . . . . . . . : globalitcertification.com
   Node Type . . . . . . . . . . . . : Unknown
```

```
   IP Routing Enabled. . . . . . . . : Yes
   WINS Proxy Enabled. . . . . . . . : Yes
   DNS Suffix Search List. . . . . . : globalitcertification.com

Ethernet adapter Local Area Connection:

   Connection-specific DNS Suffix  . :
   Description . . . . . . . . . . . : NETGEAR FA310TX Fast Ethernet Adapter
   (NG RPCI)
   Physical Address. . . . . . . . . : 00-A0-CC-61-C3-62
   DHCP Enabled. . . . . . . . . . . : Yes
   IP Address. . . . . . . . . . . . : 192.168.1.12
   Subnet Mask . . . . . . . . . . . : 255.255.255.0
   Default Gateway . . . . . . . . . :
   DNS Servers . . . . . . . . . . . : 127.0.0.1
                                       192.168.1.12

PPP adapter {E5694F3A-CBA7-4F47-994D-6602F7457176}:

   Connection-specific DNS Suffix  . :
   Description . . . . . . . . . . . : WAN (PPP/SLIP) Interface
   Physical Address. . . . . . . . . : 00-53-45-00-00-00
   DHCP Enabled. . . . . . . . . . . : No
   IP Address. . . . . . . . . . . . : 209.204.149.109
   Subnet Mask . . . . . . . . . . . : 255.255.255.255
   Default Gateway . . . . . . . . . : 0.0.0.0
   DNS Servers . . . . . . . . . . . : 208.201.224.11
                                       208.201.224.33
   NetBIOS over Tcpip. . . . . . . . : Disabled
```

You may be able to resolve the problem solely by examining the output of this utility. For instance, if the DHCP client is unable to obtain an IP address, `ipconfig` displays `169.254.x.y` for the IP address and `255.255.0.0` for the subnet mask. This may mean there are no free IP addresses in the DHCP server's scope or the DHCP server cannot be reached.

Windows Server 2003 supports automatic IP addressing even when the DHCP server is unavailable through APIPA and Alternate configuration. These features and more about DHCP are covered in *MCSA/MCSE: Windows Server 2003 Network Infrastructure Implementation, Management, and Maintenance Study Guide.*

In some cases, you may have the incorrect IP address. In others, you may have the incorrect subnet mask. We will look to verify these two cases in the following sections.

Incorrect IP Address

Take the following steps to verify that the IP address assigned is valid:

1. Verify that the IP address is not a duplicate address.
2. Verify that the IP address is from the correct subnet.
3. Verify that the IP address is not the subnet address.
4. Verify that the IP address is not a broadcast address for the subnet.

When there is a duplicate address conflict in Windows Server 2003, the first address is preserved and the duplicate reverts to all zeros.

Incorrect Subnet Mask

Diagnosing problems with an invalid subnet mask can be very tricky. Frequently, an incorrect subnet mask prevents only certain computers from communicating, while the rest of network remains operational. An invalid subnet mask can have no negative repercussions, or it can render the entire network unreachable for a certain host.

Document your subnetting strategy so you can refer to it when you need to verify that subnet and broadcast addresses have not been assigned in error to hosts and other such things. Faulty subnet mask configurations often result from errors in planning your subnetting strategy or from user error during manual configuration.

Testing IP Communications

After verifying that a host has obtained a valid IP address configuration, you can use the `ping`, `tracert`, and `pathping` utilities to test IP-level connectivity and isolate problems to specific locations on the network. We'll investigate each utility in turn.

Ping

You can test basic IP-level connectivity using the *ping* utility. `Ping` sends Internet Control Message Protocol (ICMP) echo requests to the destination host and analyzes ICMP echo replies. The utility has a number of command-line options you can use to fine-tune your analysis.

The five-step procedure for testing with `ping` is as follows:

1. Ping the loopback address.
2. Ping the IP address of the local host.
3. Ping the IP address of the default gateway.
4. Ping the IP address of the remote host.
5. Ping the remote host by name.

Depending on where the `ping` test fails, you can focus your troubleshooting efforts:

- If you can't `ping` the loopback address, reinstall the TCP/IP protocol.

- If you can't `ping` the local IP address, check for a mistyped, duplicate, or otherwise invalid address.
- If you can't `ping` the default gateway, check the subnet mask.
- If you can't `ping` the remote host by IP, check the default gateway address on the local host, verify the connection between routers, and make sure the remote computer is online.
- If you can't `ping` the remote host by host name, this indicates a problem with host name resolution.

The `ping` utility comes with a number of switches to help you isolate the problem. For instance, you can specify the number of echo requests to send or the time to live (TTL).

The syntax for the `ping` utility is listed below:

```
ping [-t] [-a] [-n count] [-l size] [-f] [-i TTL] [-v TOS] [-r count] [-s count]
[[-j host-list] | [-k host-list]] [-w timeout] [-R] [-S srcaddr] [-4] [-6]
   target_name
```

Table 2.6 lists of all of the available command-line options (available by typing **ping /?**):

TABLE 2.6 Ping Command-Line Options

Option	Description
-t	Ping the specified host until stopped.
Ctrl+Break	To see statistics and continue.
Ctrl+C	Stop.
-a	Resolve addresses to hostnames.
-n ***count***	Number of echo requests to send.
-l ***size***	Send buffer size.
-f	Set Don't Fragment flag in packet (IPv4 only).
-i ***TTL***	Time to Live.
-v ***TOS***	Type of Service (IPv4-only).
-r ***count***	Record route for count hops (IPv4 only).
-s ***count***	Timestamp for count hops (IPv4 only).
-j ***host-list***	Loose source route along host-list (IPv4 only).
-k ***host-list***	Strict source route along host-list (IPv4 only).

TABLE 2.6 Ping Command-Line Options *(continued)*

Option	Description
-w ***timeout***	Timeout in milliseconds to wait for each reply.
-R	Trace round-trip path (IPv6 only).
-S ***srcaddr***	Source address to use (IPv6 only).
-4	Force using IPv4.
-6	Force using IPv6.

Tracert

You can use the *tracert* utility to isolate problems related to an improper router configuration or link failure. True to its name, `tracert` will trace the route to a destination network and tell you exactly where a packet stopped on the journey.

Here is the command-line syntax for the `tracert` utility:

```
tracert [-d] [-h maximum_hops] [-j host-list] [-w timeout] [-R] [-S srcaddr]
[-4] [-6] target_name
```

The available command-line options (available by typing **`tracert /?`**) are listed in Table 2.7.

TABLE 2.7 Tracert Command-Line Options

Option	Description
-d	Do not resolve addresses to hostnames.
-h ***maximum_hops***	Maximum number of hops to search for target.
-j ***host-list***	Loose source route along host-list (IPv4 only).
-w ***timeout***	Wait timeout milliseconds for each reply.
-R	Trace round-trip path (IPv6 only).
-S ***srcaddr***	Source address to use (IPv6 only).
-4	Force using IPv4.
-6	Force using IPv6.

The following example shows a trace where the second router has determined that no valid path for host 172.16.0.7 exists:

```
C:\>tracert 172.16.0.7
Tracing route to 172.16.0.7 over a maximum of 30 hops
1. <10 ms  <10 ms  <10 ms 172.16.0.7
2. 172.32.8.54 reports: Destination net unreachable.
   Trace complete.
```

Here's another example in which the trace passes a network access server, a gateway, and some routers before it times out. This example demonstrates how `tracert` includes the Fully Qualified Domain Names (FQDNs) and IP addresses of the devices it encounters:

```
H:\Documents and Settings\Administrator>tracert 172.16.0.7
Tracing route to 172.16.0.7 over a maximum of 30 hops

  1   139 ms   134 ms   130 ms  nas1.oak.sonic.net [209.204.149.2]
  2   134 ms   132 ms   132 ms  gw.oak.sonic.net [209.204.149.1]
  3   140 ms   133 ms   134 ms  10.204.149.1
  4   171 ms   237 ms   209 ms  fast1-1-0.border.sr.sonic.net [209.204.191.194]
  5   132 ms   132 ms   131 ms  fast1-1-0.border2.sr.sonic.net [209.204.191.134]
  6   136 ms   133 ms   133 ms  serial1-0.gw.focal-sf.sonic.net [64.142.0.2]
  7     *        *        *     Request timed out.
  8     *        *        *     Request timed out.
  9     *        *        *     Request timed out.
 10     *        *        *     Request timed out.
 11     *        *        *     Request timed out.
 12     *        *        *     Request timed out.
 13     *        *        *     Request timed out.
 14     *        *        *     Request timed out.
 15     *        *        *     Request timed out.
 16     *        *        *     Request timed out.
 17     *        *        *     Request timed out.
 18     *        *        *     Request timed out.
 19     *        *        *     Request timed out.
 20     *        *        *     Request timed out.
 21     *        *        *     Request timed out.
 22     *        *        *     Request timed out.
 23     *        *        *     Request timed out.
 24     *        *        *     Request timed out.
 25     *        *        *     Request timed out.
 26     *        *        *     Request timed out.
 27     *        *        *     Request timed out.
 28     *        *        *     Request timed out.
```

```
29    *    *    *    Request timed out.
30    *    *    *    Request timed out.

Trace complete.
```

Both examples indicate one of two likely causes: a router is misconfigured or the `172.16.0.0` network does not exist (a bad IP address). `Tracert` is useful for troubleshooting large internetworks in which there are multiple routers or bridges such that multiple paths can lead to the same destination.

If you can `ping` across the router but you cannot establish a session, find out if the router is able to pass large packets. The `ping` utility sends its data in ICMP packets of 74 bytes, but NET requests can be significantly larger. If necessary, you can use the `ping -l` command to specify the packet size.

`Ping` will indicate that it is using only 32 bytes of data, but it reports only the data block length. The actual ICMP packet is 74 bytes and consists of a 32-byte data block and three headers: a 14-byte Ethernet header, a 20-byte IP header, and an 8-byte ICMP header.

Pathping

You can obtain statistical analysis of network traffic using the *pathping* utility. `Pathping` is essentially a hybrid of the `ping` and `tracert` tools. However, it provides even more useful information to enable you to isolate the cause of a network problem. In addition to returning the computer name and IP address for each hop, `pathping` computes the percentage of lost/sent packets to each router or link. Results are analyzed over a period of time, which can vary depending on the number of hops between the source and destination, but this is usually about 5 minutes. Here is the command-line syntax for the `pathping` utility:

```
pathping [-g host-list] [-h maximum_hops] [-i address] [-n] [-p period]
[-q num_queries] [-w timeout] [-4] [-6] target_name
```

The available options for `pathping` are listed in Table 2.8.

TABLE 2.8 Pathping Command-Line Options

Option	Description
-g ***host-list***	Allows a loose source route along host-list (consecutive computers to be separated by intermediate gateways).
-h ***maximum_hops***	Maximum number of hops to search for target. The default is 30.
-i ***address***	Use the specified source address.
-n	Do not resolve addresses to hostnames.

TABLE 2.8 Pathping Command-Line Options *(continued)*

Option	Description
`-p` ***`period`***	Trace round-trip path (IPv6 only).
`-q` ***`num_queries`***	Number of queries per hop.
`-w` ***`timeout`***	Wait timeout milliseconds for each reply.
`-4`	Force using IPv4.
`-6`	Force using IPv6.

You can use also Network Monitor to capture network traffic data and use the results from traces to help you troubleshoot and optimize your network. You will learn how to use Network Monitor in Chapter 10, "Planning Network Maintenance, Optimization, and Recoverability."

Troubleshooting DHCP

TCP/IP utilities can work together to troubleshoot connectivity problems. In this section, we will look at how you can use these utilities to address connectivity issues on the network using DHCP as the example.

Troubleshooting DHCP problems involves first isolating the problem to a client-side issue, an infrastructure issue, or a server-side issue. This is done by determining whether the problem is specific to one client or whether it affects many clients. Problems that affect one client indicate a client-side issue, while problems affecting multiple clients indicate an infrastructure issue or a server-side issue. The following sections look at areas that should be investigated, in order, when diagnosing DHCP problems.

Client-Side Issues

When checking the client-side issues, you'll want to ask the following questions:

Is the client connected? Verify that you have a link-level connection to the network. Then verify that you can reach the DHCP server using `ping`.

Are you getting a lease? Use `ipconfig /all` to find out. This will indicate whether or not a DHCP server assigned an IP address. If a DHCP server has not assigned an address, use another client to see if you can still obtain a lease from this subnet by using `ipconfig /release` and `ipconfig /renew`. Note that you may be forced to sacrifice a previously operational client if this lease request is not answered.

Where is the lease originating? The `ipconfig /all` command will tell you if the client is using an APIPA address, thereby indicating that it did not get an address from the DHCP server.

It may be necessary to disable APIPA to troubleshoot further. Use `ipconfig /release` and `ipconfig /renew` for troubleshooting.

If the problem affects more than one client, you may find it beneficial and expedient to use a sniffer, such as Network Monitor, to run a packet trace and to capture packets from different broadcast domains so that you can view all of the transactions between client, relay agent, and server.

Infrastructure Issues

When looking at infrastructure issues, you'll want to ask the following questions:

Are relay agents and routers configured properly? If the router or other relay agent is not configured properly, DHCP messages cannot be properly forwarded to the DHCP server. Network Monitor can be used to verify the proper configuration of the relay agent.

Are packets routing between subnets? Use `ping`, `pathping`, and `tracert` to find out.

Server-Side Issues

When looking at server-side issues, you'll want to ask the following questions:

Is the DHCP service operating properly? Examine the event logs to make sure DHCP is running. If the event log contains Jet database messages indicating that the DHCP database is corrupt, you can use the Jetpack program to repair the database. Failing this effort you can restore the database from the backup directory (*`systemroot`*`\system32\dhcp\backup\jet\new`; restore to *`systemroot`*`\system32\dhcp`) or from backup media. On busy DHCP servers with large databases you should compact the database monthly.

Are leases available for proper scopes? If multiple DHCP servers are configured with overlapping scopes, clients could receive duplicate IP addresses. If an address that is invalid for the subnet has been assigned, a rogue DHCP server (a DHCP server that has not been authorized in Active Directory) has probably been joined to the network.

Are options and scopes configured properly? If a router or a name server option is misconfigured in the DHCP settings, the client will appear to be unable to access resources on the network.

Summary

In this chapter, you learned:

- How to evaluate and implement network protocols. Microsoft is moving away from NetBIOS and no longer supports the NetBEUI protocol. TCP/IP is the standard network protocol. It is installed by default and is required for DNS and Active Directory.
- How to design an IP routing strategy. Designing an IP routing strategy involves choosing between hardware and software routing, as well as static or dynamic routing and the types of routing protocols to use. For large networks with high performance needs, choose a link state routing protocol such as OSPF.

- How to understand IP addressing and subnetting. Understanding the fundamentals of subnetting is critical to network design and troubleshooting.
- How to plan a strategy for TCP/IP implementation. Planning an address assignment model enables you to build a solid network infrastructure that will be easy to scale, administer, and maintain.
- How to evaluate between public and private addressing. Public addressing should be used for limited servers, while most of the workstations can use private addressing for greater protection from malicious attack. Unauthorized addresses should be avoided.
- How to evaluate IPv6, which features a 128-bit hexadecimal address space, built-in security, and automatic configuration.
- How to troubleshoot TCP/IP addressing issues. This involves asking the right questions first, then using the `ipconfig`, `ping`, `tracert`, and `pathping` utilities in logical order.
- How to troubleshoot DHCP problems. This involves using the TCP/IP utilities, the event logs, and the Network Monitor utility to isolate and diagnose problems with automatic address assignment and configuration using DHCP.

Exam Essentials

Understand network protocols. TCP/IP is the protocol of choice in modern networks. Understand how network protocols and packets work. Know the difference between connectionless (IP) and connection-oriented (TCP) protocols.

Know how to design an IP routing strategy. Considerations include hardware versus software routing, static versus dynamic routing, and distance vector (RIP v1) versus link-state (RIP v2, OSPF) protocols.

Understand how IP addressing works. Know the fundamentals of the hierarchical IP addressing scheme and the specific characteristics of each different class of network. Understand subnetting, including how to calculate and express subnet masks in decimal, binary, and CIDR notation formats. Given a subnet mask, know how to calculate the number of subnets and how to subnet each class of network.

Know how to plan a comprehensive strategy for TCP/IP implementation. Know how to plan an address assignment model, which includes choosing between classful or classless IP addressing, between classful or classless routing, and between flat routing or route summarization. It also includes planning for noncontiguous subnets, planning VLSMs, and planning supernetting and CIDR. Understand the strategic implications of IP address allocation methods, and public/private IP addressing.

Know how to evaluate IPv6. Understand the differences between IPv4 and IPv6. Know the benefits of IPv6, which include features that solve the scalability, security, and performance limitations of IPv4.

Know how to troubleshoot TCP/IP configuration. Understand the logical process of troubleshooting IP configuration and connectivity issues. Know when and how to use tools such as `ipconfig` and `ping`. Know how to isolate problems with IP address and subnet mask assignment. The `ipconfig` utility is used to verify IP address configuration. The `ping`, `tracert`, and `pathping` utilities are used to verify IP-level connectivity.

Know how to troubleshoot DHCP problems. Understand the logical flow of diagnostic questions and activities for troubleshooting IP configuration and server connectivity issues related to DHCP. Know when and how to use tools such as `ipconfig` and `ping`. Know how to isolate problems that indicate client-side, infrastructure, and server-side issues. Know when to use the event logs and Network Monitor.

Key Terms

Before you take the exam, be certain you are familiar with the following terms:

anycast address
AppleTalk
autoconfiguration
autodiscovery
autoregistration
classful IP addressing
classful routing protocols
Classless Inter-domain Routing (CIDR)
classless IP addressing
classless routing protocols
connectionless protocols
connection-oriented protocols
Denial of Service (DoS)
DHCP relay agent
distance vector routing protocol
dynamic routing
flat routing
IP spoofing
IP version 4 (IPv4)
IP version 6 (IPv6)
`ipconfig`
Link state routing protocols
link-local address
mapped address
multicast address
Network Address Translator (NAT)
Network Basic Input/Output System (NetBIOS)
noncontiguous subnets
NWLink
on-link prefix
Open Shortest Path First (OSPF)
packet authentication
packet confidentiality
packet integrity
packet payload
packets

`pathping`

`ping`

private address

protocol binding

public addresses

route summarization

Routing Information Protocol (RIP)

site-local address

sniffing

stateful configuration

stateless configuration

static routing

subnet address

subnet mask

subnets

supernetting

`tracert`

unauthorized addresses

unspecified address

variable length subnet masks (VLSMs)

Review Questions

1. You are a systems engineer designing a TCP/IP strategy for a postsecondary institution using a private Class B address. The network encompasses five buildings on a single campus. The buildings have the following numbers of computers:

Building 1	556
Building 2	101
Building 3	35
Building 4	236
Building 5	98
Building 6	187

The institution's five-year plan involves adding approximately 150 additional computers to the network. About 50 of these additional computers will be placed in Building 5 and about 100 in Building 3. For performance reasons, you will never have greater than 200 computers per subnet.

Which subnet mask should you use to meet current and future growth requirements?

A. `255.255.248.0`

B. `255.255.252.0`

C. `255.255.254.0`

D. `255.255.255.0`

E. `255.255.255.128`

2. In your network, a workstation has the IP settings shown in the following table. This computer is unable to communicate with any other computers on the network.

IP address	134.62.2.55
Subnet mask	255.255.192.0
Default gateway	134.62.89.1

Which of the following settings is the cause of this problem?

A. IP address

B. Subnet mask

C. Default gateway

D. None of the above. The problem must lie elsewhere.

3. You have a Class B network address of `166.37.0.0` with a subnet mask of `255.255.224.0`. Which of the following IP addresses are valid (choose all that apply)?

   A. `166.37.22.77`

   B. `166.37.25.77`

   C. `166.37.190.88`

   D. `166.37.200.23`

4. You are the network architect in a Class B enterprise internetwork. You are designing a new network that will have 22 subnets to start, but it will scale quickly to over 100 subnets within a year. Each subnet must support at least 350 hosts. Which of the following subnet masks will enable you to meet your objective?

   A. `255.255.0.0`

   B. `255.255.248.0`

   C. `255.255.255.0`

   D. `255.255.254.0`

5. You have a Class C network address of `192.168.7.0` with a subnet mask of `255.255.255.240`. Which of the following host IP addresses are valid?

   A. `192.168.7.16`

   B. `192.168.7.5`

   C. `192.168.7.63`

   D. `192.168.7.32`

   E. `192.168.7.17`

6. After setting up a new client on a subnet, you find that you are able to `ping` all of the other devices on the same subnet, but you cannot ping the server on a separate subnet. Which of the following steps should you take next to isolate this problem?

   A. `Ping` the loopback address.

   B. `Ping` the near side of the router.

   C. `Ping` the far side of the router.

   D. `Ping` your computer by IP address.

7. You are a systems engineer on a consulting project with a multinational corporation with a Class B network address. You are designing a WAN strategy to connect the remote field offices via a direct connection between each physical site. Each of these links must be on its own subnet or network, and each router port requires an address. Which of the following basic designs meet these criteria?

   A. Use the 255.255.255.0 subnet mask with a distance vector routing protocol such as RIP v1.

   B. Use the 255.255.255.252 subnet mask with a link state routing protocol such as OSPF.

   C. Use the 255.255.255.254 subnet mask with a distance vector routing protocol such as OSPF.

   D. Use the 255.255.255.248 subnet mask with a distance vector routing protocol such as VLSM.

   E. Use the 255.255.255.224 subnet mask with a link state routing protocol such as RIP v2.

8. You administer a network for which you are deploying DHCP. Network hosts will receive their IP configuration from the DHCP server, and network servers have been configured with static addresses. After deploying DHCP, users suddenly cannot print documents. You realize the printers have the wrong IP addresses assigned. What is the reason the printers are misconfigured?

   A. You did not enable the relay agent service.

   B. You did not reserve the IP addresses belonging to the printers.

   C. You did not authorize the scope containing the printers' IP addresses.

   D. You did not exclude the IP addresses belonging to the printers.

9. A user is experiencing difficulty connecting to some computers in different departments. You notice that all of these computers are on remote subnets, so you begin a `ping` test to troubleshoot. You succeed in pinging all of the other workstations in the subnet and most of the workstations in the remote subnets on the intranet. You cannot `ping` all of the remote subnets. However, all of the other computers can `ping` each other. What is the most likely cause of this problem?

   A. The user has a duplicate IP address.

   B. The user has an invalid default gateway.

   C. A filter is applied on the routing protocol.

   D. The user has an invalid subnet mask.

10. You add a second subnet to your network to accommodate additional users. You create a new DHCP scope for the new subnet. However, the DHCP server is not servicing any of the clients on the new subnet. What should you do to resolve this problem?

    A. Configure a WINS proxy server.

    B. Configure a DHCP Relay Agent.

    C. Authorize the scope for the new subnet.

    D. Configure a new default gateway to correspond to the appropriate router port.

11. You are a consultant specializing in network design. Your client is a small, family-run manufacturing business that uses the network only for file sharing and printing capabilities. A separate stand-alone computer is used for dial-up access to the Internet. The network has only grown by two computers in the last three years, and future growth projections are minimal. Which of the following types of IP addressing schemes would work for this client?

    A. Private IP addressing

    B. Public IP addressing

    C. Unauthorized IP addressing

    D. All of the above

12. You are the network architect for a large technical consulting firm. Your new ISP has given you a Class C address with a default subnet mask. Your job is to design a network with 16 subnets (12 are required now, and 4 are reserved for future growth) that supports 200 nodes per subnet. Which technology will support this design?

    A. Classful addressing

    B. VLSM

    C. CIDR

    D. Subnetting

13. You are the systems engineer of a large enterprise internetwork. You are planning a routing strategy and deciding which routing technologies to implement. Your objectives include scalability, ease of administration, and high performance. Which of the following options provides the best solution?

    A. Implement a combination of hardware and software routing; use dynamic routing with a link-state routing protocol such as RIPv2.

    B. Implement hardware routing; use dynamic routing with a link-state routing protocol such as OSPF.

    C. Implement a combination of hardware and software routing; use static routing with a link-state routing protocol such as OSPF.

    D. Implement a combination of hardware and software routing; use dynamic routing with a distance vector routing protocol such as RIP v1.

14. You are creating a Class A network with eight subnets. What should your subnet mask be?

    A. 255.0.0.0

    B. 255.192.0.0

    C. 255.240.0.0

    D. 255.224.0.0

    E. 255.255.0.0

15. As a network architect in a large enterprise, you are evaluating the IP addressing strategy for your company. Your objectives are to implement supernetting to fuse contiguous subnets into larger supernets. Which of the following combinations of technology choices will best enable you to achieve your objective?

    A. Classless routing protocols, dynamic routing

    B. Noncontiguous subnets and a combination of static and dynamic routing

    C. Distance vector routing protocols and classful IP addressing

    D. RIPv1 and BGP

Answers to Review Questions

1. D. The purpose of subnetting is to create a greater number of smaller networks. In this example, performance considerations dictate that you will never have more than 200 computers per subnet inclusive of future growth. Options A, B, and C allow for many more host IDs than you will ever need to support on a subnet. We know that regardless of growth, you will never have more than 200 hosts per subnet, so the default mask `255.255.255.0` with 254 hosts per subnet is the most efficient way to meet your criteria and is, therefore, the best choice. Choice E cannot be correct because it provides only 126 hosts ($2^7 - 2 = 126$) per subnet.

2. A. The problem is that this workstation's IP address is illegal given the subnet mask. When defining a subnet ID, you take the value of the lowest bit used in the subnet mask. In this example that would be `11000000`. The value of the lowest bit is 64, which means that the subnets will be in increments of 64 as follows. `134.62.1.1` through `134.62.63.254`; `134.62.64.1` through `134.62.127.254`; `134.62.128.1` through `134.62.191.254`; and `134.62.192.1` through `134.62.254.254`. However, due to conventions, the first and last set of subnet IDs are illegal and cannot be used. Microsoft adheres to this convention on the exam, so be forewarned.

3. C, D. Options C and D are the only IP addresses listed that are within the range defined by this subnet mask.

4. D. `255.255.0.0` is the default subnet mask for a Class B network that is not subnetted. `255.255.248.0` will only support up to 30 subnets. `255.255.255.0` can support up to 254 subnets, but only 254 hosts. `255.255.254.0` will give you 126 subnets and 510 hosts.

5. E. The only valid address here is `192.168.7.17`. Because subnetting, by convention, disallows you from using the first and last networks when you subnet, the first usable network in this scenario is `192.168.7.16`. Therefore, A is invalid because it uses a network address, and B is invalid because it uses an address from the first network. C is invalid because it uses the broadcast address of the second network (`192.168.7.32`). D is invalid because it uses a network address.

6. B. Pinging the default gateway, which is the near side of the router, would be the next step in isolating the problem. This enables you to verify that traffic can get to the default gateway for the subnet. Pinging the far side of the router enables you to confirm that the routing table is correct, and it would be the next step if pinging the near side of the router worked. If you are able to ping every computer on the local subnet, then pinging the loopback is unnecessary because you obviously already have good network communications. The same holds true for pinging the local computer by IP address.

7. B. The best option in this scenario is to use the 255.255.255.252 subnet mask, which gives you 16,382 subnets with 2 hosts per subnet. You must use a link-state routing protocol such as OSPF to support VLSM. VLSM allows you to run the 255.255.255.252 subnet mask on your interface to the WANs, and run the 255.255.255.0 subnet mask on the router interfaces in your LAN.

8. B. IP address reservations are required for network devices including printers and routers prior to deploying DHCP.

9. D. An invalid subnet mask, depending on how it is misconfigured, can cause connectivity problems with some remote subnets but not others.

10. B. In order to use DHCP for address assignment, each subnet must have either its own DHCP server or a DHCP Relay Agent configured.

11. D. The simplest method is to use a private IP addressing scheme. However, because this is a small, private network with no need to connect to the Internet, you could use any of the IP addressing schemes: public, private, or even unauthorized IP addressing. The stand-alone computer for dial-up access must have a registered public address.

12. C. Classful addressing will allow only one subnet with 254 nodes. VLSM will allow more subnets, but not enough hosts in each subnet. The only possible answer is CIDR. By moving the subnet mask to the left, you can create the required number of subnets (supernetting) and provide the required number of nodes. Choice D is the same as Choice B.

13. B. Enterprise internetworks will benefit most from a routing strategy that features hardware routing, dynamic routing, and link-state routing protocols such as OSPF. The fastest routing always occurs through hardware routing. To increase cost-effectiveness, software routing can also be used.

14. C. Class A networks use `255.0.0.0` as the standard subnet mask. It does not support any additional subnets. `255.192.0.0` can be used to create 2 subnets, `255.224.0.0` can be used to create 6 subnets and `255.240.0.0` can be used to create up to 14. An easy way to calculate this is to break it down into binary. The subnet mask `255.240.0.0` in binary is: `11111111.11110000.00000000.00000000`. Note the second octet, 11110000. Add up the binary values of the four 1s in the second octet, and you get 8 + 4 + 2 + 1 = 15. Finally, subtract 1 and you have the number of subnets that a given mask will support.

15. A. Supernetting requires the use of classless routing protocols. It is incompatible with RIPv1 and classful IP addressing.

Planning a Network Connectivity Strategy

MICROSOFT EXAM OBJECTIVES COVERED IN THIS CHAPTER:

✓ **Plan and modify a network topology.**

- Plan the physical placement of network resources.
- Identify network protocols to be used.

✓ **Plan a routing strategy.**

- Identify routing protocols to use in a specified environment.
- Plan routing for IP multicast traffic.

✓ **Troubleshoot TCP/IP routing. Tools might include the `route`, `tracert`, `ping`, `pathping`, and `netsh` commands and Network Monitor.**

✓ **Plan an Internet connectivity strategy.**

✓ **Troubleshoot connectivity to the Internet.**

- Diagnose and resolve issues related to Network Address Translation (NAT).
- Diagnose and resolve issues related to name resolution cache information.
- Diagnose and resolve issues related to client configuration.

The logical TCP/IP network infrastructure maps to the physical network design and is related to the tasks of planning routing and planning network connectivity. Both tasks are critical to laying a solid foundation for a stable and scalable network infrastructure.

Routing is the process of delivering traffic to the correct destination. IP routing is simple to understand at the most basic level: Packets have addresses, and the process of routing involves getting a packet from its source to its destination. In the previous chapter, you learned the general considerations when planning a routing solution in conjunction with an IP addressing strategy. Now we can delve more fully into the topic of how IP routing is actually implemented in Windows Server 2003.

Until recently, Microsoft did not offer a way for more than one person to share a single connection to the Internet. Linux and MacOS users have been able to do this for a while, and a number of third parties have shipped products like WinGate to provide this functionality. As part of Windows 98 Second Edition, Microsoft included a feature called *Internet Connection Sharing (ICS)*. The idea behind ICS is simple: If you have more than one computer and the computers are networked together, one of them can act as a gateway to the Internet. This is conceptually simple, but some behind-the-scenes magic must happen to implement it.

ICS is a simple implementation of a service called *Network Address Translation (NAT)*. Every IP packet contains address information. NAT is a service that translates between your own network's addresses and Internet-visible addresses. With NAT, your entire network uses only a single IP address on the Internet. All outgoing traffic passes through the NAT host machine on its way out. All inbound traffic is likewise addressed to the ICS host machine, which is responsible for passing it back to the proper computer on your local network.

ICS is as limited as it is simple. In a very small office, such as a home with only a few computers, ICS can be used to share one connection to the Internet. For most organizations, a more robust NAT solution is needed. Fortunately, organizations can take advantage of the more scalable implementation of NAT that is managed through the Routing and Remote Access Services (RRAS) console in Windows Server 2003.

We'll begin this chapter with a discussion of IP routing in Windows Server 2003. Then we'll proceed to NAT and how it is used to establish network, extranet, and Internet connectivity under Windows Server 2003.

The TCP/IP configuration and troubleshooting tools were introduced in Chapter 2, "Planning a TCP/IP Network Infrastructure." Network Monitor is covered in Chapter 10, "Planning Network Monitoring, Remote Administration, and Recovery."

Understanding IP Routing

Complex networks like the Internet support, and even require, routing. Consider what happens when you want to fly from one part of the country to another. If you look at a map of the physical topology of the Internet, you'll see that there are a large number of potential routes to get from one location to another. Some might be better than others; for instance, one route could take you west, across the Pacific, then Eastern Europe, then Western Europe, and then across the Atlantic Ocean to the East Coast of the U.S. That is a legal route, and it would get the data to its intended destination, but it would be terribly inefficient.

Routing combines the idea that each packet on a network has a source and destination with the idea of associating routes with costs. The concept of a route's "cost" is similar to the expenses involved in travel. A direct flight from San Francisco to New York costs less time, money, and risk than an indirect flight with intermediate stops in Phoenix and D.C. The longer, indirect flight takes passengers longer to get there and each change of planes adds to the risk that their bags will be delayed or lost in transit. In an analogous fashion, routing systems allow administrators to attach a *metric*, or cost, to each leg of a route. In a moment, you'll see how routing systems use this metric information to calculate the most efficient route for packets to take.

Although Windows Server 2003 supports routing IPX, AppleTalk, and IP, this section will cover only IP routing. It is the most widely used, and it is the one featured on the exam.

The actual way in which the metric information is used in calculations varies between RIP version 1, RIP version 2, and OSPF. The important point to remember is that all three protocols use metrics to figure out the "best" route in any situation.

In the following sections, we'll cover how routing works, including static versus dynamic routing. Then we'll cover routing in Windows Server 2003 and finish with terms you should know.

How Routing Works

In this section, we'll discuss the theory and practice of routing IP networks. The basic underlying idea is that each packet on a network has a source address and a destination address, which means that any device that receives the packet can inspect its headers to determine where it came from and where it is going. If such a device also has information about the network's design and implementation—for example, how long it takes packets to travel over a particular link—it can intelligently change the routing to minimize the total cost.

According to the OSI model, a gateway and a router are two different things. However, Microsoft uses the terms interchangeably, and so will we.

Figure 3.1 shows an imaginary network made up of six interconnected local networks. These networks, named A through F, are connected by links of varying speeds and costs. This accurately mirrors what happens in the real world, where it is common for internal networks (or Internet providers) to have multiple ways to establish a link between two points.

FIGURE 3.1 An example network

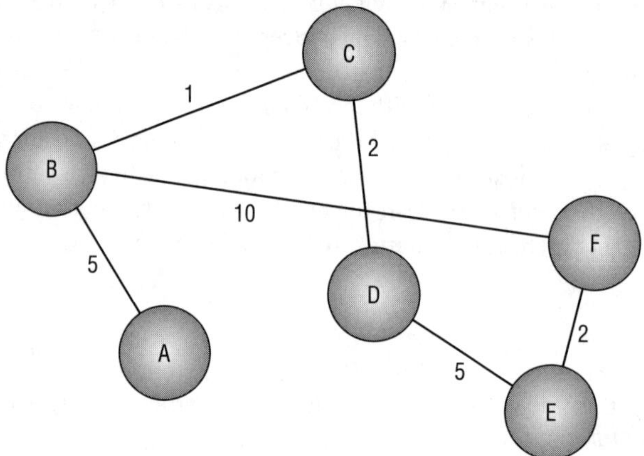

Imagine that a client machine on network B wants to send traffic to a machine on network E. The most obvious route would probably be B to F to E, but you could also use B to C to D to E. Notice the costs: B-F-E has a total cost of 12, while the seemingly longer B-C-D-E actually has a lower cost of 8. That does not appear to make sense, because the latter route has a longer path. When you consider what "cost" really means, though, you'll understand why this makes sense.

Assigning link costs is entirely up to you. Normally, you assign costs that reflect your preference for how you want traffic to flow. A high-priced, fast link would probably deserve a lower cost than a cheaper or slower link; by assigning your most financially expensive links (say, a metered ISDN connection) a high cost, they would not be used if there were more cost-efficient links available.

Now, revisit Figure 3.1 with the assumption that each circle is really a router. After all, you can hide all the complexity of the network behind a router, because only the router is in charge of moving packets. Call your client machine "X" and your server "Y." When X wants to send traffic to Y, it already knows the destination IP address of its target. X will build a packet, including its IP address as the source and Y's address as the destination. X will then use its default gateway setting to send that packet to router B.

Router B receives the packet and has both source and destination address information. By examining the IP addresses, it can determine that it does not know a direct route to the network where Y is located. However, there are two intermediate nodes that claim to know how to reach Y: C and F. Because C has the lowest link cost, the router at B will send the packet to C in a simple routing algorithm. When C receives it, it will go through the same process, forwarding the packet on to D, and so on. Eventually, the packet arrives at its destination.

The Internetwork

An *internetwork* is a network of networks. For example, Figure 3.2 shows a sample internetwork that actually contains five distinct networks: Atlanta, Boston, Orlando, Portland, and San Diego. The internetwork is the collection of all of these networks.

Do not confuse "an internetwork" with "the Internet." The Internet we all use is actually just a really large, really complex internetwork.

FIGURE 3.2 A sample internetwork

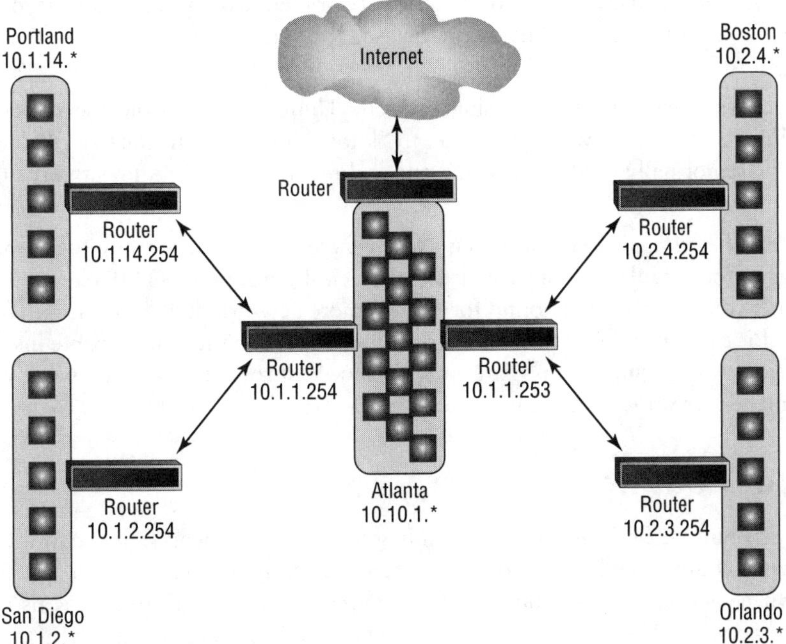

Our sample internetwork uses routers to connect the four satellite networks with headquarters in Atlanta. In this chapter, you'll examine different configuration choices for the routers and how these choices affect the overall performance and reliability of the internetwork.

Internal routing refers to the process of moving packets within as opposed to outside of an internetwork. Internal routers can use static or dynamic routing techniques to build the routing table for their local areas.

Routing Tables

A *routing table* is a database that stores route information. Think of it as a road map for the internetwork—the routing table lists which routes exist between networks, so the router or host can look up the necessary information when it encounters a packet bound for a foreign network. Each entry in the routing table contains the following four pieces of information:

- The network address of the remote host or network
- The forwarding address to which traffic for the remote network should be sent
- The network interface that should be used to send to the forwarding address
- A cost, or metric, that indicates what relative priority should be assigned to this route

For example, you could write the San Diego-Atlanta route as `10.1.1.0:10.10.1.254:ATL:1`, assuming that the interface name was "ATL" and that you wanted to use a metric of 1. The actual format of how these entries are stored is not important (in fact, it is not visible in RRAS); what's important for you to know is that every routing table entry contains that information.

Routing tables actually can contain these three different kinds of routes:

- *Network routes* provide a route to an entire network. For example, the San Diego-to-Atlanta route is a network route because it can be used to route traffic from any host in San Diego to any host in Atlanta.
- *Host routes* provide a route to a single system. Think of them as shortcuts—they provide a slightly more efficient way for a router to "know" how to get traffic to a remote machine, so they are normally used when you want to direct traffic to remote networks through a particular machine.
- The *default route* is where packets go when there is no explicit route for them. This is similar to the default gateway you are used to configuring for TCP/IP clients. Any time a router encounters a packet bound for some remote network, it will first search the routing table; if it cannot find a network or host route, it will use the default route instead. This saves you from having to configure a network or host route for every network with which you might ever want to communicate.

Types of Routing

There are different methods of routing depending on the requirements of a network or internetwork. Internal routing can be static or dynamic, as you're about to discover. Border routing is involved when packets are routed outside of an internetwork. Multicast routing is also supported in Windows Server 2003 so that packets can be sent to multiple host destinations. In the following sections, we'll discuss each of these four types of routing.

Static Routing

Static routing systems do not make any attempt to discover other routers or systems on their networks. Instead, static routes specify how to get packets to a specific network. For example, the simplest way to configure our sample internetwork is to configure each router in a remote office with a single static route entry that routes all packets for foreign addresses over the link to Atlanta. For example, assume that a user in San Diego wants to access a resource on the Boston network. The packet goes from the client machine to the San Diego router, which examines its routing table and finds no network route for the Boston network. The default route kicks in, and the packet goes to Atlanta, which *does* have a network route for Boston.

If you instead defined a static route for the San Diego-Boston hop, what would it look like? The remote network address is `10.2.4.0`, and the corresponding forwarding address is `10.1.1.254`—this combination effectively says, "All packets going to Boston should be sent to Atlanta." The interface and metric will vary according to how you set up the route.

Static routes tell the routing engine how to get data to other networks by indicating what other networks are reachable from your network. They do this by specifying their network addresses and subnet masks, along with a metric for that network. This information goes into the system's routing table, which contains a list of known routes to other networks. When an outgoing packet arrives at the routing engine, the engine can examine the routing table to select the lowest-cost route to the destination. If there is no explicit entry in the routing table for that network, the packet goes to the default route, which is then entrusted with getting the packet where it needs to go. The default route is a physical connection that is used when no explicit route is found in the routing table. For example, a router has two routes to two different sites within the same company. When a packet is addressed to an address that is not in either site, the router will use the default route that is pointing to a physical connection attached to the Internet.

Static routing is faster and more efficient than dynamic routing. Static routing works well when your network does not change much. You can identify the remote networks to which you want to route, then add static routes to them to reflect the costs and topology of your network. In Windows Server 2003, you maintain static routes with the route command, which allows you to either see the contents of the routing table or modify it by adding and removing static routes to individual networks.

Dynamic Routing

By contrast with static routing, *dynamic routing* does not depend on your adding fixed, unchangeable routes to remote networks. Instead, a dynamic routing engine can discover its surroundings by finding and communicating with other nearby routers in an internetwork.

This process, usually called *router discovery*, enables a newly added (or rebooted) router to configure itself. This is roughly equivalent to the process that happens when you move into a new neighborhood. Within a short time of your arrival, you'll probably meet most of the people who live nearby, either because they come to you or because you go to them. At that point, you have useful information about the surrounding environment that could only come from people who were already there.

The two major dynamic routing protocols in Windows Server 2003 are the Routing Information Protocol (RIP) and the Open Shortest Path First (OSPF) protocol, which we will look at in the following sections. Each has its advantages and disadvantages, but they share some common features and functionality. Each router (whether a hardware device, a Windows Server 2003 machine, or whatever) is connected to at least two separate physical networks. When the router starts, the only information it has is drawn from its internal routing table. Normally, that means it knows about all the attached networks plus whatever static routes have been previously defined. The router then receives configuration information that tells it about the state and topology of the network.

As time goes on, the network's physical topology can change. For example, take a look at the network in Figure 3.3. If network G suddenly dropped out of the air, the routers in sites A, D, and E would need to readjust their routing tables because they could no longer route traffic directly to G. The process by which this adjustment happens is what makes routing dynamic, and it is also the largest area of difference between the two major dynamic routing protocols for IP.

FIGURE 3.3 A more complex, dynamically routed network

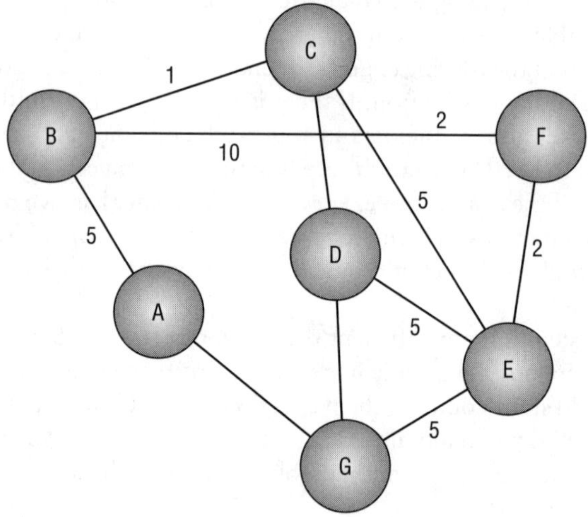

The Routing Information Protocol (RIP)

RIP is like NetBEUI: It is simple and easy to configure, but it has performance limitations that restrict its usefulness on medium-to-large networks. RIP routers begin with a basically empty routing table, but they immediately begin sending out announcements that they know will reach the networks to which they are connected. These announcements may be broadcast or multicast. Routers on other networks that hear these announcements can add those routes to their own routing tables. The process works both ways, of course; our hypothetical router will hear announcements from other routers and then add those routes to its list of places it knows how to reach.

Microsoft's RIP implementation in Windows Server 2003 supports only version 2 of RIP. The primary difference between the two versions is the manner in which updates are sent. RIPv1 uses broadcasts every 30 seconds, and RIPv2 uses multicasts only when routes change. In the real world, RIPv1 routes over seven hops are very slow and may not work at all due to time-outs. RIP v1 sends the entire table, even if there is no change. RIPv2 also supports simple (e.g., plain text) username/password authentication, which is handy to prevent unwanted changes from cluttering your routing tables.

To prevent unwanted changes to the routing table, you can use the RRAS snap-in to set up two kinds of filters that screen out some types of updates. Route filters allow you to pick and choose the networks that you want to admit knowing about and for which you want to accept announcements. Peer filters give you control over the neighboring routers to which your router will listen.

In addition to sending and receiving announcements, RIPv2 routers have the ability to receive triggered updates. When you know that your network topology is changing (perhaps because you've added connectivity to another network), you can send out a trigger that contains information about the changes. This trigger forces all the RIP routers you own to assimilate the changes immediately. Triggered updates are also useful, because routers that detect a link or router failure can update their routing tables and announce the change, making their neighbors aware of it sooner rather than later.

RIP also incorporates features that attempt to prevent route loops. Refer back to Figure 3.2. The network topology has the potential to cause a route loop. Why? Say that someone in E wants to send a packet to a machine in A, but the G-to-A and D-to-C links are down. E sends the packet to G, which recognizes that it cannot reach A. G also knows that the route D-C-B-A will work, so it sends the packet to D. When the packet reaches D, D knows it cannot talk to C, so it sends the packet to E because E-G-A is normally a valid route. You can see that the packet will never reach its destination and will loop continually. This might seem like a contrived example, but in real life, where internetwork links are often concentrated among a small number of physical links, it is a real problem.

RIP offers several methods for resolving and preventing loops, including the split-horizon and poison reverse algorithms.

Understanding how the split-horizon and poison reverse algorithms work is not important for the purposes of this book. Knowing their purpose and that RIP implements them to protect against routing loops is enough.

RIP has two operation modes:

Periodic Update Mode In *periodic update mode*, a RIP router sends out its list of known routes at periodic intervals (which you define). The router marks any routes it learns from other routers as RIP routes, which means they remain active only while the router is running. If the router is stopped, the routes vanish. This mode is the default for RIP on LAN interfaces, but it is not suitable for demand-dial connections because you do not want your router to bring up a connection just to announce its presence.

Auto-static Update Mode In *auto-static update mode*, the RRAS router only broadcasts the contents of its routing table when a remote router asks for them. Better still, the routes that the RRAS router learns from its RIP neighbors are marked as static routes in the routing table, and they persist until you manually delete them—even if the router is stopped and restarted or if RIP is disabled for that interface. Auto-static mode is the default for demand-dial interfaces, because a table update will cause a dial-up.

The Open Shortest Path First (OSPF) Protocol

RIP is designed for fairly small networks; as it turns out, it can only handle 15 router-to-router hops. If you have a network that spans more than 16 routers at any point, RIP will not be able to cache routes for it; some parts of the network will appear to be (or actually will be) unreachable. The Open Shortest Path First (OSPF) protocol is designed for use on large or very large networks. It is much more efficient than RIP, but more knowledge and experience are required to set up and administer it.

RIP routers continually exchange routing data with one another, which allows incorrect route entries to propagate. Instead of doing that, each OSPF router maintains a map of the state of the internetwork. This map, called a *link state map*, provides a continually updated reference to the state of each internetwork link. Neighboring routers group into an *adjacency* (think neighborhood); within an adjacency, routers synchronize any changes to the link state map. When the network topology changes, the router that notices it first floods the internetwork with change notifications. Each router that receives the notification updates its copy of the link map and then recalculates its internal routing table.

The "SPF" in OSPF refers to the algorithm that OSPF systems use to calculate routes: Routes are calculated so that the shortest path (e.g., the one with the lowest cost) is used first. SPF-calculated routes are always free of loops, which is another nice advantage over RIP.

OSPF is not available on 64-bit versions of Windows XP or Windows Server 2003.

OSPF networks are broken down into areas; an area is a collection of interconnected networks. Think of an area as a subsection of an internetwork. Areas are interconnected by backbones. Each OSPF router keeps a link state database only for the areas to which it is connected. Special OSPF routers called *area border routers* interlink areas. Figure 3.4 shows how this looks.

FIGURE 3.4 A simple OSPF network

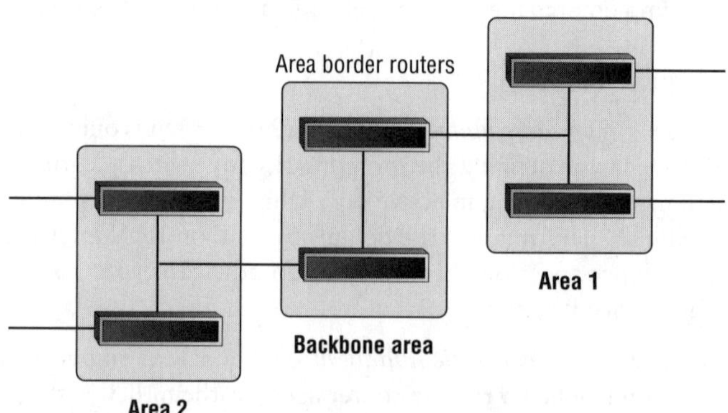

Microsoft's OSPF implementation supports (but does not require) the use of *route filters*, which allow you to pick and choose the networks that you want to admit knowing about and for which you want to accept announcements. This means that any Windows Server 2003 OSPF router can choose to accept routing information either from other OSPF routers or from other types of routers (e.g., those using RIP). In addition, a desirable feature not always found in OSPF routers is that you can change any of the OSPF settings discussed later in this chapter and have them take effect immediately without having to stop and restart the router.

Real World Scenario

Determining Whether to Use Software or Hardware Routers

For several years, your company has been growing steadily. It has grown from a small network of 50 Windows NT workstations and 5 Windows NT servers to a medium-sized network of more than 200 Windows 2000 and XP Professional workstations and more than 10 Windows Server 2003 servers. Everything functions properly, but performance is beginning to suffer. After analyzing the network traffic, you realize that you need to segment the network into subnets to control the traffic and improve the performance. You are considering using multihomed computers to save money on the purchase price of dedicated routers.

A great deal can be said about the level of sophistication in Windows Server 2003, such as the expanded support within routing protocols. For years, RIP has been used to build fairly large networks, while OSPF has been used for huge, complex networks. However, that level of functionality is cost-prohibitive for many environments. But before you leap at the cost savings of using a multihomed Windows Server 2003, you want to take a closer look.

Despite the expense, there is a notable performance advantage in using dedicated hardware routers for the connection points in networks. When there is a significant utilization of bandwidth across your network, whether or not the multihomed host will be able to provide the level of service that you need is questionable. The performance of general-purpose operating systems such as Windows Server 2003 will always pale in comparison to a specialized device that is designed to perform a singular task. In addition, with the basic routing protocol, there are many tools and services that are used to guarantee levels of service and to set up filters and access-control lists.

Windows Server 2003 has its advantages as a router when you want to connect a small satellite office to a larger network. Software routing using ws2003 will provide the basic routing functionality to make the connection, when more robust services are not necessary. Make sure you apply these Windows Server 2003 routing services in the areas that are appropriate for the particular load and scale of your situation.

Border Routing

Border routing occurs when packets leave your internetwork and go to another one someplace else. When you use your home computer to browse a Web site, TCP/IP packets from your machine go to your ISP (probably via PPP, over an analog, cable, DSL, or ISDN connection).

The ISP examines the destination address of the packets and determines that they should go to some other network to which it does not have a direct connection.

As an example, consider what happens when you want to fetch a Web page from Microsoft's Web site. You are dialed into a local ISP (such as hiwaay.net), which is connected to several upper-tier providers, including Sprint and Cable & Wireless. Microsoft uses so much bandwidth that it acts as its own ISP, but its Web server farm is located on yet another network.

Figure 3.5 shows this internetwork with a dashed border area around each piece of the internetwork: one for HiWAAY, one for Cable & Wireless, one for msft.net, and one for Microsoft proper. The thick black lines between borders indicate *backbone links*, which are links that join border areas together.

FIGURE 3.5 Networks are divided into border areas linked by backbones.

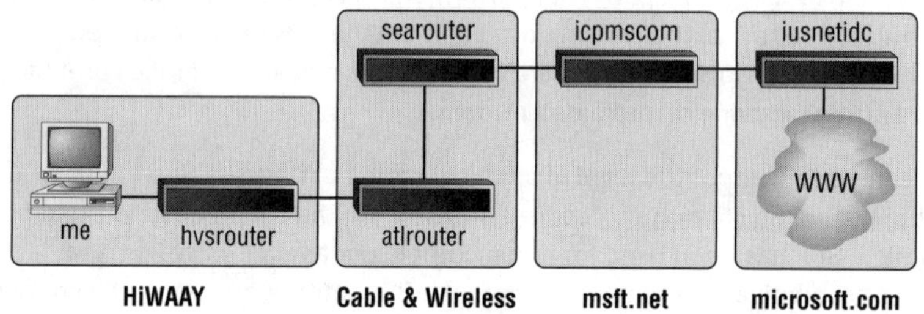

In a border routing network, some routers are responsible for handling packets inside the area, while others manage network communication with other areas. These border routers are responsible for storing routes to other borders that they can reach over the backbone. Because this represents a huge number of potential routes, border routing requires a dynamic routing protocol—OSPF. OSPF will allow a border router at HiWAAY to discover routes in the adjacent Cable & Wireless border area.

Multicast Routing

Multicast routing works by sending a packet to a single IP address that is read by many hosts. The hosts all have individual IP addresses, but they belong to a multicast group that shares a single, separate IP address. Multicast group membership is dynamic, and groups can contain unlimited hosts on separate IP networks, provided that routers between the networks support multicast traffic. In fact, computers that aren't part of a multicast group can send multicast packets.

Multicasting uses a special range of IP addresses, called the *Class D address space*, reserved exclusively for multicasting. The multicast address range contains the IP addresses 224.0.0.0 through 239.255.255.255. Each multicast group uses a single address in the Class D address space. In addition, just like regular IP addresses, the multicast address range reserves a few special addresses used for specific purposes. Table 3.1 details a partial list of these special multicast addresses.

TABLE 3.1 Special Multicast Addresses

Address	Description
224.0.0.0	Base address (reserved)
224.0.0.1	All Hosts, all systems on the same network segment
224.0.0.2	All Routers, all routers on the same network segment
224.0.0.5	All OSPF Routers, used to send routing information to all OSPF routers on the network
224.0.0.6	All Designated OSPF Routers, used to send routing information to all designated OSPF routers
224.0.0.9	All RIP 2 Routers, used to send routing information to all RIP 2 routers on the network
224.0.1.24	Used to support replication for WINS servers

Companies that specialize in routing solutions (such as Cisco and Nortel) define and use addresses within the multicast range. The lower range of Class D should be avoided when configuring a Multicast range, especially when those routers connect to the Internet.

Internet Group Management Protocol (IGMP) is used to exchange multicast group membership information between multicast-capable routers. You can configure RRAS in IGMP router mode or IGMP proxy mode as discussed here:

IGMP Router Mode IGMP router mode listens for IGMP membership report packets and tracks group membership. IGMP router mode must be attached to any interfaces that connect to multicast-configured hosts.

IGMP Proxy Mode IGMP proxy mode essentially acts like a multicast host, except that it forwards IGMP membership report packets to an IGMP router. This provides a list of multicast-enabled hosts to an upstream router that normally would not be aware of the hosts. Typically, IGMP proxy is used on single-router networks connected to the Internet. The IGMP proxy sends the list of multicast hosts to the multicast-capable portion of the Internet known as the Internet multicast backbone, or MBone, so that the hosts can receive multicast packets.

You may need to send multicast traffic across routers that aren't multicast compatible. This is made possible through the use of IP-in-IP interfaces. An IP-in-IP interface actually encapsulates packets with an additional IP header. The encapsulated packets can be sent across any router because they appear to be ordinary IP packets. You create and manage IP-in-IP interfaces in RRAS similarly to the way you configure other interfaces.

Routing in Windows Server 2003

In Windows Server 2003, routing is implemented by using the Routing and Remote Access Services (RRAS).

RRAS also handles VPN and dial-up network connectivity. RRAS was introduced in *MCSA/MCSE: Windows Server 2003 Network Infrastructure Implementation, Management, and Maintenance Study Guide* by, James Chellis, Paul Robixchaux, and Matt Sheltz.

RRAS provides a multiprotocol router—in other words, the RRAS routing engine can handle multiple network protocols and multiple routing methods on multiple NICs. When you consider that most of the T1-speed routers on the net right now are powered by Motorola 68030s running at 25MHz, you can see why a machine powerful enough to handle Windows Server 2003 should not have any trouble with routing.

RRAS provides some specific features that are of interest when the conversation turns to network routing. These features include the following:

- It can bring up connections to specific networks when the router receives packets addressed to those networks. This is *demand-dial routing*, and it allows you to use on-demand links instead of permanent connections. This is especially nice for ISDN, which combines per-minute fees in most places with really fast call setup times. PPTP connections can be demand-dialed, too, or you can use demand-dial interfaces to make long-distance connections only when they are needed.
- You can establish static routes that specify where packets bound for certain networks should go. The most common use of this feature is to link a remote network with your LAN; the remote network gets one static route that basically says, "Any traffic leaving my subnet should be sent to the router," and then RRAS handles it from there.
- It provides dynamic routing using RIPv2 and the OSPF protocol. These protocols provide two different ways for your router to share routing information with other routers "near" it in network space.
- It provides *packet filtering* to screen out undesirable packets in both directions. For example, you can create a packet filter to keep out FTP traffic, or you can add a filter to a demand-dial interface so that it will be brought up only for Web or e-mail traffic. Other traffic types will pass if the link is up, but they will not cause RRAS to open the link if it is not already open.
- It supports *unicast routing*, in which one machine sends directly to one destination address. It also supports multicast routing, where one machine sends to a group of computers or an entire network.
- It supports *network address translation (NAT)*, a service that allows multiple LAN clients to share a single IP address or multiple public IP addresses and Internet connections.

Managing IP Routing

You will manage all of the tasks in this chapter from the Routing and Remote Access console (see Figure 3.6). This is the command center from which you will actually configure such things as the static routes and routing protocols we've discussed so far in this chapter.

FIGURE 3.6 The Routing and Remote Access console

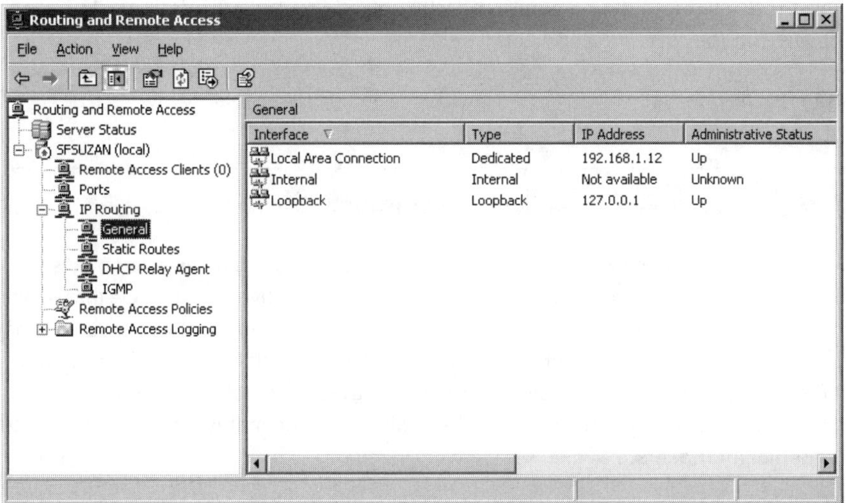

You already know from experience and prior study that the server's functionality is configured through the RRAS Setup Wizard. Just right-click the server and choose Configure And Enable Routing and Remote Access from the context menu. When the summary page of the RRAS Setup Wizard appears, it will remind you to do either two or three of the following things:

- Add demand-dial interfaces if you want to support demand dialing.
- Give each routable interface a network address for each protocol it carries. For example, if you are using TCP/IP and IPX on a computer with three NICs, each NIC that participates in routing needs to have distinct TCP/IP and IPX addresses.
- Install and configure the routing protocols (e.g., OSPF or RIP for IP in this case) on the interfaces that should support them.

These three steps form the core of what you must do to make your RRAS server into an IP router.

In the following sections, you'll learn how to create and manage interfaces, how to set IP routing properties, how to manage routing protocols, and how to manage static routes.

Creating and Managing Interfaces

The Network Interfaces node in the RRAS snap-in shows you a summary of the routable interfaces available on your machine for *all* protocols. It lists all of the LAN and demand-dial interfaces, plus two special interfaces maintained by RRAS: Loopback and Internal. Each of the interfaces displayed has a type, a status (either enabled or disabled), and a connection status associated with it.

For example, one of the machines in the internetwork displayed earlier in Figure 3.5 has two LAN interfaces—Public (HiWAAY) and Private (`192.168.0.x`). Each of those interfaces represents a potential destination for routed packets.

You can right-click each interface to get a context menu with some useful commands, including Disable, Enable, and Unreachability Reason (that command tells you why an interface is marked as "unreachable"). Some commands are specific to demand-dial interfaces, and they will be covered in the following sections.

The next sections will cover the different types of interfaces, including LAN, demand-dial, RIP, and OSPF interfaces.

What It Means When an Interface Is "Unreachable"

A demand-dial interface can have several different states. The enabled and disabled states that appear in the Status column indicate whether the link is administratively available—that is, whether you are allowing people to use it or not. The Connection State column shows you whether the connection is *working* or not, which makes the display more useful. The default state for a demand-dial connection is Disconnected. When RRAS tries to establish a connection, the state changes to Connected. In both the connected and disconnected states, any static routes tied to the demand-dial interface are available.

When RRAS tries to dial a number and fails to connect, it will continue to try until it reaches the redial limit set in the Dialing tab of the interface's Properties dialog box. If the redial limit is reached, the interface will be marked as Unreachable for a time-out period. As long as the interface is unreachable, any static routes pointing to it will be unavailable—they'll actually disappear from the routing table. After the time-out period, RRAS will try again to dial; if it fails this time, it tacks another 10 minutes onto the time-out and tries again. The time-out starts at 10 minutes and works up from there; if it reaches 6 hours, it will stop incrementing the counter so the time-out will stay there until a successful connection is made or until you restart the RRAS service.

Fortunately, you can adjust both the minimum and maximum values for this time-out from their defaults (10 minutes and 6 hours, respectively). You make this change by adding two `REG_DWORD` values to `HKLM\System\CurrentControlSet\Services\RemoteAccess\Interfaces\InterfaceName` (where *`InterfaceName`* matches the name of the interface for which you want to change the time). The `MinUnreachabilityInterval` value controls both the minimum retry interval *and* how much the retry interval is incremented after each failure; the `MaxUnreachability-Interval` sets the upper limit. Both of these values must be expressed in seconds.

Managing LAN Interfaces

Each LAN interface has properties of its own; these interfaces, which appear when you select the General node under the IP Routing node in RRAS, correspond to the interfaces you've defined in RRAS. These interfaces allow you to set general properties for the interface. You add an interface by right-clicking the General node and selecting New Interface.

Once you've added an interface, you can add specific routing protocols to the interface, and you can configure those protocols individually (as you'll see in the following text). To see the properties for an interface, just select the General node in the console, pick the interface of interest from the right-hand pane, and use the Action ➤ Properties command, or you can right-click the interface and select Properties.

The settings you'll need to configure for LAN interfaces are contained on the General tab and the Configuration tab of the interface's Properties page, so these are the tabs we'll discuss in the following sections.

The General Tab

The General tab (see Figure 3.7) allows you to set some useful parameters for the entire interface, including whether or not this interface will send out router discovery advertisements so that other routers on your network can find it.

FIGURE 3.7 The General tab of the interface Properties dialog box

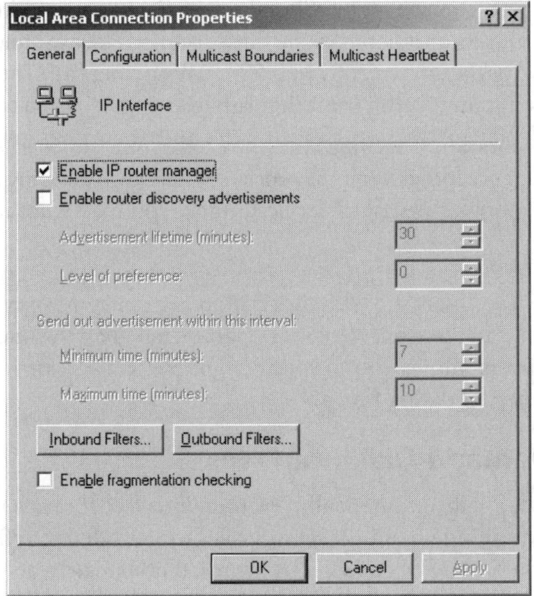

The controls on the General tab do the following:

- The Enable IP Router Manager checkbox controls whether or not this interface allows IP routing. When checked, the administrative status of this interface will appear as "Up," indicating that it is available for routing traffic. When unchecked, the interface will be marked as "Down," and it will not route any packets nor will other routers be able to communicate with it. The inability to access the Internet through a LAN connection is a symptom of being "Down."

- The Enable Router Discovery Advertisements checkbox controls whether or not this router will broadcast *router discovery messages*. These messages allow clients to find a "nearby" (in network terms) router without any manual configuration on your part. When this checkbox is enabled, the other controls below it become active so you can set the following fields:
    - The Advertisement Lifetime (Minutes) field, which lets you determine the lifetime of advertisements for client use. Clients will ignore any advertisement they receive after its lifetime has expired.
    - The Level Of Preference field, where the preference level is assigned to the use of this particular router. Clients use routers with higher preferences first. If more than one router have equal preference levels, the client can randomly select one.
    - The minimum and maximum time intervals for sending advertisements. RRAS will send out advertisements at a randomly chosen interval that falls between the minimum and maximum; with the default settings, that means RRAS will send an advertisement every seven to 10 minutes.
- The Inbound Filters and Outbound Filters buttons allow you to selectively accept or reject packets on the specified interface. You can accept all packets that do not trigger a filter, or accept only those packets that match filter criteria. Each type of filter can use the source or destination IP address and net mask as filter criteria. For example, you can construct a filter that rejects all packets from `206.151.234.0` with a net mask of `255.255.255.0`; that effectively screens out any traffic from that subnet.
- The Enable Fragmentation Checking checkbox tells your router to reject any fragmented IP packets instead of accepting them for processing. Because flooding a router with fragmented IP packets is a popular denial-of-service attack, you may want to check this box.

The Configuration Tab

The Configuration tab (see Figure 3.8) sets the IP address, subnet mask, and default gateway for an interface if you want it to use a different set of parameters than the ones defined for the interface. The Advanced button allows you to specify multiple IP addresses and default gateways, just as the TCP/IP Properties dialog box does.

Creating New Demand-Dial Interfaces

When you install RRAS, it will automatically create an interface for each LAN connection it can find. You can also create new demand-dial interfaces. Demand-dial interfaces can use a physical device (such as a modem or an ISDN adapter) or a virtual private networking (VPN) connection. For example, you can have a demand-dial connection that opens a VPN tunnel to a remote network when it sees traffic destined for that network. Following are the considerations for planning demand-dial interfaces.

In the following sections, we'll discuss considerations for connecting via a VPN, routing and security considerations, and dialing credentials.

You will see how to perform all the following tasks in Exercise 3.1.

FIGURE 3.8 The Configuration tab of the interface Properties dialog box

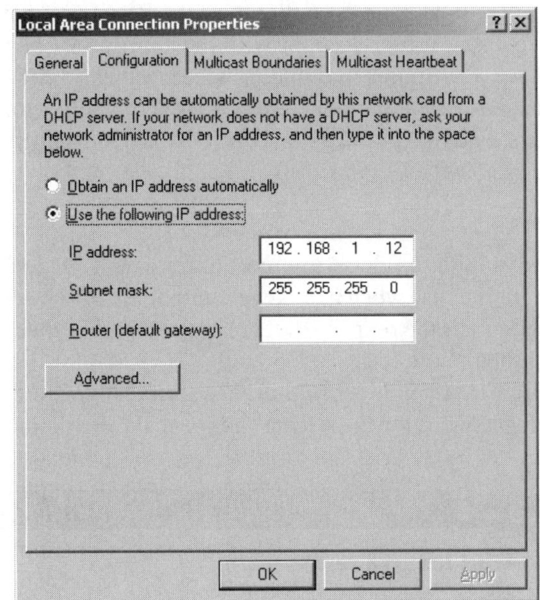

Connecting via a VPN

You must determine what type of VPN connection to use. You have the following three choices:

- Negotiate the connection type with the remote server. This is the most flexible choice.
- Always use Point-to-Point Tunneling Protocol (PPTP).
- Always use Layer 2 Tunneling Protocol (L2TP).

Routing and Security Considerations

Consider the following four items when you configure protocols and security options:

- By default, IP routing is enabled.
- You can add a user account so that a remote router (either running RRAS or not) can dial in. You can also choose to authenticate the remote router when dialing out.
- Some routers can handle PAP, CHAP, or MS-CHAP authentication, but others can only handle PAP. If your remote partner falls into this latter group, the local router must accept plain-text passwords.
- If the system that your RRAS server is calling is not running RRAS, it may expect you to manually interact with it, perhaps through a terminal window. If so, you can use scripting to complete the connection with the remote router. This enables you to open a terminal window after the modem connects so you can provide whatever commands or authenticators you need.

Dial-In Credentials

You can choose to allow remote routers to dial in to the RRAS machine you are setting up. If you do, you'll have to create a user account with the appropriate permissions. Microsoft recommends that you pick a username that makes evident which routers use the link. You can use ICAO airport identifiers, city names, or whatever else you like, so long as you as the name are easily identifiable. For example, the airport code "HSV-MCO" tells you right away that this account is used for the Huntsville-Orlando link.

Dial-Out Credentials

If you want your router to initiate calls to another router, you'll need to tell your local RRAS installation what credentials to use when it makes an outgoing call. The credentials you provide here must match the credentials the remote router expects to see, or your router will not be able to authenticate itself to the remote end.

In Exercise 3.1, you'll create a simple demand-dial interface. This requires you to have the phone number, user name, and password for the remote end (your ISP or whomever you are calling).

EXERCISE 3.1

Creating a Demand-Dial Interface

1. Open the RRAS MMC console by selecting Start ➢ Administrative Tools ➢ Routing and Remote Access.
2. Select the server you want to create the interface on, and select its Network Interfaces node.
3. Right-click the Network Interfaces node, and select New Demand-Dial Interface.

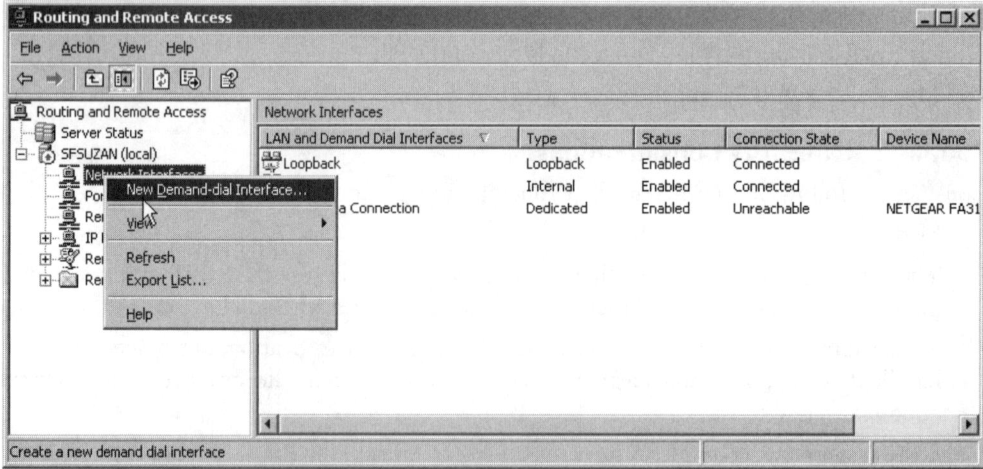

4. This starts the Demand Dial Interface Wizard.
5. Click the Next button on the Welcome To The Demand Dial Interface Wizard page. Specify a name for the interface on the Interface Name page.

EXERCISE 3.1 *(continued)*

6. The Connection Type page appears. Select the Connect Using A Modem, ISDN Adapter, Or Other Physical Device radio button if you have one of these devices installed. Select the Connect Using Virtual Private Networking (VPN) radio button if you want to connect to the remote router via a VPN interface. Alternatively, you can choose to connect through a PPPoE (broadband modem) connection. For the rest of this exercise, we will assume that you chose the Connect Using A Modem, ISDN Adapter, Or Other Physical Device. Click Next.

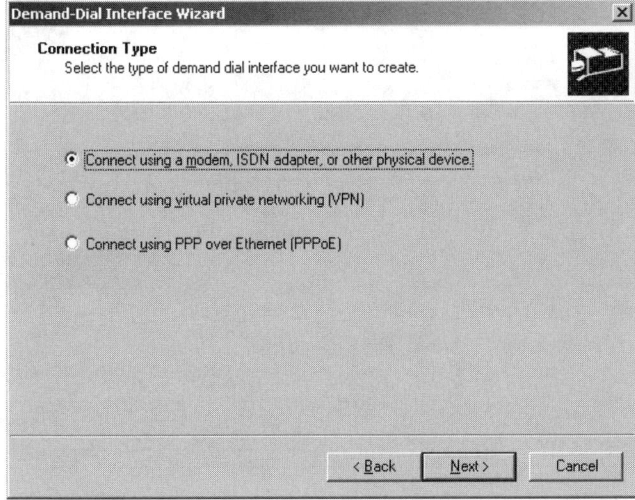

7. The Select A Device page appears. Select your device from the list of devices that appears and click Next. If this page does not appear, you do not have a modem installed and configured.

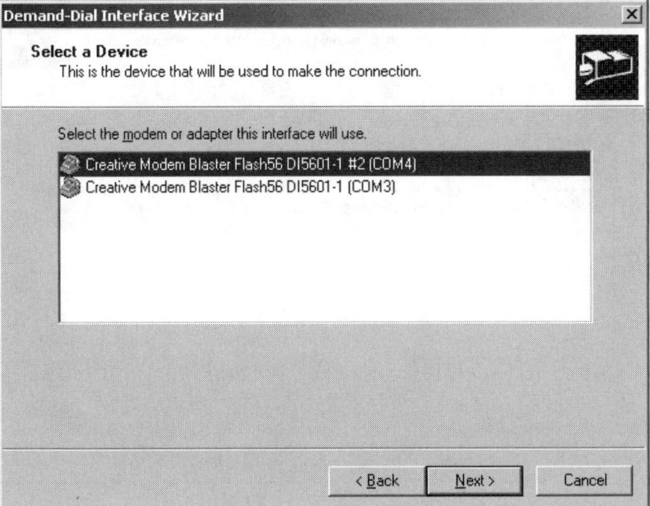

EXERCISE 3.1 *(continued)*

8. On the Phone Number page, enter the phone number of the remote server or router you are calling if prompted and click Next.

9. On the Protocols And Security page, make sure the Route IP Packets On This Interface checkbox is the only one selected, and then click Next.

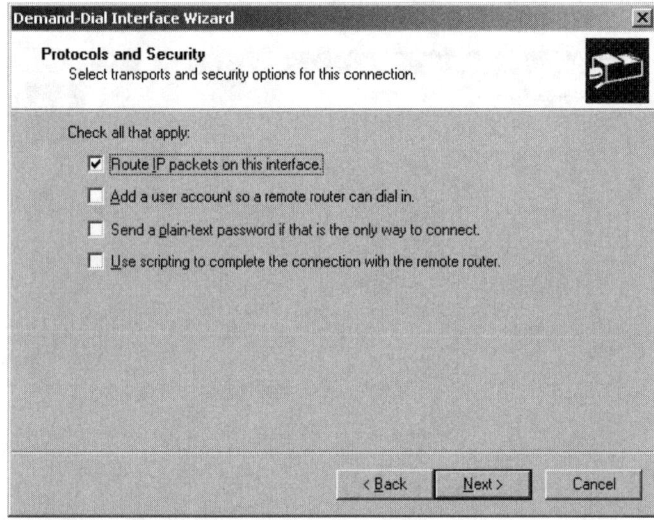

10. If you have not defined any static routes yet, the Static Routes For Remote Networks page appears and prompts you to do so before you can activate the demand-dial connection.

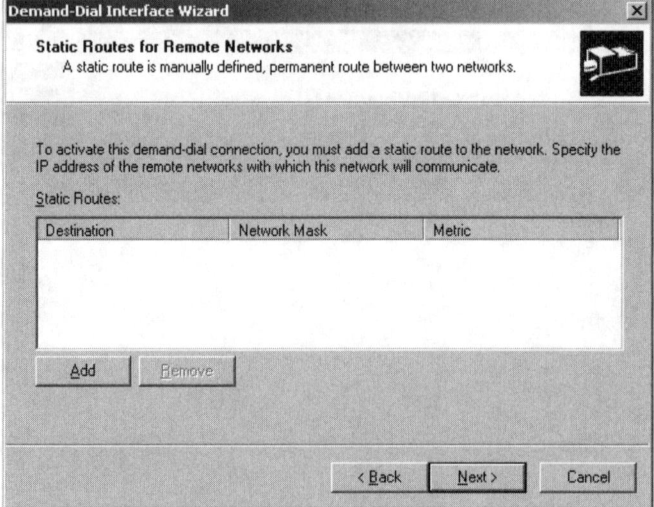

EXERCISE 3.1 *(continued)*

11. Click the Add button and enter the IP address, subnet mask, and metric of the remote router, and click OK when you are done. You will notice the new static route in the list. Click Next.

12. On the Dial Out Credentials page, fill in the username, domain (if any), and password needed to connect to the remote network. Click Next.

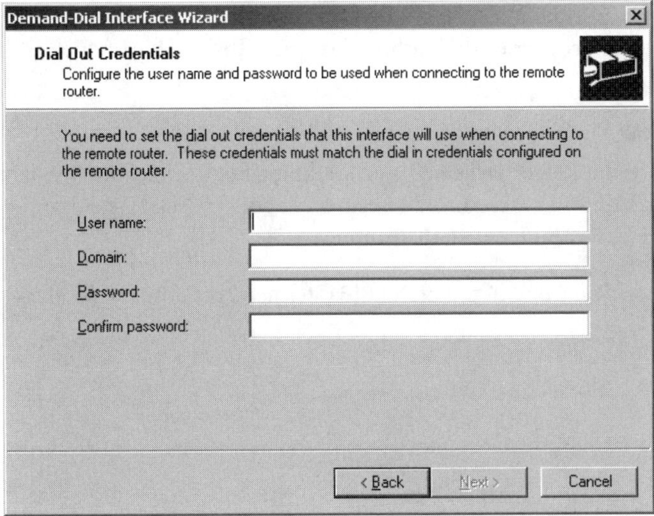

13. When the wizard's summary page appears, click the Finish button to create the interface.

Creating RIP or OSPF Interfaces

After you create the physical interface (using either demand-dial or LAN interfaces), the next thing you need to do is attach the routing protocol you want to use to that interface. To do this, right-click the General node in the RRAS and select New Routing Protocol. Next, click RIP Version 2 For Internet Protocol and click OK. Repeat this procedure, but this time add Open Shortest Path First (OSPF).

Now that the routing protocols are listed under IP Routing, the next step is to attach the routing protocol to the interface. Right-click either the RIP node or the OSPF node in the RRAS console, and choose New Interface. This displays the New Interface dialog box, which simply lists all the physical interfaces that are available for the selected protocol. For example, if you have two NICs in a computer and have already bound RIP to both of them, you can add OSPF to either or both; however, if you try to add another RIP interface, you'll get an error message.

Once you select the interface you want to use and if RRAS can create the interface, it adds the interface to the appropriate item in the console and opens the corresponding properties dialog box.

You can remove a RIP protocol or an OSPF protocol by selecting it under IP Routing and pressing the Delete key, by using the Action ➤ Delete command, or by using the Delete command on the context menu. You can remove an interface by clicking on General node and in the right pane selecting the interface and pressing the Delete key, by using the Action ➤ Delete command, or by using the Delete command on the context menu.

Setting RIP Interface Properties

RIP interfaces have their own properties, all of which are specific to the RIP protocol. You adjust these settings by selecting the RIP interface under IP Routing and using the selecting the Properties command from either the context or Action menus.

The RIP interface Properties dialog box has four tabs, each of which is discussed in the following sections.

The General Tab

The General tab of the RIP Interface Properties dialog box (see Figure 3.9) lets you control the router's operational mode, determine which protocols it uses to send and accept packets, increase the route cost, and identify the router.

FIGURE 3.9 The General tab of the RIP interface Properties dialog box

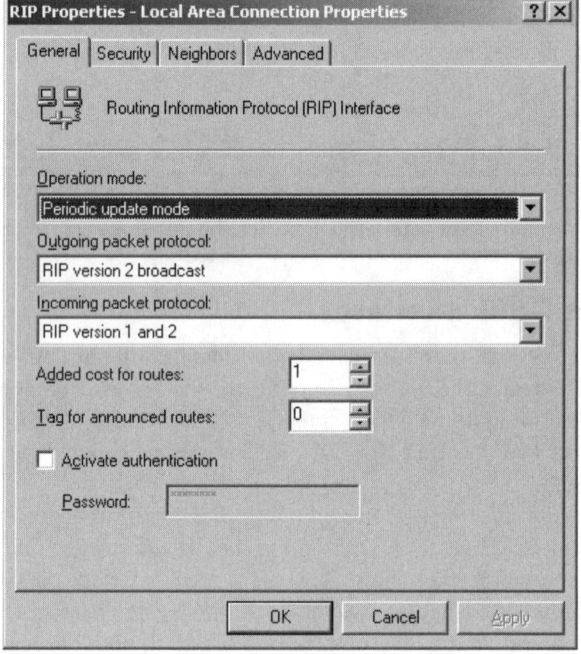

Here's what you can do with in General tab:

- The Operation Mode pull-down list controls the router's mode. By default, demand-dial interfaces will be set to auto-static update mode, while LAN interfaces will be set to use periodic update mode.
- The Outgoing Packet Protocol pull-down list controls what kind of RIP packets this router sends out. If your network has all RIPv2 routers, choose RIPv2 Broadcast or Multicast to

make RRAS send out efficient RIP multicasts. Version 1 has a selection for this, too. The fourth choice, Silent RIP, is useful when you want your RRAS router to listen to other routers' routes but not advertise any of its own. Typically, you'll use Silent RIP when you are using RRAS to connect a small network (for example, a branch office) that does not have any other routes to a larger network—the small network does not have any routes to advertise because it is only connected to one remote network.

- Use the Incoming Packet Protocol pull-down list to specify what kinds of RIP packets this interface will accept. You can choose to accept only RIPv1 packets, only RIPv2 packets, both version 1 and version 2 packets, or ignore incoming packets. The default setting is to accept both version 1 and version 2 packets.
- The Added Cost For Routes field lets you control how much this router will increase the route cost. Normally, it is best to leave this set at 1 because setting it too high may increase the interface's cost so much that no one uses it.
- The Tag For Announced Routes field gives you a way to supply a tag included in all RIP packets sent by this router. RRAS does not use RIP tags, but other routers can use them. You should tag the announced routes so that other types of routers can use them.
- The Activate Authentication checkbox and Password field give you an identification tool for use with your routers. If you turn on authentication, all incoming and outgoing RIP packets must contain the specified password. Therefore, all of this router's neighbors need to use the same password. The password is transmitted as clear text, so this option does not provide you with much security except for the fact that only routers with that password will be able to talk together.

The Security Tab

The Security tab (see Figure 3.10) helps you regulate which routes your RIP interface will accept from and broadcast to its peers. You should be careful about which routes you accept into your routing table because a malicious attacker can simply flood your router with bogus routes. Likewise, you may not want to advertise every route in your routing table, particularly if the same routers handle both Internet and intranet traffic.

You can use the controls on this tab to discard routes that fall within a particular range of addresses, or you can accept only those routes that fall within a particular range.

The default setting is to accept all routes, but you can change it using these controls:

- The Action pull-down list lets you choose whether you want to impose settings on incoming routes that your router hears from its peers or on outgoing routes that it announces. Depending on which of these options you choose, the wording of the three radio buttons below the pull-down list will change. These radio buttons control the action applied to incoming or outgoing routes.
- The default settings, Announce All Routes (for outgoing routes) or Accept All Routes (for incoming routes), are announced or accepted no matter the source.
- Selecting Announce All Routes In The Ranges Listed (for outgoing routes) or Accept All Routes In The Ranges Listed (for incoming routes) causes RRAS to silently ignore any routes that fall outside of the specified ranges. You normally use this option when you want to limit the scope of routes that your router can exchange traffic over.

FIGURE 3.10 The Security tab of the RIP interface Properties dialog box

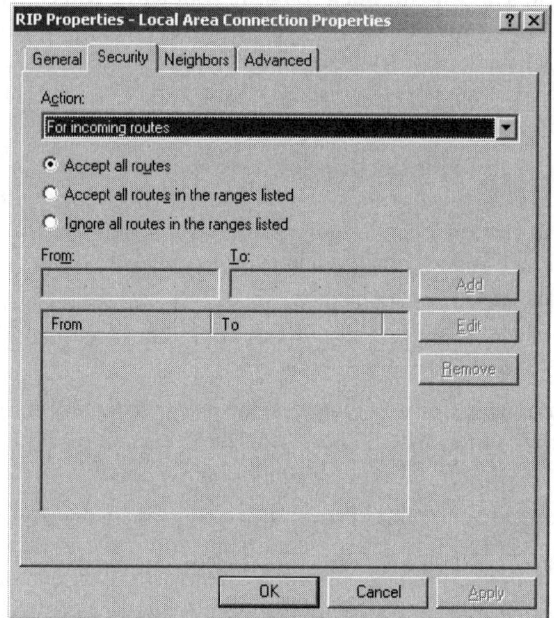

- The Do Not Announce All Routes In The Ranges Listed (for outgoing routes) or Ignore All Routes In The Ranges Listed (for incoming routes) settings tells RRAS to silently ignore any routes that fall within the specified ranges. This is useful for filtering out routes that you do not want to make available, or those you do not want to use to reach remote systems.
- The From and To fields, the Add, Edit, and Remove buttons, and the address range list are all used to specify which set of addresses you want to use with the restriction radio buttons.

The Neighbors Tab

The Neighbors tab (see Figure 3.11) gives you a finer degree of control over how this particular interface interacts with its peer RIP routers. By specifying a list of trusted neighbor routers (an OSPF concept that Microsoft has added to its RIP implementation), you can choose to use neighboring routers' routes in addition to, or instead of, broadcast or multicast RIP announcements.

You will see the following radio buttons on the Neighbors tab:

- The Use Broadcast Or Multicast Only radio button tells RRAS to ignore any RIP neighbors. This is the default setting. It specifies that any router that can successfully broadcast or multicast routes to you can load its routes into your routing table.
- The Use Neighbors In Addition To Broadcast Or Multicast radio button tells RRAS to accept routes from RIP peers as well as from the neighbors you've specified.
- The Use Neighbors Instead Of Broadcast Or Multicast radio button indicates that you do not trust RIP announcements that your router picks up from the Internet; instead, you are telling RRAS to trust only those neighbors that are defined in the neighbor list.

FIGURE 3.11 The Neighbors tab of the RIP interface Properties dialog box

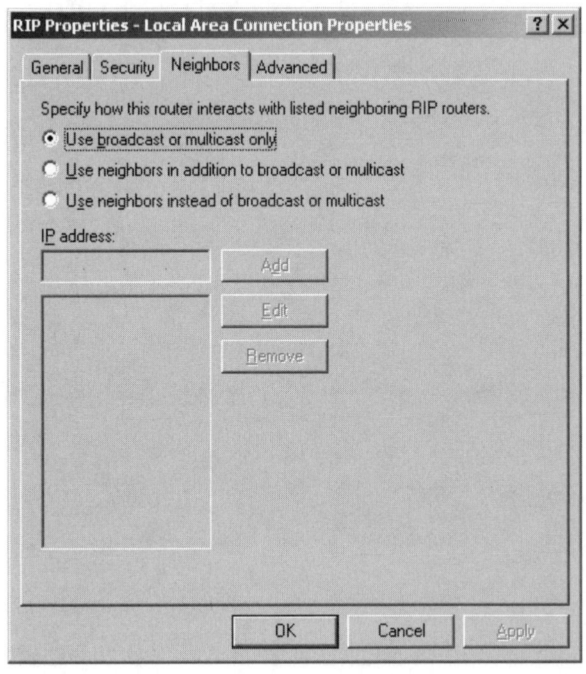

You manage the list of trusted neighbor routers using the IP Address field, the Add, Edit, and Remove buttons, and the list itself. These controls are enabled when you specify that you want to use neighbor-supplied routing information; once the controls are activated, you can add router IP addresses to the neighbor list.

The Advanced Tab

The Advanced tab (see Figure 3.12) contains 12 controls that govern some fairly complex RIP behavior.

The first three controls are only active when you turn on periodic update mode on the General tab:

- The Periodic Announcement Interval (Seconds) field controls the interval at which periodic router announcements are made. The default is 30 seconds, which equals a default RIP 1 interval. This interval is too low and can flood the connections between routers if the routers are using large tables. You should increase this interval to at least 60 seconds. The maximum interval is 86,400 seconds (24 hours).
- The Time Before Routes Expire (Seconds) field controls how long the route may stay in the routing table before it is considered to be expired. The arrival of a new RIP announcement for the route resets the timer—it will be marked as invalid only if it reaches the expiration time limit without being renewed through a new announcement.
- The Time Before Route Is Removed (Seconds) field controls the interval that may pass between the time a route expires and the time it is removed.

FIGURE 3.12 The Advanced tab of the RIP interface Properties dialog box

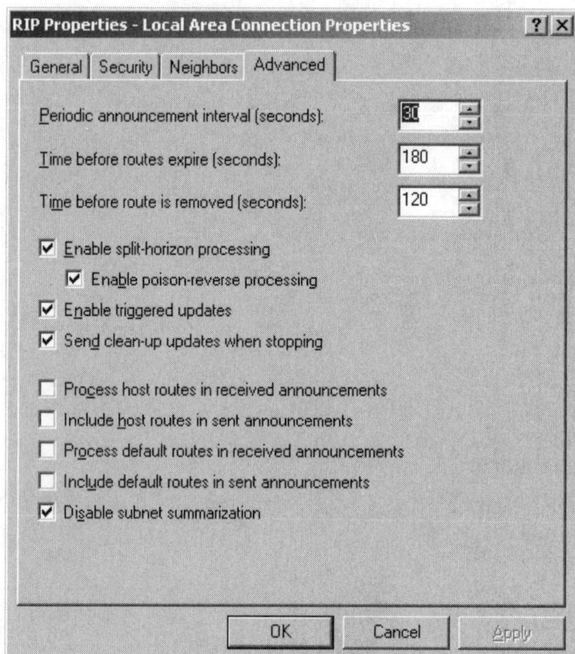

The next group of checkboxes controls update processing and loop detection:

- The Enable Split-Horizon Processing checkbox turns on split-horizon processing, in which a route learned by a RIP router on a network is not rebroadcast to that network. Split-horizon processing helps prevent routing loops, so it is on by default.
- The Enable Poison-Reverse Processing checkbox (which is only active when the Enable Split-Horizon Processing checkbox is on) modifies the way split-horizon processing works. When poison-reverse is turned on, routes learned from a network are rebroadcast to the network with a metric of 16, a special value that tells other routers that the route is unreachable. It also prevents routing loops while still keeping the routing tables up-to-date.
- The Enable Triggered Updates checkbox indicates whether you want routing table changes to be immediately sent out when they are noticed (the default) or not. Triggered updates help keep the routing table up-to-date with minimum latency. You should make sure that this setting is checked.
- The Send Clean-Up Updates When Stopping checkbox controls whether or not RRAS will send out announcements that mark the routes it was handling as unavailable. This immediately lets its RIP peers know that the routes it was servicing are no longer usable.

The last set of controls governs what happens with host and default routes:

- By default, RRAS ignores any host routes it sees in RIP announcements. Turn on the Process Host Routes In Received Announcements checkbox if you want it to honor those routes instead of ignoring them.

- The Include Host Routes In Sent Announcements checkbox directs RRAS to send host route information as part of its RIP announcements; normally it will not do this.
- The Process Default Routes In Received Announcements and Include Default Routes In Sent Announcements checkboxes have the same function as their host-route counterpart.
- The Disable Subnet Summarization checkbox is active only if you have RIPv2 specified as the outbound packet type for the router. When subnet summarization is turned off, RIP will not advertise subnets to routers that are on other subnets.

Setting OSPF Interface Properties

OSPF has its own set of properties that you can set on OSPF-enabled interfaces. These properties are both simpler and more complex than RIP—there aren't as many of them because OSPF is largely self-tuning, but the properties you *can* set tend to be somewhat more abstruse.

To set general OSPF properties, right-click on the OSPF node in RRAS and choose Properties to open the dialog box in which you can specify an IP address for the router as well as define areas, virtual interfaces, and external routing behavior. To open the Properties dialog box for a specific OSPF interface, simply highlight the OSPF node in the RRAS console. Right-click the desired interface, and choose Properties from the context menu.

This dialog box has three tabs: the General tab, the NBMA Neighbors tab, and the Advanced tab.

The General Tab

The General tab (see Figure 3.13) of an OSPF interface Properties dialog box controls, among other things, whether or not OSPF is enabled on a particular interface address.

FIGURE 3.13 The General tab of an OSPF interface Properties dialog box

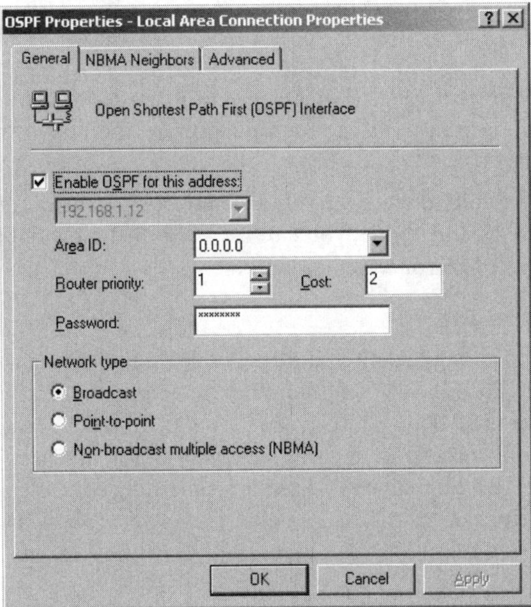

Here's what you can do with the controls on the General tab:

- The Enable OSPF For This Address checkbox, combined with the address pull-down, specify whether OSPF is active or not on the *selected* address. Because a single interface can have multiple IP addresses, you use this checkbox and pull-down to specify which IP addresses are OSPF-capable. The settings you make in the OSPF Properties dialog box apply to the IP address you select here.
- The Area ID pull-down allows you to select which OSPF area this interface is a part of. One IP address can be in one area (an area works just like a workgroup that includes only routers). However, if you have multiple IP addresses defined, each one can be in a separate area.
- The Router Priority field controls the priority of this interface, relative to other OSPF routers in the same area. OSPF supports the concept of a designated router in an area; that router serves as the default router for the area it is in. The router with the highest priority will become the designated router unless there is an existing designated router when this router joins the party.
- The Cost field controls the metric attached to this router's routes in the link state database.
- The Password field works just like it does for RIP—all routers within an area can share a common plain-text password for identification. This does nothing for access control (especially since the default password is an easy-to-guess "12345678").

The Network Type controls influence how this router interacts with its peers, but to understand what its controls do you have to know some more buzzwords:

- A *broadcast router* is one that can talk to any number of other routers—like a typical LAN router, which can see any number of other routers on the LAN.
- A *point-to-point router* is one that has only one peer. For example, a typical DSL installation will have one router on your end and one on the ISP end—that is a point-to-point configuration.
- A *non-broadcast multiple access* (NBMA) is a little harder to define. An NBMA router is one where a single router can talk to multiple peers without using a broadcast, as in an ATM or X.25 network.

You use these radio buttons to specify the kind of network in which your router is participating. If you set the router to NBMA mode, you can use the NBMA Neighbors tab to specify the routers to which your NBMA router should talk.

The NBMA Neighbors Tab

Think back to the description of RIP neighbors. You learned that Microsoft recycled an OSPF concept for use in RIP. The NBMA Neighbors tab (see Figure 3.14), therefore, is very similar to the Neighbors tab of the RIP interface Properties dialog box. The address pull-down at the top of the tab lets you pick the IP address or addresses of the neighbors you are configuring. Once you've picked an IP address, you can use the remaining controls in the tab to specify the IP addresses and priorities of the NBMA neighbors to which you want this router interface to talk.

FIGURE 3.14 The NBMA Neighbors tab of an OSPF-enabled interface's Properties page

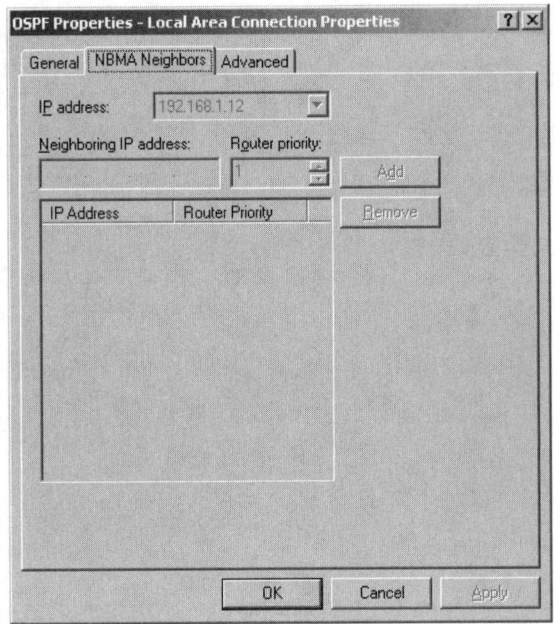

The Advanced Tab

The Advanced tab (shown in Figure 3.15) contains several advanced parameters. The first thing you'll probably notice is the IP Address pull-down list, which lets you choose the IP address you are configuring. Past that point, you'll need to use the six fields that give you access to some inner OSPF workings.

The six fields of the Advanced tab include the following:

- The Transit Delay (Seconds) field specifies how long you think it will take for a link state update to propagate outward from this router. The OSPF engine uses this value to decide how stale route information is when it arrives.
- The Retransmit Interval (Seconds) is for your best estimate of the round-trip delay required for two routers to communicate—if it takes longer than this interval for a packet to arrive, it will be retransmitted.
- The Hello Interval (Seconds) field controls how often OSPF routers send out packets to discover other routers. This value must be the same for all routers on the same network; lowering the interval will speed up the discovery of topology changes at the expense of generating more OSPF traffic.
- The Dead Interval (Seconds) field controls the interval after which a router is marked as "dead" by its peers. Microsoft recommends using an integral multiple of the hello interval for the dead interval. For example, if your hello interval is set to the default of 10 seconds, the default dead interval of 40 seconds will work fine.

FIGURE 3.15 The Advanced tab of an OSPF-enabled interface's Properties page

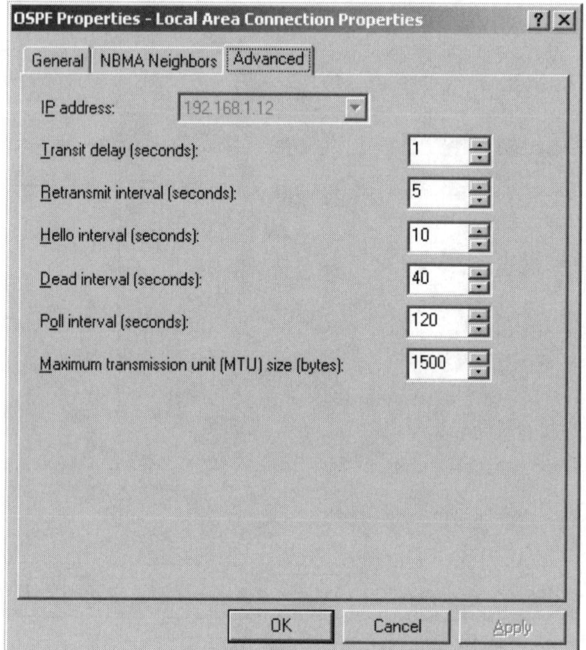

- The Poll Interval (Seconds) field controls how long an NBMA router will wait before attempting to contact an apparently dead router to see whether it is really dead or not. This interval should be set to at least twice the dead interval.
- The Maximum Transmission Unit (MTU) Size (Bytes) field regulates how large an OSPF IP packet can be. Your best bet is to leave this value alone.

Setting IP Routing Properties

The IP Routing node in the RRAS console has several subnodes, including the General subnode. When you select the General node's Properties command, you'll find that you can change some settings that apply to all installed IP routing protocols on the server. These settings give you some additional control over how routing works.

If you expand the IP Routing node, right-click General, and choose Properties from the context menu, you will encounter a dialog box with tabs for Logging, Preference Levels, and Multicast Scopes. The Multicast Scopes tab is where, not surprisingly, you configure multicast scopes. The Logging and Preference Levels tabs are discussed in the following two sections.

The Multicast Scopes tab is used for setting and managing multicast scopes, which are beyond the scope of this chapter.

The Logging Tab

The Logging tab (see Figure 3.16) contains four radio buttons that you use to control what information the IP routing components of RRAS log. These buttons include the following:

- The Log Errors Only radio button instructs the server to log IP routing–related errors and nothing else. This gives you adequate indication of problems *after* they happen, but it does not point out potential problems noted by warning messages.
- The Log Errors And Warnings radio button is the default choice; this instructs RRAS to log error and warning messages to the event log without adding any informational messages. If you get in the habit of carefully reviewing your event logs, these warning messages may give you welcome forewarning of incipient problems.
- The Log The Maximum Amount Of Information radio button causes the IP routing stack to log messages about almost everything it does. This gives you a lot of useful fodder when you are troubleshooting, but it can flood your logs with minutiae if you are not careful—do not turn it on unless you are trying to isolate and fix a problem.
- The Disable Event Logging radio button turns off all IP routing event logging.

Do not use the Disable Event Logging option because it will keep you from being able to review the service's logs in the event of a problem.

FIGURE 3.16 The Logging tab of the IP Routing, General node's Properties dialog box

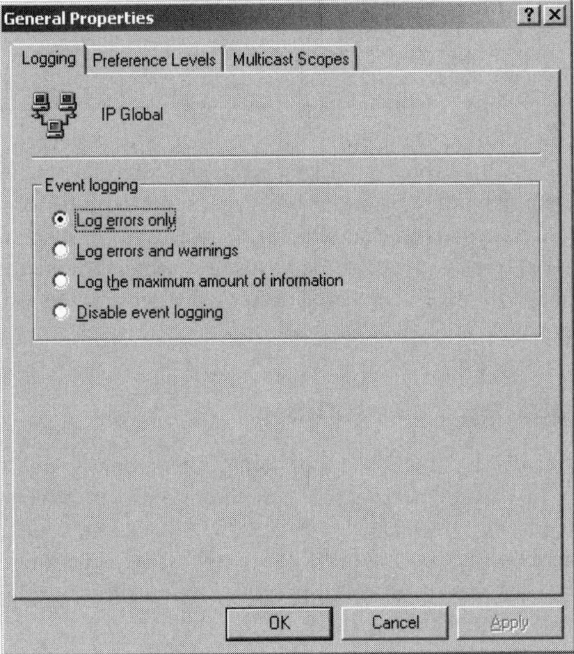

The Preference Levels Tab

The Preference Levels tab (see Figure 3.17) gives you a way to tweak the router's behavior by telling it what class of routes to prefer. You can change the router's class preference by selecting the class you want to tweak and using the Move Up and Move Down buttons.

FIGURE 3.17 The Preference Levels tab of the General node's Properties dialog box

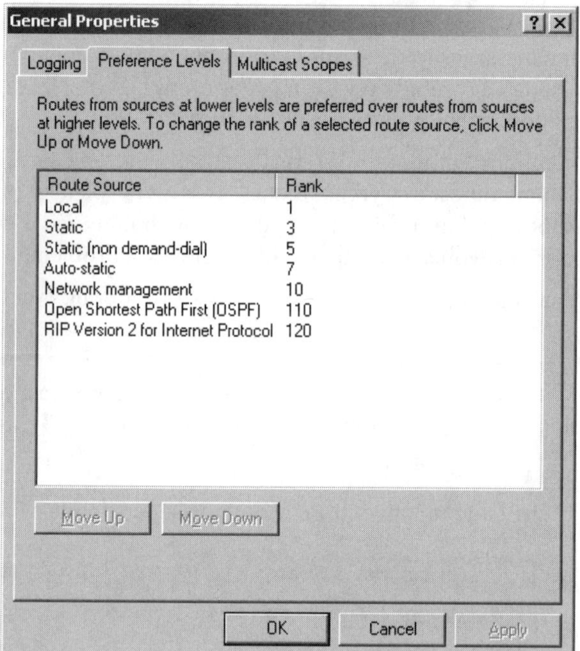

In the earlier discussion of routing, you read that the router selects routes based on cost metric information. That is true, but another factor comes into play: the preference level of the routing source. The default configuration for RRAS causes it to prefer local and static routes to dynamically discovered routes. As an example, say there are two routing table entries indicating routes to `216.80.*`—one that you've entered as a static route and one that your router has discovered via a RIP peer. In this example, the router will always try to use the static route first; if it cannot, it will try to use the RIP-generated route.

Managing Routing Protocols

Routing protocols typically do not take a lot of management; once you install RIP or OSPF, the protocol engine takes care of exchanging routes with remote routers. Unlike what you may be accustomed to with dedicated routers using a router OS like Cisco's IOS, there is no way to directly edit the contents of the routing table generated by dynamic routing protocols. That means your management of these protocols is pretty much limited to installing them, configuring them to meet your needs, and watching them as they run.

In the following sections, you'll learn how to install RIP and OSPF as well as how to configure their properties.

Installing RIP and OSPF

You add routing protocols from the General subnode beneath the IP Routing node in RRAS. This is quite different from the way you manage network protocols in Windows NT, but it makes sense—there is no reason to install RIP or OSPF unless you are using RRAS, so it is logical that you would install it from there. Exercise 3.2 explains how to install the RIP and OSPF protocols.

You'll need both RIP and OSPF installed for the later exercises in the chapter.

EXERCISE 3.2

Installing the RIP and OSPF Protocols

1. Open the RRAS MMC console by selecting Start ➢ Administrative Tools ➢ Routing and Remote Access.
2. Select the server you want to configure in the left pane of the MMC. Expand it until you see the General node beneath IP Routing.
3. Right-click the General node, and select New Routing Protocol. The New Routing Protocol dialog box will appear.

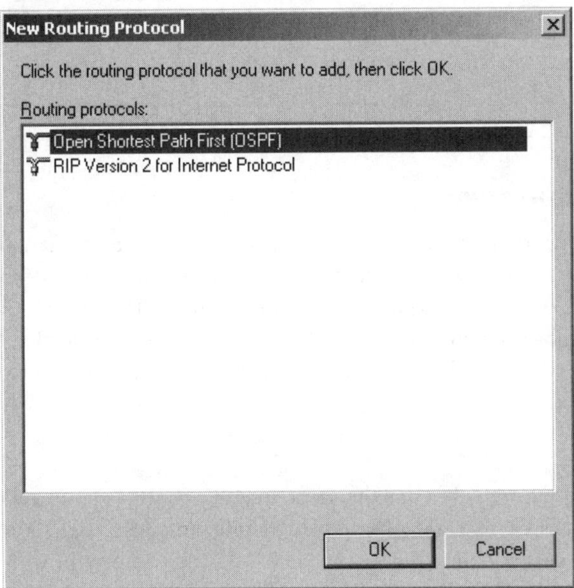

EXERCISE 3.2 *(continued)*

4. Select the routing protocol you want to install. In this case, choose RIP Version 2 For Internet Protocol. Then click the OK button.

5. The RRAS console refreshes its display, revealing a new node labeled RIP under the IP Routing node.

6. Right-click the General node and select New Routing Protocol. This time when the New Routing Protocol dialog box appears, select Open Shortest Path First (OSPF) and click the OK button.

7. The RRAS console refreshes its display, revealing a new node labeled OSPF under the IP Routing node.

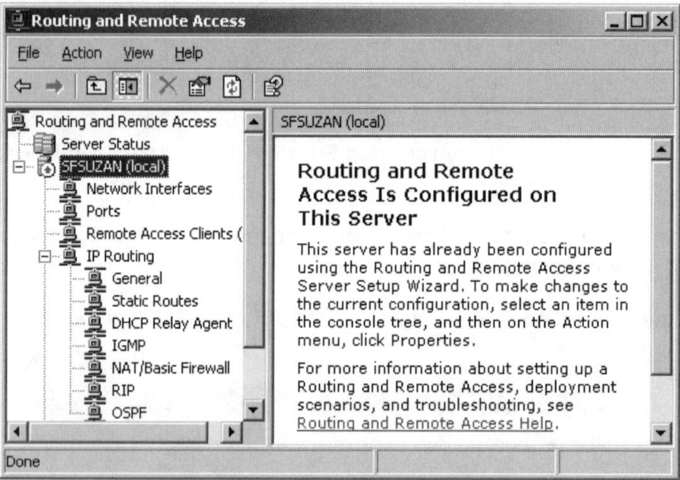

Setting RIP Properties

The RIP protocol is pretty much self-tuning. Once you configure an RRAS router to use the RIP protocol, it will look for peer routers and exchange routing information without a whole lot of effort on your part. You can change a small group of settings through the RIP Properties dialog box, which you open by selecting the RIP node under IP Routing in the RRAS console, and then selecting Action ➢ Properties. In the following sections, we will look at the two tabs of the Properties dialog box.

The General Tab

The General tab (see Figure 3.18) has the same logging controls you saw on the IP Routing Properties dialog box's General tab. However, there is an additional control you can use. The Maximum Delay (Seconds) control governs how long the router will wait to send an update notification to its peers.

FIGURE 3.18 The General tab of the RIP Properties dialog box

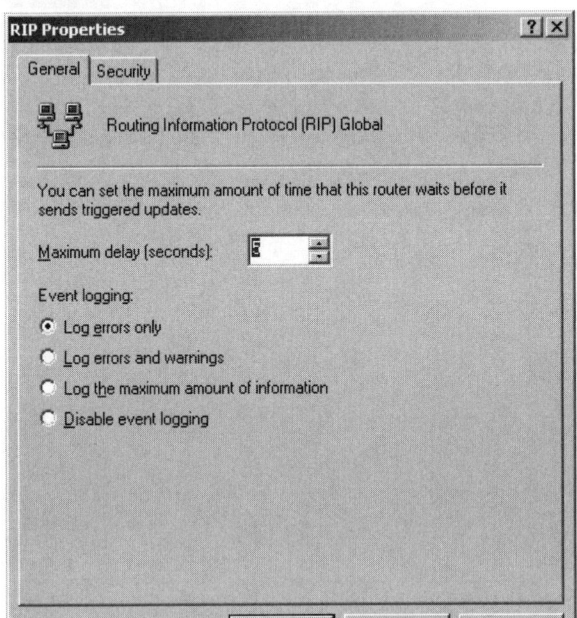

The Security Tab

The Security tab (see Figure 3.19) lets you control what router announcements your router will accept. By default, the RRAS RIP implementation will ingest routes supplied by any other router; you can restrict this behavior by supplying either a list of routers to trust or a list of routers whose routes you want to reject.

Setting OSPF Properties

You can also set some OSPF-specific properties by selecting the OSPF node under the IP Routing item in the RRAS console and opening the OSPF Properties dialog box. In the following section, we will look at the tabs of the OSPF Properties dialog box.

OSPF is a complex protocol worthy of its own book. If the descriptions in this section seem cursory, it is because you need to know simply what these settings do, and not necessarily how the guts of OSPF work, to pass the exam and to plan basic software routing using Windows Server 2003.

The General Tab

The General tab (see Figure 3.20) contains the logging controls that you've already seen twice in this chapter, plus two additional controls that you'll probably have occasion to use.

FIGURE 3.19 The Security tab of the RIP Properties dialog box

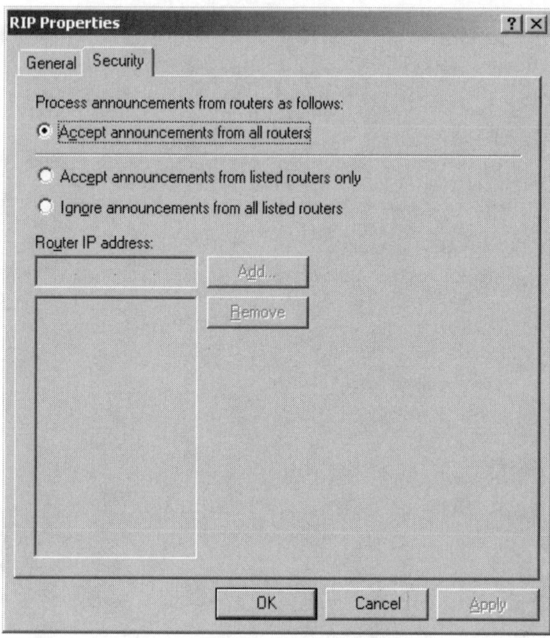

FIGURE 3.20 The General tab of the OSPF Properties dialog box

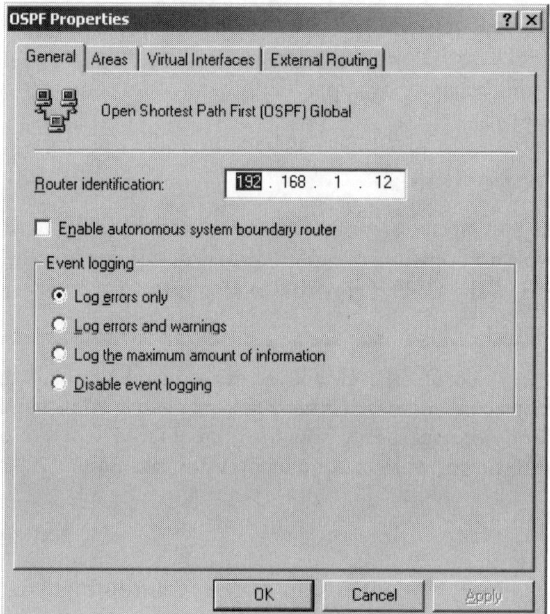

The two additional controls are listed here:

- The Router Identification field allows you to enter an IP address that your router uses to identify itself. Although it is not a good idea to assign a bogus IP address as your router's identifier, you may want to choose the public IP address, even for internal interfaces.
- The Enable Autonomous System Boundary Router checkbox controls whether or not your OSPF router will advertise routes it finds from other sources (including its static routes and routes it learns via RIP) to the outside world. The External Routing tab will not be enabled unless you check this box; check it only if you want this particular RRAS router to try to exchange OSPF routing information with its peers.

The Areas Tab

The Areas tab (see Figure 3.21) lists the OSPF areas that your router knows about. You can add, edit, or remove areas from the list using the corresponding buttons below the list box.

FIGURE 3.21 The Areas tab of the OSPF Properties dialog box

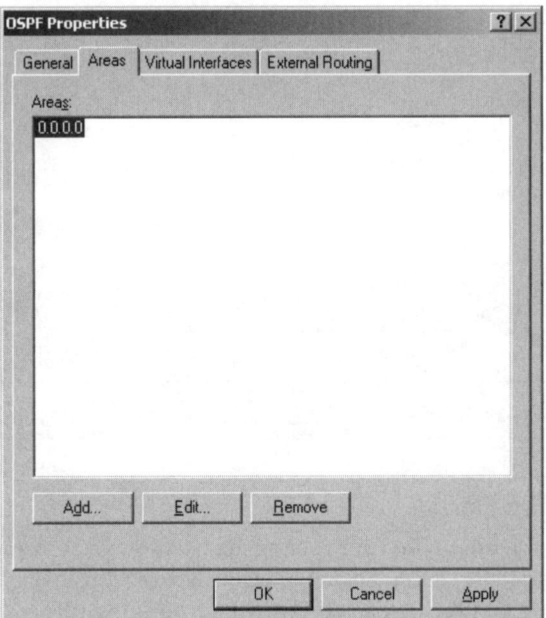

The Virtual Interfaces Tab

Recall that OSPF conceptually divides networks into areas, some of which may be part of the backbone and some of which aren't. Because a non-backbone router will not be connected to the backbone, there has to be some other way to allow backbone and non-backbone routers to share routing information. A *virtual link* is a logical point-to-point connection between a backbone *area border router (ABR)* and a non-backbone area border router. The first area is known as the transit area, the area across which the virtual link is created in order to logically connect the second area to the backbone. Once the link is created, the two routers can share routing information just as though they were connected to the same physical network. To create a virtual link, both routers, called *virtual link neighbors*, are configured with the transit area, the router ID of the virtual link neighbor, matching hello and dead intervals, and a matching password.

You use the Virtual Interfaces tab (see Figure 3.22) to create and edit these virtual links.

FIGURE 3.22 The Virtual Interfaces tab of the OSPF Properties dialog box

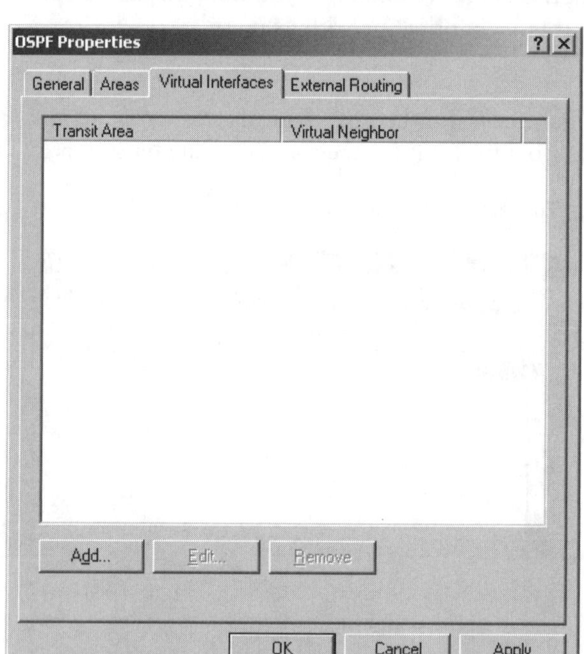

The External Routing Tab

OSPF is not the only potential source for routing information—your router can acquire routes from a number of other sources. You might not want all of those routes to be accepted and used, though. When you use OSPF, you can control which additional routing sources the OSPF components will use by checking the appropriate boxes on the External Routing tab (see Figure 3.23).

The two radio buttons at the top—Accept Routes From All Route Sources Except Those Selected and Ignore Routes From All Route Sources Except Those Selected—let you control the meaning of the checkboxes in the Route Sources list. By default, OSPF will accept all routes from all sources. To turn off individual route sources (for instance, static routes), check the appropriate box. If you want to reject all route sources *except* for a particular group, use the Ignore Routes From All Route Sources Except Those Selected radio button, and then check the route sources you do want to use.

FIGURE 3.23 The External Routing tab of the OSPF Properties dialog box

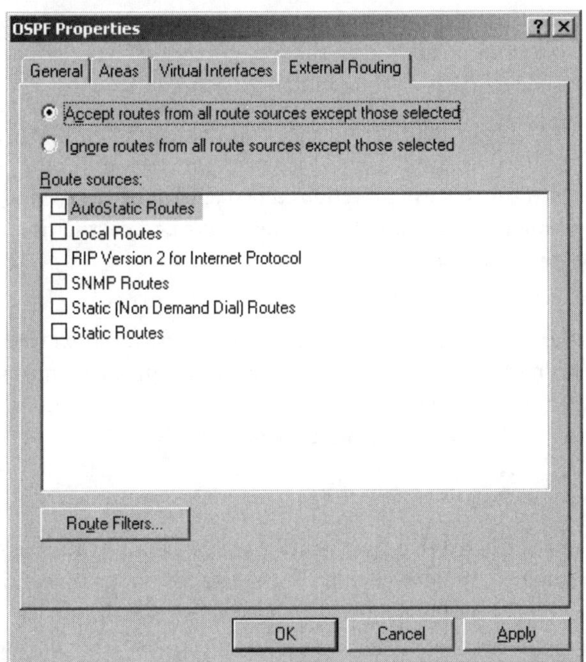

This tab will be active only if you check the Enable Autonomous System Boundary Router checkbox on the General tab.

The Route Filters button allows you to either ignore or accept individual routes. This is a handy way to screen out particular routes that you do not want without disallowing entire classes of route source information.

Defining Static Routes

When you use static routes, there is some good news and some bad news. The good news is that they are simple to manage and configure because they do not participate in any kind of automatic discover process. Static routes are conceptually very simple—they combine a destination network address with a subnet mask to provide a list of potential destinations. The destination addresses are reached through a particular interface on your router, and they are sent to a specified gateway (normally, another router, either on your end or on some remote network). Finally, a metric is associated with the static route.

You define new static routes in two ways: by using the `route add` command from the command line or by right-clicking the Static Routes node in the RRAS console and using the New Static Route command. The next sections will take a look at how those methods work.

Using *route add*

The `route add` command allows you to add new static routes; you can choose whether or not these routes remain in the routing table after the system reboots. Routes that stick around in this manner are called *persistent routes*. The command itself is simple:

```
route add destination mask subnetmask gateway metric cost interface
```

You specify the destination, subnetmask, gateway, metric, and interface name on the command line. These parameters are all required (except `interface`), and `route add` does some basic error checking to make sure that the net mask and destination match and that you haven't left anything out. For example:

```
route add 10.1.1.0 mask 255.255.0.0 192.168.1.254 metric 2
```

This command generates a static route of destination network `10.1` through the gateway of `192.168.2.254` with a metric of 2. If you use the interface entry, you must specify the interface as a number, not as a name. However, the `route print` command (which will be covered a little later) lists its interfaces and the associated numbers.

Using RRAS

When you create a new static route using the RRAS console, all you have to do is choose the New Static Route command by right-clicking Static Routes under IP Routing, and you'll see the Static Route dialog box (see Figure 3.24). You have to provide the same parameters as with the `route add` command—the interface you want to use to connect, the destination and network mask, the gateway for the outbound packets, and a metric. If you are creating a route that is not bound to a LAN interface, you can also use the Use This Route To Initiate Demand-Dial Connections checkbox to specify that the route should bring up the demand-dial connection on the specified interface.

FIGURE 3.24 Use the Static Route dialog box to create new static routes.

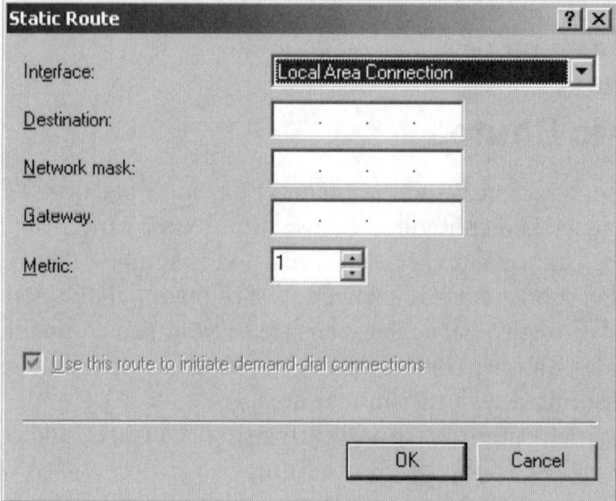

Exercise 3.3 shows you how to add and remove static routes using the RRAS. Follow these steps to add and then remove a static route (you remove it only to make sure it does not interfere with any other machines on your network).

EXERCISE 3.3

Adding and Removing Static Routes

1. Open the RRAS MMC console by clicking Start ➢ Administrative Tools ➢ Routing and Remote Access.
2. Select the server you want to configure in the left pane of the MMC. Expand it until you see the Static Routes node beneath IP Routing.
3. Right-click the Static Routes node, and select New Static Route. The Static Route dialog box will appear.
4. Select the interface you want to use from the Interface pull-down list; you can use the internal interface or any other interface you've already defined.
5. Enter the destination address (try **`192.168.1.0`**) and a net mask of **`255.255.255.0`**.
6. For the gateway address, enter the IP address of your RRAS server.
7. Click the OK button. The RRAS console will reappear.
8. Right-click the Static Routes item and choose Show IP Routing Table. The IP Routing Table window will appear. Verify that your newly added static route is present in the table.

SFSUZAN - IP Routing Table

Destination	Network mask	Gateway	Interface	Metric	Protocol
0.0.0.0	0.0.0.0	0.0.0.0	The following name ...	1	Network management
127.0.0.0	255.0.0.0	127.0.0.1	Loopback	1	Local
127.0.0.1	255.255.255.255	127.0.0.1	Loopback	1	Local
192.168.1.0	255.255.255.0	192.168.1.12	Local Area Connect...	30	Local
192.168.1.12	255.255.255.255	127.0.0.1	Loopback	30	Local
192.168.1.255	255.255.255.255	192.168.1.12	Local Area Connect...	30	Local
209.204.149.2	255.255.255.255	209.204.149.66	The following name ...	1	Network management
209.204.149.66	255.255.255.255	127.0.0.1	Loopback	50	Local
224.0.0.0	240.0.0.0	209.204.149.66	The following name ...	1	Network management
224.0.0.0	240.0.0.0	192.168.1.12	Local Area Connect...	30	Local
255.255.255.255	255.255.255.255	192.168.1.12	Local Area Connect...	1	Local

9. In the RRAS console, select the Static Routes item. Note that the right pane of the MMC changes to list all static routes that you've defined. Compare the list with the contents of the IP Routing Table window.

EXERCISE 3.3 *(continued)*

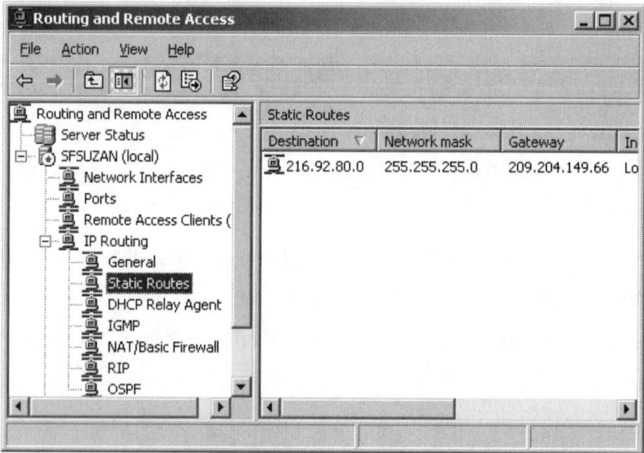

10. Right-click the static route you added, and select Delete to remove it.

Filtering TCP/IP Packets

One of the most useful features in RRAS is its ability to selectively filter TCP/IP packets in both directions. You can construct filters that allow or deny traffic into or out of your network, based on rules that specify source and destination addresses and ports. The basic idea behind packet filtering is simple: You specify filter rules, and incoming packets are measured against those rules. You have two choices:

- Accept all packets except those prohibited by a rule.
- Drop all packets except those permitted by a rule.

Filters are normally used to block out undesirable traffic. Of course, the definition of "undesirable" varies, but in general the idea is to keep out packets that your machines should not see. For example, you could configure a packet filter that would block all packets to a Web server except those on TCP ports 80 and 443. On the other hand, you could just as easily create a filter that blocks all outgoing packets on the ports used by the MSN and AOL instant messaging tools. Another example (and one that is more helpful for the exam) is the use of filters for a PPTP or L2TP server; these filters screen out everything except VPN traffic so that you can expose a Windows Server 2003 VPN server without fear of compromise. You will learn more about PPTP and L2TP in Chapter 6, "Planning Secure Network Access," but for now it is enough to know that VPN traffic is always carried on one of the two protocols.

Filters are associated with a particular interface; the filters assigned to one interface are totally independent of those on all other interfaces, and inbound and outbound filters are likewise separate. You create and remove filters by using the Inbound Filters and Outbound Filters buttons on the General tab of the interface's Properties dialog box (refer back to Figure 3.7 for a look at the tab). The mechanics of working with the filters are identical; just remember that you create inbound filters to screen traffic coming to the interface and outbound filters to screen traffic going back out through that interface.

In the next sections, you'll learn how to create packet filters in general and also specifically for VPN connections.

Creating Packet Filters

To create a filter, find the interface on which you want the filter, and then open its Properties dialog box. Click the appropriate packet filter button, and you'll see a dialog box like the Inbound Filters dialog box (see Figure 3.25).

FIGURE 3.25 The Inbound Filters dialog box

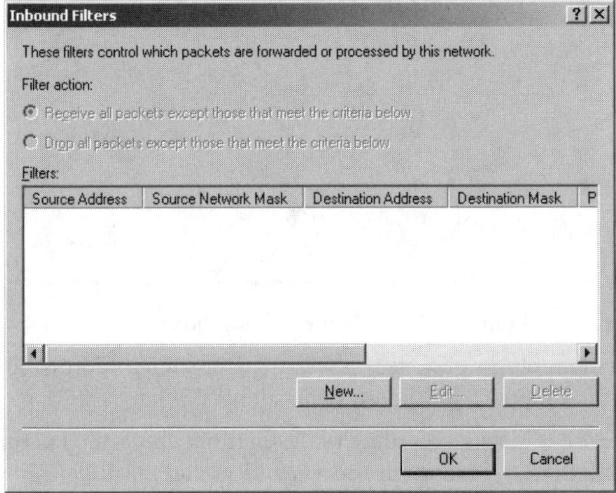

This dialog box has the following controls:

- The Receive All Packets Except Those That Meet The Criteria Below and the Drop All Packets Except Those That Meet The Criteria Below radio buttons control what this filter does. To make a filter that excludes only those packets you specify, select the Receive All Packets Except Those That Meet The Criteria Below button. To do the opposite, and accept only those packets that meet your rule, select the Drop All Packets Except Those That Meet The Criteria Below button. Note that these buttons will be inactive until you create a filter rule.
- The Filters list, which is initially empty, shows you which filters are defined on this interface. Each filter's entry in the list shows you the source address and mask, the destination address and mask, and the protocol, port, and traffic type specified in the rule.
- The New, Edit, and Delete buttons add, edit, and remove filters.

Creating a filter is straightforward. Click the New button, and you'll see the Add IP Filter dialog box in Figure 3.26. All of the conditions you specify here must be true to trigger the rule. For example, if you specify both the source and destination addresses, only traffic from the defined source to the defined destination will be filtered.

FIGURE 3.26 The Add IP Filter dialog box

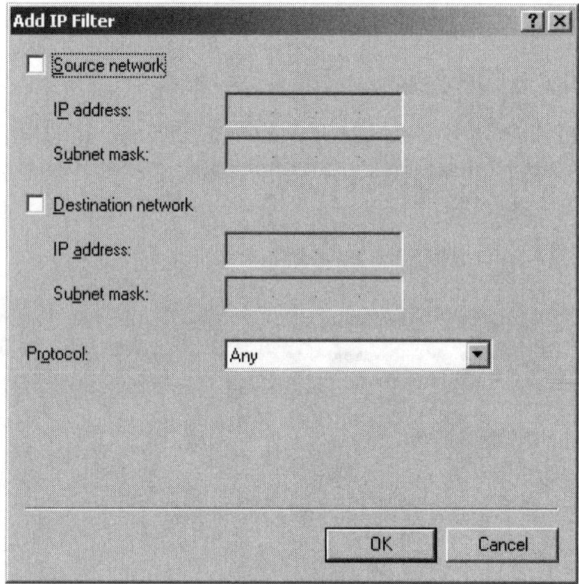

Follow these steps to fill out the Add IP Filter dialog box:

- To create a filter that blocks packets by their origin or source address, check the Source Network checkbox and supply the IP address and subnet mask for the source you want to block.
- To create a filter that blocks according to destination, check the Destination Network checkbox and fill in the appropriate address and subnet mask.
- To filter by protocol, choose the protocol you want to block or enable. For each of these protocols, you'll have to enter some additional information. For example, if you select TCP, you have to specify the source or destination port numbers (or both), while for Other you'll have to enter a protocol number (you'll see this in action in Exercise 3.4). The options for protocol filtering are listed here:
  - Any (which blocks or enables everything)
  - TCP
  - Established TCP
  - IP
  - UDP
  - ICMP
  - Other

Once you've specified the filter you want, click the OK button and you'll see it in the filter list. Filters go into effect as soon as you close the interface's Properties dialog box; you can always go back and add, edit, or remove filters at any time.

Creating VPN Packet Filters

Packet filters provide a useful security mechanism for blocking unwanted traffic on particular machines. You can use packet filters for special tasks such as to keep non-VPN traffic out of your VPN servers. The rules for doing this are straightforward. You can plan PPTP packet filters as well as L2TP packet filters. We will look at how to do this in the following sections.

PPTP Packet Filters

You need at least two filters to adequately screen out non-PPTP traffic. The first filter allows traffic with a protocol ID of 47, the Generic Routing Encapsulation protocol (GRE), to pass to the destination address of the PPTP interface. The second filter allows inbound traffic bound for TCP port 1723 (the PPTP port) to come to the PPTP interface.

You can add a third filter if the PPTP server also works as a PPTP client; in that case, the third filter needs the interface's destination address, a protocol type of TCP (established), and a source port of 1723.

Once you've created these filters, select the Drop All Packets Except Those That Meet The Criteria Below radio button in the Inbound Filters dialog box and close it. You have to repeat the process on the outbound side, creating two or three corresponding outbound filters that screen out any traffic not originating from the VPN interface and using the correct protocols.

In Exercise 3.4, you'll set up RRAS IP packet filters that block everything except PPTP traffic on the specified interface.

You should not attempt to filter traffic on your production VPN server until you've been successful in trying it on another, less mission-critical machine. Packet filters are based on complicated dependencies and sequencies of behavior, and it is essential that you know how to predict and test this behavior, both for the exam and for real-world implementations. There is no shortcut to replace hands-on practice and experience.

EXERCISE 3.4

Creating PPTP Packet Filters

1. Open the RRAS console by clicking Start ➤ Administrative Tools ➤ Routing and Remote Access.

2. Expand the server and IP Routing nodes to expose the General node of the server upon which you are working. Select the General node.

3. Right-click the appropriate interface, and then choose Properties.

EXERCISE 3.4 *(continued)*

4. In the General tab of the interface Properties dialog box, click the Inbound Filters button. The Inbound Filters dialog box will appear.
5. Click the New button, and the Add IP Filter dialog box will appear.
6. Fill out the Add IP Filter dialog box as follows:
    a. Check the Destination Network checkbox.
    b. Fill in the destination IP address field with the IP address of the VPN interface.
    c. Supply a destination subnet mask of `255.255.255.255`.
    d. Select a protocol type of TCP, and then specify a source port of **1723** and a destination port of **1723**.
    e. Click the OK button.
7. The Inbound Filters dialog box reappears, listing the new filter you created in Step 5. Repeat Step 5, but this time specify Other in the Protocol field and fill in a protocol ID of **47**. When you are done, click the OK button and you'll go back to the Inbound Filter dialog box.
8. In the Inbound Filter dialog box, click the Drop All Packets Except Those That Meet The Criteria radio button, and then click the OK button.

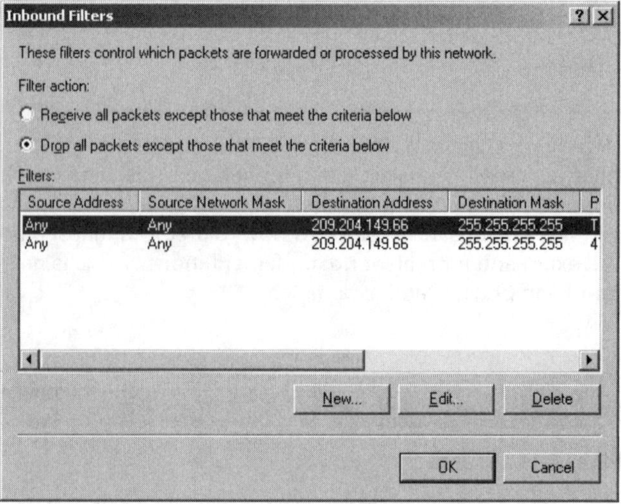

9. Repeat Steps 3 through 8, but this time create outbound filters. Make sure to specify the IP address of the VPN adapter as the source, not the destination.
10. Close the interface Properties dialog box.

L2TP Packet Filters

To plan L2TP packet filters, you have to go through the same basic process you did for PPTP, but the filters you need are slightly different. A total of four filters are required—two inbound filters and two outbound filters:

- An inbound filter with a destination of the VPN interface address and a net mask of `255.255.255.255`, filtering UDP with a source and destination port of 500
- An inbound filter with a destination of the VPN interface address and a net mask of `255.255.255.255`, filtering UDP with a source and destination port of 1701
- An outbound filter with a source of the VPN interface address and a net mask of `255.255.255.255`, filtering UDP with a source and destination port of 500
- An outbound filter with a source of the VPN interface address and a net mask of `255.255.255.255`, filtering UDP with a source and destination port of 1701

Troubleshooting IP Routing

Troubleshooting and managing IP routing is fairly simple: if you understand how the options described earlier in this chapter work, you know most of what you need to know to keep IP routing working smoothly. All of the remaining skills you need center around monitoring your routers to make sure traffic is flowing smoothly and troubleshooting the occasional problem.

A number of status displays are built into the RRAS console. Knowing that they exist, and what they display, makes it much easier to see all of the various health and status data that RRAS maintains. Each of the following commands shows you something different:

The General ➤ Show TCP/IP Information Command As you would expect, this display shows a broad general selection of IP routing data, including the number of routes in the route table, the number of IP and UDP datagrams received and forwarded, and the number of connection attempts. You can use the Select Columns command (right-click in the TCP/IP Information window) to customize what you see in this view.

The Static Routes ➤ Show IP Routing Table Command This command shows you the entire contents of the routing table, including the destination, network mask, and gateway for each route. This version of the routing table does not show you where the route came from (e.g., whether it was learned by RIP or OSPF).

The RIP ➤ Show Neighbors Command This command shows you which RIP neighbors exist; for each router, you can see how many bad packets and bad routes that neighbor has tried to foist off on your router.

The OSPF ➤ Show Areas Command This command shows you a list of all the defined areas (keep in mind that there will only be one area per interface). For each area, you can see whether that area is up or not, as well as the number of shortest-path computations performed on the link.

The OSPF ➤ Show Link-State Database Command This command presents a view of the entire contents of the link-state database, which is far outside the scope of this book.

The OSPF ➤ Show Neighbors Command This command shows you everything RRAS knows about the OSPF neighbors of this router, including the type of neighbor (point-to-point, broadcast, or NBMA), the neighbor's state, priority, and its router ID.

This OSPF ➤ Show Virtual Interfaces Command This command shows you a list of virtual interfaces for this OSPF router. Unless you have a fairly complicated OSPF network, this is likely to be blank.

In Exercise 3.5, you'll learn how to monitor the status of IP routing.

EXERCISE 3.5

Monitoring Routing Status

1. Open the RRAS MMC console by clicking Start ➤ Administrative Tools ➤ Routing and Remote Access.

2. Select the server whose status you want to monitor in the left pane of the MMC. Expand it until you see the Network Interfaces node.

3. Select the Network Interfaces node. Note that the right pane of the MMC now lists all of the known interfaces along with their status and connection state.

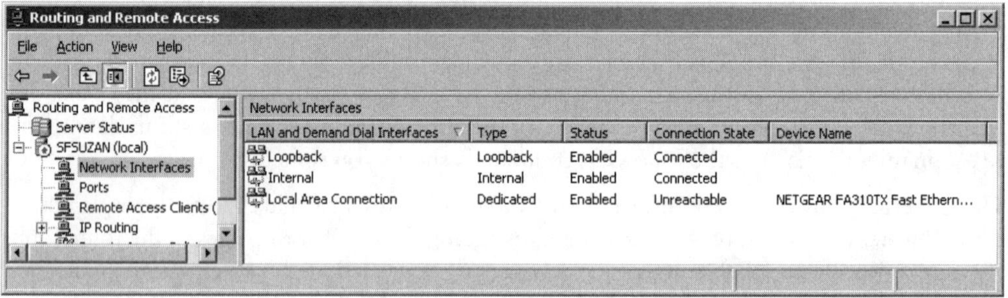

4. Select the General node beneath IP Routing. Note that the right pane of the MMC updates to show the IP routing interfaces, their IP addresses, their administrative and operational states, and whether or not IP filtering is enabled on each interface.

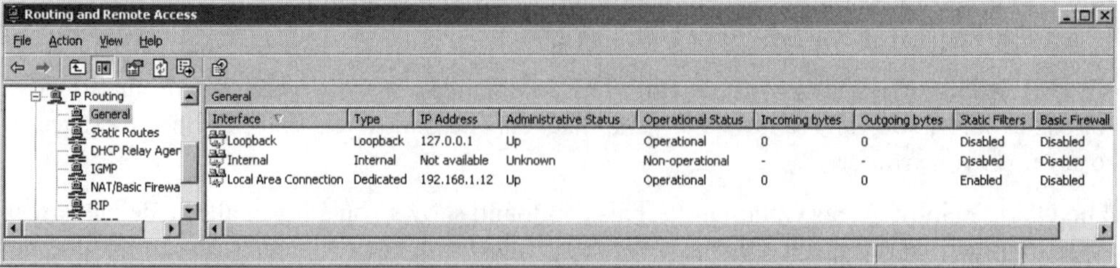

5. Right-click the General node, and choose the Show TCP/IP Information command. Check the number of IP routes shown.

EXERCISE 3.5 *(continued)*

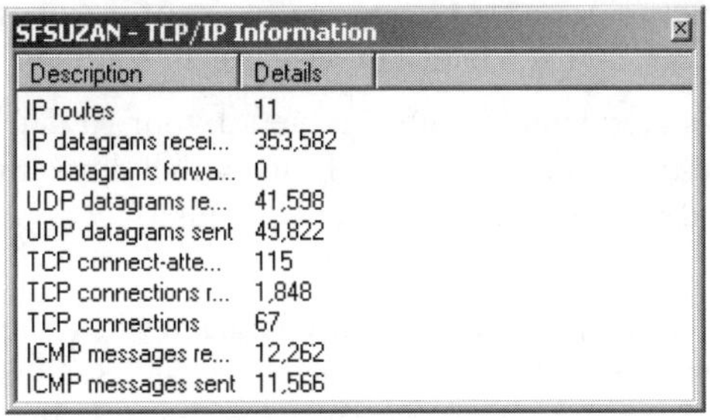

SFSUZAN - TCP/IP Information

Description	Details
IP routes	11
IP datagrams recei...	353,582
IP datagrams forwa...	0
UDP datagrams re...	41,598
UDP datagrams sent	49,822
TCP connect-atte...	115
TCP connections r...	1,848
TCP connections	67
ICMP messages re...	12,262
ICMP messages sent	11,566

6. Right-click the Static Routes node, and choose the Show IP Routing Table command. Note that the number of routes listed corresponds to the route count in the TCP/IP Information window, and that some of the routes listed are automatically generated.

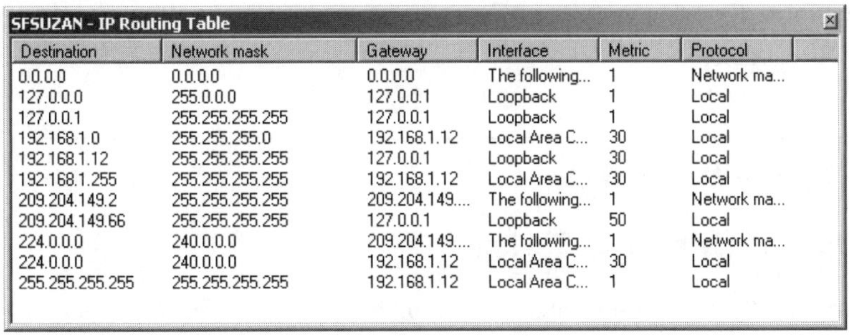

SFSUZAN - IP Routing Table

Destination	Network mask	Gateway	Interface	Metric	Protocol
0.0.0.0	0.0.0.0	0.0.0.0	The following...	1	Network ma...
127.0.0.0	255.0.0.0	127.0.0.1	Loopback	1	Local
127.0.0.1	255.255.255.255	127.0.0.1	Loopback	1	Local
192.168.1.0	255.255.255.0	192.168.1.12	Local Area C...	30	Local
192.168.1.12	255.255.255.255	127.0.0.1	Loopback	30	Local
192.168.1.255	255.255.255.255	192.168.1.12	Local Area C...	30	Local
209.204.149.2	255.255.255.255	209.204.149....	The following...	1	Network ma...
209.204.149.66	255.255.255.255	127.0.0.1	Loopback	50	Local
224.0.0.0	240.0.0.0	209.204.149....	The following...	1	Network ma...
224.0.0.0	240.0.0.0	192.168.1.12	Local Area C...	30	Local
255.255.255.255	255.255.255.255	192.168.1.12	Local Area C...	1	Local

You already learned how to use the `route add` command to add a new static route from the command line. However, the `route print` command can show you all or part of the routing table from the command line. Just typing **`route print`** into a command prompt window will give you a complete dump of the entire routing table; adding a wildcard IP address (for example: `Route print 206.151.*`) will display only routes that match `206.151`.

A comprehensive overview of IP routing troubleshooting could easily fill a book or two of this length. Microsoft's online help is pretty good at suggesting probable causes and solutions for most routing problems, and you should be familiar with the most obvious problems (and their solutions). To wit, when you suspect that your RRAS server is not routing traffic properly, begin by verifying the following:

- The RRAS service is running and configured to act as an IP router.
- The router's TCP/IP configuration is correct (including a static IP address).
- You have IP routing protocols attached to each interface where you need them.

Next, you need to verify the following routing-specific settings and behaviors:

- If you are using OSPF, make sure that the Enable OSPF On This Interface checkbox is turned on in the interface's OSPF Properties dialog box.

- Check to be sure that your router is receiving routes from its peers. Do this by opening the routing table and looking at the Protocol column. Seeing entries marked as OSPF or RIP tells you that at least some peers are getting routing information through. If you do not see any RIP or OSPF routes, that is a bad sign, because no routes are being received.
- You need to have a static default route enabled if your router hasn't received any default routes. To do this, add a new static route with a destination of `0.0.0.0`, a net mask of `0.0.0.0`, and either a demand-dial or LAN interface appropriate for your network setup.
- To test a demand-dial connection, use the `ping` command with a `-t` switch. For a demand-dial connection with a range of `208.40.3.0`, execute `ping 208.40.3.1 -t` (press Ctrl+C to halt). This command sends a continuous ping and gives the dial-up enough time to establish a connection and then send the ping. If you use a regular ping, it will fail because the connection will not have been established by the time the ping ends.

See Chapter 2 for more details on the TCP/IP configuration and troubleshooting tools.

Real World Scenario

Bringing In Experts to Help the Experts

Your company has finally realized that using its multihomed computers as routers isn't the most effective means for supporting your network. You decide to explore using dedicated routers and switches to segment and control network traffic. You also want to make sure that you have evaluated the differences between the two approaches thoroughly and professionally. How exactly should you proceed?

Part of the MCSE certification, covered in this chapter, is TCP/IP routing and the RIP and OSPF routing protocols. Those concepts are important because you are most likely placing the Windows Server 2003 information system in a routed environment. Just as it is important to understand that expertise regarding Windows Server 2003 is essential, it's also important to understand the need for experts in the world of OSPF and other routing protocols.

Although the concepts are covered in this book, and although the certification exam tests your understanding of the concepts, this book and certification don't fully prepare you to design an OSPF network with all the nuances that the operating systems from vendors such as Cisco, Nortel, and Lucent provide. This is a deep field, just as Windows Server 2003 is a deep field. Both a vascular surgeon and an orthopedic surgeon are technically proficient, and there is a great deal of cross-over knowledge between the two. However, when your bones are sticking out and the blood is flowing, you want the two doctors to cover their own specialties. The same is true in networking. If you aren't as experienced and knowledgeable in internetworking as you are in networking, you would be well served to run your routing or IP designs by an internetworking specialist. The specialist should have insight that has been honed over time. Such insight will reap benefits to your information system. No single person knows everything, and one of the hallmarks of a professional is knowing when to call in another professional. Both professionals need to work together to build an infrastructure that will support the requirements of the new services available in Windows Server 2003.

Understanding Network Connectivity

The job of a NAT server seems simple enough at first glance: Allow a group of computers to masquerade behind a single IP address. (In fact, NAT is sometimes called "IP masquerading" in the Unix world.) However, there are some subtleties that make NAT more complex than a first glance would indicate. You can start exploring the process by looking at a simple representation of a network using NAT to connect to the Internet (see Figure 3.27).

FIGURE 3.27 A small NAT network

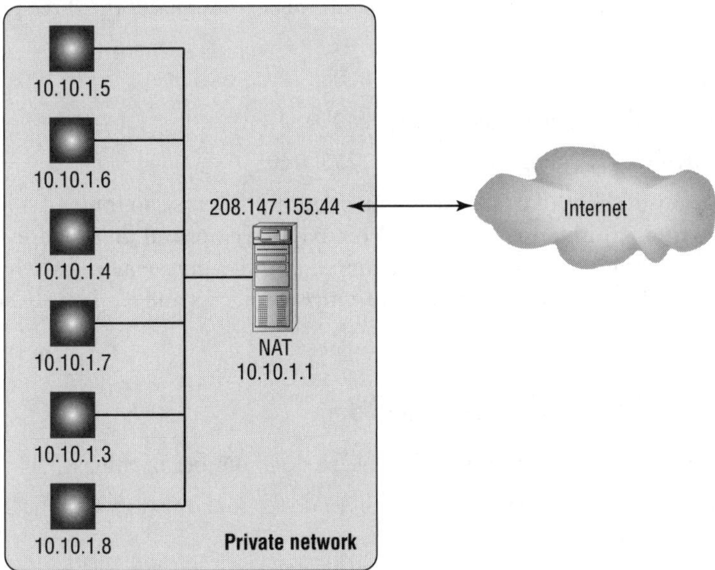

This network has six workstations and a NAT server, each with addresses in the `10.10.1.x` range. Notice that the only machine connected to the Internet is the NAT server and that it actually has a second IP address assigned—those are both small but very important details, as you'll see shortly.

In the rest of this chapter, we'll use NAT to refer to the protocol used both by the ICS and NAT services in Windows Server 2003, but we'll call those components by their correct names.

In the following sections, we'll cover the aspects of network connectivity you need to know. We'll start with private addressing, discuss NAT in Windows Server 2003, cover the flow of inbound and outbound packets, discuss NAT editors, and debate the merits of ICS versus NAT.

Understanding Private Addressing

In the early days of the Internet, the IP addressing scheme we've all come to recognize must've seemed capable of providing a large enough address space for the foreseeable future. The designers of the Internet did not, however, forsee the explosive growth of the Internet and the impending exhaustion of the IPv4 address space. Each device directly connected to the Internet normally needs its own address, and addresses have become scarce.

As a workaround, the Internet Network Information Center (InterNIC), in conjunction with the Internet Assigned Numbers Authority (IANA), designated some address ranges as *private addresses*. These addresses cannot receive traffic from or send traffic to the Internet. In every other respect, though, they are just ordinary IP addresses. The idea behind private addresses is that you can use them to configure a network that is not connected to the Internet. That seems like a useful idea, until you want to hook your network up to the Internet. That is where NAT comes in: It translates between public and private addresses.

RFC 1597, "Address Allocation for Private Internets," designates the three private address ranges:

- `10.0.0.0` with a subnet mask of `255.0.0.0`
- `172.16.0.0` with a subnet mask of `255.240.0.0`
- `192.168.0.0` with a subnet mask of `255.255.0.0`

You can use any of these address spaces with impunity, because no router is allowed to route Internet traffic to or from those addresses. You may have noticed that Figure 3.27 shows a second IP address assigned to the computer running NAT—now you know why. The NAT server uses a public IP address to communicate with the Internet and a private IP address for the local network.

NAT in Windows Server 2003

For NAT to work, the NAT server must be able to do a number of things:

- Maintain two interfaces, one with a private IP address and one with a public IP address, and route packets between them.
- Determine where outbound packets are going, and then edit their address data so that replies come back to the NAT computer (after all, Internet servers cannot send data back to the original clients).
- Receive replies sent in response to outbound packets, and then readdress them to the correct client on the private network.

You can follow each of these steps to see what really happens when a client makes a request for some data on an Internet server. For this example, you can say that a client with a private

IP address of `10.10.1.5` is trying to fetch a Web page from `www.chellis.net` (`216.92.40.80`). The NAT router has two IP addresses: `10.10.1.1` on the private side and `208.170.118.207` on the Internet.

Windows Server 2003 already understands how to route data between multiple IP addresses on the same computer—it just uses the same static routing code included with Windows NT. As you learned earlier in the chapter, static routing just moves packets among multiple interfaces that you define yourself. In reality, though, you have to install and configure the Routing and Remote Access Service (RRAS) to use NAT on a Windows Server 2003. ICS does not require RRAS, even though it does the same kind of routing.

You will learn how to install and configure NAT later in this chapter, in the "Planning NAT" section.

The Fate of the Outbound Packet

The journey of the outbound packet is shown in Figure 3.28 and is listed here:

1. The client generates its request and sends it to its default gateway—the NAT server. The packet is addressed to port 80 at IP address `216.92.40.80`, the machine you are trying to reach.
2. The NAT server receives the packet and examines it to determine where it is bound. It creates an entry in its NAT table that ties the real destination address and port number to its origin and to a substitute port number it chooses at random. It also replaces the original source address of the packet with its own address, so that replies from the target machine will come back to the NAT machine.

FIGURE 3.28 An outbound packet's journey through NAT

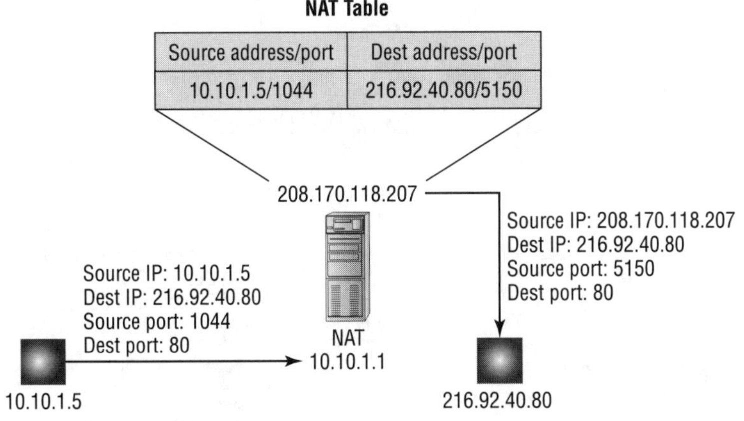

3. The NAT server sends the rewritten packet over its external interface to the Internet, where it is routed and handled normally. At this point, there is essentially no way to tell that the request came from a computer behind the NAT server, because all the network's Internet traffic originates from, and is returned to, the NAT machine.

The NAT table is the key to this whole process, because it associates the original source address and port with the destination address and port. That way, when an incoming packet arrives, the NAT software can scan the table to identify the original source for the packet.

The Fate of the Inbound Packet

So far, you've seen how the outgoing packet is rewritten so that it appears to be a request from port 5150 on a machine at `208.170.118.207` and is sent to port 80 on the machine at `216.92.40.80`. You can assume that the packet reaches the destination machine without incident and that it is able to generate a reply packet containing the requested data. This packet is addressed to `208.170.118.207`, port 5150. What happens when the packet reaches the NAT machine?

The journey of the inbound packet is shown in Figure 3.29 and is listed here:

1. The Web server sends a packet back to the source address of the original request, which happens to be the address of the NAT server.
2. When the NAT server receives the packet, it uses its table of port and address mappings to determine that the incoming packet is arriving in response to an outgoing packet sent from a particular address. In this case, the table tells the NAT software that an incoming packet addressed to port 5150 at `208.170.118.207` was sent in response to an outbound packet that reached the NAT server from `10.10.1.5`'s port 1044. In other words, the NAT table maps the original client address and source port to the destination address plus the source port that NAT used when it rewrote the packet.

FIGURE 3.29 An inbound packet's journey through NAT

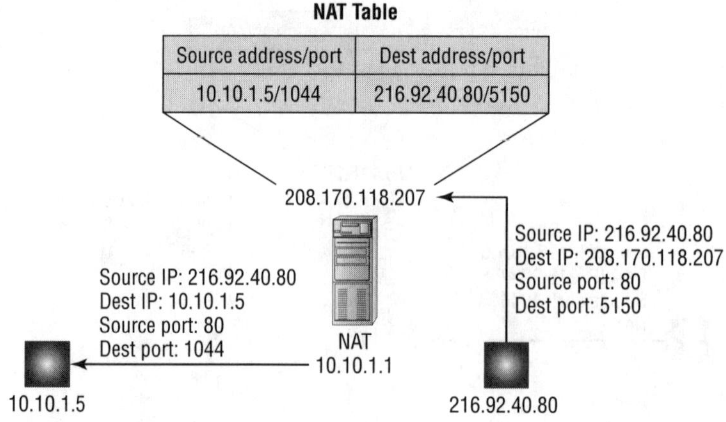

The NAT server uses the return port number as a reference into the table and re-addresses the packet to the original source address (`10.10.1.5`) and port number (1044). When that machine receives the packet, it appears to have come directly from the requested host. As far as the client and remote server can tell, NAT never even happened.

NAT Editors

The approach described above works fine for data where the IP address information is all in the packet headers, but it falls down for protocols that embed addressing information in the packet payload. For example, the File Transfer Protocol (FTP) embeds IP address data in the payload, as do NetBIOS over TCP/IP and the Point-to-Point Tunneling Protocol. The approved solution is for the NAT machine to inspect the packet payloads and change any addressing data it finds. However, this works only with certain data types; a special component called a *NAT editor* is responsible for changing data in the protocols it supports. Windows Server 2003 includes NAT editors for FTP, PPTP, NBT, and the Internet Control Message Protocol (ICMP).

ICS versus NAT

Up to this point, we've treated ICS and NAT as though they are identical. That is because they are extremely similar: They both implement NAT, but with differing levels of bells and whistles. However, Microsoft expects you to know the differences between the two, including the following:

What they run on: NAT requires Windows 2000 Server or Windows Server 2003. ICS is available on Windows 98, Windows 2000 Professional, and Windows XP Professional, as well as Windows 2000 Server and Windows Server 2003.

How you configure them: Checking one checkbox on the Sharing tab of a network adapter configures ICS. NAT requires you to use the Routing and Remote Access console, and many more configuration options are available.

How many public IP addresses they can use: With ICS, you expose a single public IP address (e.g., the address that your ISP assigns you). NAT can expose a number of public IP addresses, which is useful if you want to tie specific public IP addresses to individual machines on your LAN.

How many networks they can link: ICS links one LAN to one public IP address, but NAT can link many LANs (provided they each have their own interfaces) to many public IP addresses.

ICS was introduced in *MCSA/MCSE Windows XP Professional Study Guide, Second Edition* by Lisa Donald with James Chellis (Sybex, 2003).

Installing ICS

Now that you understand how the underlying protocol works, you might be curious to see what happens on a machine when you install Internet Connection Sharing. ICS is a NAT implementation, but it leaves out some of the more powerful features included in the full-blown NAT version.

ICS is simple to install and use, provided you make the right decisions during installation. It's easy to configure, too; this ease of use and management comes at the expense of some functionality, though.

Unlike almost every other service you've seen in this book, you don't install ICS using the Windows Components Wizard. All you do is check one box on a Properties dialog tab, and the installation process is invisible after that—save for the changes ICS makes to your existing TCP/IP configuration.

ICS is primarily intended for connecting small office/home office (SOHO) networks to the Internet. In particular, it's designed for small networks that don't already have a full network infrastructure and that have a single connection to the Internet. Because ICS installs its own DHCP server (more on that in a minute) and it requires you to use the `192.168.*` address block, it's not suitable for networks that already have their own DHCP server, that use static IP addresses, or that run DNS servers or Windows Server 2003 domain controllers.

Assuming you still want to install ICS, you must have administrative privileges on the target machine to do so.

As an example, say you have a machine that's connected to your cable modem via an Ethernet NIC. You decide to install ICS so that you can add network connections for two other machines in your house, so you buy the necessary supplies and hardware to construct a LAN for your house. As part of that process, you add a second NIC to your machine so it can run ICS. Although this isn't strictly required, ICS *does* require you to have two independent network interfaces. One can be a modem or a NIC; the other must be a NIC.

When you install ICS, you attach it to one of the adapters—the one that's connected to the Internet. When you do so, some things change in your machine and adapter configurations:

- The *other* adapter (e.g., the one connected to your LAN) gets a new IP address of `192.168.0.1` and a subnet mask of `255.255.255.0`.
- The Internet Connection Sharing service is started and set to run automatically at boot time.
- The DHCP address allocator service is enabled. The allocator gives out IP addresses in the range `192.168.0.2` through `192.168.0.254`, using the standard `255.255.255.0` subnet mask. Think of it as a simplified DHCP server without any configurable options.
- If you're using a dial-up connection on the Internet-connected adapter, automatic dialing is enabled.

These changes don't do anything special to the clients on your network; you must manually configure each of them to use DHCP so they can get the necessary settings from the *DHCP allocator*. ICS also doesn't make any changes to the adapter connected to the Internet. If you need to make changes (for example, because your ISP wants you to use DHCP with your cable modem), change them on the Internet adapter, *not* the LAN adapter.

Installing ICS is easy. Open the Properties page for the network connection for which you want to enable ICS (Start ➤ Control Panel ➤ Network Connections ➤ *the name of the connection you want to share*). Open the Properties dialog box, click the Advanced tab, and you'll see the Advanced tab of the network connections Properties dialog box (see Figure 3.30).

FIGURE 3.30 The Advanced tab of the network connection's Properties page

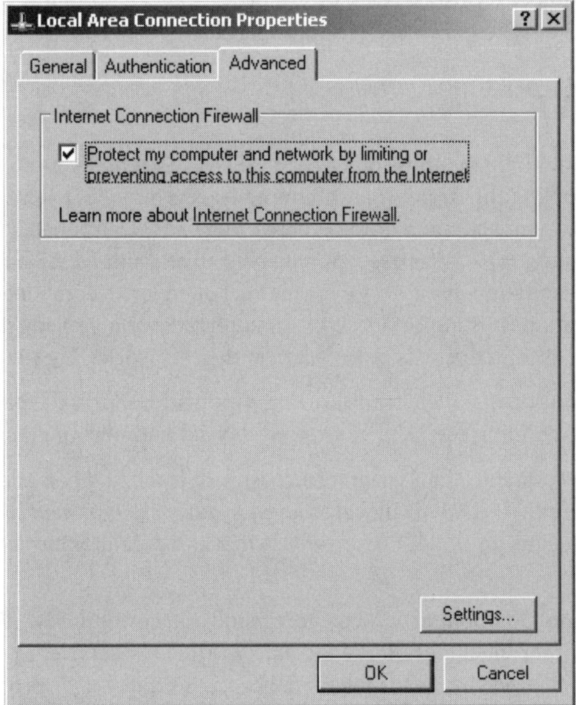

To enable ICS, just click the checkbox labeled Allow Other Network Users to Connect Through This Computer's Internet Connection, and that's it! If you want Internet traffic from other computers on your LAN to automatically bring up the connection (as you normally will), make sure the Enable On-Demand Dialing checkbox is on, too. That's all you have to do to set up a basic ICS configuration, apart from configuring each client to use DHCP.

Installing ICS interrupts any TCP/IP connection you have set up, so don't do it in the middle of any operations you don't want interrupted.

You can enable ICS on any Windows XP Professional or Windows Server 2003 computer.

Planning NAT

Earlier in the chapter, you saw that the primary differences between the ICS and NAT implementations in Windows Server 2003 are related to scale and scope. The good news is that the actual configuration is not that much more difficult—there is just more of it. In the next sections, you'll learn how to install NAT in Windows Server 2003, how to add and remove NAT interfaces, and how to configure NAT properties.

Installing NAT

Installing NAT is something of a misnomer because NAT is actually treated as another routing protocol you install using the Routing and Remote Access Service (RRAS). In that light, when you install NAT what you are really doing is activating some components that provide services within the RRAS framework. Of course, you must install and run RRAS before you install NAT.

Microsoft's documentation discusses three separate, but related, components that contribute to the NAT implementation. It is important to understand these components so that you'll understand the buzzwords used in their documents and in the real world. They include the following:

The Translation Component The translation component handles the NAT functions themselves, including maintaining the NAT table for inbound and outbound connections.

The Addressing Component This is what Microsoft calls the "DHCP address allocator" in its ICS documentation. Like the DHCP allocator, the *addressing component* is just a stripped-down DHCP server that assigns an IP address, a subnet mask, a default gateway, and the IP address of a DNS server.

The Name Resolution Component When you install and configure NAT, it begins to act as a DNS server for the other machines on the local network. That service is provided by the *name resolution component*. When a client resolver makes a DNS query, it goes to the name resolution component on the NAT server, which forwards it to the DNS server defined on the Internet-connected adapter and returns the reply. Think of this like a proxy for DNS.

Of course, installing these components does not mean you'll have to use them all. You always need the translation component because it actually implements the NAT functionality. If you are running a DHCP server *or* the DHCP relay agent on your private LAN, you cannot concurrently use the NAT addressing component. Likewise, if you are running an internal DNS server, you may not use the name resolution component.

You'll see how to turn these off a little later in the chapter in the section titled "Configuring NAT Properties."

The NAT Process

ICS hides a lot of the necessary details from you, but Microsoft assumes that if you are experienced enough to run NAT, you can take a little extra time to do some of the things ICS does for you.

Most of these steps will be familiar to you from the procedures for routing, but some of them are specific to NAT configuration. Here's what you need to do:

1. Install RRAS and enable it. If you use the RRAS Wizard (as described in the next section), this is your last step. The wizard will take care of the other steps for you. If you are installing NAT on an existing RRAS box (or if you just like to know what the wizard is doing behind your back), go to Step 2.
2. If you are not using a permanent connection (that is, not something that is always up like a dedicated analog line, ISDN line, DSL, or cable modem connection), you need to configure your dial-up connection to reach your ISP using these steps:
   a. Create a demand-dial interface to reach your ISP using the Demand Dial Wizard.
   b. Use RRAS to make the dial-up port routable.
3. Configure the local network adapter properly. This means that you need to give it an appropriate private IP address and network mask, and you need to make sure there is no default gateway specified.
4. Add a static IP route on the adapter that is connected to the Internet. The destination address must be `0.0.0.0`, and the subnet mask should also be `0.0.0.0`. This forces RRAS to send all traffic across that interface, which is what you want for Internet connectivity.
5. Add NAT as a routing protocol inside RRAS.
6. Add two NAT interfaces: one for your Internet adapter and one for the local network adapter.
7. If you want to use the addressing or name resolution components, you need to configure them.

Installing NAT Using the RRAS Console

If you've already configured RRAS to handle IP or IPX routing, you'll probably want to know how to configure NAT without deactivating RRAS (which wipes out its configuration information) and reactivating it to start the RRAS Wizard. The steps required to do this are described in Exercise 3.6—note that this only covers the installation and not the process of adding a NAT interface and configuring it.

In Exercise 3.6, you'll install NAT on an RRAS server. You should have at least two network interfaces available on your computer: one for the public side and one for the private side.

EXERCISE 3.6

Installing NAT on an RRAS Server

1. Open the Routing and Remote Access snap-in by clicking Start ➢ Administrative Tools ➢ Routing and Remote Access.
2. Locate the server on which you want to enable NAT. If its icon has a little red down-pointing arrow, right-click it and choose the Enable And Configure Routing and Remote Access Service command, and use the procedure shown in the previous section discussing

EXERCISE 3.6 *(continued)*

NAT installation. Otherwise, right-click the General node under IP Routing and select New Routing Protocol.

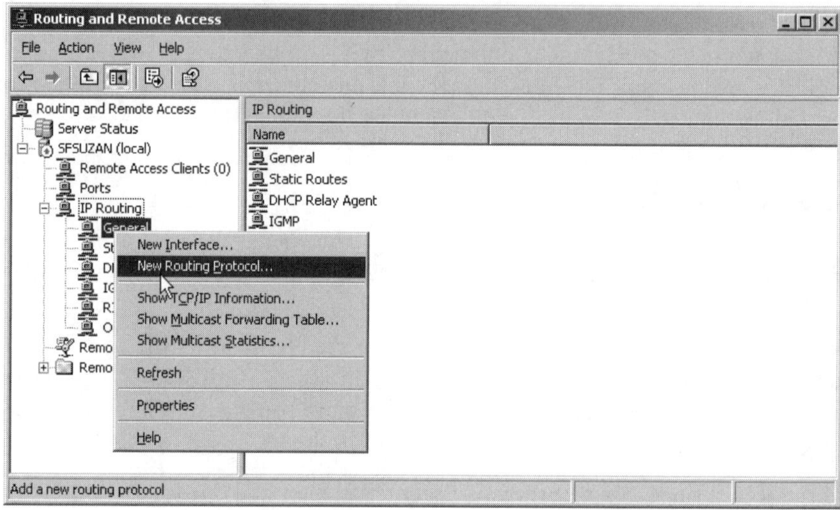

3. In the New Routing Protocol dialog box, select the NAT/Basic Firewall option and click OK. If this choice does not appear, it was already installed via the RRAS Wizard.

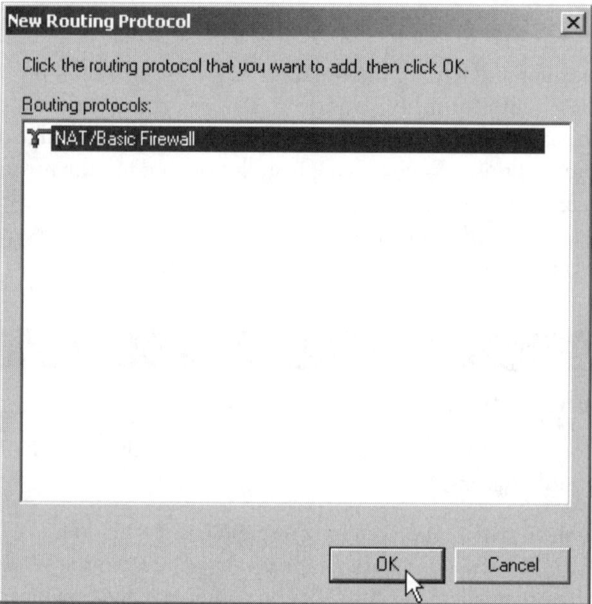

EXERCISE 3.6 *(continued)*

4. Notice that a new node called "NAT/Basic Firewall" now appears under IP Routing.

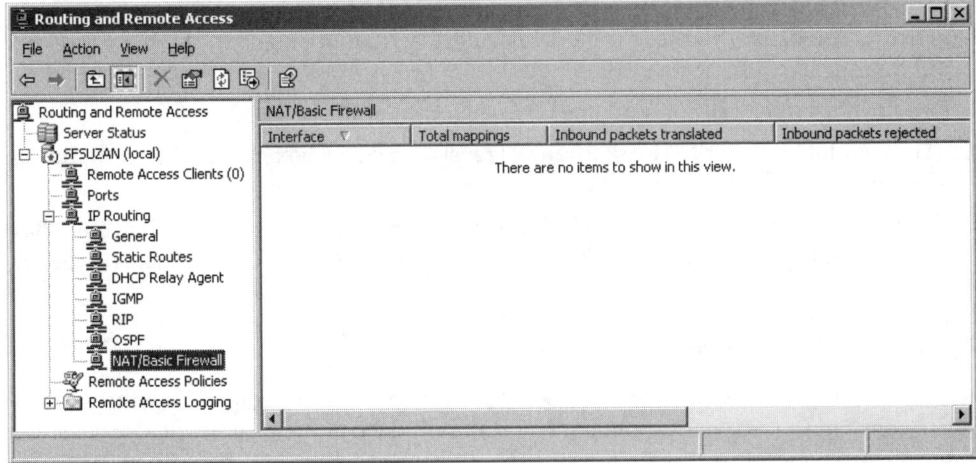

Adding and Removing NAT Interfaces

You have to add an interface in RRAS before it can do anything with packets bound to or from that interface. NAT is no different; before you can use NAT on your local network, you must add a *NAT interface* by using the RRAS console. The actual process of adding a new NAT interface is fairly simple provided you know on which adapter to put the interface. You will see how to add and remove a NAT, as well as how to set NAT interface properties, in the following sections.

Realize that the NAT process "hides" your internal network. From the Internet, a host can only see your connection to the Internet and none of the hosts on the internal network (unless you create port mappings).

Adding a NAT Interface

Just as with ICS, you have to distinguish between adapters that are connected to your local network and those connected (or that can connect) to the Internet when adding a NAT interface. NAT links these two interfaces, so you actually need to create both of them. ICS is smart enough to automatically create both interfaces for you, but RRAS\NAT requires you to do it yourself. There are some simple rules to follow:

- Create an interface for your local network adapter first, specifying it as such.
- Create the Internet adapter interface second. If you are using a dial-up connection, you need to also add some routing information.

Follow these steps to add a NAT interface. You must have an additional interface available in your computer.

1. Open the Routing and Remote Access snap-in by clicking Start ➤ Administrative Tools ➤ Routing and Remote Access.
2. Expand RRAS until you see the Network Address Translation node (RRAS, *ServerName*, IP Routing, NAT/Basic Firewall).
3. Right-click NAT/Basic Firewall and choose New Interface.
4. The New Interface For Network Address Translation dialog box appears. Select the adapter you want to use and click OK.
5. The NAT Properties dialog box (which we will discuss in the section titled "The NAT/Basic Firewall Tab.") appears. Select "Public Interface Connected To The Internet and click the OK button.

Removing NAT Interfaces

As it turns out, you can easily remove any NAT interface—just select it and use the Action ➤ Delete command (or the corresponding command on the context menu). RRAS asks you to confirm that you want to remove the interface. If you remove an interface that has active connections, they'll be immediately closed—so don't do this if you (or your network users) are in the middle of something you do not want interrupted.

Setting NAT Interface Properties

Each NAT interface has its own set of properties. You can edit these properties by right-clicking an interface and choosing the Properties command on the context menu. In the following sections, we will discuss the various tabs of the NAT Properties dialog box. The tabs that are relevant to our discussion and that you need to know how to configure are: the NAT/Basic Firewall, Address Pool, and Services And Ports tabs.

The NAT/Basic Firewall Tab

The NAT/Basic Firewall tab lets you designate what kind of NAT interface this is. Normally, you'll need to add a pair of NAT interfaces: one for the adapter that is connected to the Internet and the other for your local adapter. That means you'll have reason to use both of the radio buttons on the NAT/Basic Firewall tab (see Figure 3.31). These buttons include the following:

- The Private Interface Connected To Private Network radio button is what you use to specify that this interface is bound to the adapter on your local network.
- The Public Interface Connected To The Internet button specifies that this adapter is connected to the Internet. That means that you use it only on the adapter that you use to connect to the Internet, whatever type of adapter it is. The checkboxes allow you to enable NAT on the interface, and/or enable a basic firewall on the interface.
- The Basic Firewall Only button adds an extra layer of security to your NAT configuration by including a basic firewall that can be used in conjunction with NAT. The firewall only allows traffic to pass that is specifically requested by the private side of the network. The Inbound and Outbound Filters buttons allow you to define filters for inbound and outbound traffic.

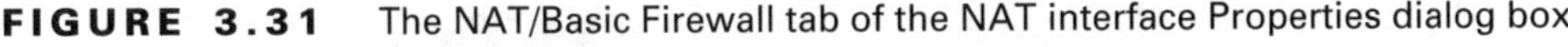

FIGURE 3.31 The NAT/Basic Firewall tab of the NAT interface Properties dialog box

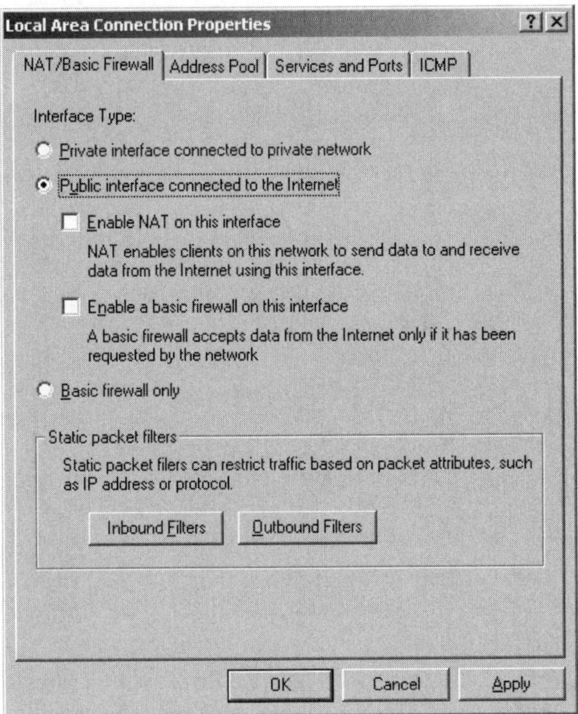

The Address Pool Tab

As you may recall, the number of supported IP addresses is one of the differences between NAT and ICS. The Address Pool tab (see Figure 3.32) is where you tell NAT which IP addresses it should expect traffic to come from. You can assign *address pool* information as a range or as a collection of individual addresses. No matter how deep the pool is, you manage it from this tab by using the list of addresses (or ranges) and the Add, Edit, Remove, and Reservations buttons.

When you add a new range of addresses, you specify the starting address, the subnet mask, and the ending address. If you are using a single address, just specify it alone. RRAS tries to be helpful and calculate the correct ending address based on the start address and subnet mask you specify. When you edit a range, you can tweak any of these settings; removing a range from the address pool removes it as part of the public IP address set that can be used to reach machines on your internal LAN.

Removing an address from the address pool *does not* prevent outside hosts from reaching your NAT server; it just prevents the NAT server from routing packets any further on your LAN.

FIGURE 3.32 The Address Pool tab of the NAT interface Properties dialog box

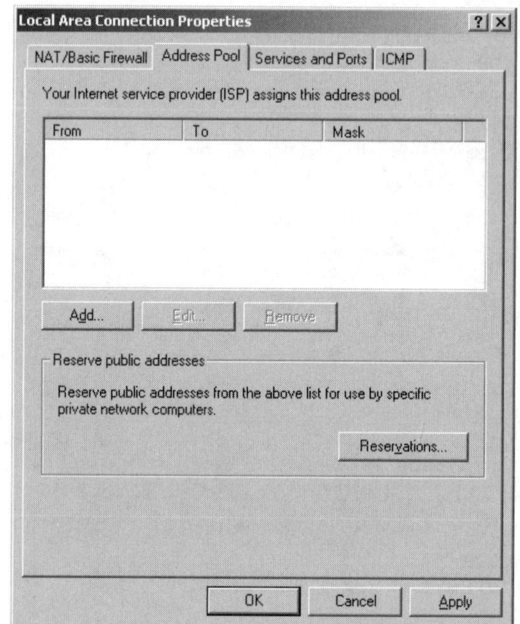

The Reservations button allows you to reserve individual IP addresses from the public range and add static mappings in the NAT table that point to particular hosts on the inside of your network. This adds a degree of efficiency to the NAT process. For example, let's say that you have a Web server whose private IP address is `192.168.0.146`. By adding a reserved address that maps that private IP to a single external public IP (say, `208.70.14.212`, if that were in your address pool), you could register a DNS record for `www.globalitcertification.com` (or whatever other name you wanted it to have). The NAT table would contain a predefined entry that would map any traffic bound for `208.70.14.212` to `192.168.0.146`. The only tricky part of adding a reservation is getting the matching addresses into the Add Reservation dialog box (see Figure 3.33). You need to specify a single public IP address that maps to a single private IP address. If you want incoming traffic to reach through the NAT box and to the target machine, you must also check the Allow Incoming Sessions To This Address checkbox.

The Services And Ports Tab

You can also edit the NAT table in a second way: You can specify which ports inbound traffic should be mapped to using the Services And Ports tab (see Figure 3.34). This allows you to take traffic coming to any port on any of your public IP addresses and direct it to the port you want on any machine on your private network.

For example, you could channel any incoming Web requests to a single machine by mapping port 80 on the public interface to port 80 on your internal Web server. Of course, you could do the same with SMTP or any other TCP or UDP protocol if you want. In the example here, the Secure Sockets Layer (SSL) port is mapped to 192.168.0.240 so that any SSL connection attempt from the outside world will automatically be channeled to a single machine on the private network. The Services And Ports tab lists the *port mappings* you have in effect, and you can add, edit, and remove them using the buttons at the bottom of the tab. Port mappings specify to which ports inbound traffic should be mapped.

FIGURE 3.33 The Add Reservations dialog box

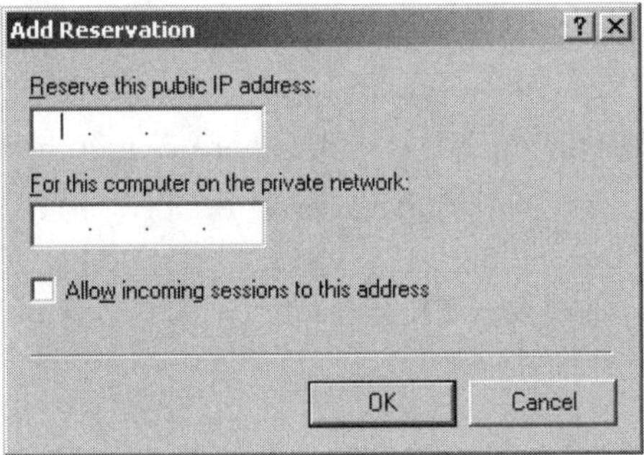

FIGURE 3.34 The Services And Ports tab of the NAT interface Properties dialog box

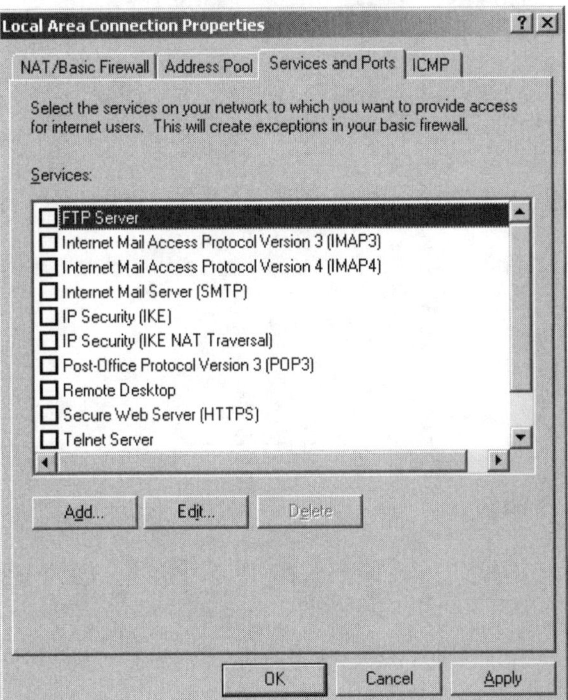

When you add or edit a service or port, you'll see a dialog box like the one shown in Figure 3.35. You use the controls in this dialog box to set up the special port mapping you want to take effect:

- The Description Of Service field is simply a text field that describes the service.
- The Public Address group lets you specify what public address can receive traffic for this specific port. The On This Interface radio button (the default choice) accepts traffic on the specified port for all public IP addresses in the address pool. If you instead select the On This Address Pool Entry radio button, the public IP address you provide is the only one for which this port mapping will be active.
- The Protocol radio buttons allow you to specify either TCP or UDP.
- Specify the port number the outside world will be using in the Incoming Port field.
- Use the Private Address field to specify the private address to which incoming traffic on the port will go.
- Use the Outgoing Port field to select the port that will be used for outbound traffic generated by hosts on your local network.

FIGURE 3.35 The Edit Services dialog box

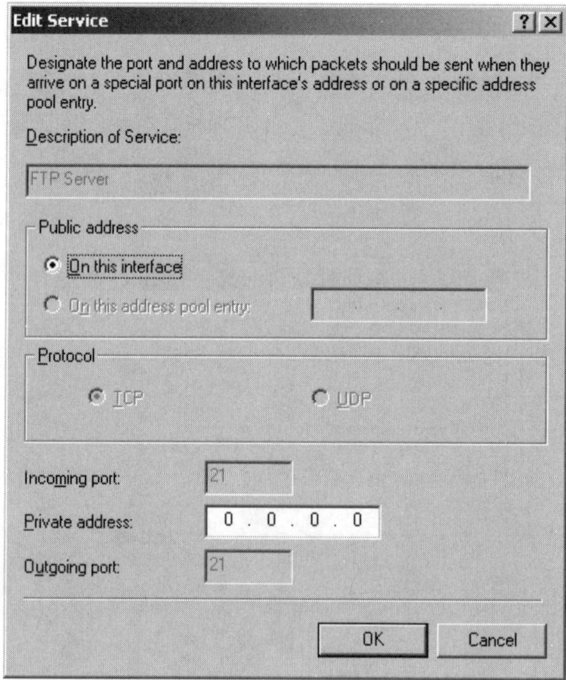

Configuring NAT Properties

In addition to the properties that configure the interfaces themselves, some properties pertain to all NAT interfaces and connections on your RRAS NAT server. You modify these settings through the NAT Properties dialog box, which you get by right-clicking the NAT/Basic Firewall node in the RRAS console and using the Properties command. The Properties dialog box has four tabs: the General tab, the Translation tab, the Address Assignment tab, and the Name Resolution tab. We will discuss each in the following sections.

The General Tab

The General tab (see Figure 3.36) allows you to change the amount of event logging information that the NAT software writes to the system event log. The default is set to log errors only, but you can choose from three other levels: no logging at all, logging errors and warnings, and logging *everything*. The more detailed log information is useful when you are trying to troubleshoot a problem, but it can bulk up your event log quickly, so do not turn up logging unless you are trying to find and fix a problem.

FIGURE 3.36 The General tab of the NAT Properties dialog box

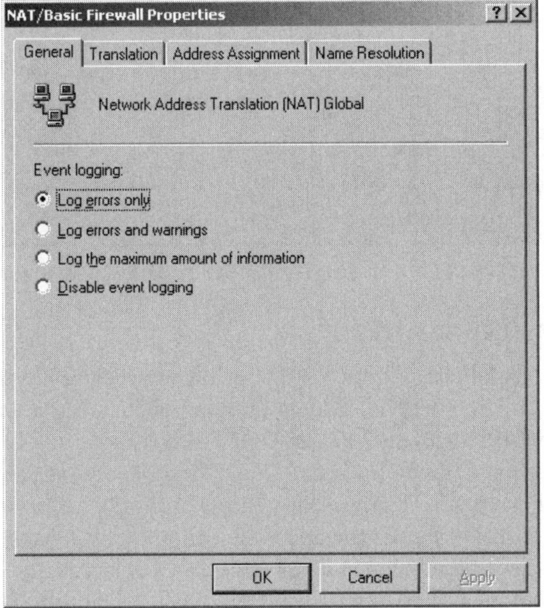

The Translation Tab

The Translation tab (see Figure 3.37) allows you to set scavenging times for port mappings. The Remove TCP Mapping After (Minutes) and Remove UDP Mapping After (Minutes) fields allow you to control how long entries remain in the NAT table after their last use. The default behavior is to keep TCP mappings for 24 hours (1444 minutes) and UDP mappings for 1 minute.

FIGURE 3.37 The Translation tab of the NAT Properties dialog box

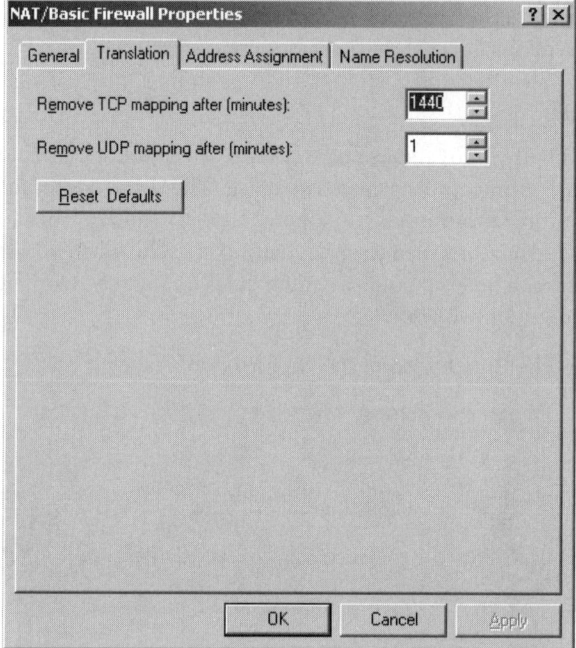

The Address Assignment Tab

The Address Assignment tab (see Figure 3.38) controls whether or not the NAT addressing component is used. Recall that the NAT addressing component is just a simplified DHCP server; you don't need to use it if you already have a DHCP server on your private network, but you can use it if you want to streamline the number and kind of services you have installed. The controls in this dialog box are simple. The Automatically Assign IP Addresses By Using The DHCP Allocator checkbox controls whether the addressing component is active or not. If it is, the IP Address and Mask fields control the address range that is handed out. There is no way to change the default gateway address (it is always the private IP address of the NAT machine), default DNS server, or any of the other DHCP options.

You can, however, exclude IP addresses that you do not want assigned by the allocator. You do this with the Exclude button, which displays the Exclude Reserved Addresses dialog box (see Figure 3.39). In this dialog box, you'll see a list of any reserved IP addresses, and you can modify the list contents with the Add, Edit, and Remove buttons. This is functionally equivalent to creating an exclusion range in the DHCP snap-in when you are using the "real" DHCP server.

FIGURE 3.38 The Address Assignment tab of the NAT Properties dialog box

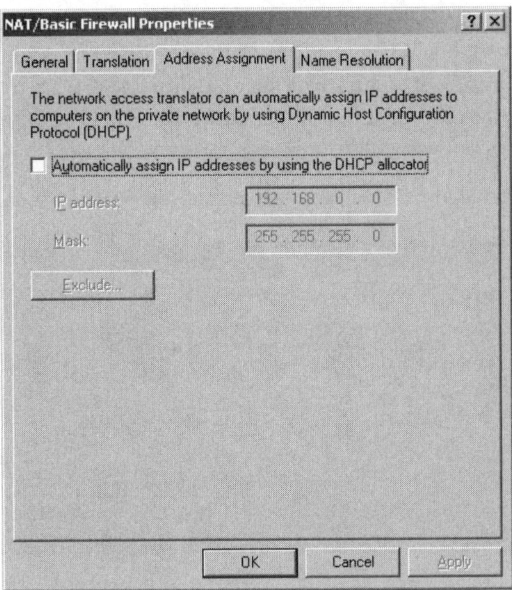

FIGURE 3.39 The Exclude Reserved Addresses dialog box

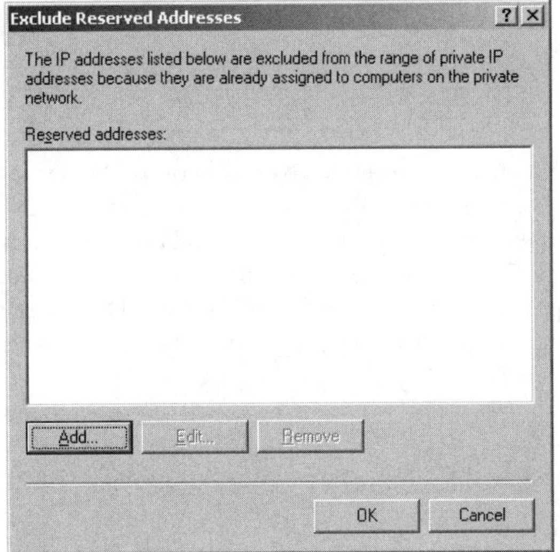

To allow inbound connections from the Internet, you need to exclude the IP address of the target machine, and then assign that IP address statically to the target. Once you've done so, you'll be able to configure a special port pointing to the target.

The Name Resolution Tab

You can choose to either use or not use the NAT name resolution component with the Name Resolution tab (see Figure 3.40). When you turn on the component, its address is distributed by the addressing component, and client computers send all their DNS queries to the NAT computer that acts as a DNS proxy. You can still configure each individual client with the IP address of an external DNS server, but then you may not be able to resolve the names of hosts on your private LAN.

FIGURE 3.40 The Name Resolution tab of the NAT Properties dialog box

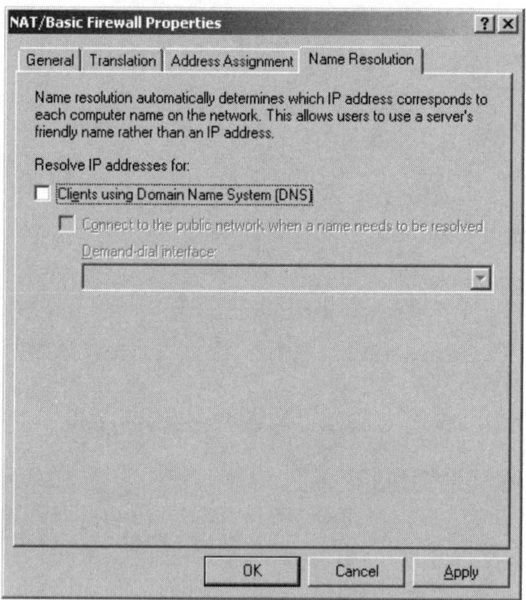

The Name Resolution tab has two checkboxes that control how resolution works. The first, Clients Using Domain Name System (DNS), is normally checked. This controls whether the name resolution component is active or not. The second checkbox, Connect To The Public Network When A Name Needs To Be Resolved, specifies whether or not you want the Internet connection brought up just for DNS queries. The Demand-Dial Interface pull-down list lets you select which demand-dial interface, if any, you want brought up when a DNS query requires bringing the link up.

Real World Scenario

The Need for NAT

Your company has a Class C address that it acquired years ago when it had 50 employees and a few network servers. Now the company has grown to over 300 employees, all of whom want to access the Internet. You have been running NWLink for internal traffic, using TCP/IP only for Internet traffic, and allowing only some of the users to connect to the Internet. So far, you have had sufficient address space for your Internet traffic. However, because you see more growth ahead, you realize that your current solution will not work much longer. As the network administrator, you have been told that everyone must have access to the Internet. Rather than chase down more Class C public addresses, you decide that you are going to implement Windows Server 2003 NAT.

Stretching the address space is particularly useful for small- to medium-sized companies that cannot acquire a public Class C address for their own private address space. Small companies can contact their ISPs and acquire a small block of IP addresses, commonly in the range of 4 to 32 individual addresses. However, this solution usually does not provide enough addresses to uniquely identify all of the devices within most networks. NAT is often seen as the solution for addressing problems, and it obviously addresses the problems rather well.

IP v6 is poised to resolve these addressing issues and other problems with a more robust protocol stack and a 128-bit address space. But even as wide-scale implementation approaches, the movement to IP v6 will cascade from the backbone and slowly radiate down to the client devices on the edge of the network. Even after the address space squeeze is solved, the rationale for NAT will still exist because of the other benefits it provides for access control in your network. NAT provides additional security for the network architecture. It can also be used to control the manageability of the enterprise network.

Summary

In this chapter, you learned:

- How IP routing works. Internal routing uses static or dynamic routing protocols to move data within an internetwork. Border routing uses IGMP to move data outside of an internetwork. Multicast routing sends data to multiple nodes.
- How to create and manage interfaces for IP routing. Interfaces are created and managed using the RRAS console.
- How to set OSPF and RIP routing parameters. RIP sends periodic announcements to discover other routers in the network topology. OSPF uses an area that is a collection of interconnected networks.
- How to manage demand-dial routing. Considerations include VPN connectivity, routing and security, and dialing credentials.
- The differences between Internet Connection Sharing and the Network Address Translation service. ICS is a simplified version of NAT that is used to share an Internet connection in small offices and home networks. NAT describes the process of translating a private, nonroutable IP address into a publicly visible and routable IP address.
- How to install and configure ICS. ICS links the computers on a LAN to one public IP address and is used to share one Internet connection between two or more computers.
- How to install and configure NAT. NAT can link many LANs to many public IP addresses, and it is used to enable secure Internet connectivity for nodes on a private IP network.

Exam Essentials

Know the difference between static routing and dynamic routing. *Static routing* systems do not make any attempt to discover other routers or systems on their networks. Instead, you tell the routing engine how to get data to other networks. Dynamic routing does not depend on your adding fixed, unchangeable routes to remote networks. Instead, a *dynamic routing* engine can discover its surroundings by finding and communicating with other nearby routers in an internetwork.

Understand routing in Windows Server 2003. RRAS provides Windows Server 2003 computers with routing capabilities. You can establish static routes that specify where packets bound for certain networks should go. RRAS provides dynamic routing using version 2 of the Routing Information Protocol (RIP) and the Open Shortest Path First (OSPF) protocol. It also provides packet filtering to screen out undesirable packets in both directions.

Understand the difference between RIP and OSPF. A RIP-capable router periodically sends out announcements while simultaneously receiving announcements from its peers. This exchange of routing information enables each router to learn what routers exist on the network and which destination networks each router knows how to reach. OSPF networks are broken down into areas; an area is a collection of interconnected networks. Think of an area as a subsection of an internetwork. Areas are interconnected by backbones. Each OSPF router keeps a link state database only for the areas to which it is connected.

Know how to install RRAS and configure IP routing. The RRAS components are installed on computers running Windows Server 2003 and Advanced Server, whether or not you choose to activate them. To enable your server to route IP packets, you have to activate and configure RRAS using the RRAS Server Setup Wizard in the RRAS MMC console. You then need to add demand-dial interfaces if you want to support demand dialing, give each routable interface a network address for each protocol it carries, and install and configure the routing protocols on the interfaces that should support them.

Know the private address range of addresses. Know the address range of each class of private addresses and when they can and should be used. Understand that it is illegal for a router to forward any of these addresses to the Internet.

Know VPN port numbers. Know the ports that must be open for a PPTP connection and an L2TP connection. Know how to configure TCP/IP packet filters.

You can construct filters that allow or deny traffic into or out of your network, based on rules that specify source and destination addresses and ports. To create a filter, find the interface on which you want the filter, and then open its Properties dialog box and click the appropriate packet filter button.

Understand the difference between ICS and NAT. ICS is a simplified implementation of NAT. NAT requires Windows 2000 server or Windows Server 2003, while ICS is available on Windows 98, Windows 2000 Professional, and Windows XP Professional and the various versions of Windows 2000 and Windows 2003 servers. ICS is much simpler to configure. ICS links one LAN to one public IP address, but NAT can link many LANs (provided each has its own interface) to many public IP addresses.

Understand what happens when you install ICS. When you install ICS, you attach it to one of the adapters—the one that is connected to the Internet. The other adapter (e.g., the one connected to your LAN) gets a new IP address of `192.168.0.1` and a subnet mask of `255.255.255.0`. The ICS service is started and set to run automatically at boot time. The DHCP address allocator service is enabled. If you are using a dial-up connection on the Internet-connected adapter, automatic dialing is enabled. The only thing you need to do is configure the machines on the LAN to use DHCP.

Understand the different components of NAT. The translation component handles the NAT functions themselves, including maintaining the NAT table for inbound and outbound connections. The addressing component is just a stripped-down DHCP server that assigns an IP address, a subnet mask, a default gateway, and the IP address of a DNS server. The name resolution component acts as a DNS server for the other machines on the local network.

Know how to install and configure NAT. First, install RRAS and enable it. Then configure the local network adapter properly. Add a static IP route on the adapter that is connected to the Internet, if port mappings will be used. Add NAT as a routing protocol inside RRAS. Add two NAT interfaces: one for your Internet adapter and one for the local network adapter. Configure the addressing or name resolution components as needed.

Key Terms

Before you take the exam, be certain you are familiar with the following terms:

address pool
addressing component
adjacency
area border router (ABR)
auto-static update mode
backbone links
border routing
broadcast router
default route
demand-dial routing
DHCP allocator
dynamic routing
host routes
inbound port mappings
internal routing
internetwork
link state map
metric
multicast routing
name resolution component
NAT editor
NAT interface
network address translation (NAT)
network routes
non-broadcast multiple access
packet filtering

periodic update mode
point-to-point router
port mappings
private addresses
route filters
router discovery messages
routing table
static routing
unicast routing
virtual link
virtual link neighbors

Review Questions

1. Your NAT configuration is shown in the following diagram.

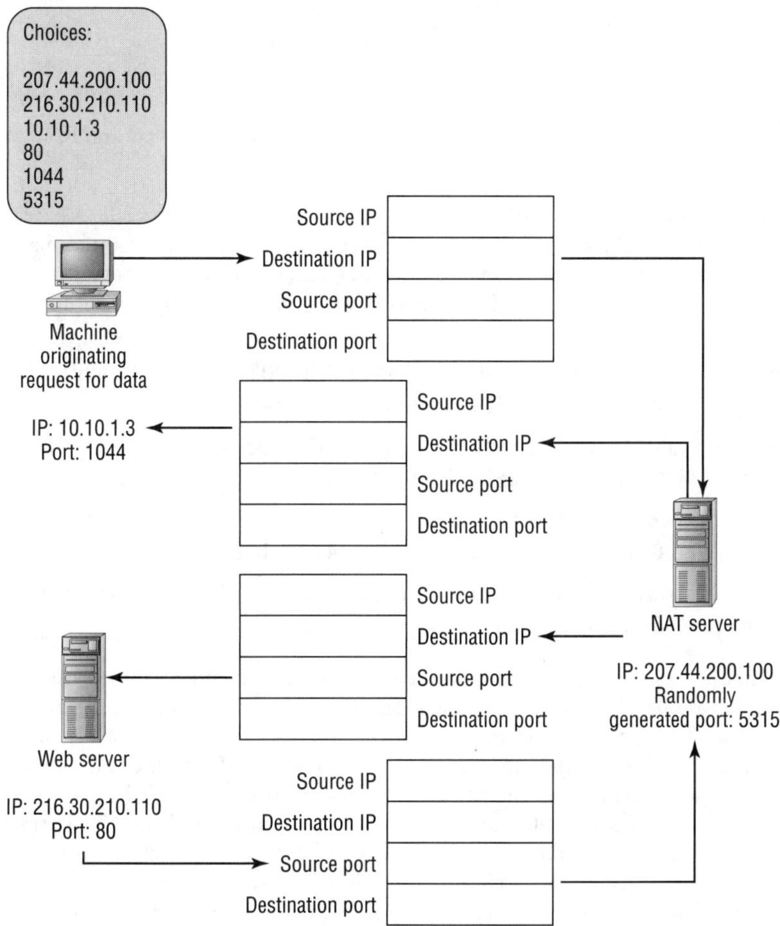

One of the computers behind the NAT server is requesting data on port 80 from a Web server that has the IP address 216.30.210.110. Select the IP addresses and port numbers in the Choices column and place them in the appropriate positions in the diagram. Note that any of the items can be used more than once or not at all.

2. You are the systems engineer in charge of a Windows network with four subnets whose addresses are `208.45.231.0`, `208.45.232.0`, `208.45.233.0`, and `208.45.234.0`. Your routers are configured with these IP addresses:

- Router 1: `208.45.231.1` and `208.45.232.1`
- Router 2: `208.45.231.2` and `208.45.233.1`
- Router 3: `208.45.232.2` and `208.45.234.1`
- Router 4: `208.45.233.2` and `208.45.234.2`

Router 2 is connected to the Internet. The connection between Router 2 and Router 4 is a very slow 56K dial-up line.

Your computer's IP address is `208.45.231.25`. Your default gateway is `208.45.231.2` because that is the address of the router that is connected to the Internet. You want to make sure that your computer always routes information to `208.45.234.0` through Router 1 unless Router 1 becomes unavailable because the 56K line is so slow. Which command should you use to accomplish this?

A. `route add 208.45.231.1 mask 255.255.255.0 208.45.234.0 metric 1route add 208.45.231.2 mask 255.255.255.0 208.45.234.0 metric 2`

B. `route add 208.45.234.0 mask 255.255.255.0 208.45.231.1 metric 2route add 208.45.234.0 mask 255.255.255.0 208.45.231.2 metric 1`

C. `route add 208.45.234.0 mask 255.255.255.0 208.45.231.1 metric 1route add 208.45.234.0 mask 255.255.255.0 208.45.231.2 metric 2`

D. `route add 208.45.234.0 mask 255.255.255.0 208.45.232.1 metric 1route add 208.45.234.0 mask 255.255.255.0 208.45.233.1 metric 2`

3. Your company has six locations that have been connected together in a hub-and-spoke design with your location as the center. The network is designed that way because it grew over time and you simply added another connection to your Windows NT RAS server every time a new one was needed. You are concerned that if your connection goes down, the entire network will go down and all your users across the country will lose connectivity. You have migrated all your servers to Windows Server 2003, and you are migrating the Windows NT workstations to Windows XP Professional. You decide that each RRAS server will have at least three separate connections to other RRAS servers in the network so that you will always be able to find a path through the network. You want to accomplish this with the least amount of administrative effort. Router update traffic and convergence time for the changes in the connections must be minimized. How should you configure the RRAS computers to ensure these objectives?

A. Configure RIP version 2 on all routing interfaces.

B. Configure OSPF on all routing interfaces.

C. Configure RIP version 1 on all routing interfaces.

D. Configure static routes.

E. Configure RIP version 2 and OSPF on all routing interfaces.

4. You work for a very large accounting company that has more than 1000 workstations in three locations over a routed network. You have upgraded all of the servers to Windows Server 2003, and you are converting all of the workstations to Windows XP Professional. Two of the locations are connected to the central office, which has a T1 connection to the Internet. All of the users on all three networks are funneled through this RRAS server for Internet access. Company policy prohibits personal Internet browsing from company equipment. The main purposes of Internet access within the company are e-mail connectivity and VPN traffic to your business partners. Some of the staff occasionally download new regulations and forms from a few government Web sites. How can you implement this policy, using the tools and services on your Windows Server 2003 network?

   A. Configure TCP/IP filters to control access to the Internet.

   B. Configure IP packet filters to control access to the Internet.

   C. Configure the Internet browsers through global policy to control which Web sites users can and cannot visit.

   D. Create static routing tables to control which Web sites, based on address, the users can reach.

5. You are the systems engineer of a Windows network that consists of four subnets. The IT Director wants to reduce costs as much as possible. You decide to configure at least one Windows Server 2003 computer on each subnet with RRAS and a nonpersistent demand-dial connection. You would prefer that routing updates not broadcast to the network, but any changes should be propagated to the other RRAS computers. Which of the following should you use to accomplish these goals?

   A. RIP version 2

   B. OSPF

   C. RIP version 1

   D. Area border routers

6. You recently upgraded all of the sites in your internetwork to Windows Server 2003 and implemented the routing capability built into the servers. Because you did not want to deal with the complexity of the OSPF routing protocol, you chose to implement RIP. After implementing the routers, you discover that routes that you do not want your network to consider are updating your RIP routing tables. What can you do to specify the networks with which the RIP routing protocol will communicate on your network?

   A. Configure TCP/IP filtering.

   B. Configure RIP route filtering.

   C. Configure IP packet filtering.

   D. Configure RIP peer filtering.

   E. There is no way to control this behavior.

7. You are the administrator of a network consisting of six subnets that are routed together through an ISP that does not support multicasting. You are connected to the ISP at all locations with Windows Server 2003 RRAS servers. The marketing department is interested in providing audio and video presentations between the corporate office and one of the other locations; these presentations will be a test of how audio and video presentations could be used throughout the entire company. Your company is growing rapidly, and you plan to build a private network to support more flexibility in your routing capability—but that is not going to happen in time for the test. What can you do on your side of the network to allow the multicasting traffic to reach the intended destinations?

   A. Configure multicast boundaries on each of the appropriate RRAS routers.

   B. Install RIP version 2 and OSPF to carry the multicast traffic.

   C. Configure an IP-in-IP tunnel interface on the appropriate RRAS routers.

   D. Configure the multicast heartbeat on the appropriate RRAS routers.

8. You are planning to upgrade the network to Windows Server 2003 to take advantage of the various new services available and the general overall stability that it promises to provide. Your network is located in one large building and is not connected to remote locations; the entire network is on one subnet, and its utilization is beginning to take its toll on performance. You want to break the network into smaller pieces, and the company does not want to spend money on a dedicated router. After you get your servers up and running Windows Server 2003, you plan to build one Windows Server 2003 server with multiple NICs so that you can break the network into four subnets. When you are ready to set up this solution for this network, what would be the best way to configure the multihomed Windows Server 2003 router?

   A. Install and configure the OSPF routing protocol, and let it figure out the routing tables automatically.

   B. Install and configure RIPv1 so that the broadcasts will fill in the tables and keep them up-to-date automatically.

   C. Install and configure RIPv2 so that the broadcasts will fill in the tables and keep them up-to-date automatically.

   D. Configure the multihomed host with a static routing table.

   E. Install and configure RIPv1 and RIPv2 so that the broadcasts will fill in the tables and keep them up-to-date automatically.

9. You are part of the small support staff of a medium-sized company that is growing. No one on your staff is experienced with routers; and because your company has a hiring freeze that extends to your support staff, you cannot bring routing experts on board in the foreseeable future. However, you are charged with connecting eight offices together. You are almost finished upgrading your servers to Windows Server 2003, and you've read that you can use them as routers. When it comes time to connect the servers between the various offices using the routing functionality offered in Windows Server 2003, what routing protocol would make the most sense for your particular situation?

   A. OSPF

   B. RIP

   C. BGP

   D. Dynamic routing file

   E. Static routing tables

10. Your network has eight subnets; each subnet has at least two connections to the other subnets, and some have three or four connections to the other subnets. This design was created because you wanted to make sure that every subnet was accessible from every other network if any connection went down. You want to implement this design as effectively as possible, and you want the network to recover as quickly as possible if a link goes down. You are going to implement this design in the near future and use Windows Server 2003 servers as the routers as you bring each subnet online. Which routing protocol supported by Windows Server 2003 would be the most appropriate for this design?

    A. RIP 1

    B. RIP 2

    C. OSPF

    D. Static routing tables as a backup to RIP

    E. Static routing tables as a backup to OSPF

11. You are building four networks—each in a different city—to support the regional activities of the Sunrise Flower Shop. Each region needs to communicate with each of the others so that it can take orders for the other regions and then transmit the delivery instructions, including JPEG images, to the appropriate location. To save costs, you decide to set up demand-dial connections with a bandwidth that is sufficient to support the images. However, you do not want routing updates to be broadcast throughout the network—although you do want any changes to the network to be sent to the 15 other routers so that communications can be reliable. Which routing protocol should you use when you configure the Windows Server 2003 servers that you are using for the connection points?

    A. OSPF

    B. RIP 2

    C. Static routing tables

    D. RIP 1

    E. CHAP

12. Your Windows Server 2003 network has 350 Windows XP Professional workstations and 5 Windows Server 2003s. You had a Class C address that you acquired from the InterNIC, but you released it when you went to a national ISP. The cost of having almost 400 IP addresses from your ISP continues to rise, and your manager has told to reduce this cost. You decide to implement NAT and use a statically configured private address space, `172.16.0.0/12`, while obtaining a single public address and DNS service from your ISP. You install another NIC in one of your Windows Server 2003s and configure the public NIC with the provided address. When you try to reach the Internet from any of the machines except the NAT server, your attempt fails. What is most likely causing this problem?

    A. You did not create any address reservations.

    B. You do not have proper name resolution.

    C. You did not enable TCP and UDP header translation.

    D. You did not create the range of ports needed for the translation.

13. You are responsible for a Windows Server 2003 network that provides sustaining engineering under a contract to a major software company. Two hundred Windows XP Professional workstations are on the network. They use a bank of 10 Windows Server 2003 computers to hold and keep track of the different versions of software that are modified as a result of technical support calls. You have implemented NAT, which will help provide security against intruders trying to get into your network while your engineers are browsing the Internet. You are told that you need to install an FTP server on the internal network, so you reserve an address on the external interface on the NAT server. When you give that address to your contacts at the other company, they cannot access the FTP server. What is the most likely reason for the problem?

    A. FTP is not supported through a NAT interface.

    B. FTP needs to be installed on the NAT server in order to be exposed to the public network.

    C. An FTP editor needs to be configured.

    D. A special version of FTP that supports NAT needs to be installed.

14. You have set up a Windows Server 2003 network for a small public relations company. They have 10 agents, 3 researchers, and 4 salespeople, all of whom use Windows XP Professional workstations. These workstations all connect to a Windows Server 2003 that is running ICS so that the workstations can access the Internet. The workstations are also running the Microsoft Office applications and Exchange Server for e-mail. Fatima, one of the researchers, has learned that Exchange supports NNTP. She wants to use this service so the staff can supply their clients and media outlets with information through Exchange Server. You configure and test Exchange for the NNTP service, and Fatima begins creating content for the server. When she is ready to publish to the world, she sends an e-mail about the new service to the company's clients. After a while, she starts getting messages that the URL she sent does not work. What is the most likely cause of this problem?

    A. You haven't added the local DNS name of the Exchange Server in the Services tab.

    B. You haven't configured the port for NNTP in the Services tab.

    C. You cannot expose internal services to the Internet through the ICS and must use NAT.

    D. You need to list the addresses of the people who will be accessing the NNTP service on the Exchange Server in the ICS service.

15. You are supporting the Widgets Unlimited network, which has 100 Windows XP Professional workstations and 3 Windows Server 2003 servers with static IP addresses. A multihomed router is being used to separate the 15 graphics workstations because they were generating so much traffic that it affected the rest of the network. Management is finally succumbing to pressure to provide Internet access for all the users, but only if you can provide it without a separate account for each user. You install the RRAS and NAT services and decide to use NAT's automatic distribution of IP addresses to help with the translation and generally to ease the administration of the IP network. You also plan to use the ISP for name resolution services to simplify administration. When you attempt to configure NAT, what is the major problem that you will encounter with this network?

    A. NAT does not allow workstations on other subnets.

    B. The DHCP on NAT supports only one scope.

    C. You need to install a full-featured DNS server when you have more than one subnet.

    D. There should be no problem with this type of environment.

Answers to Review Questions

1.

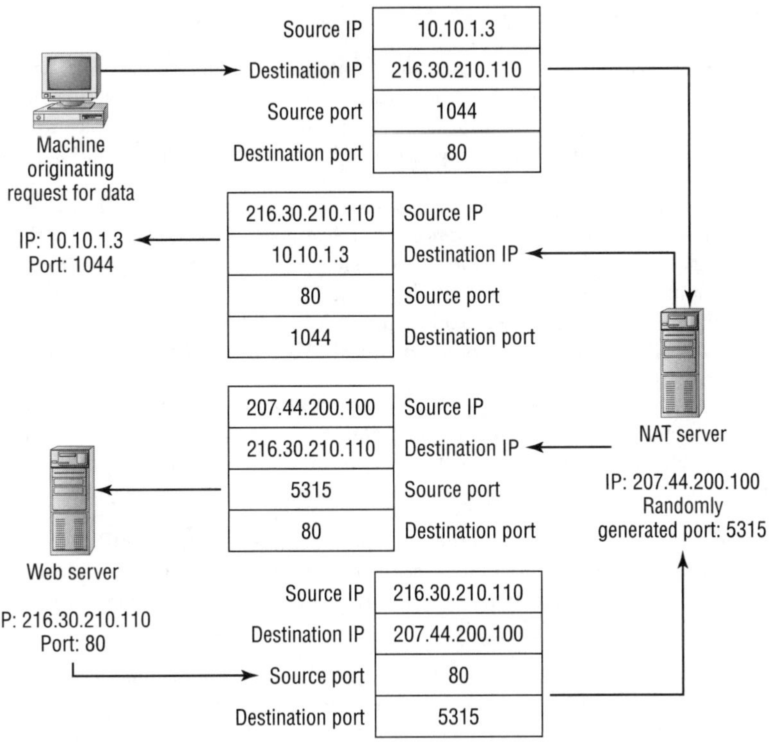

The client generates its request and sends it to the NAT server. The NAT server receives the packet and examines it to determine its destination. It creates an entry in its NAT table that ties the real destination address and return port number to the packet's originating IP via a substituted port number that NAT chooses at random. The NAT server also replaces the original source address of the packet with its own Internet address, so that replies from the target machine will come back to the NAT machine. The NAT server sends the rewritten packet over its external interface to the Internet, where it is routed and handled normally. The Web server sends the packet back to the source address of the original request, which happens to be the address of the NAT server. When the NAT server receives the packet, it uses its table of port and address mappings to determine that the incoming packet is arriving in response to an outgoing packet sent from a particular address. It then re-addresses the packet and sends it to the original IP.

2. C. The correct syntax for the `route add` command is as follows:

`route add` *`destination`* `mask` *`subnet mask gateway`* `metric cost metric`

In Answer A, the destination and gateway addresses are reversed. Answer B uses incorrect metrics. Answer D uses gateways that are not on the host's subnet.

3. B. The OSPF protocol doesn't have as much overhead on the network as either version of RIP. If the network changes, the information will be propagated to the other routers immediately instead of waiting for a specified broadcast time. Although configuring OSPF has more up-front administrative overhead than RIP has, once everything is set up, the subsequent effort will be less. OSPF propagates route changes to its neighbors immediately.

   RIP is a distance-vector protocol that periodically broadcasts routes to the other servers. It is useful for a very simple routed network; however, when you want to set up many multiple and complex routes, RIP creates a great deal of traffic. Your environment is much too complex to configure static routes. Every time something changed, you would have to modify all the routing tables manually.

4. B. IP packet filters are applied at the RRAS server and can control access based on rules that act on source and destination addresses and ports. For example, you could build a rule that specifies the IP addresses of all acceptable Web destinations while dropping all other requests, or you could create a rule that would not allow requests to reach specific sites by IP address. You could also build a rule that would not allow services such as CHAT to work through your RRAS server. By applying this governor at the RRAS server, you would not have to keep track of each individual workstation.

   TCP/IP filters are configured at each workstation. Although they can control specific communication, the administrative overhead is unacceptable for a broad-based policy. Configuring each browser through global policies is not a valid option. Using static routing tables applies only to communication between routers and is not concerned with the ultimate destinations of the packets.

5. A. The only way to accomplish all the goals is to use RIP version 2. RIP version 1 broadcasts changes to the entire network, so that choice would not work. OSPF cannot be used because the connection is a nonpersistent demand-dial interface. Area border routers are simply special versions of OSPF routers.

6. B. RIP route filters allow you to configure your routers to either ignore or accept updates from specific network addresses or a range of addresses. TCP/IP filtering is configured at each individual host to control the traffic at a granular level, such as specific address, UDP port, or TCP port. IP packet filtering is used on the router interface to control IP traffic based on subnet masks, IP address, or port. RIP peer filtering is used to control communication between individual routers rather than control the entire network address.

7. C. An IP-in-IP tunnel encapsulates IP datagrams inside other IP packets. This allows you to send packets that are not supported, such as multicasts in this situation, to other locations that *are* supported. Multicast boundaries use the multicast scope, rate of traffic, or IP header to control the forwarding of the traffic; however, this does not allow that traffic to flow across a section of the network that does not support it. This is also the case for multicast heartbeat, which is used to look for multicast support connectivity on the network. RIP and OSPF are routing protocols that manage the tables that locate routes through the network. They are not involved in the support or lack of support of multicast traffic.

8. D. Configuring the multihomed router with a static routing table is the simplest approach for this environment. Although you could spend the time configuring the server with the more sophisticated routing protocols, this situation has no compelling advantage because every subnet will always be one hop away from the others. The more sophisticated protocols become useful when multiple routes are available or there are subnets across multiple routers. Also remember that OSPF does not figure out routes automatically until you have configured OSPF properly. There is nothing automatic about it.

9. B. RIP is the easiest dynamic routing protocol among the choices you have with Windows Server 2003. RIP will automatically discover the other RIP routers and build the tables necessary for the routing to take place. Although there is broadcast traffic associated with RIP on a small network, it will not have an impact. OSPF demands up-front planning and understanding of how OSPF functions, and it is not particularly useful in a small network that is not going to change very often. Even as you add new paths to this network, RIP will update its tables appropriately. Static routing tables are a bit too cumbersome and error-prone for a network with multiple routes. There is no such thing as a dynamic routing file. BGP (Border Gateway Protocol) is used to connect large, independently managed networks and is not an option with the Windows Server 2003 product.

10. C. OSPF is best suited for routed networks that have multiple connections and that can change abruptly without severely impacting the availability of the other networks. The RIP protocols are better suited for simple networks with straightforward routes. Building static routes to back up dynamic routing protocols is self-defeating.

11. B. RIP version 2 uses a multicast method for communicating changes to the other routers when routing changes are detected on the network. This minimizes any traffic on the network, but this protocol is still easy to configure and is reliable. RIP 1 broadcasts every 30 seconds to communicate with the other routers. OSPF has a great deal of overhead and is designed to manage the convergence of large networks when links go down. Static routing tables must be edited manually and will not update other routers. CHAP is an authentication protocol, not a routing protocol.

12. C. When you have fewer public addresses than private addresses, NAT performs Port Address Translation (PAT), which uses port numbers to keep track of individual sessions. This is done through the ability of the NAT server to translate the TCP or UDP headers that address the packets. Address reservations are used when you want to map a specific private internal address to a specific public external address consistently. The NAT server provides the name resolution for the private clients using the ISP DNS server.

13. C. FTP embeds IP address information in the data component of the packet. Because NAT translates headers only, this information will not match, and the connection will not work. The NAT editor translates the IP address information in the header itself to match the translated address. FTP is supported through NAT, and there is no need to install the FTP server on the NAT server. If you did that, you could expose the FTP service on just the public side of the NAT interface, but that would be outside the realm of the NAT. There is no special NAT version of FTP.

14. A, B. The Services tab allows outside computers to access specified services on your internal network. You do this by specifying the local DNS or IP address of the machine running the service that you want to expose. You also specify the ports that the service will use, in this case port 119.

15. B. The DHCP allocator, which is what NAT provides, supports only a single scope of addresses. If you need more than one scope, you will have to disable the DHCP allocator in NAT and install a full-featured DHCP server for the network. NAT does allow workstations on other subnets to access the Internet. The DNS service in NAT will pass any name resolution request to the DNS server at the ISP; you just need to use the address of the NAT server for the DNS server.

Planning a DNS Strategy

MICROSOFT EXAM OBJECTIVES COVERED IN THIS CHAPTER:

✓ **Plan a host name resolution strategy.**

- Plan a DNS namespace design.
- Plan zone replication requirements.
- Plan a forwarding configuration.
- Plan for DNS security.
- Examine the interoperability of DNS with third-party DNS solutions.

✓ **Troubleshoot host name resolution.**

- Diagnose and resolve issues related to DNS services.
- Diagnose and resolve issues related to client computer configuration.

The Domain Name System (DNS) is one of the most important aspects of Windows Server 2003 network administration and planning. Active Directory depends on DNS, and many important system functions (including Kerberos authentication and finding domain controllers) are now handled through DNS lookups. Windows 2000 Professional and XP Professional clients use DNS for name resolution, too, but they also use DNS to find Kerberos Key Distribution Centers (KDC), global catalog servers, and other services that may be registered in DNS.

The primary specifications for DNS are defined in RFCs 974, 1034, and 1035. The Windows Server 2003 DNS server supports the requirements found in RFCs 1033, 1034, 1035, 1101, 1123, 1183, 1536, and 2136.

In this chapter, you will learn how DNS functions. You will also learn how to plan a DNS namespace, how to plan DNS zones, how to plan DNS zone replication and delegation, how to plan forwarding, how to plan the server resources to support DNS, how to integrate DNS with WINS, and how to troubleshoot host name resolution.

Fictional companies, such as Acme or Widgets, Inc., can be useful in demonstrating business and technical concepts. Microsoft uses its own fictional companies, such as Contoso, Fabrikam, and Northwind Traders. These nonexistent companies are helpful in illustrating Windows design procedures. In this chapter, we'll follow Microsoft's lead and use these companies for our examples.

Understanding DNS

The *Domain Name System (DNS)* is a hierarchically distributed database. In other words, its layers are arranged in a definite order, and its data is distributed across a wide range of machines. DNS is a standard set of protocols that defines the following:

- A mechanism for querying and updating address information in the database
- A mechanism for replicating the information in the database among servers
- A schema of the database

DNS has its roots in the early days of the Internet when the Internet was a small network created by the Department of Defense for research purposes. Host names of computers were manually entered into a file located on a centrally administered server. Each site that needed to resolve host names had to download the HOSTS file. As the number of computers on the Internet grew, so did the size of the `HOSTS` file, as did the traffic generated by the downloading of this file. The need for a new system that would offer features such as scalability, decentralized administration, and support for various data types became more and more obvious. The Domain Name System (DNS), introduced in 1984, became this new system.

With DNS, the host names reside in a database that can be distributed among multiple servers, decreasing the load on any one server and providing the ability to administer this naming system on a per-partition basis. DNS supports hierarchical names and allows registration of various data types in addition to the host-name-to-IP-address mapping used in `HOSTS` files. By virtue of the DNS database being distributed, its size is unlimited and performance does not degrade much when adding more servers.

In the following sections, we'll discuss what DNS does, features of DNS under Windows Server 2003, the terminology of DNS, and how DNS works.

What DNS Does

DNS's job is to translate between computer host names and IP addresses. DNS works at the application layer of the OSI reference model and uses TCP and UDP at the transport layer. The DNS model is pretty plain: Clients make requests ("what's the IP address for `www.chellis.net`?") and get back answers ("`209.155.222.222`"). If a particular server can't answer a query, it can forward it to another, presumably better informed, server.

To really understand how DNS works, it's important to learn about some fundamental parts of the system, which we'll do in the following sections.

Domain Naming

DNS is composed of a distributed database of names that establishes a logical tree structure called the *domain namespace*. Each node, or domain, in that space has a unique name. `chellis.com` and `chellis.net` are thus two different domains, and they can contain subdomains.

A domain name identifies the domain's position in the logical DNS hierarchy in relation to its parent domain by separating each branch of the tree with a period. Figure 4.1 shows a few of the top-level domains, where the Microsoft domain fits, and where a host called "Tigger" fits within the `microsoft.com` domain. If someone wanted to contact that host, they would use the fully qualified domain name (FQDN): `tigger.microsoft.com`.

Each node in the DNS database tree, along with all the nodes below it, is called a *domain*. Domains can contain both hosts (computers) and other domains (subdomains). For example, the Microsoft domain `microsoft.com` could contain computers, such as `betanews.microsoft.com`, and subdomains, such as `exchange.microsoft.com`. These subdomains can, and usually do, contain hosts; the host adds its name to its domain, as in `mail.exchange.microsoft.com`.

Each domain is associated with a DNS *name server*. In other words, for every domain registered in the DNS, there is another server that can give authoritative answers to queries about that domain. For example, the `chellis.net` domain is handled by a name server at an Internet provider. This means that any resolver or name server can go straight to the source if it can't resolve a query by looking in its own cache.

FIGURE 4.1 The DNS hierarchy

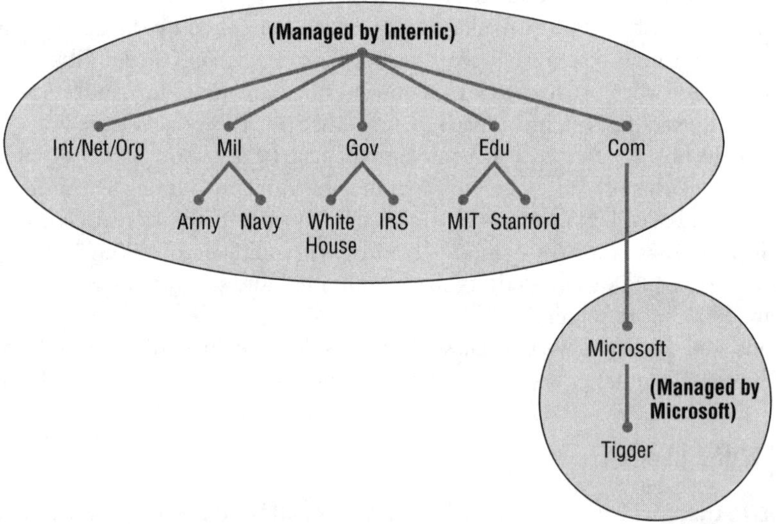

Domain names and host names must contain only the characters *a* to *z*, *A* to *Z*, 0 to 9, and the hyphen (-). Other common and useful characters, such as the ampersand (&), slash (/), period (.), and the underscore (_), are forbidden. This is in conflict with NetBIOS's naming restrictions; however, you will find that Windows Server 2003 Server is smart enough to take a NetBIOS name like Server_1 and turn it into a legal DNS name.

DNS and the Internet

You're undoubtedly familiar with how DNS works on the Internet. If you have ever sent or received Internet e-mail or browsed Web pages on the Net, you have firsthand experience using DNS. Internet DNS depends on a set of top-level domains that serve as the root of the DNS hierarchy. These *top-level domains* and their authoritative name servers are managed by the Internet Network Information Center (`www.internic.com`). The top-level domains are organized in two ways: by organization and by country. Table 4.1 shows some of the most common top-level domains.

TABLE 4.1 Common Top-Level Internet Domains

Top-Level Domain Name	Examples	Type of Organization
com	`globalitcertification.com` `microsoft.com`	Commercial organizations, such as `globalitcertification.com` for the Global IT Certification Network and Microsoft
net	`sonic.net`	Networking organizations, such as Internet Service Providers (ISPs) This domain is also used by a growing number of commercial organizations

TABLE 4.1 Common Top-Level Internet Domains *(continued)*

Top-Level Domain Name	Examples	Type of Organization
org	`ICANN.org`	Nonprofits and other noncommercial organizations, such as ICANN
edu	`harvard.edu`	Educational organizations, such as Harvard University
gov	`whitehouse.gov`	U.S. government organizations, such as the White House
mil	`af.mil`	U.S. military organizations, such as the U.S. Air Force
int	`nato.int`	International organizations, such as NATO
uk		UK companies and Web sites
au		Australian companies and Web sites
ca		Canadian companies and Web sites
us		U.S. companies and Web sites
jp		Japanese companies and Web sites

This is not an exhaustive list. You can find a complete listing of top-level domains at `http://www.icann.org` under Top-Level Domains (TLDs).

Each top-level domain can have additional subdomains beneath it. For example, commercial organizations in Japan will have `.co.jp` on the end of their domain names. The police department in Athens, Alabama has a server in the `ci.athens.al.us` domain: "ci" for city, "Athens" because the city's name is Athens, "al" for Alabama, and the top-level "us" domain.

DNS and Windows Server 2003

Windows Server 2003 Server relies on TCP/IP, and Active Directory requires DNS—even if you're not connected to the Internet. Naturally, Windows Server 2003 Server includes a DNS server, and it adds some features that are even interoperable with other DNS implementations. We will look at those features in the following sections.

Dynamic DNS

With previous versions of Windows—such as Windows NT 4—you use DHCP to assign IP addresses to clients. You have no way to keep the corresponding DNS records up-to-date. For example, a DNS entry for `minuteman.chellis.net` pointing to `192.168.0.202` will work great until minuteman's DHCP lease is released and it gets a new address. At that point, you'll get to choose between either fixing the DNS record by hand or relying on NetBIOS and WINS for name resolution. You may have a similar problem if you use a dial-up ISP—every time you dial up, you'll get a different IP address.

The *Dynamic DNS (DDNS) standard*, described in RFC 2136, was designed to solve this very problem. DDNS allows DNS clients to update information in the DNS database files. For example, a Windows 2000 Server or a Windows Server 2003 DHCP server can automatically tell a DDNS server which IP addresses it has assigned, and to what machines. Windows 2000 and XP Professional DHCP clients can do this, too, but for security reasons it's better to let the DHCP server do it. The result: IP addresses and DNS records stay in synch so that you can use DNS and DHCP together seamlessly.

Because DDNS is an Internet standard, you can even use Windows Server 2003 Server's DDNS-aware components with Unix-based DNS servers.

DNS and Active Directory

You can store DNS data in Active Directory instead of in regular disk files. Although it might seem odd to use AD to store information that AD will have to run, it makes sense. Consider a typical DNS zone data file on disk—it's plain text and easily editable. It's not replicated, it's probably not secured, and there's no way to delegate control over it. All of these limitations go away when you build what Microsoft calls an Active Directory–Integrated *(ADI) zone*. In an ADI zone, Active Directory stores all of the DNS zone data in AD, so it gains all of the benefits of AD—especially improved security and seamless replication.

To learn how to install and configure DNS in Windows Server 2003, refer to *MCSA/MCSE: Windows Server 2003 Network Infrastructure Implementation, Management, and Maintenance Study Guide* by Michael Chacon, James Chellis, and Matt Sheltz.

DNS Terminology

Before you manage a DNS server, you'll need to know a few important terms and concepts. Understanding these terms will make it easier to understand how the Windows Server 2003 DNS server works:

DNS Servers Any computer that provides Domain Name System is a *DNS server*. That being said, not all DNS servers are alike. Earlier implementations of DNS (for example, early versions of the popular Berkeley Internet Name Domain, or BIND) were originally developed for Unix, and they handled a fairly small and simple set of RFC requirements.

You must also consider the concept of primary and secondary DNS servers. A *primary DNS server* is the "owner" of the zones (which store the actual *domain name records*) defined in its database. The primary DNS server has the authority to make changes to the zones it owns. Secondary DNS servers receive a read-only copy of zones through *zone transfers*. The *secondary DNS server* can resolve queries from this read-only copy, but it cannot make changes or updates to zone records. A single DNS server may contain multiple primary and secondary zones.

Any DNS server implementation supporting Service Location Resource Records (SRV RRs, as described in an Internet Draft: "A DNS RR for specifying the location of services [DNS SRV]") and Dynamic Updates (RFC 2136) is sufficient to provide the name service for Windows 2000 and newer computers. However, because Windows Server 2003 DNS is designed to take full advantage of the Windows Active Directory service, it is the recommended DNS server for any networked organization with a significant investment in Windows or extranet partners with Windows-based systems.

DNS Clients A *DNS client* is any machine issuing queries to a DNS server. The client host name may or may not be registered in a name server (DNS) database. Clients issue DNS requests through processes called *resolvers*.

Resolvers *Resolvers* handle the process of mapping a symbolic name to an actual network address. The resolver (which may reside on another machine) issues queries to name servers. When a resolver receives information from name servers, it caches that information locally in case the same information is requested again.

When a name server is unable to resolve a request, it may reply to the resolver with the name of another name server. The resolver must then address a message to this new name server in the hope that the symbolic name will be resolved.

Queries Two types of *queries* can be made to a DNS server: recursive and iterative (we'll discuss the difference shortly).

Root Servers When a DNS server processes an *iterative query* and that query cannot be resolved from local zone files, the query must be escalated to a root DNS server. The process of escalating a query to another DNS server is called a *recursive query* (simply, DNS server to DNS server). The *root server* is responsible for returning an authoritative answer for a particular domain or a referral to a server that can provide an authoritative answer. Because each DNS server is supposed to have a full set of root hints (which point to the root servers), your DNS server can refer queries recursively to other servers with the assistance of the root servers. You can also configure a DNS server to contain its own root zone; you might want to do so if you don't want your servers to be able to answer queries for names outside of your network.

How DNS Works

Knowing how servers and resolvers communicate with each other, and what kind of queries are passed around, is critical to properly configuring your network. That knowledge begins with understanding what's actually in the DNS database itself.

In the following sections, you'll learn about the resource records stored in the DNS database, the zone database files, the process of name resolution through DNS, zone transfers, and database migrations.

What's In the DNS Database?

A *DNS zone* stores name information about one or more DNS domains. No matter where your information is stored, a DNS zone contains a variety of DNS information. Although the DNS snap-in makes it unlikely that you will ever need to edit these files by hand, knowing exactly what data are contained in there is a good idea.

The first thing to understand is the fact that each zone file consists of a number of *resource records (RR)*. Each resource record contains information about some resource on the network, such as its IP address. To effectively manage your DNS servers, you need to know about several types of resource records. We'll look at these in the following sections.

Start of Authority (SOA) Records

The first record in any database file is the *start of authority (SOA) record*, which looks like this:

```
@ IN SOA source host contact e-mail serial number refresh time retry time
   expiration time TTL
```

The SOA defines the general parameters for the DNS zone, including who the authoritative (or primary) server is for the zone. Each zone contains exactly one SOA record, which is created automatically when you create a new zone. Table 4.2 lists the attributes stored in the SOA record.

TABLE 4.2 The SOA Record Structure

Field	Meaning
source host	The host on which this file is maintained.
contact e-mail	The Internet e-mail address for the person responsible for this domain's database file.
serial number	The "version number" of this database file that will increase each time the database file is changed.
refresh time	The elapsed time (in seconds) that a secondary server will wait between checks to its primary server to see if the database file has changed and a zone transfer should be requested.
retry time	The elapsed time (in seconds) that a secondary server will wait before retrying a failed zone transfer.
expiration time	The elapsed time (in seconds) that a secondary server will keep trying to download a zone. After this time limit expires, the old zone information will be discarded.
TTL (time to live)	The elapsed time (in seconds) that a DNS server is allowed to cache any resource records from this database file. This is the value that is sent out with all query responses from this zone file when the individual resource record doesn't contain an overriding value.

Here's an example of a server-generated default SOA record (the parentheses are used to wrap multiple lines):

```
@    IN  SOA     nameserver.place.dom.  postmaster.place.dom. (
                                 1            ; serial number
                                 3600         ; refresh   [1h]
                                 600          ; retry     [10m]
                                 86400        ; expire    [1d]
                                 3600 )       ; min TTL   [1h]
```

Name Server (NS) Records

Name server (NS) records list the name servers (both primary and secondaries) for a domain; this allows other name servers to look up names in your domain. A zone file may contain more than one name server record. The format of these records is simple:

`[domain | @] IN NS nameserver host`

Domain is the name of your domain, and *nameserver host* is the FQDN of a name server in that domain. Here are a couple of interesting shortcuts that can be used in DNS records:

- In a zone file, the `@` symbol represents the root domain of the zone. `IN` stands for Internet.
- Any domain name in the database file that is not terminated with a period will have the root domain appended to the end. For example, an entry that just has the name `sales` will be expanded by adding the root domain to the end. The entry `sales.chellis.net.` won't be expanded.

Here are three examples of NS records:

```
@ IN NS ns1.chellis.net.
@ IN NS ns2.chellis.net.
example.chellis.net.    IN NS  ns1.example.chellis.net
```

NS records play a key role in the referral process that you will learn about later in the chapter.

The A Record

An *A record* (also called a *host record* or an *address record*) is used to statically associate a host's name to its IP addresses. The format is pretty simple:

`hostname IN A IP_address`

Here are three examples of A records:

```
minuteman  IN  A  192.168.0.204
titan      IN  A  192.168.3.144
aphrodite.chellis.net   IN  A  206.27.54.12
```

The A record ties a host name (which is part of a FQDN) to a specific IP address. This makes them suitable for use when you have devices with statically assigned IP addresses; in that case, you'd create these records manually using the DNS snap-in. As it turns out, if you enable DDNS, your DHCP server can create these for you; that automatic creation is what DDNS is all about.

The Pointer (PTR) Record

Host records are probably the most visible component of the DNS database, because Internet users depend on them to turn FQDNs such as `www.microsoft.com` and `www.delta-air.com` into IP addresses so that browsers and other components can find them. However, the host record has a lesser-known but still important twin: the *pointer (PTR) record*. Here's the format:

```
reverse_IP_address.in-addr.arpa.  PTR FQDN
```

The host record maps a host name to an IP address, and the PTR record does just the opposite. Having both types of records makes it possible to perform *reverse lookups*, where a resolver asks a DNS server to cough up the FQDN associated with a particular IP address. This is a useful function for, among other things, preventing people with made-up or illegal domain names from using services like e-mail or FTP servers.

Here's an example:

```
12.0.0.10.in-addr.arpa.    PTR  host.example.microsoft.com.
```

The Alias (CNAME) Record

Almost every company on the Web has a URL that uses the `www.companyname.com` construct. This is standard, but did you ever stop to consider whether all of those domains actually have machines named `www`? In fact, many (if not most) of them don't. They use DNS *alias records* (also known as *canonical name*, or CNAME, entries) that allow them to use more than one name to point to a single host. Here's the format:

```
aliasname   CNAME   truename.example.microsoft.com.
```

For example, take a URL `broadway.com` whose "real" host record name is `42ndstreet.broadway.com`. The same machine could have *CNAME records* that pointed the names `mail.broadway.com` and `ftp.broadway.com` to the same machine. A resolver that queried `broadway.com`'s DNS server for either `mail` or `ftp` would actually get the host record for 42ndstreet. Here's how it's done:

```
mail        CNAME  42ndstreet
ftp         CNAME  42ndstreet
42ndstreet  IN  A      172.30.1.14
```

Two CNAME records specify that `mail` and `ftp` both point to `42ndstreet`, and an A record resolves `42ndstreet` to its IP address.

The Mail Exchange (MX) Record

The *mail exchange (MX) record* tells you which servers can accept e-mail bound for this domain. Each MX record contains two parameters—a preference and a mailserver—as shown in the following example:

```
domain IN MX preference mailserver host
```

As an example, consider the `chellis.net` domain. Users in this organization have addresses of `someuser@chellis.net`. To make sure that mail is delivered where you want it to go—your Exchange server in this case—you have two MX records: One points to `mail.chellis.net`, and one points to your ISP's mail server. When someone on the Internet tries to send SMTP mail to any user whose address ends in `chellis.net`, their mail server will look to see if that domain contains an MX record. If it does, the sending server will use the host specified in the MX record to deliver the mail.

You will notice that we said the domain has two MX records. That's because MX records have preferences attached to them. If multiple MX records exist for a domain, the DNS server uses the mail server with the lowest preference, and then it tries the other mail servers when the most preferred host can't be contacted. For instance, suppose the two records we used above look like this:

```
chellis.net. IN MX 100 mail.isp.com.
chellis.net. IN MX 10 mail.chellis.net.
```

In this case, DNS will first attempt to use the `mail.chellis.net` mail server.

Service (SRV) Records

Windows Server 2003 Server depends on some (relatively) new services, like LDAP and Kerberos. These protocols postdate the DNS system by quite a while. Normally, clients use DNS to find the IP address of a machine whose name they already know. Microsoft wanted to extend this system by devising a way for a client to locate a particular *service* by making a DNS query.

For example, a Windows 2000 or XP Professional client can query DNS servers for the location of a domain controller; this makes it much easier (for both the client and the administrator) to manage and distribute logon traffic in large-scale networks. For this approach to work, Microsoft had to have some way to register the presence of a service (or, really, a TCP/IP protocol) in DNS, but none of the RR types you have read about so far offer any way to do so.

Service (SRV) records tie together the location of a service (such as a domain controller) with information about how to contact the service. Think of a host record: It ties a name to an IP address. The MX record extends the concept by adding another parameter, the preference. SRV records take it even further by providing seven items of information. Here's the format:

```
service.protocol.name  ttl  class  SRV  preference  weight  port  target
```

Let's look at an example to help clarify this powerful concept:

```
ldap.tcp.chellis.net  SRV  10  100  389  hsv.chellis.net
ldap.tcp.chellis.net  SRV  20  100  389  msy.chellis.net
```

The first field, `ldap.tcp.chellis.net`, contains a service name (`ldap` for LDAP or `kerberos` for Kerberos), a transport protocol (`TCP` or `UDP`), and the domain name for which the service is offered (in this case, `chellis.net`). Therefore, `ldap.tcp.chellis.net` indicates that this SRV record is advertising an LDAP server for the `chellis.net` domain. The next field is just the record type—SRV in this case.

The two numbers following are the priority and the weight. The priority field specifies a preference, just like the preference field in an MX record. The SRV record with the lowest priority will be used first. The weight is a little different: Service records with equal priority will be chosen according to their weight. Consider the case of three SRV records of priority 0 and weight 100. That tells the DNS server to answer queries by picking one of the three at random because they have equal weight. If one record had a weight of 50 (instead of 100), one of the other two records would be chosen at random. In other words, if the priority is equal, then the higher weight is used.

The next field is the port number on which the service is offered: `389` for LDAP or `88` for Kerberos.

The final entry in the record defines the DNS name of the server that offers the service (in this case, `hsv.chellis.net` and `msy.chellis.net`). You will read later how these service records are actually used in DNS queries; for now it's enough to understand that they exist.

You can define other types of service records. If your applications support them, they can query DNS to find the services they need.

Where the Zone Databases Are Located

Let's assume for a minute that you're not using an ADI zone to illustrate where the zone database files reside on a non-ADI server, as well as to describe what's in them. As it turns out, you can specify names for some, but not all, of these files when you install DNS on your Windows Server 2003 Server. We'll explore these files next.

The Domain Name File

Each domain that has a forward lookup zone on your server will have its own database file—the *domain name file*. For example, when you create a new zone named `chellis.net` on a Windows Server 2003 DNS server, you will end up with a new file named `chellis.net.dns` in the system's DNS directory (`systemroot\system32\DNS`). The file is pretty much empty when you create the zone. It contains only an SOA record for the domain and one NS record listing the name of the server you just created. As you add new host records to the domain, they're stored in this file.

The Reverse Lookup File

The *reverse lookup file* holds information on a single reverse lookup zone. These zones are usually named after the IP address range they cover. For example, a reverse lookup zone that can handle queries for the `172.30.1.*` block will be named `1.30.172.in-addr.arpa`. Notice that the network address is reversed; you will see why in a minute.

The reverse lookup file allows a resolver to provide an IP address and request a matching host name. It looks like the domain database file (e.g., it has SOA and NS records), but instead of host records, it has one PTR record for each host designated in the reverse lookup zone.

DNS reverse lookup is frequently used as a sort of backdoor authentication method. For example, most modern mail servers can be configured to refuse incoming mail from servers whose IP address can't be resolved with a reverse lookup. This prevents people with real IP addresses but fake DNS names (for example, spammers) from using those mail servers. Reverse lookups are also valuable for troubleshooting name resolution problems, because you can always find the IP address of a machine—even if you're not sure what its domain name is supposed to be.

The Cache File

The *cache file* (`cache.dns`) contains host information needed to resolve names outside of your authoritative domains. In short, it holds a list of the names and addresses of root name servers.

If your DNS server will be able to connect to the Internet, you can leave this file alone. If not, you can edit it so that it lists the authoritative roots for your private network.

The Boot File

Sometimes a de facto standard is a powerful thing. In the Unix world, the *Berkeley Internet Name Daemon (BIND)* is the de facto standard DNS server. The *boot file* is included in Windows Server 2003 DNS for compatibility with BIND-based DNS. Boot files are not used by default in Microsoft DNS implementations. You can port an existing BIND boot file to a Windows Server 2003 DNS server.

To understand the purpose of this file, consider what a primary DNS server must do when it boots. Somehow, it has to figure out what zones it's supposed to be serving, decide whether it's authoritative for any of them, and link up with other servers in the zone, if any. You can choose the method by which Windows Server 2003 DNS servers get this information: from AD, from the Registry, or from a BIND-style boot file. The boot file, which must be named `systemroot\system32\DNS\boot`, controls the DNS server's startup behavior. Boot files support only four commands:

Directory The `directory` command specifies where the other files named in the boot file can be found. This is almost always the `systemroot\system32\DNS` directory. You use the command along with a directory path, like this:

```
directory f:\winnt\system32\dns
```

Cache The `cache` command specifies the file of root hints used to help your DNS service contact name servers for the root domain. This command, and the file it refers to, must be present. For example, `cache cache.dns` points the DNS server at the default `cache.dns` file shipped with Windows Server 2003.

Primary The `primary` command specifies a domain for which this name server is authoritative, as well as a database file that contains the resource records for that domain. You can use multiple `primary` commands in a single boot file. For example:

```
primary chellis.net       chellis.net.dns
primary hsv.chellis.net   hsv.chellis.dns
```

Secondary The `secondary` command designates a domain as being one that your server handles as a secondary. That means your server is authoritative, but it pulls DNS information from one (or more) of the specified master servers. The command also defines the name of the local file for caching this zone. Multiple `secondary` command records may exist in the boot file. The `secondary` command looks like this:

```
secondary wuolukka.com    ns.pair.com    wuolukka.dns
secondary chellis.com    ns2.pair.com     chellis.dns
```

DNS Name Resolution

A client can make three types of queries to a DNS server: recursive, iterative, and inverse. Remember that the client of a DNS server can be a resolver (what you'd normally call a client) or another DNS server.

Iterative queries are the easiest to understand: A client asks the DNS server for an answer, and the server returns the best answer it has. This type of query is typically sent by one DNS server to another, after the original server has received a recursive query from a resolver. The answer may be "I don't know; go ask the server at `x.y.z.1`," or it may be an actual RR.

Most resolvers, however, use recursive queries, which are different from iterative queries. In a recursive query, the client sends a query to one name server, asking it to respond either with the requested answer or with an error. The error states one of two things: that the server can't come up with the right answer, or that the domain name doesn't exist. The name server isn't allowed to just refer the querier to some other name server. In addition, if your DNS server uses a forwarder, the requests sent by your server to the forwarder will be recursive queries.

Figure 4.2 shows an example of both recursive and iterative queries. In this example, a client within the Microsoft Corporation is querying its DNS server for the IP address for `www.whitehouse.gov`. Here's what happens to resolve the request:

1. The resolver sends a recursive DNS query to its local DNS server asking for the IP address of `www.whitehouse.gov`. The local name server is responsible for resolving the name and cannot refer the resolver to another name server.
2. The local name server checks its zones and finds no zones corresponding to the requested domain name.
3. The root name server has authority for the root domain and will reply with the IP address of a name server for the GOV top-level domain.
4. The local name server sends an iterative query for `www.whitehouse.gov` to the GOV name server.

FIGURE 4.2 A sample DNS query

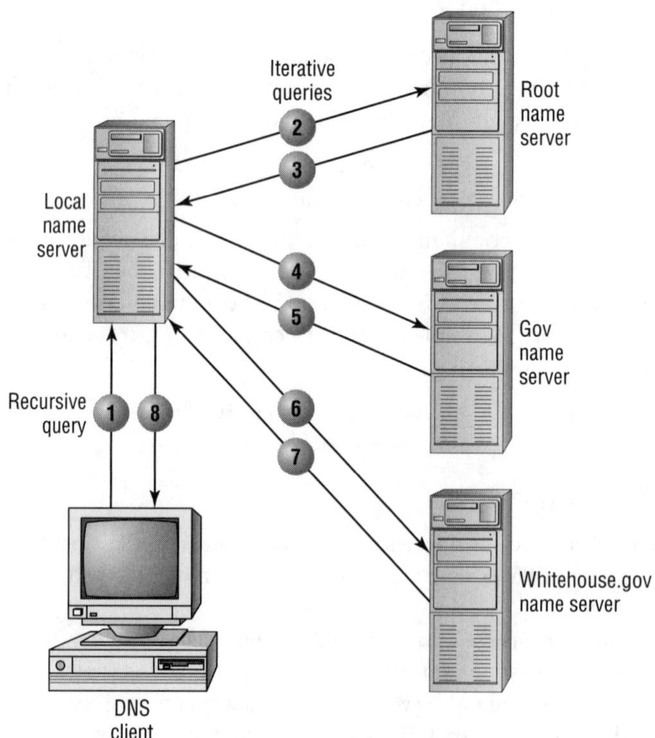

5. The GOV name server replies with the IP address of the name server servicing the `whitehouse.gov` domain.
6. The local name server sends an iterative query for `www.whitehouse.gov` to the `whitehouse.gov` name server.
7. The `whitehouse.gov` name server replies with the IP address corresponding to `www.whitehouse.gov`.
8. The local name server sends the IP address of `www.whitehouse.gov` back to the original resolver.

Inverse queries use PTR records. Instead of supplying a name and then asking for an IP address, the client first provides the IP address and then asks for the name. Because there's no direct correlation in the DNS namespace between a domain name and its associated IP address, this search would be fruitless without using the `in-addr.arpa` domain.

Nodes in the `in-addr.arpa` domain are named after the numbers in the dotted-octet representation of IP addresses. But because IP addresses get more specific from left to right and domain names get less specific from left to right, the order of IP address octets must be reversed when building the `in-addr.arpa` tree. With this arrangement, administration of the lower limbs of the DNS `in-addr.arpa` tree can be given to companies as they are assigned their Class A, B, or C subnet addresses.

Once the domain tree is built into the DNS database, a special PTR record is added to associate the IP addresses to the corresponding host names. In other words, to find a host name for the IP address `206.131.234.1`, the resolver queries the DNS server for a pointer record for `1.234.131.206.in-addr.arpa`. If this IP address is outside the local domain, the DNS server starts at the root and sequentially resolves the domain nodes until arriving at `234.131.206.in-addr.arpa`, which contains the PTR record for the desired host.

The following sections will cover more advanced considerations for resolving DNS names, including caching and TTL, load balancing with round robin and netmask ordering, BIND options, and queries for services.

Caching and Time to Live

When a name server is processing a recursive query, it may be required to send out several queries to find the definitive answer. Name servers are allowed to cache all the received information during this process; each record contains something called a *time to live (TTL)*.

The name server owner sets the TTL for each RR on their server. If your data changes a lot, you can use smaller TTL values to help ensure that data about your domain is more consistent across that network. However, if you make the TTL too small, the load on your name server will go up. That's because once data is cached by a DNS server, the server begins decreasing the TTL from its original value; when it hits zero, the server "flushes" the RR from its cache. If a query that can be satisfied by this cached data is received, the TTL that's returned with it equals the current amount of time left before flush time. Client resolvers also have data caches and honor the TTL value, so that they, too, know when to flush.

Load Balancing with Round Robin and Netmask Ordering

The Windows Server 2003 Server implementation of DNS supports load balancing through the use of round robin and netmask ordering. Load balancing distributes the network load between multiple network cards if they are available. You can create multiple resource records with the same host name but different IP addresses for multihomed computers. Depending on the options that you select, the DNS server will respond with one of the multihomed computer's addresses.

If round robin is enabled, the first address that was entered in the database is returned to the resolver and then sent to the end of the list. The next time a client attempts to resolve the name, the DNS server will return the second name in the database (which is now the first name) and then send it to the end of the list, and so on.

If netmask ordering is enabled, the DNS server will use the first IP address in the database that matches the subnet of the resolver. If none of the IP addresses match the subnet of the resolver, then the DNS server reverts to round robin. If round robin is disabled, the DNS server simply returns the first IP address in the database.

If neither round robin nor netmask ordering are enabled, then the DNS server always returns the first IP address in the database. This usually isn't very helpful, so fortunately round robin and netmask ordering are both enabled by default. You will see how to enable and disable round robin and netmask ordering in the following section.

BIND Options

Earlier we briefly hinted that BIND is a simple DNS implementation primarily used by UNIX servers. This is true to an extent, but BIND is really just a set of RFCs that standardize the way DNS operates. Windows Server 2003 Server is actually compliant with several versions of BIND (specifically, BIND 4.9.7, 8.1.2, 8.2, and 9.1.0), which makes the Windows Server 2003 DNS implementation interoperable with other DNS servers. Windows Server 2003 DNS can also be used on the Internet; BIND is the standard for DNS on almost every computer on the planet.

We don't need to get into the specifics of the different versions of BIND, but you should understand two key points about how BIND can affect your Windows Server 2003 environment:

- When Windows Server 2003 Server sends a zone transfer to a secondary DNS server, it sends several compressed resource records simultaneously. Unfortunately, BIND versions prior to 4.9.4 don't support compression, and they can receive only one RR at a time. If your secondary servers are running older versions of BIND, then you will need to disable these features, as you will see in the next section.
- Active Directory requires a SRV-based DNS server or a BIND server version 8.1.2 or higher. Usually you would use Windows Server 2003 DNS servers with Active Directory–Integrated zones, but some companies have long-established UNIX-based DNS servers that they need to continue to use. You may need to upgrade these servers if they don't meet the minimum BIND requirement and you want to use Active Directory.

Queries for Services

Windows Server 2003 uses some special domains (not unlike the `in-addr.arpa` domain you read about earlier) to make it possible for domain clients to look up services they need. RFC 2052 ("A DNS RR for specifying the location of services (DNS SRV)") specifies how this mechanism should work. However, the underscore (_) character isn't legal in domain names, so Microsoft uses it to mark its special domains and to keep them from colliding with RFC 2052-compliant domains. There are a total of four of these Windows Server 2003 domains, as listed here:

`_msdcs` This domain contains a list of all the Windows Server 2003 domain controllers in a domain. Each domain controller, global catalog, and PDC emulator is listed here. In Windows Server 2003 DNS this is actually a pointer to _msdcs.domain_name.

`_sites` Each site has its own subdomain within the `_sites` domain. In Active Directory parlance, a site is a group of connected network subnets that have high bandwidth between them.

`_tcp` This domain lists service records for services that run on TCP: LDAP, Kerberos, the `kpasswd` password changer, and the global catalogs.

`_udp` This domain lists services that run on UDP: Kerberos and the `kpasswd` service.

When any network client wants to find a service (for instance, a domain controller), it can query its DNS server for the appropriate SRV record. By making a recursive query, the client can force the local DNS server to poke around in the domain until it finds the desired information.

Zone Transfers

DNS is such an important part of the network that you simply cannot use a single DNS server. If that server fails, the network fails. Adding a secondary server provides DNS redundancy and helps to reduce the load on the primary server, because resolvers can distribute their queries across multiple DNS servers.

Secondary DNS servers receive their zone databases through zone transfers. When you configure a secondary server for the first time, you must specify the primary server (master) that is authoritative for the zone and will send the zone transfer. The primary server must also permit the secondary server to request the zone transfer. Zone transfers occur on TCP port 53.

Zone transfers occur in one of two ways: full zone transfers (AXFR) and incremental zone transfers (IXFR).

When a new secondary server is configured for the first time, it receives a full zone transfer from the primary DNS server. The full zone transfer contains all of the information in the DNS database. Some DNS implementations always receive full zone transfers.

After the secondary server receives its first full zone transfer, subsequent zone transfers are incremental. The primary name server compares its zone version number with that on the secondary server and only sends the changes that have been made in the interim. This significantly reduces network traffic generated by zone transfers.

Windows NT4 does not support incremental zone transfers.

Zone transfers are typically initiated by the secondary server when the refresh interval time for the zone expires or when the secondary server boots. Alternatively, you can configure notify lists on the primary server that notify the secondary servers whenever any changes to the zone database occur.

When you consider your DNS strategy, you must carefully consider the layout of your network. If you have a single domain with offices in separate cities, you want to reduce the number of zone transfers across the potentially slow or expensive WAN links, although this is becoming less of a concern as bandwidth seems to multiply daily.

Migrating the DNS Database Files

You can migrate the DNS database files from your older systems to Windows Server 2003 in one of three ways:

Upgrade Windows NT 4 or 2000 to Windows Server 2003 When you upgrade to Windows Server 2003 from NT 4 or 2000, all of your zone files remain intact and are stored in the same folder locations.

Manually Move the BIND Files Because the Windows Server 2003 DNS service is based on BIND, and BIND is based on standardized RFCs, you can literally copy and paste BIND files into the DNS directory on the DNS server. Be aware that Windows Server 2003 won't recognize some features of UNIX BIND files, but that's okay because you would not have been able to implement those features anyway. Be aware that the BIND files you receive from your UNIX brethren use a different naming convention, as shown in Table 4.3.

TABLE 4.3 BIND Files in Windows and UNIX

Windows	Unix
`Boot`	`Named.boot`
Domain_name`.dns`	`Db.`*domain_name*
IP_network_reverse_notation`.dns`	`Db.`*IP_network_forward_notation*

Migrate Using Zone Transfers You can set up your Windows Server 2003 DNS server with secondary zones for each of your primary zones. Then set up your current primary servers to allow the Windows Server 2003 server to receive zone transfers and immediately perform a full zone transfer. At this point, the Windows Server 2003 DNS server has everything it needs to be the primary server for the domain. All you need to do is convert the zones on the Windows Server 2003 server to primary zones. If you want your new primary DNS server to perform zone transfers, you will also need to configure the secondary servers in your network to point to the new server and specify that the secondary servers are valid in the primary server's properties.

Planning a DNS Namespace

The importance of planning a *DNS namespace* for an organization is analogous to the importance of laying a solid foundation for a building. The building could be a factory, or it could be a retail store where customers should be able to locate it. The building could be as simple as a five-room office or as large as a skyscraper—and these different buildings have different needs.

In a similar fashion, planning your DNS namespace is a task that should be customized to the needs of your business.

Planning a DNS namespace involves examining your existing network environment to see if there are any factors that could affect the DNS design or performance. You must also consider the need for Internet access as well as multiple namespace considerations. Then you can design a namespace that fits your needs.

DNS name resolution is a vital component in the Windows Server 2003 network infrastructure. Without proper name resolution, users cannot find the network resources they need without proper name resolution services. The tasks involved include identifying the DNS namespace to be registered for use on the Internet. If you don't register the name on the Internet, you should still choose a unique name. Then you create the DNS namespace with Active Directory in mind, and make sure that the namespace that resides on the Internet does not conflict with the internal namespace.

Use different internal and external namespaces. For instance, you could use a namespace such as `microsoft.com` as the name by which people outside of the network reach the company. For internal use, you could use a unique namespace such as `microsoft.net` or a subdomain of the external name such as `corp.microsoft.com`. If you already have an existing DNS namespace, using a subdomain to distinguish internal network resources is easy. You can assign different departments, sites, or organizations to different subdomains such as `marketing.microsoft.com` and `engineering.microsoft.com`.

Make sure that internal servers contain name (NS) records for only those resources that are meant for internal use, and vice versa. You should not overlap internal and external namespaces, because the usual result is that computers receive incorrect IP addresses from DNS and can't find the resources they need.

In the following sections, you will learn about domain names and options for planning a DNS namespace.

Understanding Domain Names

Domain names are simple to understand. The FQDN describes the exact path to a node and exists in a format such as `www.microsoft.com` or `mail.marketing.southwest.microsoft.com`. You will notice that the actual computer node, `www` or `mail` in these examples, is listed first. In the first example, the `microsoft` domain follows `www`, then the top-level domain. In the second example, two subdomains are in the hierarchy: `marketing` and `southwest`.

The highest domain name is the root, represented by a period (.) and followed by the top-level domain, which can be a designation such as `com`, `net`, `org` and others listed earlier in the chapter in Table 4.1.

The Internet cannot function with duplicate information, so a central authority for managing domain names is needed. The Internet Corporation for Assigned Names and Numbers (ICANN) maintains authority for the root and top-level domain names of the Internet DNS namespace. ICANN assigns globally unique identifiers, which include Internet domain names, Internet Protocol (IP) address numbers, and protocol parameter and port numbers, to organizations.

Visit ICANN's Web site at `http://www.icann.org` for more information about ICANN.

To obtain a top-level domain name, you simply request it from ICANN or another Internet naming authority. Once you are granted your domain name, you can connect to the Internet and use DNS servers to resolve the names of host devices contained within their portion of the namespace.

You can name the computers and network devices within the assigned domain and its subdivisions, or delegate subdomains of your domain to other users or customers, which you would do if you were an Internet Service Provider (ISP).

For domains and Internet-visible computers, only use characters that are part of the Internet standard character set permitted for use in DNS host names. The allowed characters are defined in RFC 1123 as: *A* to *Z*, *a* to *z*, 0 to 9, and the hyphen (-) character.

You can make sure the name is unique by using the Registry Whois tool at `http://www.internic.net` to see if a particular domain name has been registered.

The Web site `http://www.domainsurfer.com` is an invaluable aid in planning your namespace, because it lets you view a list of all registered domain names that contain the specific text you want to use in your domain name.

Your namespace needs will vary depending on how you plan to actually use DNS. For instance:

- Will the namespace only be for internal use? If so, you can implement your own DNS root, use any domain name you want, and even use illegal characters in the domain name.
- Will the namespace be used on the Internet? If this is the case now, or if there is any possibility that this will be the case in the future, then you should register a unique domain name of your own by using the Internet root servers. This means that you must ensure that the name uses only legal characters.
- Are you using or do you plan to use Active Directory? This will affect the storage of zone data, replication, security, and the types of servers you will configure.

DNS Namespace Options

When selecting a DNS namespace, you can use an existing namespace, a delegated namespace such as a subdomain, or a new, unique namespace (such as `microsoft.net` instead of `microsoft.com`).

Be forewarned that configuring hosts in separate DNS namespaces so that they can locate each other is a complicated task that requires separate devices such as proxy servers.

You can choose one of the following options when you plan your internal namespace:

- Use the existing external namespace as the internal namespace (for example, `acme.com` for both external and internal use).
- Use a unique internal namespace that is different from the existing external DNS namespace (for example, `acme.com` for external use and `acme.net` for internal use).

- Use a delegated domain of the existing external namespace as the internal namespace (for example, `acme.com` for external use and `corp.acme.com` for internal use).
- Use a DNS child domain to represent the organization for the root of Active Directory instead of using the registered DNS domain name. This method enables you to isolate all Active Directory data in its domain or domain tree.

The option you choose will depend on your business requirements and the existing DNS environment.

Using a single DNS domain name for both the external and the internal namespace makes it necessary to ensure that the internal namespace is not accessible from the Internet.

If you use an existing namespace, users can access a single domain name when they access resources both internally and externally. Additional administration is required to ensure that appropriate records are stored on internal and external DNS servers.

Using separate public and private namespaces has the following benefits:

- Resources are easy to manage and secure.
- Existing DNS zones and DNS topology can remain unchanged.
- Existing DNS server content does not need to be replicated to the DNS servers for the internal namespace.
- Internal resources are not accessible from the Internet, because the internal namespace is not exposed.

Using a *delegated namespace* resembles creating separate public and private namespaces. However, in this case you are creating a single subdomain within the namespace in which the DNS servers for the namespace will reside, rather than dividing the namespace into public and private portions. In this model, you would enable internal clients to resolve both internal and external DNS namespaces, but deny access to the internal namespace to external clients. A separate DNS server or servers is required for the delegated internal domain. This method has minimal impact on the existing namespace and requires minimal administrative effort.

Make sure that the name you use for your internal namespace is a name that you can and will register with a registrar. You also want to avoid a situation where two companies will merge and use the same name for their Active Directory namespace.

Real World Scenario

Planning a DNS Namespace for a Windows NT Server Migration

As the network administrator of Contoso, Ltd., an auto parts manufacturer, you are responsible for planning the DNS namespace. The company is planning a migration from NT Server to Windows Server 2003. The company uses WINS for name resolution and has no DNS servers at present. Contoso wants to host its Web site, `www.contoso.com`, internally after the migration. Active Directory will be implemented after the migration is completed. Clients need access to the Internet.

How will you plan the DNS namespace to meet current and future business needs?

In this scenario, you would retain the existing external namespace and host it on an externally accessible DNS server. A separate internal DNS server will service the internal namespace. The DNS servers communicate with each other to resolve external names for internal clients, but they do not resolve internal names for Internet clients. You would brainstorm on possible names for the internal namespace, such as `contosocorp.com` or `contoso.net`, that could be used for Active Directory. You would check the availability of these names, and then present the available namespace candidates to the Contoso decision makers and get buy off on the final name, which you will then register.

Planning DNS Zones

Your DNS strategy needs to include a plan for DNS zones and zone configurations. This involves determining zone requirements, identifying zone types and security requirements, and configuring zones and zone forwarding.

The zone type you choose will depend on whether or not you are running Active Directory and whether the zone will be integrated with Active Directory. If you are not running Active Directory, you will need to determine where the primary server and any secondary servers should be placed.

Determining zone security requirements involves choosing a method of secured dynamic updates: in Active Directory, dynamic updates from DNS, or dynamic updates from DNS clients.

Next, you will need to determine whether to store the zone data in an Active Directory–Integrated zone, in a traditional zone, or in a combination of the two.

Forwarding comes into play when a request needs to be resolved on behalf of a client, but the name server with the information resides in a different network.

In the following sections, you will learn how to plan for all of these requirements.

Selecting the Appropriate Zone Type

DNS offers different zone types that are suitable for different scenarios. Each zone type solves a specific requirement, so the DNS zone type you choose will influence where you locate DNS servers. Three zone types are used with the standard DNS zones that are stored on disk. These are primary, secondary, and stub zones. But before we discuss them, you should understand the standard zone file.

Standard zone files, also called *traditional DNS zone files*, are stored as text files on the server's hard drive. To use standard zone files, you create a zone on a DNS server that then becomes the primary zone server where all updates occur. These updates may include things like resource record additions or deletions. You can use secondary zone servers to provide load balancing and a certain degree of fault tolerance by pointing them to the primary zone server to get a copy of the zone file.

With *primary zones*, the default for a newly created zone, the server has a read/write copy of the zone information and acts as the point of update for the zone. The server periodically replicates its zone file to the secondary zone server to ensure that the secondary zone server's copy of the file is current. At first the server transfers a complete copy of the zone file. Later transfers consist of changes only. The primary zone server can administer zone information separately.

Secondary zones have a complete, local, read-only copy of the zone information. They are used to improve availability and performance at local and remote locations. The secondary zone can be placed in screened subnets to be accessed by Internet users. Secondary zone servers continue to respond to DNS queries, so they provide only limited fault tolerance. Furthermore, they cannot perform updates because they have only a read-only copy of the zone file. Windows Server 2003 DNS supports incremental zone transfers (IXFR), which means that the primary zone server sends only changes since the last replication.

A *stub zone* functions like dynamic delegation. The stub zone server will periodically query the target name servers for updates. This is used to keep the DNS server that hosts the parent zone aware of its child zone for more efficient name resolution. The DNS server that hosts both the parent zone and the stub zone maintains a current list of authoritative DNS servers for the child zone by regularly updating a stub zone for its child zone. Stub zones keep delegated zone information current as well as simplify DNS administration.

How Stub Zones Work

Stub zones are used to enable a DNS server to perform recursion by using a list of target name servers, instead of querying a root server for the DNS namespace. By using stub zones you can distribute a list of the authoritative DNS servers for a zone instead of using secondary zones. Stub zones and secondary zones serve different purposes, as stub zones do not provide redundancy and load sharing. Also, a DNS server configured with a stub zone is not authoritative for that zone. The stub zone only identifies the DNS servers that are authoritative for the zone.

Selecting the Zone Data Location

Depending on whether or not you are running Active Directory, you need to identify where the DNS zone files will be located. You can store DNS data by any of three methods: in traditional DNS zones, in Active Directory-Integrated zones, or in a combination of both.

Be careful not to unintentionally create root servers. The Dcpromo Wizard can create root servers, which can unintentionally allow internal clients to reach external clients or parent domains. If the "." zone exists, it means that a root server has been created and might need to be removed for proper name resolution.

Traditional DNS Zones

Traditional DNS zones store the zone information in a file on a computer running Windows Server 2003 and DNS. Traditional DNS zones have the following characteristics:

- They utilize a single master model for storing and replicating zone information. Primary zones are the only zone types that have a read/write copy of the zone information. There can be only one primary zone for each namespace. Read-only copies of the zone information can, however, be replicated to any number of secondary DNS servers.
- They replicate in two ways: incrementally or by transferring the complete zone contents.
- They function exactly the same way as BIND–based DNS servers.

Choose this zone type when you have an existing DNS infrastructure that does not support Active Directory, such as a BIND-based DNS infrastructure hosted on Unix servers.

Active Directory-Integrated Zones

Active Directory-Integrated zones store DNS zone information within Active Directory. These zones have the following characteristics:

- They utilize a multimaster model of read/write copies of the zone information. You can make updates to the original zone or to replicated copies. Fault tolerance is possible, because you can still perform updates to the DNS zone information if a DNS server fails.
- They are replicated by Active Directory.
- They are required for secured, dynamically updated DNS zones. You can also set permissions for the parties (users, groups, or computers) that can update the DNS zone information, adding an additional layer of security.
- They enable the administrator to control the scope of replication. For example, you can replicate DNS data to a DNS server within a forest, domain, or specific domain controllers, as well as traditional secondary zones outside the domain.
- They appear and are treated as a traditional primary zone by BIND-based DNS servers or for that matter any DNS server on the Internet.

Choose this zone type when you want to integrate DNS within an existing AD structure and have a single point of support for both. Use Active Directory–Integrated zones if your DNS strategy includes dynamic updates to DNS. Traditional DNS zones are not multimaster; therefore, if the DNS server hosting a primary zone fails, dynamic updates cannot occur.

A Combination of Zone Types

Active Directory-Integrated zones can replicate DNS data to traditional secondary DNS zones. This means that you can use a combination of both zone types. This is a good solution if you have DNS servers from different vendors.

Choose this zone type when the root server is running traditional DNS. This method supports Active Directory–Integrated zones as a delegated domain.

Table 4.4 compares the features of Active Directory–Integrated zones with traditional DNS zones.

TABLE 4.4 DNS Features of Active Directory–Integrated Zones versus Traditional DNS Zones

DNS Features	Active Directory-Integrated Zones	Traditional DNS Zones
Supports incremental zone transfers.	Yes	Yes
Uses Active Directory replication with a multimaster model.	Yes	No
Offers better availability, with each DNS server containing its own read/write copy of the zone data.	Yes	No
Updates to the zone information can always occur in the event that a DNS server fails.	Yes	No

Securing Zones

Securing DNS access from private and public networks is an important goal that can be accomplished through several methods. The security measures you choose will depend on how you have planned your zones. Later in the chapter, in the section titled "Securing DNS," we'll discuss the three levels of security for a DNS infrastructure. In this section, we'll discuss methods of securing DNS zones through dynamic updates and zone permissions.

Choosing a Method for Dynamic Updates

Dynamic updates enable DNS records to be updated on the fly. Because clients and servers can do this themselves, securing the method of dynamic updates is important. These methods include *secured dynamic updates* in Active Directory, dynamic DNS updates from DHCP, and dynamic updates from DNS clients, which will be discussed in the following sections.

Secured Dynamic Updates in Active Directory

Active Directory-Integrated zones can use the Active Directory security features to provide secured dynamic updates (configured as the Secure Only option in DNS). The DNS console offers access control list (ACL) editing features that can be used to add and remove users, groups, and computers from the ACL for an entire zone or for an individual resource record. Permissions to update the DNS zone are configured within Active Directory. Computers must be in the Computers folder to take advantage of dynamic updates.

Dynamic DNS Updates from DHCP

DHCP servers can dynamically update DNS when the server configures a DHCP client computer. You configure this as follows:

- On the DHCP server, specify the DNS zone or zones for which the DHCP server is responsible to automatically update.
- On the DNS server, specify the DHCP server as the only computer that is authorized to update the DNS entries.

In networks with multiple Windows Server 2003 DHCP servers and zones configured to allow secure (dynamic updates) only, you must use Active Directory Users and Computers to add the DHCP server computers to the built-in group DnsUpdateProxy group. This grants the secure rights required so that your DHCP servers will perform updates by proxy for any DHCP clients.

Dynamic DNS updates from DHCP servers can be very useful in scenarios such as the following:

- The DNS client operating system is older than Windows 2000.
- You want to protect against the security risks of unauthorized computers impersonating authorized computers. These risks could be introduced by allowing individual DNS clients to update DNS entries.
- The administrative effort it would take to assign permissions for each user, group, and computer that needs to update its respective DNS entry would be far too much effort.

Dynamic Updates from DNS Clients

Newer DNS clients running Windows 2000, XP Professional, or Server 2003 can directly update DNS automatically by themselves. This can be an appropriate solution in the following situations:

- When the client computer has a manually assigned static IP address.
- When the amount of administrative effort needed to assign the appropriate permissions to enable the client to update its own DNS entries is manageable.
- When no potential security risks are introduced by allowing individual DNS clients to update their own DNS entries. By default, dynamic updates are not allowed. This setting prevents an attacker from updating DNS zones and records, so it is the most secure option. The best solution is to store DNS zones in Active Directory and use the Secure Only dynamic update feature to enable computers to securely update DNS data.

Default Zone Permissions

Active Directory stores a *discretionary access control list (DACL)* on the DNS zones it stores. A DACL is the part of an object's security descriptor that grants or denies permission for access of the object to specific users and groups. You can thereby control the permissions for the Active Directory users and groups that may control the DNS zones.

Table 4.5 lists the default group and user permissions for DNS zones stored in Active Directory.

TABLE 4.5 Default Permissions for DNS Zones

Group/User	Permissions
Administrators	Read, Write, Create All Child objects, Special Permissions
System	Full Control, Read, Write, Create All Child objects, Delete Child objects
Authenticated Users	Create All Child objects
Everyone	Read, Special Permissions
DnsAdmins	Full Control, Read, Write, Create All Child objects, Delete Child objects, Special Permissions
Domain Admins	Full Control, Read, Write, Create All Child objects, Delete Child objects
Enterprise Admins	Full Control, Read, Write, Create All Child objects, Delete Child objects
Enterprise Domain Controllers	Full Control, Read, Write, Create All Child objects, Delete Child objects, Special Permissions
Creator Owner	Special Permissions
Pre-Windows 2000 Compatible Access	Special Permissions

Real World Scenario

Planning a Strategy for DNS Zones

As the systems engineer for Contoso, you have decided on a namespace strategy (the Active Directory root and internal namespace will be `contoso.net`). You are now turning your attention to planning the zones. Contoso is about to open a new office for the customer service call center. This office will have a redundant T-1 link back to the corporate offices. There are going to be two domain controllers at the main office, and you have the budget to add a domain controller to the call center location.

You must consider security and network traffic requirements. What kind of zone strategy should you create for `contoso.net`?

In this scenario, you should create an Active Directory-Integrated zone on the corporate network's DNS servers. This zone will replicate to all other DNS servers in the domain, including the call center, using a multimaster model. You should also make the domain controller in the call center a DNS server. Then you should specify Secure Only updates.

The built-in security features of Active Directory enable you to assign permissions and delegate control of the DNS zones. The DNS data is replicated along with the existing Active Directory replication. Local client queries can all be locally handled so that no unnecessary traffic is created across the WAN.

Another feature of Active Directory–Integrated zones is that zone transfers are encrypted, and in this case they are secured going across the WAN link.

Integrating DNS and WINS

In networks that use both DNS and WINS for name resolution, you can use WINS servers to look up names not resolved by the DNS servers. This is accomplished by sending a request that is unresolvable in the DNS namespace to the WINS server, which then checks its NetBIOS namespace. You can do this by taking a fully qualified domain name such as `mail.microsft.com` and dropping off `microsoft.com` and then forwarding `mail` to the WINS server.

By allowing DNS clients to resolve host names found in the WINS service, you can eliminate the necessity of creating DNS zone entries for every computer on the network. Forwarding for these queries can also be set on a zone-by-zone basis.

To integrate DNS and WINS, there are two special resource record types: the WINS and WINS-R records. In the following sections, we'll look at these records in turn, and then review considerations and recommendations for WINS integration.

WINS Resource Records

In a heterogeneous environment, you might have hosts such as Unix computers that are unable to query and register with WINS themselves. You might also have resources on hosts such as Windows NT 4 or Windows 95/98 that can only dynamically register NetBIOS names with WINS and cannot dynamically register with DNS. With WINS integration, the UNIX hosts could resolve the Windows hosts names through DNS.

For a cursory understanding of WINS, see the introduction to Chapter 5, "Planning a WINS Strategy."

The *WINS resource record* helps to resolve the unresolved DNS queries. It does this by listing the WINS servers to which a name query can be sent.

The WINS record applies only to the topmost level of a zone and does not apply to subdomains within the zone.

The WINS resource record follows a specific syntax as follows:

```
owner class WINS [LOCAL] [Lookup_timeout] [Cache_timeout] wins_server_ip
```

Following is an example of a WINS resource record (the zone root is assumed to be the current origin):

```
@ IN WINS 10.0.0.12
@ IN WINS LOCAL L1 C10 10.10.10.12 10.10.10.13 10.10.10.14
```

Table 4.6 describes the various fields that are used with the WINS resource record.

TABLE 4.6 WINS Resource Record Fields

Field	Description
Owner	Indicates the owner domain for this record. This field should always be set to @ to indicate that the current domain is the same as the zone origin.
Class	Indicates the class for this record. This field should always be set to "IN" because the Internet class is the only supported class for DNS servers running Windows Server 2003.
LOCAL	When used, indicates that the WINS resource record is only to be used locally at the DNS server and is not to be included during zone replication with other DNS servers. This field corresponds to the Do Not Replicate This Record checkbox that is selected or cleared during the process of configuring WINS lookup at the DNS console. If the checkbox was cleared, this field will not be included when the record is written to the zone.
lookup_timeout	This is the time-out value that is applied for this record.
Cache_timeout	This is the cache time-out value that is applied for this record.
Wins_ip_addresses	This is used to specify one or more IP addresses of WINS servers. At least one IP address of a valid WINS server is required.

WINS-R Resource Records

The *WINS-R resource record* provides the same functionality, literally in reverse. It is used in a reverse lookup zone for reverse queries that were not found in the DNS zone. DNS can't send a reverse name lookup to WINS because the WINS database is not indexed by IP. Instead, DNS queries WINS in a roundabout way. DNS sends a node adapter status request directly to the IP address, so that it can retrieve the NetBIOS name. Then it appends the DNS domain name to the NetBIOS name, and it forwards the FQDN to the requesting client.

To use the WINS-R resource record, you therefore have to specify the parent domain so that it can be appended to the NetBIOS computer name. The other fields used have the same functionality as their compatriots in the WINS forward lookup record.

This record also has a specific syntax, as follows:

```
owner class WINS [LOCAL] [Lookup_timeout] [Cache_timeout]
   Domain_to_append
```

Here's an example (once again, the zone root is assumed to be the current origin):

```
@ IN WINS-R LOCAL L1 C10 sample.microsoft.com.
@ IN WINS-R wins.sample.microsoft.com.
```

WINS Integration Considerations

WINS integration can best be accomplished by adhering to the following recommendations:

- Designate a subdomain within the DNS namespace that will be used as a placeholder for WINS names. This subdomain should contain no entries except for the WINS and WINS-R resource records. If you are using separate private and public namespaces, this subdomain belongs under the private namespace.
- Unresolved DNS queries should be forwarded to the delegated subdomain as follows:
  - For any domain names that are within the organization's namespace, you can specify that the DNS queries be forwarded to a delegated subdomain for WINS first if you want to resolve names with WINS prior to checking other domains.
  - Conversely, you can specify that the DNS queries be forwarded to a delegated subdomain for WINS last if you want to attempt to resolve names by searching other domains prior to resolving them within WINS.
- Enable WINS resolution on a zone and specify the WINS server in the zone configuration. You can specify more than one WINS server to be used for unresolved DNS queries. You can even specify the order in which to search the servers by ordering the IP addresses. Multiple WINS servers are recommended to improve the availability of your DNS solution.

If multiple WINS servers share the WINS database, you can create unique DNS zones for each of the WINS servers.

WINS Integration Examples

You work for a multinational European company that has a WINS server with records for only Amsterdam and has another WINS server with records for only London. If you create separate DNS zones for Amsterdam and London, you can also create different subdomain names for the Amsterdam and London WINS servers. If desired, you can create a single DNS zone listing both WINS servers so that the WINS resolution takes place within a single subdomain name.

Planning DNS Zone Replication and Delegation

After planning a DNS namespace and zone requirements, it's time to plan other aspects of DNS zones. Some important things that you need to consider include identifying server configurations, zone delegation, and fault-tolerance requirements. You will need to determine if a zone should be delegated to improve performance, as well as identify fault-tolerance requirements.

Additional secondary zones can be created when you want to introduce redundancy and load balancing.

You can choose to delegate management for one or more zones in order to extend the namespace, balance the load between several servers, and authorize individuals or groups to manage zones.

The important tasks that you need to complete in planning DNS zone replication and delegation are to create secondary zones where necessary, design zone transfers and replication, secure zone transfers, and delegate zones. These subjects will be covered in the following sections.

Creating Secondary Zones

Secondary zones can increase availability and fault tolerance. Different environments have different requirements. The following guidelines and best practices will help you determine the need for and placement of secondary zones.

- Add additional DNS servers to provide zone redundancy. This enables DNS name resolution in the zone to continue if a primary server for the zone stops responding. As you add servers that are authoritative for a given zone, the likelihood that queries will be unanswered for resources in that zone is reduced.
- Add DNS servers to reduce network traffic. You can benefit from adding a DNS server to the remote side of a low-bandwidth WAN link to make traffic more efficient and eliminate unnecessary traffic. In general, locate servers as close as possible to the client populations they serve.
- Add secondary servers to reduce the load on a primary server. Secondary servers should be used to service queries from only local clients and not clients throughout the network.
- When you use secondary servers, you will need to plan for secure zone replication and zone transfers. Make sure that these processes only take place with the hosts that you intend.

Zone Transfers and Replication

Maintaining the availability of zones is a critical service provided by the DNS infrastructure. You have seen that you should ensure availability and fault tolerance by using multiple DNS servers.

The replication methodology depends on whether or not you use Active Directory. If you use Active Directory, you must use zone replication. If you use the traditional DNS zone structure, you must use zone transfers. Implementing secure zone transfers will depend on your replication methodology and requirements. We'll look at these methods next, as well as how to improve performance for zone replication.

Zone Transfers

A *zone transfer* is a pull operation that begins with a secondary server within a zone. The secondary server requests a transfer of zone information from its configured master servers, which can be any other DNS server that loads the zone. Possible master servers include the primary server for the zone or another secondary server. A master server can reply with a partial transfer or a full transfer of the zone information.

Incremental zone transfers (IXFRs) are now supported in Windows 2000 Server and higher. (Older implementations of DNS required a full transfer of the entire zone database just to receive updates.) Just like an incremental backup, an incremental zone transfer enables the secondary server to pull just the changes it needs in order to synchronize its copy of the zone data with its configured source. Zone transfers are completed much more quickly and with far less network traffic generated.

Windows NT 4 does not support incremental zone transfers. Incremental zone transfers must be supported on both ends—by the server that is acting as the source for a zone and also by any servers that pull the zone changes from that source.

Active Directory Replication

Active Directory replication, the process of synchronizing the data in the Active Directory database across all Active Directory servers, is more advantageous than zone transfers, because it uses a *multimaster replication model*. This means that multiple masters can update the zone. A master is any domain controller running Active Directory–Integrated DNS. Any of the domain controllers for the domain can modify the zone and replicate changes to the other domain controllers. This is better than standard DNS replication, in which only the primary server for a zone can modify the zone.

Unlike DNS *full zone transfers*, in which the entire zone is propagated, only relevant changes are propagated in Active Directory replication.

Unlike incremental zone transfers, in which all changes made since the last change are propagated, only the final result of a series of changes to a record will be sent in Active Directory replication.

Within Active Directory, DNS zones are stored in the domain or application directory partitions.

Improving Performance for Replication Traffic

Network administrators are always looking for ways to reduce network traffic, make traffic more efficient, and improve data transmission rates. Zone replication will definitely have its impact on heavily used network segments. You can improve performance through the following methods:

- By setting the replication schedule for secondary zones so that replication only occurs during off-peak hours.
- By using fast zone transfers, which compress the zone replication data.
- By using incremental zone replication.

Windows NT 4 DNS does not perform incremental zone transfers. BIND version 8.2.1 or later is required to support incremental zone transfers. Older versions of BIND also lack support for fast zone transfers.

Securing Zone Transfers

Whether you use zone transfers or Active Directory replication to perform updates, you will need to secure the zone replication traffic. This can be accomplished by many different methods, which include:

- Restricting zone transfers to only authorized IP addresses
- Implementing IPSec and VPN tunnels to encrypt all zone replication traffic transmitted across public networks
- Using Active Directory–Integrated zones to provide encryption and authentication services.

Windows Server 2003 provides a secure configuration for DNS by default. By default the Zone Transfers tab is not checked to allow any zone transfers. When you check it, it defaults to allowing zone transfers "To Any Server." You can and should increase the level of security by changing the setting to "Only To Servers On The Name Servers Tab" to allow zone transfers only to specified IP addresses. The security administrator will still be responsible for protecting against IP spoofing so that a malicious party cannot impersonate one of the authorized IP addresses.

If you change this setting so that you allow zone transfers to any server, you will expose the DNS data to an attacker who is footprinting your network.

DNS zone replication can occur across the Internet and other public networks. When doing so, it is imperative that you protect the names and IP addresses being replicated over such inherently unsecure networks against unauthorized access from malicious parties. Methods of protecting replication traffic include using IPSec, VPN tunnels, and/or Active Directory–Integrated zones.

You must encrypt all replication traffic sent over public networks to ensure security. We recommend encrypting replication traffic by using IPSec or VPN tunnels, using the strongest level of encryption and VPN tunnel authentication.

Active Directory–Integrated zones provide inherent security by encrypting all replication traffic between DNS servers. In addition, all DNS servers that have Active Directory–Integrated zones must be registered with Active Directory.

Delegating Zones

Once you have created the DNS zones, you may benefit from delegating the zones. *Zone delegation* provides a way to assign responsibility for a part of a DNS namespace to another organization, workgroup, or department. Delegation involves assigning authority over portions of a DNS namespace to other zones. The NS record is used to specify a delegated zone and the DNS name of the server that is authoritative for that zone.

You might choose to delegate zones for a number of reasons, including:

- You want to add several subdomains so that you can extend the namespace (for example, if you need to support a new branch or site within the organization).
- You want to delegate administration of a DNS domain to different organizations or departments within your organization.
- You want to enhance performance and add fault-tolerance by using multiple name servers to distribute the load of DNS services.

Windows Server 2003 DNS servers measure round-trip intervals for name resolution queries over a period of time for every DNS server. The DNS servers develop intelligence and can find the closest DNS server. This is especially helpful in cases when multiple name server records exist for a delegated zone, and those records point to a number of available DNS servers.

The NS records identify DNS servers for each zone, and they appear in all forward and reverse lookup zones. This means that if a DNS server needs to resolve a name in a delegated zone, it will simply reference the NS records for DNS servers in the target zone.

Every time you create a new zone, you need to have delegation records in other zones that point back to the authoritative DNS servers for the new zone. You need to do this so that you can transfer authority from those zones and correctly refer to other DNS servers that are authoritative for the new zone.

Zone delegations are checked first before forwarders. However, it is possible to configure a forwarders list that may override the standard behavior of zone referrals, assuming that your zone delegations are correctly configured.

Real World Scenario

Planning Zone Replication and Delegation for a Newly Acquired Company

As the systems engineer for Contoso, you have created a namespace and zone strategy. Now you are ready to proceed to the next phase of your implementation. You need to make a plan for zone replication and delegation. Senior management advises you that Contoso has just acquired Fabrikam, an auto parts invention factory. Management may decide that Fabrikam will take on the Contoso name, but this won't happen for a while. You need to figure out a technology strategy to support the acquisition of Fabrikam.

Fabrikam has a Unix-based network infrastructure, and it uses five BIND version 8.3.3 DNS servers. You need to enable the two companies to share data and eventually merge the data infrastructures. You also need to integrate Fabrikam's DNS with Contoso's DNS infrastructure in such a way that resources can be shared securely between the two companies. You want to place a Windows Server 2003 domain controller running DNS on the Fabrikam network. However, you also want to maintain the existing DNS infrastructure. A large number of file shares will be on the Windows Server 2003 computer, and client/server traffic between the two companies will steadily increase. Fabrikam wants to reduce the DNS load on the Windows Server 2003 by utilizing the existing BIND servers.

How can you integrate the DNS infrastructures of the two companies to meet these requirements?

First, you can create secondary zones on the BIND servers. This method will allow each BIND-based DNS server to resolve names in the Contoso zone, thereby reducing the load on the Fabrikam local Windows Server 2003 server. Next, you can specify the IP addresses of the BIND secondary servers to allow them to perform zone transfers with the Fabrikam Windows Server 2003 DNS server. This method ensures security for zone transfers. To enable Fabrikam to administer its own zone information, you can create a Fabrikam subdomain within the Contoso zone and delegate the domain to the DNS servers on the Fabrikam side. This is a good method for enabling Fabrikam to autonomously administer its DNS information.

Determining DNS Caching and Forwarding

DNS caching and forwarding support different needs and target objectives. Four types of servers can be configured, depending on your business and technical objectives:

- Caching-only servers
- Stub zones
- Conditional forwarders
- Forward-only servers

In the following sections, you will learn the differences between caching-only servers, stub zones, conditional forwarders, and forward-only servers. You will also learn the situations in which you would choose each type of server.

Caching-Only Servers

Caching-only servers resolve names on behalf of clients and cache the results. The cache contains the most frequently requested names and their IP addresses, so that the information is available to speed up subsequent queries. Caching-only servers are not authoritative for a zone. They also do not store standard primary or standard secondary zones. They do, however, help to reduce WAN traffic because they do not generate zone transfer traffic, and because cached queries reduce the amount of name resolution traffic that needs to cross the WAN.

Use caching-only servers when you have a remote office with a limited bandwidth connection to corporate headquarters.

Assume that you have a remote office that needs to resolve queries for names at the corporate office, and that the connection to corporate headquarters has low available bandwidth. You can configure a caching-only server at the remote office to send recursive queries to a DNS server at the corporate office. The DNS server at corporate headquarters, which has more bandwidth available for intranet and Internet connections, assumes the responsibility for resolving the query.

Stub Zones

The purpose of a stub zone is to keep a DNS server that hosts a parent zone aware of the authoritative DNS servers for its child zone. This makes DNS name resolution more efficient. When redundancy and load balancing are not required or have already been provided through other means, stub zones can be used instead of secondary zones to distribute a list of the authoritative DNS servers for a zone.

A stub zone contains the following information:

- The IP address of one or more master servers that can update the stub zone.
- One or more DNS servers that are authoritative for the child zone can serve as master servers for a stub zone. The master server is usually the DNS server that hosts the primary zone for the delegated domain name.
- Resource records for the delegated zone, including SOA, NS, and glue A resource records.
    - The start of authority (SOA) resource record indicates the starting point or original point of authority for information stored in a zone.

  The SOA record is the first resource record that is created when you add a zone. Other computers use the parameters in this record to determine how long the information for the zone will be used and how often updates will be required.
    - In the context of zones, name server (NS) resource records designate the DNS domain names for authoritative DNS servers for the zone.
    - The *glue address (glue A) resource record* provides the address of the host specified in the NS record.
- A *delegation resource record* that is used to locate the authoritative DNS servers for a delegated zone. These records "glue" zones together and provide an effective path for delegation and referral that other DNS servers can follow in the process of resolving a name.

Use stub zones when you want a DNS server hosting a parent zone to remain aware of the authoritative DNS servers for one of its child zones. The stub zone keeps the server updated on the list of new or additional DNS servers authoritative for the child zone and also helps to resolve names from different namespaces.

Stub zones are useful when you want a DNS server hosting a parent zone to stay updated with the name servers that are authoritative for its delegated child zones.

Make sure you understand the behavior of a stub zone. A DNS server hosting a stub zone in one network will reply to queries for names in the other network with only a list of all the authoritative DNS servers for that zone. It will not respond with the specific DNS servers that are designed to handle the name resolution traffic for that zone.

Conditional Forwarders

A *conditional forwarder* will forward DNS queries for external DNS names to DNS servers outside of its own network. This type of DNS server forwards DNS queries based on the domain name in the query. You could, for example, specify that a DNS server will forward all queries for names that end in `acme.com` to the IP address of a DNS server or servers.

Using conditional forwarding, you would configure the domain names for which the DNS server will forward queries and configure one or more DNS server IP addresses for each domain name you specify.

Conditional forwarders behave this way:

1. A DNS server first attempts to resolve received queries by using its own local data: the primary and secondary zones and cache.
2. The server will forward an unresolved query to the DNS server designated as a forwarder.
3. The server sends a recursive query to the forwarder, as opposed to the iterative query used in standard name resolution without a forwarder.
4. The first DNS server waits briefly for the forwarder to reply with an answer. Then it will contact the DNS servers specified in its root hints.

Use conditional forwarding when DNS clients in separate networks resolve each others' names without having to query a DNS server on the Internet.

When would you use conditional forwarders? You may have a scenario in which clients in different networks need to resolve each other's names. In this situation, you will most likely want to enable name resolution without relying on the DNS servers sending queries to root hints servers on the Internet. What you should do, then, is create a direct method for the DNS servers in both networks to contact each other for name resolution. In each network, the DNS servers should be configured to forward queries for names in the other network to a DNS server or servers that can resolve the queries for names in that network. That server or servers will eventually build a sizeable cache, and this will decrease the amount of recursion.

Stub Zones versus Conditional Forwarders

Both conditional forwarders and stub zones allow a DNS server to respond to a query by forwarding to a different DNS server (conditional forwarders) or by providing a referral for a different DNS server (stub zones). However, they are used to accomplish very different objectives.

Conditional forwarding tells the DNS server to forward a received query to a DNS server depending on the DNS name contained in the query.

Stub zones keep the DNS server hosting a parent zone aware of all DNS servers that are authoritative for a child zone. You would not use a conditional forwarder to do this, because every time the authoritative DNS servers for the child zone changed, you would have to manually configure the conditional forwarder setting on the DNS server hosting the parent zone with the new information. This would be a cumbersome and inefficient solution.

Forward-Only Servers

A DNS server that is configured to use forwarders cannot always resolve a query, either through its local information or by using its configured forwarders. Under normal circumstances, the server then uses standard recursion to attempt to resolve the query. However, there is another way to resolve requests in this instance. If you configure a DNS server to not use recursion when forwarders fail, the server fails the query. This type of server is known as a *forward-only server*. A forward-only server builds up a cache and uses it in its attempts to resolve domain names.

A *nonrecursive DNS server* is different from a forward-only DNS server. It won't build up a cache, nor will it perform recursion if the query fails.

The different types of DNS servers that use forwarders will all attempt to resolve the query using their authoritative data before using their forwarders.

You can disable recursion on the entire DNS server, which will prevent you from using forwarders on that server, or you can disable recursion on a per–domain name basis.

Forwarders are best used to manage the DNS traffic between your network and the Internet. You can configure the firewall to permit only one DNS server to communicate with the Internet. You can then configure the other DNS servers to forward any unresolved queries to the first DNS server. The Internet-capable DNS server can then query its configured root hints servers on the Internet to attempt to resolve failed queries.

Use forwarders to manage DNS traffic between the local network and the Internet.

Planning DNS Server Resources

When designing a DNS infrastructure, make sure that you remember to plan for the server resources. This involves several considerations:

- Determine the server requirements. How many servers do you need? What system resources do they require? For instance, one of the most critical system components for a DNS server is its RAM.

- Determine how many servers you need and where to place them. Your choices will be as unique as your network topology and business structure. Factors that will affect your decisions include whether or not you are running Active Directory and the speed of interoffice connections.
- Determine the level of security you will implement based on your specified security objectives.

In the following sections, we'll discuss all of these factors to consider in planning DNS server resources.

Planning General DNS Server Requirements

To plan DNS server resources, start with the server requirements. Determine the following factors:

- Hardware requirements for new and existing DNS servers
- How many servers you need
- Whether the server will be a domain controller or a member server
- Which servers will host primary zones, and which will host secondary zones
- Where you will place the servers on the network to provide for the most efficient traffic, including replication traffic
- Whether you need to plan support for a heterogeneous deployment, including interoperability with BIND-based DNS servers

Many of these factors have been answered elsewhere in the chapter.

Planning for Server Capacity

Server capacity planning involves many factors involving the overall network, as well as individual servers. Identify the number of client queries that a given DNS server will service. Plan the size of each zone the server will service based on the size of the actual zone file and the number of resource records in the zone. Also identify the number of zones the server will host. The following sections discuss planning for hardware requirements, DNS server placement, and the number of servers.

Planning for Hardware Requirements

One of the best investments you can make in your DNS server is to provide it with plenty of RAM. The DNS server service has to load all configured zones into memory. Therefore, if a server has to load many zones, and especially if there are frequent dynamic updates of client information, you should throw memory at the problem. A typical DNS server uses memory for each zone or resource record. Resource records consume memory at the average rate of 100 bytes each, so a zone with 1,000 resource records needs about 100KB of memory.

You can use the DNS-related counters in the Windows Server 2003 monitoring tools to baseline DNS server performance and determine needs. The performance monitoring tools and counters are introduced in Chapter 10, "Planning Network Monitoring, Remote Administration, and Recovery."

Planning DNS Server Placement

Usually, you will place a DNS server on each subnet. You want the servers to be close to the users who will be serviced by them.

Make sure that clients can access at least one other DNS server in case the first DNS server fails to respond. This is especially important when some of the DNS server's clients are on remote subnets. You also want to plan for availability and balance the load of client requests across multiple servers.

In a small LAN on a single subnet, you could configure a single DNS server to simulate both the primary and secondary servers for a zone. When you have reliable high-speed links, you might be able to get away with one DNS server for a larger network area spanning multiple subnets. Conversely, if you have a single subnet with a large number of clients, the best solution may be to add a redundant DNS server to the subnet so that clients have another option for name resolution if the server stops responding.

Planning the Number of Servers

The number of servers you need will be affected by zone transfers and DNS query traffic, especially across slower links. A well-planned DNS infrastructure will help reduce broadcast traffic between local subnets. Nonetheless, traffic will be generated between servers and clients. When implementing DNS in a network that has a complex routing topology, you especially need to pay attention to how traffic is generated.

Evaluate how zone transfers across slow links will affect other network traffic. Incremental zone transfers and caching can help reduce traffic. However, if you have short DHCP leases, they will result in more frequent dynamic updates in DNS and thereby increase traffic. In situations where you need to connect a remote office across a WAN link, a good solution is to set up a caching-only DNS server at remote locations. Figure out how much fault tolerance you need for your network. Usually, you will use at least two DNS servers for each zone for fault tolerance. DNS was actually designed to use two servers for each zone, one as the primary server and the other as a backup or secondary server.

Securing DNS

Securing your DNS infrastructure is critically important in your overall DNS implementation plan. A poorly designed DNS implementation can leave your network open to a variety of attacks and is a serious compromise to your network's security. DNS has three levels of security:

- Low-level security
- Medium-level security
- High-level security

In the following sections, we'll discuss the features of each level of security so that you can make your organization's DNS infrastructure more secure.

Low-Level Security

Low-level security simply describes a standard DNS deployment with no configured security precautions. The only case in which you would use this level is when you have absolutely no reason to be concerned for the security of the DNS information. For instance, you may choose this level of security (or nonsecurity) in a private network that has no connection to the Internet and where there is no threat of someone compromising the DNS data.

Characteristics of this level of security include the following:

- The DNS data is fully exposed, so this configuration is not recommended if you have Internet connectivity.
- Every DNS server is configured with root hints pointing to the root servers for the Internet.
- UDP and TCP ports 53 are open on the network firewall for both source and destination addresses.
- All DNS zones can have dynamic updates.
- Cache pollution prevention is disabled.
- Every DNS server in the network performs standard DNS resolution.
- Zone transfers are permitted to and from all servers
- Multihomed DNS servers listen on all of their IP addresses.

Medium-Level Security

Medium-level security uses DNS security features, but not the advanced security that is available when you run DNS servers on domain controllers and use Active Directory–Integrated zones.

Characteristics of this level of security include the following:

- The DNS data has limited exposure to the Internet.
- Internal servers communicate with external servers through the firewall with a limited list of source and destination addresses allowed. The external DNS servers in front of the firewall are configured with root hints pointing to Internet root servers.
- Resolution of Internet names is accomplished through proxy servers and gateways.
- DNS servers only allow zone transfers to servers that are listed in the Zone Transfers tab of their zones.
- Every DNS server is configured to use forwarders to point to specific internal DNS servers
- Dynamic updates are not allowed for any zones.
- Cache pollution prevention is enabled.
- DNS servers listen only on specified IP addresses.

High-Level Security

High-level security uses all of the DNS security features of medium-level security, and adds the advanced security that is available when you run DNS servers on domain controllers and use Active Directory–Integrated zones. In this configuration, there is no DNS communication at all with the Internet. If Internet connectivity isn't a requirement, we recommend using this configuration.

Characteristics of this level of security include the following:

- There is no Internet communication with the internal DNS servers.
- You use an internal DNS root and namespace in which all authority for zones is internal.

- Internal servers are configured with root hints that point to the internal DNS servers that host the root zone for the internal namespace.
- Forwarding servers forward only to internal DNS servers.
- All zone transfers are limited to only specified IP addresses on every server.
- Zones are configured for secure dynamic updates except the top-level and root zones, which do not allow any dynamic updates.
- Cache pollution prevention is enabled.
- DNS servers only run on domain controllers, with a DACL configured to control administrative access to the DNS Server service.
- All zones are Active Directory–Integrated, with a DACL configured so that only certain people have access to create, delete, or modify DNS data.
- DNS servers listen only on specified IP addresses.

Real World Scenario

Securing the DNS Infrastructure

DNS services are up and running for Contoso. Now your attention turns to security. You realize that all of the DNS servers on the network are vulnerable to attack because the firewall allows DNS traffic to and from all of the DNS servers. You cannot accept the security risk of direct Internet communication with the DNS servers, and you must make some immediate changes.

You want to limit outbound DNS traffic so that it originates from a single DNS server on the network. This traffic should only come from the intranet DNS servers to the outbound DNS server.

How can you implement the desired changes? What should you do to make it so?

You should configure medium-level security in this scenario, because Contoso needs the ability to communicate with Internet servers. Configure the DNS servers on the intranet as forward-only servers. Queries that are authoritative for their own zone data will be answered, and all other queries will be forwarded to the outbound DNS server. If the forwarder fails, recursive query will not be attempted. As time goes by, the intranet servers will build up a cache, and this will help to reduce the amount of traffic sent through the firewall to answer a query.

Troubleshooting Host Name Resolution

In all phases of a DNS deployment, from the initial design stage to maintenance, you will find it necessary to troubleshoot host name resolution when DNS doesn't behave the way you expected. When troubleshooting host name resolution, start with the simplest steps applicable to a problem and progress to the more advanced tools.

The simplest test is to use the *ping* command to make sure the server is alive. A more exhaustive test uses *nslookup* to verify that you can actually resolve addresses for items on your DNS server. Before reading about troubleshooting, though, you should examine some basic monitoring and management issues.

Monitoring DNS

You can use the DNS snap-in to do some basic server testing and monitoring. More importantly, you use the snap-in to monitor and set logging options. The Event Logging tab of the server Properties dialog box (see Figure 4.3) lets you pick which events you want logged. The more of these options you turn on, the more log information you will get. This is useful when you're trying to track what's happening with your servers, but it can result in a very large log file if you're not careful.

FIGURE 4.3 The Event Logging tab of the Server Properties dialog box

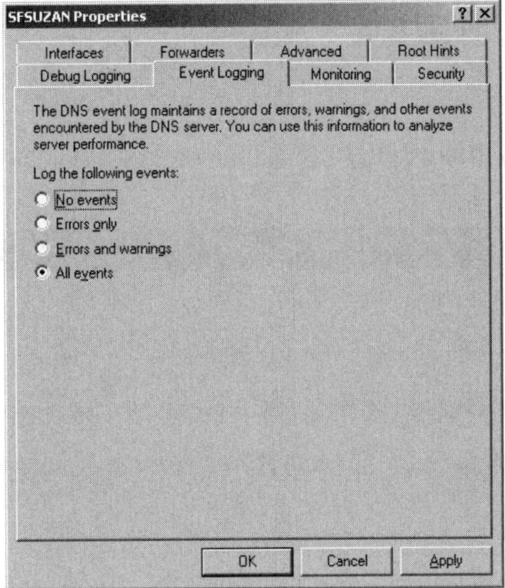

The Monitoring tab (see Figure 4.4) gives you some simplistic testing tools. The Checking A Simple Query Against This DNS Server checkbox asks for a single record from the local DNS server; it's useful for verifying that the service is running and listening to queries, but not much else. Checking A Recursive Query To Other DNS Servers uses a recursive query to see whether forwarding is working correctly. The Test Now button and the Perform Automatic Testing At The Following Interval control allows you to run these tests now or later, as you require.

If the simple query fails, check that the local server contains the zone `1.0.0.127.in-addr.arpa`. If the recursive query fails, check that your root hints are correct and that your root servers are running and accessible.

FIGURE 4.4 The Monitoring tab of the Server Properties dialog box

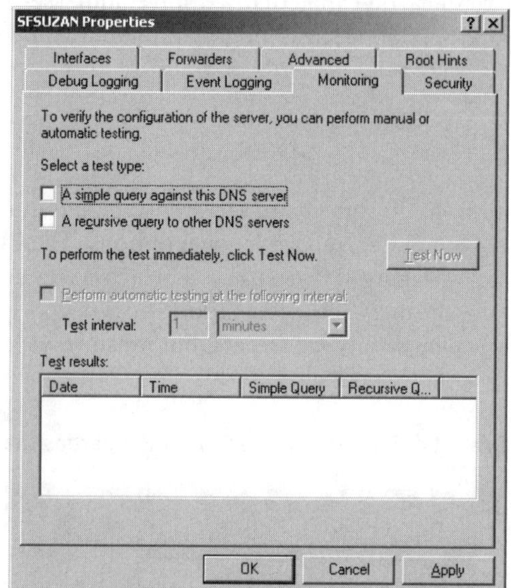

In Exercise 4.1, you will enable logging and use the DNS MMC to test the DNS server.

EXERCISE 4.1

Simple DNS Testing

1. Open the DNS management tool by clicking Start ➢ Administrative Tools ➢ DNS.
2. Right-click the DNS server you want to test and select Properties.
3. Switch to the Debug Logging tab, check all of the Debug logging options except Filter Packets By IP Address, and enter a full path and filename in the File Path and Name field. Click the Apply button.
4. Switch to the Monitoring tab, check both A Simple Query Against This DNS Server and "A Recursive Query To Other DNS Servers.
5. Click the Test Now button several times, and then click OK.

Troubleshooting DNS

When troubleshooting DNS problems, first ask yourself the following basic questions:

- What application is failing? What works? What doesn't work?
- Is the problem basic IP connectivity, or is it name resolution? If the problem is name resolution, does the failing application use NetBIOS names, DNS names, or host names?

- How are the things that do and don't work related?
- Have the things that don't work now ever worked on this computer or network?
- If so, what has changed since they last worked?

Windows Server 2003 provides several useful tools that can help you diagnose and solve problems with DNS. This section discusses the following:

- You can use `nslookup` to perform DNS queries and to examine the contents of zone files on local and remote servers.
- You can use `ipconfig` to view DNS client settings, display and flush the resolver cache, and force a dynamic update client to register its DNS records.
- You can use Event Viewer to view DNS client and server error messages.
- The network redirector allows you to stop the DNS client and flush its cache by stopping and restarting it with the `Net Stop` and `Net Start` commands.
- You can configure the DNS server to monitor certain events and log them in the DNS log for your edification.
- You can perform test queries by using the options on the Monitoring tab in the DNS console.

In the following sections, we'll explore the use of the `nslookup` and `ipconfig` utilities and the DNS log in troubleshooting name resolution problems.

Using *Nslookup*

`Nslookup` is a standard command-line tool provided in most DNS server implementations, including Windows Server 2003. `Nslookup` offers the ability to perform query testing of DNS servers and to obtain detailed responses at the command prompt. This information can be useful for diagnosing and solving name resolution problems, for verifying that resource records are added or updated correctly in a zone, and for debugging other server-related problems. You can do a number of useful things with `nslookup`:

- You can use `nslookup` in noninteractive mode to look up a single piece of data.
- You can enter Interactive mode and use the Debug feature.
- From within Interactive mode, you can:
  - Set options for your query.
  - Look up a name.
  - Look up records in a zone.
  - Perform zone transfers.
  - Exit `nslookup`.

When you are entering queries, entering FQDNs so you can control what name is submitted to the server is generally a good idea. However, if you want to know which suffixes are added to unqualified names before they are submitted to the server, you can enter `nslookup` in debug mode and then enter an unqualified name.

Let's start with using `nslookup` in plain old command-line mode:

```
nslookup name server
```

This code will look up a DNS name or address named *name*, using a server at an IP address specified by *server*.

However, `nslookup` is a lot more useful in Interactive mode because you can enter several commands in sequence. Running `nslookup` by itself (without specifying a query or server) puts it in Interactive mode, where it will stay until you type **exit** and press Enter.

While in Interactive mode, you can use the `set` command to configure how the resolver will carry out queries. Table 4.7 shows a few of the options available with `set`.

TABLE 4.7 Command-Line Options Available with the set Command

Option	Purpose
`set all`	Shows all the options available with the set option.
`set d2`	Puts `nslookup` in debug mode so you can examine the query and response packets between the resolver and the server.
`set domain=`*domain name*	Tells the resolver what domain name to append for unqualified queries.
`set timeout=`*timeout*	Tells the resolver which time-out to use. This option is useful for slow links where queries frequently time-out and the wait time must be lengthened.
`set type=`*record type*	Tells the resolver which type of resource records to search for (for example, host, PTR, or SRV). If you want the resolver to query for all types of resource records, type **set type=all**.

While in Interactive mode, you can look up a name just by typing *name* `[`*server*`]`. In this example, *name* is the owner name for the record you are looking for, and *server* is the server that you want to query.

You can use the wildcard character (*) in your query. For example, if you want to look for all resource records that have K as the first letter, just type **k*** as your query.

If you want to query for a particular type of record (for example, an MX record), use the `set type` command.

```
Set type=mx
```

This example tells `nslookup` that you're only interested in seeing MX records that meet your search criteria.

You can do a couple of other things with `nslookup`. You can get a list of the contents of an entire domain with the `Ls` command. To find all the hosts in the `apple.com` domain, you'd type **Set type=a**, and then type **Ls -t apple.com**.

You can also simulate zone transfers by using the `Ls` command with the `-d` switch. This can help you determine whether or not the server you are querying allows zone transfers to your computer.

Type the following: **`ls -d <domain name>`**

A successful `nslookup` response looks like this:

```
Server: Name of DNS server
Address: IP address of DNS server
Response data
```

`Nslookup` might also return an error. The following message means that the resolver did not locate a PTR resource record (containing the host name) for the server IP address:

```
DNS request timed out.
Timeout was <x> seconds.
*** Can't find server name for address <IP Address>: Timed out
*** Default servers are not available
Default Server: Unknown
Address: <IP address of DNS server>
```

`Nslookup` can still query the DNS server, and the DNS server can still answer queries.

The following message means that a request timed out:

```
*** Request to <Server> timed-out
```

This might happen, for example, if the DNS service was not running on the DNS server that is authoritative for the name.

The following message means that the server is not receiving requests on UDP port 53:

```
*** <Server> can't find <Name or IP address queried for>: No response
   from server
```

The following message means that this DNS server was not able to find the name or IP address in the authoritative domain:

```
*** <Server> can't find <Name or IP address queried for>:
  Non-existent domain
```

The authoritative domain might be on that DNS server or on another DNS server that this DNS server is not able to reach.

The following message generally means that the DNS server is running but is not working properly:

```
*** <Server> can't find <Name or IP address queried for>: Server failed.
```

For example, this message might include a corrupted packet, or the zone in which you are querying for a record might be paused. However, this message can also be returned if the client queries for a host in a domain for which the DNS server is not authoritative and the DNS server cannot contact its root servers, or it is not connected to the Internet, or it has no root hints. In Exercise 4.2, you will get some hands-on practice with the *nslookup* tool, a simple but effective way to troubleshoot many types of DNS problems.

EXERCISE 4.2

Using the Nslookup Command

1. Open a command prompt by selecting Start ➢ All Programs ➢ Accessories ➢ Command Prompt.
2. When the command prompt window opens, type **`nslookup`** and press the Enter key. (For the rest of the exercise, use the Enter key to terminate each command.)
3. `Nslookup` will start, printing a message telling you the name and IP address of the default DNS server. Write these down; you will need them later.
4. Try looking up a well-known address: type **`www.microsoft.com`**. Notice that the query returns several IP addresses (Microsoft load-balances Web traffic by using multiple servers in the same DNS record).
5. Try looking up a nonexistent host: type **`www.fubijar.com`**. Notice the message you get: "Non-existent domain." This is normal behavior.
6. Change the server to a nonexistent host (try making up a private IP address that you know isn't a DNS server on your network, such as `10.10.10.10`). Do this by typing **`server`** ***`ipAddress`***. `Nslookup` will take a while to think about it, because it will try to turn the IP address into a host name. Eventually, it will print a message telling you that the new default server is using the IP address you specified.
7. Try doing another lookup of a known DNS name. Type **`www.microsoft.com`**. Notice that `nslookup` is contacting the server you specified and that the lookup times out after a few seconds.
8. Reset your server to the original address you wrote down in Step 3.
9. If doing so won't disrupt your network, unplug your computer from the network and repeat Steps 4 through 8. Notice the difference in behavior.

Using *ipconfig*

You can use the command-line tool `ipconfig` to view your DNS client settings, to view and reset cached information used locally for resolving DNS name queries, and to register the resource records for a dynamic update client.

If you use `ipconfig` with no parameters, it displays DNS information for each adapter, including the domain name and DNS servers used for that adapter. Table 4.8 shows some command-line options available with `ipconfig`.

TABLE 4.8 Command-Line Options Available for the `ipconfig` Command

Command	What It Does
`Ipconfig /all`	Displays additional information about DNS, including the FQDN and the DNS suffix search list.

TABLE 4.8 Command-Line Options Available for the `ipconfig` Command *(continued)*

Command	What It Does
`Ipconfig /flushdns`	Flushes and resets the DNS resolver cache.
`Ipconfig /displaydns`	Displays the contents of the DNS resolver cache.
`Ipconfig /registerdns`	Refreshes all DHCP leases and registers any related DNS names. This option is available only on Windows 2000 and newer computers that run the DHCP Client service.

DNS Log

You can configure the DNS server to create a log file that records the following types of events:

- Queries
- Notification messages from other servers
- Dynamic updates
- Content of the question section for DNS query messages
- Content of the answer section for DNS query messages
- Number of queries this server sends
- Number of queries this server has received
- Number of DNS requests received over a UDP port
- Number of DNS requests received over a TCP port
- Number of full packets sent by the server
- Number of packets written through by the server and back to the zone

The DNS log appears in `*SystemRoot*\System32\dns\Dns.log`. Because the log is in RTF format, you must use WordPad or Word to view it.

You can change the directory and filename in which the DNS log appears by adding the following entry to the Registry with the REG_SZ data type:

```
HKEY_LOCAL_MACHINE\SYSTEM\CurrentControlSet\Services\DNS\Parameters\
  LogFilePath
```

Set the value of `LogFilePath` equal to the file path and filename where you want to locate the DNS log.

By default, the maximum file size of the `Dns.log` is 4MB. If you want to change the size, add the following entry to the Registry with the REG_DWORD data type:

```
HKEY_LOCAL_MACHINE\SYSTEM\CurrentControlSet\Services\DNS\
  Parameters\LogFileMaxSize
```

Set the value of `LogFileMaxSize` equal to the desired file size in bytes. The minimum size is 64Kb.

Once the log file reaches the maximum size, Windows Server 2003 writes over the beginning of the file. If you make the value higher, data persists for a longer time, but the log file consumes more disk space. If you make the value smaller, the log file uses less disk space, but the data persists for a shorter time.

Do not leave DNS logging turned on during normal operation because it sucks up both processing and hard disk resources. Enable it only when diagnosing and solving DNS problems.

Summary

In this chapter, you learned:

- What the Domain Naming Service (DNS) is and how it works. DNS is a hierarchical, distributed database that provides computer-name-to-IP-address mappings. DNS provides name registration and resolution services similar to those provided by WINS.
- How to plan a DNS namespace. Choices include using the same namespace for internal and external name resolution, using a delegated namespace such as a subdomain name for external versus internal traffic, and using a child domain for internal traffic.
- How to plan DNS zones. Considerations include the zone type, the location for zone data, zone security, and WINS integration.
- How to plan DNS zone replication and delegation. This may involve creating secondary zones, configuring zone transfers and Active Directory replication, securing the zone transfers, and delegating zone transfers.
- How to plan DNS forwarding. Possibilities for servers include caching-only servers, stub zones, conditional forwarders, and forwarding-only servers.
- How to plan resources for DNS servers. Considerations include planning for server capacity and securing DNS.
- How to troubleshoot host name resolution with DNS. Troubleshooting begins with monitoring the server with the DNS console and logs. Troubleshooting tools include the `nslookup` and `ipconfig` utilities.

Exam Essentials

Understand how DNS works. DNS is a distributed, hierarchical database that resolves host names to IP addresses. DNS has a variety of concepts with which you should be familiar. For example, you must know the different server and resource record types used in DNS. You must also know how the concepts of zones and forwarding fit into the big picture.

Be able to plan a DNS namespace. The namespace decisions you make will depend on your business and technical requirements. Know how to plan for internal and external namespaces as well as how and when to use delegated subdomains.

Be able to plan a DNS zoning strategy. Choose primary, secondary, and stub zones to meet different objectives. Understand the differences between traditional and Active Directory–Integrated DNS zones. Secure the zones by choosing the appropriate method of dynamic updates and by configuring DACLs on the DNS zones. Integrate DNS and WINS.

Create a plan for DNS forwarding. Choose between caching-only servers, stub zones, conditional forwarders, and forward-only servers to meet different business and technical requirements.

Plan the server resources for DNS. Plan hardware requirements, server placement, and server number based on the organization's requirements. Choose between low-level, medium-level, and high-level security configurations.

Troubleshoot DNS name resolution. Know the tools and best practices for monitoring and troubleshooting a DNS implementation. Use the `nslookup` utility to verify record registrations. Use `ipconfig` to verify DNS client settings.

Key Terms

Before you take the exam, be certain you are familiar with the following terms:

Active Directory replication	DNS zone
Active Directory–Integrated (ADI) zone	Domain Name System (DNS)
Berkeley Internet Name Daemon (BIND)	Dynamic DNS (DDNS) standard
boot files	forward-only server
cache file	full zone transfers
caching-only servers	glue address (glue A) resource record
CNAME records	high-level security
conditional forwarder	host record
delegated namespace	incremental zone transfers (IXFRs)
delegation resource record	iterative query
discretionary access control list (DACL)	low-level security
DNS client	mail exchange (MX) record
DNS namespace	medium-level security
DNS server	multimaster replication model

name server

name server (NS) records

nonrecursive DNS server

nslookup

ping

pointer (PTR) record

primary DNS server

primary zones

recursive query

resolver

resource records (RR)

reverse lookup file

root server

secondary DNS server

secondary zones

secured dynamic updates

service (SRV) records

standard zone files

start of authority (SOA) record

stub zone

top-level domains

traditional DNS zones

WINS forward lookup resource record

WINS-R resource record

zone delegation

zone transfers

Review Questions

1. You are the network administrator for your company. The company's network has a mixture of Windows NT and Unix servers.

   You are almost finished migrating the network from Windows NT to Windows Server 2003. The Unix servers and workstations are managed by a separate IT group. You are in the process of building the Windows Server 2003 DNS infrastructure. The Unix group has been running DNS BIND 2.4.1 for the organization because DNS was primarily used for Internet name resolution. Because DNS is critical to the functioning of Windows Server 2003 Active Directory, you can justify giving Windows Server 2003 DNS the authority to be the primary zone for the network. However, the Unix group will still maintain the DNS server for the group and use the Windows Server 2003 DNS as authoritative. When you finally configure the DNS servers, the Unix DNS server cannot receive zone transfers from the Windows Server 2003 DNS.

   How must you configure the Windows Server 2003 DNS to send zone transfers to the Unix DNS?

   A. Disable the dynamic updates on the Windows Server 2003 DNS server.

   B. Enable round robin on the Windows Server 2003 DNS server.

   C. Enable dynamic updates on the Unix DNS server.

   D. Configure the BIND secondaries option on the Windows Server 2003 DNS server.

   E. Enable secure updates on the Windows Server 2003 DNS server.

2. You are the network administrator for your company. The network runs Active Directory in Native mode. All servers are Windows Server 2003, and all clients are Windows XP.

   You are charged with upgrading your Windows NT network to Windows Server 2003. You plan to install Active Directory and upgrade all your client machines to Windows XP Professional. Your company does not allow Internet access for its employees. You realize that DNS is still an important component of Windows Server 2003, even though you won't be using it to locate resources on the Internet. You are committed to implementing Windows Server 2003 DNS in accordance with best practices. What DNS records must you include in the configuration of the Windows Server 2003 DNS service in this environment? (Choose all that apply.)

   A. Host record

   B. Pointer record

   C. Alias record

   D. Name server records

   E. Start of authority record

   F. Mail exchange record

   G. Service record

3. You are the network administrator for a large sales organization with four distinct regional offices situated in different areas of the United States. Your Windows Server 2003 servers are all in place, and you have almost finished migrating all the workstations to Windows 2000 and XP Professional. Your next step is to implement a single Active Directory tree, but you want to put your DNS infrastructure in place before you start building your tree. Because DNS is a critical component for the proper functioning of Active Directory, you want to make sure that each region will have service for local resources as well as good performance. What should you do to realize these requirements?

   A. Install a single DNS server at your location and create a separate domain name for each region for resolution of local resources.

   B. Install a DNS server at each regional location and create a single domain name for all the regions for resolution of local resources.

   C. Install a single DNS server at your location and create a single domain name for all the regions for resolution of local resources.

   D. Install a DNS server at each regional location and create a separate domain name for each region for resolution of local resources.

4. Acme Bowling Pin Company, with offices in 4 states, has been acquired by Roadrunner Enterprises, which has offices in 14 states and is a highly diversified organization. Although the various companies are managed independently, the parent company is very interested in minimizing costs by taking advantage of any shared corporate resources; it also wants to have overall central control. This means that you, the network administrator, will manage your own DNS namespace but will still be under the umbrella of the parent organization. Which of the following will best accomplish these goals?

   A. Have each location, including yours, register its own namespace and manage its DNS system independently.

   B. Register a single domain name for Roadrunner Enterprises and use delegated subdomains on a single DNS server at corporate headquarters to provide name resolution across the enterprise.

   C. Register a single domain name for Roadrunner Enterprises and use delegated subdomains on DNS servers installed at each location to provide name resolution across the enterprise.

   D. Have each location, including yours, register its own namespace and add it on a single DNS server at corporate headquarters to provide name resolution across the enterprise.

5. You are the network administrator for your company. The network is running in a heterogeneous environment with a mixture of Windows NT, Windows Server 2003, and Unix servers. You will migrate the NT network to Windows Server 2003.

   After upgrading your Windows NT network to Windows Server 2003, you decide that you want to implement Active Directory. Your network consists of 3 Windows Server 2003 servers, 65 Windows 2000 and XP Professional workstations, and 3 Unix workstations, with one of them running a large laser printer and another a fax server. You have been using a DNS server on one of the Unix boxes for Internet browsing only, but now you will need DNS for Active Directory. You deploy the Windows Server 2003 DNS service, replacing the DNS on the Unix box and configuring it for dynamic updates. After you deploy Active Directory, everything appears to work fine—the users can connect to resources on the network through host names. However, it becomes apparent that the fax server and the laser printer are no longer accessible via their host names. What is the most likely cause of this problem?

   A. You need to disable dynamic updates on the DNS server.

   B. You need to install WINS to resolve the host names on the Unix machines.

   C. You need to manually add host resource records for the Unix machines.

   D. You need to integrate the primary DNS zone into Active Directory.

6. You have been brought into an organization that has a variety of computer systems. Management is trying to tie these systems together and to at least minimize the administrative efforts required to keep the network-provided services running. The systems consist of 4 Windows NT servers, 7 Windows 2003 Servers, 300 Windows 2000 and XP Professional workstations, 100 Windows NT workstations, 30 Unix clients, and 3 Unix servers. Management wants to continue the migration toward the new versions of Windows and also to expand the number of Unix servers as the need arises. Presently, they are using WINS running on the Windows NT servers, and a DNS service on one of the Unix servers that points to an ISP and provides all host name resolution. What would be your recommendation for providing name resolution service for this organization?

   A. Install the Windows Server 2003 DNS service on the Windows Server 2003 server.

   B. Install the WINS service on the Unix server.

   C. Upgrade the DNS on the Unix server to the Windows Server 2003 DNS.

   D. Use the standard DNS service that is already on the Unix server.

   E. Install BIND version 8.1.2.

7. Your company has offices in six cities across the country. Each location is relatively autonomous, because the locations provide different services under a larger corporate umbrella. As a result, each network has its own support staff. Even though the locations are fairly independent, their standards and deployed technologies are still overseen by the corporate office, to minimize costs. Part of this centralization is supplying primary DNS name resolution services for all the locations. However, the company also uses slow links between the offices, which is causing name resolution performance issues when the requests are for resources across the WAN. You want to resolve this by installing an additional DNS server at each location without increasing zone transfers across the WAN links. Which type of DNS server should you deploy in each location to ensure the results you desire?

   A. Slave server

   B. Caching-only server

   C. Another secondary server

   D. Master server

8. You are the network administrator for your company. The network is running Active Directory in Native mode. All servers are Windows Server 2003, and all clients are XP Professional.

   All of the client machines are configured to use the server named `DNS1` for name resolution. Recently, users of the client computers have been complaining that they cannot access resources on the Internet, but they are still able to access all of the resources in the local domain. Identify the most likely cause of the problem.

   A. The name server is configured as a root server.

   B. The server does not support dynamic updates.

   C. The server's root hints file is not configured or updated.

   D. The name server has only one network card.

9. Your company has been extraordinarily successful with its e-commerce site. In fact, because your customers have come to expect such a high level of reliability, you want to build several servers that mirror each other; just in case one of them fails, you will still be able to provide excellent service for your customers. The name of the Web server is `http://www.stuffforyou.com`, which you are duplicating on machines on different subnets, and you have made all the necessary host records in the DNS. What else must you do so that all the mirrored Web servers can be utilized by your customers?

   A. Enable DNS sharing.

   B. Enable IIS sharing.

   C. Enable DNS round robin.

   D. Enable request redirector.

   E. Configure the proper priorities metric for this host name.

10. You are the network administrator for your company, Contoso, Ltd. The network is running Active Directory in Native mode. All servers are Windows Server 2003, and all clients are Windows XP Professional.

    The company has recently acquired a former competitor, Fabrikam, and you are charged with planning zone replication and delegation for the newly acquired company. Fabrikam's network infrastructure is Unix-based and has four BIND version 8.3.2 servers. You have added a Windows Server 2003 domain controller running DNS on Fabrikam's network. You want to enable resource sharing and name resolution between the two companies using the existing infrastructure and using the least possible administrative effort. In the future, the namespaces could be combined, so you want a plan that offers flexibility for the future.

    What type of zones should you implement on the BIND-based DNS servers, and how should you configure zone transfers and/or forwarding?

    A. Create primary zones on the BIND-based DNS servers and forward them to the DNS servers that are authoritative for the main corporate namespace at Contoso.

    B. Create secondary zones on the BIND-based DNS servers and configure them to perform zone transfers with the Windows Server 2003 DNS server on the Fabrikam local network.

    C. Create primary zones on the BIND-based DNS servers and configure them to perform zone transfers with the Windows Server 2003 DNS server on the Fabrikam local network.

    D. Create secondary zones on the BIND-based DNS servers and forward them to the DNS servers that are authoritative for the main corporate namespace at Contoso.

11. You are the network administrator for your company. The network is running Active Directory in Mixed mode. Thirty servers are Windows Server 2003, and the remaining 12 servers are Windows NT Server. All clients are Windows XP Professional. The network also has multiple DNS, WINS, and DHCP servers running exclusively on Windows Server 2003.

    Zones are configured to allow Secure Only updates. The XP clients are configured to use secure dynamic updates in Active Directory. The NT Server computers are configured to use dynamic DNS updates via DHCP. You intended for this to relieve the necessity of manually configuring permissions to enable the Windows NT Server computers to update its own DNS entries.

    Windows XP and Windows Server 2003 computers are able to update their own DNS entries. Despite your efforts, however, dynamic updates to the DNS entries are not working for the Windows NT Server computers. What should you do?

    A. Upgrade the Windows NT Server computers to Windows 2000 Server or higher. Enable secure dynamic updates on these computers.

    B. Enable secure dynamic updates on the Windows NT Server computers.

    C. Add the DHCP server computers to the DnsUpdateProxy group.

    D. On the DNS server, specify the DHCP server as the only computer that is authorized to update the DNS entries.

12. You are the network administrator for your company. The network is running Active Directory in Native mode. All servers are Windows Server 2003, and all clients are XP Professional. You want to configure a Windows Server 2003 DNS server so that it can answer queries for hosts on the local intranet but not on the Internet. What should you do? Choose two of the following options. Each option represents a partial solution.
    A. Install the DNS server inside this company's firewall.
    B. Configure this server as a root server and leave out root hints for the top-level domains.
    C. Leave forwarding turned off.
    D. Disable recursive lookups.

13. A spammer is attempting to send junk mail through an unsuspecting e-mail server. The spammer uses a fake DNS name from which he thinks the e-mail server will accept mail, but he is rejected anyway. How does the mail server know to reject the spammer's mail?
    A. The spammer's DNS name is not in the cache file of the primary DNS server that serves the mail server's domain, so it is rejected.
    B. A fake DNS name is automatically detected if the IP address is not recognized by the e-mail server.
    C. The e-mail server employs a reverse lookup to verify that DNS names are not fake.
    D. The spammer does not have an MX record in the database of the DNS server that serves the e-mail server's domain.

14. A DNS client sends an iterative query to its local DNS server, asking for the IP address of `www.bigbrother.gov`. The DNS server finds no local zones corresponding to the requested domain name, so it sends a request to a root name server. With what does the root name server reply?
    A. The IP address of the name server for the `bigbrother.gov` domain
    B. The DNS name of the GOV top-level domain
    C. The IP address of `www.bigbrother.gov`
    D. The IP address of the name server for the GOV top-level domain

15. You are the network administrator for your company. The network is running Active Directory in Native mode. All servers are Windows Server 2003, and all clients are XP Professional.

You have just deployed Windows Server 2003 DNS. You want to quickly verify that your DNS service is running and listening to queries. What should you click in the following exhibit in order to accomplish your objective?

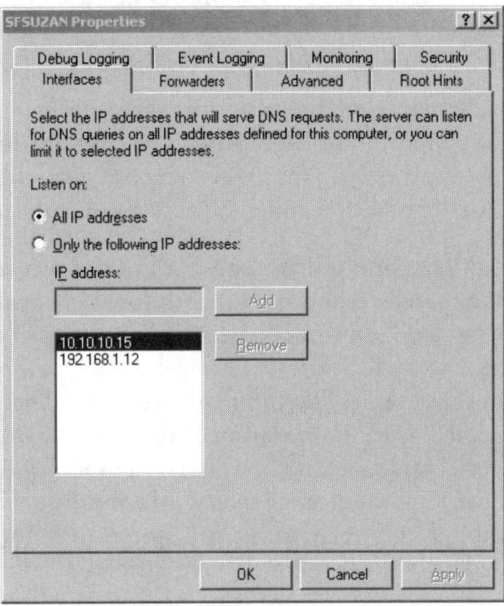

A. The Query checkbox on the Advanced tab

B. The Update checkbox on the Advanced tab

C. The Monitoring tab

D. The Interfaces tab

Answers to Review Questions

1. D. The BIND Secondaries option on the Windows Server 2003 DNS is used for backward compatibility with older versions of DNS. Before BIND version 4.9.5, only one resource record at a time could be transferred. Windows DNS supports fast zone transfers, in which multiple records are transferred simultaneously. Because the Unix DNS in this case is 2.4.1, the old transfer method needs to be used in order to accept the transfers.

   Round robin is used to load-balance multiple hosts with the same name using multiple IP addresses. Dynamic updates are not supported in DNS BIND 2.4.1 or even in most current versions of Unix DNS. Secure updates apply only to the DNS zones that are integrated into Active Directory so that access to the records can be controlled by access control lists.

2. A, D, E, G. Even though best practice is to have all of the records associated with DNS as a part of each installation, name resolution will still function properly with just the fundamental records. The host record, or A record, is the basic record that contains the mapping between the logical name and the IP address. This is the heart of DNS. The name server records identify the DNS servers that are available for this network. The start of authority record, or SOA record, contains the basic configuration of the DNS service. The service record, while not essential to a traditional DNS, is critical to Active Directory because it is used to identify the domain controllers for login and other query information. The pointer record is used for reverse lookups; although it is very useful, it is not required for standard functionality. The alias record is needed only if you plan to have different names associated with the same physical address. The mail exchange record is necessary only if you are using DNS to locate e-mail servers.

3. B. A DNS server installed at each regional location will provide name and service resolution even if the WAN links go down. The local location will also have better performance because the requests will not have to travel through the WAN links.

   A single domain name for all the locations is needed because your requirement is to have one Active Directory tree with a contiguous namespace.

4. C. DNS has the ability to create subdomains of a central corporate domain, and a subdomain can be delegated to a DNS server in each location for independent management. The entire company could use a single DNS server at corporate headquarters with the multiple domains, but then each namespace would not be managed locally at each location.

5. C. Windows 2000 and newer computers will register themselves in the DNS through dynamic updates. However, the Unix machines will not register themselves in DNS. These machines will have to be added manually into DNS so that the other clients can locate them.

   If you disabled dynamic DNS updates, you would then have to add all the workstations on the network to the DNS manually. WINS is useful only for NetBIOS name resolution to IP addresses. Integrating the DNS records into Active Directory will have no effect on retrieving the host names of machines that don't support dynamic DNS updates.

6. A. Installing the Windows DNS service on Windows 2003 Server will provide dynamic updates to allow the newer Windows machines to publish themselves and locate the Active Directory services through the SRV records that this version of DNS supports. The Windows Server 2003 DNS will also provide standard DNS services to the Unix and Windows NT machines. In addition, it can point to the DNS server that your ISP is supplying for searches beyond the local network.

   No WINS service is available for Unix. It may remain on the Windows NT server until the upgrade is complete and the NetBIOS name resolution is no longer necessary. The DNS service on the Unix server will work, but the manual updates that are necessary make it impractical to use for providing services for a Windows Server 2003 network.

7. B. Caching-only DNS servers don't perform zone transfers. They build up their information as queries are resolved and, therefore, get smarter over time. If they were deployed in each location, those specific requests would build up in the cache server, thereby reducing the number of requests that would need to be forwarded to the primary DNS server at the corporate office across the slow WAN link.

   Windows 2000 uses a slave server to forward requests it can't resolve to a DNS server that is specifically used to resolve requests outside your network. Therefore, a slave server does not apply to this situation. Another secondary server would increase performance for local resolution but wouldn't address other requests. Installing a master server would increase traffic, because it would be used to perform zone transfers to secondary servers; in this scenario those servers are already receiving zone transfers from the primary server.

8. C. When a DNS server processes a recursive query that cannot be resolved from local zone files, the query must be escalated to a forwarder or a root DNS server. Each standards-based implementation of DNS includes a cache file (or root server hints) that contains entries for root servers of the Internet domains.

9. C. The round robin option allows you to list a host name with multiple IP addresses and then, as each request comes into the DNS server, the DNS server rotates that list, presenting each of the IP addresses in turn. This will balance out the load across all the servers you have mirrored and configured in the DNS.

10. B. In this scenario, the best solution is to create secondary zones on the BIND-based DNS servers and configure them to perform zone transfers with the Windows Server 2003 DNS server on the Fabrikam local network. This method will allow each BIND-based DNS server to resolve names in the Contoso zone, thereby reducing the load on the Fabrikam local Windows Server 2003 server.

    The next logical step to take is to specify the IP addresses of the BIND secondary servers to allow them to perform zone transfers with the Fabrikam Windows Server 2003 DNS server. This method ensures security for zone transfers.

    To enable Fabrikam to administer its own zone information, you can create a Fabrikam subdomain within the Contoso zone and delegate the domain to the DNS servers on the Fabrikam side. This is a good method for enabling Fabrikam to autonomously administer its DNS information.

11. C. In networks with multiple Windows Server 2003 DHCP servers and zones configured to allow secure only updates, you must use Active Directory Users and Computers to add the DHCP server computers to the built-in group DnsUpdateProxy group. This grants the secure rights required so that your DHCP servers will perform updates by proxy for any DHCP clients. Upgrading the NT computers would work, but that option was not mentioned in the scenario.

12. B, C. Configuring the server as a root server and leaving forwarding off means that the server will either answer a query (for addresses it knows) or return a failure (for addresses it doesn't know). Answer A is valid in the real world, but it is not a requirement of the question.

13. C. Most e-mail servers can be configured to reject incoming mail from servers whose IP addresses cannot be resolved with a reverse lookup.

14. D. The root name server has authority for the root domain and will reply with the IP address of a name server for the GOV top-level domain.

15. C. From the Monitoring tab of a DNS server's Properties page, you can perform simple and recursive queries in order to see if DNS servers are running and listening to queries. You can either run the tests immediately or set a schedule on which the tests will run.

Planning a WINS Strategy

MICROSOFT EXAM OBJECTIVES COVERED IN THIS CHAPTER:

- ✓ **Plan a NetBIOS name resolution strategy.**
  - Plan a WINS replication strategy.
  - Plan NetBIOS name resolution by using the Lmhosts file.
- ✓ **Troubleshoot host name resolution.**
  - Diagnose and resolve issues related to client computer configuration.

In earlier versions of Microsoft's operating systems, NetBIOS names were used as the means of identifying computers and other resources on the network. NetBIOS names are "friendly" computer names such as SalesSrv1. A computer that needed to communicate with SalesSrv1 would send a broadcast to all nodes on the network, requesting a response from SalesSrv1. The NetBIOS naming protocol was originally designed for small, non-routed networks using the NetBEUI network protocol. Therefore, there was no need for a separate service to map NetBIOS computer names to IP addresses.

However, this method of NetBIOS name resolution creates problems in larger, subnetted networks because NetBEUI traffic is not routable and because the broadcasts generated have a significant impact on performance. Broadcasts will not pass through a router and will, therefore, not hit any clients on the other subnets.

The LMHOSTS file could be used for NetBIOS name resolution, but it is not compatible with DHCP, and the process of manually editing this file with every computer name-to-IP address listing is costly in terms of administrative effort and the potential for human error.

WINS was created to support NetBIOS traffic over the TCP/IP network protocol (NetBT) and provide a distributed server solution for NetBIOS name resolution.

The Windows Internet Name Service (WINS) uses a distributed database to register dynamic mappings of NetBIOS computer names to IP addresses. Network traffic is made more efficient because local broadcasts are no longer necessary—systems can be located through registrations with the local WINS server. Each time a client joins or leaves the network, it registers automatically in the WINS database. It is commonly implemented together with DHCP to allow for dynamic updates of address configuration changes.

In some modern Windows networks, name resolution services can be handled exclusively by DNS, but if your network has legacy clients (earlier than Windows 2000) or servers (NT 4 or earlier), or it runs services that require NetBIOS name resolution, such as Microsoft Exchange for e-mail services or uses applications that use NetBIOS computer names, you'll need to know how to implement a WINS strategy for NetBIOS name resolution.

In this chapter, you'll learn when and why you'll need to use WINS, how it works, how to plan a strategy for WINS implementation, how to monitor WINS, how to configure inter-forest replication, and how to troubleshoot WINS.

Understanding NetBIOS Name Resolution

NetBIOS works by broadcasting information about network resources, such as which shares a server offers. You learned in the introduction to this chapter that standard NetBIOS broadcasts are fine for small, non-routed networks—for instance, a boutique design office with only five computers on a peer-to-peer network. Most organizations, however, require a more scalable solution.

Microsoft solved the routability problem by offering *NetBIOS over TCP/IP (NBT)*. In the past, you could use NBT on your network without a WINS server, but the *Windows Internet Name Service (WINS)* solves the very important problem of broadcast traffic. In the absence of a WINS server, NBT broadcasts were transmitted to every node on the network. WINS clients, however, have no need to broadcast NBT information; therefore, the load on your network is significantly reduced. A WINS server is also known as a *NetBIOS name server (NBNS)* because it resolves NetBIOS names on behalf of network clients.

WINS is an advanced method of NetBIOS name resolution, but it is being phased out along with the older Microsoft operating systems. If your network has only a few clients that are running operating systems earlier than Windows 2000, and no NetBIOS-aware applications (such as Exchange Server or SQL Server), you may actually benefit by implementing a more ancient method for NetBIOS name resolution (LMHOSTS) instead of WINS.

In the following sections, we'll take a closer look at how WINS name recognition works.

How Name Resolution Works

Recall the process of DNS name resolution that was discussed in Chapter 4, "Planning a DNS Strategy." When a TCP/IP-based application needs an address, it calls the resolver, which uses the DNS query mechanism to obtain an IP address. The application then uses the address to open a communication channel. Like DNS, which maps host names to IP addresses in TCP/IP networks, WINS maps NetBIOS computer names to IP addresses in networks using Microsoft operating systems. This service works in three simple steps as follows:

1. Each time a WINS client (e.g., a machine that's been given the address of a WINS server) starts up, it registers its NetBIOS name and IP address with the WINS server.
2. When a WINS client wants to talk to another computer, the resulting NBT name query is sent directly to the WINS server instead of being broadcast across the local network.
3. If the WINS server finds the destination host's NetBIOS name and IP address in its database, it returns this information directly to the WINS client. If it doesn't, the WINS server can then make a standard NBT broadcast (if necessary) to hunt down the necessary address.

For Windows 2000, Windows 2003 Server, and XP clients, when a client tries to access a network resource by using a NetBIOS-based application, the name resolution process follows these steps by default:

1. It verifies that the name is a valid NetBIOS name. If the name is longer than 15 characters or if it contains periods (.), then it queries DNS for the name.
2. It checks the local client's NetBIOS name cache.
3. It attempts to resolve the name using any configured WINS servers. If resolved, it returns the IP address to the client. If not resolved, it goes to Step 4.
4. It makes local IP broadcasts to the subnet.
5. It parses the complete local LMHOSTS file to look for a name-to-IP match if Enable LMHOSTS Lookup is enabled in the TCP/IP properties for this connection (which is on by default).

6. It checks a local HOSTS file.
7. It queries a DNS server.

Because the WINS server receives updates from each WINS client as it starts up, its database entries reflect the current state of the network. You should set up multiple WINS servers on a network so that WINS traffic is distributed; the servers can replicate their database entries according to the method and schedule you specify. This ensures that each server contains entries for all the clients on the network and a client can resolve computer name-to-IP addresses in the event of a WINS server failure.

The NetBIOS node type describes the methods used and the order of methods used in client attempts to resolve NetBIOS names. The WINS default mode is *h-node*. The default procedure for name resolution just described is used for the h-node type of client node. The techniques a client uses for NetBIOS name resolution can be changed by specifying a different NetBIOS node type, such as *p-node*, *b-node*, or *m-node*. Node types are described in Table 5.1.

TABLE 5.1 NetBIOS Node Types

Node Type	Name Resolution Method(s)
b-node	Uses broadcast NetBIOS name queries
p-node	Uses direct queries to an NBNS
m-node	Uses b-node plus p-node methods in order
h-node	Uses p-node plus b-node methods in order

WINS in Windows Server 2003

The WINS implementation in Windows Server 2003 is largely unchanged from what Microsoft shipped with Windows NT 4. The biggest changes relate to the integration of WINS with DNS and Active Directory in Windows 2000 Server and higher.

WINS is now integrated with DNS, which means that DNS-capable clients such as Web browsers can transparently take advantage of WINS resolution (provided you've turned on this integration). This allows you to retrieve a Web page, or other resource, from a machine when all you know is its NetBIOS name. The client application uses the resolver, which makes a DNS query; the DNS server can ask the WINS server for the address after it fails to find it in its local zone. The DNS server strips the domain name off of the request, which leaves the computer name and then forwards it to WINS for resolution.

New to Windows Server 2003 are advanced database search and filtering capabilities, which help you analyze very large WINS databases, and enhanced control over replication. You can define a list used during pull replication to control incoming name records by source. This ability allows you to block name records from specific replication partners or to accept only name records owned by specific WINS servers during replication. This will help you when you're planning the replication strategy for your company.

The WINS Process

When a WINS client starts, the client exchanges WINS messages with its designated WINS server. Each client can actually hold addresses for a *primary WINS server* and a *secondary WINS server*; the secondary will be used if the primary doesn't answer. In Windows Server 2003, you can configure up to 12 WINS servers for added fault tolerance.

The intent of the message exchange is to allow the client to register its address with the server, without allowing name or address duplication. This message exchange includes four processes: *name registration*, *name renewal*, *name release*, and *name resolution*. Each of these processes will be explained in the next section.

An easy way to recall the processes of the WINS message exchange is by thinking of the *Four Rs*: name **R**egistration, name **R**enewal, name **R**elease, and name **R**esolution (otherwise known as a query).

Name Registration

When a client joins a WINS-enabled network, it's required to register its name and IP address with its designated WINS server. When the WINS server receives a *name registration request*, it must evaluate it by asking two questions:

Is the name unique? Duplicate names are not allowed, because they make it impossible to tell which computer *really* has a particular name—the computer equivalent of cloning. If the WINS server receives a request to register a name that already exists in the database, the WINS server sends a challenge to the currently registered owner of the disputed name. The challenge message is repeated three times, at 500-millisecond (half-second) intervals—less if the server receives a reply. If the current owner of the name responds (saying, in effect, "Hey, that's still my name!"), the WINS server rejects the new request by sending a negative name request back to the machine attempting to claim the already-in-use NetBIOS name. If the currently registered owner *doesn't* reply, then the name is deleted from the database, and a positive acknowledgment is sent to the requesting machine.

When the client is a multihomed system, the WINS server sends challenge and confirmation messages to each of the client's IP addresses in sequence, until the server either receives a reply or tries each address three times.

Is the name valid? NetBIOS names have restrictions: Their length must be 15 or fewer characters, and they can't contain certain characters, such as the period. The WINS server will reject any registration request for an invalid name.

Assuming the WINS server receives a request for a unique, valid name, it registers the name in its database and returns a message confirming the registration. This confirmation includes a time to live (TTL) for the WINS record; this TTL functions exactly the same as the TTL on a DNS record.

If the client sends a request to its primary WINS server and never receives an answer back, the client tries again. After three tries, the client will make three attempts to contact the secondary WINS server, if one is configured. If that fails, too, the client attempts to contact additional WINS servers if they are defined. Failing all of the above efforts, the client will attempt to register its name by sending an NBT broadcast.

Name Renewal

WINS clients must renew their names with the server at periodic intervals. With WINS, the client must notify the server that it wants to continue using its registered name so that the server will reset the TTL.

When the TTL has reached 50 percent of its original value, the WINS client sends a name renewal message to the primary WINS server. This message contains the client's name, the source, and the destination IP addresses for the client and the server. If there's no response, the message will be resent once more when one-eighth of the original TTL remains. If there's *still* no response from the primary server, the client will then attempt renewal through the secondary WINS server—if one is configured. If the effort is successful, the WINS client will attempt to register with the secondary server as though it was the first attempt. If, after three attempts, the WINS client fails to contact the secondary WINS server, it continues to try any additional WINS servers for which it is configured, and failing these, it will restart the process with the primary server.

Once successful contact is made, the WINS server will respond by sending the client a new TTL period. This process will continue as long as the client computer is powered on and as long as it remains a WINS client.

Name Release

A WINS client can relinquish ownership of its name at any time by sending a name release message, which contains its IP address and name. However, this is most often done when the client machine is cleanly shut down. When the server receives a name release message, it deletes the client's information from its database and returns a positive release message composed of the released name and a new TTL of zero to the client. At this point, the client will stop responding to its former NetBIOS name.

If the IP address and name sent by the client don't match the WINS database, the WINS server will return a negative release message. If the client doesn't get either a positive or negative release message, it will send up to three b-node broadcasts notifying all other systems, including non-WINS clients, to remove the now invalid name from their NetBIOS name caches.

Name Resolution

So far, you've learned about the communications only between a WINS-enabled computer and a WINS server. For regular network clients that obtain information from the WINS database, the client should try to exhaust other methods of resolution before it resorts to blasting network broadcasts (although, as you'll see, the process works a little differently in practice).

Here's how the process works, assuming you're trying to map a network drive on a server named DELTA:

1. You type **`net use g: \\delta\public`** into a command-line window.
2. NBT will check the system's local name cache to see if it already has an IP address on file for DELTA. If the name is found in the cache, the Address Resolution Protocol (ARP) will then be used to turn the name into a hardware address (known as a physical or MAC address). This deftly avoids adding unnecessary traffic on the network.

3. If the name isn't in the local cache, the name query goes directly to the primary WINS server. If the primary server is available, and the name is found in its database, the IP address is returned to the requestor, where it's added into the local cache. If the server fails to respond, the request is repeated twice before the client switches to the secondary WINS server and starts over. This process is repeated for all configured WINS servers.
4. If none of the WINS servers configured for the client can resolve the name, the client will resort to making a broadcast. If another node returns an address for the requested name, it goes into the local cache.
5. If the broadcast fails to generate a useful answer, NBT will search the LMHOSTS file for an answer. If that fails, NBT will then check the HOSTS file and, finally, DNS. If none of these works, the request fails.

The WINS Database

A WINS client registers names for itself and for the services that it hosts. The first 15 characters are user-specified, and the 16th character is a value from 00 to FF hex, which indicates the resource type. Group names can also be registered by multiple computers. WINS records are stored in the *WINS database*, which in the Windows Server 2003 family uses the same Extensible Storage Engine technology used in Active Directory. Therefore, the WINS database is self-maintaining, although there are administrative activities you can and should perform on the database. Administrative tasks include verifying the database for consistency, changing the database path, backing up and restoring the database, and scavenging the database. Note that consistency checking is resource- and network-intensive, so it should be performed during off-peak hours. WINS database administration will be covered later in the chapter.

Resetting the local system clock can adversely affect WINS performance, and it could compromise the integrity of the WINS database, because the replication and scavenging algorithms used rely on a reasonably consistent system clock.

Supporting Non-WINS Clients

Older Microsoft clients that predate the introduction of WINS need to use a different method for NetBIOS name resolution. These clients include Microsoft Windows 3.1 and Windows for Workgroups, and as b-nodes, they must rely on NBT broadcasts, the LMHOSTS file, or the WINS proxy agent to resolve NetBIOS names.

You can provide WINS services to clients that are not WINS-capable with one of the features included with the Windows Server 2003 WINS service. *Static mapping* enables you to manually enter IP addresses and NetBIOS names, just as you would manually create host records in DNS. This enables WINS clients to reach the non-WINS computers. You can also install and configure the WINS proxy agent, which listens for NBT broadcasts and forwards them on to a WINS server. This enables non-WINS clients to send standard NBT broadcasts, which are transparently intercepted and resolved by the WINS server.

We will look at both static mapping and the proxy agent in the following sections.

Using Static Mappings

You can create static name-to-IP address mappings for each non-WINS node on your NetBIOS-enabled network. This ensures that WINS clients can access the non-WINS computers by a "friendly" computer name.

One reason you might use static WINS entries is to make sure a mission-critical server cannot have its name usurped by another computer while the server is offline. Servers running a non-Microsoft operating system could be given a static WINS mapping, although you would most likely use DNS instead. You may want to support a temporary change on your network while you are in the process of migrating, in which case you'd leave the default setting of Overwrite Unique Static Mappings At This Server (Migrate On) active in the replication partner properties. In this way, later attempts to dynamically register a name entry will result in a challenge process. If the challenge is successful, the entry will change from static to dynamic. This feature is particularly useful for migrating records for older non-WINS clients that cannot dynamically register themselves. Therefore, it helps to simplify the update of legacy NetBIOS b-node (broadcast-only) type clients that are later upgraded to support WINS.

Static mappings add administrative hassle, so you will want to use them only for mission-critical servers and very specific objectives. If you use static mappings, it's best to configure corresponding reservations in DHCP. If the IP address or computer name changes later, you'll probably have to update other settings manually in DHCP and DNS, as well as on the actual computer.

Creating static mappings is simple. In the WINS console, expand the server and right-click the Active Registrations node. Select the New Static Mapping command, enter the name and IP address that you want to configure, and click OK. The static mapping will appear in the Active Registrations window.

You can easily import an existing LMHOSTS file to automatically create static mappings via the Import LMHOSTS File option on the Action menu of the WINS console.

There are many other administrative functions that you can perform through the WINS console. The console is launched by selecting Start ➤ Administrative Tools ➤ WINS and is pictured in Figure 5.1.

FIGURE 5.1 The WINS console

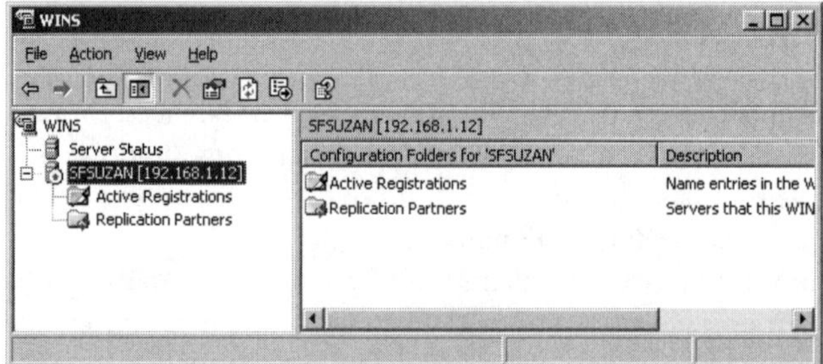

Never add static mappings for WINS-capable computers. This will create added administrative work to migrate, delete, or tombstone the mappings for WINS replication.

The WINS Proxy Agent

Non-WINS clients can still use WINS indirectly to register and resolve NetBIOS names. A WINS proxy is simply a WINS client computer configured to run the *WINS proxy agent*, which listens for NetBIOS broadcast queries and attempts to register and resolve names on behalf of b-node network clients. If the proxy agent receives a name registration request, it forwards the request to the WINS server, which then verifies the name. (It does not actually register the name in its database; you must use static mappings for non-WINS clients.) If the proxy agent receives a name query request, it searches its cache for the name. If the proxy agent cannot locate the name in its cache, it forwards the request to the WINS server.

You can configure the WINS proxy agent only on a WINS client computer. To enable the proxy agent, you must change the value of the `HKEY_LOCAL_MACHINE\SYSTEM\CurrentControlSet\Services\NetBT\Parameters\EnableProxy` key in the client's Registry from a `0` to a `1`. Only one WINS proxy should be configured per subnet to avoid overloading the WINS servers on that subnet.

Real World Scenario

Using Non-WINS Methods Of NetBIOS Name Resolution

As the systems engineer in an enterprise with a heterogeneous client environment, you want to make sure all the clients can access resources on the network. Although you have implemented a WINS strategy for NetBIOS name resolution, you know that some of the older clients are running Windows for Workgroups and are not WINS-capable. Therefore, you need to figure out a way to provide WINS services to these clients. In addition, you want to enable NetBIOS-capable clients to access resources on Unix servers by "friendly" computer names using NetBIOS-aware applications. You have created a number of scripts in which you need to be able to map drives to the Unix servers using the `net use` command.

What services can you implement in Windows Server 2003 to meet these objectives?

For the first part of your objective, you can configure the WINS proxy agent on one of the WINS client computers. The proxy agent will then listen for NetBIOS broadcasts and forward them to the WINS server as needed. The Windows for Workgroups clients can attempt to resolve NetBIOS names the old-fashioned way—by sending NBT broadcasts on the local network. The proxy agent will intercede on behalf of its older peer to ensure that the registration or query is answered.

For the second part of your objective, you can do one of two things. You can create a static mapping in WINS for each of the Unix servers, so that clients can refer to the Unix servers using a "friendly," Microsoft-style NetBIOS name. This name will be transparently resolved to the IP address, just as if the servers were running Microsoft operating systems.

If only a few clients need to reference the Unix servers, you could use the LMHOSTS file on the client to create a NetBIOS name-to-IP address mapping. Assuming the file exists, the clients will automatically check for an entry in LMHOSTS by default during the name resolution process.

Using LMHOSTS as an Alternative to WINS

LMHOSTS stands for "Lan Manager hosts," and the LMHOSTS file is the static alternative to WINS—just as the HOSTS file is the static alternative to DNS. The LMHOSTS file can provide NetBIOS name resolution for small networks that do not have a WINS server. If WINS is in use, LMHOSTS can also be used to support subnets without a WINS server, as well as for backup in case the WINS server is unavailable. LMHOSTS is usually used for file and print services, but it can also be used to locate domain controllers.

If a client is not configured to use WINS, then by default it is configured as a b-node, which is a computer that uses IP broadcasts for NetBIOS name resolution. However, this traffic is both chatty and nonroutable, so an alternative is to use a local LMHOSTS file to map NetBIOS names to IP addresses. Recall from earlier in the chapter that a local client's name cache is checked before an IP broadcast is sent in an attempt to resolve a name. Failing both, the entire LMHOSTS file is parsed in an attempt to find a name-to-IP match. This strategy enables LMHOSTS to hold a large number of mappings without requiring an equally large chunk of static memory to hold an infrequently used cache.

To use an LMHOSTS file for name resolution, create a file named `LMHOSTS` (with no extension) in the `\Windows\System32\drivers\etc` folder on Windows NT, NT Workstation, 2000, XP, or 2003 computers. On Windows 9*x* and older clients, the file is in the root `Windows` folder. The `LMHOSTS.sam` file is provided as a sample file. You can save a copy of this file as **`LMHOSTS`**, and edit it to your needs.

You edit the file with any text editor such as Notepad or Edit.com. Note that the LMHOSTS file uses very specific syntax and must be properly formatted. It requires a hard carriage return at the end of each line, as well as three to four carriage returns at the end of the file. The pound sign (#) is usually used to indicate a comment. However, in LMHOSTS (and its DNS-related equivalent, HOSTS), it is also used to designate a special keyword, which we'll discuss in just a moment. Also, if you use Notepad to edit the file, make sure you do not save it as Unicode.

You enable LMHOSTS lookup in the Advanced TCP/IP Setting dialog box, via the Enable LMHOSTS Lookup checkbox on the WINS tab (as shown in Figure 5.2). Once you enable LMHOSTS lookup (enabled by default on a Windows 2003 Server) for any TCP/IP connection, it is enabled for all connections using TCP/IP. Also note that you can import an LMHOSTS file here.

Importing an LMHOSTS file is similar to using a `#INCLUDE` statement (which we'll discuss in a moment) within LMHOSTS to point to a centralized LMHOSTS file. In the latter case, the computer on which the file is located must include the Registry entry `NullSession-Shares` for the LMHOSTS location. `NullSessionShares` is in the following Registry subkey:

```
HKEY_LOCAL_MACHINE\SYSTEM\CurrentControlSet\Services\lanmanserver\parameters
```

You load the contents of an LMHOSTS file into the NetBIOS Remote Cache Name Table using the `nbtstat -R` command, and then you view the entries using the `nbtstat -c` command.

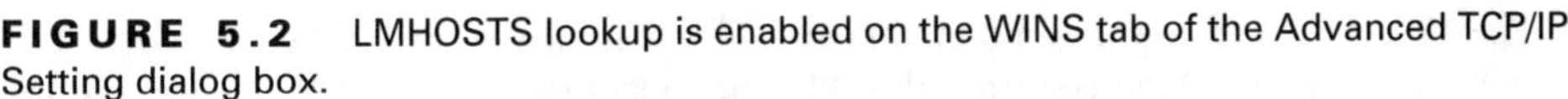

FIGURE 5.2 LMHOSTS lookup is enabled on the WINS tab of the Advanced TCP/IP Setting dialog box.

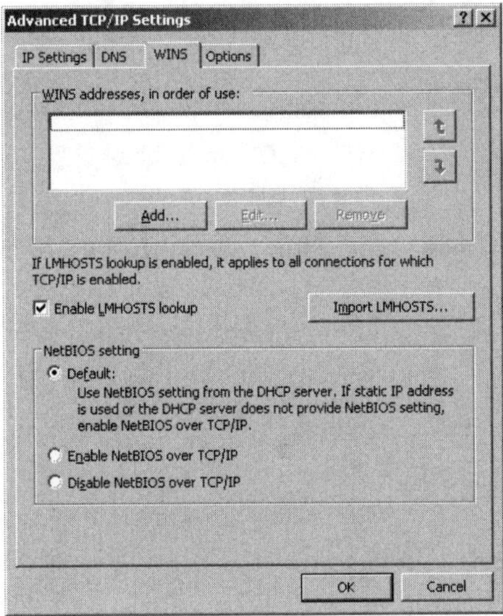

Microsoft includes a sample copy of the LMHOSTS file, called `LMHOSTS.sam` and located in Windows\system32\drivers\etc. The sample file includes useful tutorial information and examples that explain how the statements function:

This file follows a very specific format. For example, extra carriage returns appear at the end of the file. This is important in order for the file to be parsed correctly. If the last couple of entries in your LMHOSTS file are not being loaded, the most probable cause is that there are no added carriage returns, so the file is assumed to end earlier.

There are several keywords, also called extensions, that perform special functions in this file. We'll discuss each one in turn.

#PRE The `#PRE` keyword causes a NetBIOS name-to-IP address mapping entry to be preloaded into the name cache. Remember that by default, entries are not preloaded into the name cache; they are only parsed if WINS and name query broadcasts fail. If you use `#INCLUDE` statements, you must preload these entries or they will be ignored.

#INCLUDE *file name* The `#INCLUDE` *`file name`* statement forces the system to find the file specified by the filename and parse it as part of the local LMHOSTS file. Usually, the filename is specified as a UNC name, and it can include servers on remote subnets. If the server is on a remote subnet, it is necessary to reference it prior to the `#INCLUDE` statement so that the server can be located, because a local broadcast wouldn't work. Don't reference files by mapped drive letters, because different clients have different login scripts and drive mappings can change.

#BEGIN_ ALTERNATE/#END_ALTERNATE The `#BEGIN_ ALTERNATE` and `#END_ALTERNATE` keywords allow multiple `#INCLUDE` statements to be grouped together. This is known as a block inclusion, which allows multiple servers to be searched for a valid copy of the LMHOSTS file.

#DOM The #DOM keyword specifies a domain controller. Usually, you would name more than one. If you want to preload these entries, the #PRE tag must precede the #DOM tag. Here is the format:

```
102.54.94.97      rhino            #PRE #DOM:domain_name
```

#MH The #MH keyword specifies a multihomed entry and follows this format:

```
102.54.94.95      zebra            #MH #NIC1 on zebra
102.54.94.96      zebra            #MH #NIC2 on zebra
```

#SG The #SG keyword specifies a user-defined special group (for example, network-attached printers or print servers). Use this format:

```
102.54.94.94      printsrv1            #SG:printservers #Print↵
                                       server for accounting
```

Listing 5.1 shows an edited version of the LMHOSTS.sam file.

Listing 5.1: The Edited LMHOSTS File

```
102.54.94.97      rhino          #PRE #DOM:networking  #net group's DC
102.54.94.102     "appname  \0x14"                     #special app server
102.54.94.123     popular              #PRE            #source server
102.54.94.117     localsrv             #PRE            #needed for the
#                                                      include
#
#BEGIN_ALTERNATE
#INCLUDE \\localsrv\public\lmhosts
#INCLUDE \\rhino\public\lmhosts
#END_ALTERNATE
```

Notice that all unnecessary comment text has been removed. The entries are uncommented by removing the "# " (the pound symbol plus white space). The servers rhino and localsrv must be preloaded because they are featured in #INCLUDE statements as centralized sources where clients can locate an LMHOSTS file. The server rhino is also listed as a domain controller—again, with the #PRE tag preceding #DOM. It is listed first because it is more critical than the other servers listed. The server "appname \0x14" is listed in quotes because it contains both a space and a special, nonprinting character. Comments follow each entry prior to the carriage return. A block inclusion is used so that two different possible locations for a centralized LMHOSTS file can be searched.

You should be aware of some special requirements and other considerations for LMHOSTS:

- Do not add LMHOSTS entries for regular DHCP clients, which have dynamic (and therefore volatile) IP address assignments. Clients that hold permanent IP address reservations would be the exception.
- Because LMHOSTS files are searched one line at a time starting from the beginning, list remote computers accessed most frequently at the top of the file, followed by remote systems that will be listed in #INCLUDE statements.

- Use the #PRE entries to preload frequently accessed workstations and servers into the local computer's name cache, as well as to define servers listed in the #INCLUDE statements. The #PRE keyword entries go at the end of the file. These entries will be preloaded into the cache at system initialization, and they are not accessed later. Placing them at the end makes searches faster in the event that WINS queries and local broadcasts fail, and the entire LMHOSTS file needs to be parsed. Preloaded entries are limited to 100 by default.
- Note that comment text increases the time it takes to parse the file. Ideally, you'll want a very clean file of perhaps just a few entries and very minimal text comments to identify the entries.
- When names are resolved successfully, they will remain in the name cache for 600 seconds. The `nbtstat` command can remove or correct preloaded entries or any other names cached by a successful broadcast resolution. Run `nbtstat -R` to purge and reload the name cache, including any LMHOSTS entries tagged with the #PRE keyword.

Now that you've seen the added administrative hassle of using LMHOSTS files for NetBIOS name resolution, you may just choose to implement WINS to make things easier. That's entirely understandable, and the next section will explain how to keep your WINS databases in synch throughout your organization.

Introducing WINS Replication

Replication is a service that makes the WINS data stored on your servers more useful by making it available across subnets. Consider a network with two subnets and one WINS server on each. Normally, each WINS server will collect name resolution information about the hosts on its subnet; with the proper use of the WINS proxy agent, each subnet can query the other subnet's WINS server for names on that subnet. However, that's an inefficient solution because all queries from one subnet for hosts on the other must travel to the other subnet.

Replicating WINS registrations from one server to another provides a way around this problem. Because the registrations are duplicated on both servers, a host on one subnet can get the IP address for a host on the other subnet without having to actually send a resolution request to the other subnet.

For replication to work properly, a couple of additional subtleties must be considered. First, consider the concept of *convergence time*. In IP routing, *convergence* refers to the state in which every router knows about all of its peers. *Convergence* has a similar meaning in WINS. In a network with more than one WINS server, the convergence time for that network is the time it takes a change from any server to propagate to all other servers on that network. You might expect that a very short convergence time would be desirable, but actually the opposite is true. Short convergence times mean that almost every change will be replicated on all servers. WINS registrations are in constant flux, because machines release their reservations when they shut down or reboot. Longer convergence times, therefore, reduce overall replication loads by not replicating changes—like name releases—that will frequently be rendered obsolete before the convergence interval has been reached.

WINS releases don't necessarily occur every time a client disjoins from the network. Because they occur at normal shutdown, an abnormal shutdown will leave a dangling registration. Eventually, the server will purge this record, but a WINS registration doesn't carry the same authority as, say, a DNS or DHCP record.

WINS replication is established by creating push and pull replication partnerships to perform data replication. These concepts are explained in the following sections.

Push and Pull Partners

The relationship between two servers that replicate data back and forth is described as a partnership, and the servers are called *replication partners*. A single server can be involved with any number of replication partners; in fact, in large networks it's common for a single server to replicate to most of its peers.

WINS servers use two different types of replication partners: *pull partners* and *push partners*. Both provide the same result: Data from one server is copied to another. They're always paired, so that in any partnership one server pulls while the other pushes. However, the method of initiating the replication differs, and you can set different values for the parameters that govern when and how replication works for each set of partners.

A push replication partner pushes, or sends, update notification messages to its partners when the database changes. This exchange happens when the WINS server starts. You can configure it to take place when a registered client's IP address changes or when a certain number of replicated changes have arrived from other partners. This notification message is called a *push replication trigger*, and it signals the receiving server to request the changed data.

A pull partner pulls, or fetches, the database entries from its replication partner. This is accomplished by sending a request for entries with a version number higher than that of the last entry it received during the last replication with that partner. This message is called a *pull replication trigger*. When the partner receives this request, it sends back the requested data. A pull trigger can be sent either on its own or in response to a push trigger received from a partner. Pull requests are sent to a server's partners when the server starts and when the specified replication interval expires. You can also manually send a pull replication trigger to a partner at any time, as you'll see in a bit.

Push/pull partnerships are often used when you want to "pair up" servers in even groups across a high-speed LAN connection.

Establishing Replication Partnerships

Most replication partners should be configured in push/pull partnerships. Primary and backup WINS servers must be push/pull partners of each other to maintain database consistency.

Pairing servers to replicate WINS data can be accomplished using different methods. One way is to use automatic partner configuration, a feature that allows one server to seek out and link up with other WINS servers on the network. This feature works because each WINS server announces itself via periodic multicasts. When an unattached server hears a multicast call from another server, it adds the IP address of the announcing server to its list of replication partners, adding it both as a push and a pull partner of itself. It then configures pull replication at two-hour intervals. Although this process is useful, it's also temporary; automatic partnerships dissolve when either server in the pair is restarted.

You can also manually establish partnerships. Once you link two servers as replication partners, they stick together until you break up the partnership. Strategies for replication partnerships are covered in detail later in this chapter.

Best practices indicate that you should use automatic configuration of WINS replication whenever possible, particularly in small networks with three or fewer WINS servers.

Data Replication

WINS data is replicated at the record level. This means that as individual records are updated, they can be replicated, but the entire database won't be replicated. Each change to a record held by a server causes that server to increment an internal record called a *version ID*. When a replication partner asks "What's new?", it's really asking whether the partner's version ID is higher than the one it already has.

Servers know which version IDs belong to which servers because each WINS server maintains a table called the *owner-version mapping table* that keeps track of which WINS server owns (or holds) a particular registration, along with the highest version ID received from that server. When one server sends another a replication trigger, the sending server includes a copy of its owner-version mapping table; this allows the receiving server to determine what the sending server "knows" about the state of the WINS databases.

Designing a WINS Strategy

The WINS strategy you implement should be a good compromise between high availability of WINS services—which calls for redundant WINS servers—and high performance in a WINS replication architecture—which calls for the minimum number of WINS servers that will meet your needs.

You should consider a number of availability and performance optimization factors before you implement WINS in your network. You must determine the ideal number of WINS servers, plan replication partnerships, optimize replication traffic across subnets and WAN links, and plan for high availability and fault tolerance. In addition, you must make special considerations for mobile users. These topics, along with sample scenarios to help you better understand the concepts of designing a WINS infrastructure, are discussed next.

Determining How Many WINS Servers to Install

Processing overhead for WINS services is relatively low. A single WINS server can service up to 10,000 clients. A good conservative estimate is to plan for one primary and one backup WINS server for every 10,000 computers on the network. The factors that could prompt you to add WINS servers are the location of routers and subnets in your network, where clients are located within subnets, and the need for fault tolerance. You will also want to plan for additional WINS servers for locations separated by slow WAN links.

You can achieve fault tolerance by configuring a secondary WINS server. Depending on your needs, you can choose to configure up to 12 WINS servers for a client. If you choose two servers, you can easily set them up as replication partners of each other, naming one server as a pull partner and the other as a push partner. After you do so, you can set automatic replication by selecting the checkbox Enable Automatic Partner Configuration on the Advanced tab of the Replication Partners Properties dialog box.

Each WINS server can handle hundreds of requests per second. The actual number of users that can be supported will vary depending on actual patterns of usage and the capabilities of the WINS server. When you plan your solution, you should do so with a worst-case scenario in mind. For instance, plan the number and hardware capabilities of backup servers to meet requirements in the event of a large-scale power outage, after which the WINS server(s) will be inundated with client requests.

In an enterprise internetwork, you may realize a significant performance improvement by upgrading the server hardware and by making it a dedicated WINS server. WINS servers in large networks can benefit from enhancements to processor speed, RAM, disk space, and network throughput. The data records that are actually exchanged between servers and clients are small—about 40 bytes per record.

In large networks with heavy WINS traffic, one way to increase performance by up to 25 percent is to use a dual processor server. You might also use a dedicated disk drive for the WINS database, on a high-performance drive apart from the system drive or on a RAID array. Because of the heavy disk I/O inherent in a database application, WINS is a disk-intensive service. By default, the database is in `Windows\System32\Wins`, but you can change that path from within the WINS console.

A Pentium II 400MHz computer with 128MB of RAM running as a dedicated WINS server should be able to handle about 300 registration requests and 350 queries per second.

You can tune server performance by adjusting the *renew interval*, which is the amount of time that elapses between a client's initial registration and subsequent renewal of that registration. Increasing the interval will reduce the total number of registrations and, therefore, enhance server response time. Renewal intervals can be adjusted in the WINS console by right-clicking the server's name, selecting Properties, and selecting the Intervals tab. The performance of WINS servers may also be affected by other network traffic. For instance, if the WINS server is located across a router, all WINS-related traffic must go through the router queues. This can cause delays during periods of peak network traffic and, therefore, impact the ideal number and location of WINS servers in the network infrastructure.

Planning for Availability and Fault Tolerance

You've seen the value of adding a secondary WINS server as a backup for each primary WINS server. For each server on your network, you need to consider what will happen to WINS services on the network if that server is unavailable or unreachable.

You will want to plan redundancy to protect you in the event of hardware or power failures that could bring the server down and also to protect you if problems with a network link or router failure prevent clients from reaching the WINS server. Consider all possible points of failure, determine the maximum length of time a WINS server can be out of service on the network, and plan accordingly. Consider what happens to your WINS clients when the primary WINS server is unavailable.

Although processing requirements for WINS services are relatively low, redundant WINS servers are recommended. This redundancy will help, for instance, if you have a large network that experiences a power outage (resulting in a flood of WINS registration traffic as many WINS clients restart at the same time), or if a network link to one of the servers is faulty. Secondary WINS servers should be located on remote subnets, ideally in a separate building and on a separate power grid from the primary WINS server.

In a very large enterprise where high availability is key, you may choose to implement WINS in a clustered configuration using Windows Clustering. Corporate headquarters could feature a hub of clustered WINS servers with very high-speed disk arrays or a storage area network (SAN). This would enable immediate failover recovery, because the servers in the cluster use a common WINS database instead of needing to replicate among many WINS databases. This would also simplify the design for the purposes of replication to remote offices, which will become clear to you in the next few pages.

Clustering is discussed in Chapter 9, "Planning High Availability Services."

Securing the WINS Infrastructure

WINS replication frequently must occur over a public network, such as the Internet. This creates a huge security risk, which you can control by encrypting the replication traffic and by utilizing a perimeter network for WINS replication.

All WINS replication traffic sent over a public network must be encrypted for best security. You can use IPSec or a VPN tunnel. You will want to use the strongest possible level of encryption. In addition, you should implement a certificate-based authentication method.

To avoid exposing NetBIOS name-to-IP mappings, you can install a WINS server (for replication) in a perimeter network. Make sure you choose to replicate only with partners. (The option is on the Replication Partners Properties dialog box.) It is best to choose pull only replication from the intranet WINS servers. Again, make sure to encrypt all traffic across the inner firewall.

VPNs and IPSec are both covered in Chapter 6, "Planning Secure Network Access." Certificate Services is covered in Chapter 8, "Planning Certificate Services."

Monitoring WINS Client Traffic

WINS is great for reducing broadcast traffic between local subnets. However, it does generate traffic and you should consider the impact of WINS traffic types on routed networks when planning your strategy for WINS implementation. In addition, you should consider the impact of slower connections, such as WAN links, for both replication and WINS client traffic.

With baseline figures for existing WINS traffic, you'll be able to plan a WINS implementation that meets your current and future needs. You should start by monitoring network traffic generated under normal conditions between WINS clients and WINS servers. You can use Network Monitor to do this.

Using the Network Monitor utility is covered in Chapter 10, "Planning Network Monitoring, Remote Administration, and Recovery."

The following types of traffic are important to monitor:

- NetBIOS names that are commonly registered,
- Registration and renewal traffic resulting from the daily startup of clients, the movement of roving users and subsequent
- WINS traffic they generate when moving between subnets, and
- The effects of WAN links on replication and convergence time.

Especially for enterprise internetworks consisting of tens of thousands of computers, the heaviest WINS activity occurs at the beginning of the workday, as most of the clients are simultaneously booted up and initialized on the network. There are also special considerations for mobile users in routed networks.

WINS Client Traffic Generated at the Start of the Day

Different clients generate different amounts of WINS-related network traffic. When any WINS client joins the network, it submits a name registration request for its computer name. The request includes the user and domain names, as well as any additional NetBIOS-aware network client services running on the computer.

An XP client commonly registers more NetBIOS names than other WINS clients, because its initial name registration request often includes more information, such as File Server, Domain, the Replicator service, the Messenger service, the Computer Browser service, and names for additional network services as needed.

The `nbtstat -n` command is useful for calculating the total number of name registrations that a given client will need in order to predict WINS client traffic. `Nbtstat` is covered later in this chapter.

You know that an active client registration replicates to all pull partners and will eventually replicate to all WINS servers on the network. When the client is shut down at the close of the workday, it releases the name. The entire process starts fresh the next day, when the name, together with a new version ID, is reregistered. The new entry then replicates to all pull partners of the WINS server.

If you assume that this cycle repeats every day for every computer, then the total number of name registration entries that will be replicated on a given day will be approximately the number of computers starting each day times the number of NetBIOS names registered at each computer.

Considerations for Mobile Users in Routed Networks

As you've seen, the big performance hit will come at the beginning of the workday, when the largest number of name requests and the greatest amount of response traffic will be generated as computers start up for the day. This can cause delays during peak times.

Roving or mobile users also create extra name-challenge traffic as they relocate on different subnets with different primary WINS servers. This process generates name-challenge traffic.

When a mobile user reconnects on a different subnet, the computer sends a name registration request. (Let's assume the old name was replicated to the new WINS server before the move.) The server will then challenge the IP address as it is registered in its database, but it will get no reply. The server attempts the challenge a total of three times. All three attempts will fail. The new WINS server will update the name registration record in its database with the new IP address. Next, it will increment the version ID, which will prompt the need to replicate that entry to the other WINS servers.

You can see how this process generates a lot of WINS traffic. Consider the impact of mobile users on WINS traffic if you have many such users in your network.

Planning Replication Partnerships

The process of replication can be as simple as an automatically configured process between two standalone servers in a workgroup, or it can be as complicated as a multinational implementation with various replication schedules and partnerships configured on the basis of the underlying network infrastructure.

In smaller networks, enable automatic partner configuration to simplify setup and administration of WINS replication. Larger networks can be more complicated, requiring a strategy for replication across slow WAN links and even across untrusted Windows NT domains. Planning a replication topology to ensure a successful deployment of WINS across your organization is critical.

WINS server databases should be replicated often enough so that the failure or downtime of a single WINS server will not affect the reliability of the data on the others. Yet, you must ensure an appropriate time interval between replications so your network is not congested with unnecessary traffic. These issues are of particular importance when implementing WINS over a WAN. It's a trade-off: data consistency versus network throughput. You want to accomplish the ideal balance between the two, and this balance will differ depending on your organization's topology and needs.

We'll discuss the considerations in planning replication partnerships, and then you'll have an opportunity to see WINS replication scenarios for organizations with different needs.

Automatic Partnership Configuration

Each WINS server announces its presence on a network using periodic multicast announcements sent as Internet Group Management Protocol (IGMP) messages to the address `224.0.1.24`, which is the multicast group address reserved for WINS server use.

A WINS server using automatic partner configuration monitors multicast announcements from other WINS servers. Upon discovering another WINS server, it automatically adds the IP address for the new server to its list of replication partners. It configures the discovered server as a partner for both push and pull replication, and it configures pull replication at two-hour intervals. Automatic partnership configuration information is *not persistent*. This means that when WINS shuts down properly, this information is removed. To make the information persist, you have to manually set up the partnership.

Small networks, such as a single subnet LAN, can benefit from the simplicity and ease of automatic partnership configurations. You can use it in routed networks, too, by configuring routers to forward multicast traffic to the destination address `224.0.1.24`. This technique is only recommended for a small number of WINS servers, usually up to three, because of the added traffic generated by the multicast announcements.

Push-Only, Pull-Only, or Push-Pull

A number of factors should be considered when deciding whether to configure WINS servers in pull or push partnerships. You'll need to take into account how the servers are laid out at each site and the speed of the connections between partners. In addition, you'll also want to determine whether your organization needs to have updates distributed throughout the network immediately. You'll want to balance this need against the desired network performance, which will be affected adversely by heavy replication traffic.

Most of the time, push/pull replication is the simplest and most effective way to ensure full WINS replication between partners. The primary and secondary WINS servers for any given WINS client should be push/pull partners of each other so that WINS can continue to operate if the primary server fails.

In enterprise internetworks, *limited replication partnerships* (pull-only or push-only unidirectional partnerships) are the most effective choice for supporting replication over slow WAN links. WINS servers can be placed on either side of restricted-bandwidth links in order to reduce name query and registration traffic across these links. Keep in mind, though, that you are replacing WINS client/server traffic with WINS server replication traffic. In these scenarios, ensuring that every WINS server has at least one replication partner is important. In addition, you want to make sure that each unidirectional link (pull-only or push-only) is balanced by a unidirectional link somewhere else in the network that carries updates in the opposite direction. Avoid using limited replication partnerships except where needed to optimize replication traffic over slow WAN links.

Recall that a WINS server that is configured as a pull partner periodically queries the partner server to find out if there are any updates. Pull partnerships are useful in the following scenarios:

- Over a lower-speed WAN or on a LAN with heavy traffic
- When you want to reduce replication traffic by consolidating WINS database updates
- When you want to update the WINS database at scheduled intervals

A WINS server that is configured as a push/pull partner tells its partner when WINS updates are available. Push/pull partnerships are useful in these scenarios:

- Over a LAN or higher-speed WAN link
- When you're not concerned about the network traffic generated by frequent WINS replication updates
- When you want to keep WINS databases as closely in synch as possible

You should configure push/pull replication partners and avoid push-only or pull-only servers except where necessary to accommodate slow links.

LAN Replication

You'll encounter the same considerations when planning WINS replication for local area networks (LANs). Because you'll have faster network links to work with, you can increase the frequency of replication by optimizing certain push and pull parameters. You can decrease the Number Of Changes In Version ID Before Replication setting—for instance, by configuring a value from one to three changes in version ID before a push replication trigger is sent to the partner. You can also decrease the Replication interval settings to minutes instead of hours.

In a LAN, you'll want to configure WINS to use a persistent connection between the servers. (With a non-persistent connection, the standard update count threshold defaults to a minimum of 20, but you can specify a smaller value in a LAN.)

The replication schedule for the WINS server database should be frequent enough that a single WINS server failure will not affect the reliability of the information in the other WINS servers. However, you want to set the interval between replications high enough that it will not generate excessive traffic and interfere with network throughput. Again, Network Monitor can help you monitor and optimize the effects of these settings.

Figure 5.3 shows a simple LAN Replication Scenario.

FIGURE 5.3 A simple WINS replication scenario for a LAN

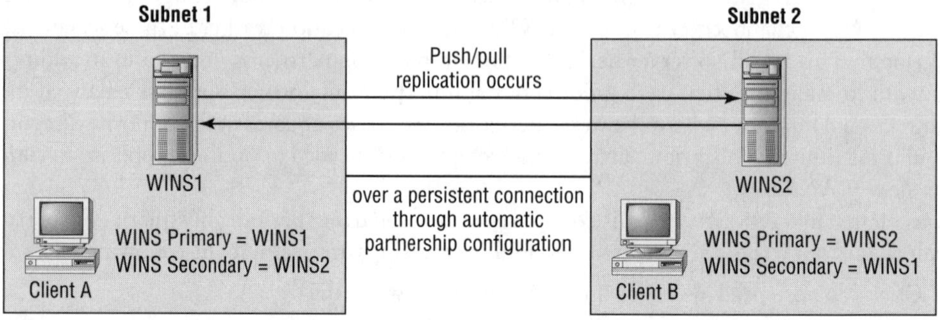

This example depicts two WINS servers on two separate subnets on the LAN. Clients on the first subnet use WINS1 as the primary WINS server and WINS2 as the secondary server; the opposite is true for clients on the second subnet. In any system design, you always want to point your clients to the closest physical resource servers (DHCP, DNS, and WINS). For WINS redundancy, point to a server on a remote subnet or network. Replication is configured automatically to result in a push/pull replication partnership.

WAN Replication

The replication strategy should map to your physical network, so that replication is optimized for the speed of the link between any given replication partners.

You have two critical considerations when you design a WINS replication strategy for wide area networks (WANs). First, you must consider the speed of the links connecting the networks together. Next, you need to consider convergence time. What is the total length of time required for all replicated changes to converge and, thereby, achieve consistency across the network?

A push/pull hub-and-spoke design using the default WINS configuration settings will usually result in the most effective strategy for WINS replication and convergence. In most cases, this model is a simple and effective design that achieves complete convergence with minimal administrative overhead. Organizations frequently have a centralized headquarters or a corporate data center (the hub) and several branch offices (the spokes). You can provide additional fault tolerance by adding a redundant hub. This can be as simple as adding a second WINS server at headquarters, or as complex as configuring a redundant hub at another physical site.

In a hub-and-spoke configuration, you can configure one WINS server as the hub and all of the other WINS servers as both push partners and pull partners of the hub. You can also configure certain servers as push-only or pull-only depending on the physical site topology.

Imagine that your network has multiple sites connected over slow WAN links. You could configure replication between servers on these links to occur less often than replication between partnered WINS servers on the LAN. Obviously, this will help reduce traffic on the slow links. Another advantage is that it reduces contention between replication traffic and WINS name query traffic.

You'll want to set replication intervals according to the proximity between servers and the availability of a high-speed link between replication partners. The network shown in Figure 5.4 illustrates such use of different replication intervals.

FIGURE 5.4 A WINS replication scenario for a WAN with different replication intervals

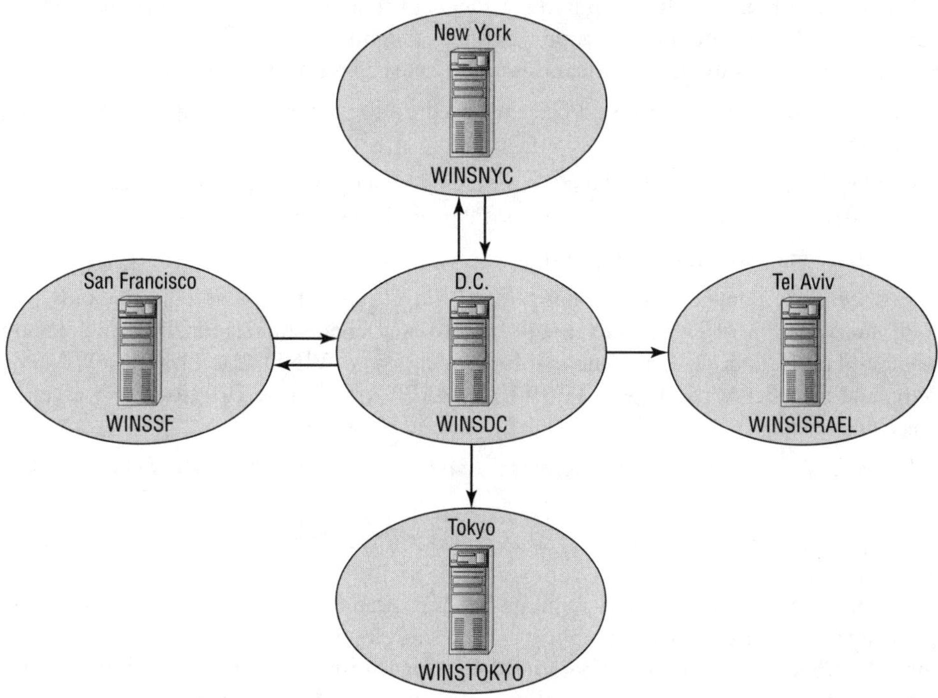

Here you see a replication topology involving three domestic WINS servers (in D.C., San Francisco, and New York) and two servers abroad (in Tokyo and Tel Aviv). The servers in D.C. and New York service large offices. D.C. is the headquarters, with 7,000 users, and the New York office has 1,500 users. The San Francisco office is a startup and currently services a modest regional sales force of 12 users. The offshore offices in Tokyo and Tel Aviv both function independently, providing design and development project services, respectively.

The domestic WINS servers are configured with push/pull partnerships, while the offshore WINS servers are configured as pull partners only. In addition, Tokyo and Tel Aviv are partnered only with D.C.

In this scenario, D.C. and New York are set to replicate once per hour, supported by the high-speed WAN infrastructure in place. Because San Franciso is such a small network, the company could have relied on NetBIOS broadcasts or even a local LMHOSTS implementation for local traffic. However, the company has positive expectations for exponential growth in a short period of time, so San Francisco gets its own WINS server. San Francisco is configured to replicate every three hours. Both Tokyo and Tel Aviv have very modest replication needs as well as exponentially slower WAN connections, so they are each configured at 12 hours.

To figure out the convergence time for the system, take the sum of the two longest convergence times to the hub. The longer the replication path, the longer the convergence time.

If a WINS client in New York, for example a server called NYCSERVER12, registers with WINSNYC, the amount of time required for clients in remote locations to query and find NYCSERVER12's current address mapping could be significant.

Here are the three ways that replications could be triggered from WINSNYC:

- A push replication trigger could be sent based on the frequency of updates made at WINSNYC.
- A pull replication trigger could be sent to other WINS servers based on the replication interval as configured in WINSNYC's Replication Partner Properties dialog box.
- You could manually force replication.

In this scenario, a new or updated name record on WINSNYC will be replicated only when the pull interval expires. This means that at remote sites, client queries for the name may not succeed until much later. The time interval for replication to WINSDC is 1 hour, to WINSSF is 3 hours, and to either WINSTOKYO or WINSISRAEL is 12 hours. Therefore, convergence time is calculated as:

> 2 × 12 hours (to/from either Tokyo or Tel Aviv) + [2 × (1 hour) between NYC and D.C.] = 26 hours

This represents the longest time interval to replicate a WINS change across the network over the worst-case path.

Practically speaking, name query requests can and often do succeed before the convergence time transpires, because entries can replicate over a shorter path. This will also happen when the Number Of Changes In Version ID Before Replication threshold as configured in push replication passes before the replication interval in pull replication expires. Therefore, the new entry is replicated earlier.

Manual replication can be used if the computer coming online is considered critical or is being added to serve as functional fault tolerance. This method will inform remote WINS servers of the addition almost immediately and severely reduce convergence time. Manual replication should be used only during nonpeak traffic times. To execute a manual replication, in the WINS console, right-click Replication Partners and select Replicate Now.

Replication between Untrusted Domains

Having a trust relationship between two domains is not necessary in order to set up WINS replication between WINS servers in either of the two domains. In fact, it's not even necessary to have a valid user account within the untrusting domain. To configure replication between the two servers, you need to have the local administrator manually configure the server via the WINS console to allow this type of replication. This must be done on each server that will participate in replication.

Forcing Replication

The Replicate Now command in the WINS console enables you to trigger an immediate replication between configured WINS servers.

Once replication has occurred, you can use the Display Records command to view records from the remote WINS database. You can also make changes to the remote WINS database, assuming that you are logged in under an account with appropriate rights in the domains for both servers.

One of the best actions you can take to optimize the WINS database and replication traffic is to disable File and Printer Sharing For Microsoft Networks on all computers that will not be used to share resources. When this service is disabled on a client node, the client does not have to register a name for the Server service, thereby reducing the size of the database and the amount of replication traffic.

Comparing WINS Deployment Scenarios

So far, you've learned how to evaluate a number of factors in designing a WINS strategy—determining the number, hardware specifications, and location of WINS servers, planning for availability and fault tolerance, securing the WINS infrastructure, monitoring WINS client traffic, and planning replication partnerships. Now it's time to see the design process in action. We'll investigate how WINS would best be deployed in scenarios featuring organizations with different needs.

Deploying WINS with Multiple Sites

The network in Figure 5.5 represents a large company with three sites of 4,000 users each. The sites are connected with multiple T1 links. Because of the large number of users at each site, each site has a primary and a secondary WINS server.

FIGURE 5.5 A multi-site WINS deployment

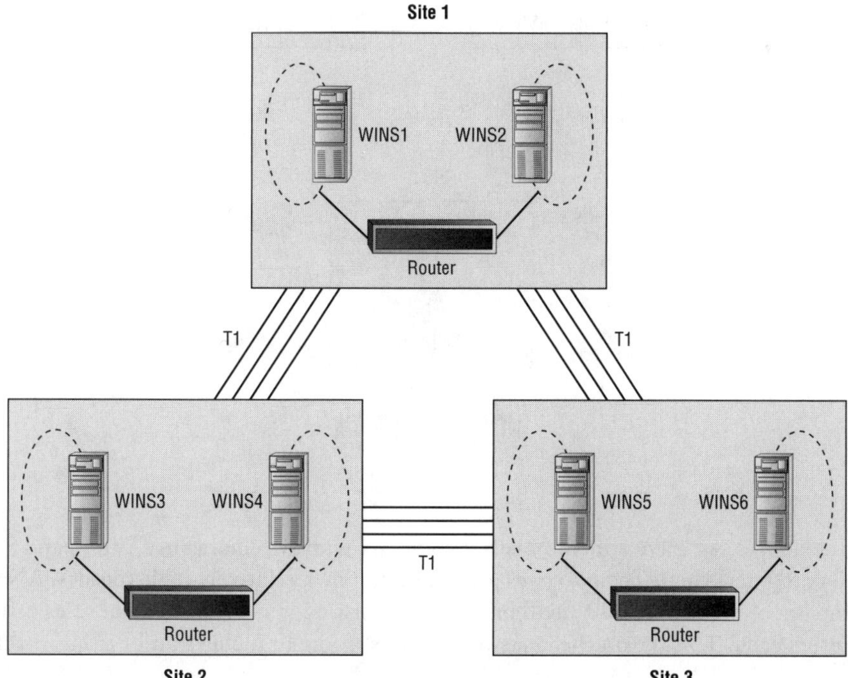

Clients here are configured with local primary and secondary WINS servers. Half of the clients point to one local WINS server as primary and the other as secondary. The other half of the clients uses the opposite configuration. This strategy results in a balanced load over both WINS servers, distributing the WINS registration and query traffic evenly between the two servers. Fault tolerance is provided as well.

The local WINS servers are configured with a pull replication interval of just 10 minutes. The replication interval between the sites is configured at 30 minutes. The result is that updates on the local networks as clients join and disconnect from the network are rapid; therefore, the list of local resources available is very current. This strategy also makes good use of the relatively fast connections between sites.

Deploying WINS with Multiple Sites and Branch Offices

Organizations often need to deploy WINS over a large number of sites, some of which are connected with high-speed links, and others which are smaller and connected with lower-speed links, like the company featured in the following scenario. Figure 5.6 shows how WINS has been deployed in this organization.

FIGURE 5.6 A multisite WINS deployment with branch offices

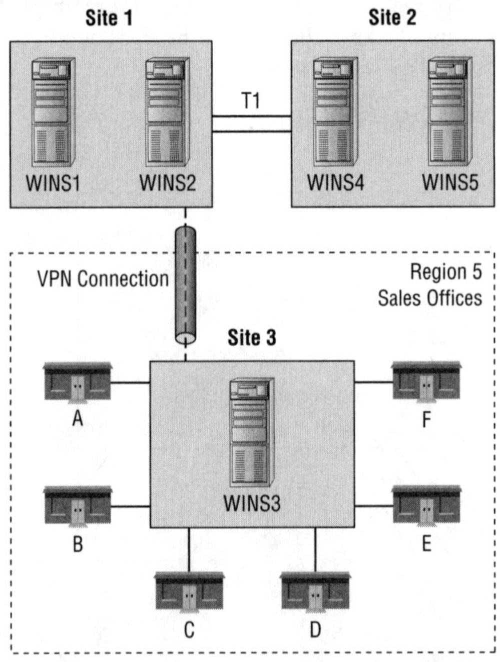

In this example, we have a medium-sized company with two main sites (Site 1 and Site 2) with 700 computers each. The two sites are connected by a relatively high-speed WAN link. This company also has over 200 small branches, consisting mainly of regional sales offices of 2 to 25 users each. To save on the costs of the links, some branches can be used to act as concentrators for a region. Here, Site 3 is acting as a concentrator for Region 5. The branch offices in Region 5, shown as A, B, C, D, E, and F, connect to Site 3 for WINS services.

Branch offices can have their own local WINS servers, but there is usually no need. The company can add regional WINS servers as mentioned when the costs of registration and query traffic increase above the cost of deploying a separate WINS server for a given branch. In such a scenario, local names can still be resolved via broadcasts if a regional WINS server is unavailable or via LMHOSTS to minimize broadcasts.

In this scenario, the regional WINS servers are optional. They increase the convergence time, thereby making the WINS deployment less efficient; therefore, they should be avoided when possible. However, they do offer a cost optimization.

The regional server at Site 3 is configured as a replication partner of the WINS servers in the main site. Clients in the main sites use the local WINS server as primary, and the WINS server in the other main site as secondary. In the branch offices, clients are configured to use the regional WINS server as primary, and WINS server from the closest main site as secondary.

Deploying WINS in a Hub-and-Spoke Design

Extremely large enterprise internetworks can feature tens or even hundreds of thousands of nodes. Figure 5.7 shows a WINS implementation designed to serve over 100,000 nodes at multiple sites.

When you're working with so many WINS servers, you may think that establishing redundancy by creating multiple push/pull relationships would be best. However, this type of strategy can result in a very complicated implementation that is a nightmare to troubleshoot. A *full-mesh* design, in which push/pull partnerships are configured between all WINS servers, results in the highest possible availability—but is a nightmare when records go bad. Databases have to be purged and clients have to be re-registered one site at a time, then replicated manually and checked. The result is usually extended system downtime.

In Figure 5.7, a central hub is used to create an orderly structure. There are four major hubs: San Francisco, New York, L.A., and D.C. Each of the hubs connects the locations with high speed links and serves as a secondary WINS server for its respective region. Replication is configured so that all of the regional primary WINS servers are push/pull partners with the hubs, and they replicate every 15 minutes. The hubs are push/pull partners with each other as depicted using a replication interval of 30 minutes.

The convergence time represents the longest it could possibly take for a WINS update to be replicated to every WINS server in the network.

Actual convergence time is reduced if a faster route is selected, or it could be increased depending on the speed and congestion of the WAN links.

Some redundancy is featured in this network; however, it has a severe limitation. Imagine, for instance, that an earthquake occurs in the greater Los Angeles area. The site loses connectivity with the outside world. In this event, the entire L.A. area is rendered incapable of replicating with the rest of this WINS system. Because all of the WINS servers have a copy of the WINS database for the entire system, name resolution can still function as usual. Any changes to WINS registration that happened after the L.A. hub went down are lost.

FIGURE 5.7 An enterprise WINS deployment in a hub and spoke topology

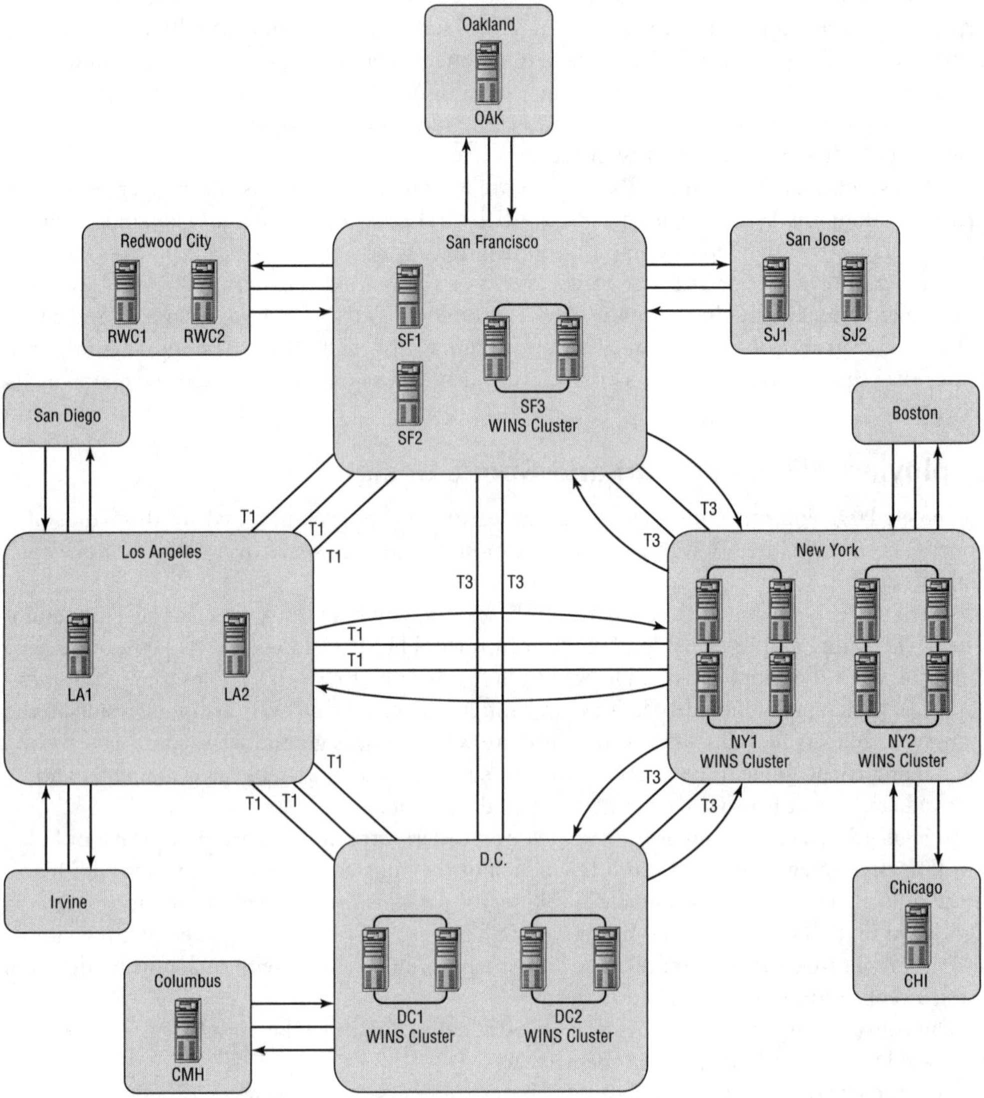

Implementing WINS

WINS is a standalone service that you manage and install like any other network service. In this case, you use the Windows Components Wizard to actually install the service, and it begins running immediately after you install it.

Exercise 5.1 covers the necessary steps.

EXERCISE 5.1

Installing the WINS Service

1. Open the Add or Remove Programs in Control Panel by selecting Start ➢ Control Panel ➢ Add or Remove Programs.
2. When the Add or Remove Control Panel window appears, click the Add/Remove Windows Components icon. This starts the Windows Components Wizard.
3. In the Components list, scroll down until the Networking Services item is visible. Click it once, and click the Details button.
4. The Networking Services window appears. Scroll down the Networking Services list until you see Windows Internet Name Service (WINS), and then select its checkbox. Click the OK button.
5. The Windows Components Window reappears. Click the Next button.
6. Insert the Windows Server 2003 CD. Click Finish to close the Wizard.

Once you've installed WINS, you can start its snap-in from the Start menu (Start ➢ Administrative Tools ➢ WINS or open the MMC and add the WINS snap-in). In the following sections, we will see how to use the WINS snap-in and how to control WINS replication.

Using the WINS Snap-In

WINS as a service is pretty simple. Its job is to listen for broadcasts from NBT clients and then answer queries for NetBIOS-to-IP mappings so that clients can get IP address data without resorting to network broadcasts.

As befits a simple service, the WINS snap-in is pretty simple. Its functionality is mostly tucked into the Properties dialog boxes for the server and its databases. However, there are more advanced skills you need to know in order to effectively manage WINS. You must be able to manage data replication between WINS servers, because the most efficient way to implement WINS is to use several servers that share data so that broadcasts and requests never have to cross from one TCP/IP subnet to another.

Setting Server Properties

Each individual WINS server has its own group of settings, including settings that govern when the service replicates its data and how often it backs up its database. You control these settings by selecting a server in the WINS snap-in and then opening its associated Properties dialog box. For controlling these settings, the Properties dialog box has four separate tabs: the General tab, the Intervals tab, the Database Verification tab, and the Advanced tab.

The General Tab

The General tab (see Figure 5.8) controls some useful server properties:

- The Automatically Update Statistics Every checkbox and the associated time controls let you govern how often your WINS server parses its logs and databases to gather statistical information (e.g., how many registration attempts have succeeded or failed). While useful in the aggregate, this statistical information isn't generally critical to the success or failure of your WINS implementation, and the default interval of 10 minutes is usually sufficient.

- The Database Backup control group lets you specify where you want your WINS database files backed up. The Windows NT WINS server had an unfortunate propensity to corrupt its databases, which is why these backup options are present. The generally accepted best practice is to keep a backup of your WINS databases on a separate physical volume on the same computer (you can't back up databases to a network drive). Keeping a database backup is a good idea, although WINS data can always be reloaded from a replication partner if it becomes necessary. The database backup will not occur until a path is chosen. Backing up the database when the server is shut down is also a good idea.
- The Back Up Database During Server Shutdown checkbox requests that the server make an additional backup of the database when the WINS server service is shut down. This is in addition to the backup that takes place at scheduled intervals.

FIGURE 5.8 The General tab of the WINS server Properties dialog box

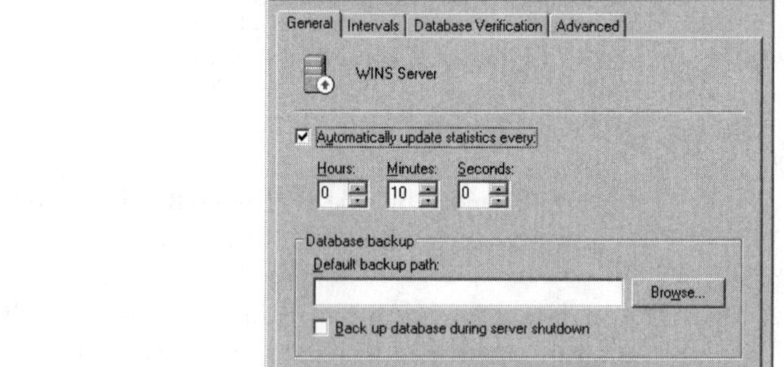

The Intervals Tab

The Intervals tab (see Figure 5.9) contains options to control the intervals at which the WINS server performs maintenance tasks on its databases. Unlike DNS, where records never expire, or DHCP, where the server handles database maintenance on its own, the WINS server allows you some measure of control over these tasks, at least to the extent of controlling how often they happen.

The dialog box has four sets of controls, and each one controls a separate maintenance activity:

- Renew Interval controls how often a WINS client must renew its registration. This is also known as the TTL or the Name Refresh Interval. The default value of six days is fine for most networks. Renewal occurs every three days for most clients, because clients attempt to renew name registrations when 50 percent of the TTL has elapsed. Shorter values increase the load on the WINS server and network and allow WINS data to become less consistent with the current state of the network, because WINS name changes can occur more frequently and out of sync with replication.

FIGURE 5.9 The Intervals tab of the WINS server Properties dialog box

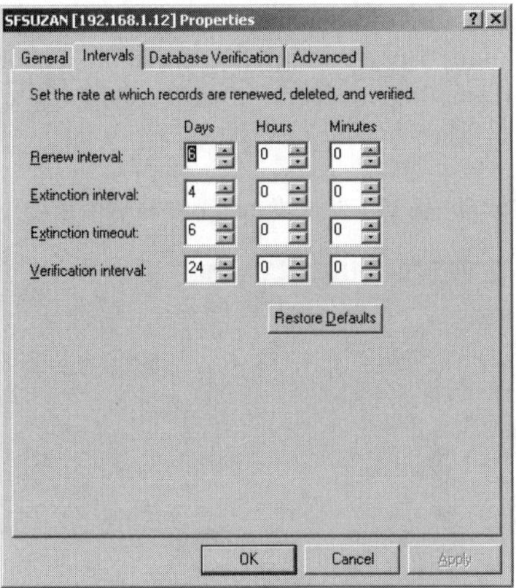

The Renew Interval influences the values of the other intervals.

- Extinction Interval controls how long a released or tombstoned WINS record will remain marked as "released" before it's marked as "extinct." This is also known as the Tombstone Interval or Name Age Timeout. It is set to four days by default.
- Extinction Timeout controls how long an extinct record may remain in the database before it's removed. This is also known as the Tombstone Timeout, and it is set to six days by default.
- Verification Interval regulates how long a stale record owned by another server can remain in the database before it's verified to see whether or not the registration is still valid. The default value is 24 days.

Note that the Database Verification tab controls the actual settings that perform the verification.

The Restore Defaults button returns these control values to their original factory default values. The default values have been carefully designed by Microsoft engineers to optimize WINS replication traffic, name resolution traffic, and synchronization. In general, they should not be modified. Exceptions may occur for special circumstances, such as renumbering the IP addressing scheme for the network.

The Database Verification Tab

The Database Verification tab (see Figure 5.10) allows you to adjust the interval at which database consistency and integrity are verified. You should always try to maintain a consistent WINS database. Because clients may depend on WINS for all their name resolution, having some way to cross-check database entries for correctness is desirable. However, doing so raises the question of what you check and what it gets checked against. Comparing two different copies of the same wrong data wouldn't do much good. Microsoft has implemented a mechanism that correlates WINS registrations between multiple servers so that conflicts or incorrect entries can be identified and flagged. Resolving conflicts or problems is still up to you, but at least you can find out where they are.

FIGURE 5.10 The Database Verification tab of the WINS server Properties dialog box

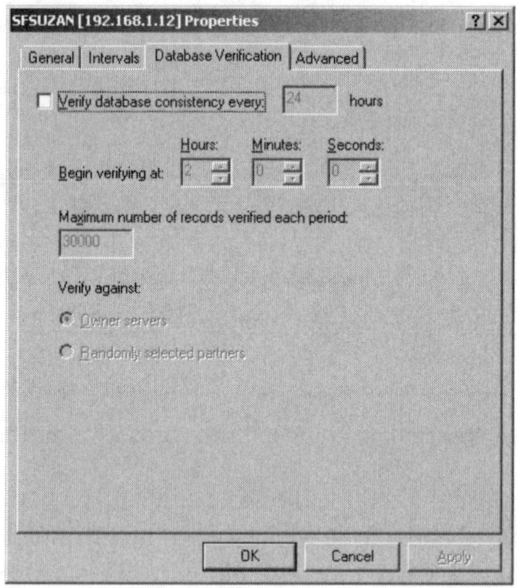

The following controls on the Database Verification tab let you specify whether or not consistency checking is done at all:

- The Verify Database Consistency Every checkbox controls whether verification is turned on or not. Consistency checking helps to maintain database integrity in large networks. When you turn it on (as it is by default), the interval you enter here will match the same interval in the Intervals tab—changing it in one place changes it in the other. If you want to, you can turn off verification altogether, although we don't recommend doing so unless you have a very small network.
- The Begin Verifying At control allows you to specify when the verification pass begins. Normally, it begins two hours after the server starts, and the interval actually starts only after that initial pass completes.
- The Maximum Number Of Records Verified Each Period control gives you a limited way to throttle back verification. A 30,000-record WINS database is still pretty large, though, and because verification always involves network chatter between the two servers involved,

you may benefit from turning this down somewhat if your WINS database has more than 1,000 or so records.

- The Verify Against radio button group allows you to compare two sets of data to see which version is correct. You have two verification choices. The first choice is to verify registrations with the server that issued them. Think of this as verifying a driver's license by calling the issuing state's license bureau. It gives you complete verification, but it may involve calling lots of different places.

  The alternative is for you to verify data by checking it against a replication partner. If your server has only a single partner, this might not be very useful. However, because many WINS implementations use several partners, this option picks a partner at random and cross-checks the subject record against it. Using the same partner all the time might lead to a failure to spot a problem record, so the WINS verifier will automatically pick a new partner for each record it verifies.

You can also verify the database manually by right-clicking the WINS server and using the Verify Database Consistency command.

The Advanced Tab

The Advanced tab of the WINS Properties dialog box (see Figure 5.11) lists all the advanced settings for a WINS server.

FIGURE 5.11 The Advanced tab of the WINS server Properties dialog box

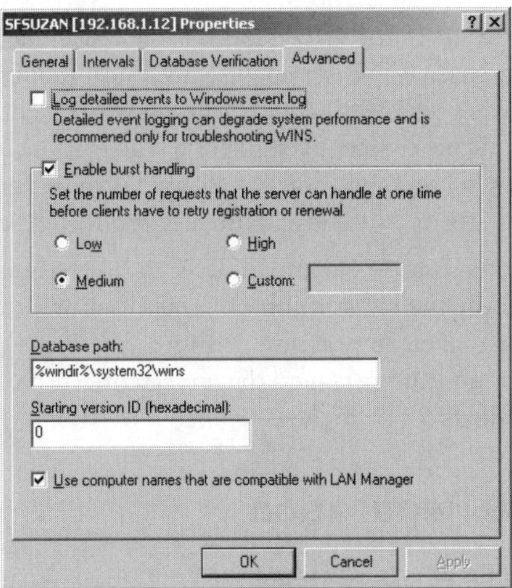

The following list describes what's in this dialog box:

- The Log Detailed Events To Windows Event Log checkbox allows you to turn on more detailed logging. Once you check this box, expect your event log to fill up pretty quickly, because the WINS service will begin logging each registration and renewal request as well as information about the request's success or failure. This should be turned on for troubleshooting only and turned off when the problem is solved.

- The Enable Burst Handling checkbox and control group give you gross (as opposed to fine) control over how many simultaneous requests your WINS server can accept. If the server is busy, any client that attempts a registration or renewal must wait until the server can handle it.

  Normally, burst handling is turned on. If you turn it off, you'll limit your server to processing a single request at a time—and that can cause a bottleneck. At the same time, you may not want your WINS server to accept lots of requests at once, so you can adjust its acceptance with the radio buttons in the control group. Selecting the Custom radio button and providing a number in the attached field will specify a firm limit on how many concurrent requests the server will accept.

  Burst mode support enables a WINS server to respond positively to a large number of simultaneous client name registration requests, even before the requests are processed and entered into the database. The server uses a burst queue size (default = 500) as a threshold value. If the value is exceeded, new registration requests are automatically granted a positive response with a shorter TTL randomized within a 5–50 minute interval, forcing the clients to reregister after the excessive WINS traffic has subsided. This comes in handy in situations such as a large-scale power failure, when multiple computers are simultaneously restarted.

- Normally, WINS databases are stored in the system's directory. The default path for the WINS database appears in the Database Path field as `Windows\system32\wins`. You can change the path (for example, to locate the database on a faster drive array). Make sure the database is regularly backed up.

- By changing the value in the Starting Version ID (Hexadecimal) field, you can tweak the version ID of your database. WINS servers use a version ID in their database. This ID, which is incremented when changes occur, can be used to identify which server in a replication partnership has the more recent version of a registration. Normally, you change only the ID in this field if you want your database to appear to be newer than the version on its partner's database (perhaps because it had already replicated some incorrect data).

- The Use Computer Names That Are Compatible With LAN Manager checkbox instructs the WINS server to allow only the registration of names that are usable with older computers still stuck with LAN Manager. In practice, this means names that are less than 14 characters and contain only letters, numbers, and the underscore (_) character. This can be ignored if your clients are Windows 95 or higher.

Controlling WINS Replication

You control WINS replication at two levels. At the highest level, you can assign settings that apply to all replication partnerships in which the target server participates. Although this is useful, it's equally useful to be able to control replication settings for individual partnerships. We will look at both of these levels, as well as adding replication partners and forcing replication, in the following sections.

Setting Properties for All Replication Partners

When you right-click the Replication Partners node in the WINS snap-in and choose the Properties command, the Replication Partners Properties dialog box appears. This dialog box has four tabs: the General tab, the Push Replication tab, the Pull Replication tab, and the Advanced tab. The defaults you set here will apply to all partners of the current server that do not have their own overriding settings in place; these settings will also apply to new partners.

The General Tab

The General tab (see Figure 5.12) has only two settings. The Replicate Only With Partners checkbox controls whether or not this server will confine its replication traffic to its defined partners. When the box is unchecked, the server will replicate with any server that asks it to (this setting is not recommended).

FIGURE 5.12 The General tab of the Replication Partners Properties dialog box

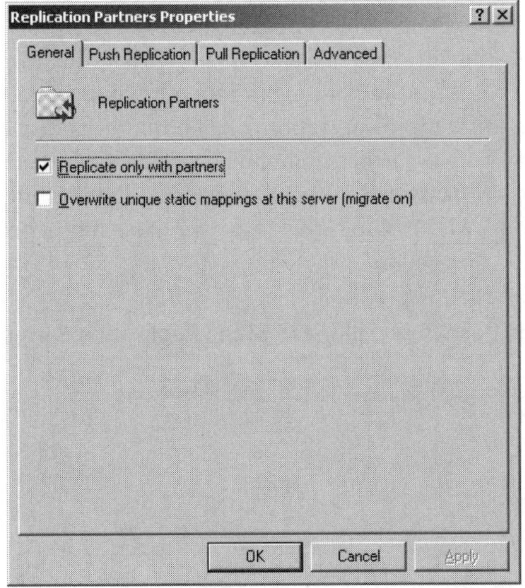

The Overwrite Unique Static Mappings At This Server (Migrate On) checkbox is included to handle situations in which the same name has both a static and a dynamic mapping attached to it. Remember that a WINS administrator can add static NetBIOS-to-IP mappings; these mappings stay in the database, as opposed to normal dynamic WINS records. They're normally used to provide WINS resolution for machines that aren't using NetBIOS, such as Macintoshes and Unix boxes. These static records normally work fine, but sometimes you'll have a need to overwrite those mappings. This can happen as you migrate from systems not using WINS to those that do—when the checkbox is on, a dynamic WINS registration request (which can only be generated by a legitimate WINS client) will always override a static mapping for the same name.

The Push Replication Tab

The Push Replication tab (see Figure 5.13) lets you control how replication works for push partners of the current server. A push trigger request tells the partner that it needs to send a pull trigger. Because this is its sole function, the controls here are all pretty easy to understand:

- The two Start Push Replication control groups let you control when this server will send push replication triggers. You can send push triggers when the WINS service starts or when a client registers a new or changed IP address with the server.
- The Number Of Changes In Version ID Before Replication control gives you a further measure of control because it allows you to specify how much drift in the owner-version mapping table you're willing to accept. For example, if you set this value to 50, you're telling your server to wait until it has accumulated 50 changes before sending a push trigger to its partners. These changes may be changes to registrations owned by the server, or they may be changes received from other replication partners.
- The Use Persistent Connections For Push Replication Partners checkbox controls the nature of the connections between push replication partners. Normally, WINS servers will establish new connections each time they initiate a replication, and they will break the connection when they are done. On some networks, this can result in bandwidth waste because the process of establishing and then breaking a connection may need to be done several times in fairly rapid succession. An alternative is to specify a persistent partner connection, in which the two partners maintain an open communication session even when they are not actively replicating data back and forth. This setting is recommended when the partners are on a LAN or when they have a *secure* high-speed connection across a WAN link.

FIGURE 5.13 The Push Replication tab of the Replication Partners Properties dialog box

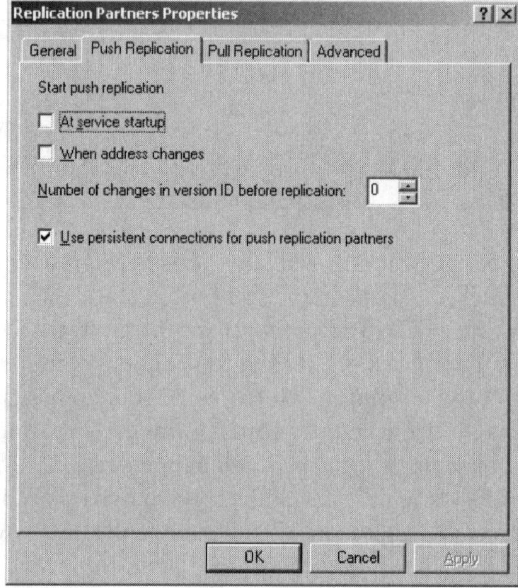

The Pull Replication Tab

A separate and completely different set of properties control pull partners, as you can see from Figure 5.14. Because pull partners seek updates from their partners, you have more options to configure when using them. The Pull Replication tab has the following controls:

- The Start Time control lets you regulate when replication starts.
- The Replication Interval control governs how often the pull partner sends pull triggers to its partners.
- The Number Of Retries control specifies how many times you want a pull partner to send pull triggers before it skips a particular partner.
- The Start Pull Replication At Service Startup checkbox, which turned on by default, gives you a way to control when the first pull trigger is sent by the service.
- The Use Persistent Connections For Pull Replication Partners checkbox controls the nature of the connections between pull replication partners, in the same way as its counterpart on the Push Replication tab.

FIGURE 5.14 The Pull Replication tab of the Replication Partners Properties dialog box

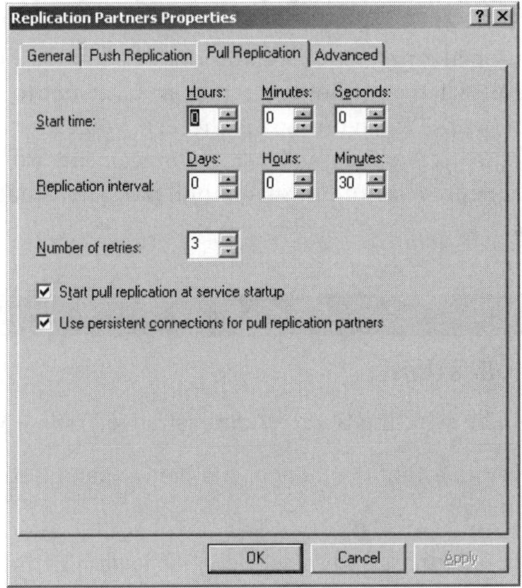

The Advanced Tab

The Advanced tab (see Figure 5.15) of the Replication Partners Properties dialog box has two primary functions. First, it allows you to block the replication of records from certain owners using the Block Records For These Owners list. This allows your servers to remain willfully ignorant of replicated data from the owners of the IP addresses specified in the list. This is an easy way to screen WINS records offered by rogue servers, or by servers in a test lab, that you don't want polluting your "real" WINS database.

FIGURE 5.15 The Advanced tab of the Replication Partners Properties dialog box

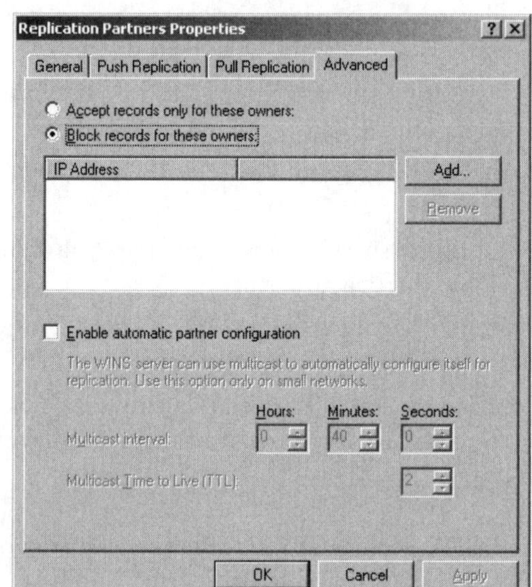

Second, it allows for automatic partner configuration. The Enable Automatic Partner Configuration checkbox controls whether or not this server will attempt to partner automatically with other servers on the network. When this box is checked, you can use the multicast interval and TTL controls to configure automatic multicast announcements from this WINS server. Automatic partners are configured as both push and pull partners. You will configure WINS replication in Exercise 5.2.

EXERCISE 5.2

Configuring WINS Replication

1. Open the WINS snap-in by selecting Start ➤ Administrative Tools ➤ WINS.
2. Choose the WINS server you want to manage, and then expand it so you can see its Replication Partners node.
3. Right-click on Replication Partners and select New Replication Partner.
4. Enter the IP address of the WINS partner to add a replication partner.
5. Right-click the Replication Partners node, and choose Properties. The Replication Partners Properties dialog box appears.
6. On the General tab, make sure the Replicate Only With Partners checkbox is marked.

EXERCISE 5.2 *(continued)*

7. Switch to the Push Replication tab, and then check both Start Push Replication checkboxes.
8. Switch to the Pull Replication tab and verify that the Start Pull Replication At Service Startup checkbox is checked.
9. Click the OK button in the Properties dialog box.

Adding Replication Partners

Once you've configured the settings you want to be applied to all the replication partners of a server, you're ready to select the partners themselves. You do this from the Replication Partners node of the server. This node enables you to turn on automatic partner configuration, manually link partners, and remove partnerships.

Changing partnership status for a server requires you to have administrative access to both servers.

Turning On Automatic Partner Configuration If you want your server to participate in automatic partner configuration with other like servers, use the controls described in the preceding section on the Advanced tab of the Replication Partners node in the snap-in.

Manually Linking Partners To add a partner manually, navigate to the partner server, right-click its Replication Partners node, select New Replication Partner, and then specify the IP address or the name of the server with which you want to partner. (If you have a choice between an IP address and a computer's name, always choose the IP address. This ensures that the connection will continue if name resolution fails. The only time you use a computer name instead of an IP address is when the computer is getting its address from a DHCP server.) This adds the new server as a push/pull partner, but you can change the replication type to match your needs after the partnership is created.

Removing a Partnership If you want to remove a replication partner from a server, open the server's Replication Partners node, right-click the server you want to remove, and choose Delete. After the **confirmation** prompt appears, click the Yes button. The partner will be deleted.

Controlling Replication for an Individual Partner

Each individual partner listed in the Replication Partners node has its own list of server settings—all of which you can change. For example, you can change from a pull partner to a push partner, or vice versa, and you can set a few of the settings you just explored at the all-servers level.

When you open the Properties dialog box for a specific replication partner, the General tab doesn't show you anything except the NetBIOS name and IP address of the partner server. However, the Advanced tab (see Figure 5.16) allows you to change the server's replication partner type from the corresponding pull-down menu. This is a fairly innocuous change, because it only affects how the server you're managing sends requests to the partner server—it doesn't actually change anything on the partner server.

FIGURE 5.16 The Advanced tab of the server Properties dialog box

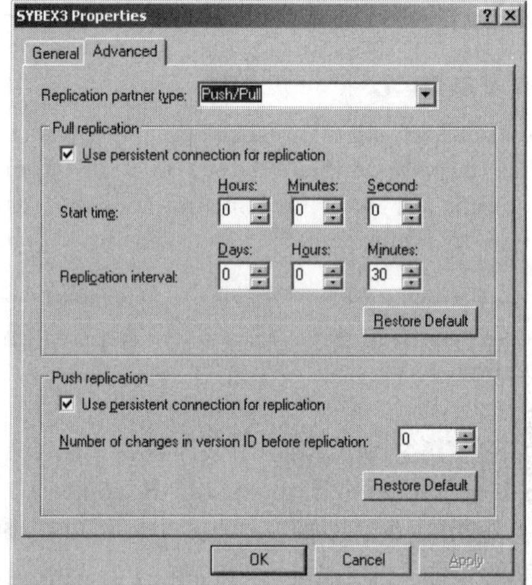

Before changing the replication type, you might want to force a replication with the target partner to ensure that you get an up-to-date replication.

Two additional control groups on the Advanced tab give you some control over pull and push replication with this particular partner. The controls in the Pull Replication group are a subset of the ones in the Pull Replication tab of the Replication Partners Properties dialog box; you can specify the start time and replication interval, as well as whether or not you want to use persistent connections. Likewise, the Push Replication control group has a pair of controls that match the Push Replication tab on the Replication Partners dialog box. In both cases, the primary difference is that you can't use the individual server's Properties dialog box to control what happens when the service starts.

Performing a Manual Replication

By right-clicking a replication partner and selecting the Replicate Now command, you can send a replication trigger request directly to that partner. This allows you to force replication at any time, not just at scheduled intervals.

 **Real World Scenario**

Migrating WINS Services from NT 4 to Windows Server 2003

As a systems engineer in a large enterprise, you are charged with the task of planning a migration of WINS services from NT 4 to Windows Server 2003. Upgrading the servers is a critical task, and you want to be sure you do it right the first time. What are the steps you will take to accomplish your objective?

Although this task may seem daunting, it's actually a relatively simple process to migrate WINS services, provided that you plan well and that you start with a stable WINS infrastructure.

Best practices indicate that you would ideally begin with a stable and functional implementation of WINS already in place on your existing network. Next, you would follow the same series of steps whether you are migrating WINS from NT 4 or Windows 2000 Server:

1. Back up vital WINS data, including the WINS databases and the following Registry key: `HKEY_LOCAL_MACHINE/System/CurrentControlSet/Services/WINS`
2. Install the WINS Server Service, either during or after the Windows Server 2003 installation.
3. Configure the WINS Service so that the server is pointing to itself for WINS. You can verify that this is the case by viewing the TCP/IP properties of the network card.
4. Convert the WINS database to Windows Server 2003.

The conversion in Step 4 can occur automatically from existing Windows NT 4 or Windows 2000 servers. Here's how:

1. Open a command prompt, and type **`net stop wins`** on both the existing and new servers.
2. Copy the contents of the `Windows\System32\Wins` folder from the existing server to the new server.
3. From the command prompt, type **`net start wins`** on both servers.
4. A message appears indicating that the conversion is in process. The conversion process can take about 30 minutes or longer to complete. The actual time will depend on the size of the database. Do not stop the process. Also, it is normal for `Jetconv.exe` to utilize the CPU heavily during the conversion process.
5. If you are prompted for additional files from the Windows Server 2003 CD-ROM during the conversion process, you will want to copy the `Edb500.dl_` file from the I386 folder on the CD-ROM to the `Windows\System32` directory on the new server.
6. Expand the `EDB500.dl_` file on the server by typing **`expand edb500.dl_edb500.dll`**.
7. Type **`net start wins`** to finish the conversion process.

At the end of the process, you can use the WINS console to verify that the database conversion was successful.

Monitoring WINS

WINS is relatively trouble-free in most implementations. From time to time you may encounter registration problems, which tend to be easy to isolate and fix. You may also encounter a corrupt database, and you should know how to recover in this event. In the following section, we will look at how to use WINS statistics, how to view records, how to compact the WINS database, and how to delete and tombstone WINS records—all of which are essential in monitoring WINS.

Using WINS Statistics

The WINS console maintains a database of statistical information that you might find useful. They include the number of successful and failed registrations, which is a good measure for how busy your WINS servers are, as well as statistics like the number of successful and failed WINS queries.

By default, the WINS statistics are hidden, but you can reveal them by selecting a WINS server in the snap-in and selecting Display Server Statistics (either from the Action menu or the context menu). This pops up a floating window that displays the pertinent statistics, shown here:

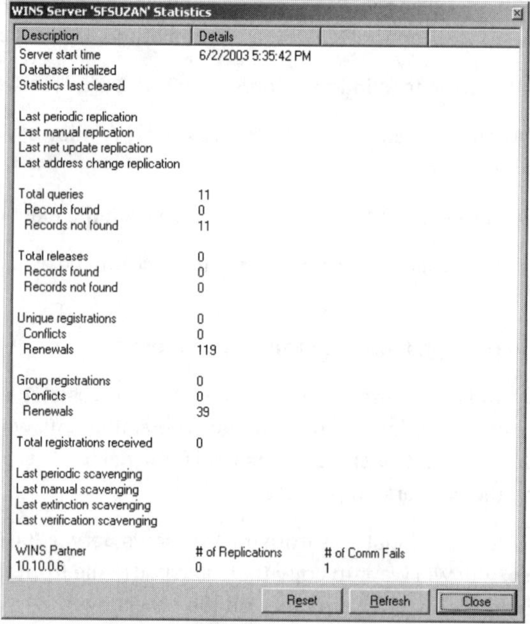

If you want to clear the statistics, perhaps because you've restarted the server or have made some other change and want a clean start, choose Show Server Statistics, and click Reset instead of Refresh or Close.

If you want to control how often the statistics are updated, check the General tab of the WINS server Properties dialog box (refer back to Figure 5.8).

Viewing WINS Records

Viewing the WINS records in your database is frequently useful, particularly if you know or suspect that something's wrong with a particular record. However, for any but a very small WINS database, sifting through the records manually will be prohibitively time-consuming. You can actually search the database in two separate ways, both of which are available by choosing the server of interest, right-clicking its Active Registrations node, and choosing Display Records from the pop-up menu, which brings up the Display Records dialog box. The following tabs control how you display the records:

Record Mapping Tab The Record Mapping tab, shown below, lets you query the database for WINS records that start with or contain a particular string of characters. For example, you can search for IP address records or all records that start with "SALES" or all that start with "SA" for that matter. You'll typically use this tab to find out whether or not there's a registration for a known name, usually as part of troubleshooting. Remember to clear the filter so that these are not the only records that you will see from now on.

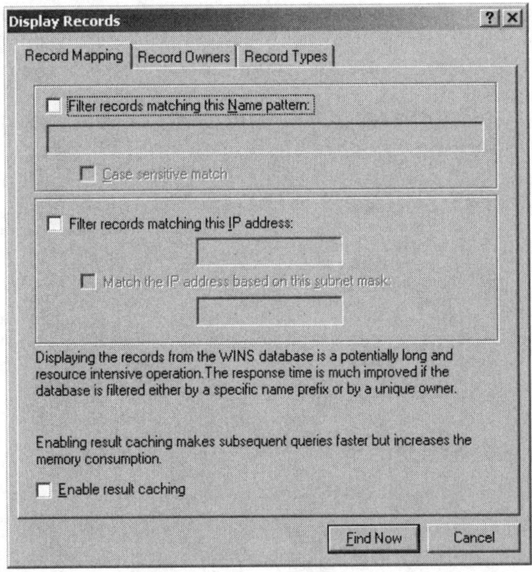

Record Owners The Record Owners tab (see Figure 5.17) lets you search for all of the WINS registrations held by a particular owner. This is the fastest way to see which records any given server owns. You can use the filtering options in the Record Mapping tab to screen out records you're not interested in.

FIGURE 5.17 The Record Owners tab of the Display Records search dialog box

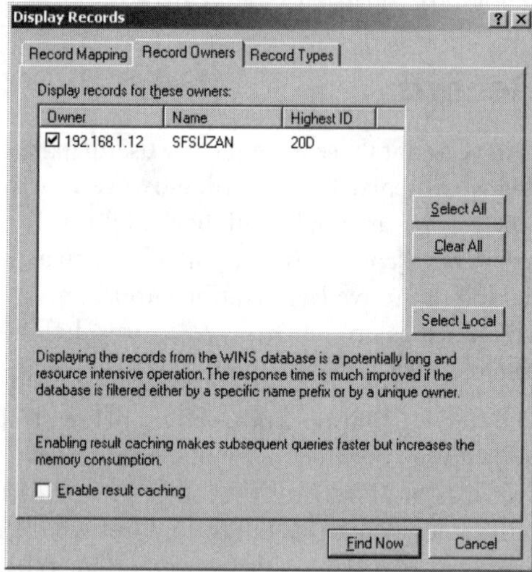

Record Types Tab The Record Types tab (see Figure 5.18) allows you to search or filter records for a particular type of server (e.g., a domain controller or RAS server).

FIGURE 5.18 The Record Types tab of the Display Records search dialog box

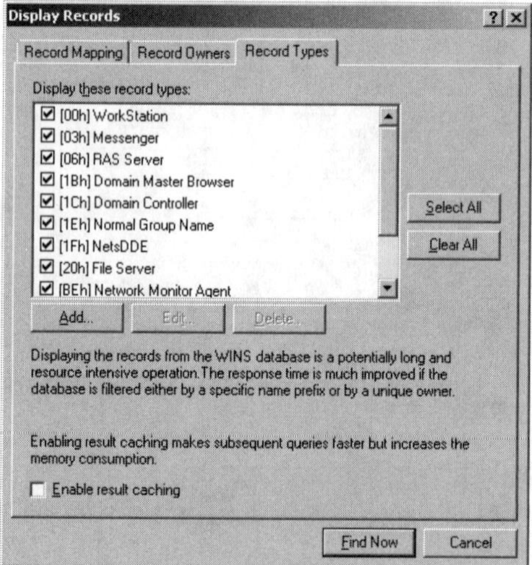

Members of the WINS Users local group have read-only access to the WINS configuration information on the WINS server.

Compacting the WINS Database

The WINS server will periodically go through its database and clean it up, deleting records that are no longer needed. This process, called *online compaction*, is a dynamic and automatic process, but it isn't as efficient at reclaiming unused space. *Offline compaction* which refers to manually compacting the database while the WINS service is stopped, is a more efficient means of reclaiming unused space in your WINS database. Monthly offline compaction is recommended for large, busy networks of more than 1,000 WINS clients. Less frequent offline compaction will be suitable for smaller networks.

The `jetpack.exe` utility allows you to perform an offline compaction. Jetpack takes two parameters: the name of the database file (normally the name is `wins.mdb`) you want to compact and the name of the temporary file you want it to use.

Take a look at the following example:

```
Jetpack wins.mdb junk.mdb
```

This code will compact the WINS database into a file named `junk.mdb`. When the database is successfully compacted, `junk.mdb` will be renamed to `wins.mdb`, and you can safely restart the WINS service.

Exercise 5.3 walks you through the necessary steps to manually compact the WINS database.

EXERCISE 5.3

Manually Compacting the WINS Database with the Jetpack Utility

1. Log on to the console of your WINS server.
2. Open the WINS snap-in by selecting Start ➤ Administrative Tools ➤ WINS.
3. Right-click the appropriate WINS server, and then choose All Tasks ➤ Stop.
4. Open a command prompt by selecting Start ➤ Run. Type **cmd**.
5. Change to the WINS database directory (by default, it's `Windows\system32\wins`).
6. Type **dir *.mdb** and note the size of the `wins.mdb` file.
7. Type **jetpack wins.mdb temp.mdb**.
8. Type **dir *.mdb** and note the size of the `wins.mdb` file. Determine whether or not the size has changed.
9. Switch back to the WINS snap-in console, right-click the server, and choose All Tasks ➤ Start command.

Deleting and Tombstoning WINS Records

You may find it necessary to remove WINS records from the database, whether they are static or dynamic. If you use a single WINS server, you can simply delete the record. If you have more than one WINS server, you can't just delete a record and assume that it has vanished forever because the server's replication partners will simply replicate the record back into the database. Fortunately, you can *tombstone* the record. The tombstoned record (which is flagged as deleted) will be replicated to the WINS partners, and they will mark their own records as tombstoned as well.

After all of the WINS servers have updated their records and the sum of the Extinction Interval, the Extinction Timeout, and the Verification Interval values have passed, the records are permanently removed from all WINS servers.

To delete or tombstone a record, right-click the record name in the WINS snap-in, and select the Delete command. The Delete Record dialog box asks you if you want to delete or replicate the deletion (tombstone) of the record. Choose the appropriate option depending on whether you have one or multiple WINS servers.

Configuring Inter-Forest WINS Replication

Windows Server 2003 supports a multitude of trust types between other forests. For example, if one forest is at the Windows 2000 Native functional level and the other forest is at the Windows Server 2003 functional level, you can create two-way nontransitive trusts between the forests. If both forests support the Windows Server 2003 functional level, you can create two-way transitive trusts between the forests. In either case, the trusts must be configured prior to setting up WINS replication partners. If you're going to set up a push/pull relationship, a two-way trust (transitive or nontransitive) must be in place.

The first steps in setting up the trust relationships are as follows:

1. Add the remote domain controller's name to the Domain Controllers folder in the Active Directory Users and Computers snap-in. If you do not accomplish this step, an error will occur in Event Viewer and the trust will not establish.
2. Repeat Step 1 on the remote domain controller.
3. Open the Active Directory Domains and Trusts snap-in. Right-click the domain name, and select Raise Domain Functional Level (to check the domain level). For this procedure, ensure the domain functional level is set to Windows 2000 Native or higher. If it is not, raise the level.
4. Right-click the Domain name, and select Properties. Select the Trusts tab.
5. Click New Trust. The Welcome To The New Trust Wizard dialog box appears. Click Next.
6. In the Trust Name field, enter the name of the remote domain (e.g., `silly.com`). Click Next.
7. If this is the first time you are running this wizard, select the two-way trust. If you receive an error at this point, it's normally because the trust was started at the remote end and not completed. Simply select the one-way trust to clear the error.
8. Click the Finish button.

Now that you have configured the trusts, you can validate them by selecting the domain name on the Trusts tab, selecting Properties and clicking the Validate button. Click Yes, validate the incoming\outgoing trust, and supply a username and password for the administrator of the remote domain. (You need to perform this task for both the trusted and trusting domains because we are using a two-way trust.) Next, execute Exercise 5.2 of this chapter on both the local WINS server and the remote WINS server to configure the Replication Partners.

The following steps are the final and most important steps of this process:

1. Open the WINS console.
2. Right-click Active Registrations, and select Display Records.
3. Click on the Record Owners tab. At this point, you should see both replication partners. If you do not see both, validate the trust relationships and add the replication partner again. (The error here is usually a mistyped computer name or an incorrect IP address—or possibly the IP address cannot be contacted. Ping the IP address using both the IP address and the computer name.)
4. Click on the server name, and click the Find Now button. Repeat this step for the other server name. The Find Now output should be the same for each server. (One server can have more names than the other due to recent registrations.) If the output is not occurring on the remote server, right-click Registration Partners and select Replicate Now.
5. If the Find Now output for both servers is identical or almost identical, you have successfully completed an inter-forest replication of two partner servers.

You should be familiar with the following additional inter-forest WINS replication information:

- If you are configuring just a pull relationship between two WINS servers, only a one-way trust relationship is required. The server that is pulling must be the trusted server.
- If you are configuring a push relationship between two WINS servers, you need to configure a two-way trust as described in this section.
- Trust relationships over WAN links should be secured by either a VPN or by IPSec, even if they are using dedicated lines.

Troubleshooting WINS

Troubleshooting WINS problems is usually simple compared to troubleshooting problems with DNS. In this section, you'll learn the general considerations for troubleshooting WINS name resolution issues, as well as how to use the `nbtstat` command to troubleshoot WINS.

General Considerations

When you have a name resolution problem, the first step is to determine where it's occurring. This is most likely on the client side, and you'll usually hear about it when a client can't resolve a particular network name. In that case, you need to begin by asking the client the following questions:

- Is the TCP/IP configuration correct? In particular, does the client have a WINS server configured?

- Can you use the `ping` command to ping the IP address of the WINS server? If not, you probably need to fix an underlying network connectivity problem.
- Is the client using DNS or WINS to resolve the name? Whichever protocol it's using, does the desired name exist on the server?
- Is the WINS server running and accepting requests?

If you determine that the problem isn't with the client, you'll want to check some common causes of server misbehavior. First, verify that the WINS server is running and accepting requests. Once you double-check and find that everything is okay, the next step is normally to search the database to see if the name requested by the client exists in the database or not. If not, you need to determine if the problem is because the name isn't registered, or if the *real* problem is that the name is registered by its owning server but the record hasn't been replicated.

If the desired name does show up in the database, the problem may be that the server is returning invalid data because an old static mapping is in place (in which case, you should remove it) or because there's a problem with the database. If the database is, or appears to be, corrupt or damaged (which is usually noted in Event Viewer), you can either run a consistency check on it or you can just stop the service and remove the database files. When you restart the service after doing so, the server will use its replication partners to get back the data it formerly owned, as well as any updates from other partners on the network.

Using the *Nbtstat* Command

During normal operation, NBT resolves NetBIOS names to IP addresses. As you saw earlier, the local machine uses one of several possible sources for this: local cache lookup, WINS server query, broadcast, LMHOSTS lookup, Hosts lookup, and DNS server query. The *nbtstat* command can help you diagnose and correct errors that occur in NBT at any of these lookup points. `Nbtstat` is run at the command prompt, and you must use several case-sensitive switches to obtain meaningful results from the command. For example, entering **`nbtstat /?`** at the command prompt lists the available options. Table 5.2 lists the `nbtstat` switches and their functions.

TABLE 5.2 *Nbtstat* Switches

Switch	Name	Function
-a *<RemoteName>*	Adapter status	Displays the NetBIOS name table and MAC address of the NIC for the remote computer name specified.
-A *<IP address>*	Adapter status	Displays the same information as -a but uses the target computer's IP address as an argument.
-c	Cache	Displays the contents of the NetBIOS name cache.

TABLE 5.2 *Nbtstat* Switches *(continued)*

Switch	Name	Function
`[Number]`	Interval	The number you enter indicates the interval, in seconds, in which to redisplay selected statistics, pausing between each display. Press Ctrl+C to stop redisplaying statistics.
`-n`	Names	Lists the names registered locally by NetBIOS applications. This can be used to calculate the number of name registrations a given client will need, which is useful in predicting WINS client traffic.
`-r`	Resolved	Shows a count of all names resolved by broadcast or WINS server.
`-R`	Reload	Purges the name cache and reloads all #PRE entries from LMHOSTS.
`-RR`	ReleaseRefresh	Releases and reregisters all names with the name server.
`-s`	Sessions	Lists the NetBIOS sessions table converting destination IP addresses to computer NetBIOS names.
`-S`	Sessions	Lists the current NetBIOS sessions and their status, with the IP address.
`/?`	Help	Displays this list.

Exercise 5.4 shows you how to use the `nbtstat` command. In this exercise, you will use the `nbtstat` command to check the status of the local name cache.

EXERCISE 5.4

Using the *Nbtstat* Command

1. Open the command prompt by selecting Start ➤ Run. Type **cmd**.
2. At the command prompt, type **`nbtstat /?`**. You should see the list of valid switches, as shown in Table 5.2.
3. Enter **`nbtstat -a`** ***name***, where ***name*** is the NetBIOS name of your computer. You should see output displaying the NetBIOS name table and MAC address of the local computer.

EXERCISE 5.4 *(continued)*

4. Try entering **nbtstat -c**. If there have been any recent successful attempts to resolve a NetBIOS name, the output of this command should include a list of names. If there haven't been any recent successful attempts, the command will return the message "No names in cache."

5. If Step 4 returns at least one name, you can use `nbtstat` to clear the name cache. Change the IP address of one of the machines that was listed in the output of Step 4, and then try pinging the NetBIOS name of that machine. You should receive a timeout message because the cache is pointing to an IP address that is no longer valid for that machine. Now enter **nbtstat -R** to purge the cache, and try pinging the NetBIOS name of that machine again. You should get a response this time.

Summary

In this chapter, you learned:

- What the Windows Internet Name Service (WINS) is and how it works. WINS provides NetBIOS computer name-to-IP address mappings for Microsoft clients. WINS provides name registration and resolution services similar to those provided by DNS.
- How WINS servers replicate their data. WINS replication occurs according to either automatic or manual configurations of replication partnerships. Replication partners can be push-only, pull-only, or push/pull.
- How to plan a strategy for WINS deployment. Designing a WINS strategy involves considering multiple factors such as security, availability, performance, replication, and network topology.
- How to configure the WINS service. WINS is managed through its MMC console, mainly through the server's Properties page, which features the General, Intervals, Database Verification, and Advanced tabs.
- How to control WINS replication. Replication is configured through the Replication Partners Properties page, which features the General, Push Replication, Pull Replication, and Advanced tabs.
- How to configure inter-forest WINS replication and the importance of trust relationships to that end.
- How to monitor and troubleshoot WINS. The WINS console enables you to view statistics and to view and manage records. The `nbtstat` command is a useful troubleshooting utility.

Exam Essentials

Understand how WINS works. WINS resolves NetBIOS computer names to IP addresses for Microsoft networks that require NetBIOS capabilities.

Understand the purpose of WINS replication. Replication is a service that makes the WINS data stored on your servers more useful by making it available across subnets. Because the registrations are duplicated on multiple servers, a host on one subnet can get the IP address for a host on the other subnet without having to actually send a resolution request to the other subnet.

Understand the difference between push partners and pull partners. A push replication partner sends its partner a notice saying in effect, "I have new data, so ask me if you want it." A pull partner sends its partner a request for new data by sending a record number and asking for any records that are newer.

Know how to plan a strategy for WINS deployment. Designing a WINS strategy involves considering multiple factors such as security, availability, performance, replication, and network topology. The ideal strategy achieves a good balance between a replication system that ensures WINS data consistency throughout the network and the elimination of unnecessary WINS-related network traffic.

Know how to configure replication for all replication partners. Understand how to use the Replication Partners Properties dialog box and its tabs to configure replication.

Know how to compact the WINS database. To effectively reclaim unused space in your WINS database, you need to perform an offline compaction. The `jetpack.exe` utility enables you to compact the WINS database after stopping the service.

Know how to use `nbtstat` to monitor and troubleshoot WINS. `Nbtstat` is a utility that enables you to view and manipulate the local name cache. `Nbtstat` has a number of useful command-line options to help you monitor WINS traffic and troubleshoot WINS issues.

Key Terms

Before you take the exam, be certain you are familiar with the following terms:

b-node
convergence time
full-mesh
h-node
limited replication partnerships
LMHOSTS
m-node
name registration
name registration request
name release
name renewal
name resolution
nbtstat
NetBIOS
NetBIOS name server (NBNS)
NetBIOS over TCP/IP (NBT)
offline compaction
online compaction

owner-version mapping table

p-node

primary WINS server

pull partners

pull replication trigger

push partners

push replication trigger

push/pull partnerships

renew interval

replication partners

secondary WINS server

static mapping

tombstone

version ID

Windows Internet Name Service (WINS)

WINS database

WINS proxy agent

Review Questions

1. You are the systems engineer of an organization that has offices in the United States and Canada. WINS is implemented so that two local WINS servers are in the NewYork office and one remote WINS server is in the Toronto office. Because the Canadian users don't need frequent updates to be replicated from N.Y., you want to configure the replication partnerships between the N.Y. and Toronto servers so that changes are replicated only after 15 changes have been made.

   Which of the following options will enable you to accomplish your objective?

   A. Create a new replication partnership for each server partner, specifying a change interval of 15.

   B. Set the Number Of Changes In Version ID Field Before Replication value on the Pull Partners tab of the Replication Partner Properties dialog box to 15.

   C. Set the Number Of Changes In Version ID Field Before Replication value on the Push Partners tab of the Replication Partner Properties dialog box to 15.

   D. Rebuild the WINS database on the Toronto server to force an update after each group of 15 changes.

2. You are the systems engineer of a heterogeneous network that consists of two subnets. Each subnet contains 200 Windows 2000 and Windows XP Professional client computers. Furthermore, the first subnet contains three Windows Server 2003 server computers and the second subnet contains two Unix-based servers and one Windows Server 2003 server computer. At least one of the Windows Server 2003 server computers on each subnet is configured as a WINS server. All of the Windows 2000 and XP Professional machines are configured as WINS clients.

   You want to enable all Windows 2000 and XP Professional computers on both subnets to access the Unix-based servers using NetBIOS names.

   Which of the following options will enable you to accomplish your objective?

   A. Enable the WINS proxy agent on the second subnet.

   B. Create a static mapping on each of the Unix computers.

   C. Create a static mapping for each of the Unix computers on each of the WINS servers.

   D. Add a name reservation for the Unix computers on one of the WINS servers. Configure the WINS servers as push/pull replication partners of each other.

3. You are the network administrator for a company with a Windows Server 2003 network in which there are multiple WINS servers. A user in Sales complains that she is unable to access departmental resources after returning from vacation. You know that she logs on using an automated script that maps file and print resources. After troubleshooting the problem, you realize that the local WINS server is failing to respond to queries for certain clients. You determine that the WINS database is corrupt.

   Which of the following options represents the most expedient way to restore WINS services to the Sales users with minimal administrative effort?

   A. Run a consistency check on the WINS database.

   B. Delete the WINS database files and let the server rebuild its database from its replication partners.

   C. Use the `jetpack.exe` utility to perform offline compaction on the WINS database.

   D. Delete the WINS database files and reboot all the WINS clients.

4. You are the lead systems engineer for a travel agency conglomerate that is acquiring boutique travel agencies at an accelerating rate. You have a stable Windows NT network with multiple routed subnets and a solid WINS configuration. Almost all of the resources that each local agency office uses are on the office's local network, which commonly consists of three to five workstations and one multihomed server that connects to the rest of the company using TCP/IP. Occasionally, the users in the local agency offices would like to connect to a server at the corporate office or at one of the other locations. None of the local agency offices has an on-site WINS server.

   You want to minimize the amount of WINS-related traffic on the network. You especially want to ensure that users can access local resources without generating unnecessary name resolution traffic across the routed network. Which of the following options will best enable you to meet your objective?

   A. Configure the local agency office computers to use h-node broadcasts.

   B. Configure the local agency office computers to use m-node broadcasts.

   C. Configure the local agency office computers to use b-node broadcasts.

   D. Configure the local agency office computers to use p-node broadcasts.

5. You are the systems engineer for a network consisting of three different locations, each with a single subnet. Each subnet contains 12 Windows Server 2003 server computers and 400 Windows 2000 and XP Professional machines. One of the Windows Server 2003 servers on each subnet is configured as a WINS server. You want WINS data to be consistent throughout the network. You also want all of the machines on all the subnets to be able to access each other by name.

   Which of the following options will enable you to accomplish both of your objectives?

   A. Configure push/pull replication partnerships between all of the WINS servers.

   B. Configure two of the WINS servers as push/pull replication partners.

   C. Configure push replication on one of the WINS servers.

   D. Configure the clients with a secondary WINS server from a different subnet.

6. The Johnson Manufacturing Company (JMC) has a total of eight locations, each with its own routed subnet. All of the servers at the JMC locations are running Windows NT 4 Server. Most of the clients are running Windows NT 4 Workstation or Windows 95; however, a few very old computers in the warehouse are still running Windows 3.1. The company wants to migrate its servers to Windows Server 2003 and its clients to Windows XP. As a consultant specializing in Windows migrations, you have been engaged to help with the migration process. Because many support issues have been brought to your attention, you want to make sure that all existing services are working properly before you start the migration.

   You discover that WINS servers are on only four of the subnets, and that the oldest clients are unable to browse to find resources across the network. What can you do to enable the warehouse clients to utilize name resolution services from the WINS servers until you complete the migration?

   A. Configure BootP on all the routers to allow the NBT broadcasts to reach the WINS servers on remote subnets.

   B. Install a DHCP server on each of the subnets; add static mappings for the older clients so that they can receive dynamic WINS configuration details.

   C. Install a WINS server on each subnet that doesn't already have a WINS server.

   D. Configure a WINS Proxy Agent on each of the subnets

7. You are the help desk specialist in a relatively small subnetted network with a single WINS server running Windows Server 2003. The client environment is heterogeneous and consists of Windows NT 4 Workstation, Windows 95, Windows 98, Windows 2000, and Windows XP Professional clients. The various clients are spread across several subnets, with NetBIOS name resolution services provided by a single WINS server.

   One morning, users begin to call with complaints that they are unable to access network resources. In the System Event log, you find a message stating that your WINS database is corrupted and that a dynamic compaction has occurred. The problems persist, and you must come up with an effective solution.

   Which of the following options should you pursue as your next step to resolve this problem?

   A. Run the Scavenge database option against the WINS database to recover the lost information.

   B. Stop the WINS service, delete the `wins.mdb` file, and then restart the WINS service and allow it to rebuild the database from the parity information in the transaction log.

   C. Copy the `wins.db` file from the `winbackup` directory over the corrupted file.

   D. Run the `jetpack.exe` program against the WINS database.

8. You are a network architect in charge of designing a WINS replication strategy for a multinational biotechnology company headquartered in the San Francisco Bay Area. After evaluating the company's physical site topology, bandwidth constraints, and data consistency needs, you have created the proposed WINS replication topology shown in the following diagram. Before you can present your solution to upper management, you must ensure that it meets the organization's needs for data consistency. What is the convergence time for the WINS replication topology shown in the diagram?

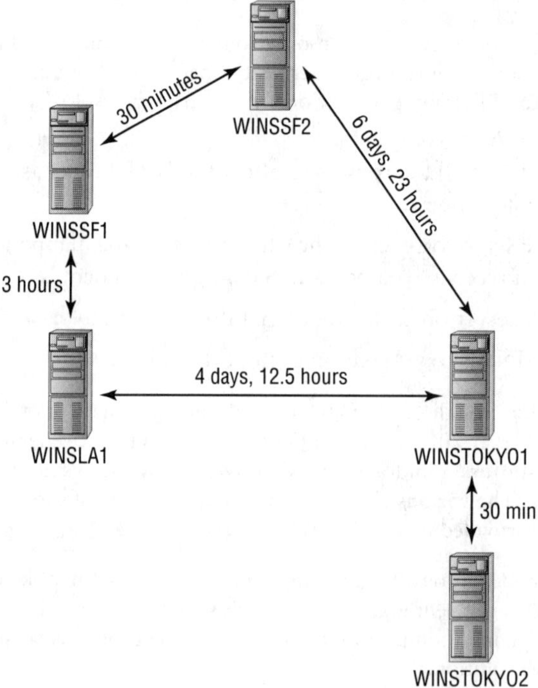

A. 11 days, 12.5 hours
B. 11 days, 13 hours
C. 7 days
D. 11 days, 12 hours
E. 4 days, 16.5 hours
F. 14 days

9. You are the new systems engineer for a company with seven distinct networks in a campus configuration. Two of the networks have been connected with routers; the remaining five exist independently, each on a flat subnet using NetBIOS-based communication. Each network has its own WINS server. You are responsible for upgrading the entire infrastructure from separate Windows NT networks to a single subnetted network running Windows Server 2003. You have installed routers to connect all of the networks, and you have upgraded the servers to Windows Server 2003, as well as implemented TCP/IP services throughout the campus. Your final objective is to make the local resources for each subnetted network available across all the networks in this campus.

   What must you do to accomplish your objective?

   A. Configure fast zone transfers between the WINS servers so that the name resolution information will be available from all of the WINS servers.

   B. Configure push/pull replication partnerships between all of the WINS servers.

   C. Configure all of the clients to support m-node so that they will first attempt to resolve names via a local broadcast first, and failing that method, will query the WINS server to locate the resources on remote subnets.

   D. Configure all of the clients to support h-node so that they will first attempt to resolve names via a query sent to the WINS server, and failing that method, will then use local broadcasts to locate the resources on the local subnet.

10. You are a consultant specializing in migrations for Microsoft networks. You have successfully migrated a Windows NT network over to Windows Server 2003 in order to capitalize on the granularity of administrative control over network security and services. The WINS service remains a necessary part of your infrastructure, and all WINS servers have been upgraded to Windows Server 2003. You now want to delegate some administrative control to key support personnel at each location. Specifically, you want to grant them the ability to view the information in the WINS database without allowing them to modify the configuration of the server. To which security group must you add the chosen support personnel in order to accomplish this objective?

    A. The WINS Users local group on the WINS servers.

    B. The Administrators group on the WINS servers.

    C. The WINS Read Only local group on the WINS servers.

    D. Instruct the support personnel to log on under the special administrative account `IUSER_computername` on the WINS servers.

11. You are a junior network administrator in an enterprise with a heterogeneous client and server environment. One of the remote branch offices is running a small NT Server 4 network using a centralized LMHOSTS file strategy for NetBIOS name resolution. You are responsible for maintaining this legacy compatibility solution until WINS can be implemented for this branch office. To provide fault tolerance in the event that the main file server is unavailable, you want to add alternate network locations for the LMHOSTS file.

    Which of the following steps would you take to edit the local clients' LMHOSTS files to accomplish this objective? Choose all that apply.

    A. Use `#BEGIN_ALTERNATE` and `#END_ALTERNATE` tags in a block exclusion to allow multiple servers to be searched for a valid copy of the LMHOSTS file.

    B. Use `#INCLUDE` <*file name*> statements to specify the location of centralized LMHOSTS files by UNC name.

    C. Use the `#PRE` tag to reference any servers on remote subnets; position these entries at the end of the file, after the `#INCLUDE` statements.

    D. Run `nbtstat -R` to purge and reload the name cache prior to editing the LMHOSTS file.

12. You are administering one of your company's remote branch offices, which consists of a small LAN of 30 nodes on a single subnet. WINS has not been implemented. A user complains that he cannot access all of the network resources, but other users have no problems. You know that the old administrator created an LMHOSTS file to store name-to-IP mappings and copied it to all the local nodes. In fact, none of the address information has changed. You open a command prompt and type **`nbtstat -c`**, which returns some invalid name-to-IP address mappings. What can you do to quickly clear and repopulate the local name cache with the right information?

    A. Recopy the LMHOSTS file from a working client, and then type **`nbtstat -R`**.

    B. Recopy the LMHOSTS file from a working client, and then type **`nbtstat -r`**.

    C. Type **`nbtstat -R`**.

    D. Point to the network share for LMHOSTS.

13. A user in Marketing complains that it takes a very long time to start up her computer and log on to the network at the beginning of the day. The problem started when she began working mornings in the Human Resources department on a special cross-functional project. She uses a laptop running Windows XP. You know that the Marketing Department was on a subnet with its own WINS server, but the Human Resources department is on a subnet without its own WINS server. You further suspect that the problem is related to a high degree of name registration traffic her particular computer is generating. You decide to use `nbtstat` to help you troubleshoot. What command line switch could you use with `nbtstat` to test your theory?

    A. Run `nbtstat -n`.

    B. Run `nbtstat -RR`.

    C. Run `nbtstat -c`.

    D. Run `nbtstat -r`.

14. You are configuring a replication partnership for a pair of WINS servers on the same subnet of the LAN. Because these servers are connected by a high-speed LAN, you want to optimize the push parameters shown in the following image to increase the frequency of replication to ensure that data is always current.

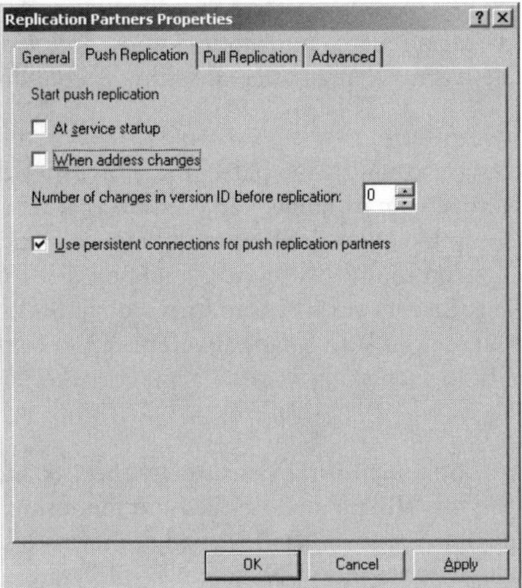

Which of the following options describes how parameters in the diagram can be configured to meet this objective? Choose two options.

A. Configure the Number Of Changes In Version ID Before Replication setting to between 1 and 3.

B. Configure WINS to use a persistent connection between the servers.

C. Configure WINS to use a nonpersistent connection between the servers.

D. Configure the Number Of Changes In Version ID Before Replication setting to 20 or higher.

15. You are the administrator in a small, routed LAN. You want to implement a WINS replication strategy that features ease of configuration and low administrative overhead. Your network has two WINS servers, each one on a separate subnet. Which of the following options describes how you could implement WINS replication to meet your objective?

A. Configure the WINS servers for automatic partnership configuration using multicasting. Configure a multicast interval and a TTL as needed.

B. Configure the WINS servers for automatic partnership configuration, but do not configure them for multicasting.

C. Configure a special push/pull replication partnership using a trusted domain.

D. Configure the Overwrite Unique Static Mappings At This Server (Migrate On) setting in the Replication Partner Properties dialog box.

Answers to Review Questions

1. C. The Number Of Changes In Version ID Field Before Replication value will enable you to configure replication according to your objective. You should set this value on the Push Partners tab. Because only push partners send change notifications, answers involving pull partner configuration are invalid. There is no change interval setting. Rebuilding the WINS database will not force replication.

2. C. Unix-based computers are not WINS-capable; therefore, they do not register themselves with WINS. In order to access them by name, you need to create static mappings for each of the Unix computers within the WINS console. You can't create a static mapping on the Unix computers, because they do not run the WINS service. Enabling the WINS Proxy Agent would not be useful in this scenario because its purpose is to forward NetBIOS traffic such as queries from older Microsoft clients that are not WINS-capable. Replication configurations are not relevant to your objective. There is no such thing as adding a name reservation for the Unix computer on the WINS server.

3. B. Database maintenance tools such as the consistency checker and the Jetpack utility will not repair corruption. Deleting the WINS database files and rebooting all the WINS clients will work in this scenario; however, this solution is costly in terms of administrative effort. The most expedient solution is to delete the WINS database files and simply allow the server to rebuild its database using its replication partners.

4. B. Using m-node on the Windows clients in the small offices will reduce name resolution traffic. M-node sends a broadcast first and, if the name can't be resolved, it will then send a request to the WINS server. Because almost every request by the local users will be to local resources, the WINS requests will be rare, which will reduce traffic, while still making it possible to request a WINS lookup.

   H-node sends a request to the WINS server and then broadcasts. This will create a great deal of unnecessarily routed traffic because the destination will probably be local.

   B-node only sends broadcasts, so it is only capable of locating resources on the local network.

   P-node will always look to the WINS server to find resources, even if the resource is in the same subnet as the requestor, and therefore will generate excessive and unnecessary network traffic.

5. A. Although each WINS server obtains the information in its own local area, all of the WINS servers need to have the same information in each database to ensure that WINS data is consistent throughout the network. You accomplish this by configuring push/pull replication partnerships between all the WINS servers. In this scenario, when a change is made to one server's WINS database, that change is replicated to the other three servers. Configuring a secondary WINS server from a different subnet increases fault tolerance, but it does not accomplish your objectives.

6. D. A WINS Proxy Agent can be configured on a client on each of the subnets to listen for the standard NetBIOS b-node broadcasts. The WINS Proxy Agent transparently intercepts name queries and refers them to a WINS server for resolution. Results are returned to the client as though they were retrieved via the normal b-node broadcast. BootP is used to transmit DHCP broadcast traffic over a router and it is not involved with NetBIOS broadcasts. Installing a DHCP server will not help the older clients resolve NetBIOS names. Adding more WINS servers does nothing to help older clients that aren't capable of querying WINS for name resolution.

7. D. The `jetpack.exe` utility can be used to perform an effective offline compaction of the WINS database, and it can recover a corrupted database. Jetpack is run dynamically as needed on Windows Server 2003 WINS servers. However, it is significantly more effective to launch Jetpack manually while WINS is offline.

   The Scavenge database option will remove records from the database that have already been marked for deletion; however, it won't run an offline compaction of the database, and it is not capable of recovering a corrupt database. WINS databases cannot be rebuilt from transaction logs and parity information. There is no `wins.db` file that will restore the database to its original state.

8. C. Convergence time represents the maximum length of time it can take for a change from any given WINS server to propagate to all other servers in the WINS infrastructure. When calculating convergence, you need to use the worst-case path for replication. In this scenario, it could take as long as seven days for the changes on WINSTOKYO2 to propagate to WINSSF1; this is the longest possible propagation time of all combinations of the servers shown.

9. B. Because all of the Windows clients are WINS-aware, you want the WINS servers to be able to share information about each subnet. This will make local resources for each subnet accessible to nodes in all subnets across the network. You can accomplish that objective by configuring push/pull replication partnerships between all of the WINS servers. Once replication has occurred, each WINS server will have the information required to resolve names and make resources from all local subnets available throughout the campus.

   M-node broadcasts start with a local broadcast, and failing that method of resolving a resource name, a query is sent to the WINS server. However, without replication, the local WINS server won't have enough information to locate resources on remote subnets.

   H-node broadcasts start by querying the WINS server, and failing that method of resolving a resource name, a local broadcast is sent. However, without replication, the local WINS server won't have enough information to locate resources on remote subnets.

   WINS servers don't support zone transfers. That feature is provided by DNS servers.

10. A. Members of the WINS Users local group have read-only access to the WINS configuration information on the WINS server. Adding support people to the Administrators group will allow wholesale power, including the ability to make configuration changes to various network services such as WINS, over the local machine. The `IUSER_`*`computername`* account is a special account used for IIS and is not relevant to the question. There is no WINS Read Only group on Windows Server 2003 computers.

11. A, B. A centralized LMHOSTS strategy involves editing the LMHOSTS file on the local clients to define a location or locations on the network where a shared LMHOSTS file or files can be found. You can use the appropriate tags to force the client to locate and parse these files as though they were part of the local LMHOSTS file. First you would use `#BEGIN_ALTERNATE` and `#END_ALTERNATE` tags in what is known as a block exclusion to allow multiple servers to be searched for a valid copy of the LMHOSTS file. These tags are wrapped around `#INCLUDE` statements specifying the actual UNC location of the centralized LMHOSTS files. Server names do not need to be preloaded into the name cache, because the entire LMHOSTS file will be parsed in this strategy. Note that if any of these servers referenced are on remote subnets, you must have entries to establish the server name-to-IP mappings prior to the `#INCLUDE` statements, or they will be ignored. Again, there is no need to run `nbtstat -R` to purge and reload the local name cache, because the entire LMHOSTS file will be parsed as the source of the name-to-IP mapping.

12. A. The problem is probably due to a bad LMHOSTS file—possibly because it was overwritten by an old copy. The easiest way to restore functionality to this client is to copy LMHOSTS from a working client, and then type **`nbtstat -R`** to purge and reload the local name cache. The **`-r`** switch is used to show a count of all of the names resolved by broadcast or WINS. Typing **`nbtstat -R`** by itself will purge the cache, but it will reload it with invalid data from the bad LMHOSTS file. In this network, there is no network share containing a centralized LMHOSTS because the file was copied to each client.

13. A. The `-n` switch can be used with `nbtstat` to list all of the names registered locally by NetBIOS applications. This feature can be very useful in calculating the total number of name registrations a given client will need in order to predict WINS client traffic. The `-RR` switch releases and reregisters all names with the name server. Using the `-RR` switch would maintain the problem rather than help you troubleshoot the problem. The `-c` option displays the contents of the name cache, showing you the name-to-IP address mappings for other, remote systems; however, it does not indicate the actual name registrations in use by the local node. The `-r` option shows a count of names resolved.

14. A, B. Because LANs feature faster network links, you can increase the frequency of replication by optimizing certain push and pull parameters to keep the data as fresh and up-to-the-minute as possible. You can decrease the Number of changes in version ID before replication setting, for instance by setting it to a value from one to three changes in version ID before a push replication trigger is sent to the partner. In a LAN, you'll want to configure WINS to use a persistent connection between the servers. With a nonpersistent connection, the standard update count threshold defaults to a minimum of 20, but you can specify a smaller value in a LAN.

15. A. The best option for implementing a WINS replication strategy that is easy to configure and features low administrative effort is to configure the WINS servers for automatic partnership configuration, in which WINS servers discover each other on the network through multicast announcements using the special multicast address of `224.0.1.24`. Configuring the WINS servers for automatic partnership configuration without using multicasting is not possible. Configuring a special type of replication partnership is not necessary. The point here is that this configuration is automatic and simple, not manual and complicated. The Overwrite Unique Static Mappings At This Server (Migrate On) setting is used to simplify the update of legacy NetBIOS b-node (broadcast-only) type clients that are later upgraded to support WINS.

Planning Secure Network Access

MICROSOFT EXAM OBJECTIVES COVERED IN THIS CHAPTER:

✓ **Plan security for remote access users.**
- Plan remote access policies.
- Analyze protocol security requirements.
- Plan authentication methods for remote access clients.

✓ **Implement secure access between private networks.**
- Create and implement an IPSec policy.

✓ **Plan for network protocol security.**
- Specify the required ports and protocols for specified services.
- Plan an IPSec policy for secure network communications.

✓ **Configure network protocol security.**
- Configure protocol security in a heterogeneous client computer environment.
- Configure protocol security by using IPSec policies.

✓ **Plan security for data transmission.**
- Secure data transmission between client computers to meet security requirements.
- Secure data transmission by using IPSec.

✓ **Configure security for data transmission.**
- Configure IPSec policy settings.

✓ **Troubleshoot security for data transmission. Tools might include the IP Security Monitor MMC snap-in and the Resultant Set of Policy (RSoP) MMC snap-in.**

With the need for connectivity expanding beyond the network to encompass a variety of remote users, the potential for security compromises is increasing. Today's networks face a number of security threats just as they face the ever-increasing need for connectivity. A critical part of your role involves planning secure network access. You can accomplish this end using two methods:

- You can ensure that all remote access connections are secured against outside attack by using remote access policies and secure protocol choices for VPN communications.
- You can provide IP-level security to defend against network attack and protect IP packets by using IPSec policies. IPSec provides data encryption, mutual authentication, packet filtering, and data integrity.

Windows Server 2003 has introduced several new tools for planning, managing, and troubleshooting IPSec. You can implement IP protocol security through the IP Security Policy Management snap-in or through the Group Policy under Computer Configuration ➢ Windows Settings ➢ Security Settings ➢ IP Security Policies on the local machine or within Active Directory. IPSec policies can be monitored through the IP Security Monitor snap-in, and you can determine how the IPSec effective policy is affecting a local machine via the Resultant Set of Policy (RSoP) snap-in. In this chapter, we'll discuss how to plan a secure solution for remote access and protocol security in Windows Server 2003. We will start with background information about remote access, and then continue through controlling access through remote access policies. Next, we'll delve into IPSec as a solution for protocol security. You'll learn how to configure policies and use the new troubleshooting tools provided in Windows Server 2003.

The behavior of both remote access and IPSec policies involves many complicated and interdependent factors. The best way to learn this subject is to practice creating policies for different objectives and then troubleshoot the policies when they fail to behave as you intend. This is an area where there really is no substitute for direct, hands-on experience—and we strongly recommend that you avail yourself of as much practice as you need.

Evaluating Remote Access Security

Some Windows 2000 and Windows Server 2003 features are simply repackaged NT functionality. Others are entirely new. The remote access service component of the Routing and Remote Access Service (RRAS) falls somewhere in between. RRAS itself dates back to the NT 4 Option

Pack, but the Windows Server 2003 implementation of remote access adds many new features not present in the older version.

The Windows 2000, XP, and Windows Server 2003 remote access client is largely unchanged from its Windows NT and Windows 98 predecessors, although the user interface is slightly different. Likewise, the server components are generally the same as they were in Windows NT—RRAS itself dates back to the NT 4 Option Pack—with added functionality. The most apparent enhancement is the ability to control remote access at a granular level through the use of a *remote access policy*, which is an ordered set of rules that defines how connections are either authorized or rejected. With Windows NT, you could control whether or not individual users could dial in, but there was no way to set that permission for groups of users. The Windows Server 2003 Group Policy Object (GPO) mechanism provides a way to apply dial-up permission and capability settings to groups of users.

We will delve further into remote access policies later in this chapter, in the section "Planning Remote Access Policies."

In the following sections, you'll learn about remote access services and remote access security.

Remote Access Services

Routing and Remote Access Service (RRAS) servers connect mobile users to the network through the Routing and Remote Access service. An RRAS server functions as a *Network Access Server (NAS)* by providing remote clients access to a network. The remote access services provided include dial-up and VPN access.

RRAS servers that are used to provide only remote access and not routing services are frequently denoted as "RAS" servers. RRAS servers that are used to provide only VPN and not dial-up or routing services are usually denoted as VPN servers.

In the following sections you'll learn about the differences between and considerations for dial-up services and VPN services.

RAS servers should *never* be configured on domain controllers. RAS policies are stored on the member server and not in Active Directory. This was designed for security reasons and allows administrators to configure multiple RAS servers in an organization each with a different configuration.

Dial-Up Services

With dial-up access, a remote access client makes a direct, temporary, physical dial-up connection to a physical port on a remote access server. This *dial-up networking* connection is accomplished by using the service of a telecommunications provider, such as analog phone service or ISDN. Dial-up networking is a direct physical connection between the dial-up networking client and the RRAS server.

You can encrypt data sent over the connection for enhanced security.

Security Risks of Using Windows NT RRAS Servers

Running Routing and Remote Access Services on Windows 2000 and higher servers within the same network as NT 4 servers that are also running either Remote Access Service (RAS) or Routing and Remote Access Service (RRAS) poses a significant security risk. Under NT 4, the RRAS service starts using `NULL` credentials, and client connections are granted certain file system and Registry access on the RRAS computer. This access is also required for compatibility in a mixed-mode RRAS implementation. If you mix NT 4 RRAS servers with Windows 2000 Server or Windows Server 2003 servers, the domain can be in Native mode as long as the RRAS servers are member servers. This will allow the use of remote access policies to control the security of remote access connections. If the domain is in Mixed mode, however, you cannot use RRAS policies. This restriction applies whether you are using NT 4, Windows 2000, or Windows Server 2003 RRAS member servers. This type of configuration represents a serious security compromise and is not recommended.

TCP/IP connections over a serial link are established using *Point-to-Point Protocol (PPP)*, which enables any two computers to establish a peer-to-peer connection. This could be a dial-up modem connection, but it could just as easily be a direct serial cable connection, an infrared connection, or any other type of serial connection. When one computer dials another, we call the computer that initiates the connection a "client," and the computer that receives the call is a "server."

There are actually at least six distinct protocols that run on top of PPP. Understanding what they do helps make the actual PPP negotiation process clearer. These protocols include the following:

The Link Control Protocol (LCP) LCP handles the details of establishing the lowest-level PPP link. In that regard, you can think of it almost as if it were part of the physical layer. When one PPP device calls another, they use LCP to agree that they want to establish a PPP connection.

The Challenge Handshake Authentication Protocol (CHAP) CHAP allows the client to authenticate itself to the server. This authentication functions much like a normal network logon; once the client presents its logon credentials, the server determines the nature of access to grant.

The Callback Control Protocol (CBCP) Once the client has authenticated itself, the server can decide whether it should hang up and call the client back. The client can also request a callback at a number it provides. Although this isn't as secure as having the server place a call to a predetermined number, it provides some additional flexibility. The CBCP negotiates whether a callback is required, permitted, and/or initiated. If a callback occurs, the connection is reestablished and reauthenticated, but the CBCP stage is skipped.

The Compression Control Protocol (CCP) CCP allows the two sides of the connection to determine what kind of compression, if any, they will use on the network data. Because PPP traffic actually consists of IP datagrams, and because IP datagram headers tend to be fairly compressible, negotiating effective compression can significantly improve overall PPP throughput.

The IP Control Protocol (IPCP) At this point in the call, the two sides have agreed to authentication, compression, and a callback. They haven't yet agreed on what IP parameters to use for the connection. These parameters, which include the maximum packet size to be sent over the link (the maximum transmission unit, or MTU), have a great impact on the overall link performance, so the client and server negotiate them based on expected traffic.

The Internet Protocol (IP) Once the IPCP negotiation has been completed, each end has complete knowledge of how to communicate with its peer, and as a result, the two sides can begin exchanging IP datagrams over the link.

Figure 6.1 shows how these protocols work together to lead up to establishing the link. Remember this diagram, because you'll see it again (with more arrows on it) when you start reading about PPTP. Here you can see what happens after the link is established and negotiation traffic begins flowing.

FIGURE 6.1 The PPP negotiation process

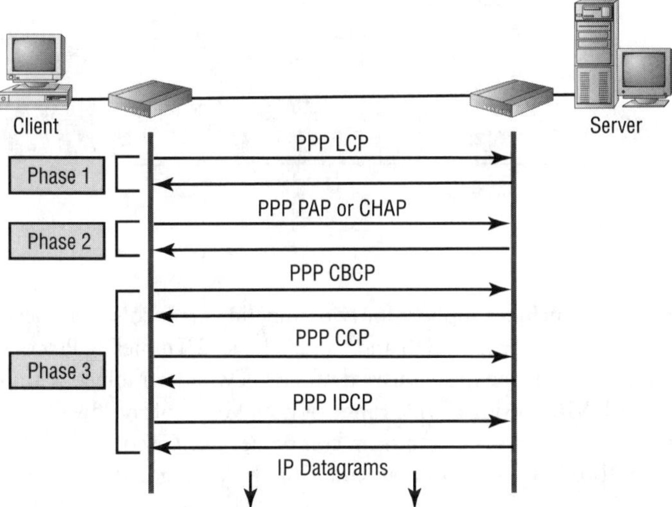

Network protocols such as TCP/IP transmit data on a hardwired LAN. Remote access protocols such as PPP negotiate the conditions for data to be transmitted across a remote connection.

The client and server can wrap other types of network traffic inside an IP datagram. This process is called *encapsulation*. The client takes a packet with some kind of content, wraps it inside an IP datagram, and sends it to the server. The server, in turn, processes the IP datagram, routing real datagrams normally and handling any encapsulated packets with the appropriate protocol. At that point, the client can communicate with the server without the need to know that its non-TCP/IP packets are being encapsulated.

Virtual Private Networks

A *Virtual Private Network (VPN)* is a secure, point-to-point connection across either a private network or a public network such as the Internet. The concept of a VPN involves the creation of a secure tunnel over an unsecure medium. A virtual private networking client uses special TCP/IP-based protocols called *tunneling protocols* to make virtual calls to virtual ports on VPN servers. The remote access server answers the virtual call, authenticates the caller, and transfers data between the VPN client and the corporate network, usually over the Internet.

VPNs offer an excellent solution for flexible, cost-effective, secure remote access. VPNs provide the security of a private network with the flexibility and low cost of the public Internet. Due to the public nature of the connection, data sent over the VPN connection must be encrypted in order to maintain security.

Any two parties can create a connection over the Internet. A VPN enables two parties to establish an encrypted *tunnel* between them using the Internet as a transportation medium. The VPN software on each end takes care of encrypting and decrypting the VPN packets. When packets leave one end of the tunnel, their payloads are encrypted and encapsulated inside regular IP packets that enable them to be delivered to the remote machine. Figure 6.2 will help you to visualize this process.

FIGURE 6.2 Creating a VPN Tunnel over the Internet

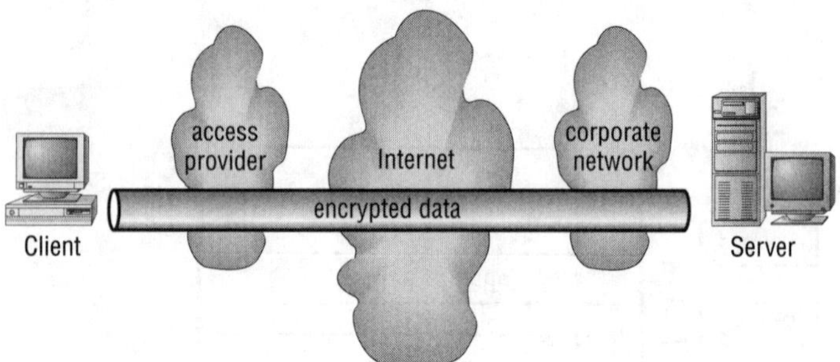

Windows Server 2003 includes support for two tunneling protocols: the Microsoft proprietary Point-to-Point Tunneling Protocol (PPTP) and Cisco's Level 2 Tunneling Protocol (L2TP). L2TP provides a more generic tunneling mechanism than PPTP; when combined with IPSec, L2TP also allows you to establish VPNs using a wide range of non-Microsoft hardware and software products, including routers and access devices from companies like Cisco and Nortel Networks.

Windows Server 2003's VPN support includes the following features:

- You can set up account lockout policies for dial-up and VPN users.
- The Extensible Authentication Protocol (EAP) allows Microsoft or third parties to write modules that implement new authentication methods and retrofit them to fielded servers. One example of EAP is the EAP-TLS module, which implements smartcard/certificate-based access control for VPN and dial-up users.
- If you're using Active Directory in Native mode, you can use remote access policies to apply and enforce consistent policies to all users in a site, domain, or organizational unit. These policies can include which encryption and authentication protocols users may, or must, use when talking to your servers.

How you enable VPN support on your Windows Server 2003 computer depends on whether you're using a server or a client. Client configuration is easy. You simply install the Dial-Up Networking service, and then use the Make New Connection Wizard to create a new VPN connection. On the server side, you'll need to install and configure the Routing and Remote Access Service, and then enable it to accept incoming VPN connections.

The client and server go through the PPP negotiation process described earlier in this chapter, because both L2TP and PPTP depend on the lower-level PPP protocols.

Real World Scenario

Implementing a VPN as a Short-Term Solution to Connect New Office Locations

You are the network administrator for a growing consulting firm. You recently migrated your company's Windows NT network to Windows Server 2003. This migration includes 150 Windows XP Professional workstations and six Windows Server 2003 servers. Your company recently acquired another firm with offices just down the street. The new firm has a Windows NT network that needs to be migrated to Windows Server 2003 as well, and you have already begun the migration. You are awaiting management approval for leased lines between the buildings. The expenses will definitely be approved; however, you need to implement a secure solution in the meantime.

You decide to create a VPN that is both encrypted and authenticated between the two facilities. This will enable users in both locations to connect using the Internet connections that already exist on each LAN.

You decide to use a combination of L2TP for authentication and IPSec for encryption for the connection. This strategy will enable both offices to communicate with guaranteed secure data transmission using the connections that already exist.

Remote Access Security

Remote access represents a persistent challenge to network security. A number of security policies, protocols, and technologies have been developed to solve this problem. In the following sections, we will look at tools used to solve the remote access problem. In particular, we will look at authentication protocols, protocol security, and access control.

The correct approach will vary depending on the unique business and technical needs of a given scenario. Understanding how to choose the appropriate configuration for user authentication including the authentication provider and authentication protocols is extremely important. The same is true for choosing protocol security and access control methods. Be certain that you understand these subjects thoroughly and have real world experience before you take the exam.

User Authentication

One of the first steps in establishing a remote access connection involves allowing the user to present some credentials to the server. User authentication involves an authentication provider and authentication methods.

The Security tab of an RRAS server's Properties page, as shown in Figure 6.3, allows you to select and configure an authentication provider (Windows Authentication or RADIUS Authentication) and an accounting provider (Windows Accounting or RADIUS Accounting). We will look at both of these providers in the following sections.

FIGURE 6.3 The Security tab of the RRAS server Properties dialog box

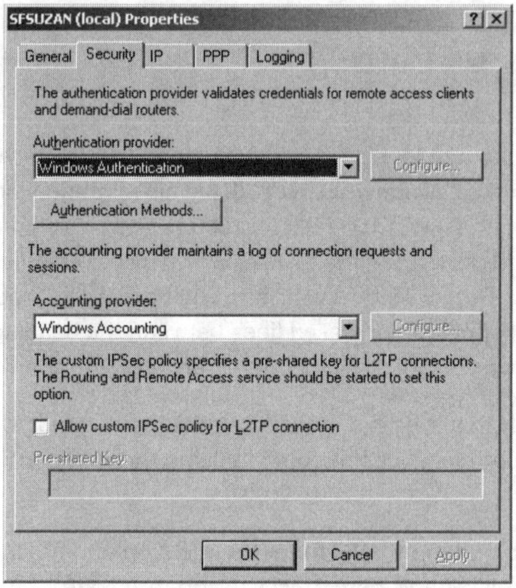

To configure the properties of an RRAS server, right-click your server in the Routing and Remote Access utility and select Properties from the pop-up menu to display the RRAS server Properties dialog box. The options with which we are concerned appear on the Security tab.

Authentication Provider

The Authentication Provider setting defines the type of server that provides authentication services for remote access or demand-dial users. You can choose one of two types of authentication providers:

- Windows Authentication uses a Windows 2003 local server, Windows 2003 domain controller, or Windows 2000 domain controller to authenticate remote access requests.
- RADIUS Authentication uses a *Remote Authentication Dial-In User Service (RADIUS)* server to authenticate remote access requests.

If you have a large network with multiple RRAS servers, your job as an administrator can be made much easier if you set up a RADIUS server, which stores a central authentication database and allows you to manage the RRAS servers from a single location. RADIUS offers a hybrid of hardware and software authentication. The Windows implementation of RADIUS is known as the Internet Authentication Service (IAS).

To configure authentication methods, click the Authentication Methods button in the Security tab. This brings up the Authentication Methods dialog box, as shown in Figure 6.4.

Windows Server 2003 supports six authentication protocols as well as unauthenticated access, for a total of seven methods. You can use any or all of the following seven authentication methods that Windows Server 2003 supports. Each is discussed in the following sections.

FIGURE 6.4 The Authentication Methods of the RRAS server Properties dialog box's Security tab

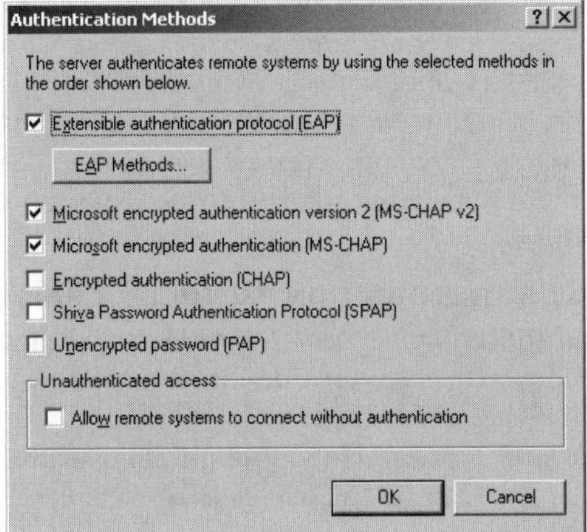

EXTENSIBLE AUTHENTICATION PROTOCOL (EAP)

A client-server pair can negotiate an authentication method using *Extensible Authentication Protocol (EAP)*. EAP extends the authentication methods available for PPP connections. This allows the use of almost any authentication method, including secure access tokens like SecurID, one-time password systems like S/Key, or ordinary username/password systems.

Each authentication scheme supported in EAP is called an *EAP type*. Each EAP type, in turn, is implemented as a plug-in module. Windows Server 2003 can support any number of EAP types at once; the RRAS server can use any EAP type to authenticate if you've allowed that module to be used and the client has the module in question.

Authentication schemes that can be selected include MD5-Challenge, Protected EAP, Secured password (EAP-MSCHAP v2), and Smart Card or other certificate. EAP MD5-Challenge implements the version of CHAP that uses the MD5 hash algorithm. The EAP version of CHAP is identical to the regular version, but the challenges and responses are packaged and sent as EAP messages. This means that if you turn EAP MD5-Challenge on and disable regular CHAP on the server, plain CHAP clients won't be able to authenticate.

The Smart Card or other certificate method is not available on a standalone RAS server.

This protocol is also designed to support emerging authentication technologies, because it extends the authentication methods available for PPP connections. EAP methods are configured through remote access policies.

MICROSOFT CHAP (MS-CHAP)

MS-CHAP is a nonreversible authentication protocol that uses an encrypted password authentication process. Microsoft has extended the CHAP protocol to allow the use of Windows authentication information (among other things, that is the purpose of the Log On With Dial-Up Networking checkbox in the Windows Server 2003 logon dialog box). There are actually two separate versions of MS-CHAP.

MS-CHAP v2 is an enhanced version of MS-CHAP that uses a higher level of security than MS-CHAP. On the server side, this version is only supported in Windows 2000 Server and

Windows Server 2003. On the client side, newer Windows operating systems support MS-CHAP version 2, including Windows 2000, XP Professional, and Windows 2003 Server.

Version 2 is newer and much more secure than version 1, and Microsoft operating systems above Windows 95 support version 1. Newer operating systems support MS-CHAP version 2, as well.

Windows 95 supports MS-CHAP v2 with the Windows Dial-Up Networking 1.3 Performance & Security Upgrade. Windows 98 supports MS-CHAP v2 with the latest service pack installed. In Windows Server 2003, remote access policies enable MS-CHAP v2 by default and MS-CHAP v1 and v2 are the only authentication protocols that support a password change during the authentication process.

CHALLENGE HANDSHAKE AUTHENTICATION PROTOCOL (CHAP)

Challenge Handshake Authentication Protocol (CHAP) is a challenge-response authentication protocol used by non-Windows clients to provide challenge-response authentication using the RSA Message Digest 5 (MD5) hashing scheme to encrypt the response that is sent from the RAS client to the RAS server. CHAP is preferable to PAP (as discussed below) because it doesn't transmit passwords as clear text. Instead, the server sends a challenge encrypted with the DES algorithm to the client, which must decrypt it and return the correct response. This allows the server to verify the user's credentials without sending those credentials across an unsecure link. CHAP is an industry standard and is widely used.

Although NT's RAS client can use MD5-CHAP when dialing into a third-party device, an unmodified NT RAS server will not support MD5-CHAP clients. This is because MD5-CHAP requires that the server store passwords in clear text. For security purposes, the SAM database stores NT passwords as a hash, never in clear text.

MD5 is the default authentication method used in IPv6.

SHIVA PASSWORD AUTHENTICATION PROTOCOL (SPAP)

Shiva Password Authentication Protocol (SPAP) is a slightly more secure version of PAP that is intended for communication with remote-access hardware devices made by Shiva (which is now owned by Intel). It is included for backward-compatibility, though it is not in wide use.

PASSWORD AUTHENTICATION PROTOCOL (PAP)

Password Authentication Protocol (PAP) is the simplest—and least secure—authentication protocol. It transmits all authentication information as clear text, making it completely vulnerable to snooping. In addition, it does not provide a means for a client and server to authenticate each other. Because other protocols offer better security, Microsoft recommends you never use PAP unless you have clients that are unable to use any other supported authentication protocol.

UNAUTHENTICATED ACCESS

This option allows the remote computers to connect to your network without any authentication. This option introduces a gaping security hole and should only be used with extreme caution by vigilant administrators!

Accounting Provider

The Account Provider setting on the RRAS server Properties dialog box allows you to choose an *accounting provider*. The accounting provider is the server that will provide accounting services for remote access or demand-dial connections. RADIUS accounting is used to charge customers for their connection time. You can specify that you will use Windows accounting, RADIUS accounting, or no accounting provider.

In Exercise 6.1, you will configure the properties for an RRAS server. This exercise assumes that you have an RRAS server installed.

EXERCISE 6.1

Configuring Security Options in the RRAS Server's Properties

1. Launch the Routing and Remote Access console by selecting Start ➤ Administrative Tools ➤ Routing and Remote Access.

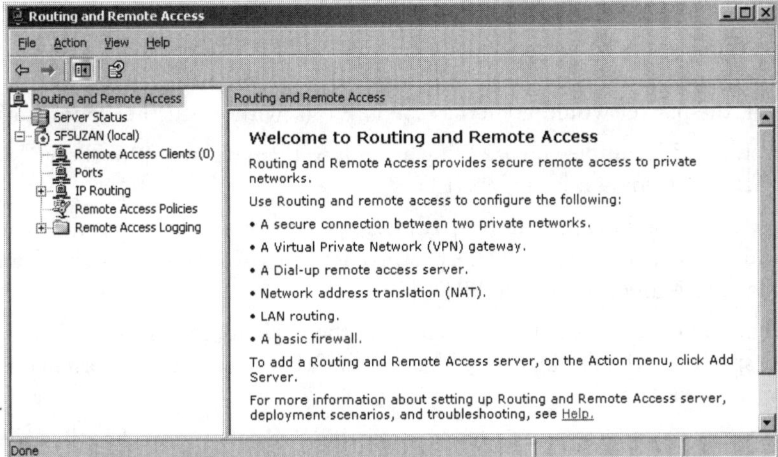

2. In the Routing and Remote Access window, right-click your server and select Properties.
3. Click the Security tab and click the Authentication Methods button.
4. In the Authentication Methods dialog box, note the defaults. Click the OK button.
5. Click the OK button again to return to the main console window.

Protocol Security

Protocol security for remote access connections is established by creating VPN tunnels using encapsulation protocols. The following sections describe how encapsulation, PPTP tunneling, and L2TP/IPSec tunneling work.

How Encapsulation Works

Early networks could carry only one kind of data. Each network vendor had its own protocol, and most of the time there was no way to use different protocols on the same network. Over time and under customer pressure, vendors began to find ways to allow a single network to carry many different types of traffic. What if there were a way to smuggle AppleTalk, IPX, or even NetBEUI traffic inside a TCP/IP packet on the Internet? Actually, there *is* a way to do that—it's called *encapsulation*.

Encapsulation works because software at each level of the OSI model requires header information to determine a packet's source and destination, but the payload contents are irrelevant to most of those components. Foreign traffic types can be routed through IP networks by fabricating header data.

VPNs depend on encapsulation, because their security depends on being able to keep the payload information encrypted. The following steps demonstrate what happens to a typical packet as it goes from being a regular IP datagram to a PPTP packet (see also Figure 6.5):

1. An application creates a block of data bound for a remote host. In this case, it's a Web browser.
2. The client-side TCP/IP stack takes the application's data and turns it into a TCP/IP packet, first by adding a TCP header and then by adding an IP header. At this point, it becomes an *IP datagram*, because it contains all of the necessary addressing information to be delivered by IP.
3. Because the client is connected via PPP, it adds a PPP header to the IP datagram. This PPP + IP combination is called a *PPP frame*. If you were using PPP instead of a VPN protocol, the packet would go across the PPP link without further modification.
4. However, in this example you *are* using a VPN, so the next step is for the VPN to encrypt the PPP frame, turning it into gibberish.
5. A Generic Routing Encapsulation (GRE) header is combined with the encrypted payload. GRE really is generic; in this case, the protocol ID fields in the GRE header tell anyone who cares that this is an encapsulated PPTP packet.
6. Now that you have a tag to tell you what's in the payload, the PPTP stack can add an IP header (specifying the destination address of the VPN server, not the original host from Step 2) and a PPP header.
7. Now the packet can be sent out over your existing PPP connection. The IP header specifies that it should be routed to the VPN server, which can pick it apart and reverse Steps 1 through 6 when the packet arrives.

Encapsulation allows the use of VPN data inside ordinary-looking IP datagrams, which is part of what makes VPNs so powerful—you don't have to change any of your applications, routers, or network components (unless they must be configured to recognize and pass GRE packets).

FIGURE 6.5 Journey of a packet

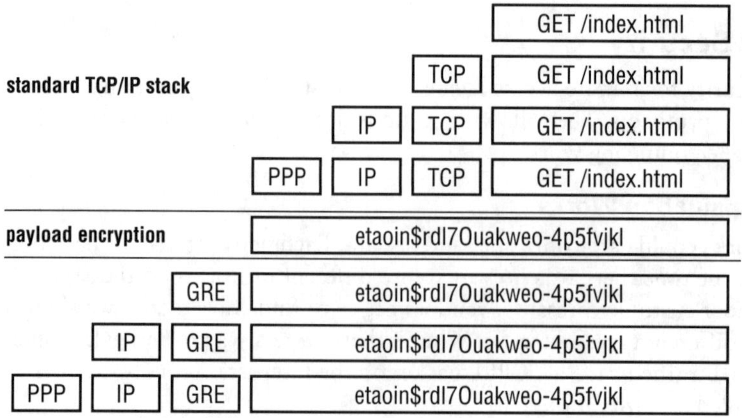

PPTP Tunneling

The *Point-to-Point Tunneling Protocol (PPTP)* is used primarily with Windows computers. PPTP works by encapsulating packets using the mechanism just described. The encryption step is performed using Microsoft's Point-to-Point Encryption (MPPE) algorithm. The encryption keys used to encrypt the packets are generated dynamically for each connection; in fact, the keys can be changed periodically during the connection.

When the client and server have successfully established a PPTP tunnel, the authorization process begins. This process is basically an exchange of credentials, with the objective of allowing the server to decide whether the client is permitted to connect or not. The server sends a challenge message to the client, and the client answers with an encrypted response. When the server gets the response, it can check to see whether the answer is correct. The challenge-response process allows the server to determine which account is trying to make a connection. Next, it determines whether the user account is authorized to make a connection. If so, the server accepts the inbound connection and applies any access controls or remote access restrictions.

L2TP/IPSec Tunneling

The *Level 2 Tunneling Protocol (L2TP)* is much more flexible than PPTP, but it's also more complicated. It was designed to be a general-purpose tunneling protocol, not limited to VPN use. L2TP itself doesn't provide security. Used by itself, it establishes an unencrypted, unauthenticated tunnel. Therefore, you would never want to use L2TP by itself to establish a VPN connection because anyone could gain access to your traffic. Instead, use L2TP in conjunction with IPSec. The flow of an L2TP/IPSec (L2TP over IPSec) tunnel session looks a little different from that of a PPTP session. Here's how the L2TP/IPSec combination works:

1. The client and server establish an IPSec security association, using the ISAKMP and Oakley protocols discussed later in this chapter. At this point, the two machines have an encrypted channel between them.
2. The client builds a new L2TP tunnel to the server. Since this happens *after* the channel has been encrypted, there's no security risk.
3. The server sends an authentication challenge to the client.
4. The client encrypts its answer to the challenge and returns it to the server.
5. The server checks the challenge response to see whether or not it's valid. If it is, the server can determine which account is connecting. Subject to whatever access policies you've put in place, at this point the server can accept the inbound connection.

Note that Steps 3 through 5 mirror the steps described for PPTP tunneling. The authorization process is a function of the remote access server, not the VPN stack. The VPN's sole purpose is to provide a secure communications channel. A separate process is required for network authentication.

Access Control

In addition to the connection-level security features you can use to prohibit illegal access to the RRAS server, there are additional ways to set restrictions on remote connections. You can allow or disallow remote access from individual user accounts as was the standard method in

Windows NT. You can also use remote access policies to limit access to users who meet a set of rules or conditions.

User Properties

You assign permissions to access an RRAS server to a user through that user's Properties dialog box, in the Local Users and Groups console on a member server, or in the Active Directory Users and Computers console on a Windows 2003 domain controller. To open the user Properties dialog box, access the appropriate utility (in our example, Active Directory Users and Computers) open the Users folder, and double-click the user account. Click the Dial-In tab to see the dialog box shown in Figure 6.6.

FIGURE 6.6 The Dial-In tab of the user Properties dialog box

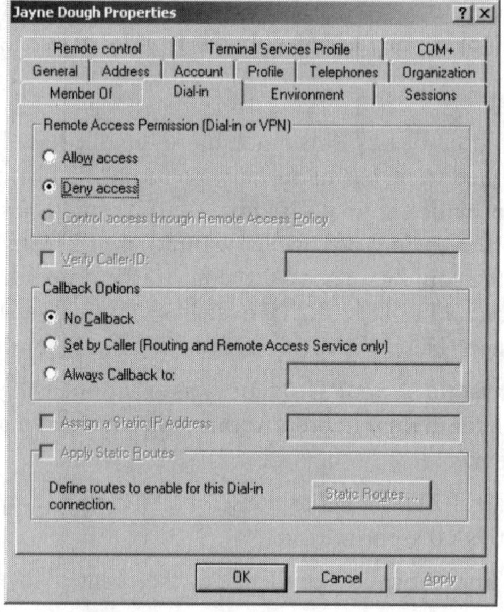

The options on the Dial-In tab allow you to configure the dial-in properties, including Remote Access Permission (Dial-in or VPN). Three radio buttons in this section enable you to configure whether to allow access, deny access, or control access through Remote Access Policy (which requires Native mode or higher). Once enabled, the Remote Access policy is based on three criteria: Conditions, Permissions, and Profile. All three criteria must be met to allow remote access.

Remote Access Policies

You can use remote access policies to limit access to users who meet a set of rules or conditions. Like group policies, remote access policies provide a means for you to apply a consistent set of policies to groups of users. Unlike group policies, remote access policies are available only in native Windows 2000 domains and Windows Server 2003 domains in Native mode or higher. Remote access policy planning is a complex subject deserving its own section. We'll discuss planning remote access policies next.

Planning Remote Access Policies

Windows NT Server offered extremely limited options for controlling remote access to the server. Many security-conscious administrators bemoaned the either/or proposition with which they were faced. They could grant access to remote users, thereby empowering the growing ranks of mobile and home office users, but in so doing, they left their network vulnerable to malicious attack. On the contrary, they could ensure a much more secure network by locking down access to permit only LAN users, yet this would prevent users from effectively working from the road or from home.

Windows 2000 Server introduced remote access policies, offering the high security every administrator wants, coupled with the remote access flexibility your users need. Windows Server 2003 continues to offer this compromise with few changes from Windows 2000 Server.

As mentioned earlier, a remote access policy is an ordered set of rules that define how connections are either authorized or rejected. Each rule has one or more conditions, a set of profile settings, and a remote access permission setting.

Remote access policies are managed through the Routing and Remote Access console.

If a connection is authorized, the remote access policy profile specifies a set of connection restrictions. The dial-in properties of the user account also provide a set of restrictions. User account connection restrictions override the remote access policy profile connection restrictions.

Remote access policies validate a number of connection settings before authorizing the connection, including: permission, group membership, type of connection, time of day, and authentication methods. Once the connection is authorized, remote access policies can also be used to specify connection restrictions, including: idle timeout time, maximum session time, encryption strength, IP packet filters, and advanced restrictions such as IP address for PPP connections and static routes.

Connection restrictions can even vary based on the client's connection settings, phone number or MAC address, or whether unauthenticated access is allowed.

In the following sections, we will see how to modify the default remote access policies and how to create a remote access policy.

Understanding the behavior of default and custom remote access policies is both complicated and extremely important. The best way to learn is to get practice, practice, and more practice working with rules.

Modifying the Default Remote Access Policies

By default, there are two remote access policies: Connections To Microsoft Routing And Remote Access server and Connections To Other Access Servers. To manage the properties of the first policy, right-click it in the RRAS console and select Properties from the pop-up menu. The Settings tab of the policy Properties dialog box will appear, as shown in Figure 6.7.

FIGURE 6.7 The Settings tab of a Remote Access Policy Properties dialog box

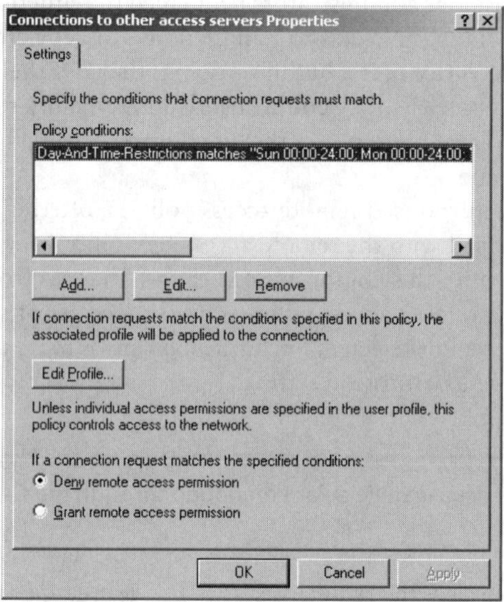

Here you specify the conditions that connection requests must match in order to either be denied or granted permission via the radio buttons at the bottom of the property page. Note that the default is to deny permission for all days and times. For any connection request that matches the policy's condition, the associated profile will be applied to the connection. Remember that the permissions from the user's profile override this policy.

Keep in mind when configuring remote access policies that the default is to deny remote access permission to all connection requests matching the specified conditions. If your objective is to define a set of criteria for legal connections, you will need to select the Grant Remote Access Permission radio button.

Notice that there is currently just one policy condition listed. The default condition specifies the Day-And-Time-Restrictions attribute defined to include all days and times. Click the Add button in the Settings tab. This brings up the Select Attribute dialog box. Choose the Windows-Groups attribute to restrict access based on membership in a group. Next try adding the Tunnel-Type attribute to specify the tunneling protocols used, such as L2TP, PPTP, ESP and/or ASH. As you add attributes, you can go back and edit or remove them from the policy.

Click the Edit Profile button at the bottom of the Settings tab to display the Edit Dial-In Profile dialog box, as shown in Figure 6.8. This dialog box has six tabs with dial-in options that you can configure, as described in Table 6.1.

FIGURE 6.8 The Edit Dial-In Profile dialog box

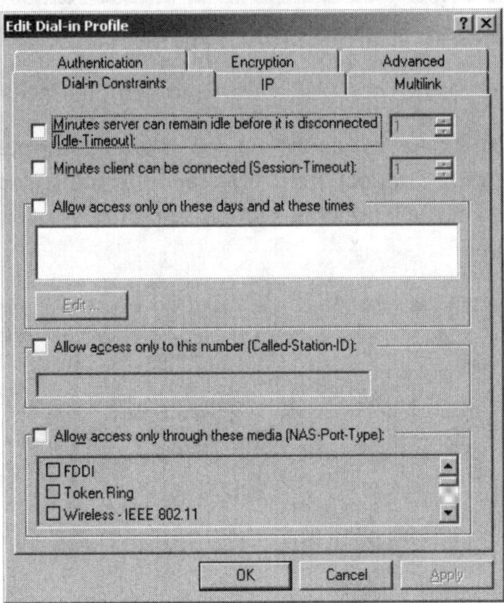

TABLE 6.1 Edit Dial-In Profile Options

Tab	Description
Dial-In Constraints	Allows you to specify when a connection is disconnected based on idle time, maximum session time, and day and time restrictions. You can also restrict dial-in access to a specific number and restrict dial-in media.
IP	Allows you to restrict IP address assignment and configure IP packet filters for the connection.
Multilink	Allows you to configure Multilink settings and BAP settings.
Authentication	Allows you to configure which authentication methods will be allowed for the connection.
Encryption	Allows you to specify the level of encryption to be used by the Routing and Remote Access Service connections.
Advanced	Allows you to specify additional connection attributes to be returned to the RRAS server.

In Exercise 6.2, you will edit the existing remote access policy and profile.

EXERCISE 6.2

Managing Remote Access Policies and Profiles

1. Select Start ➤ Administrative Tools ➤ Routing and Remote Access.
2. In the Routing and Remote Access console, expand your computer, then expand Remote Access Policies. Right-click Connections To Microsoft Routing And Remote Access server and select Properties. This accesses the Properties dialog box for the policy, and the Settings tab is displayed.

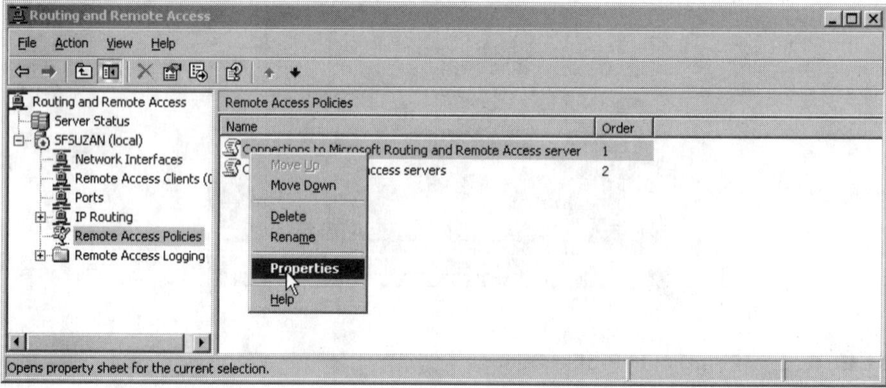

3. In the Settings tab of the remote access policy Properties dialog box, click the Add button.
4. In the Select Attribute dialog box, select the Windows-Groups attribute and click the Add button.

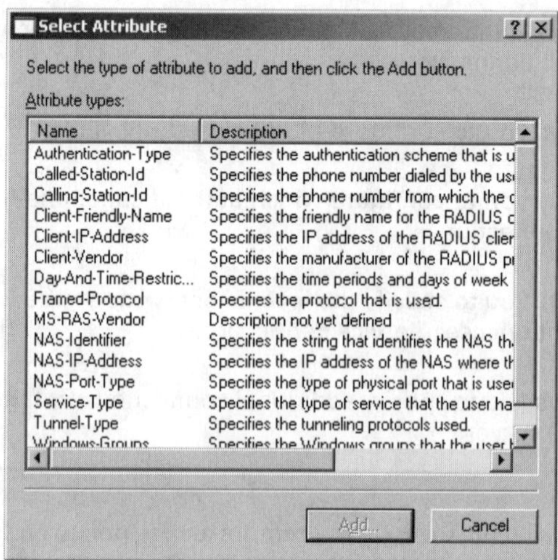

EXERCISE 6.2 *(continued)*

5. In the Groups dialog box, click the Add button.

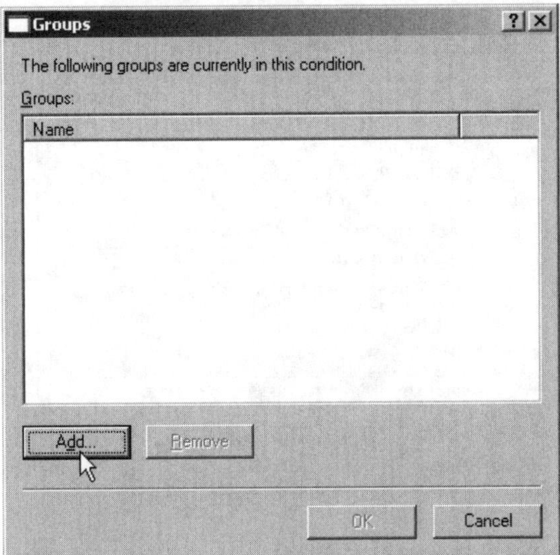

6. In the Select Groups dialog box, add the Domain Users group and click the OK button.

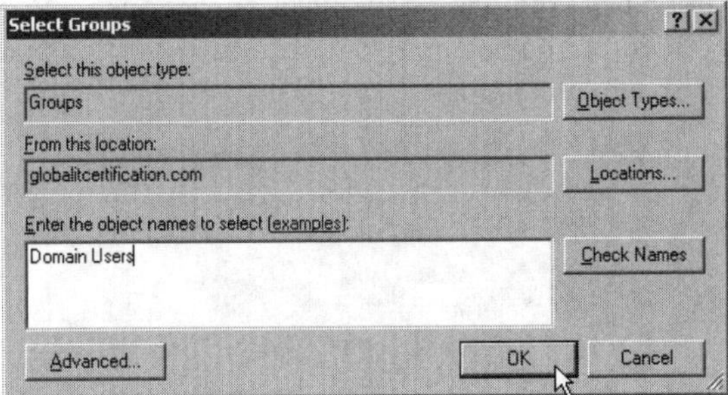

7. In the Groups dialog box, click the OK button.

8. In the If A Connection Request Matches The Specified Conditions section of the Settings tab, click the Grant Remote Access Permission radio button. Then click the Edit Profile button.

9. In the Dial-In Constraints tab of the Edit Dial-In Profile dialog box, check the Minutes Server Can Remain Idle Before It Is Disconnected (Idle-Timeout) option and set it for 10 minutes. Check the Minutes Client Can Be Connected (Session-Timeout) option and set it to 60 minutes.

EXERCISE 6.2 *(continued)*

10. Click the IP tab. Configure IP address assignment by choosing Server Must Supply An IP Address.

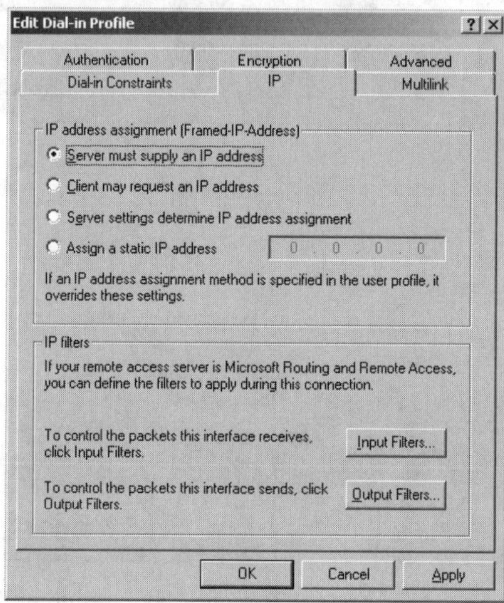

11. Click the Multilink tab. Select the Allow Multilink Connections radio button and set the Maximum Number Of Ports Allowed: to two ports. Leave the Bandwidth Allocation Protocol (BAP) settings at the default values.

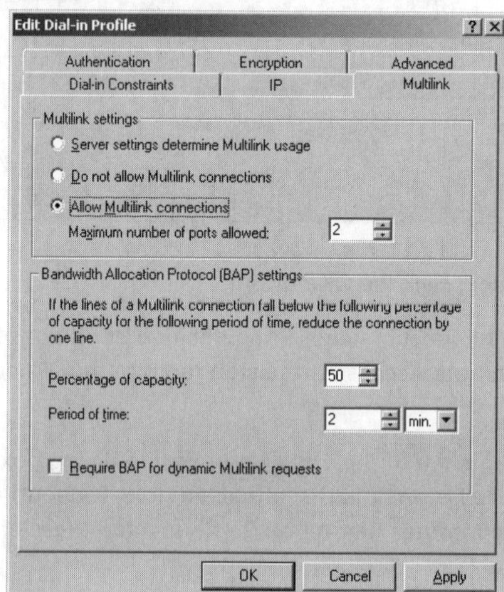

EXERCISE 6.2 *(continued)*

12. Click the Authentication tab. Deselect the default protocols and select Microsoft Encrypted Authentication version 2 (MS-CHAP v2).

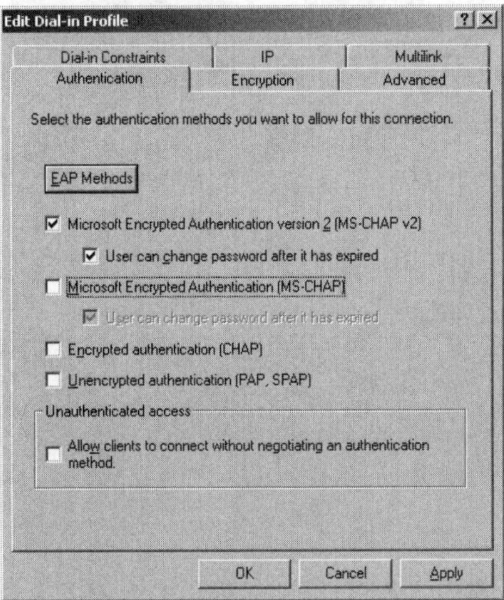

13. Click the Encryption tab and note the default settings.

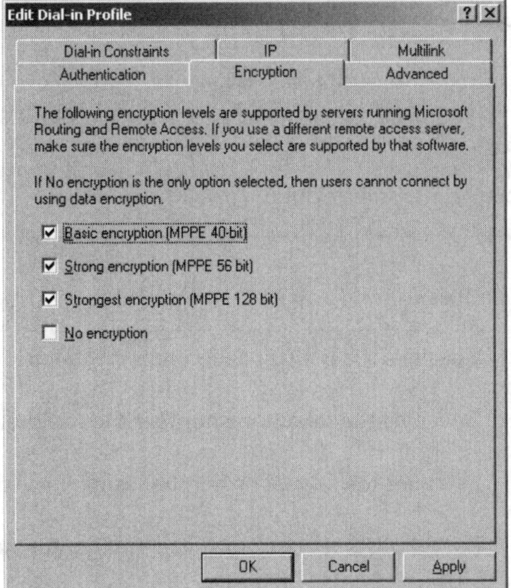

EXERCISE 6.2 *(continued)*

14. Click the Advanced tab and note the default settings.

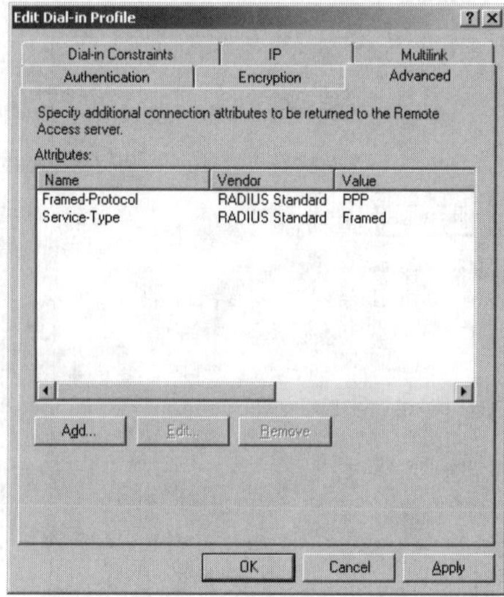

15. Click the OK button to close the Edit Dial-In Profile dialog box.

16. In the Settings tab of the remote access policy's properties, click the OK button.

Creating a Remote Access Policy

You can also create new remote access policies. When you define your policy, you can select conditions to match from a list of attributes. Table 6.2 shows the options for remote access policies.

TABLE 6.2 Remote Access Policy Options

Remote Access Policy Option	Description
Authentication-Type	Specifies the authentication scheme that is used to verify the user.
Called-Station-ID	Specifies the telephone number the remote user will dial.
Calling-Station-ID	Specifies the telephone number from which the remote user will dial.
Client-Friendly-Name	For RADIUS servers, specifies the friendly name of the RADIUS client (IAS only).

TABLE 6.2 Remote Access Policy Options *(continued)*

Remote Access Policy Option	Description
Client-IP-Address	For RADIUS servers, specifies the IP address of the RADIUS client (IAS only).
Client-Vendor	For RADIUS servers, specifies the manufacturer of the RADIUS proxy or NAS (IAS only).
Day-and-Time-Restrictions	Specifies time periods when the remote user is allowed or denied access to the RRAS server.
Framed-Protocol	Specifies the protocols that can be used for remote access.
MS-RAS-Vendor	Not in use ... *yet.*
NAS-Identifier	For RADIUS servers, specifies a string that identifies the NAS that originated the request (IAS only).
NAS-IP-Address	For RADIUS servers, specifies the IP address of the NAS that originated the request (IAS only).
NAS-Port-Type	For RADIUS servers, specifies the physical port of the NAS that originated the request.
Service-Type	Specifies the type of service that the user has requested.
Tunnel-Type	Specifies the type of tunneling protocols that can be used.
Windows-Groups	Specifies the Windows groups to which the user belongs.

To create a remote access policy, take the following steps:

1. Right-click Remote Access Policies in the Routing and Remote Access console. From the pop-up menu, select New Remote Access Policy.
2. The New Remote Access Policy Wizard appears, as shown in Figure 6.9. Click Next.
3. The Policy Configuration Method page appears, as shown in Figure 6.10. Enter a name for this policy. Click the Next button.
4. The Access Method page appears, as shown in Figure 6.11. Here you select the method of access for which you want to create a policy. Options are VPN, Dial-up, Wireless, or Ethernet. Leave it at the default of VPN, and then click the Next button.

FIGURE 6.9 The New Remote Access Policy Wizard dialog box

FIGURE 6.10 The Policy Configuration Method page

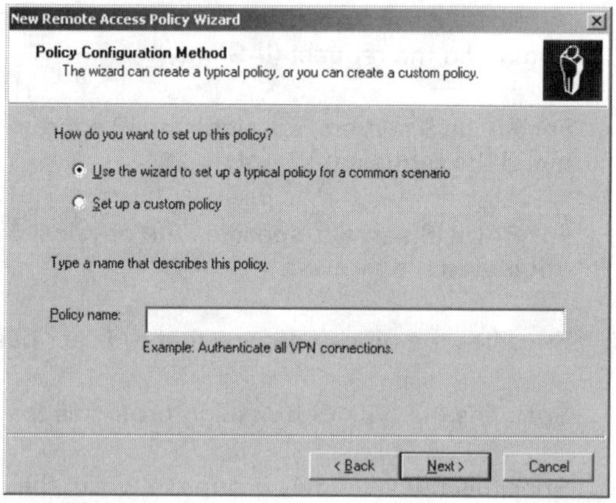

FIGURE 6.11 The Access Method page

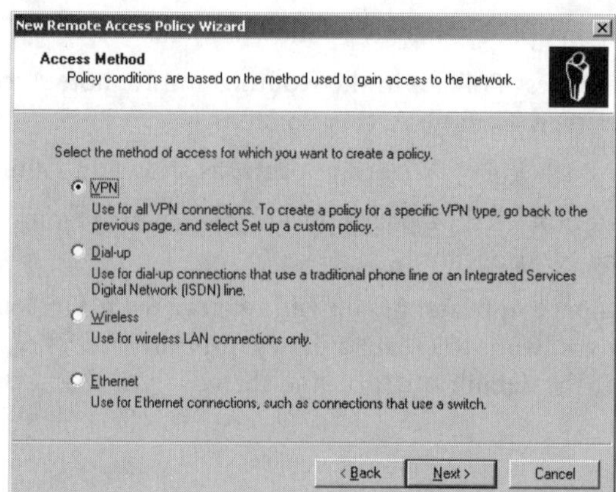

5. The User or Group Access page appears, as shown in Figure 6.12. Add a group or groups, then click the Next button.

FIGURE 6.12 The User or Group Access page

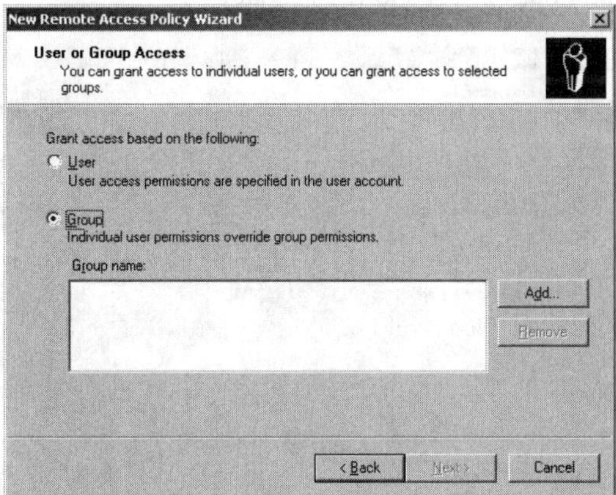

6. The Authentication Method page appears, as shown in Figure 6.13. Choose the authentication protocols to be supported by the RRAS server, and then click the Next button.

FIGURE 6.13 The Authentication Methods page

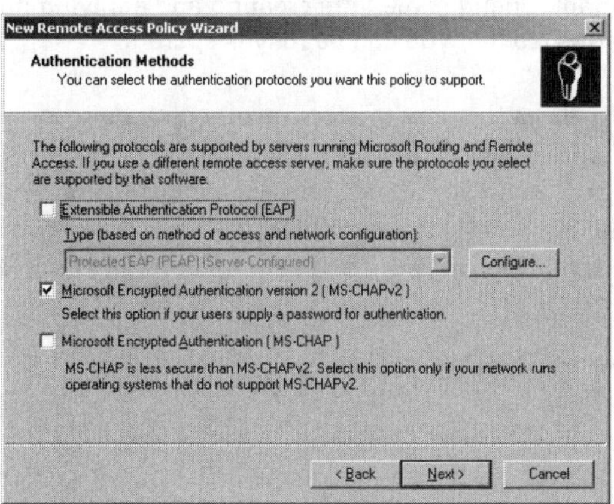

7. The Policy Encryption Level page appears, as shown in Figure 6.14. Note that the default includes all encryption levels. Select the levels of encryption to be supported in this profile, and then click the Next button.

8. The Completing the New Remote Access Policy Wizard page appears, summarizing your choices. Verify the options, and then choose Finish.

Your policy now appears in the RRAS console. You can change the order of application of the policies via the Up/Down arrows on the toolbar, or by right-clicking the policy in question and choosing Move Up or Move Down from the pop-up menu. You should ensure that the least restrictive policy is always on top and the most restrictive policy is at the bottom of the list. This speeds access for authorized remote clients, because the first policy matching the connection request is applied.

FIGURE 6.14 The Policy Encryption Level page

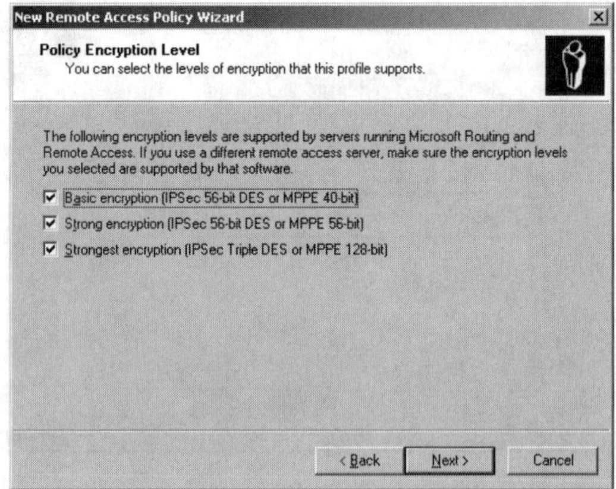

Both for the test and for your future role as a Windows Server 2003 administrator, understanding how the connection attempts are processed is very important. Spend some time creating and applying policies for a variety of scenarios, so that you can be fully prepared.

So far, you've learned about the remote access protocols, connection types, and policies. For the remainder of the chapter, we will focus on securing data transmissions through the use of IPSec Policies. You'll learn how IPSec works, how to install and configure IPSec and how to use the default security policies. You'll also learn how to define your own security policies and filters to customize the level of protection available to computers on your network.

Evaluating IP Security

The original specifications for the IP protocol made no provisions for protocol security. As the Internet expanded, it became clear that robust authentication and privacy protection were essential needs. As the installed base of IP-capable devices grew, so too did the complexity of devising a security protocol that would interoperate with those devices.

The Internet Engineering Task Force (IETF) devised a solution, and the result was the *Internet Protocol Security Extensions (IPSec)*. In the late 1990s, vendors began releasing products that applied the IP Security Extensions to *IPv4*, version 4 of the IP specification and the current version of IP for most TCP/IP networks.

Internet Protocol security (IPSec) is a framework of open standards for ensuring private, secure communications over IP networks, through the use of cryptographic security services. These services allow for authentication, integrity, access control, and confidentiality. Like

TCP/IP, IPSec is vendor-neutral. Microsoft considers IPSec to be the long-term direction for secure networking.

Major vendors, including Microsoft, Cisco, Nortel, and RSA Security, are shipping IPSec products. However, the standard itself is in transition, so if you are considering implementing IPSec in a mixed-vendor network, you must ensure that all devices can communicate with each other.

IPSec provides services that are similar to Secure Sockets Layer (SSL), but far more powerful. IPSec operates at the network layer as a set of extensions to the basic Internet Protocol (IP). This enables protocol security to extend to all protocols in the IP suite and to be completely transparent to applications. Any IP protocol can be used over IPSec. You can create encrypted tunnels (VPNs) or just encrypt traffic between computers. IPSec scales gracefully to meet the needs of networks of all sizes.

IPSec is based on an end-to-end security model that establishes trust and security from a source to a destination IP address. What this means is that only the sending and receiving computers need to know anything about the traffic being secured. They assume that the data is being transmitted over an unsecure medium, and each handles security at its own end. Other computers that would only route the data don't even have to support IPSec, assuming that there is no firewall-type packet filtering or NAT happening between the two computers. Secure end-to-end links are provided for private network users within or across the enterprise boundary. Enterprise scenarios in which IPSec can now be deployed, therefore, include:

- Client/server and peer-to-peer LANs
- Router to router and gateway to gateway across a WAN
- Remote access, including dial-up and VPN clients

An *IPSec client* is the computer that attempts to establish a connection to another machine, and an *IPSec server* is the target of that connection. Any Windows 2000, XP, or Windows Server 2003 computer may be an IPSec client or server.

IPSec provides two crucial services: a method for computers to decide if they trust each other (*authentication*) and a method to keep network data private (*encryption*).

IKE is discussed in RFC 2409. Refer to RFC 1825 for additional information on IPSec.

Windows Server 2003 implements IPSec as policy-based security through Group Policy. You can set policies that configure individual computers, groups of computers within an organizational unit or domain, or all Windows 2000, XP, or Server 2003 computers on your network. IPSec policies are applied either to the local computer or within Active Directory to objects such as computers, domains, sites, and OUs.

You create policies through a combination of rules, actions, and filters. Rules govern how and when an IPSec policy applies to communication. Through rules, you can secure communications based on the source, destination, and type of IP traffic. This is known as IP packet filtering.

IPSec can be used in one of two modes:

- *Transport mode* is the default mode and uses IPSec for end-to-end communications to encrypt or authenticate a direct connection between two computers. Network traffic is protected before it leaves the originating machine, and it remains secured until it is decrypted by the receiving machine. Transport mode encrypts only the payload. Typical IP payloads include TCP segments, UDP messages, and ICMP messages.
- *Tunnel mode* encrypts traffic that passes through a tunnel established by L2TP. Tunnel mode encrypts the entire IP packet (both the header and the payload).

In the following sections, we will look at the fundamentals of IPSec, how to use IPSec, and how to plan an IPSec Deployment.

In this chapter, and on the exam, assume that the phrase "IPSec Tunnel mode" refers to the use of IPSec for tunneling, not for VPN traffic. L2TP usually refers to "L2TP/IPSec."

IPSec Fundamentals

IPSec has two goals. First, it defends against network attacks by providing packet filtering and secure authentication to enforce trusted communication. Second, it protects IP packets by providing data encryption.

IPSec accomplishes its goals through a combination of cryptography-based protection services, security protocols, and dynamic key management. It can even be used to block receipt or transmission of specific traffic types. IPSec can be used to achieve data security by the following means:

- Data encryption
- Data integrity
- Mutual authentication
- Packet filtering

Next you'll see how IPSec provides protection through authentication and encryption.

Authentication Authentication protects your network, and the data it carries, from tampering. This tampering might take the form of a malicious attacker sitting between a client and a server, altering the contents of packets (the so-called "man in the middle" attack), or it might take the form of an attacker joining your network and impersonating either a client or a server. IPSec uses an *authentication header (AH)* to digitally sign the entire contents of each packet. This signature provides three separate benefits:

Protection against Replay Attacks If an attacker can capture packets, save them until a later time, and send them again. They can impersonate a computer after that computer is no longer on the network. This is called a *replay attack*. IPSec's authentication mechanism prevents replay attacks by including the sender's signature on all packets.

Protection against Tampering *Tampering* is a form of attack that involves altering data in transit. IPSec's signatures provide data integrity, meaning that interlopers can't selectively change parts of packets to alter their meaning.

Protection against Spoofing *Spoofing* is a form of attack in which an attacker assumes the identity of another computer. Authentication refers to the process of a client or server verifying another machine's identity. IPSec authentication headers provide authentication because each end of a connection can verify the other's identity.

Encryption Authentication protects your data against tampering, but it doesn't do anything to keep people from seeing it. For that, you need encryption, which actually obscures the payload (data) contents so that a man in the middle can't read the traffic as it goes by. To accomplish this, IPSec provides the *Encapsulating Security Payload (ESP)*. ESP is used to encrypt the entire payload of an IPSec packet, rendering it undecipherable by anyone other than the intended recipient. ESP only provides confidentiality, but it can be combined with AH to gain maximum security.

The following sections cover IPSec in Windows Server 2003, IPSec protocols, security methods, IPSec policy components, and the default policies used in IPSec.

IPSec in Windows Server 2003

The IPSec implementation in Windows Server 2003 involves a large number of changes to the TCP/IP stack. Microsoft's IPSec implementation is actually licensed from, and was written by, Cisco, and therefore it guarantees good compatibility with other standards-based IPSec clients.

In the following sections, we'll introduce new features of IPSec in Windows Server 2003, including new management consoles, Group Policy, RSoP, support for L2TP/IPSec, NAT support, certificate to account mapping, default traffic exemptions and command-line management with netsh.

Configuring IPSec with the New Management Consoles

In Windows Server 2003, IPSec policies are configured using the IP Security Policy Management MMC snap-in and monitored using the IP Security Monitor MMC snap-in. IPSecmon is no longer used to manage IP security.

You'll learn how to use the management consoles later in this chapter. The IP Security Policy Management MMC snap-in is covered in the section titled "Implementing IPSec," and the IP Security Monitor MMC snap-in is covered in the section titled "Troubleshooting Security for Data Transmission."

Applying IPSec through Group Policy

Windows Server 2003 has some other features that make IPSec more useful. In a large network of heterogeneous computers, computers can automatically take advantage of IPSec if both parties to a communication session support IPSec. You also want to ensure that the security settings you want are applied to all IPSec-capable machines. With Windows NT, and with most other operating systems, that could require hand-configuring each IPSec computer to use the settings you want.

Windows Server 2003 enables you to streamline this configuration process by using Group Policy. First, you specify the IPSec settings you want to use on your network. Then, each Windows 2000, XP, or Server 2003 computer runs a service called the *IPSec Policy Agent.* When the system starts, the Policy Agent connects to an Active Directory server, fetches the IPSec policy, and then passes it to the IPSec code.

You will learn more about the IPSec Policy Agent later in this chapter in the section titled "Deploying IPSec Policies."

Using the Resultant Set of Policy (RSoP)

The Resultant Set of Policy tool (also known as RSoP) is a new feature of Group Policy, and it enables you to accomplish two very important tasks:

- To view the results of a set of policies before you actually apply them
- To view the current policy set in effect on a remote computer

This new policy analyzer enables an administrator to forecast the effective result of multiple policies before deploying them throughout the network. This functionality will enable you to quickly and effectively implement policies that ensure secure data transmission without preventing communication from occurring.

L2TP and NAT Support

You can now use Layer Two Tunneling Protocol over IPSec (L2TP/IPSec), which enables you to implement an IPSec-based VPN, or you can allow an IPSec connection to pass through a NAT, which benefits you if you want to use IPSec-protected applications across a NAT interface.

Windows Server 2003 supports L2TP/IPSec for the highest possible protocol security. Clients that support 128-bit encryption keys can use L2TP/IPSec. You should set a standard for your remote users to encrypt data with the highest level of data encryption possible. Windows XP and the Windows Server 2003 family support 128-bit encryption keys. Older clients (such as Windows 98 with the latest service pack) can also handle L2TP/IPSec.

IPSec ESP packets can now pass through NATs that allow UDP traffic. IPSec over NAT functionality is a great new feature that allows the following deployment options:

- L2TP/IPSec VPN clients that are behind NATs can now use IPSec ESP transport mode to establish IPSec-secured communications over the Internet.
- RRAS servers can establish gateway-to-gateway IPSec tunnels when one of the RRAS servers is behind a NAT.
- Clients and servers can send IPSec-secured TCP and UDP packets to other clients or servers using IPSec ESP transport mode when one or both computers are behind a NAT.

Certificate-to-Account Mapping

When you enable certificate-to-account mapping in IPSec, IKE maps a computer certificate to a computer account in Active Directory. If you use either Kerberos or certificate authentication, you can allow or deny the following computers access to a Windows Server 2003 server:

- Computers that are members of a specific domain.

- Computers with a certificate from a specific issuing certification authority.
- A specific computer or groups of computers. In this case, you restrict access by configuring Group Policy security settings and assigning either the "Access this computer from the network" or the "Deny access to this computer from the network" user right to a computer or group of computers.

Default Traffic Exemptions

Security is dramatically improved in Windows Server 2003 because only IKE traffic, which is required for establishing secure communication, is exempted from IPSec filtering. You can set specific filters for broadcast and multicast traffic. IPSec does not negotiate security associations (SAs) for broadcast or multicast traffic.

Command-Line Management with *netsh*

The `netsh` command has a new context: the `netsh` IPSec context, which replaces the `Ipsecpol.exe` tool from the Windows 2000 Server Resource Kit. This enables you to script and automate IPSec configuration. There are many commands available that you can use to configure IPSec. Two of the security features you can configure for greatly increased security are computer startup security and persistent policy.

IPSec now provides stateful filtering of network traffic during system startup to limit traffic to DHCP traffic, outbound traffic initiated by the computer, and responses to that traffic. You can exempt other traffic types from this filtering.

You can also use `netsh` to create and apply a persistent policy that the IPSec Policy Agent will apply to the computer before any local or Active Directory–based policies. A persistent policy remains in effect regardless of whether other policies are applied. This enables you to secure a computer in the event that another policy cannot be applied.

Local or Active Directory–based policies add to the persistent policy (if configured). If there is a conflict between a persistent policy and either a domain or a local policy, the persistent policy will prevail.

IPSec Protocols

IPSec appears to be a single protocol, but it's actually implemented using three different protocols plus a number of Windows Server 2003 drivers and services, all of which will be discussed in the following sections.

ISAKMP and Oakley

The *Internet Security Agreement/Key Management Protocol (ISAKMP)* provides a way for two computers to agree on security settings and exchange a security key that they can use to communicate securely. Information is secured with a combination of an algorithm and a key.

Internet Key Exchange (IKE) services dynamically exchange and manage keys between computers. IKE also dynamically negotiates a common set of security settings, so it is not necessary for both parties to have identical IPSec policies defined. Dynamic rekeying during exchanges over unsecured session pipes blocks most impersonation and interception attacks.

A *security association (SA)* provides all the information needed for two computers to communicate securely. The SA contains a policy agreement that controls which algorithms and key lengths the two machines will use (for instance, it can say use 128-bit RC5 and SHA-1), plus the actual security keys used to securely exchange information. Think of this agreement like a contract: It specifies what each party is and is not willing to do as part of the agreement.

This process has two steps. First, the two computers use the ISAKMP to establish a security agreement. This is called the *ISAKMP SA*. To establish the ISAKMP SA, the two computers must agree on the following three things:

- Which encryption algorithm (DES, triple DES, 40-bit DES, or none) they'll use
- Which algorithm they'll use for verifying message integrity (MD5 or SHA-1)
- How connections will be authenticated: using a public-key certificate, a shared secret key, or Kerberos

Once the ISAKMP SA is in place, the two machines can use the Oakley protocol to securely agree on a shared master key. This key, called the *ISAKMP master key*, is used along with the algorithms negotiated in the ISAKMP SA to establish a secure connection. After the secure connection is brought up, the two machines start another round of negotiations. These negotiations cover the following:

- Whether the Authentication Header protocol will be used for this connection
- Whether the Encapsulating Security Payload protocol will be used for this connection
- Which encryption algorithm will be used for the ESP protocol
- Which authentication protocol will be used for the AH protocol

After *these* negotiations are finished, the two machines end up with *two* new SAs: one for inbound traffic and another for outbound traffic. These SAs are called *IPSec SAs* to distinguish them from the ISAKMP SA. At this point, Oakley is used again to generate a new set of session keys. The master ISAKMP key is used whenever new SAs are negotiated; once the SA negotiation finishes, though, the communications using that SA are protected using the SA-specific keys.

The Authentication Header (AH)

The AH protocol provides data integrity and authentication, but how? The answer lies in how the IPSec packet is actually constructed. Figure 6.15 shows a sample AH packet (note that this example shows a TCP packet, but AH works the same way for UDP).

FIGURE 6.15 An AH packet

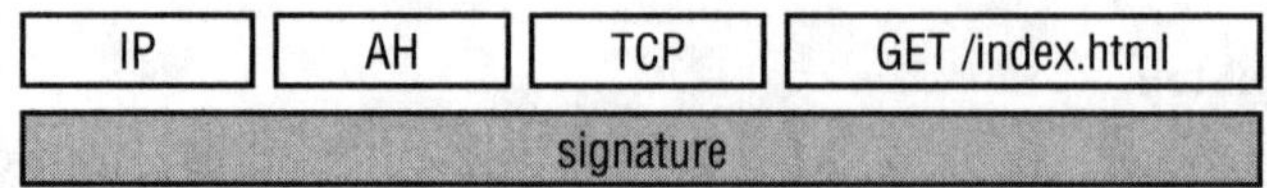

Two features lend AH its security. The first security feature is that the packet signature (which is contained in the AH itself) is computed on the entire packet: payload and headers. That means that an attacker can't modify any part of the packet, including the IP or TCP/UDP header. The second security booster is that the AH is placed between the IP header and the TCP or UDP header; this adds further tamper-proofing.

The Encapsulating Security Payload (ESP)

The ESP protocol is designed to deliver message confidentiality. Take a look at a sample ESP packet, shown in Figure 6.16, to see how it accomplishes this.

FIGURE 6.16 An ESP packet

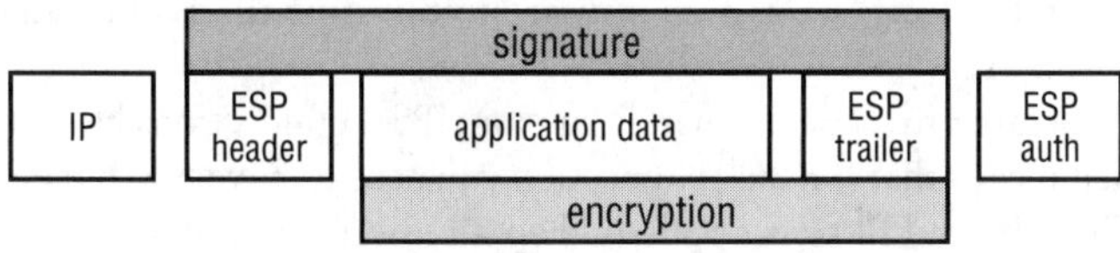

The first thing you'll probably notice is that this packet is more complex in construction than the AH packet, because ESP alone provides authentication, replay-proofing, and integrity checking. It does so by adding three separate components: an ESP header, an ESP trailer, and an ESP authentication block. Each of these components contains some of the data needed to provide the necessary authentication and integrity checking.

To prevent tampering, an ESP client must sign the ESP header, application data, and ESP trailer into one unit; of course, ESP is used to encrypt the application data and the ESP trailer to provide confidentiality. The combination of this overlapping signature and encryption operation provides good security.

Security Methods

Each IPSec connection uses a *security method*, which is a prespecified encryption algorithm with a negotiated key length and key lifetime. You can use one of the two predefined security methods (High or Medium), or you can create your own by specifying which security protocols (AH or ESP), encryption algorithms, and key lifetimes you want to use for a particular connection. When your computer is negotiating with a remote IPSec peer, the ISAKMP service works its way down the list of methods you've specified and attempts to use the most secure method first. The first method on which both ends agree is used.

Windows Server 2003 supports the DES and 3DES encryption algorithms. 3DES is more secure than DES because it encrypts each block of data three times with three different keys.

IPSec Policy Components

An *IPSec policy* is a set of one or more rules that determine IPSec behavior. There is no method for specifying the order in which to apply rules in a policy. The IPSec driver automatically orders rules based on the most-specific to least-specific filter list. For example, a rule containing a filter list specifying individual IP addresses and ports would be applied before a rule containing a filter list that specified all addresses on a subnet. Each rule contains filters and other configurable settings, which will be discussed in the following sections.

Make sure that you understand the purpose and function of the different IPSec policy components. Understand what happens when you configure filter lists and filter actions, and how they will behave in different scenarios.

IP Filter List

A security filter ties security protocols to a particular network address. The filter contains the source and destination addresses involved (either for specific hosts or networks, using a netmask), the protocol used, and the source and destination ports allowed for TCP and UDP traffic. For example, you can define a filter that specifies exactly what kind of IPSec negotiations you're willing to allow when a computer in your domain contacts a computer in the `microsoft.com` domain.

As you might remember from our earlier discussion, IPSec connections have two sides: inbound and outbound. That means that for each connection you need to have two filters: one inbound and one outbound. The inbound filter is applied when a remote computer requests security on a connection, and the outbound filter is applied before sending traffic to a remote machine.

Let's say that you want to create a rule to allow any computer in the `globalitcertification.com` domain to use IPSec when talking to any computer in the `microsoft.com` domain. For this to work, you need the following four filters:

- A filter for the `globalitcertification.com` domain for outbound packets with a source of `*.globalitcertification.com` and a destination of `*.microsoft.com`. (Yes, you can use DNS names and wildcards in filters.)
- A filter for the `globalitcertification.com` domain for inbound packets, this time with a source of `*.microsoft.com` and a destination of `*.globalitcertification.com`.
- An inbound filter in the `microsoft.com` domain that specifies a source of `*.globalitcertification.com` and a destination of `*.microsoft.com`.
- An outbound filter in the `microsoft.com` domain that specifies a source of `*.microsoft.com` and a destination of `*.globalitcertification.com`.

If any of these filters are missing or misconfigured, the IPSec negotiation process will fail and IPSec won't be used. If they're all there, though, when you try to establish an FTP connection from `delta.globalitcertification.com` to `exchange.microsoft.com`, the outbound filter on your domain will fire, and it will trigger IPSec to request a security negotiation with Microsoft's machine. Assuming everything goes well and that the filters are okay, you'll end up with two IPSec SAs on your machine, and the connection will be secured.

You normally group filters into *filter lists* for ease of management. Because you can stuff any number of individual filters into a filter list, you can easily build rules that enforce complicated behavior, then distribute those rules throughout your network as necessary. For each rule, a single filter list is selected that contains one or more predefined packet filters that describe the type of traffic to which the configured filter action for the rule is applied.

Filter Action

Filters specify a source and destination, but they also need to specify what action should take place when the criteria specified in the filter match. A *filter action* specifies how traffic matching the filter will be handled (i.e., dropped, encrypted, etc.). You can use the following actions in each filter:

- The Permit action tells the IPSec filter to take no action. It neither accepts nor rejects the connection based on security rules, meaning that it adds zero security. This action is sometimes called the *passthrough action*, since it allows traffic to pass through without modification. In general, you'll use it for applications like WINS servers, where there's no security-sensitive data involved.

- The Block action causes the filter to reject communications from the remote system. This prevents the remote system from making any type of connection, with or without IPSec.
- The Accept Unsecured and Allow Unsecured actions allow you to interoperate with computers that don't speak IPSec. The Accept Unsecured Communication, But Always Respond Using IPsec policy says that it's okay to accept unsecured connections but that your machines will always ask for an IPSec connection before accepting the unsecured request. This policy allows you to handle both unsecured and secured traffic, with a preference for IPSec when it's available. The Allow Unsecured Communication With Non-IPsec Aware Computers action allows your machines to accept unsecure connections without attempting to use IPSec; as such, we recommend that you not use it in favor of the "Accept unsecured" action.
- The Use These Security Settings option lets you specify which security methods you want used on connections that trigger this filter. This option allows you to specify custom settings for either individual computers or remote networks.

The upcoming section "Managing Rules with the Rules Tab" discusses when to use, or not use, each of these actions.

The filter action rule should be examined to ensure that the cryptographic, hashing, and session key regeneration settings are suitable for a company's needs.

Authentication Methods

IPSec supports three separate authentication methods: Kerberos version 5, certificates, and pre-shared keys. Since the first thing an IPSec client and server want to do is authenticate to each other, they need some way to agree on a set of credentials to use. The Windows Server 2003 version of IPSec supports three different authentication methods, which are used only during the initial authentication phase of building the SAs, not to generate encryption keys. We will look at each of these in the following sections.

KERBEROS V5

Kerberos v5 is the default authentication method used by Windows 2000, XP, and Server 2003 clients and servers. It's also the default authentication method for Active Directory. Kerberos replaces the older and less secure NT LAN Manager authentication scheme. Kerberos is a widely supported open standard that offers good security and a great deal of flexibility. Many third-party IPSec products include Kerberos support.

Note that only Windows 2000 and Server 2003 domain controllers support Kerberos authentication. Windows 2000 and Server 2003 member servers and NT 4 servers do not. However, if the member server is part of an Active Directory domain, an authentication request is forwarded to a domain controller (DC) and the DC will use Kerberos first to authenticate. Supported clients include Windows 2000, Windows XP Professional, and Windows Server 2003 clients that are members of the same or trusted Active Directory domains.

Kerberos engages in *mutual authentication* (also known as dual verification) to verify both the identity of the user and of network services. Tickets are granted for accessing network services. The process is transparent to the user except when entering a password or smart card credentials.

When a Windows Server 2003 is installed as a domain controller, it automatically becomes a *Key Distribution Center (KDC)*. The KDC is responsible for holding all of the client passwords and account information. Kerberos services are also installed on each Windows Server 2003 client and server.

The Kerberos v5 authentication process works as follows:

1. The client authenticates to the KDC using a password or smart card.
2. The KDC issues the client a *ticket-granting ticket (TGT)*. The client can use the TGT to access the *ticket-granting service (TGS)*, which allows the user to authenticate to services within the domain.
3. The TGS issues a service ticket to the clients.
4. The client presents the service ticket to the requested network service. This service ticket authenticates the user to the service and the service to the user, for mutual authentication.

Clients use a DNS lookup to locate the nearest DC, which then becomes the preferred KDC during the user's logon session.

Kerberos v5 is not supported on Windows XP Home clients or on any clients that are not members of an Active Directory domain.

PUBLIC KEY CERTIFICATES

A *public key infrastructure (PKI)* provides certificate-based authentication of computers and resolves many security problems by presenting security credentials without compromising them in the process.

Public key certificates (see Chapter 8, "Planning Certificate Services") are like digital passports. They are used to verify the identities of non-Windows computers, standalone computers, computers that do not belong to a trusted domain, and computers that do not support Kerberos v5. Public key certificates can be used in situations including Internet access, remote access to corporate resources, extranets, and with computers that do not run Kerberos v5.

At least one trusted certification authority and associated certificate must be configured. Windows 2000, XP, and Windows Server 2003 support X.509 version 3 certificates, including computer certificates generated by commercial certification authorities.

When you use certificate-based authentication, each end of the connection can use the other's public certificate to verify a digitally signed message. This provides great security, with some added overhead and infrastructure requirements. As you add machines to a domain in Windows Server 2003, they're automatically issued *machine certificates* that can be used for authentication. If you want to allow users and computers from other domains or organizations to connect to your IPSec machines, you'll need to explore certificate solutions that allow cross-organization certification. Certificates enable secure communication with computers that do not belong to a trusted Windows 2000 Server or Windows Server 2003 domain and with non-Windows computers, and they support restricting access to a smaller group of computers than can be accomplished with domain authentication.

You'll learn more about planning a public key infrastructure with Microsoft Certificate Services in Chapter 8.

PRESHARED KEYS

Preshared keys are essentially reusable passwords. The preshared key itself is just a word, code, or phrase that functions as a secret key that both computers share for authentication purposes. The two machines agree to use this key to establish a trust, but they don't send the plain-text phrase over the network. This method is the simplest to use and must be manually configured.

During security negotiation, information is encrypted by using a session key, which is created using a Diffie-Hellman algorithm and the shared, secret key. The same key decrypts the information on the other end. Inside the packet is a hash of the preshared key, and IPSec peers can authenticate each other's packets by decrypting and verifying the hash. Packets that fail authentication are discarded.

Preshared keys are a relatively weak authentication method because the unencrypted key is stored in Active Directory in readable hexadecimal format. It is stored in plain text in the Registry as well. Anyone who can see the key can impersonate the computer. In addition, a weaker form of encryption is produced compared to the other two methods. Microsoft recommends against using it in production. Preshared key authentication is provided for interoperability and adherence to IPSec standards. You should use preshared keys only for testing purposes and use either Kerberos or certificates in production. However, you may need to use this mode to support a third-party IPSec product that doesn't yet support certificate or Kerberos authentication.

Only one authentication method can be configured between two computers. If there are multiple rules that apply to the same set of computers, make sure that the authentication method is configured identically in all rules so that the pair can use the same method.

Be certain to know which authentication method to use to meet different technical scenarios and objectives.

Tunnel Endpoint

The *tunnel endpoint* specifies whether the traffic is tunneled and, if so, the IP address of the tunnel (destination) endpoint.

Connection Type

The *connection type* specifies whether the rule applies to LAN connections, dial-up connections, or both.

Default Policies

Windows XP and Windows Server 2003 include three default IPSec policies. These policies are intended to serve as examples and are not intended for operational use without modification. You should create new, custom policies for operational use. (In fact, you'll have to create your own policies for things like DHCP and remote access servers.) The default policies allow a computer to receive unsecured traffic and are intended for use on intranets in Active Directory domains. There are three default policies:

- The Client (Respond Only) policy enables the Windows 2000, XP, or Server 2003 computer on which it is active to respond to requests for secured communications.
- The Server (Request Security) policy provides the best balance between security and interoperability. Computers using this policy always request secure communication on outbound requests, but allow unsecured communication with non-IPSec-aware computers.
- The Secure Server (Require Security) policy mandates secure IP communications. Only the initial inbound communication request is allowed to be unsecured. In this case, DNS, WINS, Web requests, and all other IP traffic must be secured with IPSec or it will be blocked. This policy is meant for computers on an intranet that require highly secure communications.

Understanding the behavioral differences between the three default policies is extremely important, both for the exam and in real world implementations of IPSec.

The Client (Respond Only) policy has a single rule. This rule is the same as the third rule used in the other two policies. The rule enables a computer to respond to requests for secured communications.

The Server (Request Security) policy has three rules. The first rule requests security for all traffic, the second rule permits ICMP traffic, and the third rule responds to requests for security from other computers.

The Secure Server (Require Security) policy also has three rules. The first rule requires security for all traffic, the second rule permits ICMP traffic, and the third rule responds to requests for security from other computers.

Settings for rules in each of the three default policies are discussed in more detail in the following sections.

Client (Respond Only)

The Client (Respond Only) policy has the following settings:

FIRST RULE (DEFAULT RESPONSE RULE)

This is the default response rule, which can be used for all policies. The rule is activated by default for all policies and can be deactivated but not deleted.

IP Filter List: <Dynamic>

Indicates that the filter list is not configured, but that filters are automatically negotiated during the IKE negotiation exchange.

Filter Action: Default Response

The Negotiate Security filter action will be used.

Authentication: Kerberos

Tunnel Setting: None

Server (Request Security)

The Server (Request Security) policy has the following settings:

FIRST RULE

IP Filter List: All IP Traffic

Filter Action: Request Security (Optional)

Authentication: Kerberos

Tunnel Setting: None

Connection Type: All

SECOND RULE

IP Filter List: All ICMP Traffic

Filter Action: Permit

Authentication: N/A

Tunnel Setting: None

Connection Type: All

THIRD RULE

IP Filter List: <Dynamic>

Filter Action: Default Response

Authentication: Kerberos

Tunnel Setting: None

Connection Type: All

Secure Server (Require Security)

The Secure Server (Require Security) policy has the following settings:

FIRST RULE

IP Filter List: All IP Traffic

Filter Action: Require Security

Authentication: Kerberos

Tunnel Setting: None

Connection Type: All

SECOND RULE

IP Filter List: All ICMP Traffic

Filter Action: Permit

Authentication: None

Tunnel Setting: None

Connection Type: All

THIRD RULE

IP Filter List: <Dynamic>

Filter Action: Default Response

Authentication: Kerberos

Tunnel Setting: None

Connection Type: All

The best procedure is to start with the default policies, compare them to your organization's needs, and adjust the policy settings to meet your specific needs. For example, you may want to use the default policy Secure Server (Require Security) because it requires all outgoing communications to be secured. However, this policy could actually leave you open to a DoS attack. How? The computer will continue to try to negotiate security with all incoming traffic it receives.

To protect against a DoS attack while using the default policy Secure Server (Require Security), you could clear the checkbox Accept Unsecured Communication But Always Respond Using IPSec on the Filter Action, Security Methods page on the server, and configure the clients to initiate security with the server rather than use the default response rule.

You assign policies to computers in a number of ways. The easiest way is to store the policy in Active Directory and let the IPSec Policy Agent take care of applying it to the applicable machines. Once an IPSec policy is assigned to a computer through Active Directory, it remains assigned—even after the computer leaves the site, domain, or organizational unit (OU) that gave it the original policy—until another policy is provided. You can also assign policies directly to individual machines. In either case, you can manually unassign policies when you no longer want a policy in place on a specific machine.

You must be able to determine which policy to choose for computers in different roles, as well as on which computers you will apply a given default or custom policy within an Active Directory hierarchy.

IPSec in Practice

Let's see how the process actually works in practice. As an example, a computer named NYCCLIENT2 will establish a connection to a file server named NYCSERVER1. NYCCLIENT2 and NYCSERVER1 are both members of the same Windows Server 2003 domain, so they can use the Windows Server 2003 default of Kerberos authentication. Keep in mind that this entire process is utterly transparent to users on both machines, as well as applications and even most intervening routers and network devices.

When NYCCLIENT1 boots, the IPSec Policy Agent service starts. It connects to Active Directory and downloads the current IPSec policy for the domain. If this connection attempt fails, NYCCLIENT1 will keep trying until it successfully retrieves an IPSec policy.

When the policy is retrieved, policy settings are passed to the ISAKMP/Oakley subsystem and to the actual IPSec drivers in the kernel.

When NYCCLIENT1 initially attempts to make a connection to any foreign machine, its IPSec driver will check the active IPSec policy to see whether any IP filters are defined. These filters specify destination networks, traffic types, or both; for the destination or traffic type, the filter also specifies whether IPSec is mandatory, optional, or forbidden.

After NYCCLIENT1's IPSec driver determines that it's allowed to use IPSec when talking to computers on NYCSERVER1's subnet, it will use ISAKMP to establish an ISAKMP SA with NYCSERVER1.

When NYCSERVER1 sees the incoming ISAKMP request from NYCCLIENT1, its ISAKMP service replies to the request, and the two computers negotiate an ISAKMP SA as described earlier. This SA includes a shared secret key that can be used to establish connection-specific SAs.

Now that an ISAKMP SA has been established, the two computers have everything they need to establish a pair of IPSec SAs. Once those negotiations are complete, each computer has two IPSec SAs in place: one for outbound traffic and one for inbound.

NYCCLIENT1's request (whatever it is) is processed by its IPSec stack. IPSec uses AH and/or ESP to protect the outbound packets, and then it transfers them to the lower-level parts of the IP stack for delivery to NYCSERVER1. When NYCSERVER1 gets the packets, its IPSec stack will decrypt them (if necessary), verify their authenticity, and pass them up the TCP/IP stack for further processing.

Planning an IPSec Deployment

When you evaluate IPSec for your organization, you should consider some potential disadvantages. If you decide to use IPSec policies, you have many things to consider when deploying them. We'll discuss these topics in the following sections.

Considerations for Planning IPSec

The following are some factors to consider when determining whether and how to deploy IPSec in your organization:

- IPSec-knowledgeable IT staff members must be available to plan, configure, modify, assign, deploy, and troubleshoot IPSec policies.
- The sophisticated cryptographic functions IPSec performs are processor-intensive. Some network interface cards (NICs) are capable of performing these calculations on-board and can be used to speed performance and offload your CPU.
- A Group Policy plan and ideally an Active Directory infrastructure should be in place.
- Non–Active Directory environments require a public key infrastructure (PKI) or defined procedures for computers to obtain certificates.
- Non–Active Directory environments require a plan for deploying local computer policies on each computer to execute an IPSec policy.

Deployment Options for IPSec Policies

IPSec policies can be deployed by using local policies or Active Directory. Both options can be used in heterogeneous client environments. In addition, the `netsh` IPSec command can be used to configure persistent policies. This option would come in handy if you want to ensure IP security whether or not a local or Active Directory–based policy can be found.

Deploying IPSec with Local Computer Policies

Each Windows XP, Windows 2000, or Windows Server 2003 computer has a local Group Policy Object (GPO) known as the Local Computer Policy. Local policies are defined in the Registry and can include standalone computers and computers that do not belong to a trusted Windows 2000 or Windows Server 2003 domain.

Local policies can also be used in Active Directory environments, but they will be overwritten if a GPO exists for the computer's site, domain, or an OU to which it belongs. If IPSec policies are not configured in the Active Directory GPO, however, the local policy's IPSec settings will not be overwritten. Local policies can be used if there is no Active Directory infrastructure in place or if there is no need to deploy IPSec policies automatically to a large number of computers in an Active Directory environment.

Here are a few important facts to note when considering deploying IPSec through local computer policy:

- If you use local policies and choose not to use Kerberos, or if Active Directory has not been installed, then determine if there is a certificate infrastructure set up that can be used as an authentication method.
- With a Microsoft certificate authority, you can use autoenrollment to automatically store computer certificates as an actual property of an Active Directory computer account. As an alternative, you can manage computer certificates manually for any computers that need them.
- You will need to determine how to deploy IPSec policies, because you can't use Active Directory to do so. Policies have an import and export feature with which you can copy them to multiple computers.

Deploying IPSec with Active Directory-Based Policies

IPSec policies can be assigned to a GPO that is then applied to a site, domain, or OU. The IPSec policy is propagated to all computers affected by that GPO. Active Directory–based policies are managed using the IP Security Policy Management console or the `netsh` command.

Use Active Directory to deploy IPSec policies if there is an Active Directory infrastructure in place, if there is a substantial number of computers requiring IPSec policy assignment, and/or if you want to centralize the IPSec strategy for the company. Use local policies in the opposite scenarios.

Here are a few important facts to note when considering deploying IPSec within Active Directory:

- You can reduce administrative effort and configuration by using the highest possible level of the Active Directory hierarchy to assign a policy.

- The list of all IPSec policies will be available to assign at any level in the Active Directory hierarchy.
- Only one IPSec policy can be assigned at any given level in Active Directory.
- If needed, you can create new OUs to organize your computer accounts, then apply a GPO to the OU to enforce IP security.
- IPSec policies from different OUs are never merged.
- Active Directory–based policies are added to a persistent policy, if configured, and override local policies.
- IPSec policies must be included with the Group Policy backup strategy for Active Directory in order to maintain consistency.
- Policies remain in effect unless they are unassigned, so you should unassign a policy before deleting that policy object.

Active Directory–based policy can be managed using the IP Security Policy Management console or by using the `netsh` command with the IPSec context.

More considerations for Active Directory environments are discussed in the section titled "Deploying IPSec Policies" later in this chapter.

You can jump ahead to Chapter 7, "Planning Server-Level Security," for a more detailed explanation of Group Policy.

Implementing IPSec

The components necessary for a Windows Server 2003 computer to act as an IPSec client are already installed by default when you install Windows Server 2003. However—also by default—there's no policy that requires the use of IPSec, so the default behavior for Windows Server 2003 machines is not to use it. The good news is that you don't really have to "install" IPSec; you just have to open the tool you use to manage it, and then start assigning policies and filters to get the desired effect.

In the following sections, you'll learn how to use the IP Security Policy Management Console, how to manage and configure IPSec policies, and how to configure IPSec for tunnel mode.

Using the IP Security Policy Management Console

IPSec is managed through the IP Security Policy Management snap-in (which we will refer to as the IPSec snap-in from now on). There's no prebuilt MMC console that includes this snap-in, so you need to create one by opening a MMC console and adding the snap-in to it.

When you install the IPSec snap-in, you must choose whether you want to use it to manage a local IPSec policy, the default policy for the domain your computer is in, the default policy for another domain, or the local policy on another computer. This gives you an effective way to delegate control over IPSec policies, should you choose to do so.

Exercise 6.3 leads you through the process of installing the snap-in for managing a local policy and then activating IPSec on the local computer.

EXERCISE 6.3

Network Protocol Security and Enabling IPSec on the Local Computer

1. Select Start ➢ Run and type mmc to launch `MMC.exe`. An empty MMC console window appears.

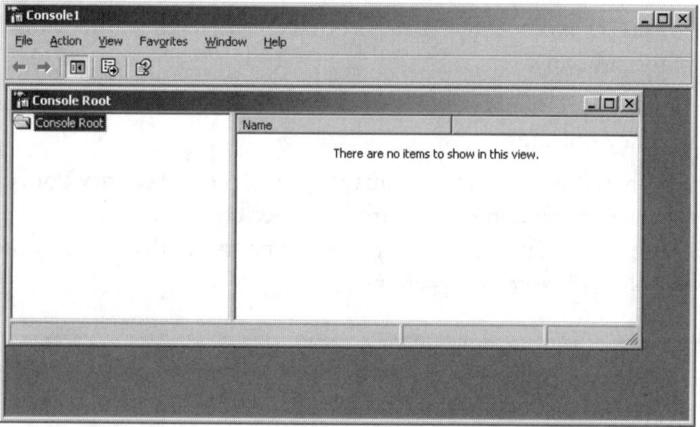

2. Select the File ➢ Add/Remove Snap-In command. When the Add/Remove Snap-In dialog box appears, click the Add button.

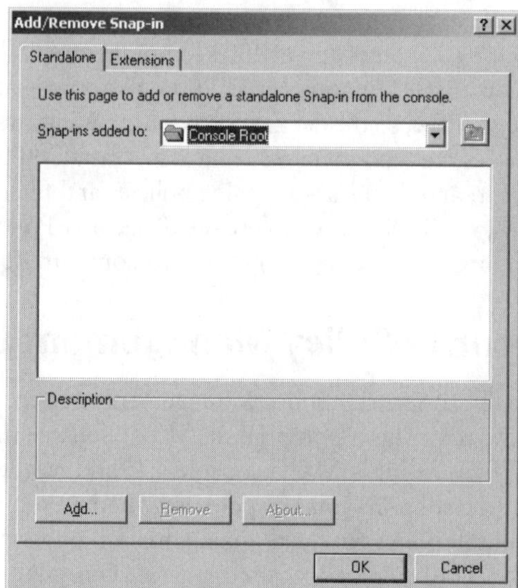

EXERCISE 6.3 *(continued)*

3. In the Add Standalone Snap-In dialog box, scroll through the snap-in list until you see the one marked IP Security Policy Management. Select it and click the Add button.

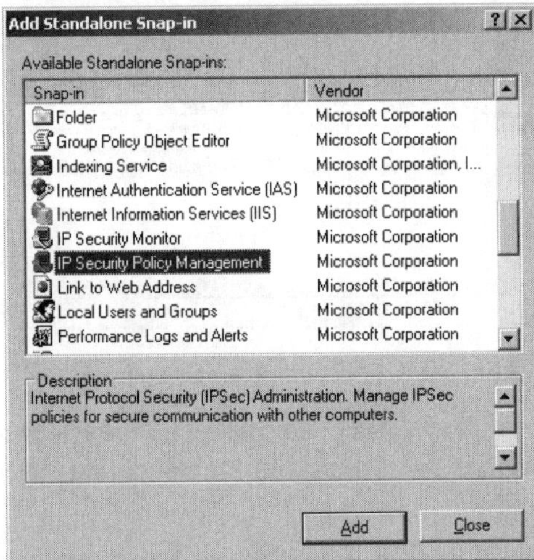

4. The Select Computer dialog box appears. Select the Local Computer (which is the default setting) radio button, and then click the Finish button.

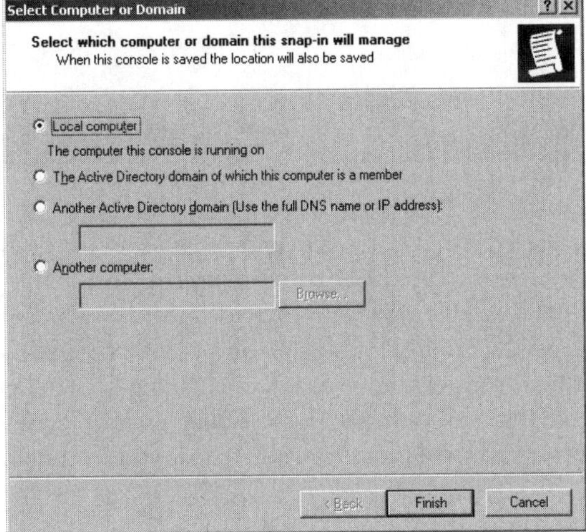

5. Click the Close button in the Add Standalone Snap-In dialog box.

6. Click the OK button in the Add/Remove Snap-In dialog box.

EXERCISE 6.3 *(continued)*

7. Select the IP Security Policies on Local Computer node in the MMC. Note that the right pane of the MMC lists the three predefined policies discussed earlier in this chapter.

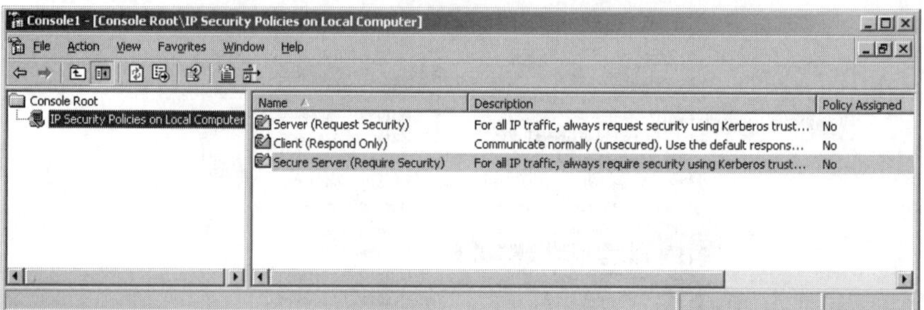

8. Right-click the Server (Request Security) policy and choose Assign.

9. Verify that the entry in the Policy Assigned column for the selected policy has changed to Yes. If the policy is assigned but not applied, a message will indicate this in the Policy Assigned column as shown.

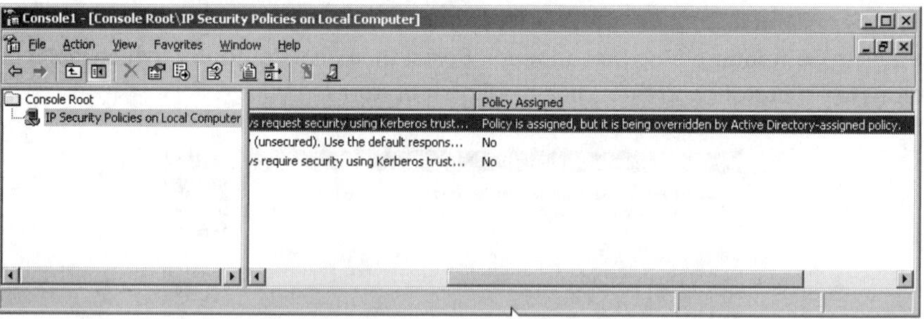

This process in and of itself doesn't do much to improve your security posture, because all it does is enable your local computer to accept IPSec connections from other computers. The real payoff comes when you start applying IPSec policies in Active Directory, which you're about to do.

You can configure IPSec by modifying the default policies, creating your own policies that embody the rules and filters you want to use, and controlling how policies are applied to computers in your management scope. Because Group Policy management is outside the range of this book, the following sections will focus instead on how you customize and control the IPSec settings themselves.

Managing Policies

You manage policies at a variety of levels, depending on where you want them applied. However, you always use the IPSec snap-in to manage them, and the tools you use to create new policies or edit existing ones are the same whether you're using local or Active Directory policy storage.

The following sections will discuss creating and deploying IPSec policies.

Creating a Policy

You create new policies by right-clicking the IP Security Policies folder in the snap-in and choosing the Create IP Security Policy command. That activates the IP Security Policy Wizard, which allows you to create a new policy, but you still have to manually edit the policy settings after it's created.

The first page of the wizard basically tells you what the wizard does. The second page allows you to enter a name and description for the policy. We will look at the rest of the IP Security Policy Wizard in the following sections.

Setting the Default Response Rule

The Requests For Secure Communication page, shown in Figure 6.17, asks you whether you want to use the default response rule or not. The default rule governs security when no other filter rule applies. For example, let's say you've set up security filters to accept secure connections from `*.microsoft.com`, `*.cisco.com`, and `*.apple.com`. When your server gets an incoming IPSec request from `delta.globalitcertification.com`, you'd probably expect IPSec to reject the connection—and it will, unless you leave the default response rule turned on. That rule will basically accept anyone who requests a secure connection. Paradoxically, for maximum security, you might want to turn it off so that you only accept IPSec connections from known hosts. However, you can customize the settings associated with the default rule; that's the wizard's primary purpose.

If you choose not to use the default response rule, the wizard will skip the steps described in the following text and take you directly to the completion page.

FIGURE 6.17 The Requests for Secure Communication page

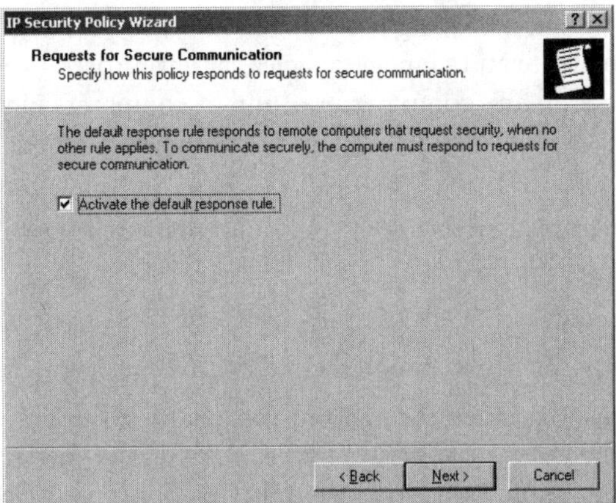

Choosing an Authentication Method for the Default Response Rule

If you choose to use the default response rule, you still have to configure an authentication method for it. To do so, you use the Default Response Rule Authentication Method page, as shown in Figure 6.18. You can choose one of the three authentication methods mentioned earlier; by default, Kerberos is selected, but you can choose a certificate authority or a preshared key instead. (If you choose to use a preshared key, make sure that you enter the same key on both ends of the connection.)

FIGURE 6.18 The Default Response Rule Authentication Method page

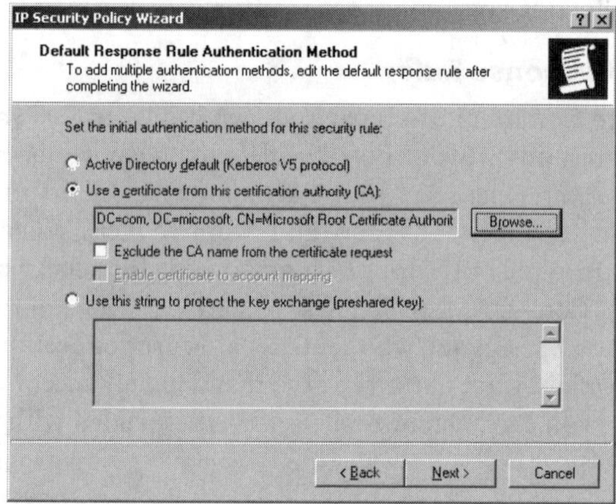

Finishing the Policy Wizard

When you complete the IP Security Policy Wizard, the completion page contains a checkbox labeled Edit Properties. This is the most interesting part of the Wizard because it gives you access to the actual settings embedded within the policy.

Deploying IPSec Policies

So far, you've read only about managing policies that apply to the local computer. You can also use the IPSec snap-in to create and manage policies that are stored in Active Directory, from which they can be applied to any computer or group of computers in the domain.

You actually accomplish this application by completing these three separate, but related, steps:

1. Target the IPSec snap-in at Active Directory, and then open it while logged on with a privileged account.
2. Edit or create the policy you want to apply using the tools in the snap-in.
3. Use the Group Policy snap-in to attach the policy to a site, domain, or organizational unit.

The first two steps are discussed throughout this chapter, but you should first take a minute to read about the third step. Because you can assign group policies to any site, domain, or organizational unit, you have the ability to fine-tune IPSec policy throughout your entire organization by using an appropriately targeted policy. For example, in Active Directory Users and Computers, you can create an organizational unit and then create a new group policy object (GPO) that applies only to that OU. Finally, you can change the settings in that GPO so they enforce the IPSec policy you want applied to computers in that OU.

You don't actually use the IPSec snap-in to assign policies; you use it to configure them and to create policies that live in Active Directory. When you want to actually apply a policy to some group in the directory, you use the group policy snap-in itself. Exercise 6.4 explains how to assign an existing policy as the default policy for a domain.

In this exercise, you will configure a default IPSec policy for all domain computers. You must have administrative access to the domain for this to work.

EXERCISE 6.4

Enabling IPSec for an Entire Domain

1. Select Start ➢ Run and type **mmc** to launch `MMC.exe`. An empty MMC console window appears.
2. Select the File ➢ Add/Remove Snap-In command. When the Add/Remove Snap-In dialog box appears, click the Add button.
3. In the Add Standalone Snap-In dialog box, scroll through the snap-in list until you see the one marked Group Policy Object Editor. Select it and click the Add button.
4. The Select Group Policy Object dialog appears. Click the Browse button to bring up the Browse for a Group Policy Object dialog box.

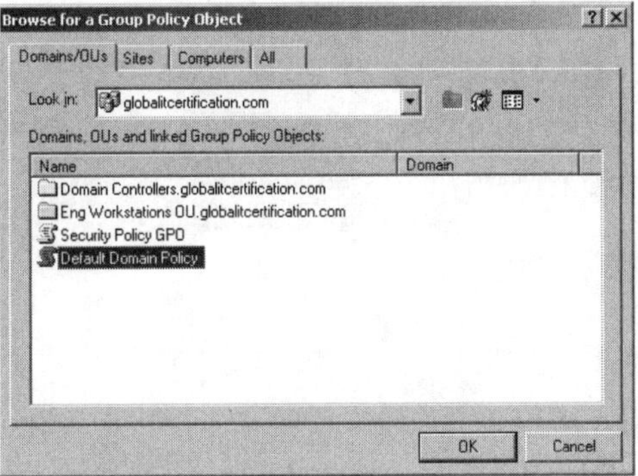

5. Select the Default Domain Policy and click the OK button. We do not recommend that you choose Default Domain Policy for testing purposes in a production environment!
6. Click the Finish button in the Select Group Policy Object dialog box.
7. Click the Close button in the Add Standalone Snap-In dialog box, and then click the OK button in the Add/Remove Snap-In dialog box.

EXERCISE 6.4 *(continued)*

8. Expand the Default Domain Policy node until you find the IPSec settings by selecting Default Domain Policy, Computer Configuration, Windows Settings, Security Settings, IP Security Policies On Active Directory (*domain name*).

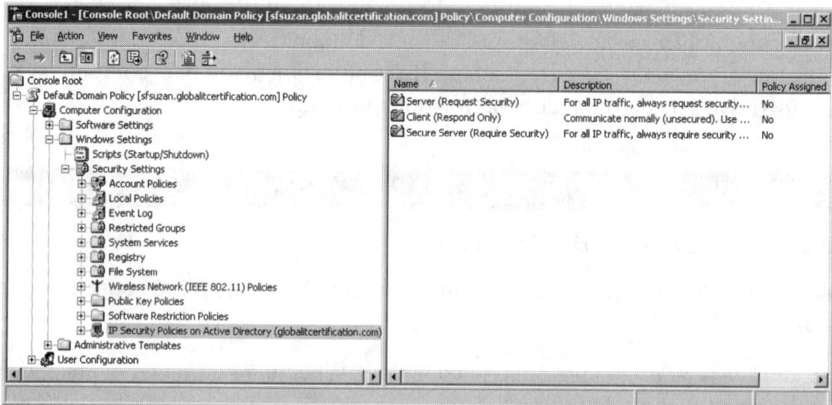

9. Select the IP Security Policies On Active Directory (*domain name*) item. The right side of the MMC window lists the available policies, including the three predefined policies and any new ones you've added using the IP Security Policy Wizard and then imported.

10. Right-click the Server (Request Security) policy and select Assign. Notice that the Policy Assigned column for that policy now reads Yes.

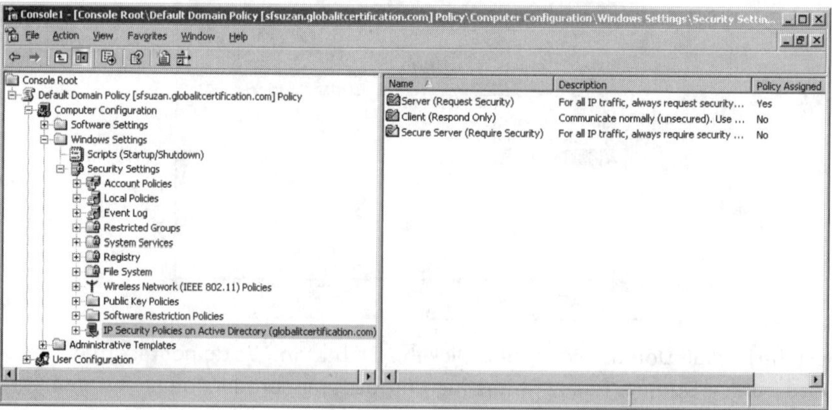

11. Save the console on the desktop (using Save As) and name it **`IPSec.msc`**. This console will be used in Exercise 6.5.

The following sections will discuss the order in which rules are applied, assigning and unassigning IPSec policies, forcing a Group Policy update, and importing and exporting IPSec policies.

The Order in Which Rules Are Applied

IPSec policies are subject to the same rules to which other objects assigned by group policy are subject. Even though this book isn't about group policy objects, understanding those rules is useful so you'll know how IPSec policy assignment really works.

The first rule is simple: A policy applied at the domain level will always override a policy assigned to the local computer (when you're logged on to the domain, of course).

The second rule is equally simple: A policy applied to an organizational unit always takes precedence over domain-level policies. That means that if you have conflicting policies at the domain and OU levels, the settings in the OU policy will be used. This of course assumes that overrides are not used.

The third rule is a little more complex: If you have a hierarchy of OUs set up in Active Directory, the policy for the lowest-level OU overrides the others. For example, let's say you have an OU named Sales, with subordinate OUs for North America and South America. If you assign two different IPSec policies to the Sales and North America OUs, the North America settings will override for the users and/or computers in this OU.

The fourth rule is subtle but important: If you assign an IPSec policy through Group Policy and then remove the Group Policy Object that assigned the policy, *the policy remains in effect.* When the IPSec Policy Agent looks for the policy while the GPO is missing, the agent assumes that the GPO server is temporarily unavailable. It then uses a cached copy of the policy, which means that you have to unassign the policy before removing the GPO that assigns it, and then either refresh the policy on each client computer or wait for the automatic refresh to take place.

Assigning and Unassigning IPSec Policies

Whether you're defining policies that affect one computer or a multinational enterprise network, you assign and unassign IPSec policies the same way—by right-clicking the policy in question and using the Assign and Unassign commands.

Assigning a policy makes it take effect the next time IPSec policies are refreshed—you may recall that the IPSec Policy Agent downloads the policy information for a computer when the computer is restarted. If you're using Group Policy to distribute your IPSec settings, you can force a policy update using the Group Policy snap-in.

Remember to unassign IPSec policies before you delete them. Otherwise the policy will remain in effect, but you will be unable to manage it.

Forcing a Group Policy Update

If you want to force one computer to update its IPSec policy, just stop and restart the IPSec Policy Agent service on that machine. When the service starts, it attempts to retrieve the newest available policy from Active Directory or the local policy store. Once the policy has been loaded, it's immediately applied.

Restarting the policy agent forces it to retrieve and reapply the correct policy—this can be useful when you're trying to troubleshoot a policy problem, or when you want to be sure that the desired policy has been applied.

By default, the IPSec Policy Agent will retrieve policies every 180 minutes anyway, although you can change that setting (as you'll see in a bit). Alternatively, you can use the `gpupdate /target:computer /force` command to refresh the local computer's policy settings.

Importing and Exporting IPSec Policies

You can take actions on IPSec policies by right-clicking IP Security Policies; the context menu that appears allows you to rename them, delete them, or import and export them. These latter commands might seem unnecessary, but they occasionally come in handy if you're not using Active Directory.

For example, let's say you have a small network of computers using Windows 2000 and XP Professional. You can create local IPSec policies on one machine, and then export them and import them on the remaining machines. Doing so ensures a consistent set of IPSec policies without requiring that you have an Active Directory domain controller present.

Real World Scenario

Planning an IPSec Strategy to Secure Communications between Business Partners

You are the system administrator of TravelSoft, a software development company specializing in applications for the travel industry. Management has just informed you that the company will be teaming up with Go2theMoon, a former rival, in a joint venture to produce a new XML-based Web portal service designed for travel agencies. This new alliance means that source code will need to be shared. This is a highly competitive area, and you are informed that it is imperative that all data transmissions between the two companies occur over a secure connection.

A conference call with the other company's IT Director gets you the rest of the technical details you need to know. You learn that like you, she is running Windows Server 2003 in Native mode and is employing IPSec to secure other data transfers.

You create inbound and outbound security filters for both domains. First, you create an outbound security filter with the source: `TravelSoft.com` and destination: `Go2theMoon.com`. The other administrator creates a security filter with the exact opposite configuration. Next, you create an inbound security filter with the source: `Go2theMoon.com` and destination: `TravelSoft.com`. The other administrator creates an inbound security filter with the exact opposite configuration. This enables both companies to control the IPSec security protocols and designate IPSec communication between the two company networks.

A final consideration is the need to ensure that service packs match. Both companies are using SMS for enterprise software configuration management, so you agree on an automated strategy for maintaining service packs to ensure compatibility.

Configuring IPSec Policies

Once you create a new policy using the IP Security Policy Wizard, you still have to customize it to make it do anything useful. You do this with the policy Properties dialog box, from which you can add, remove, and manage rules, filter lists, and security actions.

The Properties dialog box has two separate tabs. The General tab covers general policy-related settings like the policy name, and the Rules tab gives you a way to edit the rules associated with the policy. We will look at each in the following sections. We'll also explore managing filter lists and actions.

Setting General Properties

The General tab of the IPSec policy Properties dialog box (see Figure 6.19) is accessed by right-clicking the policy and selecting Properties. With this tab, you can change the policy name and description, which appear in the IPSec snap-in. It's a good idea to use meaningful names for your policies so that you'll remember what each one is supposed to be doing.

FIGURE 6.19 The General tab of the IPSec policy Properties dialog box

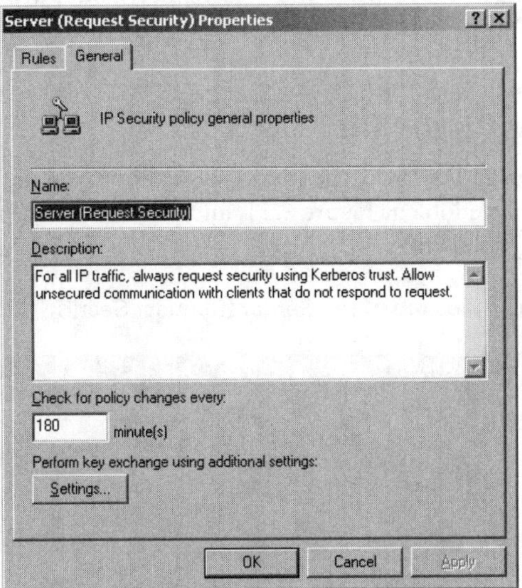

The Check For Policy Changes Every: X Minutes field lets you change the interval at which clients who use this policy will check for updates. The default value of 180 minutes is okay for most applications because you're unlikely to be changing the policies *that* frequently.

The Settings button allows you to change the key exchange settings used by this particular policy, via the Key Exchange Settings dialog box, as shown in Figure 6.20. You can use the controls in this dialog box to control how often the policy requires generation of new keys, either after a certain amount of time (8 hours by default) or a certain number of sessions. The Master Key Perfect Forward Secrecy (PFS) option specifies whether or not you want to re-authenticate the SA for every session. Enabling this option provides a higher level of security than leaving it disabled, but performance could be adversely affected.

FIGURE 6.20 The Key Exchange Settings dialog box

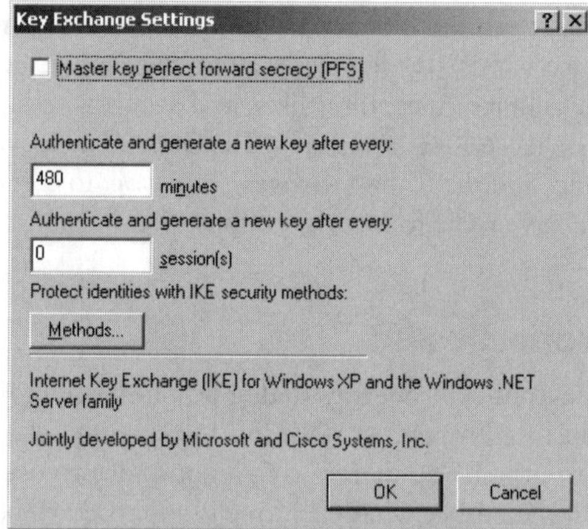

The Methods button displays a list of security methods that will be used to protect the key exchange. The method list included when you create a new policy always tries the highest-level security first, such as 3DES, and then it drops down to less secure methods if the remote end can't handle them.

Managing Rules with the Rules Tab

The Rules tab of the IPSec policy Properties dialog box allows you to change the rules included with the IPSec policy. Take a look at Figure 6.21, and you'll see what the rule set for the Server (Request Security) policy looks like.

FIGURE 6.21 The Rules tab of the Server (Request Security) Properties dialog box

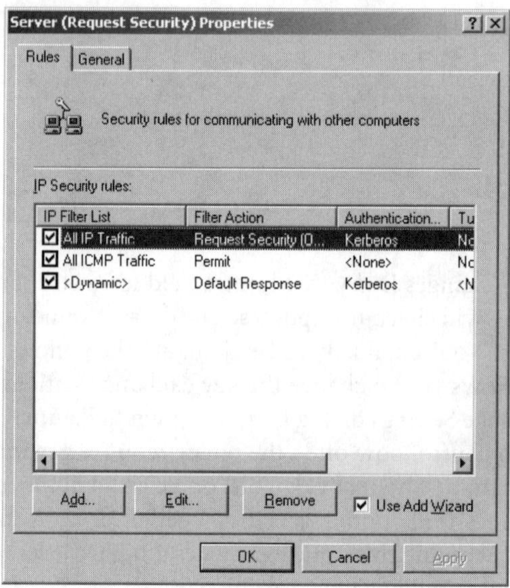

Here are the most important things to recognize on this tab:

- There are three rules, each of which ties a filter list to a filter action and authentication method. A single policy can contain an arbitrary number of rules. Having a number of rules that are applied in different situations is common. Having many different policies defined in a single Active Directory domain or local policy store is also common.
- Each rule has a checkbox next to it that controls whether or not the rule is actually applied. You can use these checkboxes to turn on or off individual rules within a policy.
- The Add, Edit, and Remove buttons let you manipulate the list of rules. Note that rules aren't evaluated in any particular order, so there's no way to reorder them.
- The Use Add Wizard checkbox controls whether or not the Security Rule Wizard is used to add a new rule (by default, this box is checked). When it's unchecked, you'll go to the rule's Properties dialog box to set up things by hand.

The Edit Rule Properties dialog box, which is associated with each rule, has five different tabs. You'll see this dialog box when you select a rule and click the Edit button, or when you create a new rule with the Use Add Wizard checkbox cleared.

The wizard basically asks you questions and fills out the tabs for you, so knowing what settings belong with each rule will enable you to successfully create them by hand or with the wizard's help. Therefore, instead of going through each step of the wizard, you should know what's on each tab.

The IP Filter List Tab

The IP Filter List tab, as seen in Figure 6.22, shows which filter lists are associated with this rule. You manage which filter lists exist using a separate set of tools, which will be covered in a later section. For now, it's enough to know that all the filter lists defined on your server will appear in the filter list; you can choose any *one* of them to be applied as a result of this rule. If you like, you can add or remove filter lists here or in the Manage IP Filter Lists And Filter Actions dialog box, which is covered in the next section.

FIGURE 6.22 The IP Filter List tab of the Edit Rule Properties dialog box

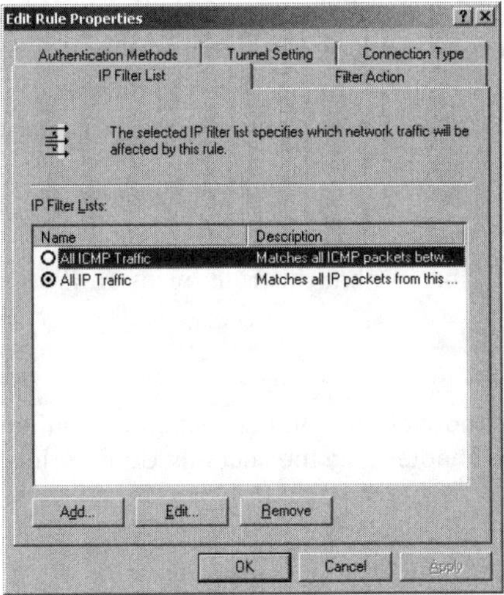

The Filter Action Tab

The Filter Action tab, seen in Figure 6.23, shows all of the filter actions defined in the policy; you can apply any filter action to the rule. Remember that you combine one filter list with one filter action to make a single rule, but you can group any number of rules into one policy. The Add, Edit, and Remove buttons do what you'd expect. The Use Add Wizard checkbox controls whether adding a new filter action fires up the corresponding wizard (which you'll get to in the next section) or dumps you into the Properties dialog box.

FIGURE 6.23 The Filter Action tab of the Edit Rule Properties dialog box

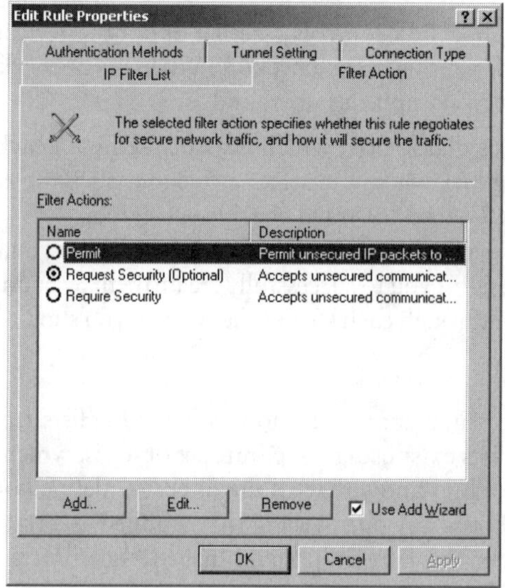

The Authentication Methods Tab

The Authentication Methods tab, seen in Figure 6.24, allows you to define one or more authentication methods that you want a particular rule to use. You can have multiple methods listed; if so, IPSec will attempt to use them in the order of their appearance in the list (thus the Move Up and Move Down buttons). You have the same three choices mentioned earlier: Kerberos, certificates, or preshared keys.

The Tunnel Setting Tab

Use the Tunnel Setting tab to specify that this rule forms an IPSec tunnel with another system (or tunnel endpoint).

You'll read more about it in the section on configuring IPSec in Tunnel mode, later in this chapter (see the section "Configuring IPSec for Tunnel Mode").

FIGURE 6.24 The Authentication Methods tab of the Edit Rule Properties dialog box

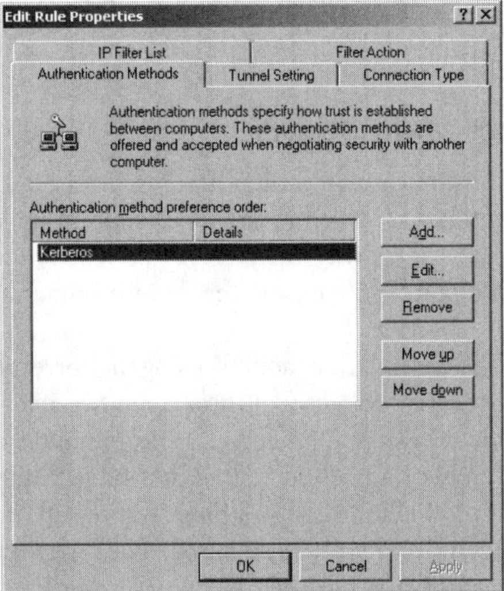

The Connection Type Tab

The Connection Type tab, as seen in Figure 6.25, allows you to specify to which kind of connections this IPSec rule applies. For example, you might want to specify different rules for dial-up and LAN connections depending on who your users are, from where they're connecting, and what they do while connected.

FIGURE 6.25 The Connection Type tab of the Edit Rule Properties dialog box

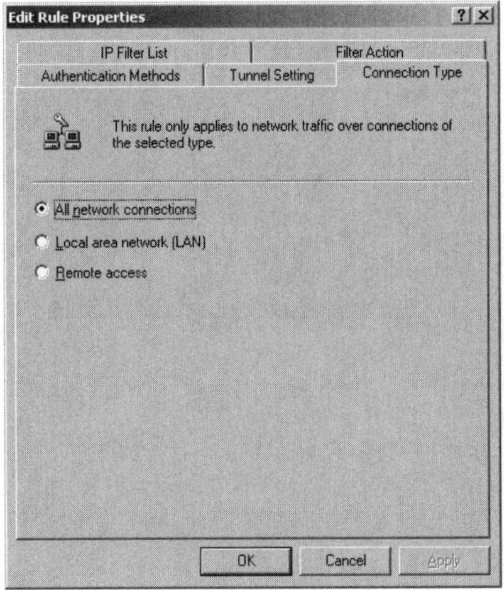

You use three radio buttons to select which type of connections this rule applies to. The All Network Connections button is selected by default, so when you create a new rule, it will apply to both LAN and remote access connections. If you only want the rule to cover LAN or RAS connections, just select the corresponding radio button.

Managing Filter Lists and Actions

Although you can manage IP filter lists and filter actions from the Edit Rule Properties dialog box, using the management tools provided in the IPSec snap-in makes more sense. This is because the filter lists and actions live with the policy, not inside individual rules, the filter lists and actions you create in one policy scope (say, the default domain policy) are available to all policies within that scope.

While you can manage filter lists and filter actions using the corresponding tabs in the Edit Rule Properties dialog box, this obscures the fact that these items are available to any policy. Instead, you can use the Manage IP Filter Lists And Filter Actions command from the context menu (right-click the IP Security Policies item or anywhere in the right-hand pane of the IPSec snap-in). This command displays the Manage IP Filter Lists And Filter Actions dialog box, which has two tabs.

Most of the items on these tabs are self-explanatory because they closely resemble the controls you've already seen. Instead of rehashing the controls in the following sections, we will look at the process of defining a new filter list and an action to go with it.

Adding IP Filter Lists and Individual Filters

Windows Server 2003 includes two IP filter lists by default: one for all IP traffic, and one for all ICMP traffic.

Perhaps you have more specific needs. For instance, you may want to create an IPSec policy to secure Web traffic between your company and its law firm. You'd first have to open the Manage IP Filter Lists And Filter actions dialog box, at which point you'd see the Manage IP Filter Lists tab shown in Figure 6.26.

FIGURE 6.26 The Manage IP Filter Lists tab

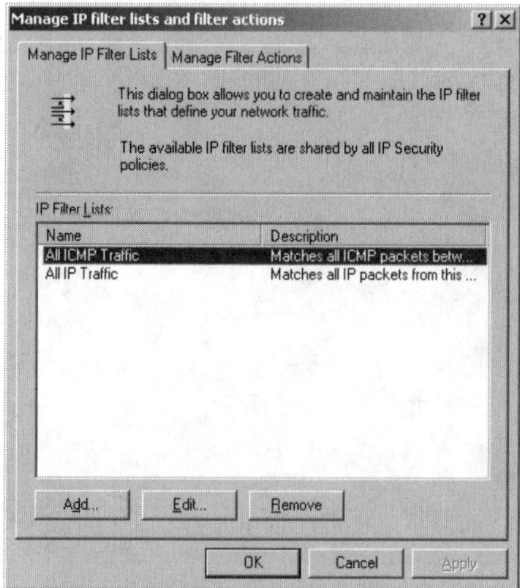

Because filter lists aren't used in order, there's no way to reorder items in the list, although you can add, edit, and remove them using the controls beneath the list. When you edit or add a filter list, you'll see the IP Filter List dialog box, as shown in Figure 6.27. This dialog box allows you to name and describe the filter list, and then add, remove, or edit the individual filters that make up the list.

FIGURE 6.27 The IP Filter List dialog box

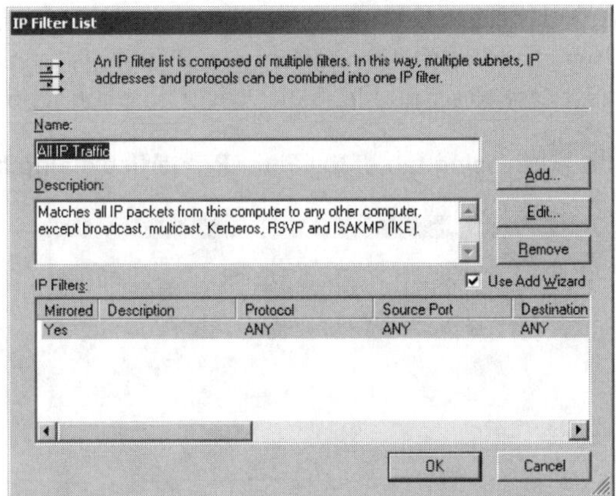

When you edit or add an individual filter, you need to know the following:

- The source and destination addresses you want the filter to use. These can be single IP addresses, single DNS names (at any level, so that `mail.globalitcertification.com`, `globalitcertification.com`, and `com` are all valid), or IP subnet. You can also use special "my" and "any" addresses (e.g., "My IP Address," "Any IP Address") to indicate the source and destination.
- Whether you want the filter to be *mirrored*. A mirrored filter automatically filters its opposite—if you set up a filter from your IP address to a remote address and configure it to allow only port 80, with mirroring you'll also get a filter that allows traffic *from* the remote end back to you on port 80.
- To which protocols and ports you want the filter to apply. You can choose any protocol type (including TCP, UDP, ICMP, EGP, RDP and RAW), and you can either select individual source and destination ports or use the "any port" buttons you'll meet in a minute.

You would use the Filter Properties dialog box to get these details. When you use the Add or Edit buttons in the IP Filter List dialog box, you'll see the Properties dialog box for the appropriate filter (the new one or whichever one you selected before clicking the Edit button). This dialog box has three tabs in it:

The Description Tab The Description tab is used for naming and describing the filter.

The Address Tab The Addresses tab, as shown in Figure 6.28, is where you specify the source and destination addresses you want this filter to match. For the source address, you can choose to use the IP address assigned to the IPSec server ("My IP Address"), any IP address, a specific DNS domain name or IP address, or a specific IP subnet. Likewise for the destination address, you can choose the IPSec computer's address, any IP address, or a specified DNS name, subnet, or IP address. You use these in combination to specify how you want the filter to trigger. For example, you could create a rule that says, "Match any traffic from my address to IP address `a.b.c.d`". You could also create a rule that does what the "All IP Traffic" filter does: match any traffic from your IP address (on any port) to any destination.

You can also use the Mirrored checkbox to specify a reciprocal rule. For example, the mirrored rule of the All IP Traffic rule matches traffic coming from any IP address on any port back to your IP address. Mirroring makes it easy to set up filters that cover both inbound and outbound traffic.

FIGURE 6.28 The Addressing tab of the Filter Properties dialog box

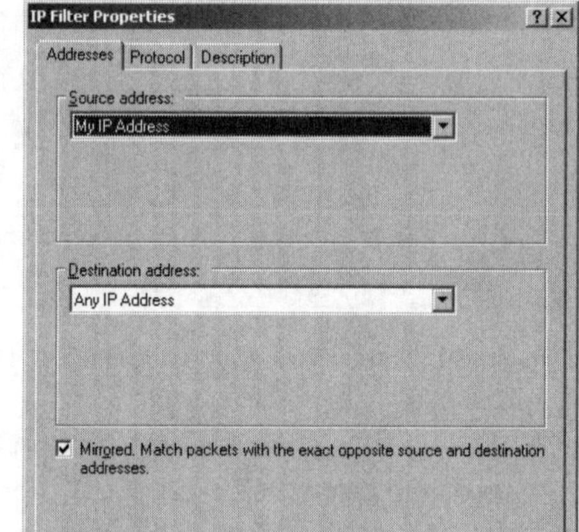

The Protocol Tab The Protocol tab, as shown in Figure 6.29, lets you match traffic coming from or sent to a particular port, using a specified protocol. This is useful, because UDP source port 80 and TCP destination port 80 are entirely different. You use the Select A Protocol Type: pull-down menu and the Set The Ip Protocol Port Control group to specify the protocols and ports you want this filter to match.

Adding a New Filter Action

The Manage Filter Actions tab, as shown in Figure 6.30, shows you which filter actions are defined in the current group of IPSec policies. You can add, edit, or remove filter actions to meet your needs.

As part of Windows Server 2003, you get three filter actions—Permit, Request Security (Optional), and Require Security—that will probably meet most of your needs, but knowing how to create policies yourself instead of depending on Microsoft to do it for you is still a good idea.

FIGURE 6.29 The Protocol tab of the Filter Properties dialog box

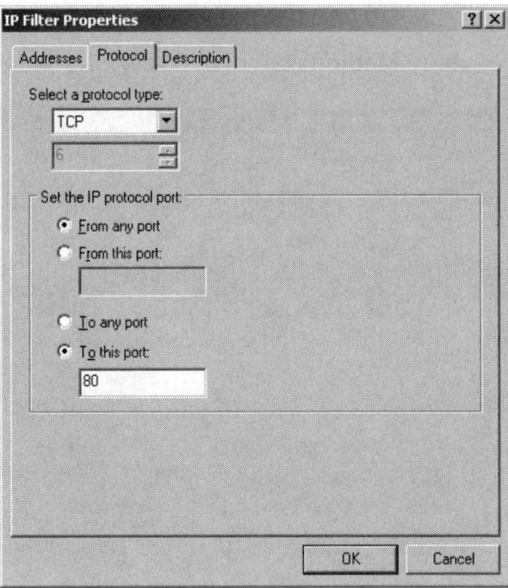

FIGURE 6.30 The Manage Filter Actions tab

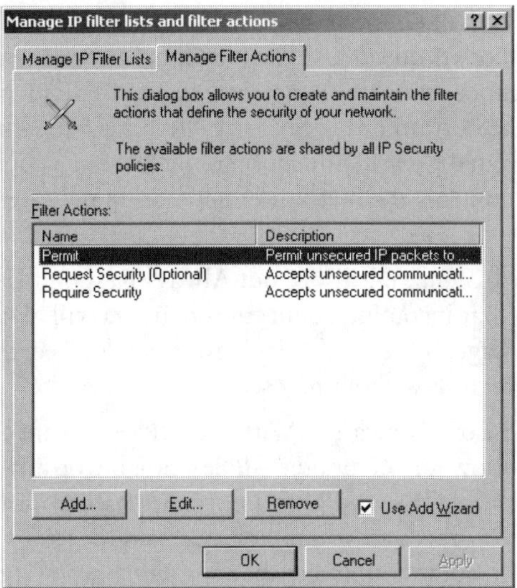

The Add button lets you add new filter actions that can be used in any policy you define. The Use Add Wizard checkbox is normally on, so by default you'll get the IP Security Filter Action Wizard. However, for now click the Add button with the Use Add Wizard checkbox

off. The first thing you see is the Security Methods tab of the New Filter Action Properties dialog box, as shown in Figure 6.31.

FIGURE 6.31 The Security Methods tab of the New Filter Action Properties dialog box

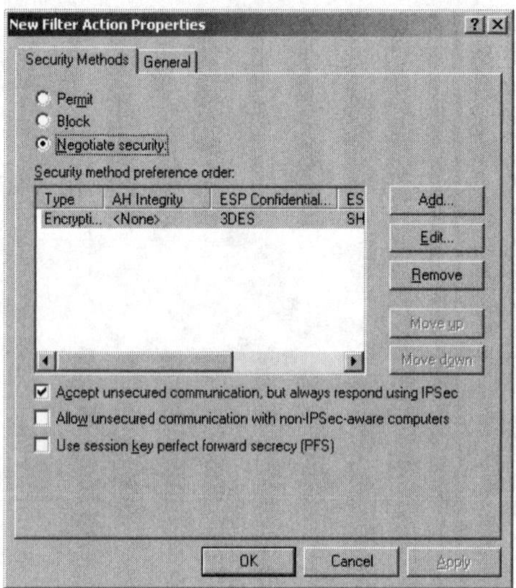

You use this tab to select which methods you want this filter action to use. In addition to the Permit and Block methods, you can use the Negotiate Security radio button to build your own custom security methods, choosing whatever AH and ESP algorithms meet your needs. The two checkboxes at the bottom of the Security Methods list control what this IPSec computer will do when confronted with a connection request from a computer that doesn't speak IPSec. A third checkbox controls the method of generating new session keys. The options include the following:

- The Accept Unsecured Communication, But Always Respond Using IPSec checkbox configures this action so that incoming connection requests will always be answered with an IPSec negotiation message. If the other end doesn't *speak* IPSec, the computer is allowed to accept the incoming request without any security in place.
- The Allow Unsecured Communication With Non IPSec-Aware Computer checkbox configures the action to allow any computer—IPSec-capable or not—to communicate. Any computer that can't handle IPSec will get a normal, unsecure connection. By default, this box isn't checked; if you check it, you must be certain that your IPSec policies are set up properly. If they're not, some computers that you *think* are using IPSec may connect without security.
- The Use Session Key Perfect Forward Secrecy checkbox configures the action to renegotiate new master key keying material every time a new session key is required, rather than deriving new session keys from current master key keying material. Configuring this option provides greater security, but this may come at the expense of performance and throughput.

In Exercise 6.4, you assigned the Server (Request Security) policy so that it would always be used. Now, Exercise 6.5 walks you through modifying the console to better meet your needs. In this exercise, you'll modify the local computer's "Server (Request Security)" policy settings to improve its interoperability. By default, all IPSec policies you create will be Transport mode (as opposed to Tunnel mode) policies. This is also true of the default local computer and domain IPSec policies.

EXERCISE 6.5

Customizing and Configuring the Local Computer IPSec Policy and Rules for Transport Mode

1. Open the IPSec policy you saved on your desktop in Exercise 6.4.
2. Select the IP Security Policies on Active Directory node in the MMC. In the right-hand pane of the MMC, right-click the "Server (Request Security)" policy and choose the Properties command. The Server (Request Security) Properties dialog box appears.
3. Select the All IP Traffic rule, and then click the Edit button. The Edit Rule Properties dialog box appears. Read the Description.
4. Switch to the Filter Action tab. Select the Request Security (Optional) filter action, and then click the Edit button. The filter action's Properties dialog box appears.
5. Click the Add button. When the New Security Method dialog box appears, click the Custom radio button, and then click the Settings button.

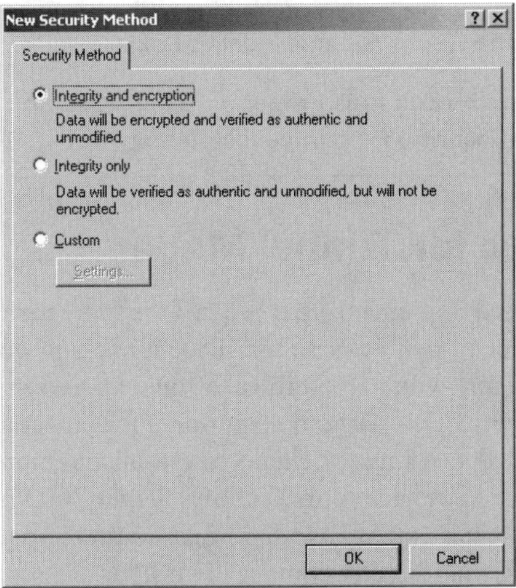

6. In the Custom Security Method Settings dialog box, check the Data And Address Integrity Without Encryption (AH) checkbox. In the drop-down list, select SHA1. Using the drop-down lists under (ESP), set Integrity to SHA1 and Encryption to 3DES.

EXERCISE 6.5 *(continued)*

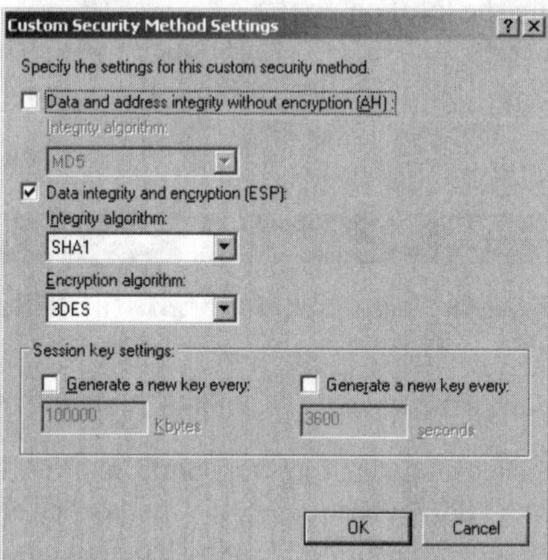

7. First check the Generate A New Key Every checkbox and set the key generation interval to 24,000KB (it must be in the range 20,480–2,147,483,647KB.) Then click the Generate A New Key Every checkbox and specify a key generation interval of 1800 seconds.

8. Click the OK button in the Custom Security Method Settings dialog box, and then click OK in the New Security Method dialog box.

9. When the Filter Properties dialog box resurfaces, use the Move Up button to move the custom filter you just defined to the top of the list.

10. Click the OK button in the Filter Properties dialog box.

11. Click the Close button in the Edit Rule Properties dialog box, and then click the OK button in the Server (Request Security) Properties dialog box.

Configuring IPSec for Tunnel Mode

To this point, we've discussed implementing IPSec in Transport mode. As you read earlier, you can also use IPSec in Tunnel mode. You can use IPSec tunnels to do a number of useful and interesting things. For example, you can establish a tunnel between two subnets—effectively linking them into an internetwork—without requiring a private connection between them. IPSec tunneling isn't intended as a way for clients to establish remote access VPN connections; instead, it's what you'd use to connect your Windows Server 2003 network to a remote device (say, a 3Com OfficeConnect ISDN LAN Modem) that doesn't support L2TP + IPSec or PPTP. You can also build a tunnel that directly connects two IP addresses.

Either way, you establish the tunnel by building a filter that matches the source and destination IP addresses, just as you would for an ordinary Transport mode. You can use ESP and AH on the tunnel to give you an authenticated tunnel (AH only), an encrypted tunnel (ESP only), or a combination of the two. You control this behavior by specifying a filter action and security method. However, when you build a tunnel, you can't filter by port or protocol; the Windows Server 2003 IPSec stack doesn't support it.

To construct a tunnel properly, you actually need two rules on each end: one for inbound traffic and one for outbound traffic. Microsoft warns against using mirroring on tunnel rules; instead, if you want to link two networks (let's say Atlanta and Seattle), you'd need to specify settings as shown in Figure 6.32. Each side's rule has two filter lists. The Atlanta filter lists specify a filter for outgoing traffic that has the Seattle router as a tunnel endpoint, and it specifies another filter for incoming traffic from any IP subnet that points back to the Atlanta tunnel endpoint. In conjunction with these filter lists, of course, you'd specify a filter action that provided whatever type of security was appropriate for the connection.

Make sure you understand the technical scenarios in which you would configure IPSec tunnels.

FIGURE 6.32 Filter lists for a simple tunnel

Filter list 1:
Filter from any IP address to specific IP subnet 10.3.*
Tunnel endpoint of 10.3.1.254
Authentication and security methods to taste
Filter list 2:
Filter from specific IP subnet 10.3.* to any IP address
Tunnel endpoint of 10.1.1.254
Authentication and security methods to taste

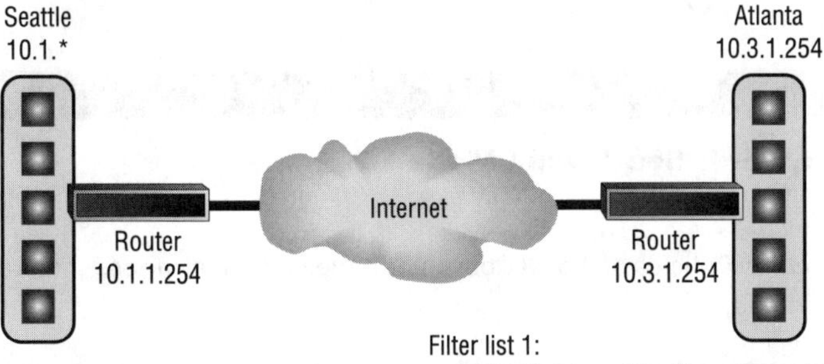

Filter list 1:
Filter from any IP address to specific IP subnet 10.1.*
Tunnel endpoint of 10.1.1.254
Authentication and security methods to taste
Filter list 2:
Filter from specific IP subnet 10.1.* to any IP address
Tunnel endpoint of 10.3.1.254
Authentication and security methods to taste

You specify whether a connection is tunneled or not on a per-rule basis using the Tunnel Settings tab of the Edit Rule Properties dialog box. Select Server (Request Security), right-click and select Properties, select All IP Traffic and click Edit, and finally click the Tunnel Setting tab, shown in Figure 6.33.

The two radio buttons specify whether this rule establishes a tunnel or not. The default button, "This rule does not specify an IPSec tunnel," is self-explanatory. To enable tunneling with this rule, select the other button, "The tunnel endpoint is specified by this IP address," and then fill in the IP address of the remote endpoint.

FIGURE 6.33 The Tunnel Setting tab of the Edit Rule Properties dialog box

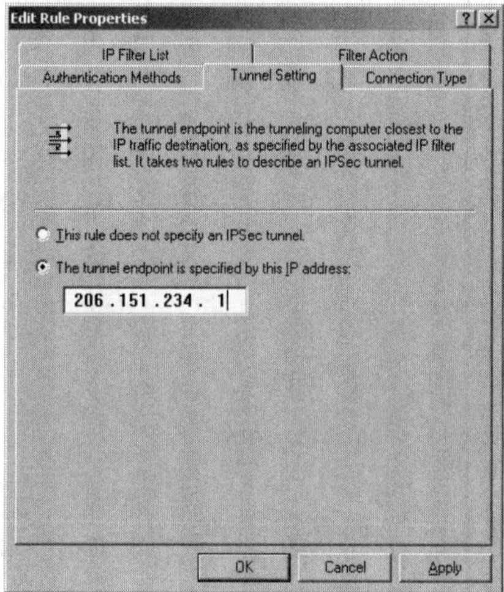

In Exercise 6.6, you'll configure a policy for IPSec Tunnel mode. This lab requires you to use two separate computers to which you have administrator access. Let's call them computer A and computer B. Before you start, you'll need their IP addresses, and you'll need to have their local IPSec policies open in an MMC console.

EXERCISE 6.6

Configuring a Policy for IPSec Tunnel Mode

Configure Computer A:

1. Right-click the IP Security Policies on Local Computer node, and then choose the Create IP Security Policy command.

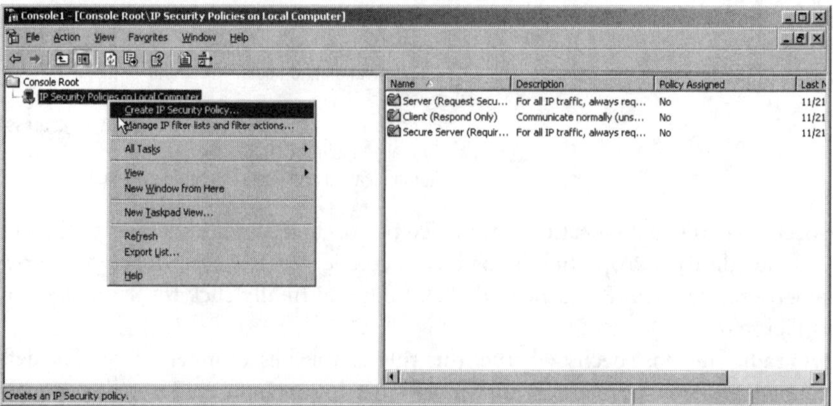

EXERCISE 6.6 *(continued)*

2. The IP Security Policy Wizard appears. Click Next.

3. Name your policy **Tunnel to B**, and then click the Next button.

4. On the Requests For Secure Communication page, turn off the Activate Default Response Rule checkbox, and then click the Next button.

5. When the Completing the IP Security Policy Wizard page appears, make sure the Edit Properties checkbox is on, and then click Finish. The Tunnel To B Properties dialog box appears. Click the Add button on the Rules tab.

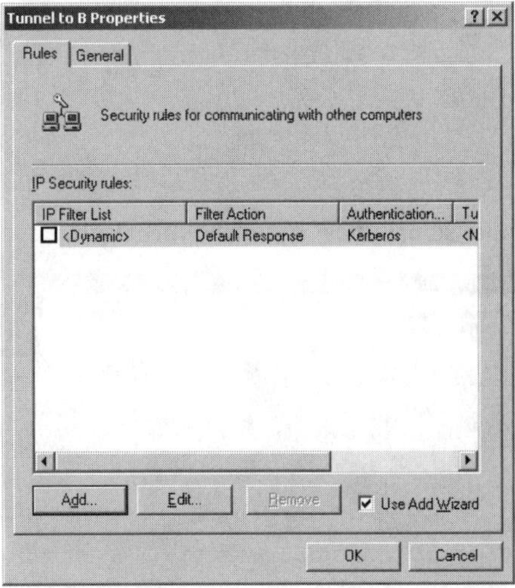

EXERCISE 6.6 *(continued)*

6. The Welcome to the Create IP Security Rule Wizard begins. Click Next.

7. In the Tunnel Endpoint page, select The Tunnel Endpoint Is Specified By The Following IP Address and enter the IP address of Computer B. Click Next.

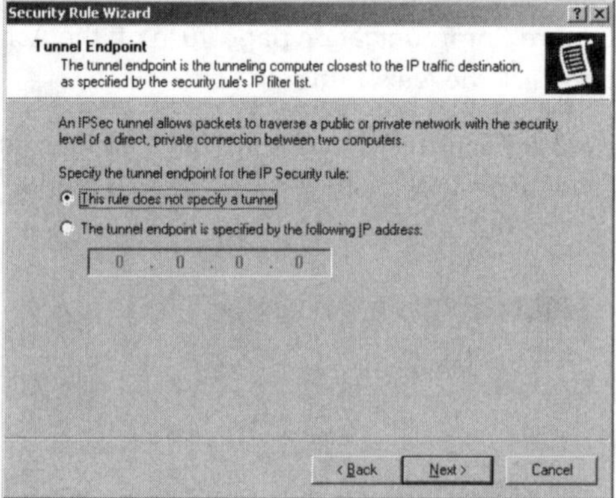

8. In the Network Type page, select Local Area Network (LAN). Click Next.

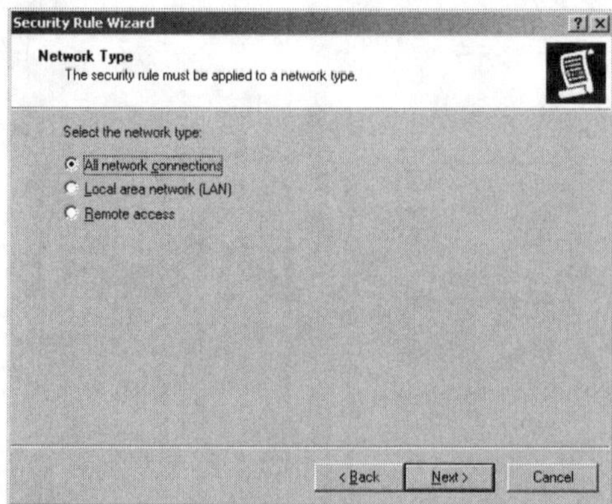

EXERCISE 6.6 *(continued)*

9. On the IP Filter List page, select the All IP Traffic radio button. Click Next.

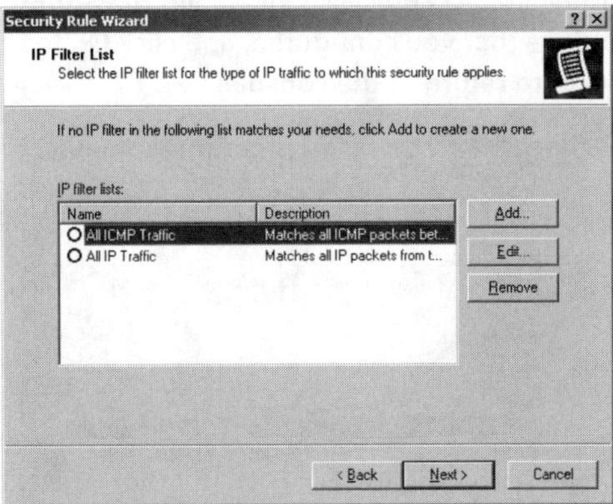

10. On the Filter Action page, select the Request Security (Optional) radio button. Click Next.

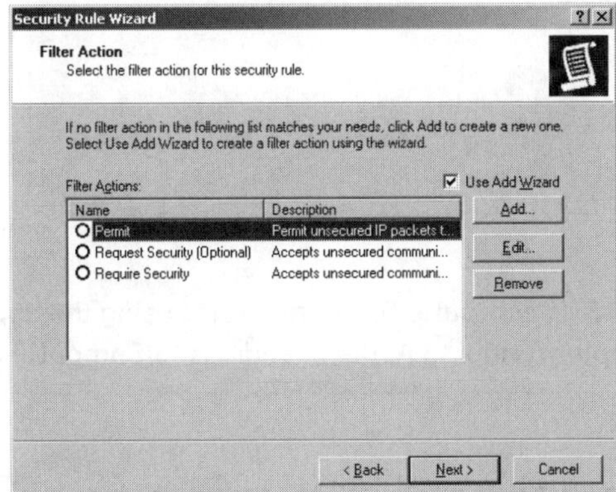

11. In the Authentication Method page, select Active Directory Default (Kerberos V5 protocol). Click Next.

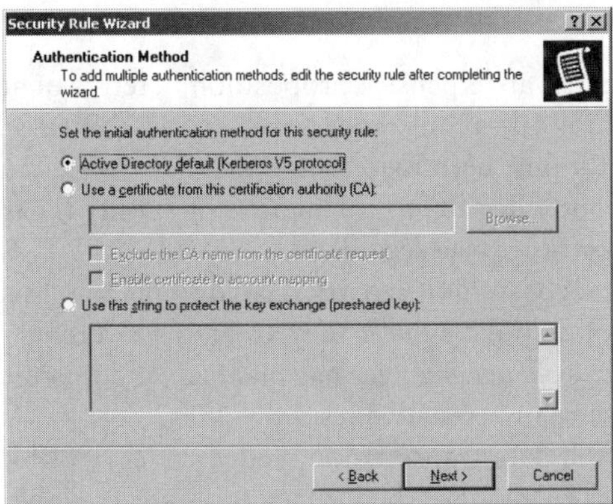

EXERCISE 6.6 *(continued)*

12. The Completing the Security Rule Wizard page appears. Make sure the Edit Properties checkbox is checked (the default) and click Finish. The New Rule Properties dialog box appears. Verify the settings that you configured, and click OK to return to the Tunnel to B properties page. Click OK to return to the console.

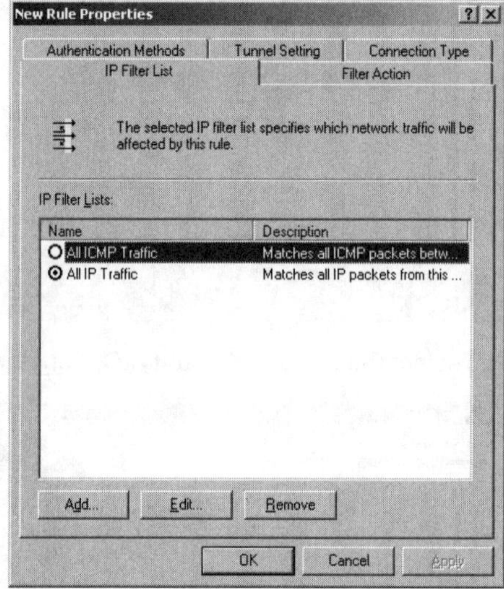

Configure Computer B:

13. Now repeat Steps 1–12 on computer B, creating rules using the appropriate IP addresses and names (for example, Tunnel to A, the IP address to Computer A in Steps 2–7).

Troubleshooting Security for Data Transmission

Implementing Group Policy is an expensive proposition in terms of administrative effort. Planning and configuring policies takes time. For remote access, this entails building remote access policies consisting of conditions, permissions, and profiles. For data transmission, this entails building filter lists, rules, and filter actions that correctly specify the traffic types and hosts you want to allow, disallow, or otherwise secure.

However, the most time-consuming activity related to planning secure network access may actually be in troubleshooting policies after they are in place. Frequently, policies do not have the effective result that the systems engineer has planned, and it is necessary to hunt down the cause of an overly permissive or restrictive result.

In Windows Server 2003, data transmission security refers to IP-level security that takes place after connectivity has been established. Many tools are available for troubleshooting data transmission security. The general tools for Group Policy management are often helpful. Windows Server 2003 provides several new tools for managing and troubleshooting IPSec and other aspects of Group Policy. Table 6.3 summarizes the tools that can be used for troubleshooting IPSec.

TABLE 6.3 Tools for Troubleshooting IPSec

Tool	Found In	Description
Event Viewer	Administrative Tools	Used for viewing IPSec policy–related events.
IP Security Policy Management	MMC Snap-in	Used for managing IPSec policies. Used to create, modify, and activate IPSec policies.
Resultant Set of Policy (RSoP)	MMC Snap-in	Used for verifying IPSec configuration. Used to determine which policies are assigned, but not applied to clients. Used to display detailed policy settings.
IP Security Monitor	MMC Snap-in	Used for monitoring the status of IP security. Used to view details about an active IPSec policy. Used to view statistics related to the key exchange process. Used to search for all matches of a specific traffic type.
Security Configuration and Analysis	MMC Snap-in	Used for verifying IPSec configuration by displaying Security Policy configuration on a target computer.
Group Policy Object Editor	MMC Snap-in; also launched when viewing the Properties for a policy	Can be used for correcting IPSec policy configuration.
Group Policy Management Console	MMC Snap-in (Download from Microsoft Web site)	Used for managing Group Policy. Used to troubleshoot policy precedence issues. Used to determine which policies are available, assigned, or applied.

You'll learn how to use the Security Configuration and Analysis snap-in and the Group Policy Object Editor in Chapter 7. Event Viewer is discussed in Chapter 10, "Planning Network Monitoring, Remote Administration, and Recovery." Group Policy concepts and management tools are discussed in more detail in *MCSE: Windows 2003 Active Directory Planning, Implementation, and Maintenance Study Guide* by Anil Desai with James Chellis (Sybex, 2003).

In the following sections, you'll learn when to use the RSoP, the IP Security Monitor, and event logs, as well as the best ways to troubleshoot IPSec.

Verifying Effective Results of IPSec Policies with Resultant Set of Policy (RSoP)

The new Resultant Set of Policy (RSoP) tool is a policy analyzer that enables a systems engineer to forecast the effective result of multiple policies. The RSoP tool is an extremely powerful tool for planning and troubleshooting Group Policy. Using this tool, you can verify the policies currently in effect on a local or remote target computer, or you can predict the effective outcome of IPSec policies before putting them into effect, thereby preventing expensive mistakes. RSoP can be used to execute queries in one of two modes:

- Logging mode queries and displays all IPSec policies that are assigned to a specific client. Logging mode is used to verify the policies currently in effect on a local or remote target computer.
- Planning mode queries and displays all IPSec policies that are assigned to a specific Group Policy container. Planning mode is used to forecast how Group Policy changes would affect a targeted user or computer.

Planning mode queries must be run on a domain controller, because data is read from the Windows Management Instrumentation (WMI) repository on the DC rather than the WMI repository on a specific target computer.

You add the RSoP tool as an MMC snap-in. Figure 6.34 shows a custom console with the RSoP tool, the IP Security Monitor, and the IP Security Policy Management tool (in the domain context).

FIGURE 6.34 The RSoP tool

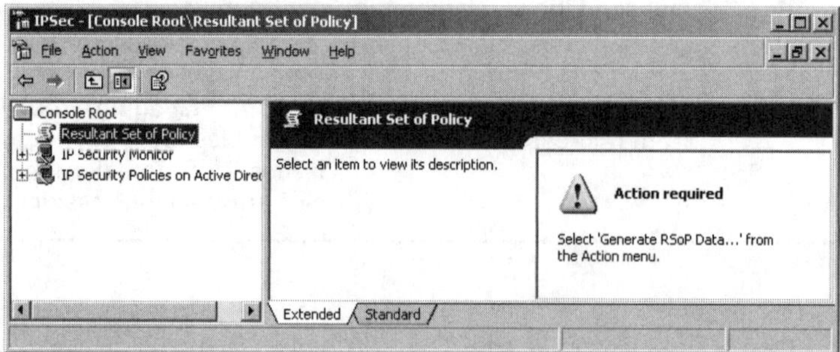

Notice the warning message that states Action Required. Before the tool can be used, you must generate data, which you do by selecting Generate RSoP Data from the Action menu (or the context menu). This launches the RSoP Wizard, which enables you to choose the mode (logging or planning), indicate the computer, and either indicate the user for whom to display policy settings, or choose to display computer policy settings only.

Because IPSec policies are specific to computers and not users, there is no need to display User Configuration settings. Figure 6.35 displays the results of a Logging mode query against the local computer.

FIGURE 6.35 The Results of an RSoP Query

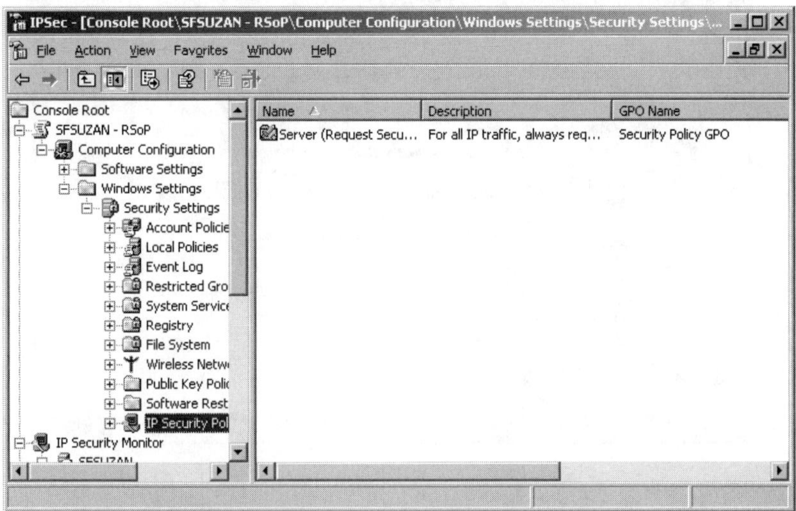

The IPSec Policy settings are located in the Computer Configuration, Windows Settings, Security Settings, IP Security Policy node. In this example, the default policy Server (Request Security) has been applied.

Monitoring IPSec Status with the IP Security Monitor

The IP Security Monitor is used for advanced troubleshooting. The tool monitors the status of IP security. The tasks you can accomplish with this tool include:

- Viewing details about an active IPSec policy
- Viewing statistics related to the key exchange process
- Searching for all matches of a specific traffic type
- Viewing security statistics

The IP Security Monitor can be used to remotely monitor computers running the same Windows OS. You can access the IP Security Monitor using Remote Desktop Connection to remotely monitor IPSec on a computer running a different version of Windows.

Remote Desktop Connection is covered in Chapter 10.

You add the IP Security Monitor as an MMC snap-in. Figure 6.36 shows the IP Security Monitor with the Active Policy node displayed.

FIGURE 6.36 The IP Security Monitor, Active Policy

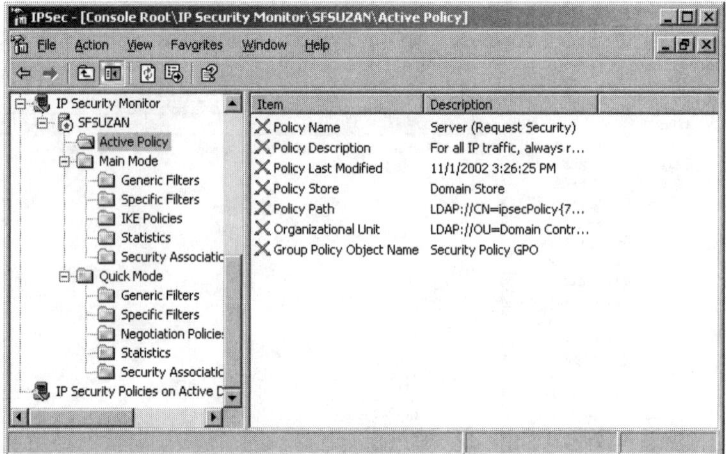

Viewing IPSec-Related Events in the Event Log

There are a number of ways to monitor IPSec traffic. The two most useful methods are viewing the security associations and traffic flowing between specific computers and checking the event log for IPSec-related events. One way that you can accomplish both tasks is through event logging.

You can use the Event Viewer to view the following events related to IPSec:

- IKE events (SA details) in the audit log
- IPSec Policy Agent events in the audit log
- IPSec policy change events in the audit log
- IPSec driver events in the system log

If you turn on auditing for logon events and object access, you'll get a wealth of logged information that can be very useful when you're trying to troubleshoot a problem. In particular, IPSec logs events when it establishes a security association. Those event messages tell you what policy, filter, and filter actions were used, plus which security methods were active on the connection. Table 6.4 lists the most common event log messages you'll see and describes what they mean.

TABLE 6.4 Common IPSec Event Log Messages

Event ID	Appears In	Description
279	System log	Generated by the IPSec Policy Agent; shows which policy was installed and from where it came.
284	System log	Generated by the IPSec Policy Agent; appears when the agent can't fetch a policy.
541	Security log	An IPSec SA was established.
542	Security log	An IPSec SA was closed. This happens when you terminate a connection to a remote machine. (May also appear as event 543, depending on the type of SA.)
547	Security log	IPSec SA negotiation failed, so no SA could be established.

In Exercise 6.7, you'll turn on auditing for logon events and object access. In order to see anything in the log, you'll need at least two IPSec-capable machines that can talk to each other. It doesn't matter which one you use to do this exercise, provided that you have administrative access on the one you use.

If you are using a domain controller, you should load the console you saved in Exercise 6.4 and skip Steps 2 through 5 of this exercise. If you are running a standalone or workgroup server, proceed normally.

EXERCISE 6.7

Monitoring IPSec Logon Activity

1. Select Start ➢ Run and type mmc to launch `MMC.exe`. An empty MMC console window appears.
2. Select the File ➢ Add/Remove Snap-In command. When the Add/Remove Snap-In dialog box appears, click the Add button.
3. In the Add Standalone Snap-In dialog box, scroll through the snap-in list until you see the one marked Group Policy Object Editor. Select it and click the Add button.
4. The Select Group Policy Object dialog box appears. Leave Local Computer set as the focus, and click the Finish button.
5. Click the Close button in the Add Standalone Snap-In dialog box, and then click the OK button in the Add/Remove Snap-In dialog box.

EXERCISE 6.7 *(continued)*

6. Find and select the Audit Policy folder by selecting Local Computer (or *domain*) Policy, Computer Configuration, Windows Settings, Security Settings, Local Policies, Audit Policy.

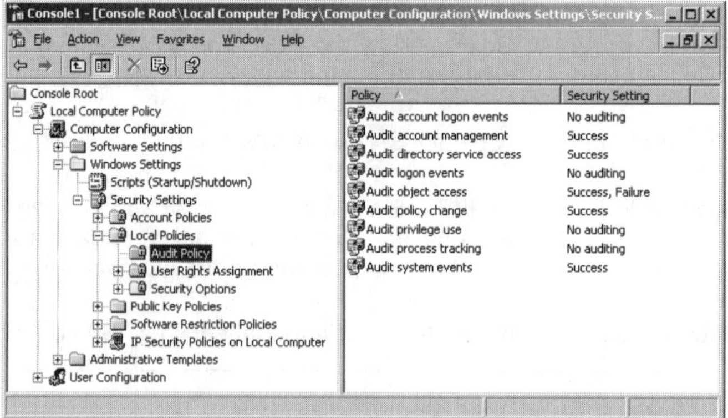

7. Double-click the Audit Logon Events entry. When the Local Security Policy Setting dialog box appears, check the Success and Failure checkboxes, and then click the OK button.

8. Double-click the Audit Object Access entry. When the Local Security Policy Setting dialog box appears, check the Success and Failure checkboxes, and then click the OK button.

9. Establish an IPSec connection from the *other* computer to the one whose local security policy you just modified.

10. Examine the system and security event logs and determine whether the IPSec negotiation succeeded or failed.

Best Practices for Troubleshooting IPSec

Before you attempt to troubleshoot IPSec, verify that you have basic, unsecured TCP/IP connectivity to the remote system. Because IPSec operates atop IP and UDP, if you can't get regular IP datagrams to the destination you won't be able to get IPSec packets there either. That means you need to perform all the standard connectivity and name resolution tests (including making sure the network cable's plugged in) before you dive into IPSec troubleshooting.

Testing Policy Integrity

Policy integrity is tested using the IP Security Monitor snap-in, which consists of three subsections. Active Policy displays the Policy Name, Description, Policy Last Modified, etc. Main Mode displays the Generic and Specific Filters, IKE Policies, Statistics (which is important for optimizing as well as troubleshooting), and the Security Associations. The last mode is Quick Mode, which has the same entries as Main mode.

Verifying that the Correct Policy Is Assigned

If you don't have an IPSec policy assigned, or if you have the wrong one in place, your communication efforts may fail. There are several ways to check the policy to see whether it's the right one or not. These checks include the following:

- Check the event log for event ID 279. The IPSec Policy Agent uses this event ID to indicate the policy it has applied.
- Check Main Mode in IP Security Monitor to determine if a Security Association was established. (If the right pane says There Are No Items In This View, an association was never created.) Then check the Statistics folder, paying close attention to any failures (negotiation failures, Authentication failures, Acquire failures, Send failures, etc.).
- Look in the appropriate group policy object (including the local computer policy) to see whether an IPSec policy is assigned. The IPSec snap-in will warn you that a group policy–based IPSec policy is assigned when you try to edit local policies on a computer.
- If event viewer displays Bad SPI, the key lifetime is set to low or the sender continues transmitting after the SA has expired.

Checking for Policy Mismatches

If you have policies applied on each end, but you still can't establish a connection, it's possible that the policies don't match. To verify whether or not this is the case, review the event log and look for event ID 547. If you find any, read the descriptive text carefully, because it may provide helpful clues. Make sure that the authentication and security methods used in the two policies have at least one setting in common. For example, if multiple rules are being applied in each policy, where some of the rules that are applicable to the connection specify Kerberos authentication and others specify certificate authentication, a connection cannot be established.

Summary

In this chapter, you learned how to install and administer remote access connections, including dial-up and VPN connections. We covered the following topics:

- How to configure appropriate encryption and security settings for remote access.
- How to configure and use remote access policies. Remote access policies consist of conditions, permissions, and profiles.
- How IPSec works. IPSec primarily provides two services: a way for computers to decide whether they trust each other (authentication) and a way to keep network data private (encryption). The Windows Server 2003 implementation of IPSec explicitly supports the idea of policy-based security.
- How to create and configure IPSec policies and filter lists. The policy's Properties dialog box contains options to add, remove, and manage rules, filter lists, and security actions.
- How to troubleshoot IPSec Policies and IPSec data transmission. Tools include Group Policy tools, Event Viewer, the Resultant Set of Policy (RSoP) tool, and IP Security Monitor.

Exam Essentials

Know how to use remote access policies. Policies determine who may and may not connect. Rules can be defined with conditions that must be met before a connection is granted. Remote access policies are managed through the Remote Access Policies folder in the RRAS console.

Know how to use remote access profiles. Each remote access policy has an associated profile. The profile determines what settings will be applied to connections that meet the conditions stated in the policy. The settings fit into six distinct areas, and each area has its own tab in the profile Properties dialog box. These tabs are named Dial-In Constraints, IP, Multilink, Authentication, Encryption, and Advanced.

Know how to configure remote access security. Remote access security configuration involves configuring methods of authentication and encryption. You can choose one of two authentication providers by using the Authentication Provider drop-down list; they are Windows Authentication and RADIUS. You can apply authentication restrictions at the server level and at the policy level.

Know how to create a remote access policy for VPNs. The simplest method is to create a policy that allows VPN access to all users. To allow VPN access to a smaller group, create a new group for the VPN users. You can then create a policy using the following conditions: Set the NAS-Port-Type attribute to Virtual (VPN), set the Tunnel-Type attribute to the appropriate protocol, and use the Windows-Groups attribute to specify the new group.

Know how to create and configure IPSec policies. You configure IPSec by modifying the default policies, creating your own policies that embody the rules and filters you want to use, and controlling how policies are applied to computers in your management scope. You customize a policy with the policy's Properties dialog box, where you can add, remove, and manage rules, filter lists, and security actions.

Know how to manage filter lists. You manage filter lists and filter actions by using the corresponding tabs in the Edit Rule Properties dialog box, which lists items that are available to any policy. You can instead use the Manage IP Filter Lists And Filter Actions command from the Context menu.

Know how to configure IPSec for Tunnel mode. You establish the tunnel by building a filter that matches the source and destination IP addresses, just as you would for an ordinary transport mode. You can use ESP and AH on the tunnel to give you an authenticated tunnel (AH only), an encrypted tunnel (ESP only), or a combination of the two. You control this behavior by specifying a filter action and security method. To properly construct a tunnel, you need two rules on each end: one for inbound traffic and one for outbound traffic.

Know how to troubleshoot IPSec Policies and secure data transmission. Know how to use the RSoP tool to troubleshoot IPSec Policies. Know how to use IP Security Monitor to determine whether or not a Security Association was established and to determine whether or not the association is receiving errors in transmission or reception. Know how to enable IPSec logging. IPSec logs events when it establishes a security association, and you can examine the event log to view IPSec statistics and auditing. Know how to manage IPSec from the command-line using the `netsh` IPSec context.

Key Terms

Before you take the exam, be certain you are familiar with the following terms:

accounting provider
authentication
Authentication Header (AH)
Challenge Handshake Authentication Protocol (CHAP)
connection type
dial-up networking
EAP type
Encapsulating Security Payload (ESP)
encapsulation
encryption
Extensible Authentication Protocol (EAP)
filter action
filter lists
Internet Key Exchange (IKE)
Internet Protocol Security Extensions (IPSec)
Internet Security Agreement/Key Management Protocol (ISAKMP)
IP datagram
IPSec client
IPSec Policy Agent
IPSec server
IPv4
Kerberos v5
Key Distribution Center (KDC)
Level 2 Tunneling Protocol (L2TP)
machine certificates
mirrored
MS-CHAP
mutual authentication
Network Access Server (NAS)
passthrough action
Password Authentication Protocol (PAP)
Point-to-Point Protocol (PPP)
Point-to-Point Tunneling Protocol (PPTP)
preshared keys
public key certificates
Public Key Infrastructure (PKI)
remote access policy
Remote Authentication Dial-In User Service (RADIUS)
Routing and Remote Access Service (RRAS)
security association (SA)
security method
Shiva Password Authentication Protocol (SPAP)
spoofing
tampering
ticket-granting service (TGS)
ticket-granting ticket (TGT)
Transport mode
tunnel
tunnel endpoint
Tunnel mode
Virtual Private Network (VPN)

Review Questions

1. As the new systems engineer for your company, you want to set up an RRAS server so that the field personnel can access the central office through a secure VPN tunnel through the Internet. You want all members of the security group Field Users to be allowed VPN access to the home office through the RRAS server. Which of the following actions can you take to accomplish your objective with the least administrative effort? (Choose two.)

   A. Enable VPN access in a Group Policy Object (GPO), and link the GPO to the Field Users group.

   B. Set the remote access permission for each user in the Field Users group to allow access.

   C. Create a remote access policy that allows VPN access to the Field Users group.

   D. Enable VPN access in the Field Users group's dial-in properties.

   E. Set the domain functional level to Windows 2000 native or Windows Server 2003.

2. You are the RAS administrator for your company and have been assigned the responsibility of setting up four RAS Policies. Policy A is for the IT department—it allows the people in the IT group permission to dial-in seven days a week, at all hours. The B Policy is for executives—it allows them to dial-in 24 hours a day, six days a week. Policy C is for most users and allows them dial-in Monday through Friday from 8 A.M. to 7 P.M. Policy D is for all personnel who are not specifically granted dial-in rights and dial-in is denied. What is the correct order list in remote access policies?

   A. Policy A, Policy B, Policy D, Policy C

   B. Policy C, Policy B, Policy A, Policy D

   C. Policy C, Policy B, Policy A, Policy D

   D. Policy C, Policy A, Policy B, Policy D

3. You want to be able to see at-a-glance all of the users who have remote access permissions. Which of the following options is the best way to create and manage the list of users who will be granted remote access permissions?

   A. Create a new group, add the authorized users to that group, then configure dial-in settings for the group, and view them on the group's Properties page.

   B. Configure the settings in the authorized users' Properties pages to Allow access, and then run an LDAP query in Active Directory to return the list of authorized users.

   C. Create a new group and add the authorized users to that group. Next, configure a remote access policy and apply it to the group. View the group's membership in the group's Properties page.

   D. Create a new group, add the authorized users to that group, and then configure the settings in the Properties page for each authorized user to Control access through Remote Access Policy. Next, configure a remote access policy and add the appropriate Windows group to it. View the group's membership in the group's Properties page.

4. You notice that users are often unable to connect to the RRAS server through dial-up networking even though one of the modems in the modem pool has never been used. Which of the following steps can you take to troubleshoot this problem? (Choose all that apply.)

   A. Check the properties of the modem using Device Manager.

   B. On the RRAS server, create a dial-up connection using that modem, and then try to use it to connect to the Internet.

   C. Configure the callback option in the modem's properties.

   D. Verify that the modem is listed in the RRAS console under Ports.

   E. Verify that the modem has been configured to accept inbound connections in the Ports Properties page.

5. You have upgraded a Windows 2000 Server to a Windows Server 2003 DNS server. You open IP Security Policies in the context of the DNS server and assign the Secure Server (Require Security) policy. You want the policy to take effect immediately, but you notice that the change is not effective. What command must you run in order to prompt policy changes to be immediately applied?

   A. `secedit /refreshpolicy machine_policy /enforce`

   B. `gpupdate /target:user /force`

   C. `gpupdate /target:computer /force`

   D. `netsh ipsec static`

6. You are the system administrator for a company that collects foreign economic information. Your company has government contracts to compile data and generate reports. The data from the reports is eventually used in congressional reports. Your company obtains this information from various subcontracted agencies in multiple countries. All data received by your company must be verified as having originated from each of the contracted organizations. You have implemented IPSec to secure data transmission. How must you configure IPSec to ensure that the information is coming from the trusted agencies?

   A. Configure AH to provide authentication of the source of each IP packet.

   B. Configure AH to provide encryption of the IP packets.

   C. Configure ESP to provide encryption of the IP payload.

   D. Configure ESP to provide authentication of the IP payload.

7. You administer a network that contains 200 Windows 2000 and XP Professional machines and 10 Windows Server 2003 computers. One of the Windows Server 2003 computers, named CLASS1, contains highly classified information, so you decide to implement IPSec on that machine. Management wants you to monitor CLASS1 frequently to ensure that data never gets into the wrong hands. Which of the following actions would allow you to monitor IPSec on CLASS1?

   A. Use System Monitor to monitor key exchange traffic.

   B. Use Network Monitor to analyze network traffic.

   C. Load IP Security Monitor in an MMC window and point it to the computer named CLASS1.

   D. Use Computer Management to verify IPSec policy assignment.

8. You are the system administrator of a financial services company that handles extremely sensitive financial information about high–net worth clients. You have gone to great lengths to secure your network by using firewalls, secured routers, and strong remote access authentication. You also have built a thorough physical security system in which all persons need badges to enter the facilities. Every door is monitored and the badge activity is tracked and reported. Although you feel comfortable that the perimeter of the network is secure, you want to make certain that no one inside the network can capture any packets on the wire and read any of the data. What IPSec component must you employ in order to achieve this objective?

   A. AH authentication

   B. IPSec packet filtering

   C. ESP encryption

   D. AH encryption

9. The security and integrity of the data on your Native mode Windows Server 2003 network is of paramount importance to the management of your company. You have seven locations that communicate with each other frequently, and all of them use their access to the Internet on a regular basis. You have been charged with securing the traffic in all communications among the managers and executive staff of the company. To accomplish this, you plan to implement IPSec to provide the authentication and encryption of the specified communications. What will you need to change in order for IPSec to function properly across your network?

   A. Modify the applications on the network that the managers and executives use to support IPSec.

   B. Upgrade the managers' and executives' NIC cards to support IPSec.

   C. Upgrade the router software to pass the IPSec traffic to the other locations.

   D. Enable IPSec on your computers to accept IPSec connections from other computers.

10. You are the system administrator in a network in which IPSec has just been implemented. You want to isolate a problem. You check the event log and find an event ID 547, which records the failure. What is the probable cause of this error?

   A. Negotiation failed because there is a policy mismatch between the two computers.

   B. The IPSec Policy Agent cannot fetch a policy.

   C. An IPSec SA was closed.

   D. An IPSec SA was not established.

11. You have just been informed that your company has signed a contract with another company to complete a joint Windows Server 2003 application software development project. This project is going to involve a great deal of source-code sharing between the two organizations, and there is considerable concern about protecting the communications between the companies. Both companies are running Windows Server 2003 in Native mode, and both have enabled IPSec to ensure the security of data transfers. Both companies want to control the IPSec security protocols and limit IPSec communication between the two company networks. Your company's domain is `panacea.com`, and the other company's domain is `hearth.com`. You create a security filter with the source of `panacea.com` and a destination of `hearth.com`. The administrator of `hearth.com` creates a security filter with a source of `hearth.com` and a destination of `panacea.com`. When you test the connection, the IPSec negotiation process fails, and the traffic is not secured. What is the most likely cause of this problem?

    A. The companies are running different service packs that relate to IPSec.

    B. Nothing. The users need to choose when to transfer data using IPSec.

    C. You need to create inbound and outbound filters.

    D. Your security filters are configured the opposite of what they should be.

12. You are troubleshooting a problem with IPSec policies. You want one policy to affect all the users in the Sales OU and all its subordinate OUs. All the users in the North America OU (a subordinate of the Sales OU) are currently being affected by a policy that's different from the one that affects the users in the Sales OU. What is the problem?

    A. The policy for the lowest-level OU overrides the others.

    B. Policies in lower-level OUs are adopted from the domain-level policy.

    C. Policies in lower-level OUs are adopted from the local computer's policy.

    D. Policies are always adopted from the next-higher-level OU. Users in the Sales OU would be affected by the domain-level policy, and users in the North America OU would be affected by the Sales policy.

13. Your human resources department is becoming increasingly concerned about liability surrounding the privacy of employee information. They have sound policies in place to control access to information such as health, salary, and other personal data; however, they have learned that if information gets out and it wasn't secured properly, the company could be liable for damages. You are told to secure the HR and accounting systems when HR employees are moving information around. However, those systems must remain open to staff in other departments. You immediately implement IPSec on the HR and accounting servers and on the machines of the employees in those two departments. In order to allow regular connections to the servers from the other departments, while requiring IPSec connections from the machines that deal with the confidential information, what security filter actions should you specify? (Choose all that apply.)

    A. Permit

    B. Block

    C. Accept Unsecured

    D. Allow Unsecured

    E. Use These Security Settings

14. You want to set up an IPSec tunnel between two sites in different cities. How should you use filter lists at each site?

A. Each site should have two filter lists. One list should specify a filter for outbound traffic that points back to itself as the endpoint, and the other list should specify a filter for inbound traffic that has the other site as an endpoint.

B. Each site should have one filter list that specifies a filter for outbound traffic that has the other site as an endpoint and a filter for inbound traffic that points back to itself as the endpoint.

C. Each site should have two filter lists. One list should specify a filter for outbound traffic that has the other site as an endpoint, and the other list should specify a filter for inbound traffic that points back to itself as the endpoint.

D. Each site should have one filter list that specifies a filter for outbound traffic that points back to itself as the endpoint and a filter for inbound traffic that has the other site as an endpoint.

15. You have been told to implement a strong security infrastructure for your hospital in preparation for the government-required HIPPA regulations. You have a secure perimeter with a firewall and access control lists on your routers. However, the only security in place on your internal LAN is the access control lists on your Windows 2003 servers that are providing applications and data. In addition, you have basic password-protected applications that are running on mainframes and Unix machines in the hospital. You do not have security on the wire throughout your network. You intend to implement IPSec so that it will provide authentication and encryption for packets going over the wire. However, you do not want to break any applications or prevent access to any applications anywhere in the hospital until you have demonstrated that IPSec can work across all the platforms within the hospital. With this in mind, you enable IPSec on all your Windows 2003 servers and workstations and then begin to implement IPSec on the other platforms within the hospital to test interoperability. Which Microsoft prebuilt policies should you assign to the Windows Server 2003 machines until you have fully tested IPSec interoperability?

A. Client (Respond Only)

B. Secure Server (Require Security)

C. Server (Request Security)

D. Client (Request Only)

Answers to Review Questions

1. C, E. Remote access is controlled by the settings on the Dial-In tab in each user's property sheet and by remote access policies. Neither security groups nor GPO's are used to control remote access. To use remote access policies, the domain functional level must be at Windows 2000 native or higher. You *could* set permissions for each user in the Field Users group; however, that would take far more effort than simply creating a remote access policy for the whole group.

2. D. Policies are ordered in least restrictive to most restrictive order. Policy C is the least restrictive and Policy D is the most restrictive. The next determination is the two groups that are remaining. Because the executive group is smaller than the IT group and the executive group has more restrictions than the IT group, the IT group would be considered less restrictive.

3. D. The best way to manage remote access permissions with the least administrative effort is by creating a remote access policy. You still need to configure the settings in the Properties page for each authorized user to control access through Remote Access Policy.

4. A, D, E. If only one of the modems in the modem pool is not accepting connections, then you want to verify that it is properly installed via Device Manager and properly configured via the RRAS console.

5. C. The new command in Windows Server 2003 to automatically refresh a computer policy change is `gpupdate /target:computer /force`.

6. A. Configuring AH to provide authentication of the source of each IP packet will ensure that the data originated from the trusted agencies. However, the ideal solution would also employ ESP to encrypt and authenticate the IP payload. Using AH with ESP provides authentication and encryption to ensure that the data you are receiving has not been seen by any unauthorized eyes, has not been tampered with, and is from the person you expect. AH provides authentication and a signature to grant integrity for the entire packet, but it doesn't provide encryption. ESP encrypts the data in the packet. It also offers a signature and authentication for the actual data. AH and ESP together virtually ensure that the packet received is from the appropriate person, that the data in the packet is from that person, and that no one has altered the packet or seen the information inside.

7. C. Because IP Security Monitor is a snap-in, it can be pointed to a local computer or any remote computer in the system. You require administrative privileges to accomplish any of these tasks.

8. C. ESP provides confidentiality by encrypting the payload (data) in each packet that transverses the network. ESP also provides other benefits, such as authentication and integrity, by signing the payload and providing dedicated sequence numbers. The main benefit in this scenario is that the payload cannot be viewed. AH authentication is used to ensure that the packet received is from the person or computer from whom you expected the packet; it protects against spoofing. AH by itself doesn't provide encryption. Packet filtering is used to control basic communication and prevent denial-of-service attacks or block protocols.

9. D. The components necessary for a Windows Server 2003 computer to act as an IPSec client are installed by default. However, also by default, the policy required for using IPSec is not turned on, and so it lies dormant. You enable IPSec through the IP Security Policy Management snap-in and choose to use it to manage local IPSec policy, your domain, or the policy of another domain. IPSec works at the network layer, and applications are no more aware of using IPSec than they would be aware of using any lower-level OSI component. If the NICs or routers support IP—and virtually all of them do—then they will support IPSec.

10. A. The presence of event ID 547 indicates that the IPSec negotiation failed. You should make sure that the authentication and security methods used in the two policies have at least one setting in common.

11. C. You need inbound and outbound filters for both domains, and only outbound filters have been created. You also need to create an inbound security filter for `panacea.com` with the source of `hearth.com` and a destination of `panacea.com`. In addition, the administrator of `hearth.com` needs to create an inbound security filter with a source of `panacea.com` and a destination of `hearth.com`. Service packs could be an issue in the future, and they should always be watched. But service packs are not an issue in this specific situation and are certainly not the most likely source of the problem. Users and applications are entirely unaware of IPSec and don't need to take any action to utilize it. The outbound filters are configured appropriately.

12. A. The IPSec policy attached to the North America OU overrides all others; it is the lowest level discussed in the question.

13. C, E. An Accept Unsecured security filter action will always request an IPSec connection before it allows an unsecured request. If all the machines that process confidential information are configured to use IPSec, these connections will be secure. The Use These Security Settings action lets you customize the behavior of the server, and you could, of course, configure it to work in the Accept Unsecured manner. An Allow Unsecured security filter action does not prefer IPSec and will not request an IPSec connection unless it's requested by the client. A Permit action tells the IPSec filter to take no action. The Block action prevents remote systems from making any type of connection.

14. C. Each side needs two filter lists: one for inbound traffic and one for outbound traffic.

15. C. Server (Request Security) is a combination of Client (Respond Only) and Secure Server (Require Security). This policy will always attempt to use IPSec by requesting it when it connects to a remote computer and by allowing IPSec when an incoming connection requests it. This will give you flexibility as you enable IPSec on the other machines, because it will allow communication even if IPSec is not utilized. Client (Respond Only) will attempt an IPSec negotiation if the other computer requests it, but it will never attempt it on its own outward-bound connections. Keep in mind that "client" in this context is not necessarily a computer workstation; it only refers to the computer that is initiating the connection. Secure Server (Require Security) specifies that all IP communication must use IPSec. Obviously, this will have an impact on a network that is not completely IPSec-enabled and interoperable. Client (Request Only) is not a valid option.

Planning Server-Level Security

MICROSOFT EXAM OBJECTIVES COVERED IN THIS CHAPTER:

✓ **Evaluate and select the operating system to install on computers in an enterprise.**

- Identify the minimum configuration to satisfy security requirements.

✓ **Plan a secure baseline installation.**

- Plan a strategy to enforce system default security settings on new systems.
- Identify client operating system default security settings.
- Identify all server operating system default security settings.

✓ **Configure security for servers that are assigned specific roles.**

✓ **Plan security for servers that are assigned specific roles. Roles might include domain controllers, Web servers, database servers, and mail servers.**

- Create custom security templates based on server roles.
- Deploy the security configuration for servers that are assigned specific roles.

✓ **Plan a framework for planning and implementing security.**

- Plan for security monitoring.
- Plan a change and configuration management framework for security.

✓ **Plan a security update infrastructure. Tools might include Microsoft Baseline Security Analyzer and Microsoft Software Update Services.**

In today's networks, it's increasingly common to find specialized servers that are dedicated to a specific task such as domain controller services, Web services, mail, or database services. Each of these functional roles carries its own unique security challenges and requirements. An effective plan for secure network infrastructure design takes into consideration the novel requirements of each server type based on its intended function. Server-level security is an important element of a secure network infrastructure.

We'll begin this chapter with an introduction of server roles, followed by an overview of the functionality of the products in the Windows Server 2003 family of server operating systems. You'll learn when the Standard Edition would suffice for a given server installation, when Enterprise Edition is needed, when you will need the Datacenter Edition for your installation, and whether or not you can employ the Web Edition for your Web application servers.

Choosing the right OS for each of your Windows Server 2003 servers is only the beginning. To establish server-level security, you will next want to create a strategy for managing customized security configurations targeted to the role in which the server will function. You'll learn how to plan a baseline for security for servers that are assigned specific roles. You'll learn how to create custom security templates based on server roles and how to analyze existing security configurations against the standardized configuration templates you've created. Once created, these standardized configurations must be effectively deployed throughout the organization, and you'll be equipped with the knowledge you need to accomplish this objective by the end of the chapter.

Security configuration management is an ongoing process. The servers and clients on your network must be kept up-to-date with the latest critical patches and operating system fixes, especially with regard to security. Many organizations employ a tool for enterprise software configuration management such as Microsoft Systems Management Server, which not only manages Windows patches, but also controls the deployment of operating systems, applications, and client configuration standards throughout an organization. If you don't already use such a tool in your network, you'll learn about two tools Microsoft provides to help you manage Windows security updates in this chapter.

Introducing Server Roles

Corporate networks exist to provide specialized services to clients. Some of these services, such as e-mail, are highly visible to the end user. However, many critical services, such as DNS and DHCP, are completely transparent to the end user.

A server that is installed to provide a specific service on the network is said to be functioning in a server role. A *server role* describes the functional purpose of a network server. There are roles for application servers, such as e-mail, Web, database, and media servers. There are roles for servers that host network resources, such as file and print servers. There are also roles for servers that provide network infrastructure services, such as name resolution and connectivity.

Although a single server can host multiple services, it is frequently desirable to plan a server strategy that employs specialized servers for mission-critical and resource-intensive functions, such as domain controller services. Some services can be provided by a single server—for example, file and print services. Other functions could present a huge security risk if they were provided by the same server—for instance, it would be a very bad idea to install a domain controller that also provided Web services to the public.

Some of the most common server roles in a Windows Server 2003 network are listed here:

File Servers File servers provide and manage access to files. You would configure a computer as a file server if you plan to use disk space on the computer to store, manage, and share information such as files or to host applications that users can access over the network.

In Windows Server 2003, file server features include the ability to implement disk quotas on NTFS volumes. This enables you to monitor disk space usage and limit the amount of disk space available to individual users.

The Indexing Service can also be implemented to enable users to quickly and securely search for information on the server or across the network. You can search for files in different formats and even in multiple languages, through the Start ➤ Search command or through a browser interface.

Print Servers Print servers provide and manage access to printers. You would configure a computer as a print server if you plan to use the server to share printers with network clients.

In Windows Server 2003, print server features include the ability to connect to network printers using Web point-and-print for single-click installation of a shared printer. This is a continuation of functionality from the Windows 2000 Server family. Network-attached printers, also known as TCP/IP printers, are installed more simply through a new standard port monitor.

There's also built-in command line functionality for print server management through the Windows Management Instrumentation (WMI) Print Provider. WMI is Microsoft's management API for monitoring local and remote system components. The WMI Print Provider enables you to use Visual Basic scripts to administer print devices and print servers. This helps you automate routine tasks and free time for more important administrative work.

Since the mid-nineties, Microsoft has referred to physical printers as "print devices" and the logical software components of the print redirector as the "printer." Adhere to the Microsoft nomenclature for the exam.

Domain Controller Servers Domain controllers store directory data and manage communication between users and domains. They service user requests for logon, authentication, and directory searches.

You must configure at least one server as a domain controller if you'll be enabling Active Directory. Additional domain controllers are recommended to provide redundancy and fault tolerance, as well as to balance the load.

It's best to locate a domain controller in each site in order to optimize network performance between sites. You want client logon processes to be handled within the local site, not crossing a slower connection and creating unacceptably slow logon times and excessive traffic between sites.

DNS Servers The Domain Name Service (DNS) is a standardized name service used on the Internet and in TCP/IP networks. The DNS service registers names and resolves queries for DNS domain name-to-IP address mappings. The service enables clients (which can be end users or other servers) to locate and access resources offered by remote computers on private networks, such as the corporate network or a VPN-connected extranet, or on public networks, such as the Internet.

If you will publish resources to be available on the Internet, for instance an internally hosted corporate Web site, you'll need to have a DNS server. Most corporate networks will require at least one DNS server, and it's best to have multiple DNS servers for fault tolerance and load balancing.

Your DNS server does not have to be a Windows Server 2003 computer—in fact, Unix servers were the first and are still the most common server providers of DNS services. The Lightweight Directory Access Protocol (LDAP) is an industry-standard protocol that allows users to query and update information in a directory service. LDAP was established by the Internet Engineering Task Force (IETF), and it has been used by Unix OSs for a very long time. Because Active Directory uses an LDAP name structure, Windows DNS services can interoperate with Unix-based DNS services.

If your network will be directly connected to the Internet (which is usually the case), you'll need to decide on a globally unique domain name. Then you must register the domain name with an authorized Internet registrar, such as VeriSign/Network Solutions, Inc. (NSI) or your ISP. The Internet Corporation for Assigned Names and Numbers (ICANN) and the Internet Assigned Numbers Authority (IANA) are responsible for ensuring globally unique domain name and IP assignments on the Internet.

In the past, DNS domain name assignment and registration was the exclusive territory of InterNIC (part of ICANN). Now it is transitioning to a shared registration system.

You can perform a `WHOIS` search to see if your desired name is available at `http://www.nsiregistry.net` or at any Internet registrar. DNS was covered in detail in Chapter 4, "Planning a DNS Strategy."

WINS Servers The Windows Internet Name Service (WINS) provides a distributed database for name resolution services in legacy Microsoft networks. The WINS service registers names and resolves queries for NetBIOS computer name-to-IP address mappings. WINS is the best choice for NetBIOS name resolution in routed networks that use NetBIOS over TCP/IP (NBT).

You should configure a WINS server if you need to support NetBIOS computer name-to-IP address name resolution in your network.

WINS is gradually being phased out in favor of networks that are entirely DNS-based, so there are no substantial improvements to WINS in Windows Server 2003. However, most Windows networks need to support older NetBIOS-aware operating systems (Windows NT/9*x*) or NetBIOS-aware applications such as Microsoft Exchange Server.

WINS was covered in detail in Chapter 5, "Planning a WINS Strategy."

DHCP Servers The Dynamic Host Configuration Protocol (DHCP) provides centralized IP address management and dynamic address allocation to client computers.

You'll almost certainly want to configure at least one DHCP server on your corporate network, and you'll likely install multiple DHCP servers for fault tolerance and load balancing.

DHCP works together with Active Directory, DNS, and WINS to efficiently allocate IP configuration information to clients.

DHCP is covered in greater detail in *MCSA/MCSE: Windows Server 2003 Network Infrastructure Implementation, Management, and Maintenance Study Guide* by Michael Chacon, Matt Sheltz, and James Chellis (Sybex, 2003).

Web Application (IIS) Servers Internet Information Services (IIS) 6 is a Web application server that is used to host Web sites and File Transfer Protocol (FTP) sites.

You will want to configure a server as a Web application server in order to host Web content on that server for internal use within a corporate intranet or for public viewing on the Internet.

For security, IIS installs only static Web server features by default. After completing the server installation, you can run the IIS Security Lockdown Wizard, which allows you to enable full server functionality.

Running IIS on a domain controller is not recommended. The networking and processor load used by domain controller processes, such as authentication, will result in severe performance degradation for IIS activities. More importantly, adding users to a group with log on locally privileges on a domain controller is a huge security risk.

IIS 6 offers an MMC snap-in management console, and can also be administered using scripts, the command-line or by editing a plain text configuration file. Remote administration is possible through the Terminal Services Web Client or Web Interface for Remote Administration (an HTML interface).

In Windows Server 2003, IIS version 6 has been enhanced to better prevent Web application failures and to keep such failures from affecting other Web sites and applications running on the same server. Features of IIS 6 include the ability to isolate a single Web application or multiple sites into a self-contained process that speaks directly to the kernel. This capability prevents one errant application or site from disrupting the Web services or other Web applications on the server. IIS also has health monitoring capabilities that enable you to prevent, discover, and recover from Web application failures.

Managing Web servers and IIS is covered in more detail in *MCSA/MCSE: Windows Server 2003 Environment Management and Maintenance Study Guide* by Lisa Donald with Suzan London and James Chellis (Sybex, 2003).

Mail (POP3) Servers Windows Server 2003 includes Post Office Protocol, version 3 (POP3) and Simple Mail Transfer Protocol (SMTP) components that can be used to provide e-mail services. The POP3 service implements the standard POP3 protocol for mail retrieval and pairs with the SMTP service for mail transfer.

You should configure a server as a mail server if you plan to use the server to provide e-mail transfer and retrieval services to client computers. The Post Office Protocol (POP3) service is used to store and manage e-mail accounts on the mail server. Users can connect to the mail server and retrieve e-mail to their local computer using an e-mail client that supports the POP3 protocol (such as Microsoft Outlook). The Simple Mail Transfer Protocol (SMTP) service is used to send outgoing e-mail.

The simple mail server provided with Windows Server 2003 is not the same as Microsoft Exchange Server, which is a standalone solution for enterprise messaging.

Routing and Remote Access Servers The Routing and Remote Access Service (RRAS) provides software routing services and secure internetworking services such as Virtual Private Networking (VPN) services.

You'll want to configure a routing and remote access server as an IP router if you plan to use software routing in your organization. If you need a secure solution for connecting remote users to the corporate network, you'll want to configure a routing and remote access server as a remote access or VPN server.

Remote access services are often used in combination with Terminal Services to support the latest Windows operating systems and applications on legacy hardware and across slow WAN links.

IP routing was covered in detail in Chapter 3, "Planning a Network Connectivity Strategy." Remote access was covered in detail in Chapter 6, "Planning Secure Network Access."

Terminal Services Servers Terminal Services provides remote computers with a centralized point of access for Windows applications and operating systems.

You'll want to configure a Terminal Services server if you want to support the latest Windows operating systems and applications on legacy systems that would otherwise not meet the minimum hardware requirements. You will also want to configure a Terminal Services server if you want to support clients that require access to remotely hosted applications and resources across slow WAN links.

It acts as a multi-user operating system to enable multiple clients to have simultaneous independent sessions that run on the Terminal Services server, not on the local node. Clients behave like dumb terminals. Users can run applications, access resources, and view the session console as though they were working on the local Desktop.

However, all processing occurs on the Terminal Services server, and only I/O data (keyboard and mouse input from the client, and video output from the server) is transmitted across the wire.

In Windows Server 2003, Terminal Services has a new tool for remote desktop administration. As in Windows 2000 Server, you can use Terminal Services for remote administration of servers and clients.

We discuss the remote administration capabilities of Terminal Services in Chapter 10, "Planning Network Monitoring, Remote Administration, and Recovery." Terminal Services is discussed in detail in *MCSA/MCSE: Windows Server 2003 Environment Management and Maintenance Study Guide*.

Streaming Media Servers Windows Media Services delivers, manages, and archives Windows Media content such as streaming audio and video over networks that range from low-bandwidth, dial-up Internet connections to high-bandwidth LANs.

You should configure a server as a streaming media server if you plan to deliver digital media content in real time over dial-up Internet connections or within LANs.

In the following sections, you'll learn about two tools that novice Windows administrators will find especially helpful for configuring and managing server roles: the Configure Your Server Wizard and the Manage Your Server tool.

Using the Configure Your Server Wizard

Server roles can be initially configured and the relevant services installed using the Configure Your Server Wizard. The Configure Your Server Wizard makes it easy for an administrator to install or remove many of the services available on a Windows Server 2003 computer. You can also use the wizard to remove a role in which you previously configured the server. You can configure a server with multiple roles.

You'll see how this wizard works in Exercise 7.1. This exercise walks you through using the Configure Your Server Wizard to add or remove a server role, depending on whether or not the role has already been configured. For instance, if a server has already been configured for a certain role, such as a file server, then you are presented with the option to remove the role.

EXERCISE 7.1

Using the Configure Your Server Wizard

1. Launch the wizard by going to Start ➤ Administrative Tools ➤ Configure Your Server Wizard. Choose Next to continue.

2. The Preliminary Steps page displays the preliminary steps, prompting you to make sure all cabling and hardware is in place, peripherals are connected, and Internet connectivity is established if the computer will be used for Internet connectivity. You are also reminded to have your Windows Server 2003 CD on hand. Choose Next to continue.

3. After the wizard detects the network settings, the Server Role page is displayed.

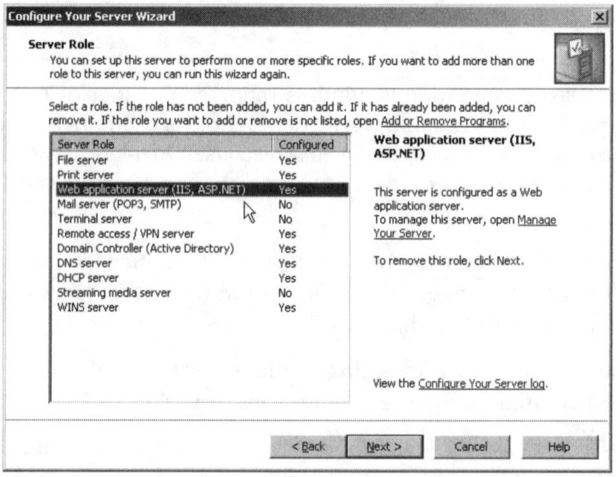

Configure Your Server Wizard

Server Role

You can set up this server to perform one or more specific roles. If you want to add more than one role to this server, you can run this wizard again.

Select a role. If the role has not been added, you can add it. If it has already been added, you can remove it. If the role you want to add or remove is not listed, open Add or Remove Programs.

Server Role	Configured
File server	Yes
Print server	Yes
Web application server (IIS, ASP.NET)	Yes
Mail server (POP3, SMTP)	No
Terminal server	No
Remote access / VPN server	Yes
Domain Controller (Active Directory)	Yes
DNS server	Yes
DHCP server	Yes
Streaming media server	No
WINS server	Yes

Web application server (IIS, ASP.NET)

This server is configured as a Web application server.
To manage this server, open Manage Your Server.

To remove this role, click Next.

View the Configure Your Server log.

< Back | Next > | Cancel | Help

Note that in this example, the Web application server role has been configured and a link to the Manage Your Server tool is provided. You can configure a server for multiple roles, as shown. Also note that there is a link to view the Configure Your Server log. Highlight a role and choose Next to add or remove that server role.

4. If you choose to remove a role, the Role Removal Confirmation page is displayed.

EXERCISE 7.1 *(continued)*

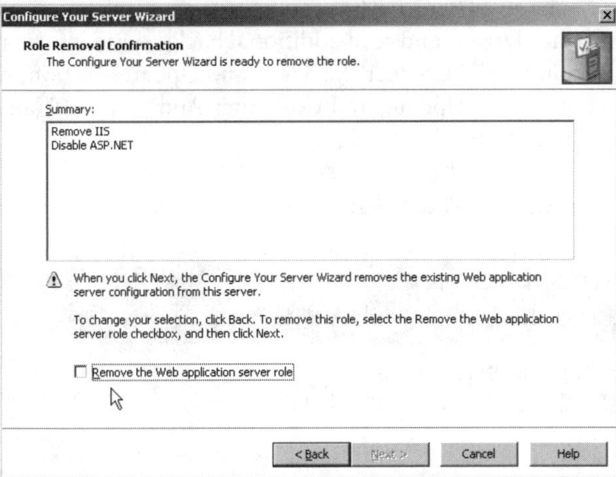

Note that you need to enable a checkbox to confirm removal of a role. Enable the checkbox, and choose Next to continue.

5. The Applying Selections page will appear, displaying a status bar. Once the removal is complete, the Windows Components Wizard appears and prompts you through any additional steps necessary in the process of applying your selections.

6. When the wizard finishes, you can view the Configure Your Server log or simply choose Finish to close the wizard.

As an alternative, you can use the Add or Remove Programs applet in the Control Panel to add or remove Windows components, including all of the services related to the server roles mentioned here with the exception of the routing and remote access server role and the domain controller server role. In addition, The Active Directory Installation Wizard (`dcpromo`) is normally used to promote or demote a domain controller, although the Configure Your Server Wizard could also be used to accomplish this task. The Routing and Remote Access MMC console is used to configure servers as IP routers and to configure servers for remote access/VPN server roles, although the remote access/VPN server role can be initially added or removed using the Configure Your Server Wizard.

Using the Manage Your Server Tool

After running the Configure Your Server Wizard, you can manage the server roles using the Manage Your Server tool located in the Administrative Tools group. The Manage Your Server tool provides a central interface from which an administrator can manage services installed through the Configure Your Server Wizard.

The Manage Your Server tool, shown in Figure 7.1, opens automatically the first time you log on to the server under an account with administrative permissions. Notice that you can search from the main window. There are links to open management consoles, launch specific tasks such as Add A Printer Driver, and read additional background information about a server role. Also notice in the upper-right corner the Tools and Updates section, which includes the Administrative Tools, Windows Update, and Computer And Domain Name Information, which are from the System Properties dialog box.

FIGURE 7.1 The Manage Your Server tool

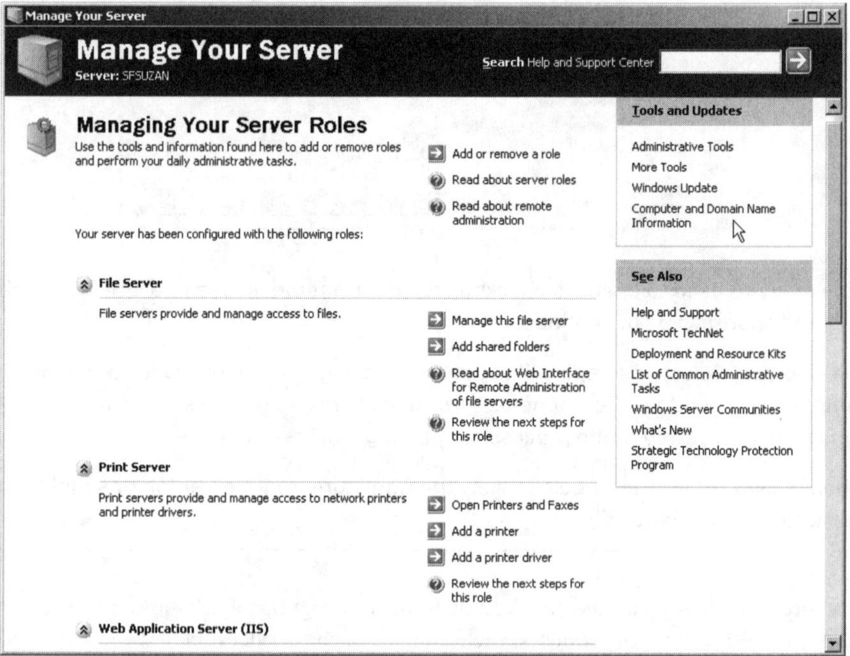

The Manage Your Server tool is a portal to the various MMC consoles and other utilities used to administer the different server functions. For junior administrators and other technical staff, using this tool is an easy way to find the relevant console for a given administrative task. For advanced Windows administrators, launching the intended console or creating custom consoles for common and delegated management tasks is usually faster.

In Exercise 7.2, you will learn how to use the Manage Your Server tool.

EXERCISE 7.2

Using the Manage Your Server Tool

1. Launch this tool on a domain controller by going to Start ➢ Administrative Tools ➢ Manage Your Server.

EXERCISE 7.2 *(continued)*

2. The main page of the Manage Your Server tool shows the roles that are configured for this server. Click Add Or Remove A Role at the top of the screen to launch the Configure Your Server Wizard. Choose Cancel to return to the main page of the Manage Your Server tool.
3. Scroll down to the Domain Controller (Active Directory) role. It has options to manage users and computers in Active Directory, manage domains and trusts, and manage sites and services. Each of these options launches the corresponding MMC console for Active Directory. Click Manage Users And Computers In Active Directory. Notice that Active Directory Users And Computers console is launched. Close the console to return to the main page of the Manage Your Server tool.
4. In the section for the Domain Controller (Active Directory) role, click Review The Next Steps For This Role. Clicking this text opens Help and displays a checklist for completing additional tasks. The checklist is populated with checks indicating the steps that you have already completed, and it shows you the steps you have yet to take to finish configuring this role. Close Help to return to the main page of the Manage Your Server tool.
5. Click Computer And Domain Name Information in the upper-right corner of the page. This opens the System Properties page with the Computer Name tab active. Click Cancel to return to the main page of the Manage Your Server tool.
6. Exit the Manage Your Server tool.

Evaluating the Windows Server 2003 Editions

The Windows Server 2003 family offers four operating system choices that you can analyze and select for installation on a target computer based on the server role or roles in which that computer will function. This section will introduce the members of the Windows Server 2003 family and provide detailed information about the functionality of the different editions so that you can make the best choice for a given server installation. Large organizations frequently have a mixture of editions installed to suit various needs.

The four different editions available in Windows Server 2003 (along with the highlights, advantages, and target markets of each) are listed here:

Windows Server 2003 Standard Edition Standard Edition is targeted for small businesses and departmental use. It is frequently used as a departmental file and print server, and it can also be used for specialized roles such as Terminal Services, Routing and Remote Access Services, and name resolution services.

Windows Server 2003 Enterprise Edition Enterprise Edition is designed for the general-purpose needs of businesses of all sizes. It is the platform of choice for applications, Web services, and infrastructures. Enterprise Edition expands the functionality of Standard Edition by including enterprise-class features such as eight-node clustering, support for up to 32GB of memory, and support for 64-bit Intel Itanium-based platforms.

Windows Server 2003 Datacenter Edition Datacenter Edition is designed for large-scale implementations that demand the highest possible reliability, availability, and scalability. The most powerful and functional server operating system Microsoft has ever offered, it runs on a minimum of eight processors. Datacenter Edition expands the functionality of Enterprise Edition with key features such as support for up to 32-way SMP and 64GB of RAM with the 32-bit version (64-way SMP and 512GB of RAM with the 64-bit version), and 8-node clustering and load-balancing services as standard features.

Windows Server 2003 Web Edition Web Edition is a cost-effective new option for Windows Server 2003. It is designed for dedicated Web serving and hosting functions as an IIS 6 Web server. It is useful for building and hosting Web applications, Web pages, and XML Web services. It can also be used as a platform for rapidly developing and deploying XML Web services and applications that use ASP.NET technology, which is a key part of the .NET Framework.

Network environments frequently feature a mix of different editions. This mixture may consist of Standard Edition for departmental file/print servers and lower-volume specialty servers such as an IP router or a Terminal Services server. Enterprise Edition can then be used for heavier-volume, mission-critical infrastructure services, such as DNS and domain controller services, and mission-critical business applications like Microsoft Exchange Server. Web Edition can be used to host corporate or departmental intranet Web pages, host lower-volume public Web sites, or build XML-based Web applications.

Both the Enterprise and Datacenter Editions are available in a 64-bit version exclusively for Intel Itanium-based platforms as well as the standard 32-bit version.

The Datacenter Edition is exclusively available as a complete hardware, software, and services solution. It cannot be purchased as a standalone operating system. Approved service providers sell a complete solution, which includes the OEM hardware, Datacenter Edition, and consulting services to design and implement a customized solution in your organization.

Whether you are installing Windows Server 2003 on a new computer or as an upgrade, ensuring that each system meets the hardware requirements for the intended edition is important. Table 7.1 displays the hardware requirements for Windows Server 2003.

TABLE 7.1 Windows Server 2003 Hardware Requirements

Requirement	Standard Edition	Enterprise Edition	Datacenter Edition	Web Edition
Minimum CPU Speed	133MHz	133MHz for x86-based computers 733MHz for Itanium-based computers	400MHz for x86-based computers 733MHz for Itanium-based computers	133MHz

TABLE 7.1 Windows Server 2003 Hardware Requirements *(continued)*

Requirement	Standard Edition	Enterprise Edition	Datacenter Edition	Web Edition
Recommended CPU Speed	550MHz	733MHz	733MHz	550MHz
Minimum RAM	128MB	128MB	512MB	128MB
Recommended Minimum RAM	256MB	256MB	1GB	256MB
Maximum RAM	4GB	32GB for x86-based computers 64GB for Itanium-based computers	64GB for x86-based computers 512GB for Itanium-based computers	2GB
Symmetric Multi-Processor (SMP) Support	Up to 4	Up to 8	Minimum of 8 required Maximum 64*	Up to 2
Disk Space for Setup	1.5GB	1.5GB for x86-based computers 2.0GB for Itanium-based computers	1.5GB for x86-based computers 2.0GB for Itanium-based computers	1.5GB

*The support for over 32 processors is only available with the 64-bit edition of Windows Server 2003, Datacenter Edition.

Although the 64-bit versions offer increased scalability and performance for critical, resource-intensive applications, the 64-bit versions also have limitations. These versions are compatible only with 64-bit Intel Itanium-based systems. You cannot install a 64-bit version of Windows Server 2003 successfully on a 32-bit system. Some of the limitations are surprising considering that 64-bit versions are intended for more advanced server environments. Hot-add memory is not supported. The .NET Framework is not supported, nor is ASP.NET.

Table 7.2 outlines support for key features in the Windows Server 2003 family.

TABLE 7.2 Key Features in the Windows Server 2003 Family

Feature	Standard Edition	Enterprise Edition	Datacenter Edition	Web Edition
Hardware Support				
64-bit support for Intel Itanium-based computers		Y	Y	
Hot-add memory		Y*	Y*	

TABLE 7.2 Key Features in the Windows Server 2003 Family *(continued)*

Feature	Standard Edition	Enterprise Edition	Datacenter Edition	Web Edition
Non-Uniform Memory Access (NUMA)		Y	Y	
Maximum RAM	4GB	32GB / 64GB	64GB / 512GB	2GB
SMP	4-way	8-way	32-way / 64-way	2-way
Directory Services				
Active Directory	Y	Y	Y	**
Metadirectory Services (MMS) Support		Y	Y	
Security Services				
Internet Connection Firewall	Y	Y		Y
Public Key Infrastructure, Certificate Services, and Smart Cards	*	Y	Y	**
Terminal Services				
Remote Desktop for Administration	Y	Y	Y	Y
Terminal Server	Y	Y	Y	
Terminal Server Session Directory		Y	Y	
Clustering Technologies				
Network Load Balancing	Y	Y	Y	Y
Cluster Service		Y	Y	
Networking Services				
Virtual Private Network (VPN) Support	Y	Y	Y	**
Internet Authentication Service (IAS)	Y	Y	Y	
Network Bridge	Y	Y	Y	

TABLE 7.2 Key Features in the Windows Server 2003 Family *(continued)*

Feature	Standard Edition	Enterprise Edition	Datacenter Edition	Web Edition
Internet Connection Sharing (ICS)	Y	Y		
IPv6	Y	Y	Y	Y
File Systems and Services				
Distributed File System (DFS)	Y	Y	Y	Y
Encrypting File System (EFS)	Y	Y	Y	Y
Shadow Copy Restore	Y	Y	Y	Y
Removable and Remote Storage	Y	Y	Y	
Management Services				
Windows Management Instrumentation (WMI) Command Line	Y	Y	Y	Y
Remote OS Installation	Y	Y	Y	Y
Remote Installation Services (RIS)	Y	Y	Y	
Windows System Resource Manager (WSRM)		Y	Y	
.NET Application Services				
.NET Framework	Y	Y*	Y*	Y
Internet Information Services (IIS) 6	Y	Y	Y	Y
ASP.NET	Y	Y*	Y*	Y
Enterprise UDDI Services	Y	Y	Y	
Multimedia Services				
Windows Media Services	Y	Y	Y	

*32-bit versions only.

**Indicates limited functionality.

You'll notice that each edition consists of those features that optimize performance for different objectives. For instance, Enterprise Edition is more scalable and robust than Standard Edition, while Datacenter Edition offers the most scalability and reliability features for mission-critical environments.

The Web Edition is intended for specialized use as a dedicated Web server and consequently has limited functionality. It supports only one VPN connection at a time. Terminal Server is not supported, but Remote Desktop for Administration can be used to administer the Desktop.

Windows Media Services is not included with the Web Edition or the 64-bit versions of the Windows Server 2003 family.

Real World Scenario

Planning a Strategy to Implement Web Services

As the network administrator for a large corporation with locations spread across North America, you are charged with planning the strategy to enable users to access localized internal corporate information. Users at each location require access to information from their human resources group. In addition, certain departments, including Marketing and Engineering, require access to departmental information, and access to this information needs to be restricted to just the users in the relevant department. Users will access the information on an occasional basis, so you do not foresee a need to plan for heavy traffic. However, critical information updates must be immediately available. This information should be easy to find and navigate, and it should be stored in a central location so users can retrieve the information on demand. Finally, you want a solution that will be cost-effective and easy to implement. The expenses will come from the local IT budgets, which were recently slashed to meet corporate efficiency objectives.

You decide to use a strategy incorporating a local Web server at each location to host localized intranet sites. To meet your cost objectives, you use a single Windows Server 2003 server running Web Edition at each location. Each intranet Web server hosts several sites: one for Marketing, one for Engineering, and two for Human Resources. Human Resources will have two sites. One site will have confidential information and will be restricted. The other HR site will be used to publish details about benefits, events, and other information that users throughout the location need to know.

You secure the solution by placing the Web servers within the local private network, using a private addressing scheme to refer to the Web servers so that they are available only from inside the corporate network. Because Web Edition supports only a single VPN connection, you use a separate RRAS server to enable remote users to reach the corporate network and access the intranet sites. Each local IT administrator can manage the Web servers and also delegate administration to authoritative users within a department by adding those users to the Web Operators group.

This strategy enables you to deploy a manageable, cost-effective solution that meets the local business needs of your organization. Web Edition is optimized for Web site hosting, and it can handle the traffic needs of multiple sites. This solution enables you to get the information to your users quickly and make it accessible through an easy-to-navigate HTML interface. Archived data, such as sales data for fiscal year 2002, is especially easy to find through a Web interface. Your plan also makes it easy to restrict data access to internal users only, and you can further restrict data access to authorized groups only.

Once you have determined the functional roles for target servers and installed the appropriate Windows Server 2003 edition according to your technical requirements, you can design a strategy to deploy standardized security configurations for each server role.

Managing Server Configurations with Security Policy

After determining which edition or editions of Windows Server 2003 to use and assigning a server role or roles to each server, you'll need a strategy for managing the security configurations on those servers. Servers in different functional roles have different security requirements that you will need to take into account.

Like its predecessor, Windows 2000 Server, Windows Server 2003 enables you to administer security at a granular level to control a panoply of options for user rights, as well as the behavior of applications and the operating system itself. This is accomplished by using Group Policy to configure the options.

Security Policy is a subset of Group Policy settings that define security configurations for computers. The policies are applied at one of two levels: the local computer level or the domain level.

Domain Security policies control security at the domain level, and they are created using the Domain Security Policy MMC snap-in. *Local Security policies* control security at the local computer level, and they are created using the *Local Computer Policy* MMC snap-in. Domain Security policies override Local Computer Security policies when the user is logged into the domain. Security policies are deployed through Group Policy Objects (GPOs) in Active Directory–enabled networks.

Security policies are defined by configuring options within security-related nodes in the appropriate GPO, which can be accessed as an MMC snap-in. Most of these options are found under Computer Configuration ➢ Windows Settings ➢ Security Settings within the Account Policies and Local Policies nodes. Account policies are used to control the logon process, such as password and account lockout configurations. Local policies are used to define Security policies for the computer, such as auditing, user rights, and security options.

Other options related to server security are configured within the Computer Configuration ➢ Administrative Templates ➢ System node.

The Security Configuration and Analysis tool is a Windows Server 2003 utility that you can use to analyze your security configuration. Using any of a set of standardized security templates, this utility compares your actual security configuration to your desired configuration.

In the following sections, you will learn how to manage security configurations in a Windows Server 2003 environment using Security policies and Group Policy Objects (GPOs). We'll start with a view of how Security Policy works with Group Policy and Active Directory. Next, we'll discuss how to configure security-related options within two nodes of the GPO: the Security Settings node and the System node.

Understanding Group Policy and Active Directory

Security policies are created by configuring a subset of options available within Group Policy. To understand how Security policies work, it's important to understand how Group Policy is applied within Active Directory, so we'll step back for a moment to get a bird's eye view of the process.

Within Active Directory, you have several levels of hierarchical structure. A typical structure will consist of domains and organizational units. Other levels exist within Active Directory, but for the purpose of discussing Security Policy, we will focus on domains and *organizational units (OUs)*.

The domain is the main unit of organization within Active Directory. Within a domain, there are many domain objects (including users, groups, and GPOs). Each domain object can have security applied that specifies who can access the object and the level of access they have.

Within a domain, you can further subdivide and organize domain objects through the use of organizational units.

Windows NT Domains versus Windows 2003 Domains

One of the key differences between Windows NT domains and Windows 2003 domains is that the NT domains were not able to store information hierarchically. Windows 2003 domains, through the use of OUs, allow you to store objects hierarchically—typically based on function or geography.

For example, assume that your company is called *ABCCORP.* You have locations in New York, San Jose, and Belfast. You might create a domain called `ABCCORP.COM` with OUs called NY, SJ, and Belfast. In a very large corporation, you might also organize the OUs based on function. For example, the domain could be `ABCCORP.COM` and the OUs might be SALES, ACCT, and TECHSUPP. Based on the size and security needs of your organization, you might also have OUs nested within other OUs. As a general rule, however, you will want to keep your Active Directory structure as simple as possible.

In Active Directory–enabled networks, Group Policy settings that you specify are contained in a *Group Policy Object (GPO)*, which is linked to target Active Directory objects—sites, domains, or organizational units.

Group Policy applies not just to users and client computers, but also to member servers, domain controllers, and any other Windows Server 2003 computers within the scope of management.

Group Policy can be used to define configuration settings within one or both of two nodes within a GPO: Computer Configuration and User Configuration. Users settings are applied to users and can be used to control such things as logon scripts and Desktop behavior; computer settings are applied to computers and can be used to control such things as startup/shutdown scripts and a wide variety of security-related settings.

Group Policies cannot be applied directly to security or distribution groups. In keeping with Microsoft's nomenclature, Group Policy Objects are applied not to groups, but to domains, sites, and organizational units (OUs). See Chapter 6 to find out how to apply Group Policy to actual groups.

In the following sections, we'll show you how GPOs are applied to objects within Active Directory, review the legacy compatibility considerations for Group Policy, identify the Security Policy management consoles, demonstrate the Group Policy Object Editor console, and demonstrate how to create a custom MMC console to manage Security Policy for a new GPO.

Group Policy Objects and Active Directory

In Active Directory–enabled networks, Security policies can be deployed by creating GPOs in which you specify the desired security configuration, and then assigning those GPOs to computers. Policies can apply to users or computers. The focus of this discussion is server-level security, so we'll focus on policies that apply to computers.

You can create GPOs through the Active Directory Users And Computers MMC snap-in from the Group Policy tab of the Properties page (see Figure 7.2). GPOs can also be created from the Group Policy Object Editor when adding snap-ins to the MMC console. The MMC consoles for Local Computer Policy, Domain Security Policy, and Domain Controller Security Policy are actually GPOs themselves, and they appear in the Administrative Tools group.

FIGURE 7.2 The Group Policy tab of an OU's Properties page

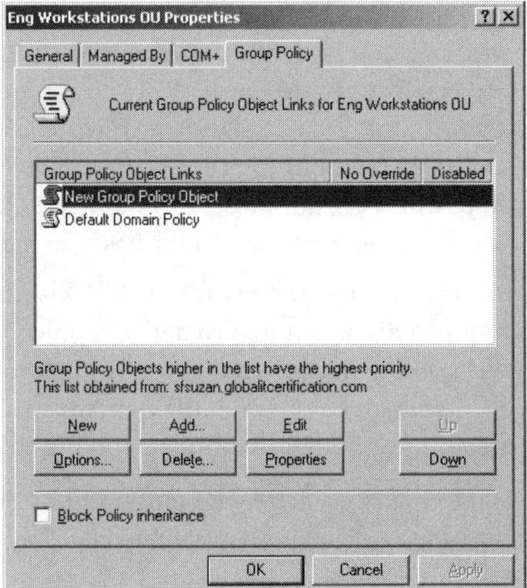

By default, certain information about GPOs is stored within Active Directory on all domain controllers in the *windir*\Sysvol folder. A policy file called gpt.ini that contains information about the Group Policy is stored in each root folder.

When GPOs are created within Active Directory there is a specific order of *inheritance* (meaning how the policies are applied within the hierarchical structure of Active Directory). When a user logs on to an Active Directory domain, depending on where GPOs have been applied within the hierarchical structure of Active Directory, the order of application is as follows:

1. Local computer
2. Site (group of domains)
3. Domain
4. OU

If there are any conflicts between settings, the Site policy overrides the Local policy. Next, the Domain policies are applied. If the Domain policy has any additional settings, they will be applied to the configuration. If there are any conflicts in the settings, the Domain policy overrides the Site policy. Next, the OU policies are applied. Again, any additions to the settings will be applied. If there are any conflicts in settings, the OU policy overrides the Domain policy. Finally, if there are conflicts between the Computer and User Policy settings, the User Policy settings are applied. Computer policy is applied for the machine at network initialization, prior to a user logon. Because Group Policy is cumulative, the User Policy settings will override any conflicting Computer Policy settings.

The following options are available for overriding the default behavior of application of GPOs:

Block Policy Inheritance The Block Inheritance option is used to allow the child container to block GPO inheritance from parent containers. You would use this option if you did not want child containers to inherit GPO settings from parent containers and only wanted the GPO you had set for your container to be applied. This option is enabled through a checkbox on the Group Policy tab of the object's Properties page.

No Override The No Override option is used to specify that child containers can't override the policy settings of higher-level GPOs. In this case, the order of precedence would be that site settings override domain settings, and domain settings override OU settings, assuming that No Override is set at both levels. You would use the No Override option if you wanted to set corporate-wide policies without allowing administrators of lower-level containers to override your settings. This option can be set on a per-container basis, as needed.

Disabled The Disabled option is used to specify that the GPO is not applied to this container. You would use the Disabled option if you wanted to define a policy on a higher-level container to be applied to all down-level containers, without actually applying the policy to the parent container itself. For instance, you may set a policy at the domain level mandating configurations that will apply to all computers in the domain without applying to the actual domain object.

The No Override and Disabled options are each configured by clicking the Options button on the Group Policy tab of the object's Properties page and enabling a checkbox in the Options window, as shown in Figure 7.3.

FIGURE 7.3 The GPO Options window

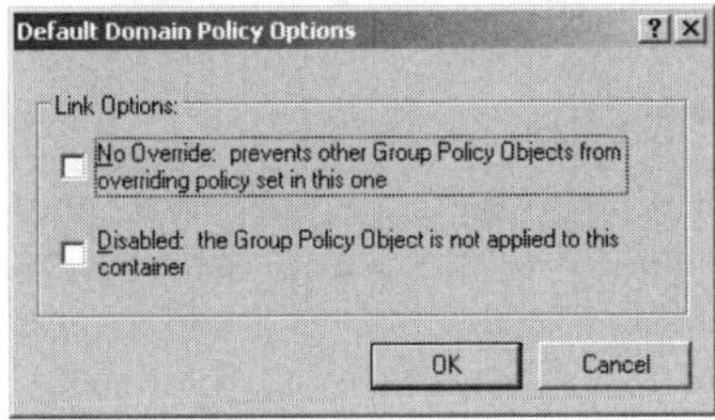

If there is a conflict between the No Override and the Block Inheritance settings, the No Override option is applied.

Understanding the order in which policies are applied for GPOs is essential.

Legacy Compatibility Considerations for Group Policy

Under NT, system configuration management was accomplished by creating *System Policy* files. System Policy was limited in the scope of settings that could be controlled. In addition, settings could not be easily backed out because they were written to various locations in the local Registry.

For instance, you might set a policy that forced the use of chartreuse wallpaper for all Desktops or a picture of the company mascot. As you can probably imagine, setting such features might not sit will with everybody on the company. Unfortunately, even after you changed the setting to allow users to change the wallpaper, you would have to visit each computer or instruct every user to change this setting. This behavior is known as "tattooing," because configurations are permanently written to the local system's Registry. With Active Directory, you can simply remove the policy and all related settings will be backed out.

Domain-level security under NT involved storing these `config` files (`NTCONFIG.POL`) in the `NETLOGON` directory of a domain controller. `NETLOGON` is the predecessor to the `Sysvol` directory, which was introduced in Windows 2000. Unlike `Sysvol`, `NETLOGON` required you to set up file replication using the often-unreliable and inconsistent NT Directory Replication Service. Under Active Directory, Security Policy is now stored mostly in Active Directory and partly in files, and replication occurs automatically with no intervention from the administrator.

If your network consists of only Windows 2000 and higher computers, you can use GPOs to manage your computer's configuration settings. Backward compatibility for NT4-based system policy is maintained in Windows Server 2003. If you want to manage configuration settings for NT 4 users within the domain, you would use NT System Policy files; these files can be configured from the `Poledit` command, which calls the System Policy Editor utility.

Administrative templates provide policy information for the items that appear under the Administrative Templates folder in the console tree of the Group Policy Object Editor. By default, the administrative templates (that is, `.adm` files) listed in Table 7.3 are used by Windows Server 2003. These templates are used to apply Group Policy settings to the Registry.

TABLE 7.3 Administrative Templates Defined

Administrative Template	Description
System.adm	Template used by Windows 2000 and higher clients to configure general system settings from the Administrative Templates node.
Intres.adm	Template used to set Internet Explorer (IE) settings for Windows 2000 and higher clients.
Winnt.adm	User interface options used by Windows NT clients. To configure options for Windows NT clients, use the System Policy Editor (Poledit.exe).
Windows.adm	User interface options used by Windows 95/98 clients. To configure options for Windows 95/98 clients, use the System Policy Editor (Poledit.exe).
Common.adm	User interface options that are common to both Windows NT 4 and Windows 95/98 clients.

The Security Policy MMC Consoles

You have seen that Security Policy is administered through GPOs. GPOs can be managed through MMC consoles or through the Group Policy tab of an object's Properties page within Active Directory. Default consoles are listed in the Administrative Tools group, and you can also add a GPO to a custom MMC console. Two consoles are created by default in the Administrative Tools program group on a domain controller: the Domain Security Policy and Domain Controller Security Policy. On a Windows Server 2003 computer without Active Directory enabled, you will instead find the Local Computer Policy MMC console (see Figure 7.4) in the Administrative Tools program group. You can add these or other GPOs to a custom MMC console by adding the Group Policy Object Editor snap-in and browsing to a GPO that the snap-in will modify.

Figure 7.4 displays the Local Computer Policy console window, expanded to show the layout of configurable options, which you view by expanding Local Computer Policy ➢ Computer Configuration ➢ Windows Settings ➢ Security Settings. Security Settings includes the subsets Account Policies and Local Policies. Also note the differences between Security Settings, which is a container that holds options that can be configured for Security Policies, and Security Options, which is a subset of the Local Policies set of configurable options. You launch this console on a non-domain controller by selecting Start ➢ Administrative Tools ➢ Local Security Policy.

Figure 7.5 displays the Default Domain Controller Policy console window, expanded to show the layout of configurable options, which you again view by expanding Default Domain Controllers Policy ➢ Computer Configuration ➢ Windows Settings ➢ Security Settings. In both examples, note that there is also a Security Settings option in the User Configuration node, but it does not contain the Security Options to manage security configurations on server computers in the network. You launch this console on a domain controller by selecting Start ➢ Administrative Tools ➢ Domain Controller Security Policy.

FIGURE 7.4 The Local Computer Policy MMC console window

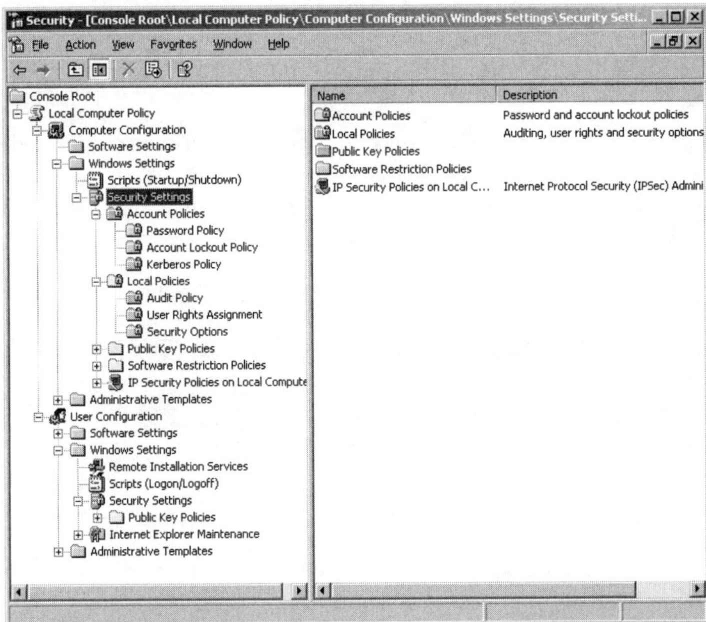

FIGURE 7.5 The Default Domain Controller Policy MMC console window

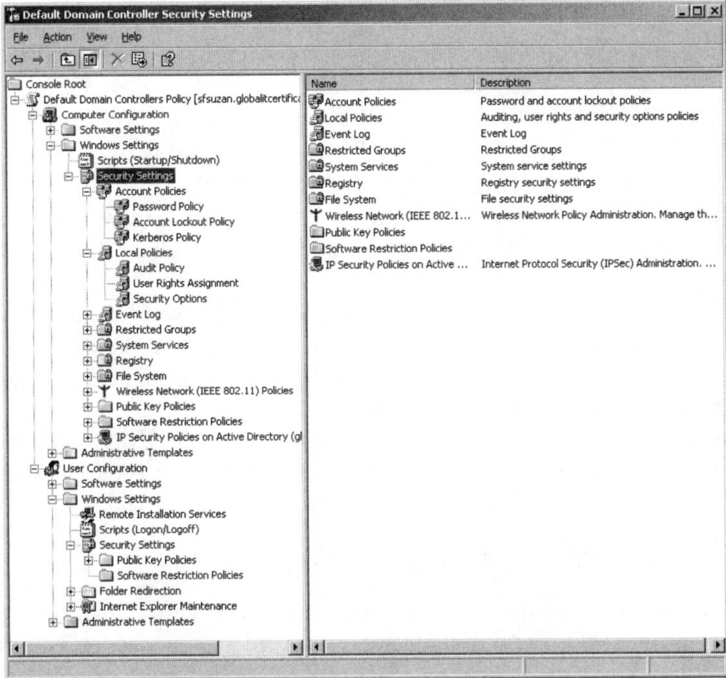

Note that Security Settings also includes Public Key Policies and IPSec Policies, which are beyond the scope of this discussion. IPSec Policies are discussed in detail in Chapter 6. Public keys are discussed in Chapter 8, "Planning Certificate Services."

Figure 7.6 displays the Default Domain Policy console window, expanded to show the layout of configurable options, which you view by expanding the same series of nodes as in the previous two examples. You launch this console on a domain controller by selecting Start ➢ Administrative Tools ➢ Domain Security Policy.

FIGURE 7.6 The Default Domain Policy MMC console window

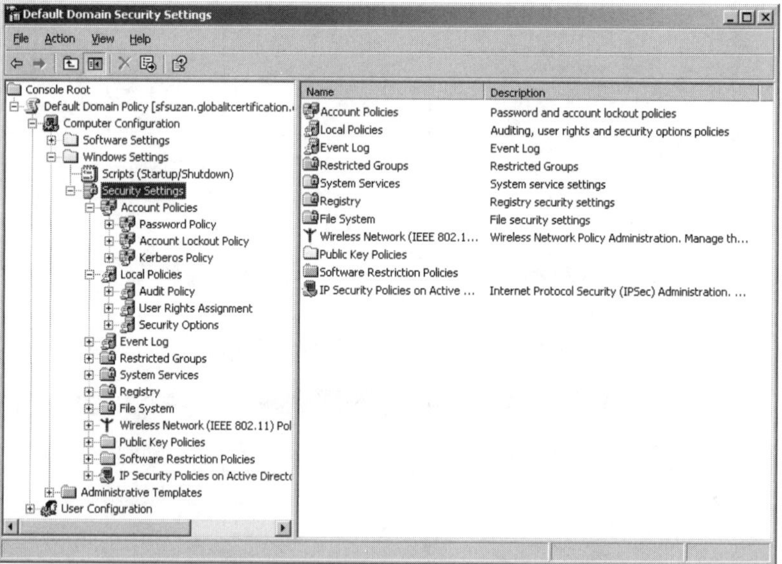

Note that there are more configurable options in the Security Settings node for the Default Domain Controller Policy and Default Domain Policy objects because they relate to domain controllers.

Figure 7.7 again displays the Default Domain Policy console window, but this time it is expanded to show the layout of configurable system options within the Computer Configuration ➢ Administrative Templates ➢ System node. This node has the same layout and options for the three consoles discussed so far in this section.

The most common Security Settings and System options that you would configure are defined in the following sections. You may want to refer back to this image to better understand where in the hierarchy particular policy settings can be found.

The Group Policy Object Editor Console

The standard MMC consoles found in the Administrative Tools program group can be used to manage the associated GPOs. As an alternative, you could manage these GPOs through the

Group Policy tab of the associated object's Properties page within Active Directory Users and Computers. This launches the Group Policy Object Editor console.

FIGURE 7.7 The Default Domain Policy MMC console window again, this time expanded to show the Administrative Templates, System options

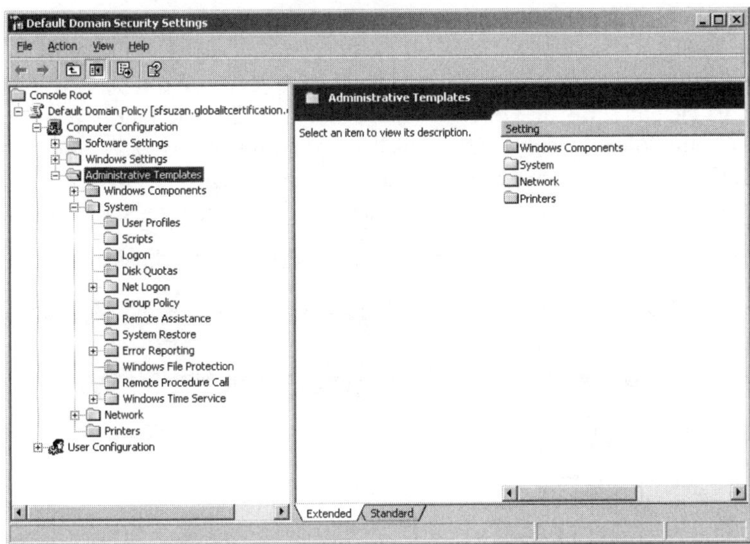

For instance, to manage the Default Domain Policy, you could launch the Administrative Tools, Domain Security Policy console. An alternate way to accomplish the same task is within Active Directory Users and Computers. Right-click the object whose GPO you want to manage (in this case, the domain) and choose Properties. Click the Group Policy tab, as shown in Figure 7.8.

FIGURE 7.8 The Group Policy tab of the domain object's Properties page

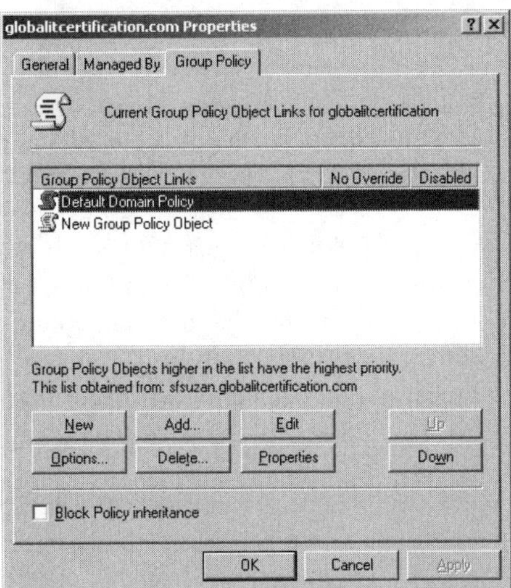

The Group Policy Management Console (GPMC) is a new tool for Group Policy management in Windows Server 2003 and can be downloaded from the Microsoft web site. This tool integrates the management of Group Policy into a single console. If you are using the GPMC, then an object's Group Policy tab would have a single button for Group Policy which you would click to launch the GPMC console.

Notice that this Group Policy tab shown in Figure 7.8 is very similar to the one shown earlier in the chapter in Figure 7.2, which displayed the Properties page of an OU. The Group Policy tab displays all current Group Policy Object links for the object. From here, you would either double-click the Default Domain Policy or highlight it and click the Edit button; either action launches the Group Policy Object Editor console, as shown in Figure 7.9. Notice that it is the same as the Default Domain Policy MMC console shown in Figure 7.6. In fact, if you open both at the same time and change a setting in one, the change will appear instantly in the other.

FIGURE 7.9 The Group Policy Object Editor for the domain object

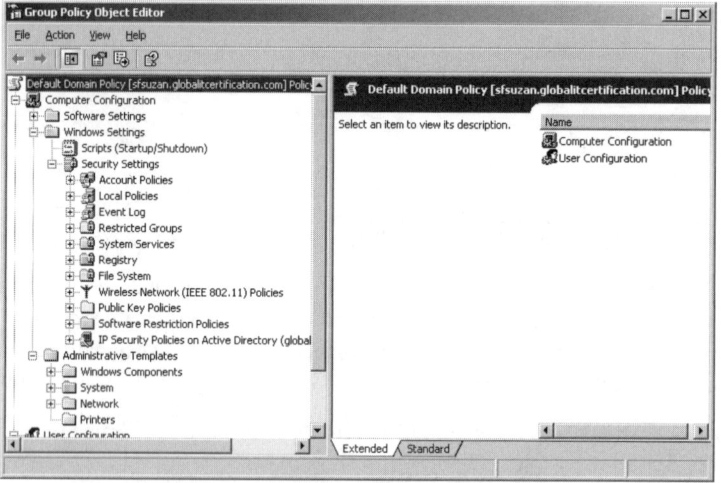

The Group Policy tab is only available on valid objects within the Active Directory Users And Computers utility (that is, objects that can have a Group Policy defined). Valid objects include domains, sites, and OUs.

Figure 7.8 also shows a New Group Policy Object. GPOs can be created to apply to a valid object by clicking the New button on the Group Policy tab of the container object to which the new policy will apply. For instance, assume that a parent container called *Engineering OU* contains the child containers Engineering Workstations OU and Engineering Users OU. You want to create a new policy to apply to all Engineering workstations and users. Create the policy on the Group Policy tab of the Engineering OU object, and it will apply to itself and all objects in the child containers also, by default.

You can link an existing GPO to a new object by clicking the Add button on the Group Policy tab for the new object. When multiple GPOs are linked to an object, you can use the Up and Down arrows to change the priority of GPOs in the list.

Creating a Custom MMC Console to Manage Security Policy for a New GPO

You've seen that GPOs can be managed through the MMC as well as from within the Active Directory Users and Computers utility. To conduct your policy management tasks, you can create a custom MMC console with the relevant snap-ins for your task. In Exercise 7.3, you'll create a management console for a new GPO named *Security Policy GPO*, and customize it by adding Event Viewer. This exercise should be performed from a domain controller. The Security Policy GPO will be used for the remaining exercises in the chapter.

For the remaining exercises in this chapter, you should be logged on as the Administrator.

EXERCISE 7.3

Creating a Custom MMC Console to Manage Security Policy for a New GPO

1. Select Start ➤ Run, type **MMC** in the Run dialog box, and choose OK to open the MMC.
2. From the main menu, select File ➤ Add/Remove Snap-in.
3. In the Add/Remove Snap-in dialog box, choose Add. The Add Standalone Snap-in is displayed.

4. Highlight the Group Policy Object Editor snap-in and choose Add. The Group Policy Wizard is displayed.

EXERCISE 7.3 *(continued)*

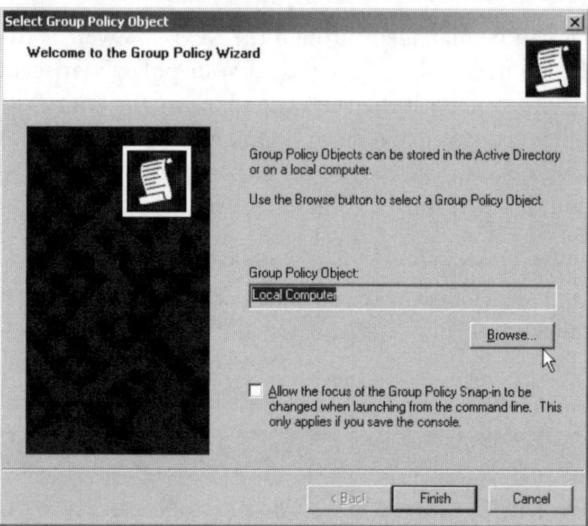

5. The Group Policy Object specifies Local Computer by default. Choose Browse to browse for a Group Policy Object.

6. The Browse For A Group Policy Object dialog box is displayed. The Domains/OU tab is the default, showing the current domain. Notice that you can choose the Default Domain Policy here, and that you have a Create New Group Policy Object button to the right of the drop-down list of domains (it's the middle icon). In the Domains/OUs tab, click the Create New Group Policy Object button. Name the GPO **Security Policy GPO**. Choose OK, then choose Finish to return to the Add Standalone Snap-in window.

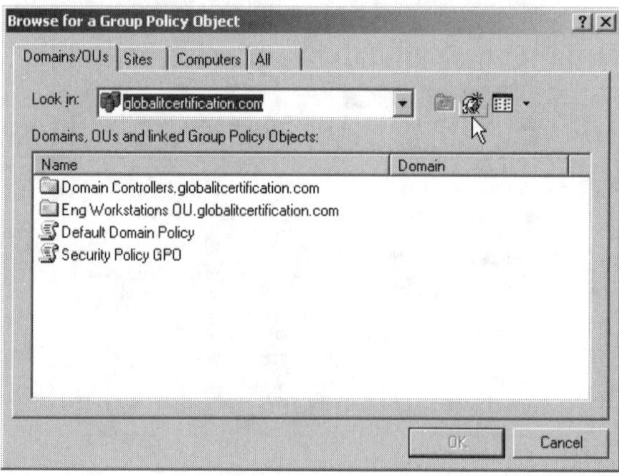

7. Highlight the Event Viewer snap-in and choose Add.

EXERCISE 7.3 *(continued)*

8. The Select Computer dialog box appears with Local Computer selected by default. Choose the Another Computer radio button, and type the name of the domain controller computer from which you are doing this exercise.

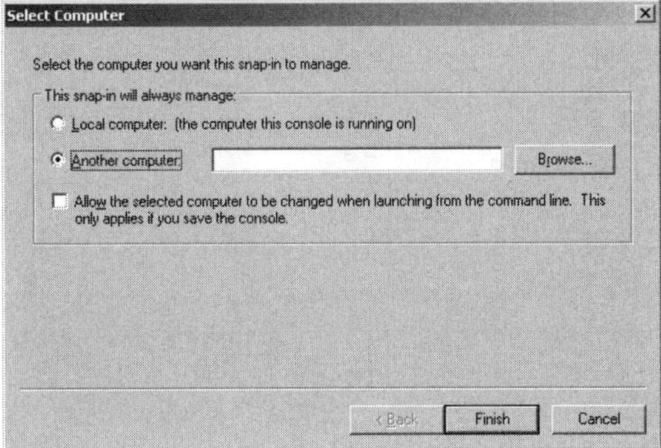

9. Click Finish, then Close.

10. In the Add/Remove Snap-in dialog box, notice that the new GPO is now listed, along with Event Viewer.

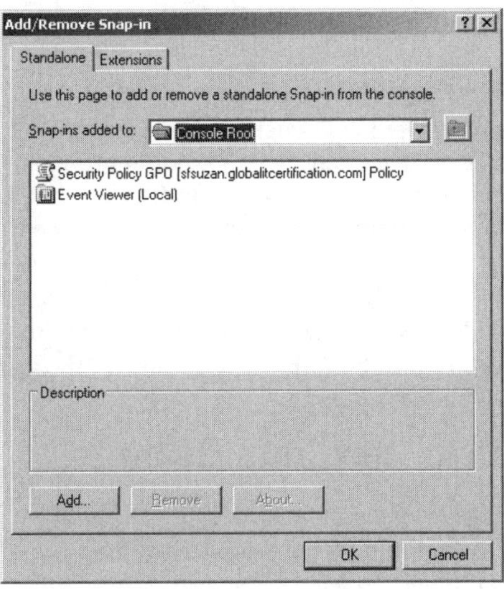

11. Choose OK to return to the main console window.

12. Select File ➢ Save As. Save the console as **Security Policy GPO** in the `All Users\Start Menu\Programs\Administrative Tools` folder and choose Save.

EXERCISE 7.3 *(continued)*

13. You can now access this console by selecting Start ➤ Administrative Tools ➤ Security Policy GPO.

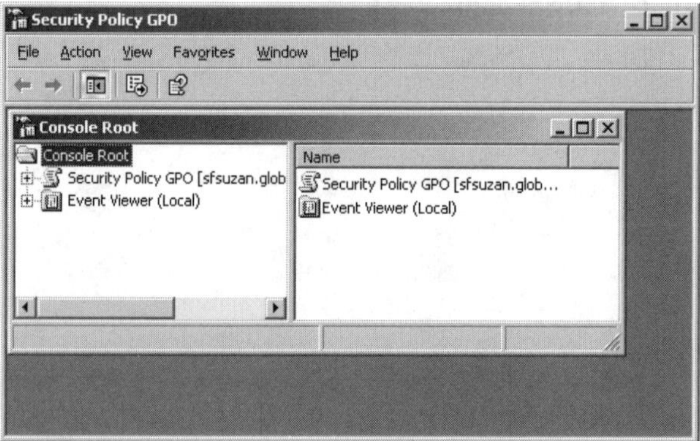

You can edit Local Computer Settings by using the command-line utility `Gpedit.msc`. To use this utility, select Start ➤ Run and at the Run dialog box, type **Gpedit.msc** and click the OK button.

Do *not* use the Default Domain Security Policy object or the Default Domain Policy object to test Security Policy configurations. Due to the default settings on these objects, it is possible to render an Active Directory network inaccessible even to Domain Admins and force the need to restore Active Directory from backup.

In the next section, we will look at how to configure security options within the Security Settings node, and enforce security configurations on servers throughout your network.

Configuring Security Settings Options

You configure security settings by expanding Security Policy GPO ➤ Computer Configuration ➤ Windows Settings ➤ Security Settings. We are concerned with two nodes that are under this option: Account Policies and Local Policies.

Configuring Account Policies

Account policies are used to specify the user account properties that relate to the logon process. They allow you to configure computer security settings for passwords, account lockout specifications, and Kerberos authentication within a domain.

To access the Account Policies folders, expand Security Policy GPO ➤ Computer Configuration ➤ Windows Settings ➤ Security Settings ➤ Account Policies.

If you are on a Windows Server 2003 member server, you will see two subfolders: Password Policy and Account Lockout Policy. If you are on a Windows Server 2003 computer that is configured as a domain controller, you will also see the Kerberos Policy subfolder. The Account policies available for member servers and domain controllers are described in the following sections.

Password Policies

Password policies ensure that security requirements are enforced on the computer. Note that the Password policy applies to computers only, and it cannot be configured for specific users.

The Password policies that are defined on Windows Server 2003 domain controllers are described in Table 7.4. On Windows Server 2003 domain controllers, the Password Policy settings are defined with the defaults shown in Table 7.5.

TABLE 7.4 Password Policy Options

Policy	Description	Default	Minimum	Maximum
Enforce Password History	Keeps track of user's previously used passwords	Remember 3 passwords	Do not keep password history	Remember 24 passwords
Maximum Password Age	Determines maximum number of days user can keep valid password	Keep password for 42 days	0 Password will not expire	Keep password for 999 days
Minimum Password Age	Specifies how long password must be kept before it can be changed	0 days (password can be changed immediately)	Same as default	998 days
Minimum Password Length	Specifies minimum number of characters password must contain	0 characters (no password required)	Same as default	14 characters
Passwords Must Meet Complexity Requirements	Allows you to install password filter	Disabled	Same as default	Enabled
Store Password Using Reversible Encryption for All Users in the Domain	Specifies higher level of encryption for stored user passwords	Disabled	Same as default	Enabled

The Password policies are used as follows:

- The Enforce Password History option is used to prevent users from reusing a password. Users must create a new password when their password expires or is changed.
- The Maximum Password Age option is used to force users to change their passwords after the maximum number of days has passed.
- The Minimum Password Age option is used to prevent users from changing their password several times in rapid succession in order to defeat the purpose of the Enforce Password History policy.
- The Minimum Password Length option is used to ensure that users create a password, as well as to specify that it meets the length requirement. If this option isn't set, users are not required to create a password at all.
- The Passwords Must Meet Complexity Requirements option is used to prevent users from using items found in a dictionary of common names as passwords. This setting requires the use of at least three of the following four characters: uppercase letters, lowercase letters, numbers, or symbols in the password.
- The Store Password Using Reversible Encryption for All Users in the Domain option is used to provide a higher level of security for user passwords.

In Exercise 7.4, you will configure Password policies for your computer. This exercise and the remaining exercises in this chapter assume that you have completed Exercise 7.3 to create the Security Policy GPO management console.

EXERCISE 7.4

Setting Password Policies

1. Select Start ➤ Administrative Tools ➤ Security Policy GPO and expand the Security Policy GPO object.
2. Expand the folders as follows: Computer Configuration ➤ Windows Settings ➤ Security Settings ➤ Account Policies ➤ Password Policy.
3. Double-click the Enforce Password History policy to open its Properties page. In the Effective Policy Setting field, specify **5** passwords remembered. Click the OK button.

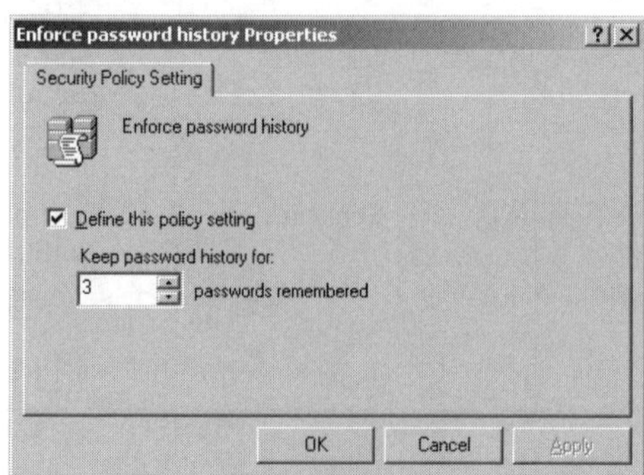

EXERCISE 7.4 *(continued)*

4. Double-click the Maximum Password Age policy to open its Properties page. In the Password Will Expire In field, specify that the password expires in **60** days. Click the OK button.

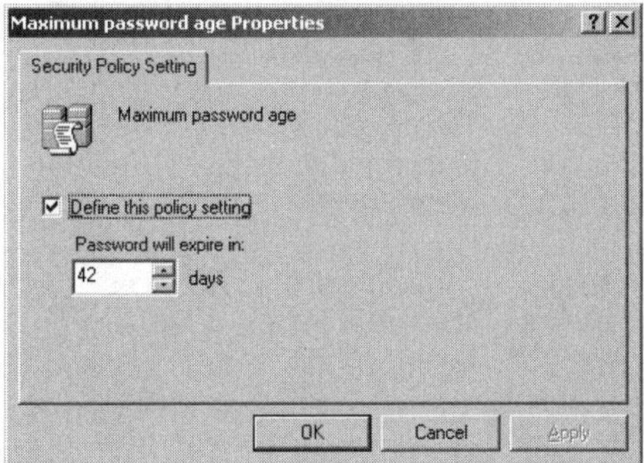

5. Select Start ➢ Command Prompt. At the command prompt, type **gpupdate** and press Enter. This will update the Group policies. Exit the command prompt.

6. At the command prompt, type **exit** and press Enter.

If you edit your Group policies and notice that your changes have not taken effect, it is most likely because the Group policies are only applied every 90 minutes to computers by default. You can force your policies to be updated by typing **gpupdate** at a command prompt.

Account Lockout Policies

The *Account Lockout policies* are used to specify how many invalid logon attempts should be tolerated. You configure the Account Lockout policies so that after a specific number of unsuccessful logon attempts within a certain period of time (in minutes), the account will be locked for a specified amount of time or until the administrator unlocks the account.

The Account Lockout policies work similarly to the way banks handle ATM access code security. You have a certain number of chances to enter the correct access code. If someone steals your card, they cannot continue to guess your access code until they get it right. Typically, after three unsuccessful attempts at your access code, an ATM machine takes the card. After a bank machine confiscates a card, the owner can request a new card from the issuing bank. Account Lockout policies work in the same fashion.

The Account Lockout policies for a domain controller are described in Table 7.5.

TABLE 7.5 Account Lockout Policy Options

Policy	Description	Default	Minimum	Maximum	Suggested
Account Lockout Duration	Specifies how long account will remain locked if Account Lockout Threshold is exceeded	Not Defined. (Defaults to 0; but if Account Lockout Threshold is enabled, 30 minutes)	Same as default	99,999 minutes	30 minutes
Account Lockout Threshold	Specifies number of invalid attempts allowed before account is locked out	0 (disabled, account will not be locked out)	Same as default	999 attempts	5 attempts
Reset Account Lockout Counter After	Specifies how long counter will remember unsuccessful logon attempts	Not Defined. (Defaults to 0, but if Account Lockout Threshold is enabled, 5 minutes)	Same as default	99,999 minutes	30 minutes

In Exercise 7.5, you will configure Account Lockout policies and test their effects. This exercise and the remaining exercises in this chapter assume that you have already created user accounts for James and Matt. You can create these users, or you can choose two other users of you choice.

Creating user accounts is outside the scope of this book. It is covered in *MCSA/MCSE: Windows Server 2003 Environment Management and Maintenance Study Guide.*

EXERCISE 7.5

Setting Account Lockout Policies

1. Select Start ➤ Administrative Tools ➤ Security Policy GPO and expand the Security Policy GPO object.
2. Expand the folders as follows: Computer Configuration ➤ Windows Settings ➤ Security Settings ➤ Account Policies ➤ Account Lockout Policy.

EXERCISE 7.5 *(continued)*

3. Double-click the Account Lockout Threshold policy to open its Properties page. In the Local Policy Setting field, enter **3** to specify that the account will lock after three invalid logon attempts. Click the OK button.

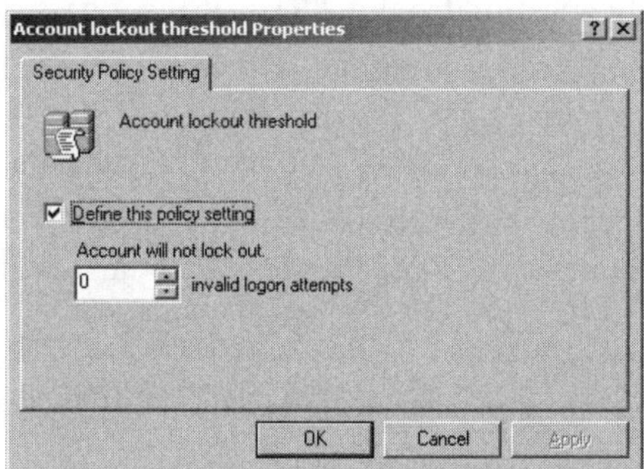

4. The Suggested Value Changes dialog box will appear. Accept the default values for Account Lockout Duration, and reset the account lockout counter by clicking the OK button.

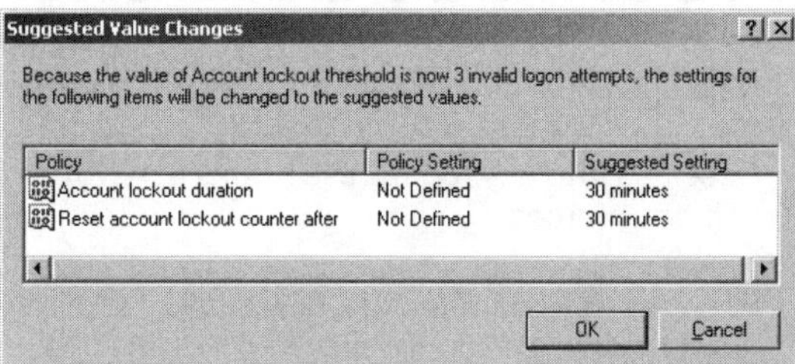

5. Select Start ➢ Command Prompt. At the command prompt, type **gpupdate** and press Enter. Exit the command prompt.

6. Log off as Administrator. Try three times to log on as James with an incorrect password.

7. After you see the error message stating that account lockout has been enabled, log on as Administrator.

8. To unlock James' account, open the Local Users and Groups snap-in in the MMC, expand the Users folder, and double-click user James. In the Account tab of James' Properties dialog box, uncheck the Account Is Locked Out checkbox. Then click OK.

Kerberos Policies

Kerberos version 5 is a security protocol that is used in Windows Server 2003 to authenticate users and network services. This is called *dual verification*, or mutual authentication.

When a Windows Server 2003 is installed as a domain controller, it automatically becomes a key distribution center (KDC). The KDC is responsible for holding all of the client passwords and account information. Kerberos services are also installed on each Windows Server 2003 client and server.

The basic steps of Kerberos authentication are as follows:

1. The client requests authentication from the KDC using a password or smart card.
2. The KDC issues the client a ticket-granting ticket (TGT). The client can use the TGT to access the ticket-granting service (TGS), which allows the user to authenticate to services within the domain. The TGS issues service tickets to the clients.
3. The client presents the service ticket to the requested network service. This service ticket authenticates the user to the service and the service to the user, for mutual authentication.

Authentication services are discussed in Chapter 8.

The Kerberos policy options for a domain controller are described in Table 7.6.

TABLE 7.6 Kerberos Policy Options

Policy	Description	Default Local Setting	Effective Setting
Enforce User Logon Restrictions	Specifies that any logon restrictions will be enforced	Not defined	Enabled
Maximum Lifetime for Service Ticket	Specifies the maximum age of a service ticket before it must be renewed	Not defined	600 minutes
Maximum Lifetime for User Ticket	Specifies the maximum age for a user ticket before it must be renewed	Not defined	10 hours
Maximum Lifetime for User Ticket Renewal	Specifies how long a ticket may be renewed before it must be regenerated	Not defined	7 days
Maximum Tolerance for Computer Clock Synchronization	Specifies the maximum clock synchronization between the client and the KDC	Not defined	5 minutes

Configuring Local Policies

As you learned in the previous section, Account policies are used to control logon procedures. When you want to control what a user can do after logging on, you use *Local policies*. With Local policies, you can implement auditing, specify user rights, and set security options.

To access the Local Policies folders, expand Security Policy GPO ➢ Computer Configuration ➢ Windows Settings ➢ Security Settings ➢ Local Policies.

Local Policies contains three folders: Audit Policy, User Rights Assignment, and Security Options. These policies are covered in the following sections.

Audit Policies

You audit events that pertain to user management through the implementation of *Audit policies*. By tracking certain events, you can create a history of specific tasks, such as user creation and successful or unsuccessful logon attempts. You can also identify security violations that arise when users attempt to access system management tasks that they do not have permission to access.

When you define an Audit policy, you can choose to audit the success or failure of specific events. The success of an event means that the task was successfully accomplished. The failure of an event means that the task was not successfully accomplished.

By default, auditing is not enabled, and it must be manually configured. Once auditing has been configured, you can see the results of the audit through the Event Viewer utility.

Auditing too many events can degrade system performance due to the high processing requirements. Auditing can also use excessive disk space to store the audit log. You should use this utility judiciously.

The Audit policies are described in Table 7.7.

TABLE 7.7 Audit Policy Options

Policy	Description
Audit Account Logon Events	Tracks when a user logs on, logs off, or makes a network connection
Audit Account Management	Tracks user and group account creation, deletion, and management actions
Audit Directory Service Access	Tracks directory service accesses
Audit Logon Events	Audits events related to logon, such as running a logon script or accessing a roaming profile
Audit Object Access	Audits access to files, folders, and printers
Audit Policy Change	Tracks any changes to the Audit policy
Audit Privilege Use	Audits each instance of a user exercising a user right
Audit Process Tracking	Tracks events such as activating a program, indirect object access, and exiting a process
Audit System Events	Tracks system events such as shutting down or restarting the computer, as well as events that relate to system security or the Security log within Event Viewer

In Exercise 7.6, you will configure Audit policies and view their results.

EXERCISE 7.6

Setting Audit Policies

1. Select Start ➢ Administrative Tools ➢ Security Policy GPO and expand the Security Policy GPO object.
2. Expand the folders as follows: Computer Configuration ➢ Windows Settings ➢ Security Settings ➢ Local Policies ➢ Audit Policy.
3. Double-click the Audit Account Logon Events policy to open its Properties page. In the Local Policy Setting field, under Audit These Attempts, check the boxes for Success and Failure. Click the OK button.

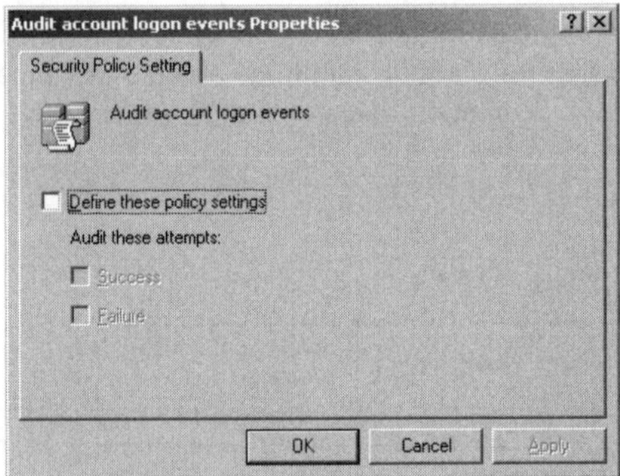

4. Double-click the Audit Account Management policy to open its Properties page. In the Local Policy Setting field, under Audit These Attempts, check the boxes for Success and Failure. Click the OK button.

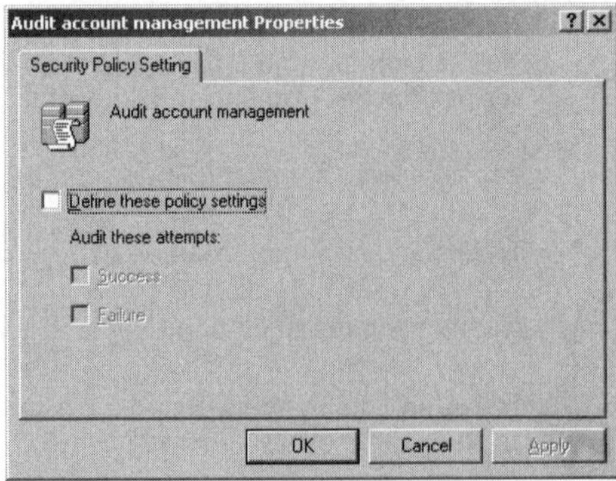

5. Select Start ➢ Command Prompt. At the command prompt, type **gpupdate** and press Enter. Exit the command prompt.

EXERCISE 7.6 *(continued)*

6. In Active Directory Users and Computers, create a new account named **JamesC** for user James Chellis with password **wRxtV23@**.
7. Open the MMC, and expand the Event Viewer snap-in.
8. From Event Viewer, open the Security log. You will see the audited events listed in this log, such as Event ID 642.

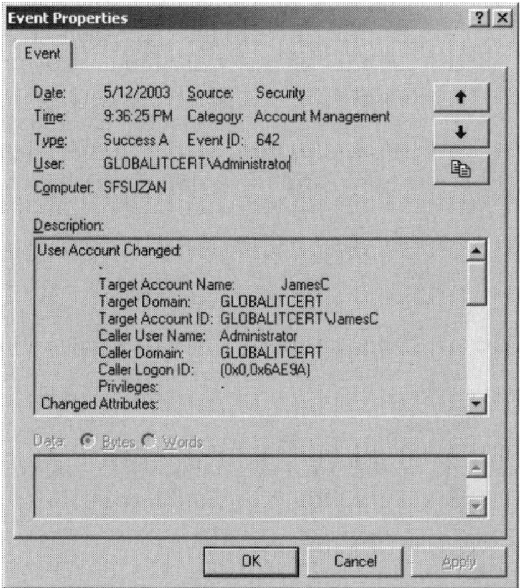

User Rights Assignment Policies

The *User Rights Assignment* policies determine what rights a user or group has on the computer. User rights apply to the system. They are not the same as permissions, which apply to a specific object.

An example of a user right is the Back Up Files And Directories right. This right allows a user to back up files and folders, even if the user does not have permission through the file system. The other user rights are similar in that they deal with system access as opposed to resource access.

The User Rights Assignment policies are described in Table 7.8.

TABLE 7.8 User Rights Assignment Policy Options

Right	Description
Access This Computer From The Network	Allows a user to access the computer over the network.
Act As Part Of The Operating System	Allows low-level authentication services to authenticate as any user.

TABLE 7.8 User Rights Assignment Policy Options *(continued)*

Right	Description
Add Workstations To Domain	Allows a user to create a computer account on the domain (valid only on domain controllers).
Adjust Memory Quotas For A Process	Allows a user to change the maximum memory that can be consumed by a process.
Allow Log On Locally	Allows a user to interactively log on to this computer. This is required by logons initiated by pressing the Ctrl+Alt+Del sequence and may be required by some service or administrative applications that can log on users. If you define this policy for a user or group, you must ensure that the Administrators group also has this right.
Allow Log On Through Terminal Services	Allows a user to log on as a Terminal Services client.
Back Up Files And Directories	Allows a user to back up all files and directories, regardless of how the file and directory permissions have been set.
Bypass Traverse Checking	Allows a user to pass through and traverse the directory structure, even if that user does not have permission to list the contents of the directory.
Change The System Time	Allows a user to change the internal time of the computer.
Create A Pagefile	Allows a user to create or change the size of a page file.
Create A Token Object	Allows a process to create a token if the process uses the NtCreateToken API.
Create Permanent Shared Objects	Allows a process to create directory objects through the Windows Server 2003 Object Manager.
Debug Programs	Allows a user to attach a debugging program to any process.
Deny Access To This Computer From The Network	Allows you to deny specific users or groups access to this computer over the network.
Deny Logon As A Batch Job	Prevents specific users or groups from logging on as a batch job.
Deny Logon As A Service	Prevents specific users or groups from logging on as a service.
Deny Logon Locally	Prevents specific users or groups from accessing the computer locally.

TABLE 7.8 User Rights Assignment Policy Options *(continued)*

Right	Description
Deny Log On Through Terminal Services	Prevents specific users or groups from logging on to the computer as Terminal Services clients.
Enable Computer And User Accounts To Be Trusted For Delegation	Allows a user or group to set the Trusted for Delegation setting for a user or computer object.
Force Shutdown From A Remote System	Allows the system to be shut down by a user at a remote location on the network.
Generate Security Audits	Allows a user, group, or process to make entries in the Security log.
Increase Scheduling Priority	Specifies that a process can increase the priority that is assigned to another process.
Load And Unload Device Drivers	Allows a user to dynamically unload and load Plug and Play device drivers.
Lock Pages in Memory	Forces data to be kept in physical memory and does not allow the data to be paged to the page file.
Log On As A Batch Job	Allows a user to log on to the system and run batch jobs, for example a task in Task Scheduler.
Log On As A Service	Allows a service to log on in order to run the specific service.
Manage Auditing And Security Log	Allows a user to manage tobject access auditing and the Security log.
Modify Firmware Environment Variables	Allows a user or process to modify firmware environment variables.
Perform Volume Maintenance Tasks	Allows a user or group to run maintenance tasks on a volume (for instance, remote defragmentation). Beware that this provides file system access and is, therefore, a security risk.
Profile Single Process	Allows a user to monitor nonsystem processes through tools such as the Performance Logs and Alerts utility.
Profile System Performance	Allows a user to monitor system processes through tools such as the Performance Logs and Alerts utility.
Remove Computer From Docking Station	Allows a user to undock a laptop through the Windows Server 2003 user interface.

TABLE 7.8 User Rights Assignment Policy Options *(continued)*

Right	Description
Replace a Process Level Token	Allows a process to replace the default token that is created by the subprocess with the token that the process specifies.
Restore Files And Directories	Allows a user to restore files and directories, regardless of file and directory permissions.
Shut Down The System	Allows a user to shut down the local Windows Server 2003 computer.
Synchronize Directory Service Data	Allows a user to synchronize data associated with a directory service.
Take Ownership Of Files Or Other Objects	Allows a user to take ownership of system objects.

In Exercise 7.7, you will apply a local User Rights Assignment policy.

EXERCISE 7.7

Setting Local User Rights

1. Select Start ➢ Administrative Tools ➢ Security Policy GPO, and expand the Security Policy GPO object.
2. Expand folders as follows: Computer Configuration ➢ Windows Settings ➢ Security Settings ➢ Local Policies ➢ User Rights Assignment.
3. Double-click the Log On As A Service user right to open its Properties page.
4. Click the Add User or Group button. The Select Users Or Groups dialog box appears.
5. Enter user **Matt**. Click the Add button. Then click the OK button.

Security Options

Security options are used to configure security for the computer. Unlike User Rights policies, which are applied to a user or group, Security Option policies apply to the computer.

Windows Server 2003 features over 70 potential security options, depending on how your server is configured. Unlike its predecessor, Windows 2000 Server, which lumped all of the nearly 40 options together, Windows Server 2003 organizes the security options under subcategories. Table 7.9 describes the new categories of security options.

TABLE 7.9 Security Options Categories

Category	Description
Accounts	Options that allow the enabling or disabling of the Administrator and Guest accounts, as well as an option to limit local account use of the blank password to local logon only.
Audit	Options that control security related to auditing, including the option to shut down the system immediately if unable to log security audits.
Devices	Options that control access to removable media, printers, docking stations, and unsigned driver installation behavior.
Domain Controller	Options that apply specifically to security on domain controllers.
Domain Member	Options for digital encryption, machine account passwords, and session keys.
Interactive Logon	Options for logging on interactively, including whether to display the last user name, whether or not to require Ctrl+Alt+Del, whether to display a custom message for users attempting to log on, and the number of previous logons to cache in the event a domain controller is not available.
Microsoft Network Client	Options to configure digitally signed communications and unencrypted passwords.
Microsoft Network Server	Options to configure digitally signed communications, session idle time, and whether to disconnect clients when logon hours expire.
Network Access	Options to configure 10 anonymous network access settings.
Network Security	Options to configure network security at a granular level.
Recovery Console	Options to configure behavior of the Recovery Console, including floppy access and automatic administrative logon.
Shutdown	Options to allow system shutdown without requiring a logon and/or to clear the virtual memory pagefile on shutdown.
System Cryptography	Options related to encryption, hashing, and signing.
System Objects	Options to configure the behavior of system objects, including whether to require case insensitivity for non-Windows systems.
System Settings	Options to configure additional settings. (It is unlikely that you will need to change them.)

In Exercise 7.8, you will define some Security Option policies and see how they work. This exercise assumes that you have completed all of the previous exercises in this chapter.

EXERCISE 7.8

Defining Security Options

1. Select Start ➤ Administrative Tools ➤ Security Policy GPO, and expand the Security Policy GPO object.
2. Expand folders as follows: Computer Configuration ➤ Windows Settings ➤ Security Settings ➤ Local Policies ➤ Security Options.
3. Double-click the policy named Interactive Logon: Message Text For Users Attempting To Log On to open its Properties page. Enable the Define This Policy Setting In The Template checkbox. In the message box, type **Welcome to the ACME network. Unauthorized access is prohibited by law and will be prosecuted**. Click the OK button.

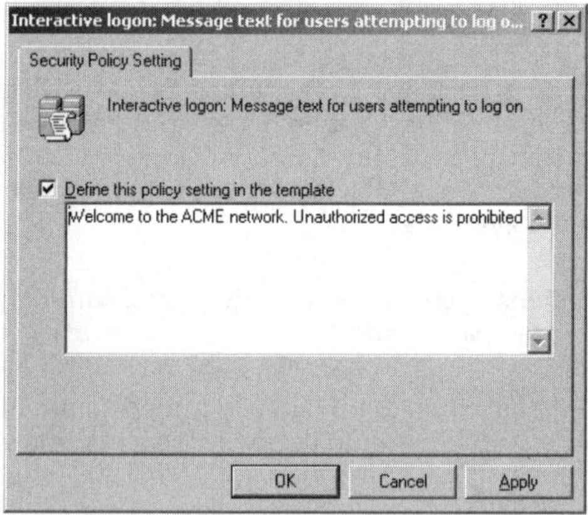

4. Double-click the policy named Interactive Logon: Prompt User to Change Password Before Expiration to open its Properties page. Enable the checkbox to Define This Policy Setting. In the Local Policy Setting field, specify **3** days. Click the OK button.
5. Select Start ➤ Command Prompt. At the command prompt, type **`gpupdate`** and press Enter. Exit the command prompt.
6. Log off as Administrator, and log on as Matt.
7. Log off as Matt, and log on as Administrator.

Configuring Public Key Policies

Public Key Policies allow you to set options so that computers can automatically submit requests to Certificate Authorities in order to install and access public keys, which are associated with cryptography.

You can also specify the Encrypted Data Recovery Agents that are used in conjunction with the Encrypting File System (EFS).

Public keys are covered in Chapter 8. EFS is covered in greater detail in *MCSA/MCSE: Windows Server 2003 Environment Management and Maintenance Study Guide.*

Configuring System Options

Other settings that are related to server security can be accessed through the GPO's MMC snap-in under Computer Configuration ➤ Administrative Templates ➤ System.

Policy settings you are likely to configure within the Administrative Templates ➤ System node include:

- User Profiles policies
- Logon policies
- Disk Quotas policies
- Group Policy policies
- Windows File Protection policies

User Profiles Policies

User Profile policies control the behavior of network connections and roaming profiles. In Windows 2000 Server, these policy settings were grouped with the Logon policy settings. Windows Server 2003 separates them under a new category, User Profiles, for a cleaner administrative interface. Table 7.10 describes the most commonly configured options.

TABLE 7.10 User Profiles Policy Options

User Profiles Policy	Description
Delete cached copies of roaming profiles	Specifies that a local copy of the roaming profile should not be saved to the local computer. Normally, you want to save a local copy of a roaming profile, because loading a copy locally is faster than loading from a network drive. The copy is saved when the user logs off.
Do not detect slow network connections	By default, the system will try to detect slow links and respond to slow links differently than it does to faster links. Setting this policy disables the detection of slow links.
Slow network connection timeout for user profiles	Allows you to specify what a slow network connection is. When enabled, the default speed of a low speed connection is 500Kbps.

TABLE 7.10 User Profiles Policy Options *(continued)*

User Profiles Policy	Description
Wait for remote user profile	Specifies that if a roaming profile is used, the roaming (network) copy of the profile should be used rather than a locally cached copy of the profile. The system will wait for the remote copy.
Prompt user when slow link is detected	Notifies users of a slow link, and prompts users to select whether they will use a locally cached copy of a user profile or the roaming (network) copy.
Timeout for dialog boxes	Allows you to configure the default timeout value that will be used to display dialog boxes. Sets the length of time the system will wait for a user response before it uses default values.
Log users off when roaming profile fails	Specifies that if a roaming profile is not available, the user should be logged off. If you do not enable this option and a roaming profile fails to load, the user will use a locally cached copy or the default user profile.
Maximum retries to unload and update user profile	Determines the number of retries the system will take if it tries to update the portions of the Registry that store user profile information and the update is not successful.

Logon Policies

Logon policies are used to specify how logon events, such as logon scripts are configured. The Logon Option policies are described in Table 7.11.

TABLE 7.11 Logon Policy Options

Logon Policy	Description
Don't display the Getting Started welcome screen at logon	Suppresses the welcome screen.
Always use classic logon	This setting forces the user to log on to the computer using the classic logon screen. By default, a workgroup is set to use the simple logon screen. This setting only works when the computer is not on a domain.
Run these programs at user logon	Specifies additional programs or documents that Windows starts automatically when a user logs on to the system.
Do not process the Run Once list	Ignores customized Run Once lists. This is a customized list of additional programs and documents that are started automatically the next time the system starts (but not thereafter).

TABLE 7.11 Logon Policy Options *(continued)*

Logon Policy	Description
Do not process the Legacy Run list	Ignores the customized Run list. This is a customized list of additional programs and documents that the system starts automatically when it runs on Windows XP, Windows 2000, Windows NT 4 and earlier. These programs are added to the standard Run list of programs and services that the system starts.
Always wait for the network at computer startup and logon	Determines whether Windows XP waits for the network during computer startup and user logon. By default, Windows XP does not wait for the network to be fully initialized at startup and logon. Existing users are logged on using cached credentials, which results in shorter logon times. Group Policy is applied in the background once the network becomes available.

Disk Quota Policies

Disk Quota policies are used to specify how the computer will be used for disk quota configuration. The Disk Quota policies are described in Table 7.12.

TABLE 7.12 Disk Quota Options

Disk Quota Policy	Description
Enable disk quotas	Forces the system to enable disk quota management on all NTFS volumes for the computer.
Enforce disk quota limit	Specifies that if disk quotas are configured, they should be enforced.
Default quota limit and warning level	Allows you to configure the default quota limit for quota management and the threshold for disk use at which users see a warning message.
Log event when quota limit exceeded	Specifies that if users reach their quota limit, an entry will be added to the Event Viewer Application log.
Log event when quota warning level exceeded	Specifies that if users reach their warning limit, an entry will be added to the Event Viewer Application log.
Apply policy to removable media	Extends the Disk Quota policies that are applied to fixed disks to removable media that are formatted as NTFS.

Group Policy Policies

Group Policy policies are used to specify how group policies will be applied to the computer. The Group Policy options that are commonly configured are described in Table 7.13.

TABLE 7.13 Group Policy Options

Group Policy	Description
Turn off background refresh of Group Policy	Prevents Group policies from being updated if the computer is currently in use.
Group Policy refresh intervals for computers	Specifies the interval rate that will be used to update the computer's Group Policy. By default, this background operation occurs every 90 minutes, with a random offset of 0–30 minutes.
Group Policy refresh intervals for domain controllers	Specifies the interval rate that will be used to update the domain controller's Group Policy. By default, this background operation occurs every 5 minutes.
User Group Policy Loopback processing mode	Specifies how Group policies are applied when a user logs on to a computer with this option configured. You can specify that the group policy is replaced or merged with other policy settings.
Group Policy slow link detection	Defines what a slow link is for the purpose of applying and updating Group policies.
Registry policy processing	Specifies how Registry policies are processed, such as whether Registry policies can be applied during periodic background processing.
Internet Explorer Maintenance policy processing	Determines when Internet Explorer Maintenance policies can be applied.
Software Installation policy processing	Determines how often Software Installation policies are updated. This option does not apply to Local policies.
Folder Redirection policy processing	Specifies how Folder Redirection policies are updated.
Scripts policy processing	Specifies how Shared Script policies are updated.
Security policy processing	Specifies how Security policies are updated.
IP Security policy processing	Specifies how IP Security policies are updated.
EFS Recovery policy processing	Specifies how Encryption policies are updated.
Disk Quota policy processing	Specifies how Disk Quota policies are updated.

Windows File Protection Policies

The *Windows File Protection policies* are used to specify how Windows file protection will be configured. The Windows File Protection Option policies are described in Table 7.14.

TABLE 7.14 Windows File Protection Options

Windows File Protection Policy	Description
Set Windows File Protection scanning	Determines the frequency of Windows File Protection scans.
Hide the File Scan Progress window	Suppresses the display of the File Scan Progress window.
Limit Windows file protection cache size	Specifies the maximum amount of disk space that can be used by Windows File Protection.
Specify Windows file protection cache location	Specifies an alternate location to be used by the Windows File Protection cache.

Analyzing Security Configurations with the Security Configuration and Analysis Tool

Windows Server 2003 includes a utility called *Security Configuration and Analysis*, which you can use to analyze and help configure the computer's local security settings. This utility works by comparing your actual security configuration to a security template configured with your desired settings.

The following steps are involved in the security analysis process:

1. Using the Security Configuration and Analysis utility, specify a working security database that will be used during the security analysis.
2. Import a security template that can be used as a basis for how you would like your security to be configured.
3. Perform the security analysis. This will compare your configuration against the template that you specified in Step 2.
4. Review the results of the security analysis.
5. Resolve any discrepancies indicated through the security analysis results.

The Security Configuration and Analysis utility is an MMC snap-in. After you add this utility to the MMC, you can use it to run the security analysis process, as described in the following sections.

Specifying a Security Database

The *security database* is used to store the results of your security analysis. To specify a security database, take the following steps:

1. In the MMC, right-click the Security Configuration and Analysis snap-in and select the Open Database option from the pop-up menu, as shown in Figure 7.10. (You'll add this tool to the Security Policy GPO custom MMC console in Exercise 7.9 later in this chapter).

FIGURE 7.10 Opening a security database

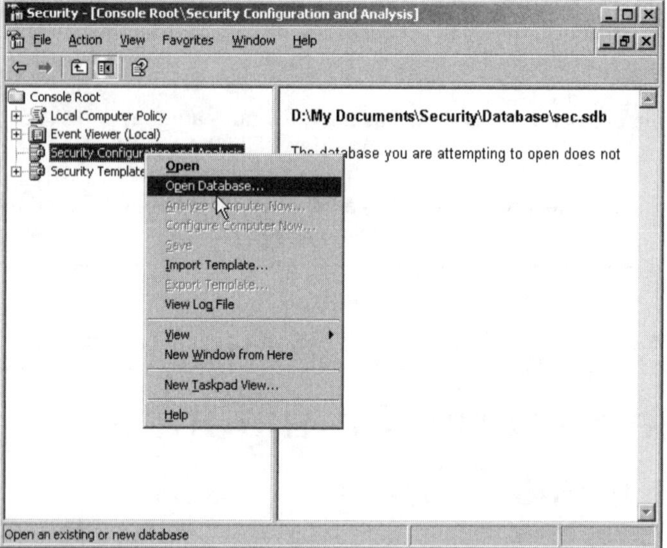

2. The Open Database dialog box appears. In the File Name text box, type the name of the database you will create. By default, this file will have a `.sdb` (for security database) extension. Then click the Open button.
3. The Import Template dialog box appears. Select the template that you want to import. You can select a predefined template through this dialog box. In the next section, you will learn how to create and use a customized template file. Make your selection and click the Open button.

Importing a Security Template

The next step in the security analysis process is to import a security template. The *security template* is used as a comparative tool. The Security and Configuration Analysis utility compares the security settings in the security template to your computer's current security settings. You do not set security through the security template. Rather, the security template is where you organize all of your security attributes in a single location.

As an administrator, you can define a base security template on a single computer and then export the security template to all the servers in your network.

Creating a Security Template

By default, Windows Server 2003 ships with a variety of predefined security templates, which are stored in *windir*\Security\Templates. Each of the templates defines a standard set of security values based on the requirements of your environment. The template groups that are included by default are defined in Table 7.15.

TABLE 7.15 Default Security Templates

Standard Security Template	Description	Default Templates
Default security (Setup security.inf)	Created during installation for each computer. Used to set security back to the default values as configured during installation, with the exception of user rights. User rights are modified by some applications so that the application will run properly. If user rights were also set back to default values, some of the applications that were installed on the computer might not function.	Setup security
Compatible (Compatws.inf)	Used for backward-compatibility. This option relaxes the default security used by Windows 2000 and higher so that applications that ran under Windows NT and are not certified for Windows 2000 and higher will still run. This template is typically used on computers that have been upgraded and are having problems running applications.	Compatws
Secure (Secure*.inf)	Implements recommended security settings for Windows 2000 and higher in all security areas except for files, folders, and Registry keys.	Securedc, Securews
Highly secure (Hisec*.inf)	Defines highly secure network communications for Windows Server 2003 computers. If you apply this security template, Windows Server 2003 computers can communicate only with other Windows Server 2003 computers. In this case, the computers would not communicate with clients such as Windows 95/98 or Windows NT 4 computers.	Hisecdc, Hisecws

TABLE 7.15 Default Security Templates *(continued)*

Standard Security Template	Description	Default Templates
Dedicated domain controller (`DC Security.inf`)	Provides a higher level of security for dedicated domain controllers. This option assumes that the domain controller will not run server-based applications, which would require a more lax security posture on the server.	`DC security`
System root security (`rootsec.inf`)	Defines the root permissions. By default, these permissions are defined for the root of the system drive. Can be used to reapply root directory permissions if they are inadvertently changed, or the template can be modified to apply the same root permissions to other volumes. This template propagates only the permissions that are inherited by child objects and does not overwrite permissions explicitly defined on child objects.	`Rootsec`

You create security templates through the Security Templates snap-in in the MMC. You can configure security templates with the items listed in Table 7.16.

TABLE 7.16 Security Template Configuration Options

Security Template Item	Description
Account policies	Specifies configurations that should be used for Password policies, Account Lockout policies, and Kerberos policies
Local policies	Specifies configurations that should be used for Audit policies, User Rights Assignments, and security options
Event log	Allows you to set configuration settings that apply to Event Viewer log files
Restricted groups	Allows you to administer local group memberships
Registry	Specifies security for local Registry keys
File system	Specifies security for the local file system
System services	Sets security for system services and the startup mode that local system services will use

After you add the Security Templates snap-in to the MMC, you can open a sample security template and modify it, as follows:

1. In the MMC, expand the Security Templates snap-in and then expand the folder for `\systemroot\Security\Templates`.
2. Double-click the sample template that you want to edit. There are several sample templates, including `securews` (for secure Windows servers) and `securedc` (for secure domain controller).
3. Make any changes you want to the sample security template. Changes to the template are not applied to the local system by default. They are simply a specification for how you would like the system to be configured.
4. Once you have made all of the changes to the sample template, save the template by highlighting the sample template file, right-clicking, and selecting the Save As option from the pop-up menu. Specify a location and a filename for the new template. By default, the security template will be saved with an `.inf` extension in the `\systemroot\Security\Templates` folder.

Opening a Security Template

Once you have configured a security template, you can import it for use with the Security Configuration and Analysis utility, assuming that a security database has already been configured, or you can open it as a database. To import a security template, in the MMC, right-click the Security Configuration and Analysis utility and select the Import Template option from the pop-up menu. Then highlight the template file you want to import and click the Open button.

Performing a Security Analysis

The next step is to perform a security analysis. To run the analysis, simply right-click the Security Configuration and Analysis utility and select the Analyze Computer Now option from the pop-up menu. You will see a Perform Analysis dialog box that allows you to specify the location and filename for the error log file path that will be created during the analysis. After this information is configured, click the OK button.

When the analysis is complete, you will be returned to the main MMC window. From there, you can review the results of the security analysis.

Reviewing the Security Analysis and Resolving Discrepancies

The results of the security analysis are stored in the Security Configuration and Analysis snap-in, under the configured security item (see Table 7.16). For example, to see the results for Password policies, double-click the Security Configuration and Analysis snap-in, double-click Account Policies, and then click Password Policy. Figure 7.11 shows an example of security analysis results for Password policies.

FIGURE 7.11 Viewing the results of a security analysis

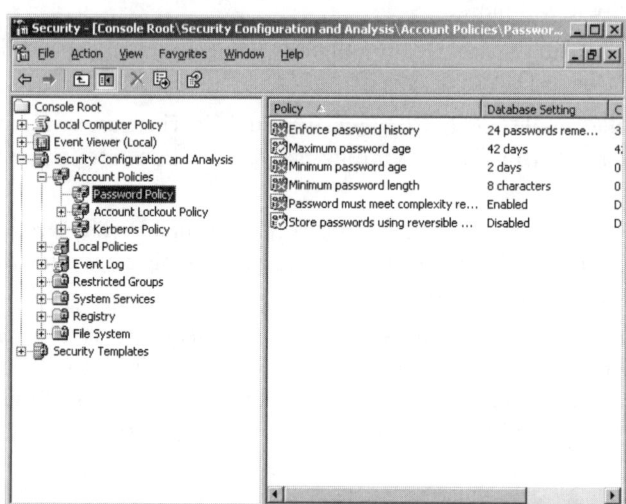

The policies that have been analyzed will have an X or a checkmark next to them, as shown in Figure 7.11. An X indicates that the template specification and the actual policy do not match. A checkmark indicates that the template specification and the policy do match. If any security discrepancies are indicated, you should resolve the security violation. One way to reconcile the differences is to use the Group Policy snap-in. As an alternative to using the Group Policy snap-in to resolve the discrepancies, you can modify the settings in the template, store them and launch them through Security Configuration and Analysis.

In Exercise 7.9, you will use the Security Configuration and Analysis utility to analyze your security configuration. In this exercise, you will add the Security and Configuration Analysis snap-in to the MMC, specify a security database, create a security template, import the template, perform an analysis, and review the results. This exercise assumes that you have completed all of the previous exercises in this chapter.

EXERCISE 7.9

Using the Security Configuration and Analysis Tool

Adding the MMC Snap-ins

1. Select Start ➢ Administrative Tools ➢ Security Policy GPO.
2. Select File ➢ Add/Remove Snap-in.
3. In the Add/Remove Snap-In dialog box, click the Add button. Highlight the Security Configuration and Analysis snap-in, and click the Add button. Highlight the Security Templates snap-in and choose Add. Then choose Close.
4. In the Add/Remove Snap-In dialog box, choose OK to return to the main console window.

EXERCISE 7.9 *(continued)*

Creating the Security Template

5. Expand the Security Templates snap-in, and then expand the *systemroot*`\Security\Templates` folder.

6. Double-click the securews file to view the configurable options.

7. Expand Account Policies, and then highlight Password Policy.

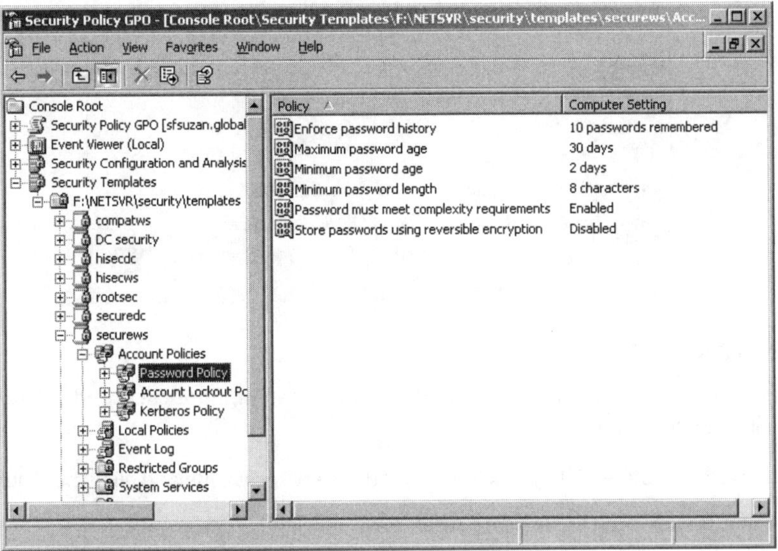

8. Edit the Password policies as follows:
   - Set the Enforce Password History option to **10** passwords remembered.
   - Enable the Passwords Must Meet Complexity Requirements option.
   - Set the Maximum Password Age option to **30** days.

9. Highlight the securews file, right-click, and select the Save As option.

10. In the Save As dialog box, place the file in the default folder and name the file **`servertest`**. Click the Save button.

Specifying the Security Database

11. In the MMC, right-click Security Configuration and Analysis and select Open Database.

12. In the Open Database dialog box, type **`sampledb`** in the File Name text box. Then click the Open button.

EXERCISE 7.9 *(continued)*

13. In the Import Template dialog box, select the template `servertest.inf` and click the Open button.

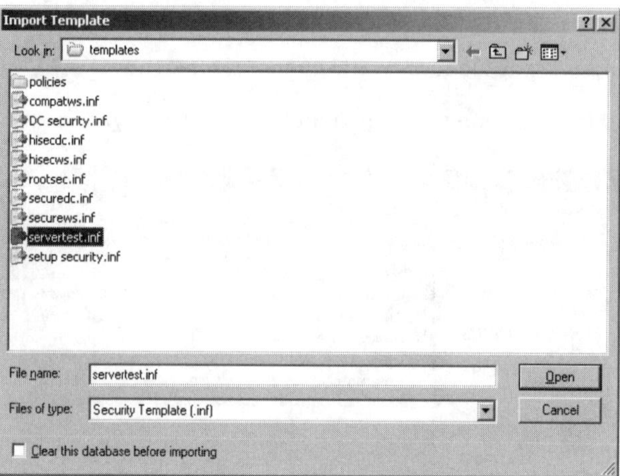

Importing the Security Template

14. Highlight the Security Configuration and Analysis snap-in, right-click, and select the Import Template option.

15. In the Import Template dialog box, highlight the `servertest` file and click the Open button.

Performing and Reviewing the Security Analysis

16. Highlight the Security Configuration and Analysis snap-in, right-click, and select the Analyze Computer Now option.

17. In the Perform Analysis dialog box, accept the default error log file path and click the OK button.

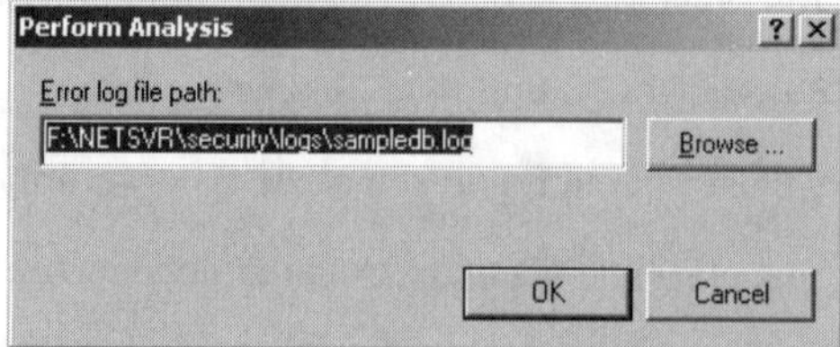

18. When you return to the main MMC window, double-click the Security Configuration and Analysis snap-in.

19. Double-click Account Policies, and then double-click Password Policy. You will see the results of the analysis for each policy, indicated by an X or a checkmark next to the policy.

Real World Scenario

Creating Customized Security Templates for Multipurpose Servers

You are the network administrator in a small company with a mixture of Windows NT 4 and Windows Server 2003 servers. You have already decided to upgrade all servers to Windows Server 2003. Eventually, all clients will be XP. Several NT 4–based applications are used for accounting, inventory, and payroll. As the budget permits, all applications will be upgraded to the latest version to run under Windows Server 2003. However, only one of the application vendors has released a new version for Windows Server 2003, so it is necessary to maintain backward compatibility with NT4.

You have tested all of the applications, and you know that they will run on Windows Server 2003. However, you know that running older applications has security implications, and you want to ensure that you maintain the highest possible security while still allowing older applications to run.

You can use security templates to configure sets of customized security options that will allow the applications to run under the most secure possible conditions. The Security Analysis and Configuration tool will help you compare the templates and create a unique Security policy based on the server and application requirements.

The `compatws.inf` template will relax the default permissions so that NT 4-based applications can run.

The Setup `security.inf` template will enable you to compare any changes made by installing applications after Windows Server 2003 is initially installed.

As servers and applications are upgraded, you can apply the `secure.inf` template to implement the recommended security settings for Windows Server 2003 servers. Because it does not change file system or Registry security, you can use the `rootsec.inf` template to enable you to reapply root directory permissions that may have been changed by older applications.

Finally, once the environment has been upgraded to exclusively Windows Server 2003-based applications and servers and XP clients, you can deploy the `hisecure.inf` template to eliminate any security holes that resulted from introducing legacy compatibility and establish the most secure network possible.

Deploying Security Policies

Deploying Security policies is easy with Active Directory. You simply configure a GPO with the desired settings and link it to the target object (OU, site, or domain).

For example, to create a Security policy that will apply to the entire domain, follow these steps:

1. Configure and apply the Default Domain Security Policy GPO.

2. Modify this GPO within Active Directory by right-clicking the domain within Active Directory Users and Computers and choosing Properties from the context menu.
3. In the Properties dialog box for the domain, click the Group Policy tab and highlight the Default Domain Policy GPO. The Group Policy Object Editor launches. Notice that it looks just like the MMC console, because it is essentially the same thing. Configure the changes that you want to make.

Another way you can modify the Default Domain Security Policy GPO is by using the Domain Security Policy MMC console, located in the Administrative Tools program group. The Domain Security Policy MMC is simply an interface to the Default Domain Security Policy GPO, so changes made to the console are made directly to the GPO. If you open both the Domain Security Policy MMC console and the Default Domain Policy GPO at the same time, you can see that changes made to one will automatically appear in the other. In the same fashion, changes to the Domain Controller Security Policy MMC console are made directly to the Default Domain Controller Security Policy GPO linked to the Domain Controllers OU in Active Directory Users and Computers.

Best practices indicate that you should create OUs to group computers that will share the same configuration settings, and then configure the settings in a GPO linked to the OU. This provides for ease of administration. You could also create a security group with those computers as members, and then give that group permission to apply a GPO that is linked to a domain, site, or OU in which the security group is contained. Note that a GPO must be read in its entirety for all of the computers and users to which it applies. This can significantly increase the amount of time it takes to log on to the domain.

Do not use the Default Domain Policy object to test settings. Because it applies to domain controllers, the Domain Admins group, and all other objects in the domain, inappropriately configuring the Default Domain Policy object can propagate changes that force the need for an authoritative restore of Active Directory.

To apply settings from the Security Settings node of a preconfigured security template to a group of computers, follow these steps:

1. Add the computers to an OU.
2. Create a GPO to apply to the OU.
3. Highlight the Security Settings node.
4. Right-click the node, and choose Import Policy from the context menu.
5. Finally, specify the template that you want to use to apply to the computers.

As an alternative method of applying a preconfigured security template to a group of computers, you could apply a GPO that specifies a login script with the following command:

```
secedit /configure /db security_database_name.sdb /cfg security_template_name.inf↵
/overwrite /log log_file_name.log
```

where `security_database_name` names the database to load and `security_template_name` names the security template to use. The `/overwrite` command option indicates that the database should be emptied prior to importing the security template. If this parameter is not specified, the settings in the security template are accumulated into the database. If this parameter is not specified and there are conflicting settings in the database and the template being imported, the template settings win. The `/log` command option specifies that configuration processing information should be stored in a log file other than the default `windir\security\logs\scesrv.log` file.

To quickly copy settings from individual nodes within a Security policy to a new policy object, you can highlight a node, such as Password Policy, and choose Export List from the context menu. This saves the configuration settings in ASCII format to a text file located by default in the `windir\security\templates` directory.

On Windows networks, computers log in the same way that users log in. Computers log in automatically during the network initialization phase at boot, whereas users log in manually at the prompt. GPOs that apply to a computer, therefore, can be used to apply to all users on a computer. *Machine accounts* are special accounts that computers use to transparently log in to a domain during network initialization and before user login. They do not have to be on the same domain as the user accounts for users logging in to a particular machine.

The Resultant Set of Policy (RSoP) tool will be of invaluable aid when determining the effective policy settings for specific computers and users on those computers. RSoP was covered in Chapter 6.

See Chapter 6 for more details on how to deploy and troubleshoot Group Policy.

So far in this chapter, you've learned how to plan and deploy Windows Server 2003 server installations based on server roles and how to implement standardized security configurations for different server roles and business requirements using Security Policy and security templates. The next step in planning server security configurations is to design a strategy for managing critical updates, which we turn to in the next section.

Planning a Security Update Infrastructure

Operating systems, just like hardware drivers and user applications, are constantly being improved. Patches and updates are frequently published on the Internet, where home and corporate users can download them. Staying current with the latest up-to-date fixes from the vendor is important in order to ensure the best performance and administrative efficiency.

Unix and other OS vendors often use the terms "patch" or "fix" to describe singular or bundled improvements to an operating system version. Microsoft prefers the euphemistic terms "update" or "service pack." These terms are used interchangeably and essentially mean the same thing.

Good practice includes using current patches, services packs, and critical security fixes for configuration management. Standardizing security configurations is also considered to be good practice.

One of the biggest advantages to maintaining the current versions of all OS patches is that it makes troubleshooting easier. In fact, keeping current with Windows updates frequently eliminates problems before they arise. Every veteran administrator carries battle scars from various esoteric problems that he spent hours troubleshooting, only to find that the issue was fixed in an existing patch.

In addition, security plays an increasingly important role in today's networks. Because security holes are constantly being discovered and exploited, staying current with the latest critical security patches is essential. The wise network administrator will also have a plan for maintaining standardized security configurations across all clients and servers in the network.

Earlier in this chapter, you learned how to use security templates to deploy standardized security configurations to servers and clients across the network. Windows Server 2003 has two more tools to assist you in planning for and maintaining the most current operating system updates and security configurations: Microsoft Software Update Services (SUS) and Microsoft Baseline Security Analyzer (MBSA).

Using Microsoft Software Update Services

Microsoft *Software Update Services (SUS)*, is a simplified solution targeted for medium-sized enterprises as a means to manage and distribute critical Windows patches. You can think of SUS as an intranet-hosted version of the Windows Update service.

Advantages of SUS include more efficient administration of critical updates. In the past, it was necessary for an administrator to check the Windows Update Web site or the Microsoft Security Web site to see what was new. Then she had to manually download and deploy the patches to each affected node. For those users with Windows Update rights, additional administrative effort was required to stop the downloading of patches and updates that were not tested or approved by the system administrators. SUS solves these problems by dynamically downloading and automatically distributing critical Windows updates. SUS is particularly powerful in combination with Active Directory, though AD is not a requirement.

SUS or SMS?

SUS was created to get critical Windows 2003, 2000, and XP updates to distributed nodes in your network as quickly as possible. You may already have a solution for enterprise software distribution in place in your organization. For example, you may be using Microsoft Systems Management Server (SMS) to manage configurations and deploy new software. If this is the case, you should continue using that solution—you don't need SUS.

SUS features server-side and client-side components. An intranet-hosted Windows Update server hosts the updates and services client HTTP requests for those updates. The administrative interface is web-based and, therefore, allows for internal remote administration via HTTP or HTTPS using Internet Explorer 5.5 or higher.

SUS Server-Side Components

The synchronization service enables an administrator to define a schedule for retrieving updates from the public Windows Update service. You can also synchronize the hosting server manually (through the Synchronize Now button). An administrator can also control deployment—he can test and approve updates before deploying them on the corporate intranet.

For multiserver deployments, you can employ server-to-server synchronization, so that one authoritative server downloads the updates, and other servers point to it instead of Windows Update for the latest patches. This enables you to bring the updates closer to your desktops and servers. You can also download to a central site for testing, and then point clients to the Microsoft download sites for approved updates. This is an ideal strategy for large networks spread over geographically disparate sites.

SUS Client-Side Components

The client-side components are based on the Windows Automatic Updates technology, which was significantly enhanced in XP. Automatic Updates is the proactive pull service that enables users with administrative rights to automatically download and install Windows updates such as critical Windows security patches and operating-system fixes.

Client-side features include customized installation of only those updates that are applicable to the computer. Bandwidth-throttling keeps updates from interfering with other network tasks by using only idle bandwidth. Chained installation enables multiple updates to be installed in a bundle so that a single restart will suffice (if a restart is necessary). Administrative security can be handled through Group Policy.

The basic procedures for setting up Software Update Services are listed here:

1. Download the Software Update Services program from Microsoft's Web site.
2. Install and configure SUS on the server.
3. Point Windows Update on the client machines to the SUS server.
4. On the server, run Windows Update.
5. Approve the updates.

For more detailed information on implementing SUS, refer to *MCSA/MCSE: Windows Server 2003 Environment Management and Maintenance Study Guide*.

Real World Scenario

Implementing Microsoft Software Update Services

You are the IT administrator for a regional division of a large corporation headquartered in Madison, Wisconsin. The regional division is located in New York City. The task of keeping all Microsoft operating systems up-to-date with the latest critical security patches and operating system fixes has been delegated to you. You are to handle the updates independently from the main corporation at a regional level. You want to design a strategy for implementing Microsoft Software Update Services in the regional division to meet specific objectives. These objectives include:

- Testing all critical updates before deploying them to client computers on the network
- Ensuring that all users are up-to-date with the latest fixes and security patches from Microsoft as soon as they are available

You decide to use the following approach to meet these objectives.

On the server-side, you design a strategy to enable you to review, test, and approve updates before they are deployed to client computers across the network. You set up two servers running Software Update Services. The first is used as a test server and the second is used a production server. You configure an Automatic Updates policy so that a small number of computers specifically designated to test updates point to the test server to download updates. You set up another Automatic Update policy to point the rest of the network computers to the production server to download updates. The production server points to the test server to download updates.

Using the synchronization feature of Software Update Services, you schedule an interval to download updates from the Windows Update Web Web site. Then you use the test server to approve updates for testing on the target computers. Upon successful completion of the tests, you approve the updates for the production server.

To ensure that all fixes are downloaded and updated as soon as they are available from Microsoft, you set up a synchronization schedule to check the Windows Update server for new updates every day at 5:30 P.M. EST. At 5:45 P.M., you deploy the updates from the test server onto the test computers. After confirming that the updates were successfully deployed, you approve the updates on the test server so that they can be downloaded to the production server.

The production server is scheduled to query for updates from the test server daily at 7:00 P.M. EST. After the updates are downloaded, they are available to be deployed to servers and clients throughout the network. All production computers are set up to automatically synchronize with the production SUS server daily at 9:00 A.M. EST.

The following morning, clients will query the SUS server after booting up to find out if there are any new updates. If a client does not boot up or connect to the network that day prior to 9:00 A.M. EST., synchronization will occur at the next scheduled interval.

For added fault tolerance and load balancing, you could implement multiple production SUS servers and/or randomize the synchronization schedule.

Software Update Services will help you manage general operating system patches. You also need a tool for managing security updates and configurations, which we consider next.

Using Microsoft Baseline Security Analyzer

The *Microsoft Baseline Security Analyzer (MBSA)* is a tool that can be used to perform local or remote scans of servers and workstations. It's commonly used to check for security updates, verify service pack status, and identify common security misconfigurations.

SMS 2.0 has a Software Update Services Feature Pack that provides enterprise customers with a security patch management solution using MBSA technology.

How MBSA Works

MBSA and Windows Update analyze systems in different ways. For instance, Windows Update manages critical updates for the Windows operating system only, whereas MBSA (through HFNetChk) will report missing security updates and security misconfigurations for the Windows operating system and other Microsoft products such as IIS, Exchange, and SQL Server.

Previously, the Microsoft Personal Security Advisor (MPSA) was used to scan for misconfigured system settings, and HFNetChk was used to scan for missing security updates and service pack status. With the release of MBSA v1.1, all of this functionality and more is integrated into one tool.

In addition to handling security updates and service packs, MBSA examines Windows computers for common security best practices such as the use of strong passwords, guest account status, the type of file system to use (NTFS is preferred), available file shares, and members of the Administrators group. It checks for misconfigured security zone settings in Internet Explorer, Outlook, and Microsoft Office. It also scans IIS and SQL servers for common security misconfigurations.

The MBSA tool includes graphical (`mbsa.exe`) and command line (`mbsacli.exe`) interfaces that run on Windows Server 2003, 2000, and XP systems. Also required are IE 5.01 or later and the Workstation and Server services. The MBSA is available for download from Microsoft's download site (`http://download.microsoft.com`). Updates are associated with Microsoft security bulletins, which are numbered in the format "MS02-008."

MBSA uses the HFNetChk tool technology to scan for missing security updates and service packs for the following products: Windows NT 4, 2000, 2003, and XP; IIS 4 and 5; SQL Server 7 and 2000; IE 5.01 and later; Exchange 5.5 and 2000; and Windows Media Player 6.4 and later.

MBSA runs its checks against the file `mssecure.xml`, which is downloaded from Microsoft upon MBSA's initial run and is continuously updated afterward. This file contains product-specific information about which security updates are available. The information includes references to relevant security bulletins, the files in each update package and their versions and checksums, Registry changes, information about which updates supersede others, and related Microsoft Knowledge Base article numbers.

As an alternative, you can use MBSA to perform the security updates portion of a scan against a local SUS server. This portion of the scan will then be performed against the list of approved security updates on the local SUS server, rather than against the complete list of available security updates listed in the `mssecure.xml` file downloaded by the tool at runtime. This includes updates that have been superseded. You would choose to run the scan in this way because it enables you to test updates and deploy only approved updates from a centralized distribution point.

MBSA will also scan for system misconfigurations in the following products: Windows NT 4, Windows 2000, Windows Server 2003, Windows XP, Internet Information Server (IIS) 4, 5, and 6, SQL Server 7 and 2000, Internet Explorer (IE) 5.01 and later, and Office 2000 and 2002.

If you intend to perform remote scans of IIS servers, you must install the IIS Common Files on the computer from which you will run the MBSA tool.

Target systems must have the Server service, Remote Registry, and File & Print Sharing enabled.

The MBSA tool will create and store individual XML security reports for each computer scanned and will display the reports in HTML format when using the GUI. By default, security reports are stored as XML files in the *`userprofile`*`\SecurityScans` directory.

The `mbsacli` command (located in `\Program Files\ Microsoft Baseline Security Analyzer`) is run in the following format:

```
mbsacli.exe [/hf] [-baseline] [-v] [-nosum]
```

Table 7.17 shows the common command-line switches used with MBSA.

TABLE 7.17 Common Command-Line Switches Used with MBSA

Option	Description
`/hf`	Indicates an HFNetChk-style scan
`-baseline`	Scan for updates that are marked as critical security updates on Windows Update
`-v`	Provides additional details on file versions found for each missing security update
`-nosum`	Does not perform checksum checks

The MBSA GUI version (`mbsa.exe`) automatically uses the following switches: `-baseline`, `-v`, and `-nosum`.

The command-line interface `mbsacli.exe` has a new flag (`/hf`) to indicate an HFNetChk-style scan. This means that if you already have scripts that call `hfnetchk.exe`, you can just replace it with a call to `mbsacli.exe /hf` followed by any valid HFNetChk v3.81 flag(s).

Troubleshooting MBSA Scans

When planning the combination of tools to use for your security update infrastructure, you need to understand some behavioral quirks of the various tools.

MBSA makes sure that the latest version of the update is always installed on the target system. A target computer may have the original version of a security update that has been re-released, such as the MS02-008 or MS02-009 update, in which case MBSA will tell you that the update isn't installed, because a newer release of that particular update is available.

However, Windows Update, SUS, and SMS use different rules to identify elements on the system that indicate whether or not an update is present. Therefore, inconsistencies can occur if you are managing updates using multiple tools. You may not be informed that a newer version is available, or different tools may return different results.

Eventually MBSA, Windows Update, Microsoft Software Update Services, and SMS security patch management will all use the same rules for determining the presence of an update on Windows systems. For now, if MBSA reports an update as missing, view the security bulletin for those updates to ensure that you actually have installed the most recent version.

You may also receive incorrect security update reports from MBSA or HFNetChk even after you install updates flagged in the scan results. This can happen when the update includes a warning or workaround rather than a patch. For instance, some updates, such as MS99-041, provide a tool to modify a specific service. In these cases, the tool itself cannot finish applying the update—additional action is required.

These types of security bulletins are referred to as "note" or "warning" messages, and they are marked with yellow Xs in the scan reports to indicate that the tool could not confirm if the security bulletin fix was applied. They will continue to be included in the scan results unless you override the default display options, because the tool cannot directly confirm that they were applied.

Finally, updates can be flagged as having greater file versions than expected. This happens when files are updated by non-security related updates after a previous security-related update was applied to the system. MBSA scans for security updates only, using file versions and checksums from the `mssecure.xml` file. Therefore, it cannot determine if files have been patched by other non-security updates.

Understanding the seemingly incomprehensible behavior of the update tools will help you determine how best to plan for automated security updates in your network.

For more information on using MBSA, refer to *MCSA/MCSE: Windows Server 2003 Environment Management and Maintenance Study Guide*.

Summary

In this chapter, you learned:

- How to plan server installations based on functional server roles. Server roles include providing specialized file, print, DNS, DHCP, WINS, Web, and domain controller services.

- How to determine which OS edition to install based on functional requirements. Windows Server 2003 is available in Standard, Enterprise, Datacenter, and Web editions.
- How to use Security policies to create standardized security configurations, which can be applied at the local or domain level using Group Policy Objects (GPOs). To manage Local Security policies, use the Local Computer GPO. To manage Domain Security policies, use the Default Domain Controllers Policy and Default Domain Policy GPOs.
- How to configure options within Security Policy. Security options that are found under the Security Settings node include Account policies and Local policies. Other security options are found under the System node.
- How to analyze your security configuration and create custom security templates using The Security Configuration and Analysis utility. You run this utility to compare your existing security settings to a security template configured with settings you are examining.
- How to deploy security configurations to computers using Group Policy Objects (GPOs).
- How to plan a security update infrastructure. Microsoft Software Update Services and the Microsoft Baseline Security Analyzer tool are used to manage critical OS and security updates.

Exam Essentials

Know how to plan server installations based on functional server roles. Server roles include providing specialized file, print, DNS, DHCP, WINS, Web, and domain controller services. The Configure Your Server Wizard provides an easy interface for adding server roles, and the Manage Your Server tool provides a portal to management consoles and utilities and help information organized by server role.

Know how to determine the OS edition to install based on functional requirements. Considerations include what server roles will be required from a target computer. Windows Server 2003 is available in Standard, Enterprise, Datacenter, and Web editions. The 64-bit versions are available exclusively for Intel Itanium-based platforms.

Know how to use security policies to create and deploy standardized security configurations. Security policies are a subset of Group Policy and can be deployed by creating GPOs and attaching them to objects in Active Directory. You can manage Security Policy GPO's by creating custom MMC consoles.

Know how to configure security settings options. Security settings options include Account policies and Local policies. Account policies control the logon process. The three types of Account policies are Password, Account Lockout, and Kerberos policies. Local policies control what a user can do at the local computer. The three types of Local policies are Audit, User Rights Assignment, and Security Options policies.

Know how to configure system options. System options include policies that control the behavior of User Profiles, Logon, Disk Quotas, Group Policy, and Windows File Protection.

Know how to use the Security and Analysis Configuration snap-in. The Security and Analysis Configuration snap-in is used to analyze your security configuration and create custom security databases. You can compare existing security configurations to default or custom databases that represent varying levels of security for different types of servers, such as general Windows servers and domain controller servers.

Know how to plan a security update infrastructure. Understand the tools that are available to manage critical OS and security updates. These tools include Microsoft SMS, Microsoft Software Update Services, and the Microsoft Baseline Security Analyzer tool.

Key Terms

Before you take the exam, be certain you are familiar with the following terms:

Account Lockout policies

Account policies

Audit policies

Disk Quota policies

Domain Security policies

Group Policy Object (GPO)

Group Policy policies

inheritance

Local Computer Policy

Local policies

Local Security policies

Logon policies

Machine accounts

Microsoft Baseline Security Analyzer (MBSA)

organizational units (OUs)

Password policies

Security Configuration and Analysis

security database

Security options

Security Policy

security template

server role

Software Update Services (SUS)

System Policy

User Profile policies

User Rights Assignment

Windows File Protection policies

Review Questions

1. You recently made changes to the GPOs on your Windows Server 2003 domain controller. You notice that the changes are not being applied automatically when new users log on. Using the following exhibit, which option can you set so that new changes to the GPO are applied within 10 minutes for any computers that are logged onto the network?

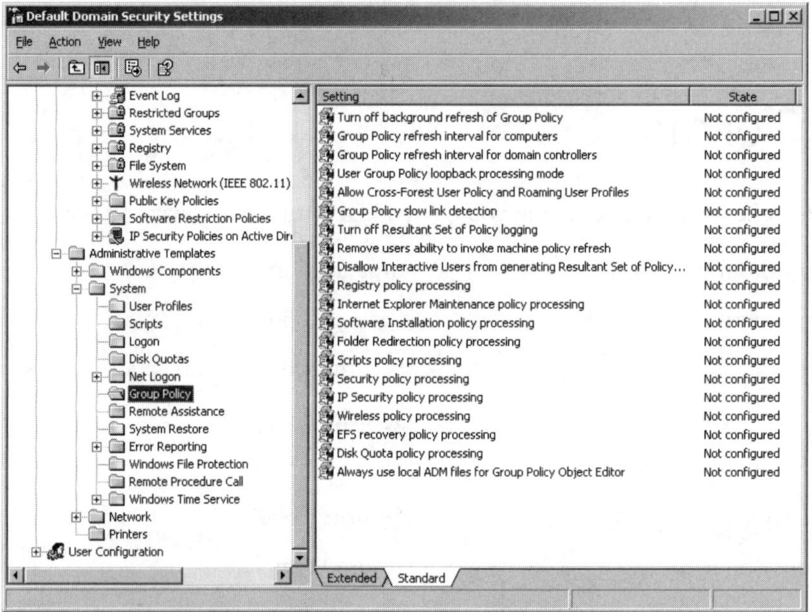

A. Enable and configure the option for Group Policy, Apply Group Policy for computers asynchronously during startup.

B. Enable and configure the option for Group Policy, Apply Group Policy for users asynchronously during startup.

C. Enable and configure the option for Group Policy, Group Policy Refresh Interval for computers to 10 minutes.

D. Enable and configure the option for Group Policy, Group Policy Refresh Interval for domain controllers to 10 minutes.

2. You are a member of the Enterprise Administrators of the TESTCORP.COM domain. You have configured Local Security Options for the Default Domain Policy object. You have delegated administrative control to the DENVER.TESTCORP.COM domain and the BELFAST.TESTCORP.COM domain to the respective local administrators. You want to make sure that the local administrators do not define any Group Policies that might conflict with the settings you have specified. What should you configure?

   A. Configure the No Override option on the TESTCORP.COM domain GPO.

   B. Configure the Block Inheritance option on the TESTCORP.COM domain GPO.

   C. Configure the Always Apply Root Level GPO option on the TESTCORP.COM domain GPO.

   D. Nothing. Your options will override any local options by default.

3. You suspect that someone is attempting to log on to your domain using the Administrator account. You want to track all user attempts (successful and unsuccessful) to log onto the domain. Based on the following exhibit, which auditing event should you enable?

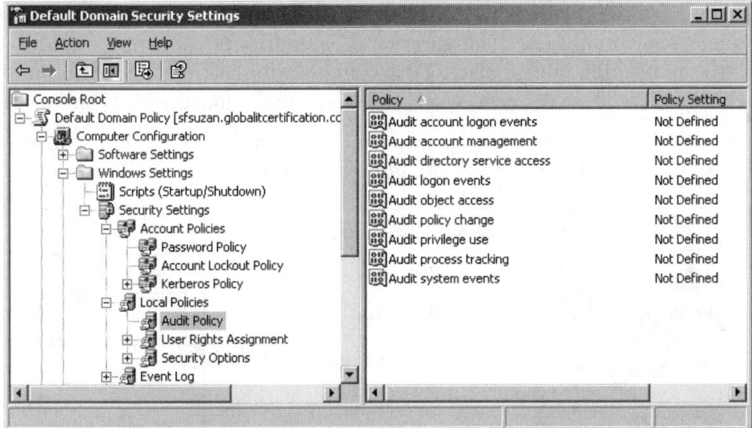

   A. Audit Account Logon Events

   B. Audit Account Management

   C. Audit Logon Events

   D. Audit Process Tracking

4. You are the administrator of a Windows Server 2003 network that uses Active Directory. Your network includes Windows Server 2003 domain controllers, Windows Server 2003 member servers, and XP Professional computers. You are concerned that the security on your network is susceptible to network attacks. You want to use the Security Configuration and Analysis Tool snap-in to tighten the network's security. Which of the following options can be applied using this tool? Choose all that apply.

   A. Track changes to security options

   B. Create and apply Group policies

   C. Set a working database of security options

   D. Import an existing security template

5. You are the system administrator of your network. You use two user accounts, one with administrative rights and one regular user account. When you attempt to log on to the domain controller with your regular user account, you receive an error message that you are not allowed to log on interactively. Which user right must you configure in order to enable you to log on interactively at the domain controller under the regular user account?

A. Log on Locally

B. Log on Interactively

C. Log on Natively

D. Log on as a Local User

6. You are the network administrator for your company. The network is running Active Directory in native mode. All servers are Windows Server 2003 and all clients are Windows XP.

There are four dedicated domain controllers. There are seven servers in the Marketing OU and four servers in the HR OU, all of which require strong security.

You are responsible for planning a strategy to secure the servers and clients on the network using Group Policy. You want to use the highest level of security possible that will still enable the necessary communication to take place. To accomplish this task with the least amount of administrative effort, you will use the default security templates included with Windows Server 2003.

Choose the correct items from the list and place them in the correct locations within Active Directory. An item may be used more than once, and not all items will be used.

Items	Location	
Setup security.inf rootsec.inf securedc.inf securews.inf hisecdc.inf hisecws.inf compatws.inf basicdc.inf basicws.inf DC security.inf ocfiless.inf ocfilesw.inf	Domain	
	Built-in	
	Computers	
	Domain Controllers	
	Foreign Security Principals	
	HR OU	
	Marketing OU	
	Users	

7. You are the network administrator for your company. The network is running Active Directory in native mode. All servers are Windows Server 2003 and all clients are Windows XP.

A branch office has two domain controllers and six departmental servers configured as shown. This location shares files hosted on the departmental servers with a business partner on a heterogeneous Windows and Unix network. The business partner gains access to the network through the VPN server.

You are responsible for planning a strategy to secure the servers and clients at this site. You want to use the highest level of security possible that will still enable the necessary communication to take place. To accomplish this task with the least amount of administrative effort, you will use the default security templates included with Windows Server 2003.

Choose the correct items from the list and apply them to the correct servers. An item may be used more than once, and not all items will be used.

Server name	Configuration
DC1	Domain Controller, Exchange Server 2003
DC2	Domain Controller, SQL Server 2000
SRV1	File and application server
SRV2	File and application server
SRV3	File and application server
SRV4	File and application server
SRV5	File and application server
SRV6	VPN server

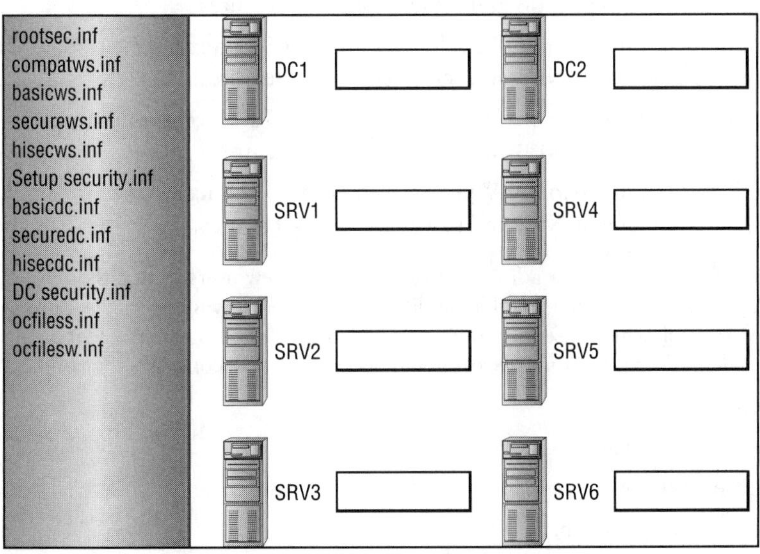

8. Your network requires an extraordinary level of security. You want to configure the Windows Server 2003 domain controllers so that only Windows 2000 clients can communicate with them. Based on your requirements, which of the following security templates should you apply to your servers?

   A. `securedc.inf`

   B. `hisecdc.inf`

   C. `dedicadc.inf`

   D. `w2kdc.inf`

9. You are the administrator of the TESTCORP.COM domain. You have configured a GPO for your domain so that users need to change their passwords every 45 days. You want to ensure that users do not immediately reuse their old password. Which Password policy must you configure in order to specify that users cannot reuse passwords until they have cycled through a specified number of unique passwords?

   A. Enforce Password History

   B. Use Unique Passwords

   C. Require C2/E2 Encryption Standards

   D. All Passwords Must Use High Level Standards

10. You are the system administrator of a large corporation that is planning to implement a mission-critical enterprise application that is based on a SQL database engine. You need to deploy the most scalable, robust solution you can implement, using the newest high-availability features, including hot-swappable memory. Cost is no object to ensure that the application will always be fast and available. Which of the following options will enable you to meet your objective?

   A. Install the 64-bit version of Windows Server 2003 Enterprise Edition, and cluster the servers to implement NLB and server clustering features.

   B. Install the 32-bit version of Windows Server 2003 Enterprise Edition, and cluster the servers to implement NLB and server clustering features.

   C. Install the 64-bit version of Windows Server 2003 Datacenter Edition, and cluster the servers to implement NLB and server clustering features.

   D. Install the 32-bit version of Windows Server 2003 Datacenter Edition, and cluster the servers to implement NLB and server clustering features.

11. You suspect that one of your administrators is creating new users so that those users can look at the Payroll folder, which has folder auditing enabled. You want to enable a policy that will allow you to track when a user or group is created, deleted, or has management actions generated. Which of the following Audit policies should you enable to accomplish your objective?

   A. Audit Object Access

   B. Audit Logon Events

   C. Audit Account Management

   D. Audit Process Tracking

12. One of your junior administrators needs to monitor the system processes of three servers through the Performance Logs and Alerts utility. What user right should be assigned to the junior administrator so that he can accomplish this task?

   A. Profile System Performance

   B. Monitor System Performance

   C. Manage System Monitoring

   D. Monitor Performance Logs and Alerts

13. You are installing a new Windows Server 2003 server computer as a member server in a mixed-mode domain with two Windows Server 2003 and two Windows NT 4 domain controllers. The new server will be used to host the company Web Web site. Therefore, you want to use the highest possible security for this server. Which of the following default security templates should you use to configure the server-level Security policies?

    A. `securews.inf`

    B. `hisecws.inf`

    C. `compatws.inf`

    D. `hiseciis.inf`

14. You have recently applied security options for your Windows Server 2003 computer. When you attempt to verify the security settings, they appear as if they have not been applied. What command-line utility can you use to force an update of the new security policies?

    A. `secupdate`

    B. `secedit`

    C. `gpupdate`

    D. `secpol`

15. You are the system administrator for a large corporation with regional branches. You want to ensure that the branches are kept up-to-date with the latest critical operating system and security updates from Microsoft. However, you also want to ensure that all updates are tested before they are deployed to clients. You are currently using Microsoft SMS for enterprise-wide software configuration management. Which of the following solutions is needed to test, deploy, and manage Windows updates and security updates from Microsoft's Web Web site?

    A. A centralized Software Update Services solution, employing a test server at the main site and production servers at regional branches.

    B. A centralized Software Update Services solution, employing test and production servers at the main site and production servers at regional branches that are separated by slow WAN links.

    C. A decentralized Software Update Services solution, employing test and production servers at each regional branch. The Baseline Security Analyzer can be used on all SUS servers to further manage security configurations across the network.

    D. None of the above.

Answers to Review Questions

1. C. The Group Policy Refresh Intervals For Computers option specifies the interval rate that will be used to update the computer's Group Policy. By default, this background operation occurs every 90 minutes with a random offset of 0 to 30 minutes.

2. A. The No Override option is used to specify that child containers can't override the policy settings of higher-level GPOs. In this case, the order of precedence would be that site settings override domain settings, and domain settings override OU settings. The No Override option would be used if you wanted to set corporate-wide policies without allowing administrators of lower-level containers to override your settings. This option can be set on a per-container basis, as needed.

3. A. The Audit Account Logon Events policy is used to track events such as when a user logs on or logs off using an Active Directory account. The Audit Logon Events policy is used to track events such as running a logon script or accessing a roaming profile.

4. C, D. Through the Security Configuration and Analysis snap-in, you can analyze an existing template against your current configuration to identify any weakness in your security settings. This utility does not configure any security options. The Configure Computer Now utility actually changes the security settings and should only be used with extreme caution.

5. A. In order to log on to a local computer, a user must have the Log on Locally user right. This is usually accomplished through membership in a group that has this right. By default, regular user accounts cannot log on to a domain controller.

6.

Templates	Containers	Applied template
Setup security.inf	Domain	
rootsec.inf	Built-in	
securedc.inf	Computers	
securews.inf	Domain Controllers	DC security.inf
hisecdc.inf	Foreign Security Principals	
hisecws.inf	HR OU	hisecws.inf
compatws.inf	Marketing OU	hisecws.inf
basicdc.inf	Users	
basicws.inf		
DC security.inf		
ocfiless.inf		
ocfilesw.inf		

In this example, you would apply the `DC security.inf` template to the domain controllers since they will not be running any other applications. You would apply the `hisecws.inf` template to the OUs containing the Marketing and HR servers. The other templates meet different needs and do not apply to this scenario. For example, Windows 2000 introduced the ocfiless template for file servers and the ocfilesw template for workstations.

7.

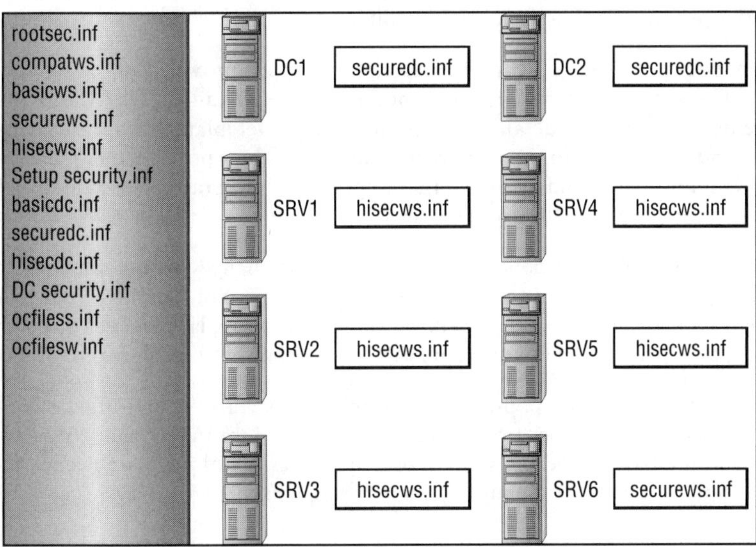

In this example, you would apply the `securedc.inf` template to the domain controllers since they will be running other applications and will not be dedicated domain controllers. You would apply the `hisecws.inf` template to the departmental servers since they will all be running exclusively Windows Server 2003. You would apply the `securews.inf` template to the VPN server to maintain compatibility with the heterogenous operating systems of the computers that may connect to the VPN server.

The other templates meet different needs and do not apply to this scenario. For example, Windows 2000 introduced the ocfiless template for file servers and the ocfilesw template for workstations.

8. B. The `hisecdc.inf` security template defines highly secure network communications for Windows Server 2003 computers. If you apply this security template, Windows Server 2003 computers can only communicate with other Windows Server 2000 or 2003 computers. In this case, the computers would not communicate with older clients such as Windows 95/98, nor could they communicate with Windows NT 4 computers.

9. A. The Enforce Password History option is used to prevent users from reusing the same password. Users must create a new password when their password expires or is changed.

10. D. This scenario calls for Datacenter Edition as the most scalable, robust solution for your mission-critical database application. Because you want to take advantage of hot-swappable memory, you must use the 32-bit version. Hot-add memory is not supported in the 64-bit version.

11. C. The Audit Account Management policy is used to track user and group creation, deletion, and management actions.

12. A. The Profile System Performance user right is used to monitor system processes through tools such as the Performance Logs and Alerts utility.

13. B. The `hisecws.inf` template is the most secure template provided and should be used in this instance. The `securews.inf` template is not as secure as `hisecws.inf`. The `hiseciis.inf` template does not exist by default. The `compatws.inf` template is the least secure template provided and is only used for backward-compatibility. This option relaxes the default security used by Windows 2000 and higher so that applications that ran under Windows NT and are not certified for Windows 2000 and higher will still run.

14. C. If you edit your security policy and notice that your changes are not taking effect, it may be because the Group policies are only applied periodically. You can force your policies to be updated by issuing the command `gpupdate`. This command replaces `secedit /refreshpolicy machine_policy` for computers and `secedit /refreshpolicy user_policy` for user settings.

15. D. Microsoft SMS is a comprehensive solution for enterprise-wide software configuration management. It is a standalone product that includes all of the functionality of Software Update Services and the Baseline Security Analyzer, so no additional tools are needed to manage Windows updates or security configurations in environments where SMS is already in use.

Planning Certificate Services

MICROSOFT EXAM OBJECTIVES COVERED IN THIS CHAPTER:

- ✓ **Configure Active Directory directory service for certificate publication.**
- ✓ **Plan a public key infrastructure (PKI) that uses Certificate Services.**
  - Identify the appropriate type of certificate authority to support certificate issuance requirements.
  - Plan the enrollment and distribution of certificates.
  - Plan for the use of smart cards for authentication.
- ✓ **Plan security for wireless networks.**

A secure network infrastructure requires a means of keeping messages and data secure. Cryptographic systems are used to validate the identity of parties to a transaction (authentication), verify that data was not altered in transit (integrity), and ensure that data is secret to all except the authorized parties (confidentiality).

Cryptography is as old as the art of communication. In times of war, transmissions can be secured from enemy interception by using a cipher to scramble the data. Unlike a code, such as Morse code or ASCII, which merely represents a signal without any intention of secrecy, a *cipher* conceals the true meaning of data by disguising it in a new form. For example, the sideband frequencies of the voice signals in a telephone conversation can be inverted to scramble the data so that an unauthorized party listening in on the conversation can't make out what is said. The inversion of frequencies is a cipher that makes the contents of the conversation secret except to the parties on either end, who know how to undo the cipher. Simple ciphers might rotate the sequence of letters in the alphabet or substitute letters for numbers. The most advanced ciphers rely on complex algorithms to rearrange the actual data bits contained in digital signals.

Secure modern networks incorporate a comprehensive system of cryptographic services known as a public key infrastructure (PKI). In a PKI, digital keys are used to lock (encrypt) and unlock (decrypt) data transmissions, and digital certificates are used to prove identity and transmit keys in a secure fashion. Certificates can be issued by trustworthy public authorities such as VeriSign, or they can be issued and used internally by an organization. Certificate services are one component of a PKI, and all of the components work together to provide a level of security that meets the specific requirements of an organization.

Microsoft Certificate Services (MCS) began as part of IIS and evolved to include e-mail, e-commerce, business partner communications, and other enterprise security needs in addition to secure Web site access and secure Web transactions. Microsoft introduced their Certificate Services implementation several years ago with Internet Information Server (IIS) 3. MCS enabled organizations to issue and manage their own digital certificates to secure Web transactions with SSL. From the beginning, MCS could also be used with Exchange 5 to provide users with e-mail security. With each subsequent release of IIS, the Certificate Services functionality has become more robust and flexible. In Windows Server 2003, MCS is now completely integrated into the operating system and directory service structure.

This chapter starts with the basic terms and concepts that underlie MCS. You will learn why encryption is important and how it is used to meet everyday business needs. You will understand how certificates fit into the big picture of a public key infrastructure. You will also learn the concepts of a certificate service and how a certificate service can be a part of an overall security solution for your organization.

You must consider many factors when you are planning a certificate solution, including planning for different certificate issuance requirements, planning for certificate enrollment and distribution, and planning for special needs such as smart card authentication and security for wireless networks. MCS can be fully integrated with Active Directory, and you will learn how to configure Active Directory for certificate publication.

Understanding the Public Key Infrastructure

A *public key infrastructure (PKI)* enables users of a basically unsecure public network such as the Internet to securely and privately exchange data and even money through the use of a public and private cryptographic key pair that is obtained and shared through a trusted authority. The PKI uses digital certificates to identify an individual or organization and directory services to store, manage, and revoke the certificates. PKI involves emerging standards and approaches.

A PKI is used to provide several security benefits, including authentication, data integrity, confidentiality, and nonrepudiation:

Authentication *Authentication* is used to validate the entity and the origin of data. Data communications implicitly assume that there is more than one party. Parties to a transaction are known as *entities*, and they can be users, organizations, computers, or devices. Cryptographic systems verify each party's identity to the other party. For example, secure Web sites allow users to verify that the server's identity is as claimed. The client can encrypt a challenge message and send it to the server. If the server can decrypt it and answer correctly, the server can prove its identity.

Integrity *Integrity* provides the means of verifying that data was not altered in transit. Data integrity is provided by using a digital signature.

Confidentiality Cryptographic systems can ensure *confidentiality*, meaning that data is secret to all except the authorized parties to a data transaction. Even complete strangers can communicate privately with assurance using cryptographic technologies.

Nonrepudiation *Nonrepudiation* is one aspect of conventional business that can now be brought to e-commerce. If one party signs a paper contract and gives you a copy, you now have protection against that party later claiming that he/she/it didn't agree to the terms of the contract. Digital signatures can provide the same assurance and even legal binding for electronic transmissions.

Deploying a PKI allows you to perform tasks such as:

- Digitally signing files such as documents and applications
- Securing e-mail from unintended viewers
- Enabling secure connections between computers, even if they are connected over the public Internet or through a wireless network
- Enhancing user authentication through the use of smart cards

In the following sections, we'll discuss key PKI concepts, the elements of a PKI, and special terms you'll need to understand.

Key PKI Concepts

In a secure transaction, there must be a means of disguising the information communicated between two parties so that it cannot be intercepted and used by an unauthorized third party. Methods such as firewalls, Network Address Translation (NAT) and Port Address Translation (PAT) can protect data from being intercepted by unauthorized parties. Methods of encryption, including IPSec and Certificate Services, prevent intercepted information from being understood and used.

Encryption is the conversion of data into a disguised form, called a *ciphertext*, for the purpose of protecting communications from unauthorized parties. *Decryption* is the conversion of encrypted data back into its original form.

The introduction to the chapter discussed how a cipher is created using a computer algorithm. To recover the contents of an encrypted signal, the correct *key* is required in order to decrypt the data. The key is actually another *algorithm* that "undoes" the work of the encryption algorithm. A computer can be used to "break" the cipher, but the more complex the encryption algorithm, the longer it takes to break the cipher.

Security experts assume that any unauthorized party with sufficient time, resources, and motivation can break an encryption algorithm. The goal is to increase the amount of time it will take to such an extent—years, decades, centuries—that by the time the data could be read, the security risk would no longer exist. However, as the strength of the cipher increases, so does the cost in terms of processing power.

As technology advances and computing power increases, stronger encryption algorithms are needed. Secure desktop clients today use 128-bit encryption, while a secure server may use 4096-bit or stronger encryption.

Encryption is essential to any type of sensitive transaction, such as a credit-card purchase over the inherently unsecure Internet, or an e-mail exchange concerning a corporate secret at the highest executive levels. Encryption assumes critical importance for communications over wireless LANs (WLANs). Wireless circuits are vastly easier to "tap" than their hard-wired counterparts.

There are two forms of encryption:

- *Symmetric encryption*, which uses the same key to encrypt and decrypt data. Symmetric encryption is used in preshared secret key systems.
- *Asymmetric encryption*, which uses one key to encrypt data and a different key to decrypt data. Asymmetric encryption is used in public key systems.

Cryptographic systems can employ secret keys or public keys. In the next sections, you'll learn the differences between these cryptographic systems. We'll then explore the advantages of public key cryptography systems, including the uses of digital signatures and digital certificates.

Secret Key Cryptography

In a *secret key cryptography* system, two people who want to communicate use a single shared key that must be kept secret. This is the equivalent of a secret password on which both parties agree. The same key is used to encrypt and decrypt data, so if the secret key is compromised through loss or theft, then the data encrypted with that key becomes vulnerable. Secret key systems tend to be fast and flexible, but their dependence on a single key makes them better suited for applications like IPSec where you can change the key frequently. In addition, secret-key systems can only be used for encryption, not authentication.

Public Key Cryptography

As opposed to the single secret key used in a secret-key system, *public key cryptography* systems use a pair of keys:

- A *public key*, which is designed to be freely distributed
- A *private key* (also called a *secret key*), which is known only to its owner and should never be revealed to any other party

These keys complement each other. If you encrypt something with your public key, it can be decrypted only with the corresponding private key (which only you hold), and vice versa. This means that anyone can use your public key to encrypt something, but only you can decrypt the same data—because only the private key can decrypt data encrypted by the public key, and only you have the private key.

The security of these keys depends on the mathematical relationship between the public and private keys. You can't derive one from the other, so passing out the public key doesn't introduce any risk of compromising the private key. For this reason, a remote party's public key is frequently used to encrypt data sent to that party, because it is freely available, yet the data can be decrypted only with the private key, which only the remote party knows.

Two fundamental operations are associated with public key cryptography: encryption, which we have already discussed, and signing.

Digital Signatures

Signing uses encryption to prove the origin and authenticity of a data transaction. A sender can use a private key to digitally sign a message, thereby creating a digital signature that proves to a recipient that the sender is indeed the true source of the information.

Digital signatures differ from handwritten signatures and even fingerprints because they are different every time they are generated. Producing two different messages that have an identical hash is virtually impossible. A special type of algorithm called a *hashing algorithm*, also known as a message authentication algorithm, calculates a unique mathematical value, known as a *digest*, from the actual message contents. The digest is then encrypted using the private key and either added to the end of the message or sent as a separate file attachment. The public key can be sent along with the message, either on its own or as part of a certificate.

If Jane wants the world to know that she is the author of a message, she signs it by encrypting it with her private key. She can then post the message publicly. This obviously doesn't provide any privacy, because anyone can decrypt the data using her public key. However, the fact that it can be decrypted using Jane's public key means that it must have been encrypted using Jane's private key, which only she holds—so it must have come from Jane.

Perhaps you want to digitally sign an e-mail message announcing a critical security flaw in one of your company's existing software products. You could use the built-in functionality of the Eudora e-mail client to do the following:

1. The encryption process examines the message content you provide and passes it through a hashing algorithm to generate a unique "fingerprint."
2. It encrypts the message and the fingerprint using your private key, thereby creating the digital signature for this specific message.

If someone wants to verify that the message is from you, you can perform the same steps in reverse. First, your software decrypts the message using your public key. Then it computes a hash for the message and comes up with a value for the digest. If the new digest and the decrypted version match, it proves that you actually sent the message, and the message hasn't been modified.

A digital signature does not provide confidentiality, because anyone can check the signature and read the data.

Digital Certificates

Digital certificates are the passports of the electronic world. Like your passport booklet, which contains the unique passport I.D. number, a digital certificate serves as a carrying case for a public key. A certificate contains the public key and a set of attributes, such as the key holder's name and e-mail address. These attributes specify something about the owner, such as the owner's identity, what the owner is allowed to do with the certificate, and so on. The attributes and the public key are bound together because the certificate is digitally signed by the entity that issued the certificate. Anyone who wants to verify the certificate's contents can verify the issuer's signature.

Your passport contains a unique key (the passport number) and some attributes (an expiration date, your name, date of birth, etc.). A passport is issued by a trusted agency and sealed to prevent alteration. Any third party (such as a country or the local DMV) that trusts the agency that issued your license (the U.S. government) and verifies that the lamination is intact can rely on its authenticity.

The entire system is based on a trust model. Although the U.S. government verifies the validity of its citizen's passports, the passport itself is not issued by the top brass in Washington. The process of issuing passports is delegated to trusted agencies of the government, such as post offices, clerks of court, and public libraries. A guy in Seattle doesn't need to fly to D.C. to get a passport—he can simply submit an application through the local post office.

Foreign entities (countries) can validate the identity of an unknown individual based on *their* trust in a known entity, the U.S. government. Because my passport carried the recognized and trusted seal of the U.S. government, Australia and Japan granted me permission to enter their countries even though neither country knew who I was. However, a country that does not have relations with the U.S. would not recognize me because it does not recognize the U.S. as a trusted entity, and there my passport would be useless.

A public key infrastructure is built on the same type of trust model. You'll understand the analogy in a deeper way as you read further, but for now, here are a few important concepts to remember:

- Certificates are digital passports that contain a unique key and a collection of attributes used to identify an individual.
- Certificates operate within a system which is based on a hierarchy of trust and authority.
- Certificates are issued to individuals by entities, which are often trusted representatives of a higher-level entity to whom the process of issuing certificates is delegated by that higher-level entity.

- Entities that issue certificates can therefore exist at different levels within a hierarchy of authority (like the U.S. Post Office as an agency of the U.S. government).
- Foreign entities can validate the identity of an unknown individual based on their trust in a known entity (like the government of Australia recognizing my U.S. passport).

Elements of a PKI

A public key infrastructure is a comprehensive system of security methodologies. A PKI has many components, including the following:

- Digital certificates, which form the foundation of a PKI. They provide the electronic credentials (the public keys) that are used to sign and encrypt data.
- *Certificate authorities (CAs)*, which are trusted entities or services that issue certificates, revoke certificates they've issued, and publish certificates for their clients. CAs, such as VeriSign and Thawte, can do this for millions of users; with MCS, you can set up your own CA for each department or workgroup in your organization if you so desire. Each CA is responsible for choosing what attributes it will include in a certificate and what mechanism it will use to verify those attributes before issuing the certificate. Multiple CAs can be used in a hierarchy to perform specialized tasks, such as issuing certificates to subordinate CAs or issuing certificates to users.
- *Certificate revocation*, which enables a proactive response to a situation in which a certificate has been compromised in some way.
- *Certificate revocation lists (CRLs)*, which are lists of certificates that have been revoked before reaching the scheduled expiration date. The CAs build and maintain these lists.
- *Certificate publishers*, also known as certificate repositories, which make certificates and CRLs publicly available, inside or outside an organization. This allows widespread availability of the critical material needed to support the entire PKI. A good certificate publisher will allow clients to automatically get the certificates they need. Microsoft's CA and clients support certificate publishers, such as Active Directory, that use the Lightweight Directory Access Protocol (LDAP).
- The certificate management system, which controls which certificates are published, temporarily, permanently suspended, renewed, or revoked. In Windows Server 2003, the Certificate Services snap-in accomplishes this function.
- *PKI-aware applications*, which allow you and your users to do useful things with certificates, such as encrypt e-mail or network connections. An effective security system works transparently, and the user doesn't need to be aware of what the application is doing to effect security. The best-known examples of PKI-aware applications are Web browsers, such as Internet Explorer, and e-mail applications, such as Outlook and Outlook Express. Windows Server 2003 includes the *Encrypting File System (EFS)*, a PKI-aware file system that can automatically encrypt and decrypt files for IT staff and end users. These applications don't have any "knowledge" per se about the underlying PKI services. They are simply able to use the certificates to implement PKI functions such as validating identity.

- *Certificate policy and practice statements*, which outline how the CA and its certificates are to be used, the degree of trust that can be placed in these certificates, legal liabilities if the trust is broken, and so on.

In the following sections, we'll explore the certificate authority, including CA types and roles. You'll then get to see the process of certificate services in action. We'll also discuss methods for certificate publication.

EFS, an Example of a PKI-Aware File System

EFS is a PKI-aware file system used in Windows Server 2003 to encrypt files and folders transparently to you and your applications so that when you're logged in, everything in an EFS-encrypted folder looks like a normal document. When an unauthorized user attempts to access another user's EFS-encrypted files, Windows Server 2003 produces an "access denied" message.

EFS files are always encrypted on disk. This happens because EFS is actually a file system driver that sits between the standard disk drivers and the applications. When Word (for example) requests a block of data from an EFS-protected file, EFS reads an encrypted block from disk, decrypts it in memory, and passes it back to Word without storing the unencrypted text on disk. EFS supports recovery so that you always have a way to recover access to files that have been encrypted. It does this by encrypting the key used to protect the file twice: once for the owner and once for the Administrator account (or whatever other account has recovery authority). The Administrator account is defined as the recovery agent by default, but you can customize recovery access and define additional recovery agents in MCS.

The Certificate Authority

A certificate authority controls the issuance and use of digital certificates for the users and computers in a defined group. You could set up a CA for a single organizational unit, a Windows Server 2003 domain, or an entire enterprise. CAs such as VeriSign and Thawte also function within the international public domain.

The CA actually has several distinct functions. Besides issuing certificates when it receives a legitimate request, it also allows administrators to revoke certificates once they're no longer needed. You can control what newly issued certificates may be used for; for example, you could apply a restriction that would permit anyone to request a certificate for secure e-mail but that wouldn't allow those certificates to be used for encrypting files.

These functions are all controlled by a robust set of permissions. For example, you can control who can request new certificates and which computers may be used to request them. As with almost any other setting in Active Directory's Group Policy Objects (GPOs), you can delegate control over these settings to whatever part of your organization needs to have it.

The CA can stand alone, but you'll normally use it to generate machine certificates for IPSec and end-user certificates for smartcard logon or EAP-TLS authentication.

Microsoft's CA can stand alone, or it can act as part of a *certificate hierarchy*. This hierarchy, also known as a certification chain, can contain CAs from inside and outside a single organization. That allows you to have secure communications with business partners and suppliers without necessarily having to issue your certificates to them or generate a user account on your server.

Consider the passport analogy. You can travel to any countries that recognize the U.S. government as a valid authority. In some countries such as Germany, you can even use a California driver's license to prove your identity. There is essentially a hierarchy of trust going on here—Germany trusts the U.S., Germany knows that the U.S. has delegated authority to the state of California to issue identity cards, the state of California trusted the Santa Barbara DMV to issue identity cards bearing the California state seal, so Germany trusts the I.D. card that you got at the local DMV office as proof of your identity.

In a hierarchy, as shown in Figure 8.1, each certificate authority signs the certificates it issues using its own private key. How can you determine whether a certificate is valid or not? Each CA actually has its own certificate, which contains the CA's public key. This CA certificate is itself signed by a higher-level CA. You can stack up any number of CAs in a hierarchy, with each CA certifying the authenticity of the certificates it has issued. Eventually, though, there must be a top-level CA, called a *root certificate authority*. Because there is no authority above the root CA in the hierarchy, there's no higher authority to vouch for its certificate. Instead, the root CA signs its own certificate, asserting that it is the root. Root CA's require far greater physical and electronic security measures to ensure the integrity of the total system. Companies, such as VeriSign, that provide certificates to the public need very strong security for the root CA. Their root CAs exist as independent computers that are taken offline and kept under lock and in vaults behind layers of physical security measures. In a highly secure environment, the root CA should never be a network-attached computer.

FIGURE 8.1 A simple certificate hierarchy

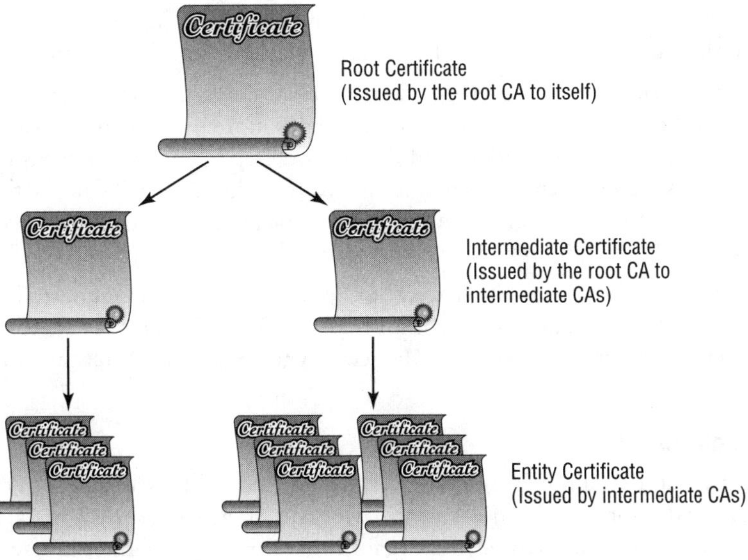

The root CA is the CA at the top of the hierarchy. CAs lower in the hierarchy are variously called *intermediate* or subordinate CAs (or sometimes, child CAs). We will discuss the different CA roles later in this chapter in "CA Roles."

CA Types

MCS supports two different *types* of CAs: enterprise and stand-alone. Each type can operate in one of several different *roles*. The difference between types and roles is simple to understand. Cars and trucks are different types of vehicles. A single car or truck can be used in different roles: to carpool, to race, and so on.

The type of CA you install determines to whom you can issue certificates and what the certificates can be used for, so it's important to understand the distinctions between them. The only real configuration difference between the two types is which set of policies is enforced, but the operational differences between them are important.

The Enterprise CA

The *enterprise CA* acts as part of the PKI for an enterprise. It issues and revokes certificates for end users *and* intermediate CAs according to the policy and security settings that you apply to the CA. As you'd expect from something labeled "enterprise," enterprise CAs require Active Directory access, although they don't necessarily have to be installed on an AD domain controller.

MCS machines acting as enterprise CAs have these five special attributes:

- All users and computers in their domains always trust them.
- Certificates issued by an enterprise CA can be used to log on to Windows Server 2003 domains if you're using smartcards (those little credit-card-looking things that actually pack an embedded microprocessor and cryptographic software).
- Enterprise CAs publish certificates and CRL information to Active Directory, where any client in the enterprise can retrieve the certificates and CRL information.
- Enterprise CAs use certificate types and templates to construct the content of newly issued certificates. You'll read about types and templates more in "Certificate Templates," but for now it's important to understand that they deliver some useful capabilities. First, enterprise CAs can use templates to automatically fill in new certificates with the right set of attributes. Second, enterprise CAs can automatically fill in the holder's name for new certificates by looking it up in Active Directory.
- Enterprise CAs will always either reject or approve a certificate request. They'll never mark a request as pending and save it for human inspection. The CA makes this decision based on the security permissions on the security template and on permissions and group memberships in Active Directory.

The Stand-alone CA

Stand-alone CAs don't require Active Directory access, because they're designed to do nothing but issue certificates for external use. In other words, a stand-alone CA is made to issue certificates to people who aren't part of your organization (for example, Internet users or business partners). Stand-alone CAs are very similar to enterprise CAs in most respects, with a few differences:

- Stand-alone CAs automatically mark incoming certificate requests as "pending," because the CA doesn't have access to Active Directory information to verify them.
- Certificates issued by a stand-alone CA can't be used for smartcard logons (though you may store them on a smartcard).
- Certificates and CRLs generated by the stand-alone CA aren't published anywhere—you must *manually* distribute them.

You *can* install a stand-alone CA on a server that participates in an Active Directory organization. The CA will be able to publish certificate information if its server is a member of the Certificate Publishers group.

CA Roles

Whether your MCS servers are acting as enterprise or stand-alone CAs, they can assume one of four distinct roles. These roles govern the conditions under which the CA will issue certificates, as well as what those certificates can be used for once issued. In addition, the role your CA will play has some bearing on the questions you need to answer when you're installing the CAs in your network. Here are the role types:

- *Enterprise root CAs* sit at the top of a certificate hierarchy. While they can issue certificates to end users or subordinate CAs, the enterprise root normally is used only to issue certificates to subordinate CAs. That's because delegating issuance powers to the subordinates gives you maximum flexibility in setting permissions and choosing which templates to use. For the most secure environments, the root CA at the top of a hierarchy is an offline, stand-alone computer under tight security.
- *Enterprise subordinate CAs* live in an enterprise CA hierarchy below the root. They typically issue certificates to computers and users, not to other subordinate CAs. By setting appropriate permissions at the enterprise subordinate CA level, you maintain granular control over who can request and revoke certificates.
- *Stand-alone root CAs* stand alone, just like the name implies. They may or may not be physically connected to the network. They may or may not be part of the Active Directory infrastructure. Because stand-alone roots can be physically and logically disconnected from the network, they can be made pretty much impervious to network attacks, making them well suited for use in issuing your most valuable certificate types.
- *Stand-alone subordinate CAs* normally issue certificates to end users. They usually don't take part in Active Directory, although they can. For example, if you were setting up a PKI for a company with offices in several countries, you could set up a separate, stand-alone, subordinate CA in each country. This would allow you to issue certificates to end users in each country without being able to cross-verify certificates issued in different countries.

How Certificate Services Work

The process of issuing a digital certificate is something only a cryptographer could love. It involves a lot of arcana necessitated by the demand for high security. However, the overall flow of data between the client and the CA is fairly easy to understand (refer to Figure 8.2). The following steps explain what happens:

1. The CA receives a certificate request from a client. This request can be generated through a Web page offered by the CA, manually by the end user, or automatically by various system components.
2. The CA checks the incoming request to see that it is complete and correct (e.g., to see whether or not the requestor already has a certificate, to see whether or not the name on the certificate is a duplicate, and so on).
3. The CA checks whatever policies the group administrator has chosen to apply to make sure the request is in line with those policies. Sometimes this means that the CA must push the request off to a queue, where it sits and waits for human approval. If you configure the CA to do so, it can automatically approve requests that meet the specified policy.
4. The CA takes the attributes specified in the certificate request, adds in some of its own data (such as the name of the CA and a copy of its own certificate), and asks a system cryptographic service to sign it. This signature, equivalent to the seal on a driver's license or a college diploma, serves as both protection against tampering and an assertion of validity. (Which cryptographic service actually does the signing is up to you.)
5. The CA returns a copy of the new certificate to the requestor.
6. Optionally, it publishes the new certificate in Active Directory or in a shared folder. This allows other users, computers, and programs to look up certificates in a domain- or organization-wide directory.

FIGURE 8.2 The flow of certificate data between client and CA

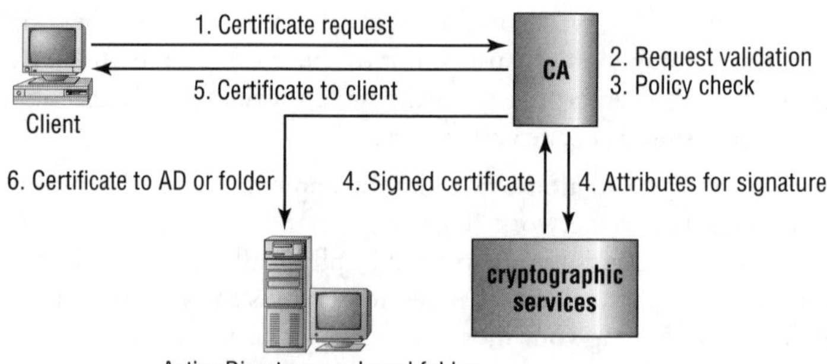

Certificate Publication Methods

One of the fundamental tasks of a PKI system is to publish certificates so that users and other entities can use them. For instance, the recipient of data that has been encrypted with a party's private key must be able to obtain the public key in order to decrypt the data.

Certificates are often published in the equivalent of an electronic phone directory. Certificates can also be physically sent through e-mail or other physical media such as floppy disks and smart cards.

Certificate directories are databases that are X.500/LDAP-compliant. Certificates are in the X.509 format. Directories can be public or private (meaning that they are only used internally by an organization).

In Windows Server 2003, Microsoft Certificate Services is fully integrated with Active Directory. Certificates are published to Active Directory by default. You can also use the `certutil -dspublish` command to publish certificates and CRLs.

Make sure you understand how to apply certificates within an Active Directory hierarchy.

PKI Terminology

Cryptographic systems and PKIs are comprised of a set of technologies. Different vendors may use different cryptographic and PKI technologies. This section discusses some additional terms and concepts related to Microsoft's implementation of PKI technologies.

Cryptographic Service Providers

We've mentioned the need for PKI-aware applications as a component of the PKI. How do these applications actually work within the PKI infrastructure?

Microsoft ships a set of cryptographic libraries with every copy of Windows NT, Windows 95/98, Windows 2000, Windows XP, and Windows Server 2003. The libraries are known as *cryptographic service providers (CSPs)*.

The libraries implement basic, low-level crypto operations, including both secret and public key encryption. They expose a set of application programming interfaces that Microsoft calls the CryptoAPI. Applications, and the operating systems themselves, make CryptoAPI calls when they need cryptographic work performed.

Any system can have any number of CSPs installed, including encryption-only CSPs and CSPs with signature capability. MCS can use installed CSPs that have the capability to sign and issue certificates.

The end result is that PKI-aware applications integrate seamlessly with the PKI infrastructure in a way that is transparent to end users and other entities.

Policy and Exit Modules

MCS supports using predefined sets of instructions that tell the CA what to do with incoming requests and how to proceed after a request is approved. The rules that govern how the CA handles an incoming request are built into *policy modules*, and rules that specify where and how a newly issued certificate is published are built into *exit modules*. Although you can write your own policy and exit modules, you'll probably use the ones Microsoft provides with Windows Server 2003.

A policy module is a set of instructions that tells the CA what to do with incoming certificate requests. A policy module can automatically approve or reject a request, based on any rules built into the module. It can also mark a request as "pending" and leave it for a human operator to approve or reject. Policy modules can also change the attributes listed in a certificate, adding or removing them according to its design. Microsoft's standard policy module does three things:

- It processes each incoming request or marks it as pending, depending on whether you're operating an enterprise or a stand-alone CA.
- It adds an attribute to the certificate that specifies where the issuing CA's certificate may be obtained. This allows clients who want to verify the new certificate to get the issuer's certificate at the same time.
- It adds an attribute that specifies where the issuing CA's CRLs are available to clients.

An exit module allows the CA to do something with a certificate after it's been issued. For example, Microsoft's standard exit module can publish new certificates to Active Directory, store them in a shared folder, or e-mail them back to the requestor. It also publishes CRLs for the issuing CA, if you enable that feature.

Certificate Trust Lists

The *Certificate Trust List (CTL)* is a way for PKI administrators to decide whom they trust. When you put a CA certificate on the CTL for your domain, you're explicitly telling your users' PKI clients that it's okay to trust certificates issued by that CA. The CTL resides in Active Directory, and as an administrator you can control who may (and may not) make changes to the CTL for a site, domain, or organizational unit through Group Policy.

Certificate Attributes

Each certificate includes a combination of attributes that provide information about the certificate holder. The X.509 standard defines which attributes are mandatory and which are optional. Optional attributes are known as *extensions*. MCS uses nine significant attributes, as shown in Table 8.1. The certificate template used when the certificate was generated determines the exact combination and contents of these attributes in a certificate—but more on that in a minute.

TABLE 8.1 Certificate Attributes

Attribute Name	Description
Basic constraints	Specifies whether this certificate can be used to sign other certificates. If so, it also specifies how many levels deep the resulting hierarchy can be.
Default CSP list	Provides a list of CSPs that can be used with this type of certificate. For example, EFS requires certificates generated with the Microsoft RSA CSP.
Display name	Displays the name when someone views the certificate's information; this is a "friendly" name that's less complex than the certificate's distinguished name (DN).

TABLE 8.1 Certificate Attributes *(continued)*

Attribute Name	Description
E-mail name	Specifies the e-mail address associated with the holder of this certificate.
Extended key usage	Specifies a list of extended functions (including signing a CTL, encrypting e-mail, and establishing secure network connections) for which this certificate can be used. The extended key usage information coexists with, but doesn't override, the standard key usage fields.
Key usage	Specifies the combination of basic operations (digital signatures, encryption, and key exchange) for which this certificate can be used.
Machine certificate template	Specifies whether certificates that use this template are intended for use by people or by computers.
Security permissions	Specifies who can request a particular kind of certificate. For example, the default permissions for the Administrator template allow only users with administrative access to request administrator-level certificates.

Certificate Templates

Like user templates, certificate templates are used to create new certificates based on the desired functionality. Windows Server 2003 includes 22 different certificate templates. There's no supported way for you to build your own templates. The most useful certificate templates are listed in Table 8.2.

TABLE 8.2 Certificate Templates in Windows Server 2003

Template Name	What Certificates Based on the Template May Do	Who Gets Certificates Issued Using this Template
Administrator	Sign code, sign CTLs, secure e-mail and EFS file systems, authenticate clients	Domain administrators
Authenticated Session	Signature-only operations for authenticating clients	Network clients
Basic EFS	Encrypt EFS intermediate keys and files	Users who have access to EFS volumes
Code Signing	Sign executable code to assert its trustworthiness	Users who have authorization to sign executable objects
Computer	Authenticate computers to servers and vice versa	Computers in a domain

TABLE 8.2 Certificate Templates in Windows Server 2003 *(continued)*

Template Name	What Certificates Based on the Template May Do	Who Gets Certificates Issued Using this Template
Domain Controller	Authenticate clients to servers and vice versa	Active Directory domain controllers
EFS Recovery Agent	Recover encrypted files when the original key material is unavailable	Users who have EFS recovery privileges
Enrollment Agent	Request certificates for users or computers	Users who are authorized to request certificates
Exchange Enrollment Agent (Offline request)	Generate offline certificate requests for Exchange mailbox owners	Users who can request new certificates for Exchange users
Exchange Signature Only	Signature-only certificate for Exchange users	Exchange users
Exchange User	Signature- and encryption-capable certificate	Exchange users
Smartcard Logon	Authenticate a client to a logon server	Smartcard holders who use smartcards to log on; cannot be used for secure e-mail or EFS security
Smartcard User	Client authentication and e-mail security	Smartcard holders who have permission to use their smartcards to log on *and* secure e-mail and EFS files
Subordinate Certification Authority	Issue and revoke certificates while acting as a subordinate CA	Computers acting as subordinate CAs
Trust List Signing	Sign the certificate trust list	Administrators who have authorization to modify the CTL
User	Authenticate client-to-server, sign and encrypt e-mail, encrypt EFS data	Ordinary, unprivileged users
User Signature Only	Sign e-mail; sign client-to-server authentication messages	Users whom you don't want to have encryption capability

Server Gated Cryptography (SGC)

U.S. export law forbids exporting strong encryption services. This restriction would make international banking extremely difficult if not for *Server Gated Cryptography (SGC)*. SGC, an extension of SSL, is an encryption protocol that uses a digital certificate and is most commonly used to protect sessions such as online banking sessions.

Most operating systems and browsers today employ SCG encryption capability. SGC works by allowing 40-bit exportable versions of Internet Explorer to use 128-bit encryption. SGC is included with all versions of Windows since Windows 95 and NT 4. The catch is that only approved financial institutions may use SGC on the server side, so SGC is not a loophole for all international encryption needs. The very nature of SGC certificates means that they cannot be generated by your stand-alone or enterprise CA. They must come from a commercial CA such as VeriSign.

Recovery Keys

Ordinarily, if you lose the key associated with a certificate, you're in trouble—it's like losing the combination to a bank vault. You might be able to locate a safecracker who could break in, but the odds aren't good. The risk of permanent data loss has precluded the adoption of encryption in many businesses, so Microsoft has provided a solution in the form of *recovery keys*. The idea behind recovery keys is that if the key used to encrypt a piece of data (on an EFS volume, e-mail message, or wherever else) is lost, the recovery key can be used to decrypt the data. Signing keys aren't recoverable, so no one can surreptitiously pretend to be you by recovering your key.

Windows Server 2003 allows you to define a recovery policy that specifies who may recover data and under what conditions. Users who have recovery authority are called *recovery agents*, and they use special certificates and keys to enable recovery. The Administrator account is automatically set up as the default recovery agent, and additional recovery agents can also be named through MCS.

Key Recovery versus Key Escrow

Some cryptographic systems use *key escrow*, in which a third party holds a copy of your encryption keys. In some escrow scenarios, this third party is a government agency, such as the National Security Agency or the Treasury Department; in others, it's an industry organization, such as the American Bar Association or the American Banking Association. If you think of recovery as using one of those magnetic key holders, you can consider escrow to be storing a copy of your key in a safety deposit box. A simple way to remember this difference is that recovery lets *you* recover *your* keys, and escrow lets *someone else* recover *your* keys. Windows Server 2003 does not implement key escrow.

Smart Cards

Support for cryptographic smart cards is a key feature of the PKI. A smart card is a credit card–sized device that is used with an access code to enable certificate-based authentication and single sign-on to the enterprise. Smart cards securely store certificates, public and private keys, passwords, and other types of personal information. A smart card reader attached to the computer reads the smart card. Smart cards are a tamper-resistant and portable way to provide security solutions for tasks such as logging on to a Windows Server 2003 domain, client authentication, code signing, and securing e-mail.

Smart cards provide the following benefits:

- Tamper-resistant storage for protecting private keys and other forms of personal information.
- Isolation of security-critical computations involving authentication, digital signatures, and key exchange from other parts of the computer that do not have a "need to know." These operations are all performed on the smart card.
- Portability of credentials and other private information between computers at work, home, or on the road.

Planning to Use Smart Cards

As the systems engineer in an enterprise internetwork with a large base of roaming users, you want to ensure security by providing the strongest possible form of authentication available. You want to use a cryptography-based identification system that can also ensure proof of possession when authenticating a user to a domain.

Smart cards are the logical choice. They provide a very strong form of hardware-based authentication. An additional benefit is that they add a layer of security through the use of a Personal Identification Number (PIN). A malicious person would have to obtain both the user's smart card and the PIN to impersonate the user and gain access to the network. Smart cards are also resistant to undetected attacks because the user will probably know when the card is missing.

Smart cards can in this way be integrated as an important component of a PKI.

Planning and Managing the Certificate Server

Managing the certificate server involves first installing MCS, configuring the CA service, configuring the CA itself, and then configuring revocation and trust. We'll explore each of these topics in the next sections.

Installing Microsoft Certificate Server

The actual process of installing and configuring MCS is pretty straightforward, especially when you compare it with the steps required to set up the equivalent service under Windows NT.

However, some prior planning is necessary to avoid making the wrong configuration choices at installation—MCS doesn't allow you to change some of its settings once it's installed.

Planning the CA Installation

Before you install a CA anywhere on your network, you must know the answer to three questions that the setup program is going to ask you:

What role do you want the CA to play? At one point in the installation process, you pick between stand-alone and enterprise CAs, and after that point, the installation options diverge. Also, you can't install an enterprise CA unless you've already set up and tested Active Directory.

Do you want to use any CSPs other than the default Microsoft modules? If you install the optional (and North America–only) High Encryption Pack for Windows Server 2003, you can take advantage of CSPs that are cryptographically stronger than the ones included with Windows Server 2003.

Do you want to allow end users to request certificates using the Web interface included with MCS? This interface makes it easier for users to get certificates, which may or may not be what you want to accomplish.

Installing the CA

You install the Certificate Server using the Windows Components Wizard. When you run the wizard, you can install the CA service itself, the Web enrollment component, or both.

When you're ready to install the CA on a computer (after answering the questions listed earlier in the section, of course), you can do the follow the steps to perform the installation:

1. Open the Windows Components Wizard by clicking Start ➤ Control Panel ➤ Add or Remove Programs and clicking the Add/Remove Windows Components icon. The wizard opens and lists all the components it knows how to install or remove.
2. Select Certificate Services from the component list. You'll see a warning dialog box telling you that you can't change the name of the computer, or move it into or out of an AD domain, after installing the CA. If you want the machine you're installing on to function as an enterprise CA, make sure you promote it to a domain controller before continuing with the installation.
3. Click the Details button and uncheck any component you don't want installed. For example, if you want to install only the Web enrollment components on a network kiosk, uncheck the Certificate Services CA option. Click OK when you're done, and then click the Next button to move on to the next wizard step.
4. The CA Type page appears (see Figure 8.3). Notice the Use Custom Setting To Generate The Key Pair And CA Certificate checkbox—you'll need to check it if you want to change the CSPs this CA can use, if you want to reuse an existing key pair, or if you want to change the default hash algorithm. Click Next once you've filled out the page.

FIGURE 8.3 The CA Type page

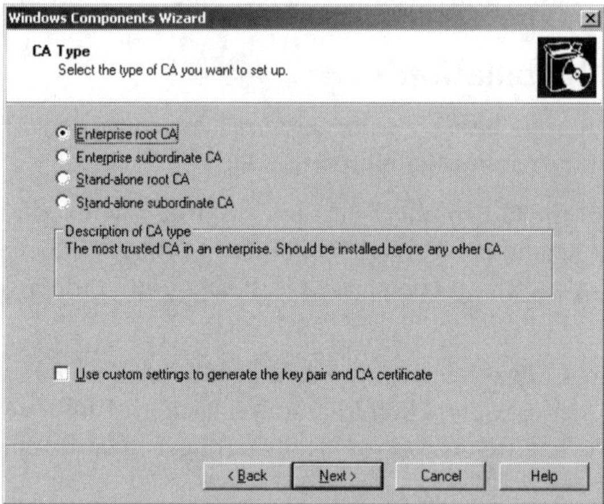

5. If you checked the Use Custom Setting To Generate The Key Pair And CA Certificate checkbox, you'll see the Public And Private Key Pair Selection page (see Figure 8.4). Apart from selecting the key pair you want to use, this page allows you to choose the CSP, hash algorithm, and key length you want to use with its controls. By default, the Microsoft Base Cryptographic Provider is the standard CSP, although you may have others available depending on what hardware and software you have installed on your server.

FIGURE 8.4 The Public and Private Key Pair Selection page

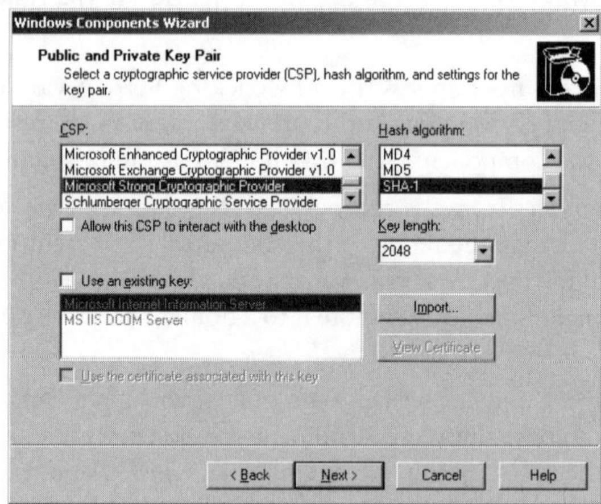

6. The fields on this page do the following:

- The CSP list shows all the CSPs on your machine. Choose the one you want this CA to use. Be forewarned that if you choose a CSP that doesn't support the RSA algorithm suite (such as the Microsoft Base DSS CSP), your CA may not interoperate properly with CAs from other vendors.

- The Hash Algorithms list allows you to choose the hash algorithm you want to use for computing digital signatures. Don't use MD4. If you can avoid it, don't use MD5 either—both algorithms have known weaknesses. Instead, accept the default setting of SHA-1.
- The Key Length drop-down list lets you select a key length if you're generating a key pair. You can take the default value of 1024 bits or you can go all the way up to 4096 bits if you need to, provided your CSP supports longer keys.
- The Use An Existing Keys checkbox allows you to reuse an existing key pair for the CA's key, as long as it was generated with algorithms compatible with your selected CSP. As you choose different CSPs, you'll see that this checkbox (and the contents of the list below it) changes to reflect the keys you could potentially use.
- The Import button lets you import certificates from a PFX/PKCS#12 file.
- The View Certificate button shows you the properties for the selected certificate.
- The Use The Certificate Associated With This Key checkbox lets you use an existing certificate if the key pair you've selected has one associated with it *and* if it's compatible with your chosen CSP.

7. Once you've set the options you want to use, click the Next button.
8. The CA Identifying Information page (see Figure 8.5) appears, allowing you to specify the information needed to uniquely identify this CA. You must specify a unique name for the CA in the Common Name field. The Distinguished Name Suffix field contains LDAP naming information. There is also a preview field to enable you to preview the distinguished name as it will be. The Validity Period controls at the bottom of the dialog box allow you to set the validity interval for your CA's certificate.

FIGURE 8.5 CA Identifying Information page

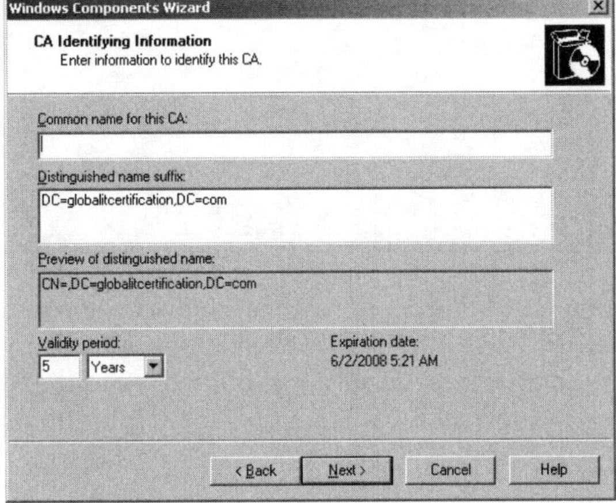

You *cannot* change any of this identifying information once the CA is installed, because it's all encoded into the CA's certificate. Make sure the information you enter here is correct!

If you choose an organization name that includes special characters (i.e., &, *, [,], etc.), the CA has to encode them with Unicode, because the X.509 standard for PKI certificates requires it. This might make some older (or broken!) applications unable to verify your CA certificate, so Setup will warn you and give you a chance to change the CA name before proceeding.

9. Click the Next button after you've filled in enough information to identify your CA.
10. The Certificate Database Settings page (see Figure 8.6) allows you to choose where on your server these database files reside. The CA stores its certificates in a database file, and you get to choose where that database resides on the disk. Note that this database contains the CA's certificates, not the certificates it issues—those are published in Active Directory or wherever else you specify. The Store Configuration Information In A Shared Folder checkbox allows you to force the CA to use a shared folder for storing the certificates it emits. This is handy if you're not using Active Directory or if you have clients that expect to get certificates only from a file on disk somewhere.

FIGURE 8.6 Certificate Database Settings page

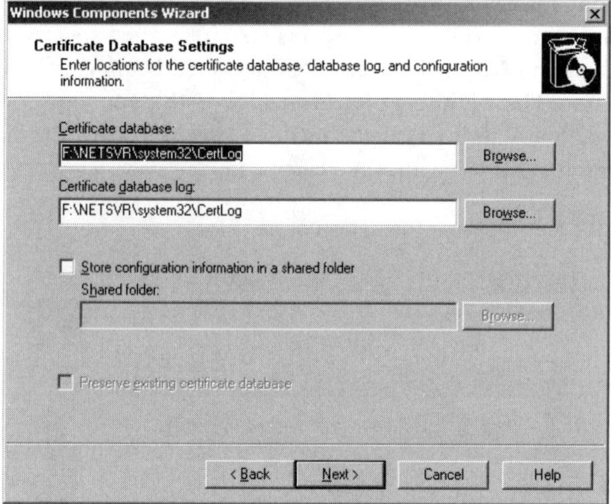

11. The Preserve Existing Certificate Database checkbox lets you reinstall the CA on top of an existing installation. For example, if you have a machine that you want to convert from stand-alone to enterprise mode, or if you need to reinstall to change the CA's name or Active Directory membership, checking this box tells setup not to erase the old certificates.

Make sure whatever location you specify is on an NTFS disk volume and that it gets backed up regularly. If you lose a CA's certificates, you'll have to reissue all the certificates ever issued by that CA.

12. Once you're happy with the settings on all of the preceding pages, click the Next button. If you're currently using the Internet Information Service (IIS) WWW service, setup will stop it for you so it can finish the installation. If you are not using IIS, Setup will inform you that you must install it if you want to use the Web enrollment component of certificate services. Once the setup is complete, you'll need to restart your machine. From then on, the CA service will automatically start whenever the server does.

Installing the Certificates and Certification Authority Snap-Ins

Managing Microsoft Certificate Server involves using two different, but related, Microsoft Management Console (MMC) snap-ins: the Certificates snap-in for managing certificates and the Certification Authority snap-in for managing the CA itself. The process for installing the two snap-ins is identical, and you can usually keep them together in a single console file so that you can quickly manage all certificate-related functionality on a machine at once.

Certificate Templates are managed separately through the Certificate Templates snap-in, as well as through the Certificate Templates node in the appropriate Active Directory snap-in for the object to be managed.

You have already seen how to install MMC snap-ins earlier in this book, and you install the certificates and CA snap-ins using the same procedure. One slight difference is that you must specify the CA to manage. The local server is selected by default, but you may need to change this if you need to manage a remote CA. You should install the snap-ins before proceeding to the next section.

To manage all three certificate types—for user, computer, and service accounts—from a single MMC, just add three instances of the Certificates snap-in.

Once you've installed the Certificate Server and the CA snap-in, you're ready to configure and manage your CA. The snap-in interface is shown in Figure 8.7, and it looks very much like every other MMC snap-in. In the left half of the console window, you'll see one node for each CA running on the server you're managing.

FIGURE 8.7 The Certification Authority snap-in

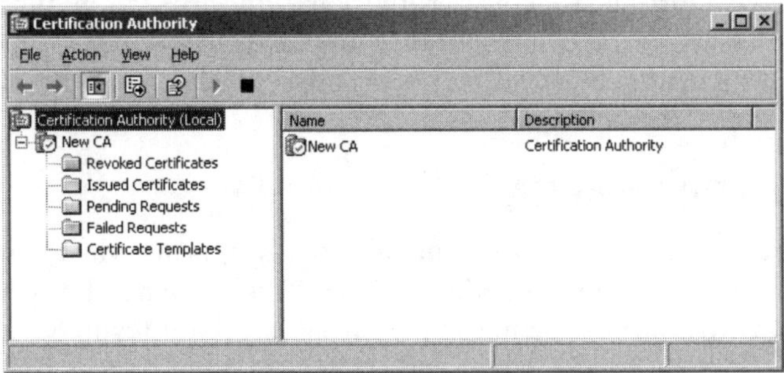

If you expand any one of those CA nodes, you'll see the following five folders below it:

Revoked Certificates This folder holds all certificates that have been revoked by this CA. Once revoked, a certificate can't be unrevoked; it will stay on the CRL forever.

Issued Certificates This folder lists the certificates that this CA has issued since its installation. Double-clicking a certificate shows its properties, and right-clicking a certificate allows you to revoke it.

Pending Requests This folder lists the requests that are queued on the CA, waiting for you to approve or disapprove them. Enterprise CAs will never have any items in this list, but standalone CAs may display zero or more requests at any given time.

Failed Requests This folder lists all the requests that failed *or* were rejected, including the CN, e-mail address, and submission date of the failed request.

Certificate Templates This folder shows the certificate templates that are available for use on this server. You may change the set of available templates by right-clicking the Policy Settings folder and using the New ➤ Certificate To Issue Or Delete commands. Double-clicking a template shows you the certificate purposes available with that certificate, but there's no way to change the template directly.

Each folder actually expands into a list, and you can customize the list's columns and fields using the View submenu on the context menu. To do this, right-click the folder, and then select the Choose Columns and Customize commands until you have the list configured the way you want it. You can also define filters using the View ➤ Filter command; for example, you could create a filter that showed only certificates that were due to expire after a particular date.

Controlling the CA Service

Because MCS is just another Windows Server 2003 service, you can configure it to start whenever you want. The installer automatically configures the service to start when the system starts; for extra security, you can set it to start manually so that it can only issue certificates when you want it to do so.

As with every other Windows Server 2003 service, you can use the Services item in the Computer Management snap-in to start and stop the services, set recovery options for it when it stops, and change the account used to run it. You can also do most of these functions, plus some other useful ones, directly from the Certification Authority snap-in. When you right-click a CA, you gain access to several commands that simplify your day-to-day management tasks; commands to perform the following tasks appear under the All Tasks submenu of the Context menu you get when you right-click the CA.

Switching to a Different CA

The Retarget Certification Authority command actually appears when you right-click the Certification Authority node, not an individual CA. This command lets you point the snap-in at a different CA; you may remember that during installation you have to specify which CA you want to manage, and this is how you change it. When you use this command, you'll be able to browse the network and change to any CA to which you have management rights.

Starting/Stopping the Service

In addition to starting and stopping the CA from the Services item in Computer Management or from the command line, you can use the Start Service and Stop Service commands from the context menu or simply right click your CA's name, select All Tasks and then Start or Stop Service. These operations take effect immediately; you don't get a chance to change your mind or confirm your command.

Backing Up and Restoring CA Data

Performing a solid backup of the CA's data is a two-step process, and it involves two separate tools. Although this seems more complicated than necessary, performing good backups is critical. If you lose the CA's certificates, you won't be able to issue, renew, or revoke certificates for that CA's domain. Of course, backing up data is pointless unless you have the ability to restore it when you need to do so.

Backing Up the CA

The two-step process of backing up the CA is conceptually simple. First, you use the Certification Authority Backup Wizard to make a usable copy of the CA's data. Because the CA keeps its files open when it's running, you can't just copy the files unless you stop the service; however, the wizard can copy the needed data while the service is running.

To begin this first step, right-click the CA's name, select All Tasks, and then use the Backup CA command. After an introductory wizard page, you'll see the Items To Back Up page, as shown in Figure 8.8. Use it to specify what you want backed up.

FIGURE 8.8 The Items To Back Up page

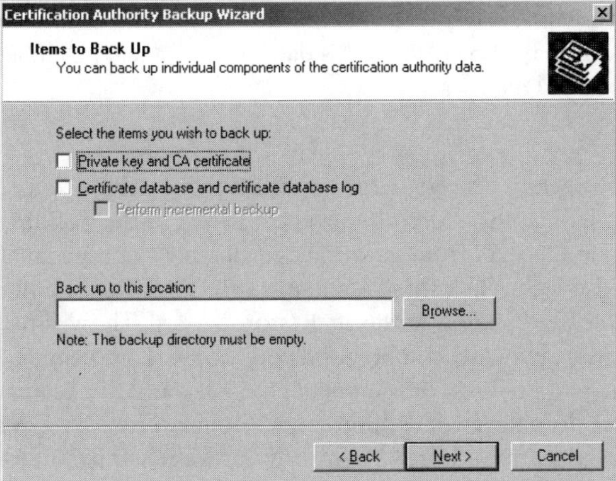

The following settings specify what should be backed up:

- The Private Key And CA Certificate setting specifies that you want to back up the CA's private key and the associated certificate. If you choose this option, the wizard will ask you for a password that it uses to encrypt the private key and certificate data and store it in a PKCS#12 file.
- The CA keeps log files that record certificate issuance and revocation. It also keeps a queue of pending requests. If you want these backed up (and you should, because losing the queue means end users will have to resubmit their requests, and losing the logs means you lose historical information about certificate issuance), check the Certificate Database And Certificate Database Log checkbox.

  If you choose to back up the log and queue files, you can further specify whether you want to back up the entire set of files at each backup (the default) or only those items that have changed since the previous backup (by checking the Perform Incremental Backup checkbox.) Incremental backups reduce the amount of data required for your regular backups, but you must still do at least one nonincremental backup. We recommend doing incremental backups during the week, with full backups either at the week's beginning or its end.
- The Back Up To This Location field (and the associated Browse button) lets you specify where you want the backed-up data to go. You must specify an empty directory; the wizard will put a file named `caName.p12` (containing the private key and certificate) and a directory named `DataBase` (which contains the actual logs, queues, and CA database) in the location you provide. You can't store multiple backups in the same directory.

Once you've chosen the appropriate settings, click the Next button. If you chose to back up the private key material, you'll be prompted to enter a password to secure the data on disk. Once you've done that (if necessary), you'll see a summary page; clicking its Finish button will actually perform the backup.

Once you've used the Certificate Authority Backup Wizard to make a backup of your CA data, the second necessary step is to use Windows Server 2003 Backup tool (or another backup tool, such as ARCserve or BackupExec) to back up your CA data to disk, tape, CD-RW, or whatever media you use for backup. Don't skip this step—all the Certificate Authority Backup Wizard does is make a clean copy of the CA's data on your local machine where it's no more protected than the original data was.

Restoring the CA

A restore reverses the backup process, returning the target machine to its original backed-up state. Restoring CA data is, therefore, the reverse process of the backup process. First you restore your backed-up CA data from its storage media, for example, by using the Windows Backup tool. Then you right-click the CA's name, select All Tasks, and use the Backup CA command to launch the Certification Authority Restore Wizard. The wizard allows you to restore whatever you've backed up, in any combination you choose. For example, you can restore just the queue; the queue and the logs; or the queue, the logs, and the key material.

The actual process does have some differences, though. First, the CA service has to be stopped to use the Certificate Authority Restore Wizard; the wizard offers to do this for you. The most important page of the wizard is the Items To Restore page, shown in Figure 8.9. You can specify what you want to restore; you must also use the Restore From This Location controls to tell the wizard where to find the specific backup from which you want to restore.

FIGURE 8.9 The Items To Restore page

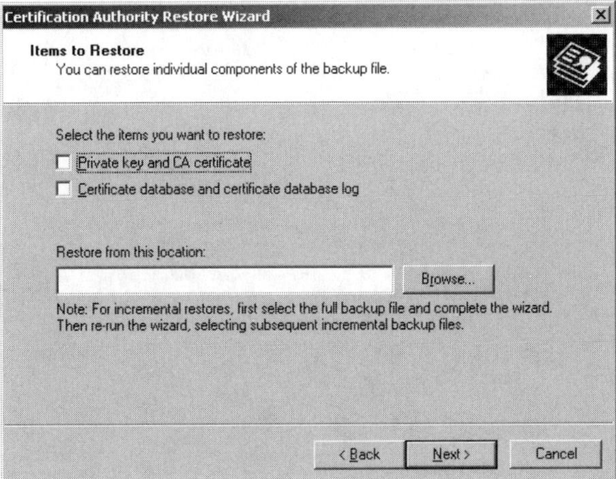

If you want to restore several incremental backups in a row—as you might need to if it's been awhile since your last full backup—you must first restore the correct full backup, then restore each of the incremental backups that match it, in the right order. To facilitate this process, you might want to name your CA backups with a code that indicates the date when the backup was made.

Renewing the CA Certificate

Like real-world credentials, certificates eventually expire. When you control the CA, you get to control the expiration interval for certificates it issues, which can be pretty handy. CA certificates aren't exempt from this process, so it's likely that you'll need to renew your CA certificates periodically. For subordinate CAs, renewal is accomplished by requesting a new certificate from the issuing CA, but root CAs get to renew their own certificates. There are two ways to accomplish this:

- The CA can take its existing keys and bind them to a new certificate. This is the most common option, because it allows you to keep reusing the existing keys for signature verification and signing. If you do this enough times, though, the CA's CRL can grow very large, and that slows performance of all your PKI components.
- The CA can generate a new key pair and use it to create a new certificate. This option is useful when you want or need to generate a new key (say, because you fear the old one has been compromised). In essence, this is equivalent to creating a brand-new CA because there's a new key and certificate.

To begin the renewal process, just right-click the CA whose certificate you want to use and select the Renew CA Certificate command. You'll be reminded that the CA must be stopped to renew the certificate, then you'll see a dialog box like the one shown in Figure 8.10. You use this dialog box to specify whether or not you want to create a new key pair for the new certificate. You can't change the CSP but you can increase the key length in this dialog box.

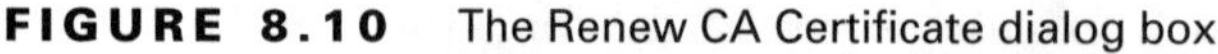

FIGURE 8.10 The Renew CA Certificate dialog box

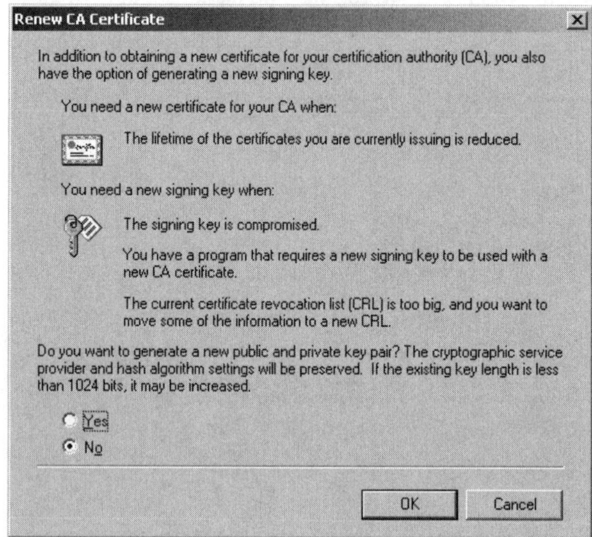

Configuring the CA

CAs have a number of configurable properties that control how they behave. Most of these settings have reasonable default values, but there are times when you might need to change them. All of the CA's properties, including its policy and exit module settings, are available through the Properties dialog box that appears when you select a CA and use the Properties command (either from the Action menu or the context menu).

In the following sections, we will look at the various CA properties and how to set them. In additon, we will see how to configure CA templates and CAs.

Setting General Properties

The first thing you'll see in the CA Properties dialog box is the General tab, shown in Figure 8.11. Most of the information here is strictly for reference—although the tab shows you the name and description for the CA, along with the CSP and hash algorithm in use, you can't change them. You can view the CA certificate's details with the View Certificate button.

Setting Policy Module Properties

The Policy Module tab, as seen in Figure 8.12, shows you which policy module is active, and it lets you configure the current module or change to another one altogether. The selected policy module will almost always be the Enterprise And Stand-alone Policy module that Microsoft supplies with Windows Server 2003 (unless you wrote your own or bought a replacement from a third party). In that case, use the Select button to pick a new policy module from the list of those registered with the system.

FIGURE 8.11 The General tab of the CA Properties dialog box

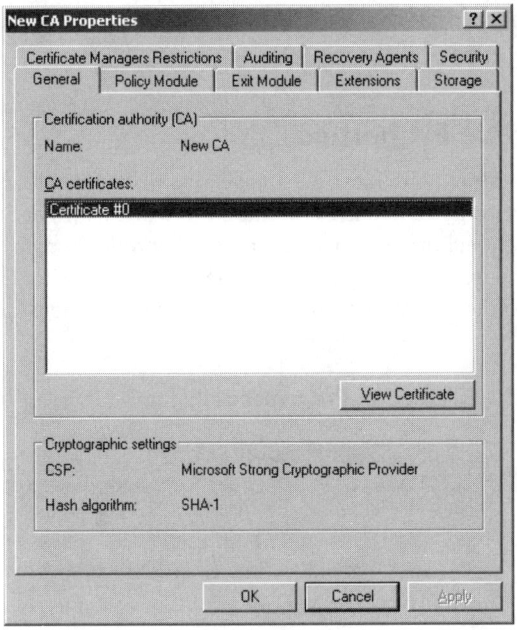

FIGURE 8.12 The Policy Module tab of the CA Properties dialog box

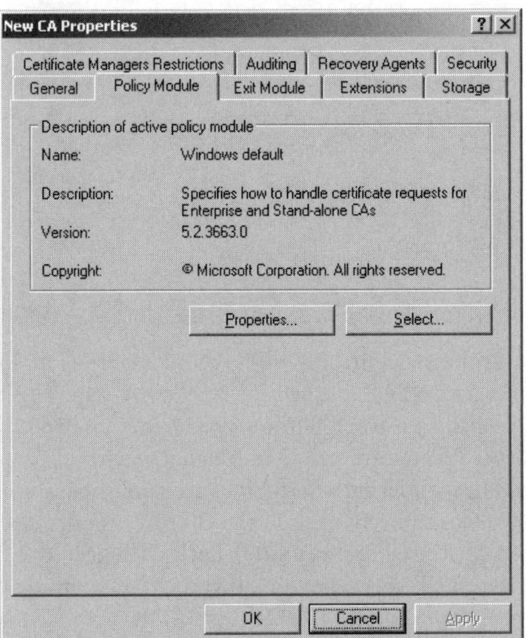

The Properties button allows you to set options for whichever policy module you have installed. The properties in this dialog box change according to what module is installed.

Setting Exit Module Properties

The Exit Module tab, as shown in Figure 8.13, is very similar to the Policy Module tab; it shows you which exit modules you've currently configured to work with your CA. A CA can use only one policy module at a time, but it may use several exit modules, which are executed in a series. For example, you could use the Microsoft policy module to publish newly issued certificates to Active Directory and the file system, then use your own module to publish certificates on a Web page or in an Exchange public folder.

FIGURE 8.13 The Exit Module Properties dialog box

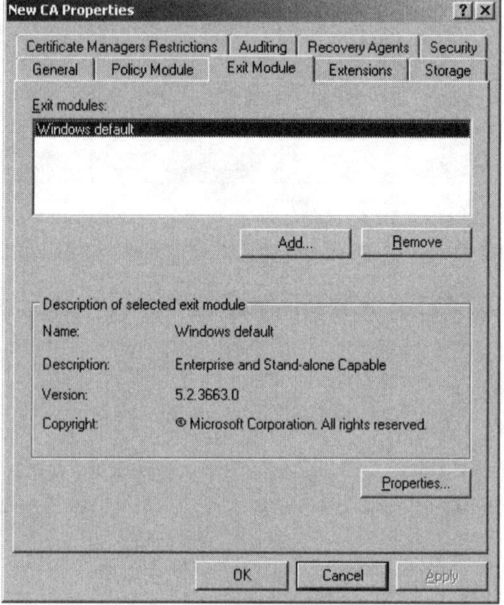

When you click the Properties button, you'll see a Properties dialog box with only one checkbox: Allow Certificates To Be Published To The File System. This checkbox lets you specify that you want new certificates stored in the shared folder you specified when you installed the CA. Otherwise, the certificates are stored in Active Directory.

At this point, you may be wondering where CRLs are published, since there's no explicit way for you to specify their disposition. By default, the CA always puts newly generated CRLs in `systemroot\system32\certserv\certEnroll`. Each CRL gets a name that starts with the letter "c" and includes the date it was generated. If you generate multiple CRLs on one day, the CA adds a suffix number. For example, `c030214.crl` is the only CRL published on 14 February 2003, while `c030311.crl` is the fifth CRL published on 11 March 2003. The CRLs will be available to LDAP and HTTP clients (according to the CDPs you specified), and you can take the generated files and publish them wherever you like.

Viewing Storage Properties

The Storage tab, shown in Figure 8.14, shows the paths where the CA is keeping its configuration and certificate database files. You can't change these values after the CA is installed, but it might be useful to have a way to double-check the file locations in case you need them, and this is the quickest way to do so. There *is* one thing you can change here: If your CA is a stand-alone CA running on a computer with Active Directory access, checking the Active Directory checkbox will move the CA's configuration information into the directory.

FIGURE 8.14 The Storage tab of the CA's Properties page

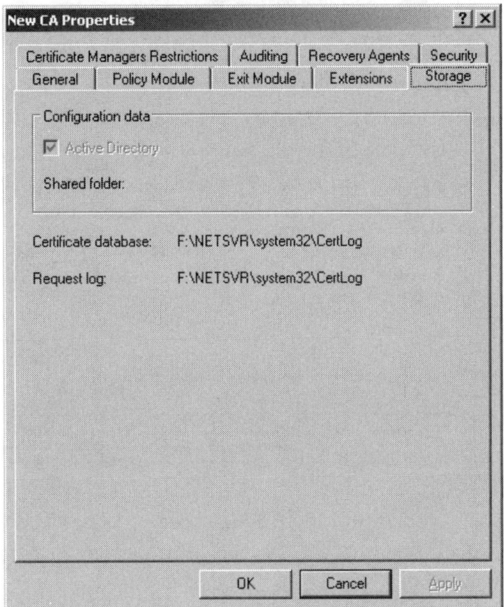

Setting Security Properties

Like practically everything else in Windows Server 2003, MCS servers can be assigned their own set of permissions that control who can see and change the information the CA owns. These permissions are managed through the Security tab, shown in Figure 8.15. Table 8.3 shows the 12 permission settings that you can apply to the CA; each permission allows someone who holds it to do something specific with the CA. Right out of the box, the following four groups have permissions to use the CA:

- The Administrators, Domain Admins, and Enterprise Admins groups have the Issue and Manage Certificates and Manage CA permissions.
- The Authenticated Users group has Request Certificates permissions.

There are also permissions for both CAs and certificate templates that you can configure in Active Directory. You access these permissions within the domain's Services ➢ Public Key Services ➢ Certificate Templates node or within the domain's Services ➢ Public Key Services ➢ Certification Authorities node. You can also set certificate-related permissions within the domain's Services ➢ Public Key Services ➢ Enrollment Services node.

FIGURE 8.15 The Security tab of the CA's Properties page

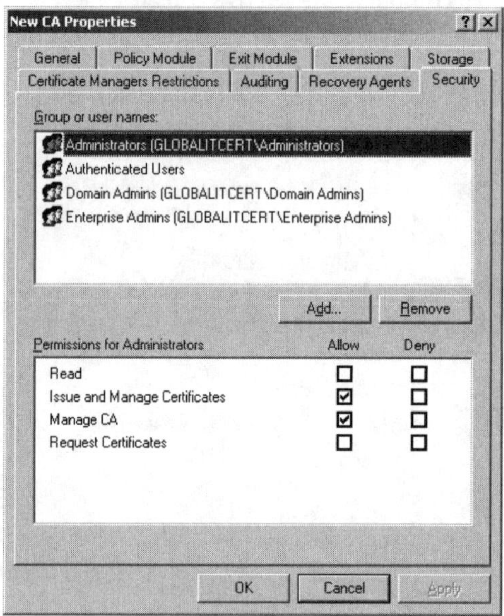

TABLE 8.3 CA Permissions that May Be Assigned to Users and Groups

Permission	Description
Read	Read certificates only from the database.
Request certificates	Request new certificates (for users or computers).
Issue and Manage Certificates	Issue, revoke, approve, and otherwise manage certificates.
Manage CA	Perform all tasks necessary to manage the CA.

Configuring Certificate Templates

Part of configuring the CA is telling it which certificate templates can be used and who can use them. When someone requests a certificate from your CA (as described in the "Requesting

New Certificates" section later in this chapter), they can request that the CA use any of the templates you've made available, and the issued certificate will be filled out according to the rules in the template. By adding and removing templates, and by setting permissions on the templates that are installed, you get control over what people can do.

Assigning Permissions to Templates

You set permissions on the CA itself using the CA Properties dialog box; however, to set permissions on the certificate templates, you have to leave the familiar environment of the Certification Authority snap-in. The Active Directory Sites and Services snap-in is where you actually adjust permissions for enterprise-wide services, including the use of certificate templates and other PKI components. You will adjust template permissions in Exercise 8.1.

You should perform this exercise on an enterprise CA.

EXERCISE 8.1

Assigning Permissions to Templates

1. Open the Active Directory Sites and Services snap-in.
2. Highlight the main node for the domain, then right-click the node and choose View ➢ Show Services Node.

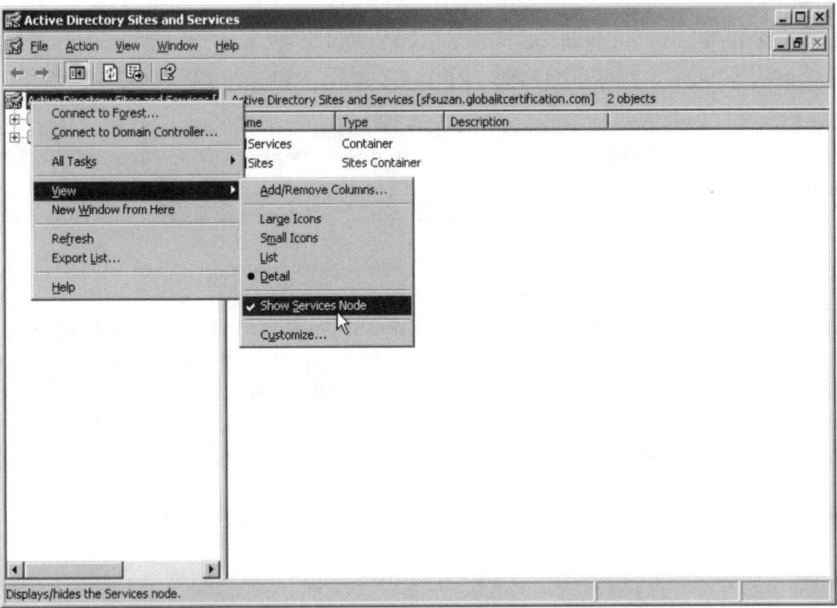

EXERCISE 8.1 *(continued)*

3. Click Services, Public Key Services, and choose Certificate Templates node. This fills the right half of the MMC window with a list of installed templates.

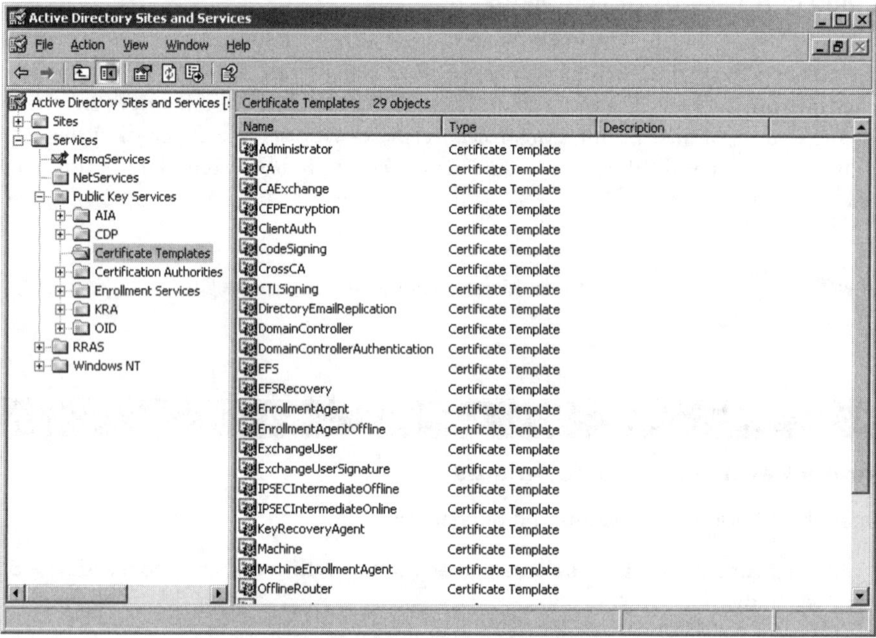

4. Right-click the template whose permissions you want to set, and then choose the Properties command. When the Properties dialog box appears, switch to the Security tab.

5. Adjust the permissions to suit your needs. To keep users from using the template to request new certificates, make sure that you deny the appropriate groups the Enroll permission.

Enabling Automatic Enrollment

Users aren't the only ones who have certificates; Windows 2000, XP, and Windows Server 2003 computers have them, too. Normally, you'd have to manually issue certificates for new computers as they join your AD domain, but this is a pain. Instead, you can use automatic enrollment to have the CA automatically generate a new certificate for each computer that joins the domain. To do this, you have to adjust a setting in the Group Policy Object (GPO) for your domain.

Exercise 8.2 shows you how to enable automatic enrollment for the CA.

You must use an enterprise CA in order to complete this exercise.

EXERCISE 8.2

Enabling Automatic Enrollment

1. Open the appropriate Group Policy snap-in, and use it to select the GPO for which you want to turn on automatic enrollment.

2. Open the GPO's Computer Configuration node, then open the Windows Settings, Security Settings, and select the Public Key Policies node. This exposes four subfolders beneath the Public Key Policies node.

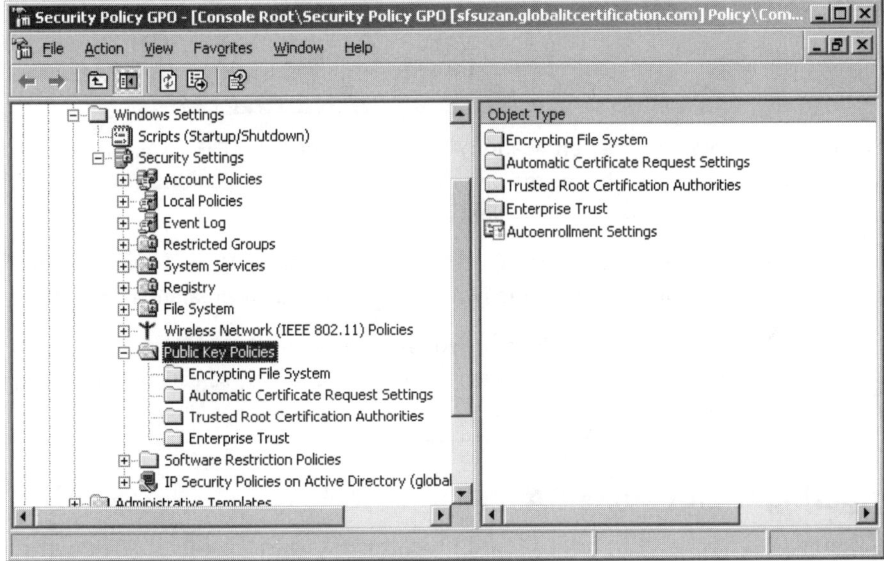

3. Right-click the Automatic Certificate Request Settings folder under the Public Key Policies node, and select New ➢ Automatic Certificate Request. This starts the Automatic Certificate Request Wizard.

4. Click Next to get past the wizard's introductory page. When the Certificate Template page appears, it lists all the types of certificates that can be automatically issued to computers. Normally, you'll use the basic Computer type, but separate types exist for domain controllers and devices that participate in IPSec. Select the template type you want to use, and then click the Next button.

EXERCISE 8.2 *(continued)*

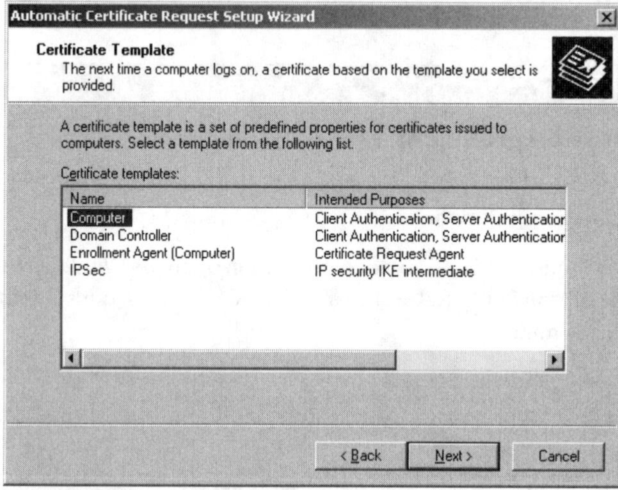

5. If there are multiple CAs, the Certification Authorities page lists all the CAs available in the Active Directory domain. Choose the one that you want to issue certificates for newly added computers, and then click the Next button.

6. When the Completing the Automatic Certificate Request Setup Wizard page appears, review your choices and then click the Finish button to actually create the request.

Once you've completed these steps, the new request appears as an item in the Automatic Certificate Request Settings folder; you can edit or remove it later by selecting it and using the commands in the Action menu.

Configuring Stand-alone CAs

Stand-alone and enterprise CAs have a few differences, about which you've already read. You need to know how to perform two additional tasks in order to configure a stand-alone CA, both of which pertain to handling incoming certificate requests.

Enterprise CAs always process incoming requests automatically. By default, though, stand-alone CAs tag inbound requests as "pending" and place them in the Pending Requests folder under the CA's node in the Certification Authority snap-in. Once queued, the requests will sit there until you either approve or reject them.

Configuring stand-alone CAs therefore requires setting the default action for new requests, and handling pending requests.

Setting the Default Action for New Requests

If you don't want requests to automatically be marked as "pending," you can change the arrival behavior by adjusting the controls on the Default Action tab, which you get to by clicking the Configure button in the Policy Module tab of the CA Properties dialog box (see Figure 8.8 earlier in this chapter).

Once you make this change, newly arrived requests will be treated in accordance with your instructions, but you'll still need to approve or reject any previously queued requests.

Handling Pending Requests

The process of approving or rejecting a pending request is fairly easy. Navigate to the Pending Requests folder in the CA snap-in and select it. When you do, all pending requests appear on the right side of the snap-in window. Right-click the request you want to approve or reject, and you'll see commands for either action.

Configuring Revocation and Trust

Issuing certificates is necessary if you want to use a PKI, but it's not the only thing you have to do. To get ongoing use and security out of your PKI, you have to decide which certificates and issuers you trust, and you need to be able to revoke certificates once their useful life span is over. You do these things by using two separate mechanisms:

- The Certificate Trust List (CTL) for a domain holds the set of root CAs whose certificates you trust. You can designate CTLs for groups, users, or an entire domain. If a CA's certificate isn't on the CTL, its trustworthiness depends on how you've configured your clients (either explicitly or through a GPO) to behave when presented with an untrusted certificate.
- The revocation function adds the targeted certificate to the CA's certificate revocation list (CRL), and a new CRL is published. Clients are required to check the CRL before using a certificate; if the certificate appears on the CRL, clients can not use it. This mechanism is very similar to the authorization mechanism stores use to verify credit cards.

In the following sections, we'll discuss trusting other CAs, managing the CTL, and managing revocation.

Trusting Other CAs

The Trusted Root Certification Authorities folder under the Public Key Policies node in the Group Policy snap-in contains a list of root CAs that you trust. Note that this isn't the same as a CTL (more on this in the next section); it's just a list of CAs that individual sites, domains, or organizational units may or may not trust. Because the set of trusted CAs for an Active Directory object is defined as part of the GPO for that object, you can designate exactly which Active Directory objects trust which CAs.

You can modify the Trusted Root Certification Authorities list in three ways:

- You can add new CA root certificates to it by importing them.
- You can remove a certificate from it.
- You can change the purposes for which the foreign CA is trusted.

You do all three of these things from the Public Key Policies node in the Group Policy snap-in. You can then do the following:

- To import a new root CA certificate and add it to the trust list, right-click the Trusted Root Certification Authorities folder and select All Tasks ➢ Import. Tell the Certificate Import Wizard how to find the new certificate; it will then load the certificate into the store and add it to the trust list.

We'll discuss certificate stores below in the Managing Certificates section.

- To remove a certificate from the folder, right-click it and choose Delete. You'll see a confirmation dialog box that warns you of the consequences of removing the certificate.
- To edit the list of purposes that a CA's certificates may be used for, right-click the CA's entry in the Trusted Root Certification Authority folder and open its Properties dialog box. By default, all purposes are enabled for newly added certificates, but you can control how these purposes are used by choosing either the Disable All Purposes For This Certificate radio button or the Enable Only The Following Purposes radio button.

The list of trusted root CAs is distributed by the GPO, which means that it is automatically available to all members of the group. Don't confuse this list with the CTL.

Real World Scenario

Planning a PKI Deployment with Active Directory

As the systems engineer for your organization, you are charged with the responsibility of setting up a PKI that allows for a hierarchy of trust that varies for different departments in your company. Specifically, the Marketing department has a business partner whose certificates they need to trust. However, the Engineering department must not trust any CAs other than the internal CAs. How will you provide a customized solution using Microsoft Certificate Services and Active Directory?

You could set up one GPO for your Marketing department that allows them to trust external CAs and another for the Engineering team that allows them only to trust internal CAs. Once you've added the foreign CA certificate to your local certificate store, you've instructed your clients to trust any certificate issued by that CA as much as they trust certificates issued by their own CA. This is a useful capability, because it allows you to trust CAs operated by other organizations without requiring that they share a common root. Because Windows Server 2003 Active Directory forests allow you to do essentially the same thing with domains, the combination of the two features allows you to selectively trust business partners, suppliers, or other "outside-the-fence" entities that need access to some, but not all, of your network resources.

Managing the CTL

The Trusted Root Certification Authorities list shows which foreign CAs you trust at all. The CTL shows that you trust how those CA's certificates will be used. Normally, you use CTLs to designate trust when your enterprise doesn't have its own CAs. If you do have your own CAs, you'd use the Trusted Root Certification Authorities list to establish the trust list.

When you add a foreign CA to your CTL, you're actually generating a new, digitally signed list that is stored in Active Directory and distributed throughout the domain. You manage CTLs with the Enterprise Trust folder under the Public Key Policies component in the Group Policy snap-in; although this may seem odd, it does make sense because the CTL is stored in Active Directory.

You can do two things with CTLs from the Group Policy snap-in: import a CTL from another machine, or create a new one. Both actions are available by right-clicking the Enterprise Trust folder. Then select All Tasks ➢ Import to use the Import Certificate Wizard (covered in more detail in the "Importing, Exporting, and Finding Certificates" section later in this chapter), or select New ➢ Certificate Trust List to create a new CTL.

Exercise 8.3 shows you how to create a new CTL.

You must perform the steps of this exercise on a domain controller.

EXERCISE 8.3

Creating a New CTL

1. Open the GPO snap-in. Right-click the Enterprise Trust folder. Then select the New ➢ Certificate Trust List command to start the Certificate Trust List Wizard. Click the Next button, and you'll see the Certificate Trust List Purpose page.

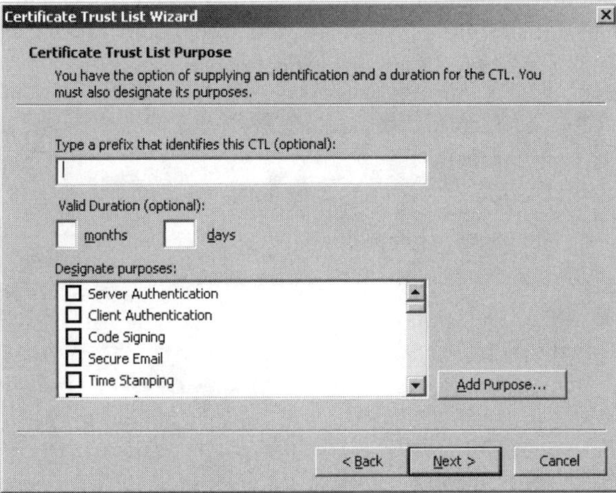

2. If you want to identify this CTL, enter a prefix for it in the provided field. If you want the CTL to be valid for a fixed period, enter its life span in the Valid Duration fields. If you want to restrict the purposes for which the certificate can be used, check the appropriate boxes in

EXERCISE 8.3 *(continued)*

the Designate Purposes list. By default, none of these purposes is specified; you must check at least one purpose to create the CTL. Click the Next button.

3. The Certificates In The CTL page appears. The Current CTL Certificates list shows you which certificates are on the CTL. A newly created CTL will be blank until you add some certificates by using the Add From Store and Add From File buttons. Click the Next button once you're done.

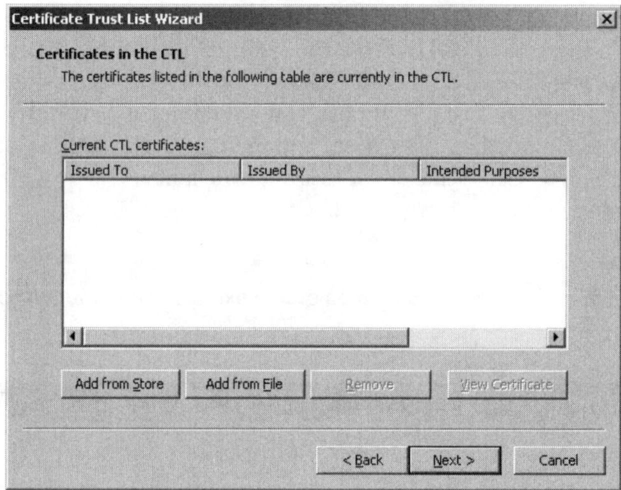

4. Next, the Signature Certificate page appears. You use this page to designate which certificate will sign the CTL. The Select From Store and the Select From File buttons allow you to riffle through your certificate stash until you find a certificate that's marked for use in CTL signing (look for the purpose marked "Microsoft trust list signing"). Click the Next button once you've identified the certificate you want to use.

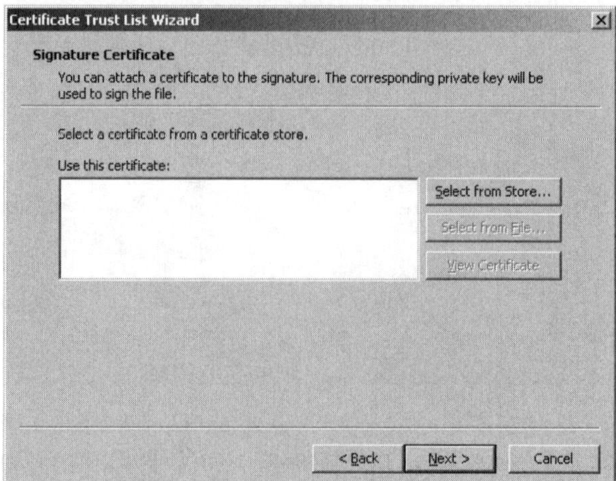

EXERCISE 8.3 *(continued)*

5. On the Secure Timestamp page you may choose to have the CTL marked with a secure timestamp, which guarantees the authenticity and integrity of the date and time recorded in the CTL. However, you must have access to, and the URL of, a secure timestamp service.

6. The Friendly CTL Name page allows you to enter a friendly name and description for the CTL; these items are displayed in the Group Policy snap-in whenever the CTL itself is shown in a list.

7. Once you've completed the wizard, you get the usual summary page. Clicking the Finish button will create the CTL and store it in Active Directory.

Managing Revocation

Certificate revocation is not something to be done lightly, because there's no way to reverse the procedure. Once revoked, a certificate stays revoked forever. Sometimes, though, revocation is necessary. For example, you typically need to revoke certificates issued to employees when they leave your organization or when they no longer need the particular certificate type you issued them. Whenever you have some reason to think that a private key may have been compromised, naturally you'll want to revoke the associated certificate as soon as possible.

In the following sections, we'll cover revoking certificates, publishing CRLs, and changing CRL distribution points.

Revoking Certificates

You can revoke any certificate issued by the CA you're managing; you cannot revoke certificates issued by other CAs because you don't have the ability to sign a new CRL for them. To revoke one of the certificates you've issued, open the Issued Certificates folder in the Certification Authority snap-in, then right-click the certificate and select All Tasks ➢ Revoke Certificate. You'll have the opportunity to choose a reason code for the revocation (the default is "unspecified," but you can also mark a certificate revoked for a specific reason, like a change of the user's affiliation or cessation of operations). Once you click OK, the certificate is *immediately* revoked.

Don't revoke a certificate unless you're sure you won't need it anymore! Your best bet is to first create a new test certificate, and then revoke the old certificate.

In Exercise 8.4 you will revoke a certificate.

EXERCISE 8.4

Revoking a Certificate

1. Open the Certification Authority administrative tool by selecting Start ➢ Administrative Tools ➢ Certification Authority. Expand the CA folder.

2. Open the Issued Certificates folder, and then select the certificate you want to revoke.

EXERCISE 8.4 *(continued)*

3. Right-click the certificate, and choose All Tasks ➤ Revoke Certificate.

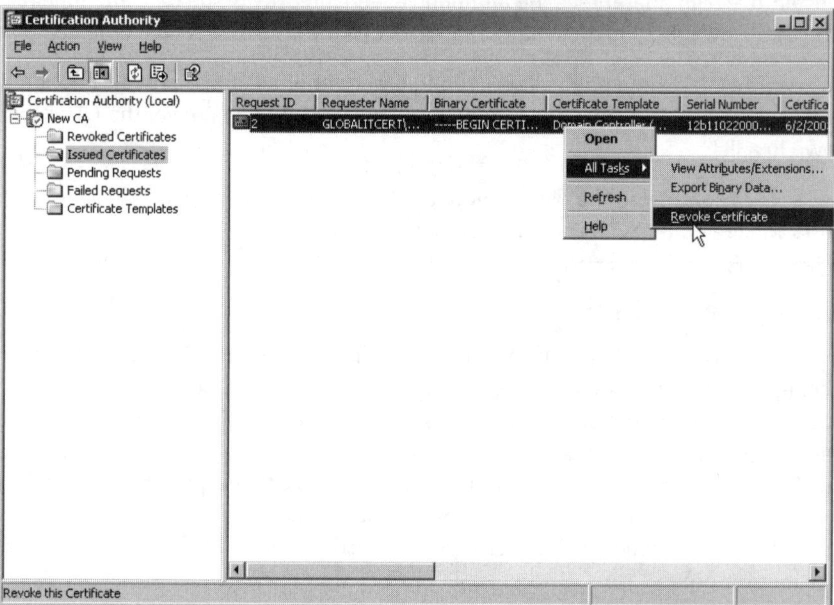

4. Select a reason code for the revocation, and then click the OK button.

Publishing CRLs

The CRL is simply a signed list of certificate serial numbers for those certificates that have been revoked. When you revoke a certificate, it's immediately added to the CRL, which is then resigned by the CA. However, the CRL isn't republished at that instant. The CA will automatically publish an updated CRL according to its schedule.

The CA's schedule is determined by the publication interval. When you right-click the Revoked Certificates folder in the Certification Authority snap-in, you can open the folder's Properties dialog box. The CRL Publishing Parameters tab, shown in Figure 8.16, provides options for the CRL publishing schedule. You can use these controls to adjust the publication interval for CRLs to anywhere from 1 hour to 9999 years (the default is 1 week).

Microsoft helpfully included some code that tells you when the next scheduled update will take place, so you can judge when that's going to happen. You can also configure the delta CRL schedule. *Delta CRLs* contain incremental CRL information; they only contain data that has changed since the last publication. This helps reduce network traffic if you have a large CRL. The default publication schedule for the delta CRL is one day.

You can see the list of CRLs in the View CRLs tab, shown in Figure 8.17. Each full and delta CRL is listed, unless the CA key is reused during a renew. To view the contents of a CRL, select it in the list and click the View CRL button.

FIGURE 8.16 The CRL Publishing Parameters tab

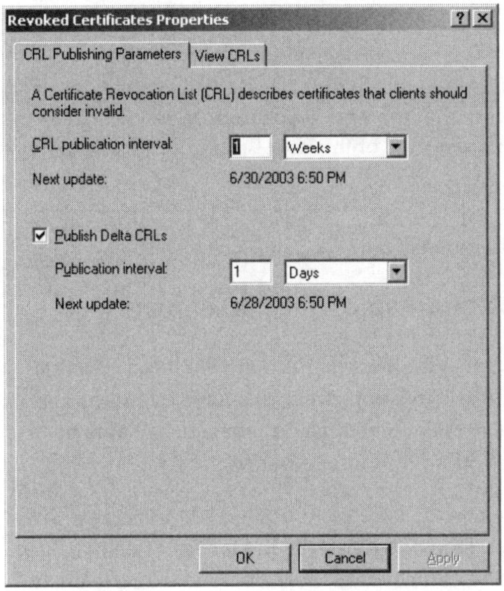

FIGURE 8.17 The View CRLs tab

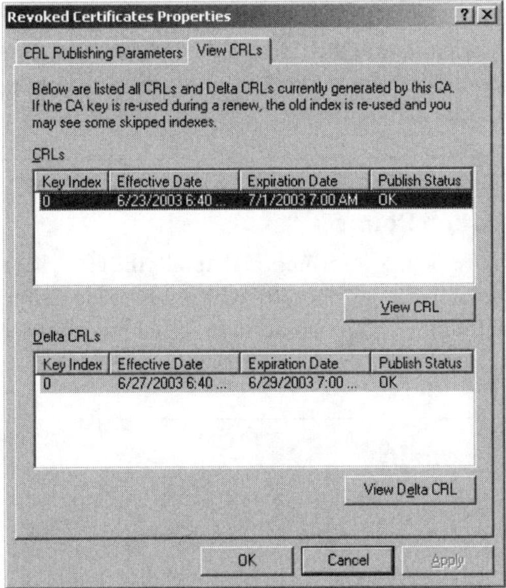

If you need to publish a CRL manually, you can do so by right-clicking the Revoked Certificates item in the CA snap-in and selecting All Tasks ➢ Publish command. You can choose to publish either the full CRL or the Delta CRL. The snap-in asks you to confirm that you want to overwrite the existing CRL; if you agree, the CA will publish the CRL to the set of CDPs that you've defined.

Clients still have to pick up the CRL from the CDPs, and that can take some time. Be aware that the time elapsed between selecting the Publish command and the actual arrival of the new CRL on client machines may vary.

Real World Scenario

Using Delta CRLs to Improve Client Performance

You are the systems engineer for an organization with large CAs that have experienced significant amounts of certificate revocation. The CRLs have become very long as a result, and this is causing a degradation in client response time because clients have to frequently download lengthy CRLs. What can you do to improve performance?

To resolve the burden on clients of frequent downloads of lengthy CRLs, you can publish delta CRLs. This enables the client to download the most current delta CRL and combine it with the most current base CRL to have an exhaustive list of revoked certificates. The client will ordinarily have a locally cached CRL, so publishing the delta CRLs can potentially improve performance.

The client applications must support the CryptoAPI in order to use delta CRLs. If the clients do not support the use of delta CRLs, you must take one of two actions: either do not configure the CA to publish delta CRLs or configure the CA to publish CRLs and delta CRLs on the same interval. This solution provides current CRLs to all applications and enables those applications that do support delta CRLs to use them.

Changing CRL Distribution Points

Certificate requests normally include information that tells the CA where to publish (or distribute) the certificate when it's done. However, because CRLs are solely a function of the CA, there's no external source for defining CDPs. You do that yourself with the X.509 Extensions tab of the Policy Module Properties dialog box.

Real World Scenario

Planning Is the Key to a Successful CA

Your network has a commercial Web site. Your manager also wants to support encrypted and signed e-mail in addition to the other methods of protecting your information resources. In the past you have helped people obtain VeriSign certificates for mail, but you think it's time to create your own certificates. You now plan to build a PKI to support the necessary certificates.

A CA is one of the most forward-looking services that you can deploy in your network. The concept of a validated digital identity is central to a distributed global information system. In the near future, a CA will be as ubiquitous in the enterprise network as a DNS or DHCP, and, of course, a directory service. Some organizations will outsource their CA service, just as they outsource their DNS service. However, as local services' dependency on certificates grows, most likely a local PKI authority will always be available.

The keys to a solid CA, as with a closely coupled directory service, are to plan, experiment, plan, and experiment some more. Remember that every time you create a certificate for an entity, it can be revoked, but the certificate itself should be kept and not deleted. This is part of the security and auditable architecture. For example, if you build a CA hierarchy and create certificates based on a specific directory structure and you then change that structure, you will most likely have to revoke all the certificates affected by the change and then create new ones. This will result in an ever-expanding CRL, which eventually will affect the performance of the CA.

One of the better strategies is to build a flat directory tree that is associated only with identity and then use other OUs of the tree to add the attributes that can define the identity with more clarity. For example, as users move around the organization, you can create a geographical OU with values representing the various locations and then have an identity attribute point to one of the location attributes in the geographical OU. This is the type of experimentation that needs to take place before you put a CA hierarchy into production.

Managing Certificates

Apart from the intricacies of managing your CA, you also need to be able to manage certificates for your account—including those issued to you. Windows Server 2003 implements a database of certificates, or a *certificate store*, for each user and computer account. This database contains end user and CA certificates and CRLs. (The certificates themselves may be stored in the local computer's Registry, in Active Directory, or in a database file, but they all appear as a single, seamless store.)

The Certificates snap-in allows you to manage the certificate store associated with your account, with a service account, or with a local computer. The snap-in also allows you to import and export certificates, request new certificates, renew existing certificates, and change various certificate properties. This particular snap-in is intended for use by end users and administrators; some of what it can do is duplicated in Internet Explorer 4 and later.

In the following sections, we'll introduce the Certificates snap-in and discuss how to manage certificates, including viewing and changing certificate properties, requesting new certificates, rekeying an existing certificate, renewing certificates, and importing and exporting certificates.

Introducing the Certificates Snap-In

Once you install the Certificates snap-in, you can begin managing certificates in the store you associated with the snap-in when you installed it. For example, if you install the snap-in to manage your certificates, you'll see it listed as Certificates–Current User in the MMC, as shown in Figure 8.18. The snap-in works the same way no matter whose certificate store you're managing, but (depending on the account you use) you may not have permission to do everything described in this section.

FIGURE 8.18 A Certificates MMC console window

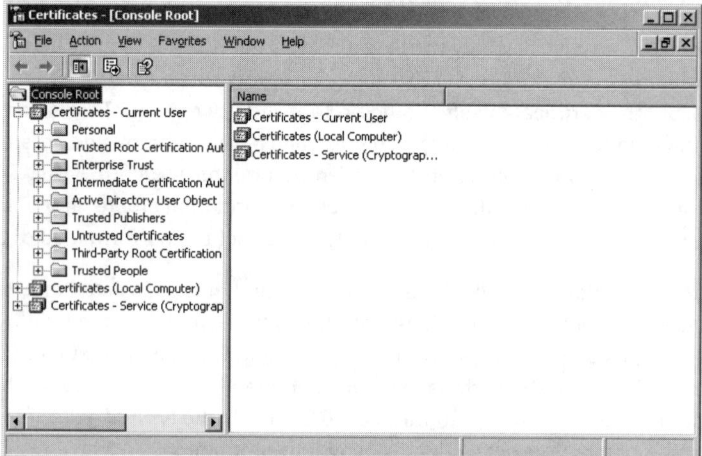

When you open the snap-in, you'll see a number of folders. The folders relevant to our discussion including the following:

Personal Folder This folder contains a subfolder named "Certificates," which contains certificates that belong to you (both those issued to you and those you've imported from elsewhere).

Trusted Root Certification Authorities folder This folder also contains a Certificates subfolder; it lists the roots you trust. Whether or not you can modify the contents of this list depends on the settings in the GPOs that apply to your account.

Enterprise Trust Folder This folder contains one subfolder, labeled "Certificate Trust List." Your GPO determines its contents, as it's loaded with whatever CTLs the GPO administrators have defined for you.

Intermediate Certification Authorities This folder contains separate Certificates and Certificate Revocation List subfolders. CA certificates and CRLs from CAs other than your own end up here.

Viewing and Changing Certificate Properties

The most common task you'll perform in the Certificates snap-in is probably viewing, and maybe even changing, properties for a particular certificate. Because the certificate contains a large amount of attribute data signed by the CA, many interesting properties are contained in each certificate. Viewing them and changing what you can change are two separate tasks:

- To see the certificate's properties, including the full path back to the top of the hierarchy and the certificate's attributes, double-click it or use the Open command on the context menu.

- To change the purposes the certificate may be used for, use the Properties command from the Actions or context menus.

This split in behavior seems a little confusing—after all, it would make more sense to view all of the certificate's properties with the Properties command. It makes more sense when you recall that the certificate's attributes are vouched for by the CA, so there's no way for you to change them without invalidating the CA's signature. You can view and change certificate properties on the General, Details, and Certification Path tabs of the Certificate Information dialog box, or in the Properties page of a personal certificate.

The General Tab

The General tab of the Certificate Information dialog box (obtained by double-clicking an issued certificate) appears in Figure 8.19. It summarizes what purposes the certificate can be used for by listing each purpose as a plainly worded bullet point. In addition, it shows the name of the holder, the name of the issuer, and the validity period for the certificate.

FIGURE 8.19 The General tab of a certificate lists the purposes for which the certificate is intended.

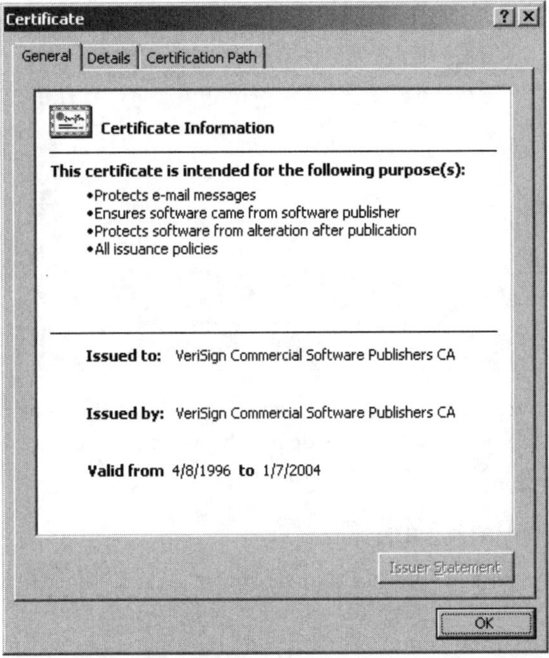

This page has a couple of interesting things to note. At the bottom of the display area, you may see a lock-and-key icon, along with a text message, if you have the private key that matches the certificate. The Issuer Statement button at the very bottom of the dialog box area allows you to view any message encoded into the certificate by the issuer. These statements, often called *certification practices statements (CPSs)*, normally set forth the terms and conditions under which the CA will issue certificates. Most large commercial CAs (like VeriSign and GTE) include CPSs in their certificates, and they can make interesting reading if you don't mind wading through lots of legalese.

The Details Tab

The Details tab contains the majority of the certificate information. Because each certificate object is a combination of an attribute name and a value, the centerpiece of this tab is a list of the attribute names and values. You can view the full contents of any field by selecting it; in Figure 8.20 you can see the full canonical name of the CA that issued the certificate.

FIGURE 8.20 The Details tab of a certificate lists its attribute names and values.

You can use the Show pull-down menu to control which attributes are displayed. By default, all of them are shown, but you can limit the display by asking to see only required extensions, all extensions, or old-style X.509 version 1 attributes.

The Certification Path Tab

Every certificate will be part of some kind of certificate hierarchy, even if it's a self-signed root certificate. Viewing the full hierarchy for a certificate is often useful, so you can see its exact provenance—much like you'd want to see the pedigree on an allegedly purebred puppy before taking it home.

The Certification Path tab, shown in Figure 8.21, shows you the complete ancestry of the selected certificate. The tab also warns you when one, or possibly more, of the ancestors of the current certificate isn't trusted. If it's displaying a certificate that isn't trusted, the Certificate Status field at the bottom of the tab explains exactly what's occurring.

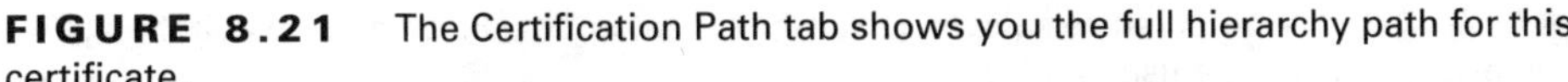
FIGURE 8.21 The Certification Path tab shows you the full hierarchy path for this certificate.

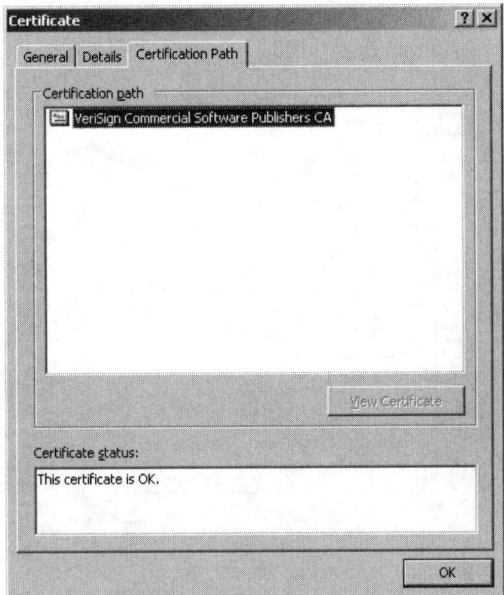

When you select a CA that's above you in the hierarchy, the View Certificate button in the dialog box becomes active. Clicking it displays a separate Certificate Information dialog box for the selected certificate.

Changing Certificate Purposes

If you use the Properties command on a personal certificate you'll see a dialog box very similar to the one in Figure 8.22. By choosing the appropriate radio button, you can change the specific tasks for which this certificate can be used:

- The Enable All Purposes For This Certificate button is set by default. When it's on, the certificate can be used for any purpose that's allowed by its issuer. That restriction exists because the issuer has control over which purpose flags are encoded into the certificate, so it's not possible for an end user to use a certificate for any purpose not provided for by the issuer.
- The Disable All Purposes For This Certificate button essentially shuts off the certificate, preventing its use for anything at all, without revoking or deleting it. This is a useful way to temporarily disable a certificate.
- The Enable Only The Following Purposes radio button, in conjunction with the list box below it, allows you to mix and match only the purposes for which you want the certificate to be used. The note above the list box explains that the listed purposes will be drawn from the purpose flags encoded into the certificate.

FIGURE 8.22 A personal certificate's Properties dialog box allows you to edit the list of purposes for which it can be used.

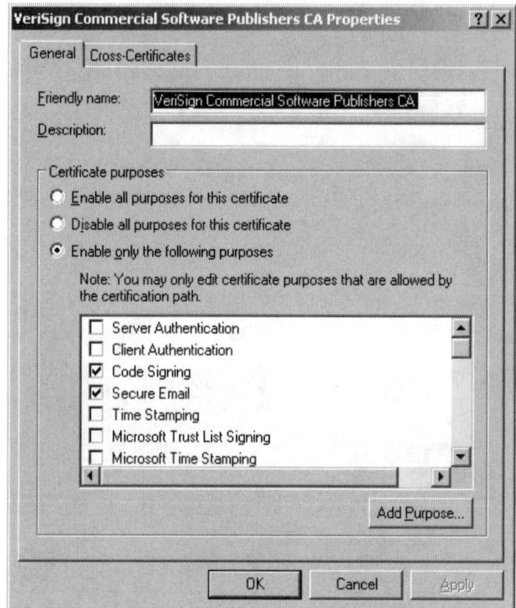

Requesting New Certificates

Requesting a certificate is simple, because you normally request one only for yourself. When you right-click the Personal folder, or its Certificates subfolder, you'll notice that the All Tasks submenu has an additional command: Request New Certificate. When you choose that particular command, you're actually starting the Certificate Request Wizard.

In Exercise 8.5, we will show you how to request a certificate using this wizard.

EXERCISE 8.5

Requesting a Certificate

1. Open the Certificates snap-in from an MMC console session using the Add/Remove Snap-In utility.

2. Right-click the Personal folder, and choose All Tasks ➢ Request New Certificate. The Certificate Request Wizard appears.

3. Skip the introductory page by clicking the Next button.

4. The Certificate Types page appears, listing all of the available certificate types that you can access. The contents of this list depend on what permissions have been set for templates in your domain. Pick a template from the list. If you want to specify that the private key for

EXERCISE 8.5 *(continued)*

this certificate should be protected, click the Advanced checkbox (do so for this exercise). Click the Next button when you're done.

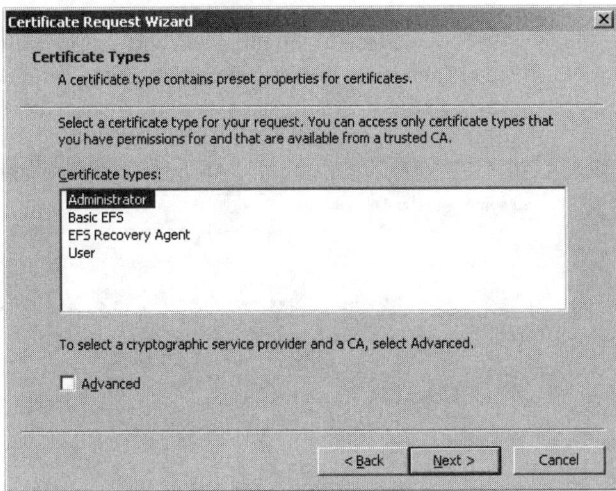

5. If you checked Advanced in the Certificate Types page the next thing you'll see is the Cryptographic Service Provider page, which lists all of the available CSPs. If you want to use a particular CSP to request this certificate, choose it from the list. More likely, you'll want to check the Enable Strong Private Key Protection checkbox, which forces the OS to alert you any time an application attempts to use your private key. You can also increase or decrease the key length from 1024 bits. Click Next when you've made the appropriate changes.

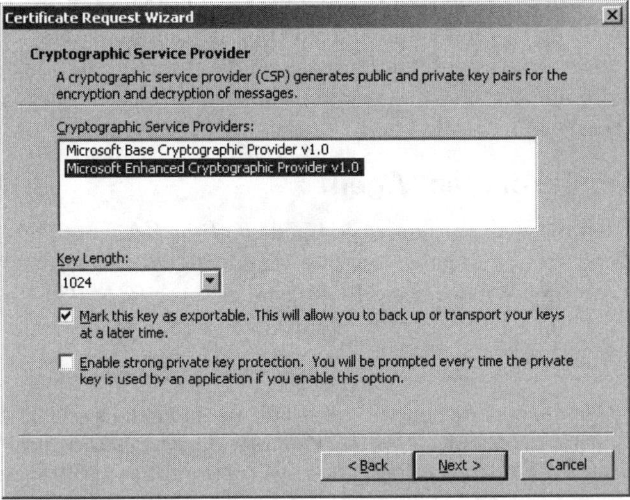

EXERCISE 8.5 *(continued)*

6. If you checked Advanced, the Certification Authority page appears, allowing you to choose the CA and computer to which your request will be sent. You can change them if you like. Click Next when you're done.
7. The Certificate Friendly Name And Description page lets you supply a friendly name and description for the certificate. These data won't be encoded into the certificate, but they will be stored with it so you can edit them later if necessary. Click Next to continue.

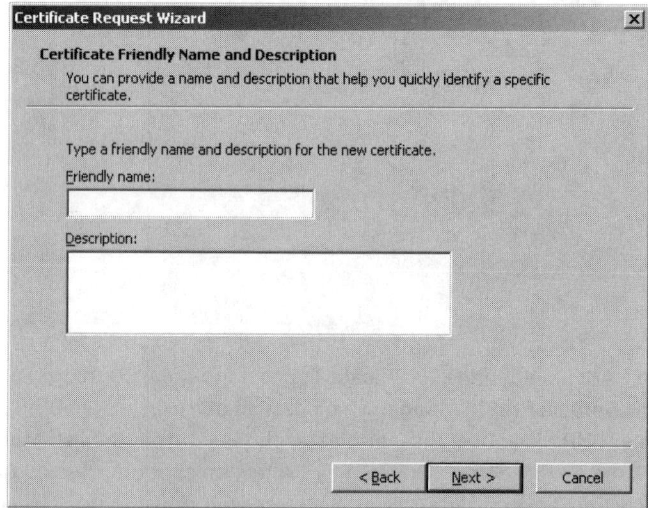

8. The Wizard Summary dialog box appears. Click Finish to send the request to your CA.

What happens next depends on your CA. If it's set to automatically process requests, you'll get either an error dialog box indicating that the request failed for some reason or a dialog box offering to automatically install the certificate in the store for you. If you're using a stand-alone CA that's set to mark requests as pending, you'll have to come back later and check the status of the request.

Using the Web Enrollment Agent

If you chose to install the Web enrollment component of the CA, your CA can also issue certificates to Web clients via a Web-based interface—assuming, of course, that your clients are all using Internet Explorer for Windows and IIS is installed on the CA. IIS is the web server built into Windows Server 2003. IIS is installed in much the same way as certificate services.

IIS is beyond the scope of this book. For full details on installing and configuring IIS, see the *MCSA/MCSE: Windows Server 2003 Environment Management and Maintenance Study Guide* by Lisa Donald with Suzan Rupp and James Chellis (Sybex, 2003).

By default, the CA pages are at `http://ca-name/certsrv/`, where *ca-name* is the name of the CA server in question. When you load that page, you see a welcome page that gives you three choices:

- The Download A CA Certificate, Certificate Chain, Or CRL task takes you to a set of pages from which you can download the current CRL, the CA's certificate, or the CA's entire certification chain.
- The Request A Certificate task leads you through a series of pages very similar to the ones in the snap-in's Certificate Request Wizard. One interesting difference is that you can use the Web interface to feed the CA a PKCS#10-format certificate request generated by another application; you can also take a private key that's already on a smartcard and request a certificate using that key pair.
- The View The Status Of A Pending Certificate Request task looks up any pending requests and tells you whether they've been approved or not.

You will see exactly how to issue a certificate with the web enrollment component in Exercise 8.6. Your server must be configured to use IIS in order to continue.

EXERCISE 8.6

Issuing Certificates

1. Install the CA and Web components, following the instructions in the previous "Installing the CA" section.

2. Open a Web browser and load the CA enrollment page (`http://ca-name/certsrv/`). If you're using Windows 2000, XP, or Windows Server 2003, the browser will identify you to the CA. If not, you'll have to log on to the domain; the browser will prompt for credentials.

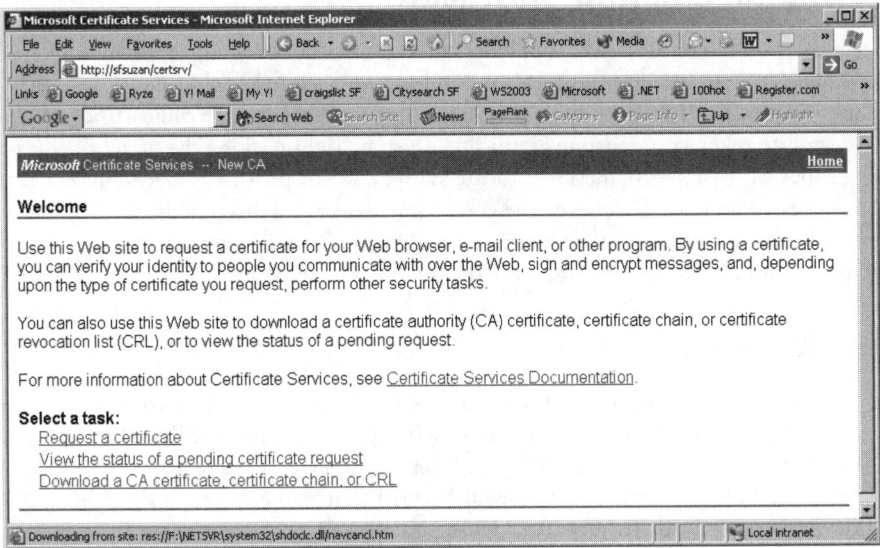

EXERCISE 8.6 *(continued)*

3. When the Microsoft Certificate Services page appears, click Request A Certificate.

4. In the Request A Certificate page, click User Certificate.

5. The User Certificate—Identifying Information page will appear. Click Submit and a summary page will appear telling you that the CA has all the information it needs.

6. If you have automatic certificate approval turned on, you'll see a page titled Certificate Issued with a link reading Install This Certificate. Click it and your new certificate will be downloaded and installed; if your CA requires approval, you'll have to go back and manually approve the request.

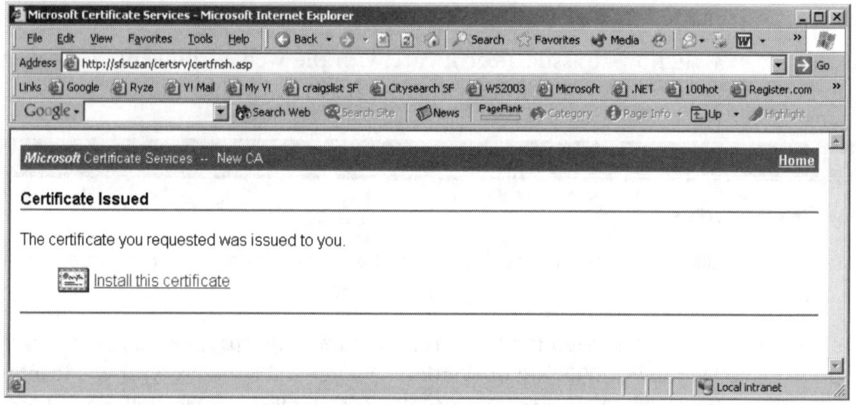

Rekeying an Existing Certificate

If you need to, you can request that your existing certificate be reissued, either with the same key or a new one. You might want to do this if you lose the private key, but not if you suspect it's been compromised (in that case, the right thing to do is to revoke the old certificate).

If you want to rekey your existing certificate, do so by right-clicking the target certificate and choosing either All Tasks ➤ Request Certificate With New Key or All Tasks ➤ Request Certificate With Same Key command. Whichever one you pick will take you through the Certificate Request Wizard again; the difference is that internally the wizard remembers that you want to change the key pair bound to the certificate, not issue an entirely new one.

Renewing a Certificate

Just as when you rekey a certificate, you can renew a certificate in one of two ways—by keeping the existing key pair or by requesting a new one. When you rekey, the certificate attributes stay the same, but the key pair may change. When you renew, some certificate attributes change.

Microsoft includes a Certificate Renewal Wizard that you can get to by right-clicking a certificate and using the All Tasks ➤ Renew Certificate with Same Key and All Tasks ➤ Renew

Certificate with New Key commands. In either case, the wizard starts by asking you to choose whether you want to use your CA's default settings or buck the trend by setting your own. While you might think the dialog box's text about "settings" and "values" applies to the expiration interval, it doesn't—it's really just a pair of radio buttons that act like the Advanced checkbox in the Certificate Request Wizard. If you choose the No, I Want To Provide My Own Settings radio button, you'll get to pick a CSP and a CA, just like you do when Use Custom Setting To Generate The Key Pair And CA Certificate is checked.

Importing, Exporting, and Locating Certificates

Your certificates can be added to your store when you request them. However, moving certificates in and out of your own personal store is frequently desirable. For example, assume that one of your users needs to exchange encrypted e-mail with a business partner. Neither you nor the business partner wants to cross-certify your CAs, so the easiest way to make the communications happen is to have your user export their certificate and send it to the other party, and vice versa.

The following sections discuss exporting and importing certificates.

Exporting Your Certificates

You may find it necessary to export a certificate from your store so that you can import it someplace else. The Certificates snap-in can export certificates and private keys in a wide variety of formats.

Exercise 8.7 shows you how to export a certificate to a file. In Exercise 8.8, you will import the certificate that you just exported.

EXERCISE 8.7

Using the Certificate Export Wizard

1. Right-click your certificate, and use the All Tasks ➢ Export command to start the Certificate Export Wizard. Click Next to dismiss the wizard introduction page.

2. If you're exporting a certificate for which you have a corresponding private key, you'll see the Export Private Key page asking you whether you want to export the private key or just the certificate. If you created your certificate with the Enable Strong Private Key Protection checkbox set, the Yes, Export The Private Key radio button will be grayed out because you can't export protected private keys.

3. Next, the Export File Format page appears so that you can choose the format for the exported certificate. If you're only exporting a certificate, your choices are as follows:

   - Plain binary X.509 format (labeled as DER Encoded Binary X.509 (.CER)). This format is just a bunch of binary data, so it's well suited for copying around on the network, onto removable disks, and so on. Most programs can accept CER files in this format, so this is a pretty portable choice.

EXERCISE 8.7 *(continued)*

- X.509 format, encoded using the base-64 encoding system. Base-64 encoding is used for moving binary data around in e-mail messages; in addition, some PKI components expect to see only base-64 certificates.
- PKCS#7 binary format (.P7B). This is the format used by most e-mail security tools, and it can contain many certificates in a single file—something that the CER files can't do. The Include All Certificates In The Certification Path If Possible checkbox causes the exporter to include as many of the intermediate and root CA certificates as possible in the output file, which makes it possible to deliver a complete end-to-end certificate chain to someone in a .P7B file.

4. If you're exporting a certificate with a private key, you get only one choice—PKCS#12 format (in the form of a .PFX file)—because the PKCS#12 standard defines a secure way to encrypt a private key and store it along with the certificate. When you use PKCS#12 format, you can use three checkboxes to control what else goes in the .PFX file:

- The Include All Certificates In The Certification Path If Possible option puts as much of the certificate chain as possible in the .PFX file.
- The Enable Strong Protection option turns on strong protection for the exported private key. A protected private key can't be exported, and the operating system will notify you whenever an application requests access to the key. This only works if you have Windows NT 4 SP4 or later, Windows 2000, XP Professional, or Windows Server 2003, all with Internet Explorer 5 or later.
- The Delete The Private Key If The Export Is Successful option removes the private key from your local store. Check this option when you want to permanently move a key pair someplace else (unchecking it will leave the certificate in place for future use) or you want to test export/import capability. Make your choices, and then click Next.

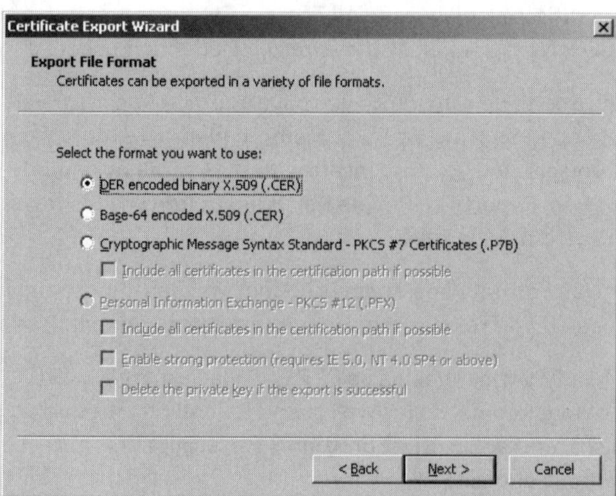

EXERCISE 8.7 *(continued)*

5. If you're exporting a .PFX file, you'll be prompted to enter and confirm a password on the Password page.

6. You must enter a filename for the exported certificate on the File to Export page. The default path on most machines is `C:\Documents and Settings\`*`username`*`\`.

7. Check the Confirmation page to double-check what the wizard is about to do, and then click the Finish button when you're done. The certificate will be exported, and you'll receive notice of the operation's success or failure.

Importing a Certificate

Importing certificates is the best way to move your certificates from some other computer or program into the Windows Server 2003 PKI. For example, if you have a VeriSign certificate that you've been using with Netscape Navigator on your home PC, you can export it and then import it onto your laptop so you can use it with Internet Explorer.

The Certificates snap-in can import certificates in several different formats. In general, the hardest part of using the Import Certificate Wizard is remembering where on the disk you put the file—the wizard takes care of all the details for you.

Exercise 8.8 shows you how to use the Certificate Import Wizard to import the certificate that you exported in the previous exercise.

EXERCISE 8.8

Using the Certificate Import Wizard

1. Start the wizard by right-clicking the appropriate certificate storage folder, and choose the All Tasks ➢ Import command from the context menu.

2. Skip the introductory page by clicking its Next button.

3. On the File To Import page, provide the full path and filename of the certificate file that you exported in the previous exercise, and then click the Next button. Alternatively, you can browse to the file by selecting the Browse button. You can import certificates in three formats:

   - PKCS#12 (.PFX or .P12) files are used to store certificates with their associated private keys. Outlook, Outlook Express, and Netscape's tools all produce PKCS#12 files when you export a certificate, as do many third-party PKI components.

   - PKCS#7 (.P7B, .P7C, or .CRT) files are used to store certificates without keys. A PKCS#7 file can contain an entire certificate chain (including CA certificates) or just a certificate—the application that creates the file gets to decide what goes in it. Almost every PKI component that runs on Windows can produce PKCS#7 files.

EXERCISE 8.8 *(continued)*

- Microsoft's own SST format, which is sparsely used.

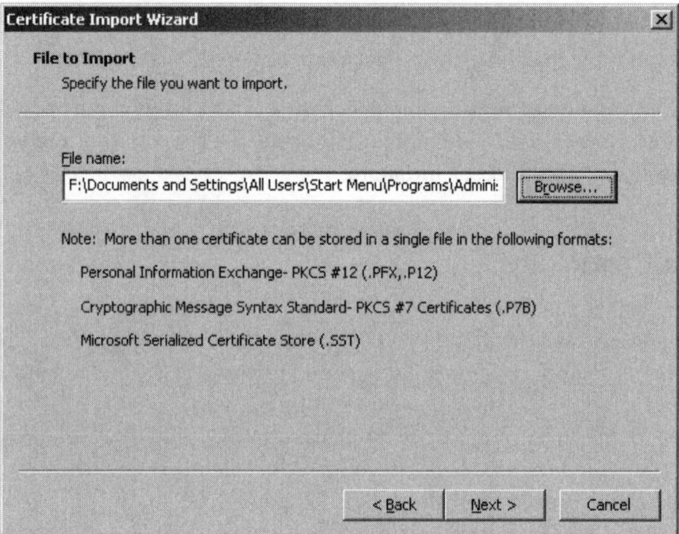

4. If you are importing a PKCS#12 file, the Password page appears and you will be prompted to enter the correct password. Use the password that you specified in Step 4 of the previous exercise. You can also enable strong private key protection and mark the key as exportable from the Password wizard page. Click Next to continue.

5. The Certificate Store page allows you to choose the store in which you want to put the certificate. You have two choices:

   - Choose the Automatically Select The Certificate Store Based On The Type Of Certificate radio button to let the snap-in determine the proper store for the certificate based on its type, issuer, and owner information. This is probably the easiest choice for ordinary use, especially since PKCS#12 and PKCS#7 files can contain multiple certificates.

   - Choose the Place All Certificates In The Following Store radio button, and then use the Browse button to locate the store you want to use. If you're sure where the certificate goes, this is the better choice (in fact, the snap-in sets this as the default choice if you select a certificate folder before you use the Import command).

EXERCISE 8.8 *(continued)*

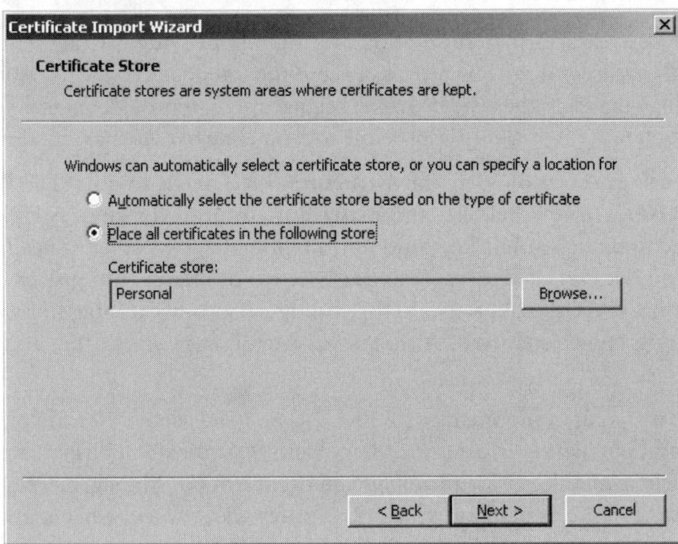

Once you've chosen the destination for the certificate, click the Next button.

6. The Completing the Certificate Import Wizard page is displayed. Click Finish to actually import the certificate. You'll get a dialog box indicating whether the import attempt succeeded or not.

Summary

In this chapter, you learned:

- The fundamental concepts of certificate-based authentication services, including what a certificate authority is, what solutions it provides, and how Microsoft's CA works.
- How to plan and manage a PKI using MCS. The planning process involves considering different certificate issuance requirements, planning for certificate enrollment and distribution, and planning for special solutions including the use of smart card authentication and security for wireless networks.
- How to install and configure the certificate server included with Windows Server 2003.
- How to configure Active Directory for certificate publication. Certificates are published to Active Directory by default. You can also use the `certutil -dspublish` command to publish certificates and CRLs.

Exam Essentials

Understand the key features that encryption and signing provide. Confidentiality ensures that encrypted data can't be read by anyone except the intended recipients. Authentication is used to verify the identity of the sender. Digital signatures can provide integrity as well as non-repudiation, which make it virtually impossible for someone to deny having signed a document.

Know the four things the public-key infrastructure (PKI) needs to do. The PKI needs to make it easy to issue, review, revoke, and manage trust levels for keys. A PKI offers a way for clients to find and fetch public keys and information about whether a specific key is valid or not. A PKI provides an easy-to-use way for users to use keys—not just by moving keys around where they're needed, but also by providing easy-to-use applications that perform public-key cryptographic operations for securing e-mail, network traffic, and other types of communication.

Understand the different components of a PKI. CAs issue certificates, revoke certificates they've issued, and publish certificates for their clients. Certificate publishers make certificates and CRLs publicly available, inside or outside an organization. Management tools allow you, as an administrator, to keep track of which certificates were issued, when a given certificate expires, and so on. PKI-savvy applications allow you and your users to do useful things with certificates, such as encrypt e-mail or network connections.

Understand the difference between an enterprise CA and a stand-alone CA. The enterprise CA acts as part of the PKI for an enterprise. It issues and revokes certificates for end users and intermediate CAs according to the policy and security settings that you apply to the CA. Stand-alone CAs don't require Active Directory access, because they're designed to do nothing but issue certificates for external use. A stand-alone CA is made to issue certificates to people who aren't part of your organization, such as Internet users or business partners.

Understand what certificate templates are. Certificate templates act like rubber stamps. By specifying a particular template as the model you want to use for a newly issued certificate, you're actually telling the CA which optional attributes to add to the certificate, as well as implicitly telling it how to fill in some of the mandatory attributes. Templates greatly simplify the process of issuing certificates, because you don't need to memorize the names of all the attributes you might potentially want to put in a certificate.

Understand CA roles in Windows Server 2003. Enterprise root CAs sit at the top of a certificate hierarchy. Although they can issue certificates to end users or subordinate CAs, normally they are used only to issue certificates to subordinate CAs. Enterprise subordinate CAs live in an enterprise CA hierarchy below the root. They typically issue certificates to computers and users, not to other subordinate CAs. Stand-alone root CAs stand alone, just as the name implies. They don't necessarily take part in your network at all, although they can be physically connected. Stand-alone subordinate CAs normally issue certificates to people. They usually don't take part in Active Directory, although they can.

Understand recovery keys. If the key used to encrypt a piece of data (on an EFS volume, in an e-mail message, or elsewhere) is lost, the recovery key can be used to decrypt the data.

Know how to install the Certificate Server. You install the Certificate Server using the Windows Components Wizard. After installing the server, you need to install the Certificates snap-in and the Certificate Authority snap-in management tools.

Know how to control the CA service. The Retarget Certification Authority command lets you point the snap-in at a different CA. You can use the Start Service and Stop Service commands from the context menu. The two-step process of backing up the CA is conceptually simple. First, you use the Certification Authority Backup Wizard to make a usable copy of the CA's data. Next, you use Windows Server 2003 Backup tool to back up your CA data to disk, tape, CD-RW, or whatever you use for backup. It's likely that you'll need to renew your CA certificates periodically.

Understand certificate revocation and trust. The Certificate Trust List (CTL) for a domain holds the set of root CAs whose certificates you trust. You can designate CTLs for groups, users, or an entire domain. The revocation function adds the targeted certificate to the CA's certificate revocation list (CRL), and a new CRL is published. Clients are required to check the CRL before using a certificate; if the certificate appears on the CRL, clients may not use it.

Know how to use the Certificates snap-in. The most common task you'll perform in the Certificates snap-in is probably viewing properties, and maybe even changing them, for a particular certificate. To request a new certificate, right-click the Personal folder and choose All Tasks ➢ Request New Certificate. The Certificate Request Wizard appears. You can request that your existing certificate be reissued, with either the same key or a new one. Just as when you rekey a certificate, you can renew a certificate in two ways: by keeping the existing key pair or by requesting a new one. Sometimes the easiest way to make communication happen is to have your user export their certificate and send it to the other party, and vice versa.

Be able to plan a PKI using MCS. Plan an MCS solution that meets specific needs. This involves considering different certificate issuance requirements, planning for certificate enrollment and distribution, and planning for special solutions including the use of smart card authentication and security for wireless networks.

Know how to configure Active Directory for certificate publication. Certificates are published to Active Directory by default for a CA that uses Active Directory. To publish certificates in a domain, the server on which the CA is installed must be a member of the Certificate Publishers group in Active Directory. The server is automatically a member of the Certificate Publishers group for the domain of which it is a member. You can also use the `certutil -dspublish` command to publish certificates and CRLs.

Key Terms

Before you take the exam, be certain you are familiar with the following terms:

algorithm
asymmetric encryption
authentication
certificate hierarchy
certificate policy and practice statements
Certificate Revocation Lists (CRLs)
certificate store
Certificate Trust List (CTL)
certification practices statements (CPSs)
cipher
ciphertext
confidentiality
cryptography
decryption
digest
digital certificates
digital signatures
Encrypting File System (EFS)
encryption
entities
exit modules
hashing algorithm
integrity
key
key escrow
Microsoft Certificate Services (MCS)
nonrepudiation
policy modules
private key
public key
public key cryptography
public key infrastructure (PKI)
recovery agents
recovery keys
root certificate authority
secret key cryptography
signing
symmetric encryption

Review Questions

1. You are the network administrator for a financial services company that has many prominent clients with vast sums of money. Information regarding the company and its clients must be managed with the utmost confidentiality. Your client contract guarantees this confidentiality. You have been charged with making sure that every internal transmission on the network between the employees associated with a particular client is accessible only to people who are appropriately involved with that client's information. You install an enterprise root CA with an enterprise subordinate–issuing CA and then deploy IPSec and EFS on all the systems in the company. This gives you encryption and authentication of all communication between employees, as well as security on the hard drive of each machine. In implementing EFS, you have created the recovery agent certificate and the necessary private keys on the initial Active Directory domain controller. What else can you do to protect the recovery agent private key for the entire domain in case it is needed to recover encrypted data from a person's computer after he leaves the company?

   A. Log on to the domain controller using the domain Administrator account and export the default recovery agent certificate to removable storage. Select the Delete The Private Key If Export Is Successful option.

   B. Log on to the domain controller using the local Administrator account and export the default recovery agent certificate to removable storage. Select the Delete The Private Key If Export Is Successful option.

   C. Log on to the domain controller using the domain Administrator account and export the default recovery agent certificate to removable storage. Select the No, Do Not Export The Private Key option.

   D. Log on to the domain controller using the local Administrator account and export the default recovery agent certificate to removable storage. Select the No, Do Not Export The Private Key option.

2. The security policy at your organization has been modified to include mutual authentication on all connections between servers and workstations on the private network. You have upgraded your network to Windows Server 2003 running in Native mode. Because you know that you have to implement certificates for the authentication, you install an enterprise root CA and an enterprise subordinate CA to issue the individual certificates for the network. You want each user's machine to automatically enroll for the computer certificate that's necessary for mutual authentication within the Active Directory domain. With this objective in mind, you configure a Public Key Group Policy for the domain. What do you need to include in this policy to meet your objective?

   A. Enable mutual authentication.

   B. Issue Enrollment Agent certificates for the domain computer users.

   C. Publish the CTL that includes the use of computer certificates in the domain.

   D. In the computer certificate template, grant Enroll permission to all domain computers.

3. You administer a Windows Server 2003 domain on which you have installed an enterprise root certificate authority and an enterprise subordinate certificate authority for secure e-mail. You believe that one of the private keys may have been compromised, and you need to invalidate the associated certificate as soon as possible. Which of the following actions must you take to invalidate the certificate? (Choose all that apply.)

   A. Publish a CRL without revoking the certificate.

   B. Enable strong private key protection.

   C. Revoke it using the Certificate Revocation dialog box from the Certification Authority MMC snap-in.

   D. Export the certificate to a floppy disk and lock it in a safe.

   E. Delete the certificate.

4. One of your users, Tammy, suffered a disk failure and lost her private key. She wants to continue using her existing certificate. This requires which of the following actions?

   A. Her certificate must be revoked.

   B. Her certificate must be reissued.

   C. Her certificate must be rekeyed.

   D. Her certificate must be renewed.

5. The Acme Investment Company is developing a whole new range of financial services on their Web site. They are going to offer their services to the public, and they want to have all the transactions done over the Internet to keep costs down. Their internal network is composed of 100 Windows XP Professional workstations and three Windows Server 2003 servers, one of which runs an Internet Information Server. The IIS Server is a stand-alone server because it isn't considered part of the internal network and it contains a database with client personal information. You want to provide a high level of security when users access the Web site. You also want to create the feeling that your site is a legitimate financial institution and you are in fact who you claim to be. To provide a solution, you plan to install a SGC certificate for your site. How can you obtain a SGC certificate for this situation?

   A. Install a stand-alone root CA and then obtain the SGC server certificate from that CA.

   B. Install an enterprise root CA with a child subordinate and obtain the SGC.

   C. Obtain the SGC from a commercial CA.

   D. Install a stand-alone root CA with a child subordinate and obtain the SGC from that CA.

6. The Risk and Mitigation Insurance Company has a Web site that is hosted on an Internet Information Server running on Windows Server 2003. This IIS server is a member of the single Active Directory domain network. The main pages on the IIS server are a series of personal questions (including medical, financial, and other personal history questions) that are needed to obtain insurance quotes. Before a potential customer fills out the application for the quotes, you guarantee that the information will remain confidential and that only the appropriate people within your company will evaluate the information. To ensure that only certain people in your organization can see the information, you need to build a CA. To provide this level of service, what kind of CA hierarchy look should you use?

   A. An enterprise subordinate child CA of an enterprise root CA

   B. A stand-alone child subordinate CA of a commercial CA

   C. An enterprise child subordinate CA of a commercial CA

   D. A stand-alone child subordinate CA of a stand-alone root CA

7. The Codeworks Company develops Java applets and ActiveX controls for Web browsers. These applications are sold over the Internet and are downloaded immediately after customers enter their credit card information. You obviously have a CA to provide security for the transaction, but you also want to offer signing so that customers can be sure that the software is coming from your organization. Your CA is set up with a root CA with an enterprise subordinate CA for issuing certificates. What should you do to provide the signing capability for your Web site?

   A. Request a User Signature Only certificate from your enterprise subordinate CA.

   B. Request a User Signature Only certificate from a commercial CA.

   C. Request a Code Signing certificate from your enterprise subordinate CA.

   D. Request a Code Signing certificate from a commercial CA.

8. Rajesh, one of your systems engineers, has set up a stand-alone subordinate CA for his users. Users started requesting certificates as soon as the CA was activated, but no user has received a certificate. What is the most likely cause of this problem?

   A. The CA is misconfigured.

   B. User requests have been going to the wrong CA.

   C. The certificates have been issued and published, but they have not yet returned to the users.

   D. The requests are marked as pending, so they're sitting in a queue for approval.

9. The Acme Law firm deals daily with very sensitive information about public figures. You have upgraded the firm's network from Windows NT to Windows Server 2003, and it consists of 200 Windows 2000 Professional workstations and 10 Windows Server 2003 servers. Although you have solid perimeter security, the partners are concerned about liability from internal people who are not related to clients and who obtain information improperly. Most of the employees aren't technically savvy, but the firm still wants the highest level of security to demonstrate good faith, in case a problem should develop. You plan to create a certificate authority hierarchy that will only be used internally to support IPSec encryption and mutual authentication. How should you set up the root CA so that it is most secure from internal access?

   A. Install a stand-alone root CA connected to the domain and then remove it.

   B. Install an enterprise root CA that is not connected to the domain.

   C. Install an enterprise root CA on a computer connected to the domain and then remove it.

   D. Install a stand-alone root CA on a computer not connected to the domain.

10. Acme revoked a user's certificate because she left the company. Then she came back. What's the best way to reintegrate the user into Acme's PKI?

   A. Issue her a new certificate.

   B. Rekey her old certificate.

   C. Manually remove her old certificate from the CRL.

   D. Regenerate a new CRL.

11. Your company is preparing to downsize in the wake of a merger with another company. You are the administrator of the Windows Server 2003 network that has Active Directory running. You are running an enterprise root certificate authority and an enterprise subordinate CA to issue certificates for authentication and access to internal Web sites. In order to protect the resources on the network, you need to invalidate the certificates for the people who will be leaving the company so that they can't access the network. How do you invalidate the users' certificates?

   A. Export their certificates.

   B. Rename their certificates.

   C. Revoke their certificates.

   D. Enable certificate protection.

12. You are responsible for protecting the data on your Windows Server 2003 network, which is used for the development operations lab of an aeronautics firm that is working on government contracts. Your perimeter is secure, as there is no outside access to the network at all. The network is used for internal purposes only, and there is no need to move raw data outside the building. However, the government requires that the data be kept secure at all times, which means that it must be secure on the wire and on the disks. To provide this level of security, you have implemented IPSec and EFS on the entire network. One of the researchers at the facility has vanished, and critical information that you need to obtain immediately is on his hard drive. Because you have configured the administrator as a recovery agent, you attempt to recover the data, but your attempt fails. What can you do to get the encrypted information from the hard drive?

    A. Install another instance of Windows Server 2003 and then retrieve the data.

    B. Delete all the recovery keys.

    C. Create a new recovery key with the missing user's certificate stored in the CA.

    D. Use the recovery agent's EFS private key.

    E. You can't recover the data, because back doors, even for special circumstances, defeat the whole purpose of truly secure data.

13. One of your systems engineers needs to restrict certain user accounts so that users can request only User certificates. To do this, she must use the ______________ snap-in to ______________.

    A. Active Directory Sites and Services; deny the users Enroll permission on everything except the User template

    B. Active Directory Users and Computers; deny the users Enroll permission on everything except the User template

    C. Certificates; remove the users' certificates

    D. Certification Authority; turn off enrollment for those users

14. John wants to restrict who can request certificates for users. What does he need to do to accomplish this?

    A. He needs to remove the Enroll permission from the Authenticated Users group.

    B. He needs to remove the Enroll permission from the Administrators group.

    C. He needs to remove the Issue Certificate permission from the Administrators group.

    D. He needs to remove the Enroll and Manage permissions from any groups he doesn't want to be able to issue certificates.

15. Ashley, a systems engineer in your organization, installed a CA on a Windows Server 2003 member server. She now wants to join an Active Directory domain. What effect will this have on the CA installation?

    A. It will have no effect.

    B. The CA will need to be removed and reinstalled.

    C. The CA will need to have its certificate reissued.

    D. The parent CA will need to be reinstalled.

Answers to Review Questions

1. A. Storing the key in the secure location is another step you can take that adds an extra layer of security. This also removes the recovery agent account. Selecting the Delete The Private Key If Export Is Successful option removes the key from the domain controller after it is exported. Obviously, you need to take care in where and how you store this key—a CD-ROM or Zip disk is preferable to a standard floppy. You need to log on with the domain account because you are dealing with the recovery agent for the domain. If you wanted the key for a specific machine, you would use the local administrator account for that machine.

2. D. Granting enrollment privileges to all the domain computers eliminates the need for the administrator to log on to each computer and request a computer certificate for the machine. With this privilege in place, each member machine of the domain has its own certificate that can be used to verify itself to other machines. Mutual authentication is the goal, but there is no switch that you turn on in the policy to accomplish this. Computer certificates by definition can be issued only to computers, not to users. Publishing the CTL only informs what certificates have been created; it doesn't convey the privileges or issue the certificates themselves.

3. C. When you want to invalidate a certificate, you must revoke it using the Certificate Revocation dialog box from the Certification Authority MMC snap-in. You must specify a reason for revoking the certificate; in this case, it is Key Compromise. After you revoke the certificate, you should manually publish the CRL, letting users know that the certificate is no longer valid.

4. C. Rekeying causes the CA to resign the existing certificate after its key material has been regenerated.

5. C. An SGC certificate is an extension of SSL and is used to provide added encryption between client sessions and Web servers. You cannot obtain an SGC certificate from a stand-alone or enterprise CA, as it must come from a commercial CA that is guaranteeing that you are authentic.

6. C. An enterprise CA will work in conjunction with Active Directory and will allow you to control employee access to particular areas or files on the IIS server. If it's set up as a subordinate child of a commercial CA, it will allow a certificate that can be verified as authentic by the commercial CA to be created by your enterprise CA. If you use your own root CA, the client will have to trust you from a self-referential source. A root CA is recommended for certifying subordinate CAs, not for issuing certificates.

7. D. Many Internet browsers are configured not to accept programs and scripts unless they are signed by a trusted authority. A commercial CA is more trustworthy than your CA because by definition it's not self-referential. User certificates are used to identify, through signatures and encryption, users' communication, such as e-mail. An enterprise CA is used to identify an organization's own users, rather than the enterprise itself as an entity.

8. D. Stand-alone CAs can mark requests as "pending," in which case the requests will be queued until the administrator approves or rejects them.

9. A. Installing the root CA on a computer connected to the domain ensures that the CA updates Active Directory and that all the domain member computers and users will trust the certificate it issues. You then remove the root CA, configuring it as an offline CA, and store it in a secure location. An enterprise CA is best suited for issuing certificates within an organization because it is closely tied to Active Directory. You can't take an enterprise CA offline—it would not be able to issue certificates without the link to Active Directory.

10. A. Once the certificate is revoked, it can't be unrevoked, even by removing its serial number from the CRL. The only way to get the user back into the PKI is to issue her a new certificate.

11. C. Revoking a certificate permanently renders the certificate invalid. You can also place a certificate on hold until it expires, but this method doesn't give you the opportunity to add the certificate to a Certificate Revocation List and give a reason for the action. This latter action is preferred because you immediately inform others about the action and you have a history of why it occurred. Exporting a certificate only copies it to another location and doesn't remove it from the CA. Renaming a certificate is not an option. Enabling certificate protection forces the user to enter a password each time the user wants to encrypt information.

12. D. A recovery agent should use their private key to gain access to data that has been encrypted. By default, the administrator is designated as the recovery agent for a computer the first time the administrator logs on to the machine. Therefore, you are free to modify recovery settings by adding recovery agents that modify policies on who can initiate recovery. One of these modifications is to remove all the recovery keys from the local machine. Installing another instance of Windows Server 2003 won't help you see data encrypted by another system; that method would work for bypassing file permissions but not encryption. Creating a new recovery key from the user's certificate isn't a valid option.

13. A. To restrict which templates certain users can use, set permissions for those users in the Active Directory Sites and Services snap-in.

14. D. Enroll permission allows a user to issue certificates. By default, the Authenticated Users group has this permission, as do all of the Administrators groups. To restrict access, you have to remove this permission from all groups, and then grant it only to the users you want to have it.

15. B. You can't rename a computer or join or leave a domain once the CA is installed.

Planning High Availability Services

MICROSOFT EXAM OBJECTIVES COVERED IN THIS CHAPTER:

✓ **Plan services for high availability.**

- Plan a high availability solution that uses clustering services.
- Plan a high availability solution that uses Network Load Balancing.

✓ **Implement a cluster server.**

✓ **Monitor Network Load Balancing. Tools might include the Network Load Balancing Monitor Microsoft Management Console (MMC) snap-in and the WLBS cluster control utility.**

✓ **Recover from cluster node failure.**

Most organizations run mission-critical business applications (such as corporate e-mail and databases) that require a high degree of availability. The system engineer's goal is to maximize the availability and scalability of network servers. High availability ensures minimal downtime, while scalability ensures that systems can grow to meet increasing demands. Downtime is bad for business because it results in lost productivity and can also result in lost faith from customers and business partners. Increasing availability is one area where IT solutions can have a direct impact on the bottom line.

Both availability and scalability can be increased by using fault-tolerant hardware solutions and, in general, by using best practices in your network infrastructure planning. Windows Server 2003 also offers two types of clustering technologies to help you meet your availability and scalability goals. Server clustering is a solution that increases availability, and Network Load Balancing (NLB) is a special type of clustering that increases scalability. A cluster is simply a group of independent computers that work together to provide a common set of services. If one computer in the cluster fails, the others take over so that there is no loss of service.

In this chapter, we'll cover the essential factors in planning an availability and scalability solution. We'll begin with an evaluation of these solutions, discuss planning server clusters and NLB, discuss monitoring NLB, and cover the techniques for recovering from cluster node failure.

Evaluating Availability and Scalability Solutions

Clustering technologies can be combined depending on the needs of the company. You should be familiar with two types of clustering technologies:

Server Clusters *Server clusters* provide high availability for more complex, *stateful applications* and services. Stateful applications (such as SQL Server) have data that is constantly being updated. Other examples of stateful applications include back-end databases, messaging, and file and print services. Server clusters are used to enable resources to be dynamically relocated in the event of a failure. This process is transparent to the client.

Server clusters run only on Windows Server 2003, Enterprise Edition or Windows Server 2003 Datacenter Edition. They can contain up to eight nodes.

In server clusters, individual computers called *nodes* share access to data. Nodes can be either active or passive, depending on the operating mode (active or passive) and how failover is configured in the cluster. Each node is attached to one or more cluster storage devices, which allow different servers to share the same data.

This means that increasing the number of nodes in a server cluster will proportionally increase the availability of the services and applications running on that server cluster. This is because spreading the workload over a greater number of nodes allows each node to run at a lower capacity. In addition, a failover is less likely to result in a decline in performance, because more servers are available to accept the workload of the failed node and because the servers involved will be running at lower capacity.

Network Load Balancing *Network Load Balancing (NLB) clusters* are groups of identical, typically cloned computers that can operate independently. All of the nodes in an NLB cluster are active. You can use NLB for applications that are stateless or can otherwise be cloned with no decline in performance. Stateful applications such as Exchange Server or SQL Server are frequently updated, making them difficult to clone and therefore not acceptable for hosting on NLB clusters.

NLB is supported on all editions of Windows Server 2003. Up to 32 nodes are supported on all editions.

NLB is designed for *stateless applications*, such as front-end Web servers, FTP servers, and VPNs. Stateless applications treat each client request as an independent operation. This type of application can independently load-balance each client request. Stateless applications often have read-only data or data that changes infrequently. Groups of clustered computers can be used to load balance traffic requests.

You can scale out NLB clusters by adding additional servers as demand on the cluster increases.

The applications are usually cloned, so that multiple instances of the same code run against the same dataset.

Table 9.1 compares the number of nodes supported in both server clustering and NLB.

TABLE 9.1 Windows Server 2003 Support for Clustering

Operating System Edition	Server Clusters	Network Load Balancing
Windows Server 2003, Web Edition	N/A	32
Windows Server 2003, Standard Edition	N/A	32
Windows Server 2003, Enterprise Edition	8	32
Windows Server 2003, Datacenter Edition	8	32

Component Load Balancing (CLB) is a third type of clustering that address the unique scalability and availability needs of middle-tier business applications that use the COM+ programming model. CLB is a feature of Microsoft Application Center 2000 and is not covered on the exam or in this book.

Sometimes it's appropriate to run all three types of clustering. For example, assume that a business runs an e-commerce Web site, in which the front-end Web servers are configured in NLB clusters that receive client requests. Middle-tier applications, such as Microsoft's BizTalk Server, use CLB clusters running on Windows Application Center 2000. The applications integrate with SQL database servers on the back-end. The SQL servers are configured in a server cluster.

Availability is the ability to provide end users with access to a service for a high percentage of time while reducing unscheduled outages. Availability can be expressed as:

Percentage of availability = (total time – downtime)/total time

Different applications will have different availability needs. Print servers usually don't require 24/7 availability; however, an e-commerce site cannot afford any downtime, because a company would lose sales and might also lose the faith of its customers. If you strive to achieve 99.9 percent availability, then this allows you 8 hours and 45 minutes of downtime per year.

Reliability is related to availability, and it describes the time between failures, expressed as:

Mean time between failures (MTBF) = (total elapsed time – sum of downtime)/number of failures

Fault tolerance increases the reliability of a system. It describes the ability of a system to continue functioning when part of the system fails. This is achieved by designing the system with a high degree of hardware redundancy.

In the following sections, you'll be introduced to concepts of *server clustering*. You'll also learn how to evaluate clustering solutions. We'll start by identifying the potential threats to availability.

Identifying Threats to High Availability

The idea behind high availability is to make sure that no single point of failure can render a server or network unavailable. To ensure availability, you must guard against several types of failures, including:

Application or Service Failures When an application or service fails, you can have another instance of the application or service running on another server in order to provide continual service to end users.

Hardware and System Failures A Redundant Array of Inexpensive Disks (RAID) is one of the most common ways to protect against storage device failures. Third-party solutions for hardware redundancy should be implemented. Hot-swapping components (such as hard disks and memory) will enable you to replace failed devices and other hardware without affecting system uptime.

RAID-5 describes disk striping with parity. RAID-1 describes disk mirroring.

Most enterprise server platforms provide internal hardware redundancy through redundant power supplies, fans, and other hardware components. Hot-swappable components ensure that failed hardware can be replaced without system downtime.

Network Connectivity and Site Failures Site failures are caused by events such as natural disasters, power outages, and connectivity outages. Your network topology should provide redundant links and hardware, such as routers and cabling, so that connectivity is ensured in a failure scenario. In such events, mission-critical applications can be deployed across geographically dispersed sites. Data centers are frequently deployed in this way.

Sites can be active-active (where all sites carry some of the load) or active-passive (where one or more sites are on standby).

Evaluating Scalability Methods

Scalability describes the ability of a network service or application to grow to meet increasing demands. In the context of clustering, scalability describes the ability to incrementally add systems to an existing cluster when the overall load of the cluster exceeds the cluster's capabilities. The two types of scalability are listed here:

Scaling Up *Scaling up* involves adding redundant or more robust system resources (such as processors, RAM, disks, and network adapters).

Scaling Out *Scaling out* involves adding servers to meet demand.

Both methods help you to improve application and server response time.

Evaluating Clustering Technologies

As stated above, a *cluster* consists of two or more computers working together to provide higher availability, reliability, and scalability than can be obtained by using a single system. The *failover* process ensures the continuous availability of applications and data. Failover automatically redirects and redistributes the workload of the failed server.

Server clusters do have limitations, including:

- They are designed to keep applications available, rather than keeping data available. Cluster technology does not protect against failures caused by viruses or software errors.
- Applications and services must be compatible with the *Cluster Service* (the service that runs server clusters) in order to respond appropriately to a failure.
- Administrators must be able to configure where an application stores its data on the server cluster.

- The clustered application or service must allow clients that are accessing it to reconnect to the cluster virtual server after a failure has occurred and a new cluster node has taken over the application.
- Services and applications must be TCP-IP based.
- The File Replication Service (FRS) isn't supported.
- Third-party tools are required if you want to use dynamic disks on shared cluster storage.

For more information about using dynamic disks on shared cluster storage, see Microsoft Knowledge Base article 237853, "Dynamic Disk Configuration Unavailable for Server Cluster Disk Resources."

Both clustering and fault-tolerant hardware protect your system from failures of components and are frequently used together. Clusters can also be used to maintain availability during an upgrade, service pack installation, or hotfix without taking a cluster offline.

Planning Server Clusters

As you've seen, server clusters ensure the availability of network services and applications in the event of any type of system downtime. This includes both unexpected failures and planned maintenance.

Each organization has different availability needs. Applications or services that will be hosted on a server cluster will also have requirements that you'll have to consider.

In Windows Server 2003, clusters require:

- Two or more computers
- Windows Server 2003, Enterprise Edition or Windows Server 2003, Datacenter Edition
- Hardware that is listed in the Windows Server Catalog
- Consistent hardware architecture. (You cannot use x86-based and Itanium architecture–based computers in the same server cluster.) Two or more network cards are required for each node.

An ideal configuration puts the clustered computers on their own private network. Private network traffic is limited to traffic related to intra-cluster communication and configuration. This method uses one network adapter to connect a node to the other nodes in the cluster on a private network. The second adapter connects the cluster to both an external network, such as the corporate intranet, and the private network.

Server clusters now support the Kerberos version 5 authentication protocol. Windows Server 2003 also adds remote management functionality to the server cluster.

The Cluster Service *is* supported on 64-bit versions of Server 2003. You cannot, however, use GUID partition table (GPT) disks for shared cluster storage. A GPT disk is an Itanium-based disk partition style in the 64-bit versions of Windows Server 2003. For these versions, you must partition cluster disks on a shared bus as master boot record (MBR) disks and not as GPT disks.

In the following sections, you'll learn the terminology relevant to server clusters. We'll cover what you need to know to consider business and application requirements and application deployment, how to choose a cluster model, how to plan multisite clusters and what to consider for networking the cluster.

Understanding the Terminology

You need to know several terms in order to understand how to plan a server cluster deployment, so we'll tackle those terms now:

- A *node*, also known as a *cluster host*, is an individual computer that is a member of a server cluster. Windows Server 2003 supports up to eight nodes in a server cluster.
- A *resource* is any physical or logical entity that is capable of being managed by a cluster, brought online, taken offline, and moved between nodes. At any point in time, a resource can be owned only by a single node.
- A *resource group* is a collection of one or more resources that can be started and stopped as an indivisible unit and independently from other groups. Resource groups are hosted on only one node and are moved to a different mode in a failover scenario. Resources can have dependencies, just like services in Windows Server 2003.
- A *virtual server* is a collection of services that appear to clients as a physical Windows-based server but are not associated with a specific server. A virtual server is typically a resource group that contains all of the resources needed to run a particular application and can be failed over like any other resource group. All virtual servers must include a Network Name resource and an IP Address resource.
- *Failover* describes the process of taking resource groups offline on one node and bringing them back online on another node. The order of processes is important because of resource dependencies. Resources upon which other resources are dependent are brought online before or taken offline after the resources that are dependent on them.
- *Failback* describes the process of relocating resources back to their original node after the failed node (which had previously failed) rejoins the cluster and comes back online.
- The *quorum resource* (also called the quorum disk) is a disk that stores the configuration data and all of the changes that have been applied to the cluster database. This data is needed to recover the cluster in the event of failure. The quorum resource is generally accessible to other cluster resources so that each cluster node has access to the most recent database changes. By default, each cluster has only one quorum resource.
- In *majority node set clusters*, the quorum data is stored on each node. This model is used for geographically dispersed clusters.

- A *Storage Area Network (SAN)* is a set of interconnected storage devices (for instance, disks and tapes) and servers that are connected to a common data transfer infrastructure to provide a pool of storage with multiple server access.

Analyzing Business and Application Requirements

A company's high availability needs depend on a few different factors, such as the length of acceptable downtime, contractual obligations with business partners (for instance, a Quality of Service or QoS agreement), and the need to prevent lost sales and lost employee productivity resulting from system downtime.

Start by answering questions such as the following:

- How much downtime can you allow for a given application?
- How many total node failures does the cluster need to protect against?
- How many users depend on a particular application?

If multiple applications will be running on the server cluster, which ones (if any) take priority? This may become critical if more than one node fails and the remaining ones do not have the capacity to take on the entire workload.

After evaluating business needs, you need to make sure your application can run on a server cluster. Good candidates for clustering share the following characteristics:

- The application is IP-based.
- The application attempts to recover from network failures, such as reconnecting user sessions.
- You can configure where application data is stored.

You need to have a good understanding of an application's needs and behavior. Make sure you know where application data is stored and whether or not the application can be upgraded while the cluster is online. Also make sure that you can anticipate how the application will behave during failover.

Keep in mind that not all applications will react to cluster events. An application must be *cluster-aware* (meaning that it can communicate with the Cluster API). Otherwise, it will not receive the necessary status and notification information from the cluster.

Most older applications are not cluster-aware; however, they can still run in a server cluster and even failover. Such applications are capable of only rudimentary failure detection and cannot interact with the cluster, so they would not be as highly available as cluster-aware applications.

Make sure that you contact the software vendor or consult the software documentation to verify that an application can be run in a clustered configuration. This will determine how you install the application, as well as how you upgrade the application after installing it in the cluster.

If you install Exchange 2000 Server or Exchange Server 2003 Server on a server cluster, the log files and database in each storage group must be on the cluster's shared disk. Otherwise, the log files and the storage group databases cannot failover to another node if the virtual server goes offline.

Make sure to test a server cluster before deploying it in a production environment. You need the certainty that your failover policies actually work, and that there is enough capacity available to allow for failover of resources.

Evaluating Application Deployment Considerations

Applications can be deployed through one of two methods (the method you choose depends entirely on the application itself):

Single-Instance Applications With *single-instance applications*, only one application instance is running on the cluster at any time, and the application typically has data sets that cannot be partitioned across multiple nodes. The Dynamic Host Configuration Protocol (DHCP) service is an example of a single-instance application. The set of leased IP addresses that the application provides is small, but they would be complicated to replicate across a cluster. Therefore, the DHCP instance exists as a single instance, and high availability is provided by failing over the instance to another node in the cluster.

Multiple-Instance Applications With a *multiple-instance application*, either multiple instances of the same code, or different pieces of code that cooperate to provide a single service, can run on a cluster. In both cases, the client or end user sees only one partition of an application. Applications can be either cloned or partitioned to create multiple instances in a cluster.

Multiple-instance applications can be cloned or partitioned. *Cloned applications* work best in NLB clusters of stateful applications, where they can run against the same, relatively static dataset. Figure 9.1 shows an example of a cloned application.

FIGURE 9.1 A cloned application

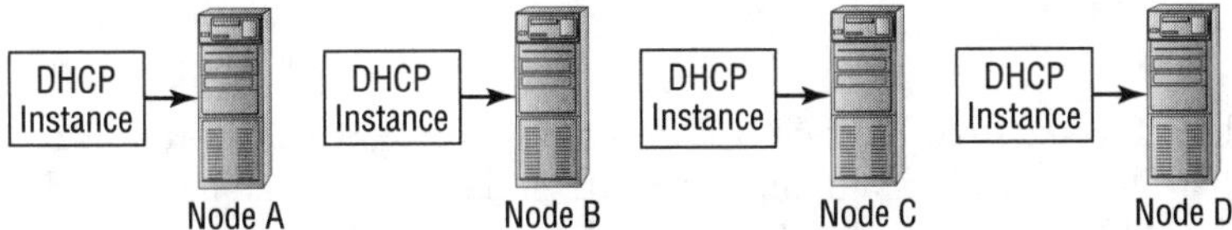

Partitioned applications work well for server clusters of stateless applications that have frequent updates to memory. An example is a database, where records A through M can reside on one partition, and N through Z can reside on another partition. Other types of applications can partition the functionality rather than the actual data. For instance, billing inquiries could be directed to a separate billing node, which has sole access to the billing database. Catalog inquiries could be directed to a separate catalog node, which has sole access to the catalog database. This example would provide scalability, but not availability because there is no option for failover. Figure 9.2 shows an example of a partitioned application.

In all of these deployment types, client requests are transparently split across the instances. You could host one or several single-instance applications, and you could host one or several multiple-instance applications in your server cluster.

Additional considerations for application deployment include planning storage methods, server capacity, and failover policies. We'll discuss each in turn in the following sections.

FIGURE 9.2 A partitioned application

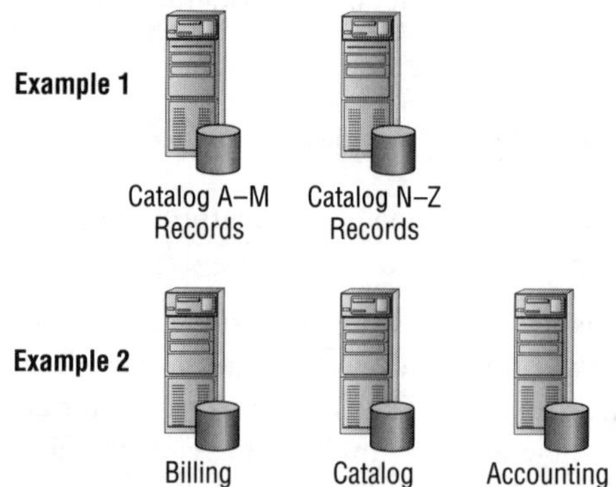

Determining Storage Methods

In a cluster, two types of information must be stored:

- The application information, which will be shared between nodes
- The cluster configuration data

Most Windows Server 2003 clusters use either parallel SCSI or Fibre Channel. The only supported storage interconnect technology supported for clusters greater than two nodes is switched Fibre Channel fabric (FC-SW).

SCSI is supported only on 32-bit versions of Windows Server 2003, Enterprise Edition.

You need a dedicated disk to use for the quorum resource, which stores the cluster configuration data. The disk must be a minimum of 50MB and ideally should have 500MB or more of space. You should use hardware RAID to provide fault tolerance.

Ideally—and especially in deployments of greater than two nodes—you should use a SAN for data storage so that you have the optimal level of fault tolerance. Many third-party vendors (such as Network Appliance, IBM, EMC, and Hewlett-Packard) provide SAN solutions, including the actual hardware as well as software management tools.

The `Mountvol` utility can be used to configure a server cluster in a SAN. It provides a means of creating volume mount points and linking volumes without requiring a drive letter.

In a SAN deployment, you can use either zoning or LUN masking to isolate and protect server cluster data.

Zoning allows you to create clouds, or storage entities, in order to control host access to storage devices as well as to control traffic flow within the SAN. Zoning is implemented at the hardware level and also provides security for SANs. Figure 9.3 demonstrates how zoning works.

FIGURE 9.3 Zoning is used to control access to devices in a SAN.

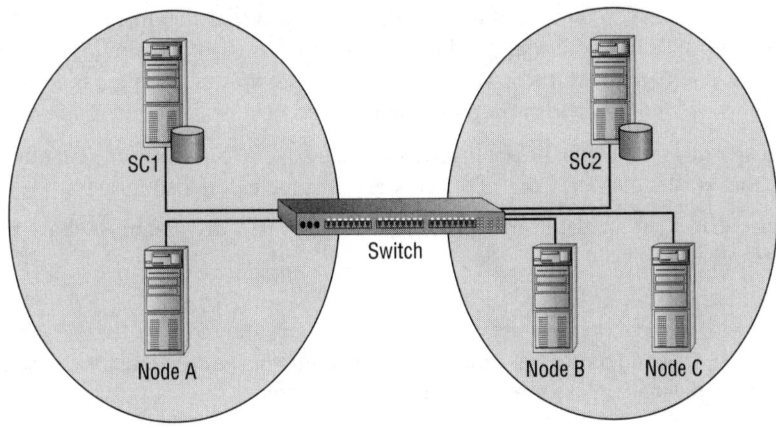

This is a logical diagram of two SAN zones, each with their own controller. In this example, Node C can access data only from SC2 and not from SC1. Traffic between ports would be routed to only the segments of the fabric that are in the same zone.

LUN masking refers to logical disks implemented at the controller level to provide access control. The controller enforces access policies for specific devices. This allows for zoning at the port level, so it is a more granular level of security than zoning. Figure 9.4 shows a sample deployment where Zones A and B overlap, and the storage controller resides in both zones. The LUNs on Cluster A can be shared with or masked (that is, hidden) from Cluster B.

FIGURE 9.4 LUN masking is used to control access to devices in a SAN with overlapping zones.

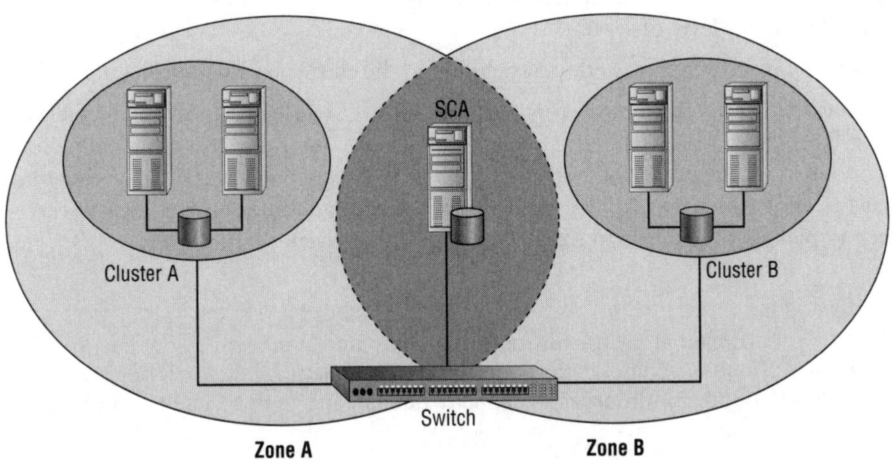

If you deploy clustering in a SAN, keep in mind the following requirements and recommendations:

- Host bus adapters (HBAs) are interface cards that connect a cluster node to a SAN, just as a network adapter connects a server to a LAN. For best results, use matching HBAs throughout the SAN. You would use multiple HBAs so that the host sees multiple paths to the same disks, and you must load the multipath driver so that the I/O subsystem can see the devices correctly. Otherwise, the second device will be disabled because the OS thinks they are two disks with the same signature.
- Each cluster on a SAN must be deployed in its own zone so that you can separate the cluster traffic from traffic coming from other clusters or nonclustered computers.
- All device drivers in a cluster, including storage and HBA drivers, must share the same software version.

To avoid data corruption, never allow multiple nodes access to the same storage devices unless they are in the same cluster.

- When using hardware snapshots with cloned disks, it is critical that only one disk with a given disk signature be exposed to the server cluster at one time. Otherwise, using multiple disks with the same disk signature can degrade performance. It could also result in data corruption if you expose a hardware snapshot to a node on the cluster.

Planning Server Capacity

You need to answer some important questions before you can deploy the clustered application:

- What is the number of servers you can use in the cluster?
- How much capacity does each server have?
- What is the acceptable level of performance in the event of a failover, and for how long can you tolerate this level of service?
- From how many separate node failures should the cluster be able to recover?

The workload of a server both before and after failover is closely tied to your server resource planning. The way your application adapts to the server cluster depends on how much of the server resources it consumes. The consumption of server resources affects the number of servers you need to ensure high availability for the application, in addition to how many servers are required to pick up the workload for a given node in the event of a failover.

To best allow for future growth and increased capacity needs, try increasing your initial estimates for server capacity by 30 percent (to give you a buffer for unforeseen capacity needs), and then add a little more for future growth.

For example, imagine that you have a two-node cluster, consisting of Node A and Node B. If Node A fails over, Node B must continue processing its own jobs in addition to processing the jobs that failed from Node A. This means that prior to failover, both nodes can operate at a maximum of 50 percent capacity. After failover, Node B operates at 100 percent capacity. When any server operates under maximum capacity, performance is severely reduced. However, reduced performance is better than losing all of Node A's workload.

If you add a third node to the above example and all three nodes operate at 50 percent, the two remaining nodes can divide the workload of a failed node. If Node A fails over, Node B and Node C assume Node A's work and operate at 75 percent capacity, which provides better application performance than a single server operating at 100 percent capacity (which is referred to as *bottlenecked*). However, if two nodes in this cluster were to failover, the remaining node would not be able to take on the entire cluster's workload.

As previously mentioned, Windows Server 2003 (Datacenter and Enterprise editions) supports up to eight nodes in a cluster. With additional nodes, you have more options for distributing the workload in a cluster.

The following illustrations of a simple four-node cluster demonstrate how server load can be balanced across nodes. These examples also demonstrate the relationship between hardware resources, fault tolerance, and availability.

Figure 9.5 shows a cluster in which all four nodes are operational, each running at 25 percent capacity.

FIGURE 9.5 A four-node cluster

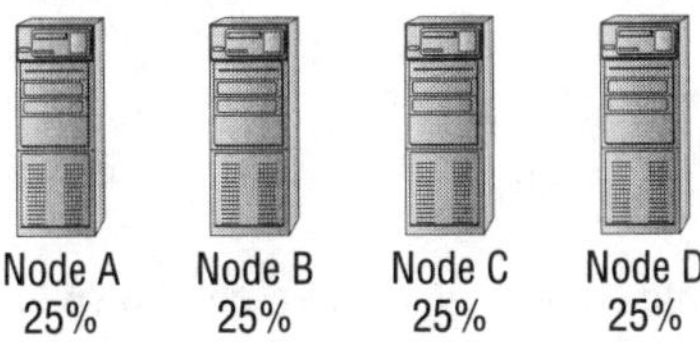

Figure 9.6 shows what happens after one of the nodes fails. The remaining three nodes each receive a share of the failed node's work.

FIGURE 9.6 A four-node cluster with one failed node

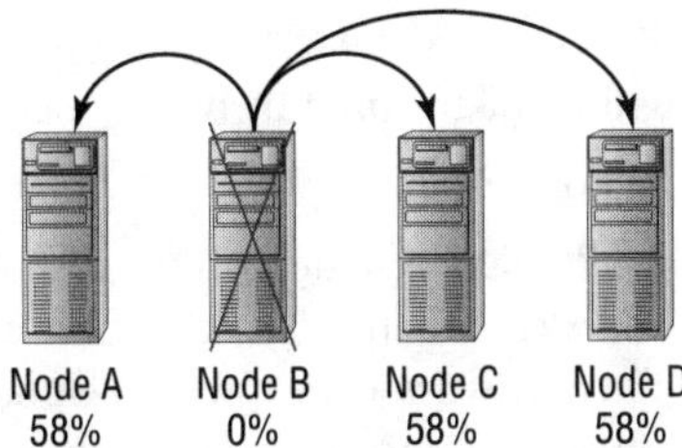

Figure 9.7 shows what happens after two nodes fail. The remaining two nodes are each operating at 50 percent capacity.

FIGURE 9.7 A four-node cluster with two failed nodes

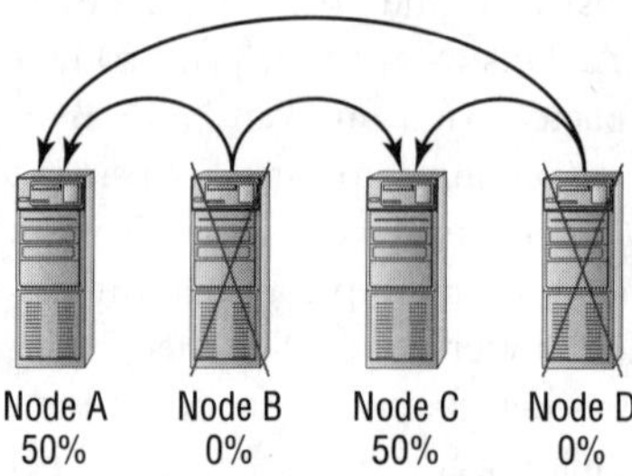

Figure 9.8 shows what happens after three nodes fail. The remaining node has barely enough capacity to take over the clusters' entire workload. However, application performance will be seriously compromised now that the server is operating at 100 percent capacity.

FIGURE 9.8 A four-node cluster with three failed nodes

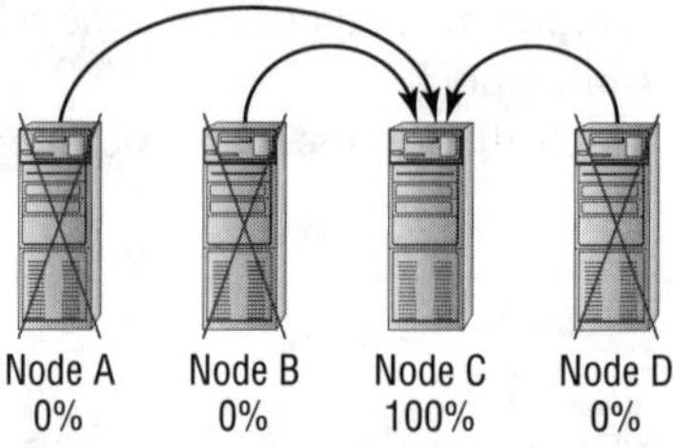

Planning Failover Policies

When there is a failure in a simple two-node cluster, the failover process is simple—redirect the resources of the failed node to the surviving node. When you have three or more nodes in a cluster, you can configure failover policies to control the behavior of the cluster. You can choose different solutions, such as:

- The number of nodes available for failover
- The specific resources to be failed over, and the nodes to which the resources will be redirected
- How the application load will be distributed or partitioned
- How resource groups will be configured

One of the biggest decisions you'll make is in determining a balance between availability and cost. For instance, you can use a dedicated standby server for each active node in a cluster—but this will double the cost of the hardware investment. The hardware used must be almost identical, because any latency between the cluster updates can queue to the point that the entire cluster fails.

In the following sections, we'll cover the different types of failover policies you can configure.

N+I Configuration

In the *N+I configuration*, there are active nodes and standby nodes. N nodes are hosting applications and I (idle) nodes are on standby. This is the most common type of failover policy. For the highest level of availability, you could have a standby server for each active node, but this would double the investment in hardware.

The benefit of N+I configurations is that they are scalable and can gracefully handle multiple failures.

Figure 9.9 shows an example of a simple 3+3 N+I configuration. This example would allow an application to keep running with no decrease in performance, because the application will failover to a node that is 100 percent available and that is not already in use.

FIGURE 9.9 N+I Configuration

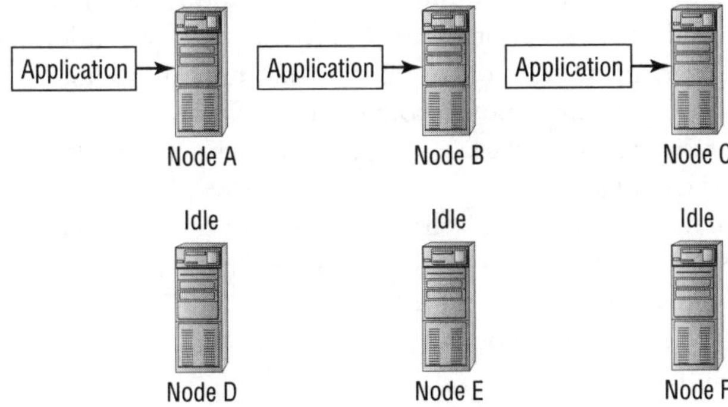

Real World Scenario

Planning an N+I Server Cluster for Exchange 2003 Server

You are the network administrator for a large organization. You need to come up with a high availability solution for the organization's messaging services. The company uses Exchange 2003 Server for e-mail.

Exchange Server 2003 is well-suited for an N+I server cluster deployment. Exchange 2003 supports both Active/Active clustering and Active/passive (N+I) clustering.

You decide to implement a four-node cluster in a 3+1 configuration, with three active nodes and one node on standby. Although only one node failure can be supported in this configuration, this cluster enables failover to a node that has 100 percent available resources. This is a good approach, because Exchange Server is a resource-intensive application.

Standby Server Configuration

A *standby server configuration* is a type of N+I that ensures a certain performance level and response time after failover. Figure 9.10 shows a three-node version of this type of failover policy.

FIGURE 9.10 Standby server configuration

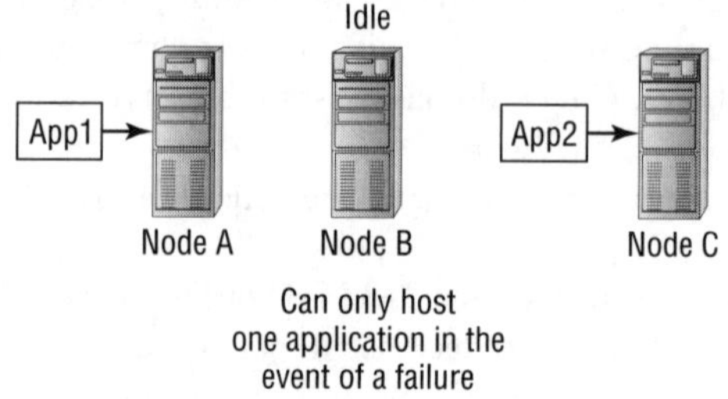

Standby servers are a good choice for resource-intensive applications, because applications are hosted on separate servers. In the example, App1 and App2 need to run on separate servers, because one server would not have enough capacity to run both applications. Assume that Node A fails. App1 would be relocated to Node B, keeping the applications hosted on separate nodes. Planning server capacity for this failover policy is easy. Spare servers need to have enough capacity to take on the workload of the largest node, and each active node needs enough capacity for the application it will host.

A disadvantage of the standby server is that it introduces a single point of failure. For example, assume that both Node A and Node B fail. There is nowhere else for App1 to go, so the application can't be relocated. Node C doesn't have the resources to run both applications at the same time. To resolve this problem, you can combine up to eight nodes so that you avoid having a single point of failure.

Failover Pairs Configuration

A *failover pairs configuration* is usually used with four or more nodes. These configurations set up pairs of nodes so that each application can failover between two nodes. Figure 9.11 shows an example using a four-node cluster.

FIGURE 9.11 Failover pairs configuration

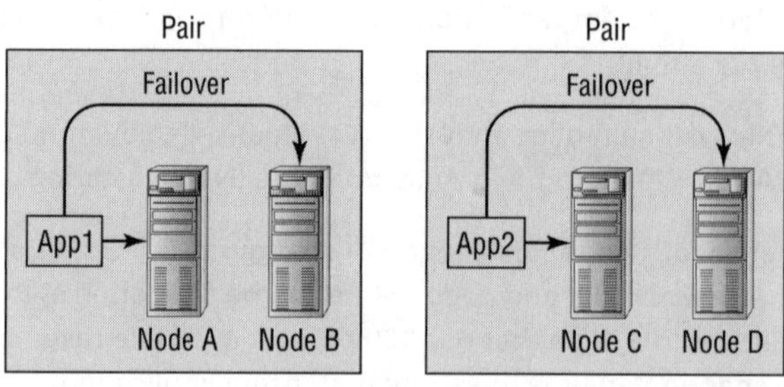

Failover pairs improve upon standby servers, because they allow a different failover node to be dynamically assigned. They tend to work well for databases and other resource-intensive applications.

The disadvantage with failover pairs is that as little as 50 percent of the cluster resources will be used at a given moment. Also, when you have multiple failures you may have to manually failback the cluster resources when you bring the nodes back online.

Random and Customized Failover Policies

Windows Server 2003 has the ability to randomly failover an application to a new location. This is a good solution when you have multiple application instances running in a two or three node cluster and when each node has enough capacity to host several of these application instances at once. With clusters of four or more nodes, there are too many possible failure scenarios that could result in unequal workload distribution, so random failover policies would not be a good solution.

Benefits of random failover policies include the ability to handle multiple failures and the ability to load balance applications.

Disadvantages of random failover policies include the inability to predict where applications will failover or the performance of the applications after failover.

When the node hosting a resource group fails, the Cluster Service will randomly assign the failover target for a resource group when the group has an empty preferred owners list.

With large and complex server clusters, you may want to exert stronger control over failover by configuring customized policies. This enables you to target specific applications to specific nodes when there is a failure. This gives you full control and makes it easy to plan capacity. Customized failover policies work with a feature known as group affinity.

Group affinity describes a dependency between groups that determines the groups' relative location in the server cluster. Some resource groups can be hosted anywhere on the cluster because they have no specific configuration requirements or hardware needs. In some circumstances, however, the location of one group can affect the location of other groups. Groups can have strong or weak affinity. Groups with strong affinity are located together on the same node, if possible. Groups can also be configured with strong or weak anti-affinity. With strong anti-affinity, groups will be kept apart if at all possible. Running more than one instance of Exchange on the same node is not recommended, so Exchange virtual servers are a good example of groups that use anti-affinity.

A disadvantage of customized failover policies is that they are difficult to configure for multiple applications, because accounting for all the possible combinations of application and server failures in the event of multiple failures is difficult.

Determining the Cluster Model

After determining failover policies, you should next consider the type of cluster model you will use. A *cluster model* describes how the quorum resource is accessed in a server cluster. This method is important because the entire point of a cluster is to have several physical servers that act as a single virtual server, and therefore every server must share the same understanding of the cluster's configuration.

The quorum resource has a critical role to play because it enables the nodes in a cluster to keep their databases in sync. After a failed node comes back online, the other nodes will update the failed node's copy of the cluster database.

The cluster database is part of the Windows Server 2003 Registry on each cluster node.

The quorum resource can be owned by only a single node at any given moment in time. A node has to have control of the quorum resource before it can form a cluster. A node cannot join or stay in a cluster unless it can communicate with the node that has ownership of the quorum resource. Servers in a cluster negotiate with each other for ownership of the quorum resource.

Clustered servers try to avoid split-brain scenarios. A split-brain happens when some of the nodes fail and the cluster loses quorum. Nodes lose communication with one another. The result is that each partition thinks it's the only instance of the cluster, which will ultimately cause data corruption.

A quorum ensures that only the partition that owns the quorum resource will survive a split-brain scenario. All other partitions of the cluster, which have "lost quorum", will not survive, and Cluster Service is terminated on those nodes.

The actual cluster configuration data is stored within the quorum log file, which contains configuration details about the servers and resources in the cluster. The log file also identifies the state (online or offline) of resources. This file acts as the definitive version of the cluster configuration, and will ordinarily be located on a shared disk that all nodes in the cluster can access.

A quorum resource must be located on an NTFS file system.

You choose the type of quorum resource based on your cluster model, and there are three types of cluster models you can use:

- Local quorum cluster
- Single quorum device cluster
- Majority node set cluster

A *local quorum cluster* has only one node and is usually used for testing.

You might also use a local quorum cluster to host file shares for home directories.

The *single quorum device cluster*, also known as the standard quorum model, is the most common cluster model. Figure 9.12 shows how the cluster configuration data is stored on a single device connected to all nodes in the cluster.

FIGURE 9.12 A single quorum device cluster

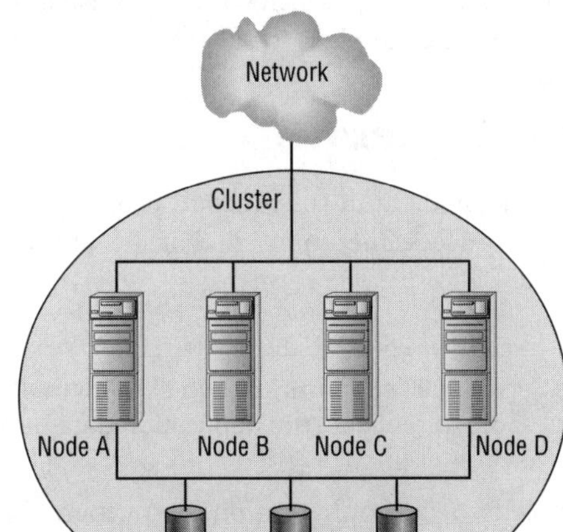

Windows Server 2003 introduced a new type of cluster model, the *majority node set cluster* (also called a majority node set quorum), which is commonly used in geographically dispersed clusters. In this model, every node maintains its own copy of the cluster configuration data. The quorum resource maintains the consistency of this data on all nodes. With a majority node set cluster, you can take a quorum disk offline without interfering with the cluster operation.

Unlike single quorum device clusters, which can survive with a single node, majority node set clusters require that a majority of the cluster nodes survive a failure or the server cluster stops working. Figure 9.13 shows an example of the majority node set cluster.

FIGURE 9.13 A majority node set cluster

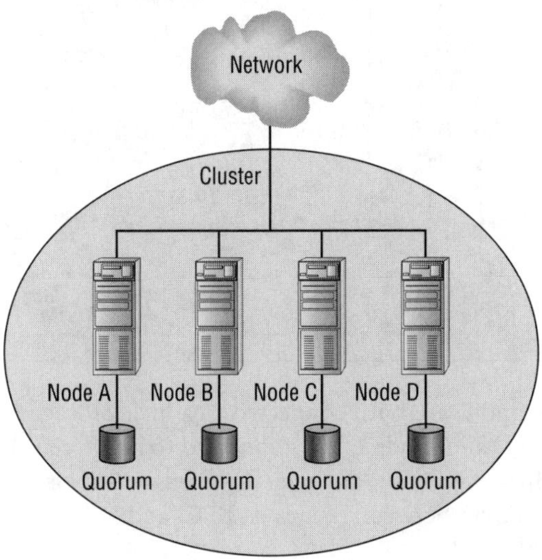

You would use majority node set clusters when you have a customized configuration in which you need to ensure strong consistency and in which you are not using shared disks. We've already discussed multisite clusters. Another example is for file replication of relatively static data.

Planning Multisite Clusters

Multisite clusters are used to provide fault tolerance to protect against a single site failure. The nodes in one site can directly access the storage in that site without any dependencies on the other site.

Windows Server 2003 supports just two-sites for multisite clusters, and requires third-party tools to replicate the application data between sites.

Figure 9.14 shows a simple two-site configuration for a geographically dispersed server cluster.

FIGURE 9.14 A geographically dispersed server cluster

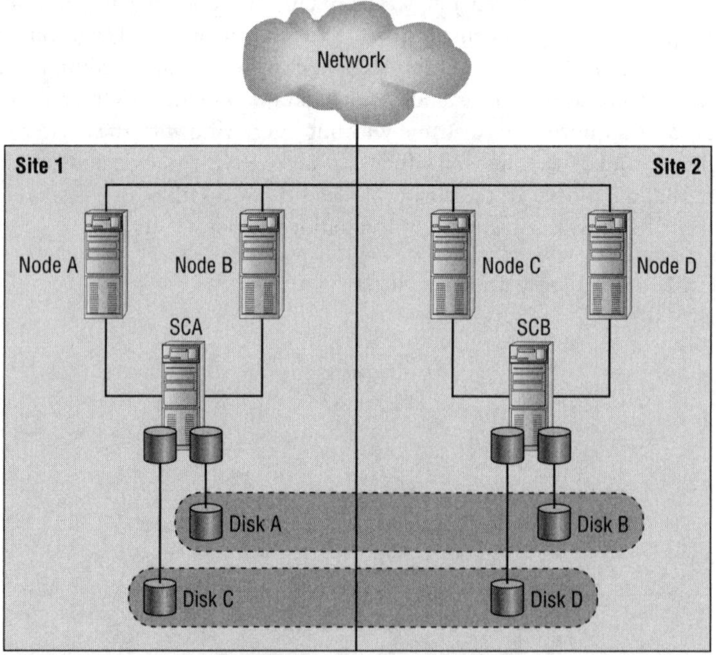

Notice how Nodes A and B are both connected to a local storage array hosted by Storage Controller A, and Nodes C and Node D are connected to a different local storage array on Storage Controller B. Mirroring is used to make the disks in the storage array appear as a single logical device that can failover between Nodes A, B, C, and D.

Mirroring can be implemented either at the controller level or at the host level.

There are three critical requirements for a multisite cluster. First, both sites need a separate copy of the data. If data is read-only, then it can simply be cloned, with a single instance running at each site. If data will change, then you must consider how replication will occur between sites. Second, the application must be restarted at a site when there is a failure at the other site. Third, you must ensure that all hardware is supported, and you will most likely need some third-party software to make the multisite cluster work.

All nodes have to be located on the same subnet. This is a network requirement of all server clusters and is especially important for multisite clusters. Clusters are usually located on a private network connected to the public network. You can create VLANs so that the public and private network connections appear as a single LAN even though the nodes are on different physical networks. Make sure that there is not a single point of failure at the network level. Each VLAN should fail independently of any of the other cluster networks.

Make sure that the roundtrip communication latency between any two nodes does not exceed 500 milliseconds, otherwise the Cluster Service will assume that a node has failed.

There are three levels at which data can be replicated between sites:

- Replication at the block level, which is known as disk-device-level replication or mirroring and is handled by the storage controllers or by mirroring the software.
- Replication at the file-system level
- Replication at the application level

In the following sections, we will discuss different methods for data replication.

Synchronous versus Asynchronous Replication

There are two types of data replication: synchronous replication and asynchronous replication.

Synchronous replication occurs when an operation is not considered to be complete until the change has made it to the other site. A change is made on one node at one site, but the operation is not completed until the change is made on the other site. Assume that you have a multisite cluster, and that you are using synchronous block-level replication. In such a scenario, an application at Site 2 could write a block of data to a local resource that is mirrored to Site 1. Until the change has been made to the disk at Site 1, the I/O operation will not be completed. Application performance can be much slower for synchronous replication because of the latency between the time an operation is executed and when it is completed.

Asynchronous replication occurs when a write operation is performed at Site 2 and considered completed before the change is also written to disk at Site 1. The I/O operation is complete the moment the write to the local disk is completed. With asynchronous replication, data can therefore be out of sync between the sites at any given moment in time.

Make sure that the vendor for your replication solution preserves the order of operations, because some vendors do not do this. In Windows Server 2003, ensuring that the order of I/O operations is preserved is critical for multisite clusters using asynchronous replication. This method ensures crash consistency between sites rather than applying I/O operations in an arbitrary order that can cause the application to think that the replicated data is corrupt.

Third-party vendors also provide a variety of solutions for mirroring and replication. These solutions always involve a disk for which there is a master copy, which is written to first, and at least one secondary copy to which changes are then propagated. Master disks can be located at either site. If the master, or primary, disk fails, it is demoted to a secondary and a secondary disk is promoted to the master.

Majority Node Set Quorum

Majority node set quorum clusters are the most common cluster model for multisite clusters. This method stores the quorum on the local hard disk of each node.

Failover is much more complex in a multisite cluster than it is in a single-site cluster. In addition, a split-brain scenario is much more likely to happen in a multisite cluster. With a loss of communication between two sites, the cluster nodes don't know whether the other site is still alive and the communication link is down, or whether the other site is dead. A single-quorum resource in the cluster needs to serve as the tiebreaker in order to avoid split-brain scenarios.

As in a single-site, single-quorum cluster, one of the partitions needs to take control of the quorum resource. Unlike a single-site, single-quorum cluster, however, a server cluster configured as a majority node set quorum can only start or continue running if a majority of the nodes are operational, and if all of those nodes can still communicate with each other. This requirement means that you need to carefully plan the number of nodes in the server cluster.

Single Quorum

You can use a single quorum disk resource in a multisite cluster by using a method such as disk mirroring to replicate the quorum across sites. You cannot, however, use asynchronous replication for the quorum data because this method could result in data corruption during the replication.

Networking the Cluster

In server clusters, a network can perform one of the following roles:

- The private network role is used for internal cluster communication.
- The public network role enables clients to access clustered applications and services.
- A mixed network role combines the functionality of the private and public networks.
- No role (otherwise known as disabling the network for cluster use)

Anticipating the cluster-related network traffic will be helpful to the planning process. With single quorum device clusters, there is no need for the Cluster Service to use the network for internal traffic. You may, however, need to plan for other traffic related to the cluster. For instance, traffic may need to pass the network in both directions to reach a domain controller for authentication.

You should use identical network adapters on all nodes within a cluster network. This means using the same make, model, and firmware version. As for throughput, the public network can require 10Mbps to 100Mbps of throughput, although the private network can require 400Mbps to 1 Gbps of throughput.

QLogic's new HBA system is 2Gbps.

Considerations for networking clusters include ensuring network availability and establishing domain controller access.

Ensuring Network Availability

A good design for the cluster network will ensure network availability.

Avoid having a single point of failure by configuring two or more cluster networks for internal cluster communication. In fact, Windows Server 2003 does not even support a server cluster with nodes that are connected by just one network.

Make sure that each cluster network fails independently of other cluster networks. This means you must use different hardware components for any two networks.

With multihomed nodes, the adapters must also reside on separate subnets. The Cluster Service can only see one network adapter per node per subnet, so don't connect multiple adapters on a single multihomed node to the same network.

You can team network adapters (meaning to group them together on multiple ports to a single physical network segment) in order to provide fault tolerance. In fact, this is the single best method to provide fault tolerance to your cluster network. However, teaming network adapters is supported only on networks that aren't dedicated to internal cluster traffic.

For those networks that are dedicated to intra-cluster traffic, there are other ways to provide redundancy, such as by adding a second private network dedicated to the internal cluster traffic.

If you have a communication problem on a cluster network on which you have teamed network adapters, try disabling teaming to see if that resolves the problem.

Establishing Domain Controller Access

The Cluster Service account must be validated in the local domain, or the Cluster Service will not start. You must therefore make sure that every node can locate a domain controller. Clustered applications (for example, Exchange Server and SQL Server) may also require account validation. There are three ways in which you could provide domain controller access:

- Install cluster nodes as member servers in a Windows Server 2003 domain. Make sure they have a fast, dependable connection to a domain controller.

- Put a domain controller within the server cluster if you can't otherwise provide fast and reliable access.
- Install the cluster nodes themselves as domain controllers.

You really want to avoid installing the cluster nodes as domain controllers. A node could be busy functioning as a domain controller, and this could prevent the Cluster Service from accessing the quorum. The Cluster Service might interpret this as a resource failure and initiate a failover. In addition, running too many services takes system resources away from clustered applications. However, if you must configure the cluster nodes as domain controllers, consider the following important points:

- At least two nodes in a cluster must be configured as domain controllers, so that you can have failover assurance for the domain controller services.
- You have to first run `dcpromo` to promote a server to a domain controller before adding the node to a cluster.
- An idle domain controller also running the Cluster Service can use between 130MB and 140MB of RAM. If replication is required, replication traffic can saturate bandwidth and degrade overall performance.
- Cluster nodes which are the only domain controllers need to also be global catalog and DNS servers. The DNS servers must support dynamic updates.
- If you redistribute the single-master operation roles among the nodes, and a node fails over, the single-master operation roles that the failed node was providing will be unavailable. (By default, the first domain controller takes on the single-master operation roles in a Windows Server 2003 domain.)
- Be very, very careful if you have to demote a domain controller that also happens to be a cluster node, because this action changes the security settings and causes certain domain accounts and groups to revert back to the default built-in accounts and groups. For example, the SID for the Domain Admins group will change to the local Administrators group. This can create problems validating the Cluster Service.

Be cautious when applying global policy settings to a domain controller; these settings could interfere with the cluster role.

Planning Network Load Balancing

NLB is a special type of server clustering that provides availability and scalability for TCP- and UDP-based applications by distributing application load across multiple servers. NLB is frequently implemented to load balance Web applications. For instance, server farms of IIS servers can be created to balance the load of client requests as well as to provide fault tolerance. Unlike standard server clusters, NLB works on all editions of Windows Server 2003.

With NLB, each node runs a separate instance of the application. NLB transparently distributes client requests across the various cluster hosts. NLB can also work together with round robin DNS to distribute client traffic across multiple clusters. Clients access the cluster through one or more virtual IP addresses. The cluster appears to clients as a single server.

Round robin DNS was introduced in Chapter 4, "Planning a DNS Strategy."

Real World Scenario

NLB and Round Robin DNS

You are the network administrator for Contoso. The company is going to expand its Internet presence and will deploy a new high-volume Web site for e-commerce running on IIS 6. You need to determine how to make this happen.

Remember that NLB offers scalability through one of two methods. You could scale out applications within a single cluster, or you can scale out by using multiple clusters. In the case of multiple clusters, you would then distribute the client traffic across the multiple NLB clusters in the Web farm by using round robin DNS.

You build a test lab and determine that your current network infrastructure can support up to seven clustered hosts on each VLAN. Client traffic is expected to be very heavy, so you want to reserve 45 total cluster hosts to handle the traffic. This means you'll need to scale out to seven clusters.

The Web farm is listed in DNS as `www.contoso.com`. The DNS zone for contoso.com contains multiple entries for `www.contoso.com`, with each entry pointing to an NLB cluster in the Web farm. In this system, round robin DNS distributes client traffic among the separate clusters, and NLB then distributes client traffic within the clusters.

With this solution, you can take individual cluster hosts offline, but you need to make sure that you do not take entire clusters offline, because round robin DNS will continue directing traffic to those clusters and clients will experience service interruptions.

The most important distinction between planning server clusters and planning NLB is that NLB is intended for stateless applications such as Web applications and VPNs.

NLB provides fault tolerance through redundant cluster hosts that provide the same applications and services. You should also include application-level monitoring, for instance with Microsoft's Application Center 2000. To provide a complete high-availability solution, you should include the following components in addition to NLB:

- Use fault-tolerant hardware, such as redundant and hot-swappable components
- Ensure that the network infrastructure itself is fault tolerant
- Use only signed device drivers and software within the cluster
- Employ application-level monitoring for clustered applications

We'll discuss monitoring and remotely administering NLB next.

Monitoring NLB

NLB can be monitored by using the Network Load Balancing Manager, as shown in Figure 9.15. You open the NLB Manager from the Start menu by choosing Start ➤ Administrative Tools ➤ Network Load Balancing Manager.

FIGURE 9.15 The Network Load Balancing Manager

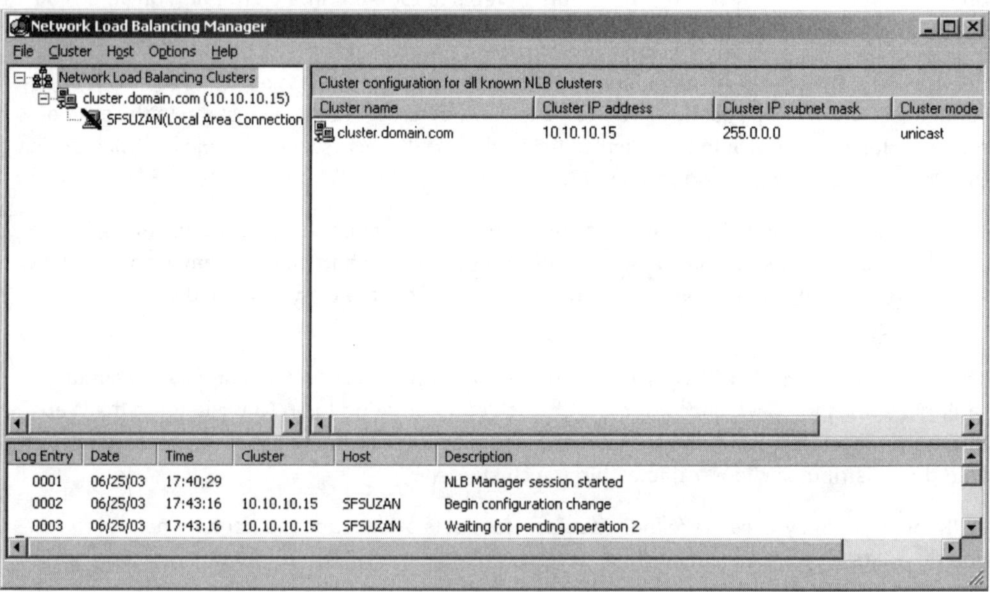

By right-clicking the server, you can access its Properties dialog from the context menu (see Figure 9.16). You can configure host parameters, cluster parameters, cluster IP addresses, and port rules using the various tabs of the Properties dialog box.

Notice that you can configure properties at the cluster level or at the individual node level. By right-clicking the cluster, you can access its Properties dialog from the context menu (see Figure 9.17). You can configure cluster parameters, cluster IP addresses, and port rules using the various tabs of the Properties dialog box.

FIGURE 9.16 An NLB Cluster Node's Properties page

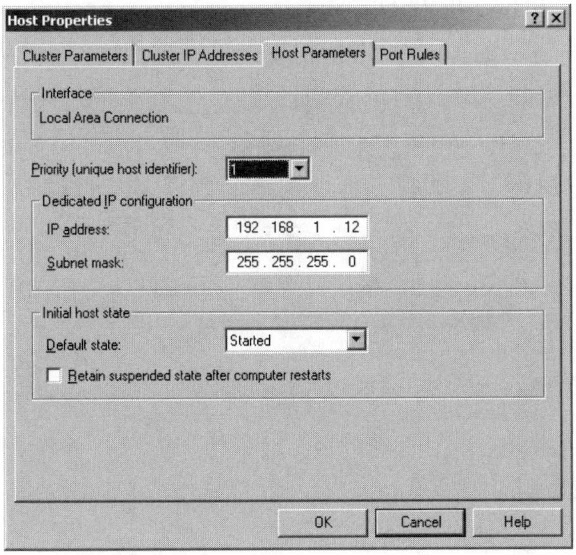

FIGURE 9.17 An NLB Cluster's Properties page

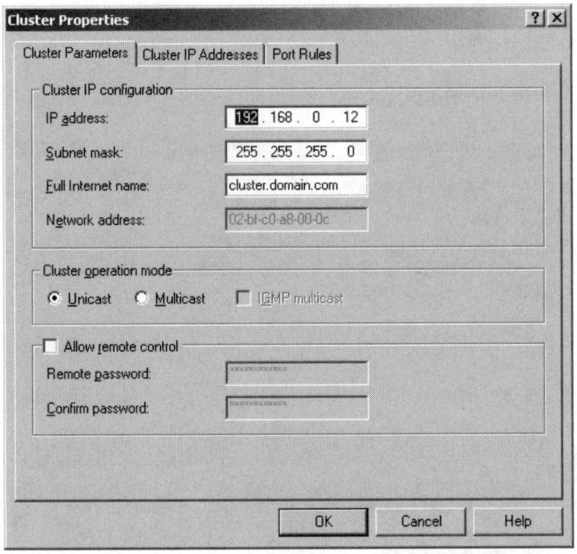

The first tab shown is the Cluster Parameters tab. On this tab, you can set the IP address and subnet mask for the cluster as well as the full Internet name in the format `cluster.domain.com`. You can also set either Unicast or Multicast mode. Notice that this tab is where you enable the checkbox to Allow Remote Control.

The Cluster IP Addresses tab, shown in Figure 9.18, is simply where you would add the IP addresses of additional nodes in the cluster.

FIGURE 9.18 The Cluster IP Addresses tab

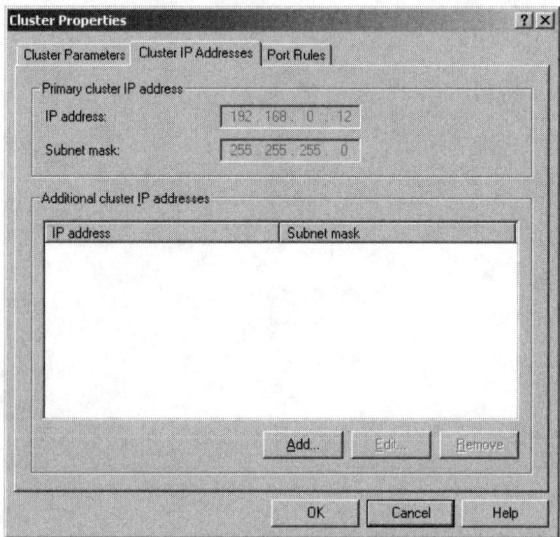

The Port Rules tab, shown in Figure 9.19, is where you can define port rules to direct TCP and UDP traffic. A single default rule is shown, and you can edit or add rules as needed.

FIGURE 9.19 The Port Rules tab

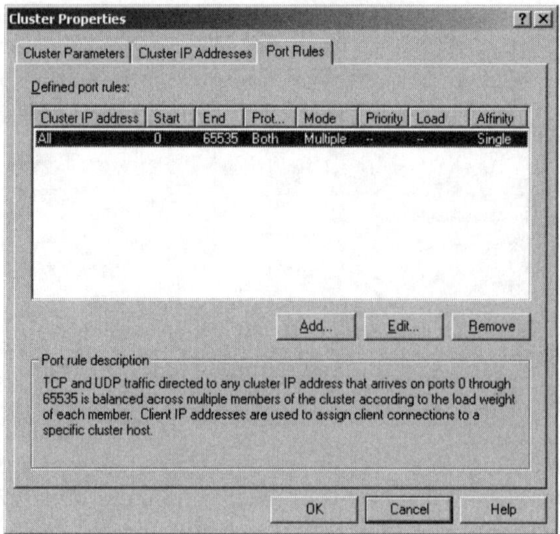

Figure 9.20 displays the Add/Edit Port Rule dialog box, reached by clicking either the Add or Edit button. You can choose to apply the rule to a single IP address within the cluster or to

all addresses in the cluster. You can specify a port range (the default includes all 65,536 ports, from 0 to 65,535). You can choose to apply the port rule to TCP, UDP or both types of traffic.

FIGURE 9.20 The Add/Edit Port Rule dialog box

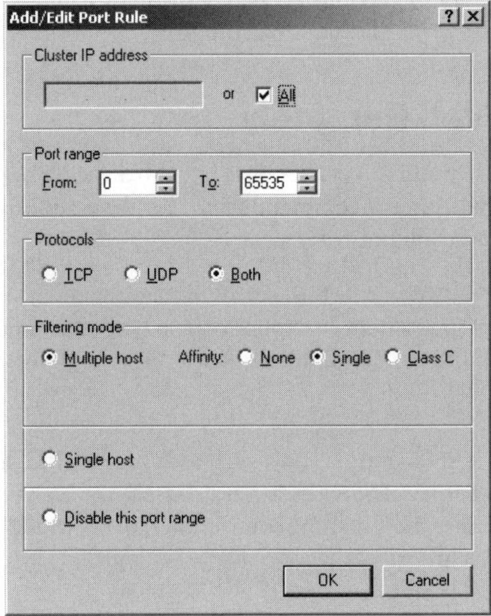

The radio buttons in the Filtering Mode section allow you to choose three options:

- Multiple Host Filtering specifies that multiple hosts in the cluster handle network traffic for the port rule. This filter mode provides scalable performance in addition to fault tolerance, because you can distribute the network load among the hosts. You can do this equally, or you can indicate that each host should handle a specific load weight.
- Single Host Filtering specifies that network traffic for the rule will be handled by a single cluster host according to the specified handling priority. This mode provides port-specific fault tolerance but not scalable performance.
- Disabling specifies the port range blocks all traffic to the specified ports and is used to increase security.

Selecting Multiple Host filtering enables you to specify one of the Affinity options: None, Single, or Class-C. *Affinity* describes how the cluster handles multiple connections from the same client. These options should be chosen as follows:

- Use None (disable affinity) when you want multiple connections from the same client to be able to be handled by any of the nodes in the cluster. This option maximizes scaled performance and provides the most effective load balancing. Use this option with the TCP option and not with the UDP or Both options.
- Use Single (the default) to direct connections from the same client to the same cluster host. You need to use this option for applications that maintain session state, such as server cookies.

- Use Class-C to direct requests from a Class-C address range to the same cluster host. This option is used when you have multiple proxy servers at use at a client site, making it look as though the client requests are coming from multiple computers. Class C affinity can also be used for applications that maintain session state, such as server cookies; however, you should use Single affinity to maximize scaled performance unless you need the capabilities of Class C.

Administering NLB Remotely

You can remotely administer an NLB cluster by using either the Network Load Balancing Manager or by calling `nlb.exe` from the command line. The Network Load Balancing Manager is the preferred tool for remote administration.

Enabling the remote control option so that you can use `nlb.exe` for remote administration of NLB introduces a number of security risks and is not advisable.

Other types of remote administration tools such as Windows Management Instrumentation (WMI) can also be used. Terminal Services is not an effective means of administering a node within an NLB cluster because the incoming connection request would simply be assigned to the next available node in the cluster.

Recovering from Cluster Node Failure

Performing regular backups of a server cluster is critical to ensure availability. The following sections describe the type of data you'll need to back up as well as the steps you'll take in different cluster failure scenarios using the Windows Backup and Recovery Wizard and Automated System Recovery (ASR) to restore data.

Backup Operators do not by default have the necessary rights to create an ASR backup on a cluster node. To grant the group permission to perform this task, add the group to the security descriptor for the Cluster Service by using Cluster Administrator or `cluster.exe`.

Backing Up Cluster Data

A server cluster requires four critical groups of data to operate:

Cluster Disk Signatures and Partitions You can back up the cluster disk signatures and partitions using Automated System Recovery in the Backup Wizard. Do this before you back up the actual data on the server cluster nodes. This is needed to restore the signature of the quorum disk. For example, you may later experience a complete system failure, and the signature of the quorum disk may have changed since the last backup.

Cluster Quorum Data When you back up data on a server cluster node, you should also back up the cluster quorum data. The cluster quorum contains the current cluster configuration, Registry information, and the cluster recovery log. You can back up this data by using the Backup Wizard to perform a System State data backup from any node on which the Cluster Service is running.

Data on the Cluster Disks To back up all cluster disks owned by a node, perform a full backup from that node. You cannot back up a cluster disk on a remote computer, only on a local node.

Data on the Individual Cluster Nodes You don't need to back up the quorum on all nodes; you can back up the cluster quorum disk on just one node. A System State Data backup automatically backs up the quorum data as long as the Cluster Service is running. You'll want to make sure to back up application data as well.

Recovering from Cluster Failure

You might encounter several different failure scenarios that will require you to restore the cluster. The steps you must take are determined by the type of failure experienced. If the cluster just isn't functioning as it should after a configuration change, you can simply roll back the cluster to an earlier configuration by using Windows Backup.

In the following sections, you'll learn how to recover from many different types of cluster node failure.

Cluster Disk Data Loss

If you've lost files and folders on one of your cluster disks, but not on the disk containing the cluster quorum, you can use the Windows Backup and Recovery Wizard to restore that data. You must restore the cluster disk data from the node that owns the cluster disk.

Cluster Quorum Corruption

In the case of corrupted files on the quorum disk, or a failed quorum disk, the cluster nodes will be able to boot, but the Cluster Service will fail to start because the quorum resource cannot come online. You must follow the steps in the appropriate scenario listed below to recover.

If you've recovered from quorum corruption by creating a new quorum log, some resources may fail to come online and the configuration data may be out of sync. This means you'll have to restore the matching checkpoints before the quorum resource can come back online. One way you can do this is by restoring the cluster quorum as described in the following scenarios.

Cluster Disk Corruption or Failure

If a cluster disk cannot come online, you can run the `chkntfs` command to determine if the disk is corrupted.

The Windows Server 2003 Resource Kit contains utilities that will enable you to restore a corrupted cluster disk without any downtime. Otherwise, you can simply use Windows Backup to restore the cluster disk, but this procedure will have to be performed offline.

If you have an ASR backup for the node, use the `confdisk` utility from the Windows Server 2003 Resource Kit, along with Windows Backup to restore the data on the cluster disk.

If you use the `confdisk` utility to restore your cluster disks, the checkpoints may not match.

If you do not have an ASR backup for the node, use the Cluster Recovery utility from the Windows Server 2003 Resource Kit and start the Cluster Service with the `/fixquorum` start up parameter.

After the restored node comes back online, restart the Cluster Service on the remaining nodes.

In a cluster quorum disk failure, the cluster nodes can boot up, but the Cluster Service fails to start because the quorum resource cannot come online. Entries in the Event Log indicate hardware failures. To recover from this failure, you would use the same tools and methods as for a cluster disk failure. As an alternative, you can create a new quorum on another node, restart the cluster using the `/fixquorum` Cluster Service start up parameter, and switch to the new quorum resource.

Single Cluster Node Corruption or Failure

If a node cannot join the cluster and the Event Log indicates that the cluster database on the local node is corrupted, you can perform a System State data restore on that node to replace the local cluster database. As an alternative, copy the latest checkpoint file (named *CHK###*`.TMP`) from the quorum disk to the `Windows\Cluster` directory. Next, rename the file as **`clusdb`**, and finally, restart the Cluster Service on that node.

If the node failure is due to system disk or other hardware failure, follow these steps to rebuild the node and rejoin the cluster:

1. Move all cluster resource groups to other nodes.
2. Replace the failed hardware.
3. Perform an ASR restore on the failed node.
4. Restore the files or application data for that node.
5. For each cluster group and resource, verify that the newly recovered node appears as a possible owner in Cluster Administrator. Then move a resource group to the newly recovered node and verify that the move is successful.

In the event that you do not have an ASR backup of the node, you would evict the node and then add a new node to the cluster.

Majority Node Set Cluster Failure

The majority node set cluster model does not use cluster disks. Instead, the cluster database is stored locally on each node rather than on a cluster disk central to all nodes. To restore the data for individual nodes, simply use the backup set for the node. The Cluster Service will automatically replicate the latest version of the cluster database to all other nodes in the cluster.

If you need to restore an older version of the cluster database, follow these steps:

1. Stop the Cluster Service on all nodes of the cluster.
2. Delete the local copies of the database on those nodes. This includes all the files under the `\MSCS\` folder.
3. Restore the cluster database to just one node and restart the Cluster Service on every node.

The Cluster Service will automatically replicate the restored version of the cluster database to all other nodes.

A *split-brain* occurs when some of the nodes fail and the cluster loses quorum. In this instance, you can force the remaining nodes to form a quorum and restart the cluster.

If the cluster database is not backed up or the database files are corrupt, you can create new cluster database files on a node by starting the Cluster Service on that node with the `/resetquorumlog` parameter. Then simply restart the remaining nodes.

Complete Cluster Failure

Even in the unlikely event that all nodes fail in a cluster and the quorum disk cannot be repaired, you can still recover the cluster. None of the nodes will be able to boot, so you must follow these steps to recover:

1. Use Automated System Recovery on each node in the original cluster to restore the disk signatures and the partition layout of the cluster disks (quorum and nonquorum).
2. Re-create the original cluster, join all nodes to the cluster, and re-create the original cluster group.
3. Using the Backup and Recovery Wizard, restore the cluster quorum on all nodes.
4. Install cluster applications on each cluster node and re-create the cluster resources using the same names as before.
5. Restore your application data from backup data sets.

If you do not have an ASR backup of each node, you cannot restore the cluster. Instead, you must re-create your cluster from scratch.

Summary

In this chapter, you learned:

- The uses of server clusters and Network Load Balancing (NLB). Server clusters are used to increase availability. NLB clusters are used to increase scalability.

- How to evaluate clustering technologies. The technology you choose depends largely on the applications to be hosted.
- How to plan a server clustering deployment. Important considerations include the type of failover policies, cluster model, and quorum type you will implement in your server cluster.
- How to plan an NLB deployment. You must understand how to plan the default port rules and how to plan unicast or multicast methods of balancing incoming client requests.
- How to monitor NLB clusters, which you accomplish by using the Network Load Balancing Monitor MMC snap-in or the WLBS cluster control utility.
- How to recover from a cluster node failure. Recovery tools include Windows Backup, ASR, the `chkntfs` and `confdisk` Resource Kit utilities, and the `/fixquorum` and `/resetquorum` startup parameters for the Cluster Service.

Exam Essentials

Understand the different purposes for server clusters and NLB clusters. Server clusters are used to increase the availability of services and stateful applications such as back-end database and messaging applications. NLB clusters are a special type of clustering technology and are used to increase scalability of services and stateless applications such as front-end Web servers.

Know the key considerations in planning a clustering solution. Key considerations include the type of application to be hosted and the levels of availability and reliability and scalability required.

Plan a server clustering deployment. Plan a server cluster using given business and availability requirements. Choose failover policies, the cluster model, and quorum type.

Plan an NLB deployment. Understand the behavior of the default port rules and when to create a custom port rule. Know whether to balance incoming client traffic using the unicast or the multicast method.

Know what tools and services are available to monitor NLB clusters. NLB clusters can be monitored using the Network Load Balancing Monitor MMC snap-in or the WLBS cluster control utility.

Be able to recover from a cluster node failure. Know the types of data to backup for clusters. Know how to recover from various types of cluster node failures by using Windows Backup and Restore Wizard and ASR. Know when to use the `chkntfs` and `confdisk` utilities and when to use the `/fixquorum` or `/resetquorum` startup parameters for the Cluster Service.

Key Terms

Before you take the exam, be certain you are familiar with the following terms:

affinity

asynchronous replication

availability

cloned applications

cluster

cluster host

Cluster Service

cluster-aware

failback

failover

failover pairs configuration

fault tolerance

group affinity

local quorum cluster

majority node set cluster

majority node set clusters

multiple-instance application

N+I configuration

Network Load Balancing (NLB) clusters

node

partitioned applications

quorum resource

reliability

resource

resource group

scaling out

scaling up

server clusters

single quorum device cluster

single-instance applications

split-brain

standby server configuration

stateful applications

stateless applications

Storage Area Network (SAN)

synchronous replication

virtual server

Review Questions

1. You are the system administrator for your company. The company runs Active Directory in Native mode. All servers are Windows Server 2003 and all clients are Windows XP.

   You must plan a solution for the Web application server farm to provide higher availability and complete fault tolerance, including recoverability of data. Additionally, you must ensure a strong level of client response time even in the event of a single node failure in order to meet your Quality of Service (QoS) agreement with your business partner. Money is no object; however, you want to spend the least amount necessary to accomplish your objectives.

   Which of the following options should you implement?

   A. Use a four-node server cluster in an N+I configuration with hardware-based RAID-0.

   B. Use a two-node server cluster in an N+I configuration with hardware-based RAID-5.

   C. Use a four-node NLB cluster with hardware-based RAID-5.

   D. Use a four-node NLB cluster in an N+I configuration.

2. You are the system administrator for your company. The company runs Active Directory in Native mode. All servers are Windows Server 2003 and all clients are Windows XP.

   You must plan a solution for the Web application server farm to provide high availability and scalability for the e-Commerce operations of the company's Web site. Additionally, you must ensure that incoming client requests are evenly distributed among available nodes in a way that is transparent to end users. You also want to use existing infrastructure services to accomplish your objective.

   Which of the following features of DNS will help you to accomplish your objective?

   A. Stub zones with conditional forwarding

   B. Zone transfers with LUN masking

   C. Round robin DNS

   D. LUN masking with stub zones

3. You are the system administrator for your company. The company runs Active Directory in Native mode. All servers are Windows Server 2003 and all clients are Windows XP.

   You must plan a solution for the SQL Server database application server farm to provide high availability for the order processing operations of the company's e-Commerce Web site. Additionally, you must ensure that the incoming client requests for data are evenly distributed among available nodes in a way that is transparent to end users. You want to configure the disks to allow for fast data access and data recoverability. You want to use the lowest-cost solution that will enable you to meet your objectives as well as provide for future scalability.

   Which of the following options should you implement?

   A. Install Windows Server 2003, Standard Edition and configure a two-node server cluster. Configure the application to store configuration and user data on a hardware-based RAID-5 array.

   B. Install Windows Server 2003, Enterprise Edition and configure a four-node server cluster. Configure the application to store configuration and user data on a hardware-based RAID-5 array.

   C. Install Windows Server 2003, Web Edition and configure a four-node server cluster. Configure the application to store configuration and user data on a hardware-based RAID-5 array.

   D. Install Windows Server 2003, Standard Edition and configure a four-node NLB cluster. Configure the application to store configuration and user data on a hardware-based RAID-5 array.

   E. Install Windows Server 2003, Enterprise Edition and configure a four-node NLB cluster. Configure the application to store configuration and user data on a hardware-based RAID-5 array.

   F. Install Windows Server 2003, Web Edition and configure a two-node NLB cluster. Configure the application to store configuration and user data on a hardware-based RAID-5 array.

4. You are the system administrator for your company. The company runs Active Directory in Native mode. All servers are Windows Server 2003 and all clients are Windows XP.

   You must plan a solution to implement high availability for the back-end database application that your company uses. The application is a proprietary accounting application from a third party vendor. You must choose the appropriate server cluster configuration.

   Which of the following server cluster configurations is not supported in Windows Server 2003?

   A. Two-node server clusters on Enterprise Edition

   B. Four-node server clusters on the 64-bit version of Datacenter Edition

   C. Four-node server clusters on the 32-bit version of Datacenter Edition

   D. Two-node server clusters on the 32-bit version of Enterprise Edition

5. You are the system administrator for your company. The company runs Active Directory in Native mode. All servers are Windows Server 2003, and all clients are Windows XP.

   You must plan a solution to implement high availability for the back-end database application that your company uses. The application is a proprietary accounting application from a third-party vendor. You must choose the appropriate server cluster configuration.

   Which of the following options describe benefits of the N+I configuration for a server cluster? Choose two.

   A. Achieves the highest level of availability of all failover policies.

   B. Optimizes the hardware investment.

   C. Good for handling multiple failures.

   D. Each node is guaranteed an idle failover node.

6. You are the system administrator for your company. The company runs Active Directory in Native mode. All servers are Windows Server 2003 and all clients are Windows XP.

   You must plan a solution to implement high availability for a back-end database application used for order processing. You decide to implement a four-node server cluster. Because of severe budgetary restrictions, you are forced to use two existing domain controllers as part of the solution.

   Which of the following options describes a recommended configuration for this deployment? (Choose all that apply.)

   A. Ensure that a minimum of 128MB of RAM on the nondedicated servers.

   B. The servers must also be global catalog servers.

   C. You must configure all four servers as domain controllers in order to have failover assurance for the domain controller services.

   D. You must promote a cluster node to a domain controller by using the Active Directory Installation Wizard before you create a cluster on that node or add it to an existing cluster.

   E. You can easily demote the domain controllers when the budget permits you to buy new, dedicated servers.

7. You are the system administrator for your company. The company runs Active Directory in Native mode. All servers are Windows Server 2003 and all clients are Windows XP.

   You must plan a solution to implement high availability for the messaging application servers. You need to ensure that you design the cluster network appropriately.

   Which of the following options describes a configuration recommendation for the cluster network?

   A. You can configure multihoming nodes as long as the adapters reside on the same subnet.

   B. Teaming network adapters on all cluster networks concurrently will provide fault tolerance and load balancing.

   C. You should design each cluster network so that it fails independently of other cluster networks.

   D. Windows Server 2003 does not support grouping network adapters on multiple ports to a single physical segment to provide fault tolerance to your cluster network.

8. You are the system administrator for your company. The company runs Active Directory in Native mode. All servers are Windows Server 2003 and all clients are Windows XP.

   You must plan a solution to implement high availability for the database application servers, which are located at two sites. You need to ensure that you design the cluster network appropriately. You are choosing between the synchronous and asynchronous methods of replication.

   Which of the following options describes a configuration recommendation for replication?

   A. Geographically dispersed server clusters must never use asynchronous replication unless the order of I/O operations is preserved.

   B. For every disk, there are two master copies in asynchronous replication.

   C. In synchronous replication, I/O operations are completed immediately.

   D. With asynchronous replication, the data at one site can never be out of date with respect to the other site at any point in time.

9. You are the system administrator for your company. The company runs Active Directory in Native mode. All servers are Windows Server 2003 and all clients are Windows XP.

   You need to plan a strategy for remote administration of your NLB cluster using the least amount of administrative effort. The security administrator advises you that you must plan the securest possible remote administration strategy that provides the least amount of privilege necessary to accomplish all of the server administration tasks. She further advises you that it is not acceptable to introduce any new security risks such as a Denial of Service (DoS) attack on the clustered computers. Which of the following options should you implement?

   A. Use a scripted solution with Windows Management Instrumentation (WMI) to call the `nlb.exe` program. Monitor the servers only from a Windows Server 2003 computer.

   B. Enable the remote control option on all nodes in the cluster. Use the Network Load Balancing Manager to call the `nlb.exe` program.

   C. Enable the remote control option on only the primary node in the cluster. Use the Network Load Balancing Manager to call the `nlb.exe` program.

   D. Use the Network Load Balancing Manager to remotely monitor the clustered servers.

10. You are the system administrator for your company. The company runs Active Directory in Native mode. All servers are Windows Server 2003 and all clients are Windows XP.

    You are planning the recovery strategy for your server farm of SQL Server 2003 computers. The SQL Server computers are configured in a four-node server cluster. Your current backup plan includes a System State data backup for all servers, including the clustered computers.

    Choose three of the following options to ensure that all of the data is backed up on the SQL Server 2003 computers. Each option represents a partial solution.

    A. The disk signatures and partitions of the cluster disks

    B. The cluster quorum data

    C. The data on the cluster disks

    D. The data on the individual cluster nodes

11. You are the system administrator for your company. The company runs Active Directory in Native mode. All servers are Windows Server 2003 and all clients are Windows XP.

    You have a server farm of Exchange Server 2003 computers configured in a four-node server cluster. Performance has suddenly degraded, and you confirm that one of the cluster disks cannot come online.

    Which of the following steps should you take first to attempt to resolve this problem?

    A. Use the `confdisk` utility to restore your cluster disks.

    B. Use the Cluster Recovery utility from the Windows Resource Kit and start the Cluster Service with the `/fixquorum` start up parameter.

    C. Create a new quorum on another node, restart the cluster using the `/fixquorum` Cluster Service start up parameter, and switch to the new quorum resource.

    D. Create a new quorum on another node, restart the cluster using the `/resetquorum` Cluster Service start up parameter, and switch to the new quorum resource.

    E. Run the `chkntfs` command to determine if the disk is corrupted.

12. You are the system administrator for your company. The company runs Active Directory in Native mode. All servers are Windows Server 2003 and all clients are Windows XP.

    You have a server farm of SQL Server 2003 computers configured in a majority node set cluster. A split-brain occurs, and the cluster loses quorum. The Event Log indicates that the cluster database on the local node is corrupted.

    List the two steps you must take in the order in which you must take them in order to resolve this problem. Each step represents a partial solution.

    Force the remaining nodes to form a quorum and restart the cluster.

    Restore the cluster database to just one node.

    Restore the cluster database to all nodes.

    Replicate the restored version of the cluster database to all other nodes.

    Start the Cluster Service on that node with the `/resetquorumlog` parameter to create new cluster database log files.

    Start the Cluster Service on all nodes with the `/resetquorumlog` parameter to create new cluster database log files.

    Start the Cluster Service on that node with the `/fixquorumlog` parameter to create new cluster database log files.

    Start the Cluster Service on all nodes with the `/fixquorumlog` parameter to create new cluster database log files.

    Stop the Cluster Service on all nodes of the cluster.

    Restart the remaining nodes.

    Delete the local copies of the database on those nodes.

13. You are the system administrator for your company. The company runs Active Directory in Native mode. All servers are Windows Server 2003 and all clients are Windows XP.

    You have a server farm of SQL Server 2003 computers configured in a four-node server cluster. Performance has suddenly degraded, and you confirm that one of the cluster disks cannot come online. Further troubleshooting indicates that the problem is due to a disk controller failure. You do not have an ASR backup of the node.

    List the two steps you must take in the order in which you must take them to resolve this problem. Each step represents a partial solution.

    A. Run the `chkntfs` command to determine if the disk is corrupted.

    B. Create a new quorum on another node, restart the cluster using the `/fixquorum` Cluster Service start up parameter, and switch to the new quorum resource.

    C. Create a new quorum on another node, restart the cluster using the `/resetquorum` Cluster Service start up parameter, and switch to the new quorum resource.

    D. Evict the node.

    E. Use the `confdisk` utility to restore your cluster disks.

    F. Use the Cluster Recovery utility from the Windows Resource Kit and start the Cluster Service with the `/fixquorum` start up parameter.

    G. Add a new node to the cluster.

14. You are the system administrator for your company. The company runs Active Directory in Native mode. All servers are Windows Server 2003 and all clients are Windows XP.

    You have a server farm of Exchange Server 2003 computers configured in a four-node server cluster. One of the nodes cannot join the cluster. You isolate the problem to a system board failure on the local node. You have an ASR backup of the node.

    Indicate the five steps you must take in the order you must take them to recover from this problem. Each step presents a portion of the solution.

    Perform an ASR restore on the failed node.

    Perform a System State Data restore on the failed node to replace the local cluster database.

    Replace the failed hardware.

    Evict the node on which the failure occurred.

    Rename the checkpoint file to **`clusdb`**.

    Move a resource group to the newly recovered node and verify that the move is successful.

    Move all cluster resource groups to other nodes.

    Restart the cluster service on that node.

    Add a new node to the cluster.

    Copy the latest checkpoint file from the system quorum disk to the Windows\Cluster directory.

    For each cluster group and resource, verify that the newly recovered node appears as a possible owner in Cluster Administrator.

    Restore the files or application data for that node.

15. You are the system administrator for your company. The company runs Active Directory in Native mode. All servers are Windows Server 2003 and all clients are Windows XP.

    You have a server farm of Exchange Server 2003 computers configured in a four-node server cluster. One of the nodes cannot join the cluster. The Event Log indicates that the cluster database on the local node is corrupted. You have an ASR backup of the node. You need to recover this node as quickly as possible.

    Indicate the three steps you must take in the order you must take them to recover from this problem. Each step presents a portion of the solution.

    Perform an ASR restore on the failed node.

    Perform a system state restore on the failed node to replace the local cluster database.

    Replace the failed hardware.

    Evict the node on which the failure occurred.

    Rename the checkpoint file to **`clusdb`**.

    Move a resource group to the newly recovered node, and verify that the move is successful.

    Move all cluster resource groups to other nodes.

    Restart the Cluster Service on that node.

    Add a new node to the cluster.

    Copy the latest checkpoint file from the system quorum disk to the Windows\Cluster directory.

    For each cluster group and resource, verify that the newly recovered node appears as a possible owner in Cluster Administrator.

    Restore the files or application data for that node.

Answers to Review Questions

1. C. NLB clusters are designed for stateless applications, such as Web application servers, and provide greater scalability and availability, but they do not provide fault tolerance for data. For this reason, you should implement a four-node NLB cluster with hardware-based RAID-5.

   Options A and B are incorrect because server clusters are designed for stateful applications such as back-end database and messaging applications. Option D is wrong because it does not provide for the recoverability of data. For this you need a separate solution, ideally hardware-based RAID-5.

2. C. Round robin DNS is the feature of DNS that distributes client traffic to the clusters, and then NLB distributes client traffic within the cluster.

   LUN masking is a method used to configure server clusters to allow for port-level zoning. It uses logical disks implemented at the controller level to provide access control.

   Stub zones, conditional forwarding, and zone transfers are all features of DNS, but they are not related to distributing incoming client traffic within an NLB cluster.

3. B. Stateful applications such as back-end database server applications are good candidates for server clustering. Server clusters are only supported on 32-bit versions of the Enterprise and Datacenter Editions of Windows Server 2003.

   NLB is used for stateless applications such as Web application servers.

4. B. Windows Server 2003 supports up to eight nodes in a server cluster on the 32-bit versions of Enterprise and Datacenter Editions.

5. A, C. Benefits of the N+I configuration include providing the highest level of availability of all failover policies, and providing good failover for handling multiple failures.

6. B, D. Ideally, you should not run domain controller services within a cluster of database application servers. However, if you cannot use fully dedicated servers, you must promote a cluster node to a domain controller by using the Active Directory Installation Wizard before you create a cluster on that node or add it to an existing cluster.

7. C. Best practices for designing cluster networks include designing each cluster network so that it fails independently of other cluster networks.

8. A. Geographically dispersed server clusters must never use asynchronous replication unless the order of I/O operations is preserved. If this order is not preserved, the data that is replicated to the second site can appear corrupt to the application and be totally unusable.

9. D. The Network Load Balancing Manager is the best solution for remote administration of an NLB cluster. Other potential options include WMI or the `nlb.exe` program. However, the `nlb.exe` program requires that you enable the remote control option and introduces security risks such as data tampering, denial of service (DoS), and information disclosure.

10. A, C, D. A System State data backup includes the cluster quorum data. In order to ensure that all data is backed up, you must add the following to the backup plan: the disk signatures and partitions of the cluster disks, the data on the cluster disks, and the data on the individual cluster nodes.

11. E. The first step you should take when a cluster disk cannot come online is to run the `chkntfs` command to determine if the disk is corrupted.

12. Start the Cluster Service on that node with the `/resetquorumlog` parameter to create new cluster database log files.

    Restart the remaining nodes.

    A split-brain occurs when some of the nodes fail and the cluster loses quorum. In this instance, you can force the remaining nodes to form a quorum and restart the cluster.

    If there is no backup of the cluster database or the database files are corrupt, you can create new cluster database files on a node by starting the Cluster Service on that node with the `/resetquorumlog` parameter. Then simply restart the remaining nodes.

13. D, G. In the event that a node cannot join the cluster due to a hardware failure, and you do not have an ASR backup of the node, you would evict the node and then add a new node to the cluster.

14. Move all cluster resource groups to other nodes.

    Replace the failed hardware.

    Perform an ASR restore on the failed node.

    Restore the files or application data for that node.

    For each cluster group and resource, verify that the newly recovered node appears as a possible owner in Cluster Administrator, then move a resource group to the newly recovered node and verify that the move is successful.

    Because the problem has been isolated to a hardware failure, you would follow these steps to recover: First, move all cluster resource groups to other nodes. Next, replace the failed hardware. Perform an ASR restore on the failed node. Restore the files or application data for that node. Finally, for each cluster group and resource, verify that the newly recovered node appears as a possible owner in Cluster Administrator, and then move a resource group to the newly recovered node and verify that the move is successful.

    If you did not have an ASR backup of the node, you would evict the node and then add a new node to the cluster.

15. Copy the latest checkpoint file from the system quorum disk to the Windows\Cluster directory.

    Rename the checkpoint file to **`clusdb`**.

    Restart the Cluster Service on that node.

    If a node cannot join the cluster and the Event Log indicates that the cluster database on the local node is corrupted, you can copy the latest checkpoint file (named `CHKxxx.TMP`) from the quorum disk to the Windows\Cluster directory. Next, rename the file as **`clusdb`**, and finally, restart the Cluster Service on that node. As an alternative, you could perform a System State Data restore on that node to replace the local cluster database. However, in this situation, you need to recover as quickly as possible, so the first option is preferable.

Planning Network Monitoring, Remote Administration, and Recovery

MICROSOFT EXAM OBJECTIVES COVERED IN THIS CHAPTER:

✓ **Plan network traffic monitoring. Tools might include Network Monitor and System Monitor.**

✓ **Troubleshoot TCP/IP routing. Tools might include the route, tracert, ping, pathping, and netshcommands and Network Monitor.**

✓ **Monitor servers that provide network services. Tools include System Monitor, Event Viewer, and service logs.**

✓ **Identify system bottlenecks, including memory, processor, disk, and network related bottlenecks.**

- Identify system bottlenecks by using System Monitor.

✓ **Plan secure network administration methods.**

- Create a plan to offer Remote Assistance to client computers.
- Plan for remote administration by using Terminal Services.

✓ **Plan a backup and recovery strategy.**

- Identify appropriate backup types. Methods include full, incremental, and differential.
- Plan a backup strategy that uses volume shadow copy.
- Plan system recovery that uses Automated System Recovery (ASR).

With all of the other elements of the network infrastructure now in place, it's time to turn our attention to planning how to keep the network running at peak performance and protected from potential disaster.

Monitoring network performance enables the administrator to anticipate problems and proactively resolve them before they even occur. Monitoring network traffic, servers, and services is accomplished using tools that are familiar from all the way back to Windows NT. If you are an experienced Windows administrator, you'll recognize Network Monitor, System Monitor, and Event Viewer. The service logs are the same as they were in Windows 2000 Server—depending upon whether a server is a member server or a domain controller, the logs may include Directory Service, DNS Server, and File Replication Service logs, among others.

Remote administration functionality has improved as the Windows server operating systems evolved, making it easier for an administrator to keep tabs on his network even from his own desktop. Windows Server 2003 now offers two new remote administration features: Remote Desktop and Remote Assistance. Remote Desktop is used to administer both server and client computers, and it enables you to take remote control of a remote computer. Remote Assistance is a type of help desk tool that offers a means for end users to request assistance from an expert user.

Designing the perfect network infrastructure, with all systems optimized for best performance, would do you no good if you failed to plan a disaster recovery strategy. Although most enterprise internetworks will require a more robust backup solution, the Windows Backup utility resurfaces in Windows Server 2003. This time, however, it has a couple of twists: Automated System Recovery (ASR) and volume shadow copy. ASR is a tool that is integrated with Windows Backup, and it provides a means of rapidly recovering System State data, system services, and disk configuration information. Volume shadow copy is another nice feature that enables users to view and restore previous versions of files that have been modified, overwritten, or deleted—without IT intervention.

In this chapter, we'll round out our coverage of planning a network infrastructure in Windows Server 2003 by exploring the techniques and best practices for network monitoring and optimization, remote administration, and recoverability of network-related services.

The tools for performance monitoring (Network Monitor, System Monitor, Event Viewer, and the service logs), remote administration (Remote Desktop and Remote Assistance), and disaster recovery (Windows Backup, volume shadow copy, and Automated System Recovery) were covered in *MCSA/MCSE: Windows Server 2003 Environment Management and Maintenance Study Guide* by Lisa Donald with Suzan London and James Chellis (Sybex, 2003) and in *MCSA/MCSE: Windows Server 2003 Network Infrastructure Implementation, Management, and Maintenance Study Guide* by Michael Chacon, James Chellis, and Matt Sheltz.

Monitoring Network Traffic

Sometimes the best way to see what's happening on your network is to watch the traffic as it passes. The *Network Monitor* tool enables you to capture and analyze network traffic. This tool is a direct descendant of the Windows NT Network Monitor, which in turn is based on the same-named tool provided with the Systems Management Server (SMS) product.

Network Monitor is an example of a type of program called a "network analyzer" (or *sniffer*, named after the Network General Sniffer toolset). Network analyzers capture raw traffic from the network and then decode it just as the protocol stack would. Because they don't depend on a protocol stack, you can use an analyzer to monitor traffic for protocol types you don't actually have installed. For example, you might use Network Monitor to capture and decode AppleTalk packets while troubleshooting a Mac connectivity problem, even without having AppleTalk on your workstation.

Network Monitor has two components:

- The application, which you install on Windows Server 2003
- The driver, which you install on any Windows 2000 or XP client machine

Before you can monitor traffic on a particular computer, the driver must be installed on that computer. The driver is automatically installed when you install the application. The driver is required because it puts the network card into *promiscuous mode*, in which the card will accept packets not addressed to it—an obvious requirement for monitoring network traffic intended for remote destinations.

Before you install and use Network Monitor, you should be aware of a couple of caveats. First, the Windows Server 2003 Network Monitor works only with Windows 2000 or XP clients. If you want to use it to monitor Windows NT, 95, or 98 clients, you need the Network Monitor drivers from the SMS product CD. More importantly, the Windows Server 2003 version of Network Monitor allows you to watch traffic to and from only the server on which it is installed. The SMS version of Network Monitor supports watching traffic anywhere on your network.

Network Monitor allocates a sizeable chunk of RAM to use as a capture buffer. When you tell Network Monitor to start capturing network packets, it copies every packet it sees on a particular network interface card (NIC) to the buffer, gathering statistical data as it goes. When you stop the capture process, you can analyze the buffered data in a variety of ways. You'll find it useful to apply capture filters, filters that screen out packets in which you're not interested, so that you can ensure that you are not overwhelmed by a blizzard of meaningless data.

In the following sections, we'll cover how to install Network Monitor. Next, you'll learn how to use Network Monitor to capture and view data about network traffic. You'll then learn to work with capture filters and display filters to target specific sets of data about network traffic. The section closes with a discussion on how to manage Network Monitor from the command line.

The Help and Support Center also includes a Network Diagnostics tool that can be used to scan a system and provide detailed information about network connections and network-related hardware and software.

Installing the Network Monitor Driver and Application

If you want to use the Network Monitor to capture packets from a machine that doesn't already have Network Monitor on it, you need to install the Network Monitor driver on the target machine. Once you've installed the Network Monitor driver on at least one other machine, you can install the Network Monitor application itself and start monitoring.

Exercise 10.1 walks you through this process. In this exercise, you'll install the Network Monitor driver and the Network Monitor application. You may be prompted for the Windows Server 2003 CD, too, so have it handy.

Be forewarned that many organizations watch their network very closely for signs of network analyzer use, so completing this exercise in a corporate network may raise an alarm in the IT department.

EXERCISE 10.1

Installing the Network Monitor Driver and Application

Installing the Network Monitor Driver

1. Open the LAN connection in the Network Connections folder by selecting Start ➢ Control Panel ➢ Network Connections ➢ Local Area Connection. The Local Area Connection Properties page appears as displayed.

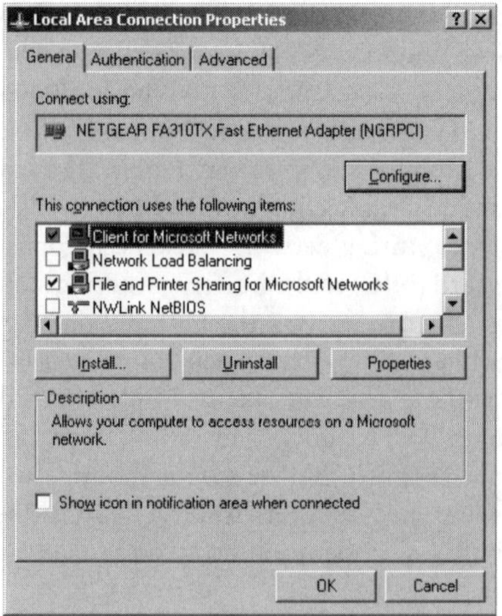

2. Click the Install button. The Select Network Component Type dialog box appears. Click Protocol in the component list, and click the Add button.

EXERCISE 10.1 *(continued)*

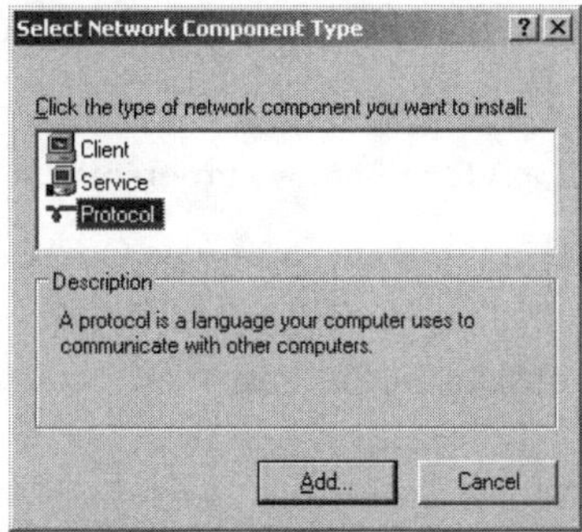

3. The Select Network Protocol dialog box appears. Select Network Monitor Driver, and click the OK button.

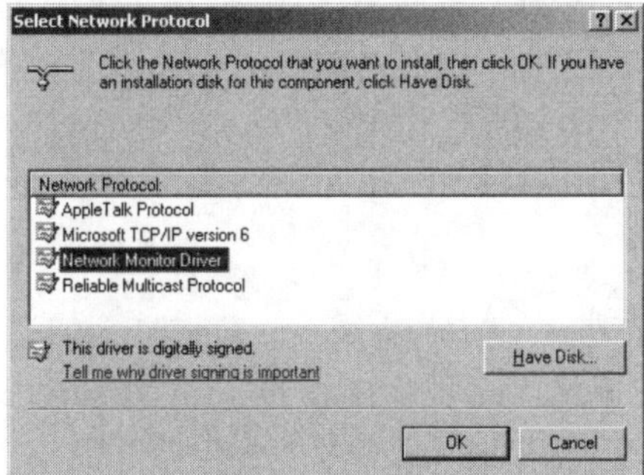

4. Once the driver is installed, the Local Area Connection Properties dialog box reappears with the Network Monitor Driver now displayed.

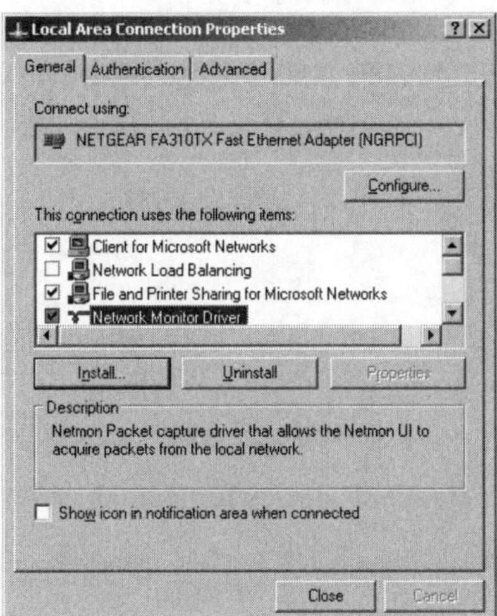

EXERCISE 10.1 *(continued)*

5. Click the OK button.

Installing the Network Monitor Application

6. Select Start ➤ Control Panel ➤ Add or Remove Programs.

7. When the Add or Remove Programs dialog box appears, click the Add/Remove Windows Components button. The Windows Components Wizard will appear.

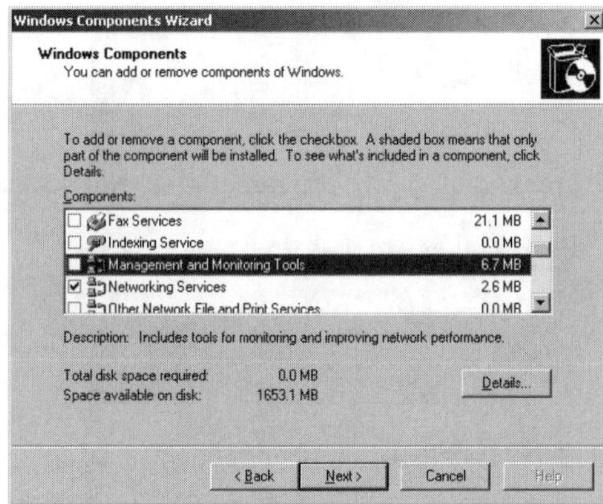

8. Select the Management and Monitoring Tools item, and then click the Details button. The Management and Monitoring Tools dialog box is displayed.

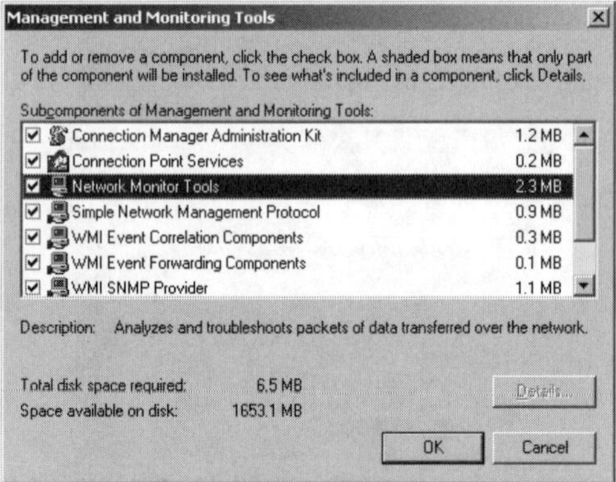

9. Check the box next to the Network Monitor Tools item, and then click OK.

10. Click Next when you return to the Windows Components Wizard.

11. After the necessary files are copied, click Finish to close the wizard.

12. Click the Close button to close the Add or Remove Programs dialog box.

Using Network Monitor

Network Monitor is a complicated tool; it's made for complicated tasks, and its interface reflects that fact. When you first start Network Monitor, it will ask you to choose a network to monitor, as shown in Figure 10.1. The list of networks you see will depend on the number of NICs you have installed; if you only have one NIC, Network Monitor will automatically select the correct network for you.

FIGURE 10.1 The Select A Network window

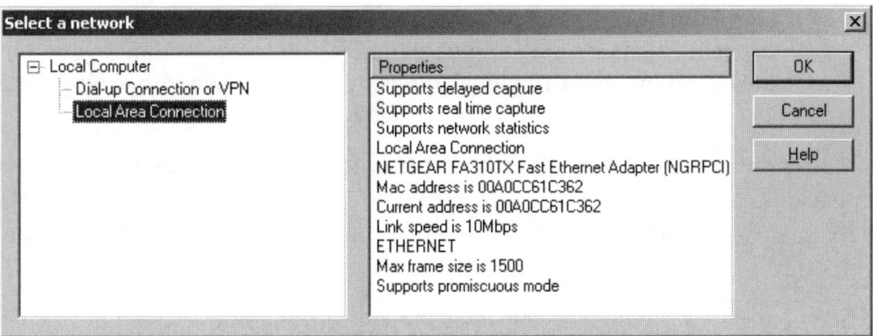

Once you've done that, you'll see the Network Monitor window, as shown in Figure 10.2. Although the screen may seem overwhelming, there is logic to what you see.

FIGURE 10.2 The main Network Monitor window

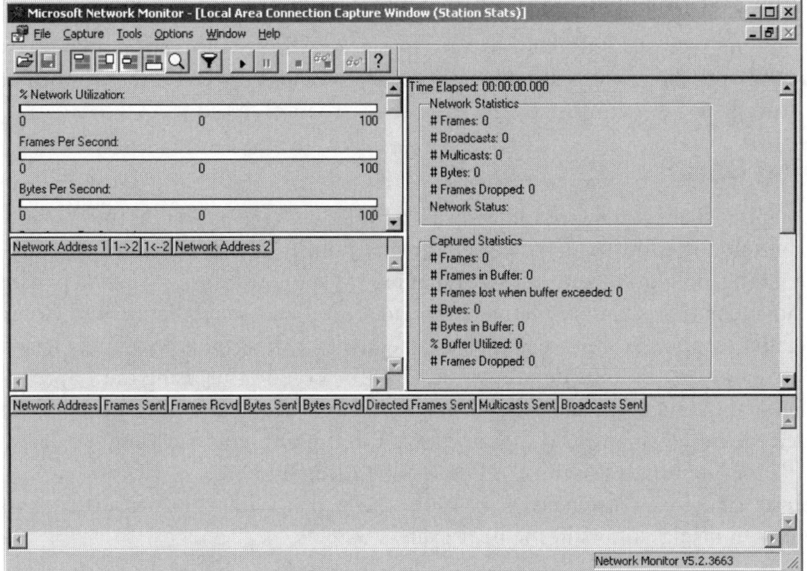

The following list explains what you'll see in the main Network Monitor window (you can turn specific panes on and off with the Window menu):

The Graph Pane This pane is located in the upper-left corner. It displays bar graphs of current network utilization, including the % Network Utilization and the number of frames, bytes, broadcasts, and multicasts per second. This pane updates only when a capture is in progress.

High % Network Utilization values can be caused by high-volume printing and high Ethernet collisions due to bad wiring or a bad NIC. When satin cables are exposed, cleaning staff can damage the cables by running over them when they vacuum, and this can also result in high % Network Utilization values.

The Session Stats Pane This pane is located in the center of the left side. It shows information about data packets captured during the current session. This information includes the source and destination network addresses and how many packets have gone in each direction between the two endpoints.

The Total Stats Pane This pane encompasses the entire right side of the window and lists a variety of interesting statistics (including the total number of unicast, broadcast, and multicast frames, plus the amount of data currently in the capture buffer). Like the Session Stats pane, this pane's contents are continuously updated during a capture.

The Station Stats Pane This pane is located at the bottom portion of the window. It contains statistics such as Frames Sent, Frames Rcvd., Bytes Sent, and Bytes Rcvd. that tell you what's been happening on the computer on which you're running Network Monitor.

The following sections will demonstrate Network Monitor in action. We'll cover capturing and viewing data, working with filters, and managing Network Monitor from the command line.

Capturing Data

When you capture data, you're just filling up a big buffer with the packets as they arrive. Network Monitor does not attempt to analyze them at that point. To control capture activity, you can use either the toolbar buttons (the ones that use the standard start, stop, and pause symbols) or the commands in the Capture menu: Start, Stop, Stop and View, Pause, and Continue.

Starting and stopping a capture is pretty straightforward, although you may need to adjust the buffer size upward from its default value of 1Mb. You do this using the Capture ➢ Buffer Settings command. Once you start the capture, Network Monitor will continue working until you've filled the buffer or stopped the capture. At that point, you can view the data or save it to a disk file for later analysis with the File ➢ Save As command.

In Exercise 10.2, you'll use Network Monitor to gather a full capture buffer so you can experiment with display filters in the next exercise.

EXERCISE 10.2

Capturing Data with Network Monitor

1. If you have not already installed Network Monitor, do so as described in Exercise 10.1.

2. Open the Network Monitor application by selecting Start ➢ Administrative Tools ➢ Network Monitor. The first time you use the Network Monitor application you will be prompted to select an interface to monitor. Select the Local Area Connection to continue with this exercise.

3. Use the Capture ➢ Buffer Settings command to increase the capture buffer size to 2Mb as shown. This gives you room for 4,096 frames of data. Click OK when done.

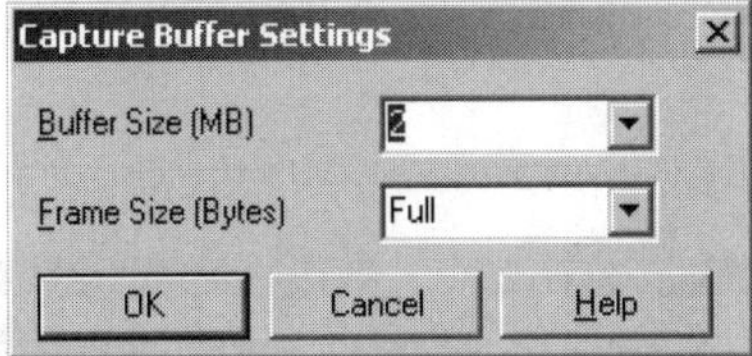

4. Start a capture with the Capture ➢ Start command. While the capture is going, use a Web browser to request a Web page from the machine upon which you are running Network Monitor. (This step is necessary for the next exercise.)

5. Let the capture run until the buffer is full; you can tell by watching the # Frames In Buffer line in the Captured Statistics pane. Then click the Stop button to stop the capture.

6. Save the capture buffer to disk with the File ➢ Save As command. (You'll need it for the next exercise.)

Viewing Data

After you stop a capture, you can view the accumulated data with the Capture ➢ Display Captured Data command. This opens the Frame Viewer, as shown in Figure 10.3. This window lists every captured frame, summarizing its source and destination address, the time at which it was captured (relative to the start of the capture operation), the network type, and the protocol in use. Although this data display is certainly interesting, picking out useful detail is difficult unless you have *impeccable* timing. You'll probably need to use Network Monitor's filtering functions to pick out just the data you want.

If you want to see the full contents of an individual frame, just double-click it. This causes two new panes to appear in the Frame Viewer window. The Detail pane is in the middle, and the Hex pane is at the bottom, as shown in Figure 10.4. This gives you an easy way to inspect, bit by bit, the contents of any captured frame in the buffer.

FIGURE 10.3 The Frame Viewer window

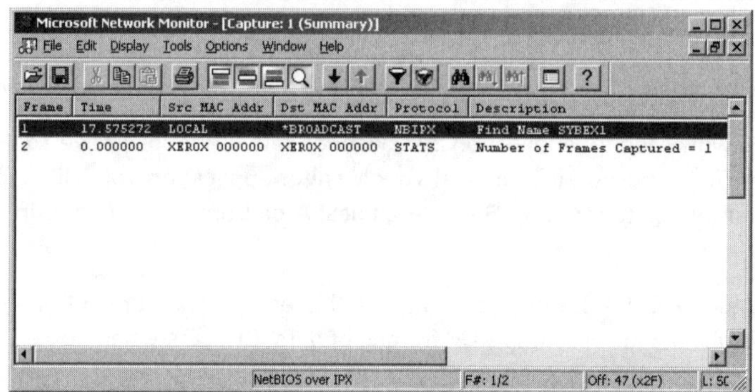

FIGURE 10.4 The Frame Viewer window with the Detail and Hex panes visible

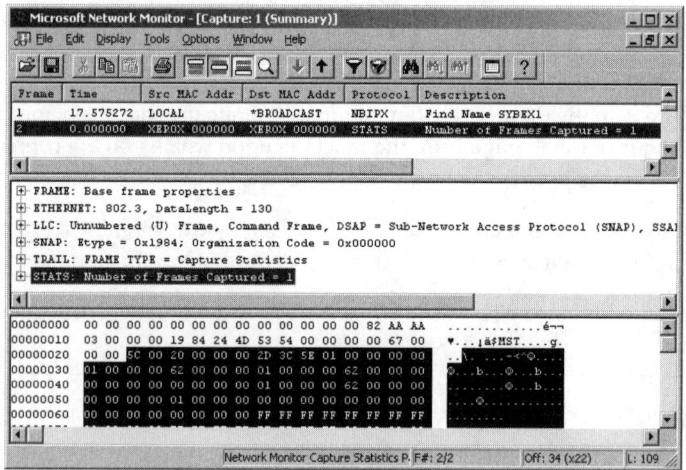

Using Filters

You can create two types of filters in Network Monitor: *capture filters* and *display filters*. Capture filters screen out unwanted packets before they're recorded to the capture buffer, and display filters display some packets, but not others. We will look at each in the following sections.

Working with Capture Filters

You create and manage capture filters using the Capture ➤ Filter command, available from the standard Network Monitor window. This displays the Capture Filter dialog box, as shown in Figure 10.5.

FIGURE 10.5 The Capture Filter dialog box

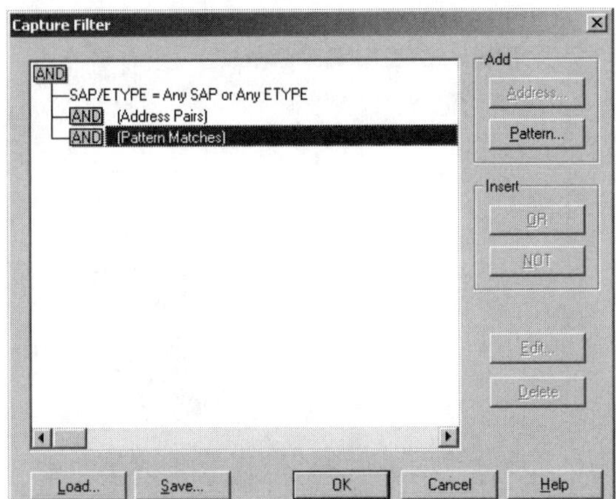

When working with capture filters, you need to remember that filters are grouped in a tree. The default filter says that any Service Access Point or Ethernet Type (SAP/ETYPE) will be captured. (Both of these tags mark packets with the protocol they're using.) They are captured because all three conditions under the root of the tree use the `and` modifier. While you can use `and`, `or`, and `not` for your own filters, you can't remove the original tree branches.

For example, suppose you want to create a filter that captures traffic going to port 80 on a particular machine. Capture filters don't care about ports, but you could create a filter based on the address by selecting the SAP/ETYPE branch and using the Edit button to capture only IP packets. Next, edit the (Address Pairs) item so that you've specified the proper destination address. If you were looking for packets with a particular payload, you could specify a pattern to capture that traffic with the (Pattern Matches) branch, too.

The capture filters feature in the Windows Server 2003 version of Network Monitor is fairly limited; many additional features work only in the SMS version.

Working with Display Filters

Once you've captured some data, you can create display filters that give you much finer control over what you see. This is useful because it's difficult to pick out the few frames you're looking for from a full capture buffer.

You create display filters while you're looking at the Frame Viewer window; use the Display ➢ Filter command to bring up the Display Filter dialog box, as shown in Figure 10.6. The mechanics of this dialog box work just as they do in the Capture Filter dialog box, with some additional features.

FIGURE 10.6 The Display Filter dialog box

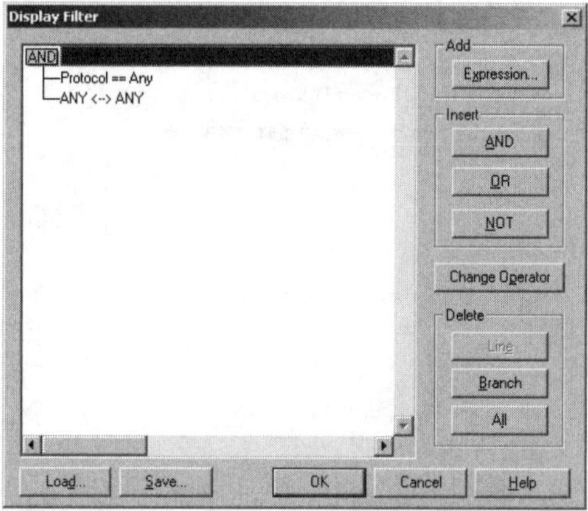

Now revisit the earlier example. You want to create a filter that only displays traffic to the Web server on a specific machine. Using the capture buffer from Exercise 10.2, you can create a display filter to limit what appears in the Frame Viewer, which you'll do in Exercise 10.3.

EXERCISE 10.3

Creating a Capture Filter with Network Monitor

1. Open Network Monitor, then reopen the capture buffer you saved by using the File ➢ Open command. If Network Monitor was left open, you could alternatively select Capture ➢ Display Captured Data to open the Frame Viewer window. The capture information should be intact from the previous exercise.

2. When the Frame Viewer window appears, use the Display ➢ Filter command to open the Display Filter dialog box.

3. Select the Protocol = Any line, and click the Edit Expression button. The Protocol tab of the Expression dialog box is displayed.

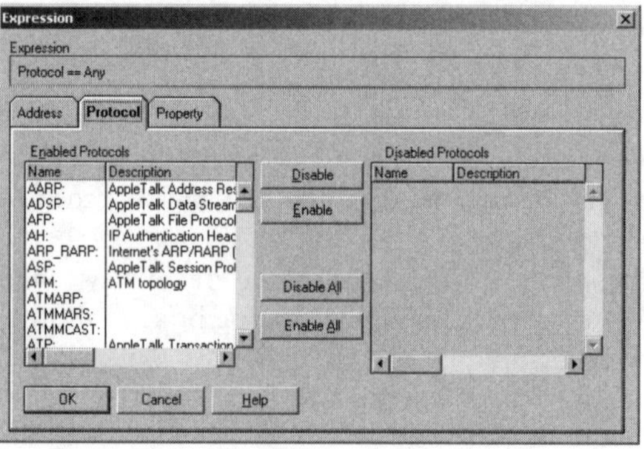

EXERCISE 10.3 *(continued)*

4. Click the Disable All button to remove all of the protocols. The filter screens out any protocol that's disabled.
5. Select HTTP in the Disabled Protocols list, and click the Enable button. HTTP should be the only enabled protocol. Click the OK button.
6. Optionally, select the ANY <--> ANY filter and use the Edit Expression button to add an address rule to the filter. Normally, you don't need to do this because the Windows Server 2003 version of Network Monitor monitors only traffic between your computer and one other at a time.
7. Click the OK button in the Display Filter dialog when you're done. The Frame Viewer window will reappear, but notice that the frame numbers (in the leftmost column) are no longer consecutive—the filter is screening out any traffic that doesn't match its criteria.
8. Double-click a frame to see its contents. Because you're looking at unencrypted HTTP packets, you can clearly see the requests and responses.

The best way to learn to use Network Monitor is to install it and get real-world practice using the tool. Practice setting up filters to capture and display different sets of data.

Managing Network Monitor from the Command Line

You can launch the Network Monitor user interface from the command line by using the `start netmon` command. The command line also lets you specify the parameters for capturing and filtering frames. The syntax is as follows:

```
start netmon [/net Number] [/capturefilter Path] [/displayfilter Path]
[/buffersize:Number] [/quickfilter {ATM | ETHERNET | IP | IPX | VINES
|TOKENRING | FDDI}, Address] [/quickfiltername FilterName]
[/autostart][/autostop]
```

For example, you may load a saved capture filter when you launch Network Monitor by typing the following command:

`start netmon /capturefilter d:\netmon\captures\http.cf`

You could set the capture buffer size to 4 megabytes with the following command:

```
start netmon /buffersize:4
```

Table 10.1 describes the parameters that you can specify for this command.

TABLE 10.1 Command-Line Parameters for the `start netmon` Command

Parameter	Description
`/net` *`Number`*	Specifies the number of the network from which you want to capture frames. You can specify any of the network segments to which your computer is connected.
`/capturefilter` *`Path`*	Specifies a capture filter to be used when Network Monitor starts. You can abbreviate `/capturefilter` as `/cf`.
`/displayfilter` *`Path`*	Specifies a display filter to be used when Network Monitor starts. You can abbreviate `/displayfilter` as `/df`.
`/buffersize:`*`Number`*	Specifies the size (in megabytes) of the capture buffer.
`/quickfilter {ATM | ETHERNET | IP | IPX | VINES | TOKENRING | FDDI},` *`Address`*	Specifies that Network Monitor should capture frames only of a particular type and from a particular address. You can specify up to three types at a time. You can abbreviate `/quickfilter` as `/qf`.
`/quickfiltername` *`FilterName`*	Specifies the name of the filter that you describe with the `/quickfilter` command. This parameter is ignored if you do not specify any `/quickfilter` options. You can abbreviate `/quickfiltername` as `/qfn`.
`/autostart`	Specifies that Network Monitor should begin to capture data at interface startup.
`/autostop`	Specifies that Network Monitor should stop capturing data when the capture buffer is full.

Real World Scenario

Capturing IPSec Traffic with Network Monitor

As the network engineer for a company that specializes in infrastructure applications for e-commerce companies, you want to ensure that the security implementation on your network is thorough. You are creating a plan to enforce protocol security on the network. Specifically, you want to periodically check the traffic between two Windows Server 2003 nodes that are configured to use the default IPSec policies. You are using a third-party network sniffer to analyze traffic. However, your sniffer is unable to interpret IPSec-specific portions of the IP packets.

You can use Network Monitor to capture IPSec traffic by creating a capture filter on one of the nodes and specifying the address pair of the two nodes between which the IPSec traffic will be generated. You can use `ping` to generate traffic between the nodes. You will need to execute several `ping`s because `ping` has a short time-out, and there will be a brief delay as the IPSec association is established between the two computers.

Packets that are secured with an Authentication Header (AH) will be displayed as a TCP, ICMP, or UDP packet with an AH header. The Next Header field shows AH as IP protocol number 51. Packets that are encrypted with Encapsulating Security Payload (ESP) will be displayed as ESP packets, instead of TCP, ICMP, or UDP packets, because ESP encrypts the original header. Furthermore, you will be unable to read the data payload in the ESP packet because it is encrypted (just view the Hex pane to see that the data fields of the frame are encrypted). The Next Header field shows ESP as IP protocol number 50. ISAKMP/Oakley packets can also be viewed, and the Next Header field shows ISAKMP/Oakley as UDP port number 500.

As you can see from this scenario, Network Monitor can be implemented as an important part of a security enforcement system.

Monitoring and Optimizing System Performance

Maintaining a healthy network involves monitoring the performance of network servers and optimizing the system performance of servers in different roles. Unlike Unix, which has a variety of settings you can configure in order to tune the kernel for better performance under different roles and requirements, Windows Server 2003 is a largely self-tuning operating system. This means that the operating system kernel is "generally optimized" for a wide variety of scenarios, and there aren't nearly as many possible actions you can take to optimize a system. The benefit is more simplified administration and less likelihood of unwittingly damaging a system due to overly enthusiastic meddling with configuration at the kernel level.

To accurately measure the performance of a server, you'll do best by starting with a performance *baseline*, which is a moment-in-time snapshot of a system's performance. Start with a minimal or default configuration, take performance measurements, and get a reliable average. Then you can start adding hardware and changing settings such as the page file settings. Take new readings after the fact to measure whether you have a net positive or net negative result in performance. Having a baseline from which to start can also help you isolate the cause of a gradual decline in server performance.

The idea is to baseline exactly where you stand at a default configuration with no load, capture data at regular intervals during typical usage as well as during and after changes to the system's hardware or software configuration, and watch for trends. This procedure has the benefit of informing you of the exact result of changes you make to a system, such as adding memory or increasing the number of file shares hosted on that system.

You can baseline a system by using the Performance Logs and Alerts utility to create a baseline counters log file. This procedure will be described in the section "Creating Baseline Reports."

The purpose of performance monitoring is to isolate bottlenecks in a system. A *bottleneck* is the least efficient point in a system. A server can perform only to the limits of its weakest link.

For instance, the server might have gigahertz quad processors; however, if it has only 128MB of RAM, the added processing power ends up being a disadvantage rather than a benefit. Data is processed much too quickly in this memory-deficient system. The resulting backlog taxes the memory subsystem to the extent that the system is crippled.

You must isolate the cause of a bottleneck in order to correct the problem. Throwing money and resources into upgrading processor speed can actually have a disadvantageous effect if the root problem is insufficient memory.

In the next sections, you'll learn how to use the System Monitor tool to resolve bottlenecks and optimize the performance of the servers on your network. First, we'll review the System Monitor utility. Next, we'll turn to analyzing server performance, and you will learn strategies to optimize the performance of four crucial resource subsystems: the memory subsystem, the processor subsystem, the disk subsystem, and the network subsystem. You'll also learn how to optimize the performance of network services. We'll wrap up the section with a discussion of how to use Event Viewer and log files to isolate and anticipate performance problems.

Understanding System Monitor

Like its predecessors since NT, Windows Server 2003 comes bundled with performance monitoring software. The *System Monitor* program is used to capture and analyze real-time performance data for a local or remote computer on the network. You can also view historical data by importing a log file from a previous capture session.

System Monitor enables the systems engineer to systematically measure the performance of the various resource subsystems and identify system bottlenecks in a logical fashion. The tasks you can perform with System Monitor include:

- Capturing data from either one computer at a time or concurrently from multiple computers
- Sampling data by collecting data points at specified intervals over a specified time period
- Displaying data in graph, histogram, or report view
- Displaying data on HTML pages
- Creating data capture configurations that can be exported to other computers

Windows 2000 granted access to System Monitor to the Administrators and Server Operators security groups. In addition to those groups, Windows Server 2003 has two new security groups whose members can use System Monitor on a local or remote system:

- Performance Log Users can manage performance-related counters.
- Performance Monitor Users can view performance-related counters.

The following sections describe System Monitor concepts and display formats.

System Monitor Concepts

You can launch System Monitor by opening Start ➢ Administrative Tools ➢ Performance. As an alternative, you can go to Start ➢ Run and type **perfmon** or **perfmon.msc**. The Performance utility contains the System Monitor and Performance Logs and Alerts.

System Monitor will have a performance impact on the computer on which it is run, so it is best to run it against a remote computer. As an alternative, you could use the command **start /low perfmon** to start the program with a low priority and thereby mitigate the performance hit of running the program locally.

Performance Logs and Alerts can be used to create a baseline of system performance and to store data collected in System Monitor for historical analysis. Custom consoles can be created to track performance for different server roles, such as Web servers, by saving the settings with a .msc file extension. The System Monitor console displays real-time data, as shown in Figure 10.7.

FIGURE 10.7 System Monitor

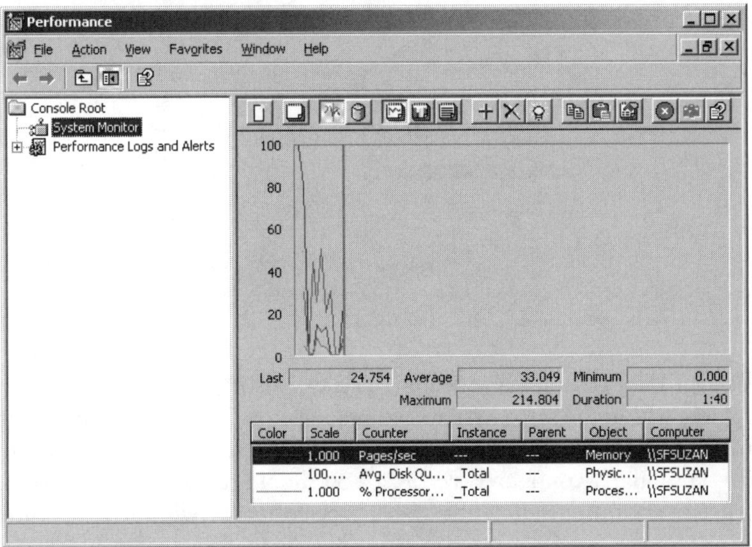

Previous versions of Windows did not track any counters by default, but in Windows Server 2003, three counters are tracked by default. These counters are tracked by default because they capture the most useful performance data for the widest variety of scenarios. The default counters include:

- Memory > Pages/Sec
- Processor > % Processor Time
- PhysicalDisk > Avg. Disk Queue Length

In describing objects and counters, we follow the format *performance object > counter*. For example, Network Interface > Bytes Total/Sec measures the Network Interface performance object and the Bytes Total/Sec counter.

You add counters by clicking the Add button (which looks like a plus sign) on the System Monitor toolbar. The Add Counters dialog box appears, as shown in Figure 10.8. Counters are defined based on four criteria:

- The local computer or counters from another computer
- The performance object
- All counters or specific counters
- All instances or selected instances

Let's explore these criteria and how they work together to define the data to be captured.

FIGURE 10.8 Add Counters dialog box

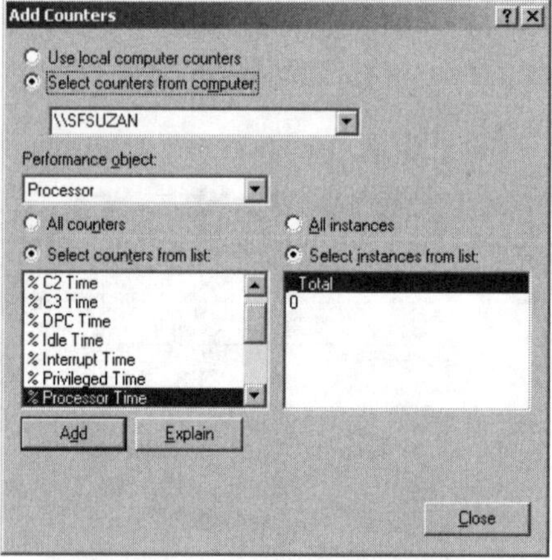

Computer

Counters track the local computer by default. You can also track counters on one or more remote computers within the same System Monitor session. This enables an administrator to track performance of a server relative to other servers, which can be useful when troubleshooting a problem on similarly configured systems. You should run System Monitor remotely so that you can get an accurate reading of a system's performance without the additional load of running System Monitor itself.

Performance Object

Performance objects are categories that organize all of the system resources that can affect performance. A system is essentially the sum of all of its performance objects. Different performance objects are listed depending on the configuration of a server. Examples of performance objects include Paging File, Memory, Process, Processor, and Network Interface.

Counter

Each performance object has an associated set of counters. A *performance counter* is a data item that is associated with a performance object and that carries a value corresponding to a particular aspect of performance for its object. Counters are used to track specific information regarding the performance object. For example, the Pages/sec counter provided by the Memory object tracks the rate of memory paging.

Each counter is listed at the bottom of the System Monitor window. For the counter that is highlighted in the list, the fields just above the counter list contain the following data:

- The Last field displays the most current data.
- The Average field displays the average of the counter.
- The Minimum field displays the lowest value that has been recorded for the counter.
- The Maximum field displays the highest value that has been recorded for the counter.
- The Duration field displays how long the counter has been tracking data.

To learn more about a specific counter, highlight the counter and click the Explain button in the Add Counters dialog box.

To select multiple counters for a performance object, Shift+click the contiguous counters or Ctrl+click the noncontiguous counters.

When you select a performance object, the most useful counter for that object is automatically highlighted for you. This is an extremely useful feature when learning how to performance tune a particular type of server, such as a Web server.

You will learn how to choose the right counters to monitor in order to performance tune different resource subsystems in "Monitoring Server Performance with System Monitor."

Instance

A performance object may consist of one or more instances. Performance objects such as Memory and Cache can have only one instance. Performance objects such as Processor or Print Queue can have multiple instances if multiple processors or print queues are on a system. Data can be tracked for all instances, such as all print queues or for specific instances, such as the HPLaserJet5N print queue.

Choosing a Display Format

The System Monitor toolbar includes three buttons that enable you to vary the view in which data is displayed:

Graph View The graph view, shown earlier in Figure 10.7, is the default view. Graph view is the view of choice when you want to see a small number of counters in a graphical format. The advantage of graph view is that you can see trends in the data over time. This view is ineffective for tracking a large number of counters, because it is difficult to view more than a few counters against each other in line chart form.

Histogram View The histogram view, shown in Figure 10.9, shows System Monitor data in bar graph form. Histogram view is the view of choice when you want to view large amounts of data. The disadvantage of histogram view is that it shows performance for only the current period. Histogram view does not display performance over time, as does graph view.

FIGURE 10.9 The histogram view in System Monitor

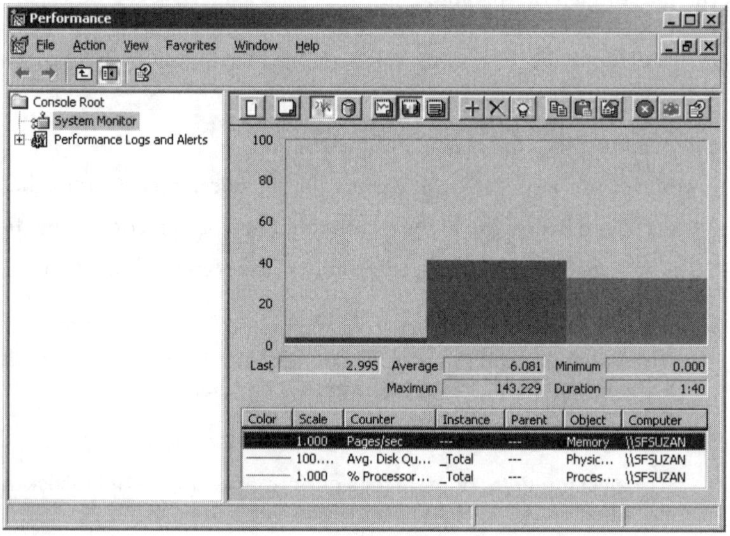

Report View The report view, shown in Figure 10.10, displays moment-in-time data for all of the tracked counters in a logical report. The data that is displayed is for the current session and is constantly refreshed in real time. The impact of this view is similar to watching people dance under a strobe light as they strike a sequence of poses. Sometimes there is no detectable change in the movement of one or more people, but in the next instant a person or group of people can be in a completely different position. You miss all of the movement between poses. The advantage of report view is that it provides a real-time snapshot of a large number of counters.

FIGURE 10.10 The report view in System Monitor

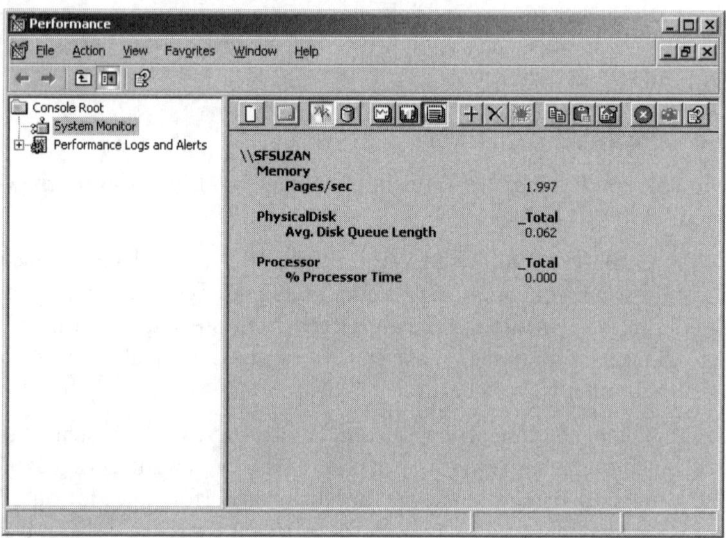

Here's a tip to help you quickly reload System Monitor with default counters. Click the bottom X in the upper-right corner of the console window to close the System Monitor console. A generic MMC console window is shown. Then open the `perfmon.msc` file listed in the File menu to open a System Monitor console with the default counters.

Monitoring Server Performance with System Monitor

By analyzing data, you can determine whether any resources are placing an excessive load on your computer and resulting in a system slowdown. Common causes of bottlenecks include insufficient system resources, insufficient network bandwidth, and misbehaving applications.

You should monitor these four main resource subsystems:

- The memory subsystem
- The processor subsystem
- The disk subsystem
- The network subsystem

In addition, you'll want to monitor the performance of network services. We'll explore how to monitor and optimize each of the subsystems, as well as network services, in the following sections; however, you must start with a performance baseline.

Counters must always be checked under a machine's full load, and the average statistic tells the story. Every device in a system has peaks and valleys. Monitoring a peak instance will not provide the overall performance of a selected device and basing an upgrade on peak performance data will not provide any increase in performance.

Creating Baseline Reports

A baseline gives you a snapshot of a server's performance at a given point in time. Your performance-tuning plan should include taking baseline reports at the following times:

- When a new system is first installed and configured
- At regular intervals after initial configuration, such as on a weekly or monthly basis
- Upon changing the system's configuration, such as after adding memory
- When troubleshooting a resource-related problem

This strategy works at all levels of IT staff and management. The help desk specialist can pinpoint resource problems on the user's computer and target users and departmental computers for potential upgrades. The hands-on administrator is better able to proactively resolve resource-related server problems. The network engineer can evaluate load on various servers and redesign the deployment of network services like WINS or implement high availability services, such as clustering and Network Load Balancing (NLB) to balance the load. The IT manager or director can use the data to justify IT expenditures for IT departments with tight budgets. The consultant can also use the data in a similar fashion to prove the effectiveness of a particular systems implementation, as well as to validate the need for a client to upgrade. The usefulness of the data is greatly enhanced when it is part of a data set that shows trends over time.

You can create baselines in the Performance Logs and Alerts utility by setting up a counter log file. In Exercise 10.4, you will create a baseline report for your Windows Server 2003 server.

EXERCISE 10.4

Creating a Baseline Report

1. Open System Monitor by launching Start ➢ Administrative Tools ➢ Performance.
2. Expand Performance Logs and Alerts.
3. Right-click Counter Logs, and select New Log Settings....
4. In the New Log Settings dialog box, type **Counter*mmddyy*** as the log name. (Replace *mmddyy* with the current month, date, and year.) The log file should be stored in the `C:\PerfLogs` folder by default. Click the OK button. In the General tab of the counter log Properties dialog box, click the Add button and add the following counters:

   Memory > Available Mbytes

   Memory > Pages/Sec

   Paging File > % Usage

   Processor > % Processor Time

   Processor > Interrupts/Sec

   PhysicalDisk > % Disk Time

   PhysicalDisk > Current Disk Queue Length

   Network Interface > Bytes Total/Sec

   TCPv4 > Segments/Sec

   Server > Bytes Total/Sec

EXERCISE 10.4 *(continued)*

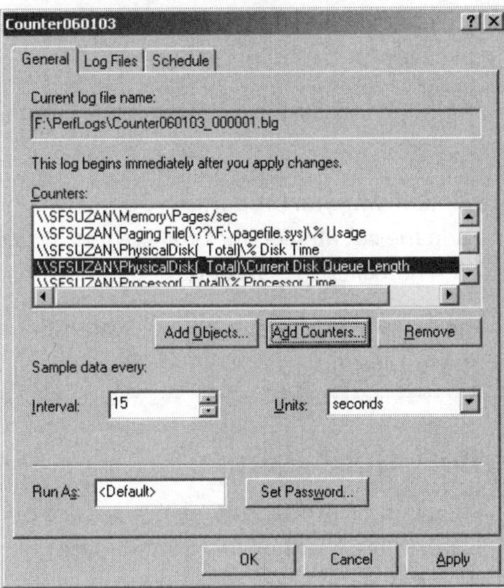

5. Set the interval for sampling data to 5 seconds.

6. Click the Log Files tab. Uncheck the End File Names With checkbox. This will prevent the filename from being appended with the current *nnnnnn* (month/day/hour). Click the OK button to close the Properties dialog box and start the log file.

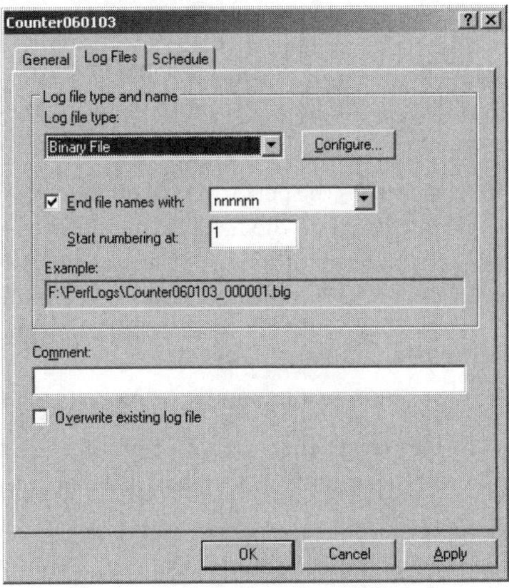

EXERCISE 10.4 *(continued)*

7. Generate system activity by launching and closing several applications, and running a graphics-intensive screen saver for two minutes.

8. Now view the log file by highlighting System Monitor in the left pane and clicking the View Log Data button on the toolbar.

9. On the Source tab of the System Monitor properties page, select the Log files: radio button. Click the Add button and add the counter log that you created, `C:\PerfLogs\Countermmddyy`, and click the Open button. Then click the OK button.

10. Add the counters from the log file you created to the System Monitor display to see the data that was collected in your log.

Monitoring the Memory Subsystem

When data is required by a program or process, the first place the operating system (OS) looks for the data is in physical memory. If the data is not found in physical memory, the next place the OS will look is in logical memory (also known as the page file). If the data is not found in logical memory, the OS will need to retrieve the data from the hard disk. It can take from 100,000 to 1,000,000 times longer to access information from the hard disk than it takes to access it from physical RAM.

Insufficient memory is the single most likely cause of any system bottleneck. The memory-related performance objects provide excellent data points for analysis even in instances when you have an idea what is causing a bottleneck. There are two performance objects directly related to memory usage:

The Memory Object This is the physical memory (or RAM). You can never have too much memory. Always ensure that there is significantly more memory available than you estimate that you will need on a given server.

The Paging File Object This measures the performance of the page file. The *page file* is logical or virtual memory that physically exists on the hard drive and is used to extend the physical memory space. Heavy disk thrashing and other symptoms of excessive *paging* (swapping between the page file and physical RAM) indicate the need to add more physical memory.

Tracking Key Counters for the Memory Objects

The following are the four most important counters for monitoring memory:

Memory > Available Mbytes Measures the amount of physical memory that is available to run processes on the computer. If this number is less than 4MB on average, you should consider adding more memory.

Memory > Pages/Sec (Added to System Monitor by Default) Shows the number of times that the requested information was not in memory and the request had to be retrieved from disk. This counter's value should be below 20 on average. For optimal performance, this counter's value should be 4 to 5 on average.

Paging File > % Usage Indicates how much of the allocated page file is currently in use. If this number is consistently over 99 percent on average, you may need to add more memory.

Paging File > % Usage Peak (Bytes) Indicates the peak usage of the page file instance in percentage.

These counters work in concert to tell a story about the memory usage patterns on a computer. Use the Paging File > % Usage counter value in conjunction with the Memory > Available MBytes and Memory > Pages/Sec counters to determine how much paging is occurring on your computer.

If you suspect that one of your applications has a memory leak, you should monitor the following counters:

- Memory > Available Bytes
- Memory > Committed Bytes
- Process > Private Bytes (for the application you suspect is leaking memory)
- Process > Working Set (for the application you suspect is leaking memory)
- Process > Handle Count (for the application you suspect is leaking memory)
- Memory > Pool Nonpaged Bytes
- Memory > Pool Nonpaged Allocs

Optimizing the Memory Subsystem

If you suspect that you have a memory bottleneck, the following options can be used to tune or upgrade memory:

- Use very fast memory, ideally 100MHz SDRAM or higher. Make sure the bus on the motherboard is 100MHz or higher to fully take advantage of the fast memory bus. Newer machines use DDR RAM. This RAM type can produce access times of 6 nanoseconds (ns).
- Increase the amount of physical memory that is installed on the computer.
- If your computer has multiple disk channels, create multiple page files across the disk channels.
- Verify that your paging file is sized correctly. Although the OS will automatically increase the size of the paging file if it is exceeded, you want to avoid this because it is an expensive operation. You can check the Memory > Commit Limit counter to verify page file sizing and extension.
- Try to run less memory-intensive applications.
- Try to avoid having your paging file on the same partition as the system files.

Typically, if your computer is experiencing excessive paging, the best way to optimize memory is to add more physical memory. However, some other options for managing the paging file for better performance are available. They include:

- Spreading the page file across multiple hard disks, which allows the disk I/O associated with paging to be spread over multiple disk I/O channels, for faster access.

- Increasing the size of the page file, if you have sufficient disk space. By default, 32-bit Windows operating systems create a page file (`pagefile.sys`) that is 1.5 times the amount of physical memory. You would want to consider increasing the page file size if the Paging File > % Usage counter was consistently near 100 percent.

If a paging file reaches the maximum size, the user will see a warning displayed, and the system might halt. This is another reason to monitor the page file and increase the size.

You will learn how to view and manage the page file later in this chapter in the section titled "Managing Performance-Related Options in the System Applet in the Control Panel".

In Exercise 10.5, you will monitor your computer's memory subsystem.

EXERCISE 10.5

Monitoring System Memory

1. Open System Monitor by launching Start ➢ Administrative Tools ➢ Performance.
2. In the System Monitor window, click the Add button on the toolbar.
3. In the Add Counters dialog box, select the following performance objects and counters:

   Select Memory from the performance object drop-down list, select Available MBytes in the counter list box, and click the Add button.

   Select Paging File from the performance object drop-down list, select % Usage in the counter list box, and click the Add button.

4. Click the Close button. You should see a chart showing how your computer's memory is being used.
5. To generate some activity, select Start ➢ Help and Support. Close Help and Support. Open Help and Support again, and then close Help and Support. The first time you opened Help and Support, you should have seen your Memory > Pages/Sec counter spiked. The second time you accessed Help, the spike should have been much lower. This is because the first time you accessed the program, it needed to be retrieved from disk; the second time you accessed this program, it was already loaded in memory.
6. Note the Paging > % Usage counter. If this counter is below 99 percent on average, you are not using excessive paging.
7. Note the Memory > Available MBytes counter. If this counter is above 4MB on average, you should have sufficient RAM.

Real World Scenario

Identifying System Bottlenecks on a Remote Computer with System Monitor

As a systems engineer in a Windows environment with dozens of Windows servers, you appreciate the tools that enable you to identify and fix problems from your office. System Monitor is best used to monitor resources on a remote computer, and can help you to isolate the true problem when users complain about slow response time from a server.

When server performance begins to degrade, you can use System Monitor to connect to the server and determine why the computer is responding less efficiently than normal. For instance, you install a new application on an application server. You then notice that the processor utilization is low but that the system is engaged in excessive paging. Based on this information, you determine that the server needs a memory upgrade in order to have the horsepower to run the application.

Monitoring the Processor Subsystem

Although processors are usually not the source of bottlenecks, you should still monitor this subsystem to make sure that processor utilization is at an efficient level. If your Windows Server 2003 computer has multiple processors, you can monitor them through System Monitor and configure them through Task Manager.

Tracking Key Counters for the Processor Object

You can track processor utilization through the Processor and System objects to determine whether a processor bottleneck exists. The following are the three most important counters for monitoring the system processor:

Processor > % Processor Time (Added to System Monitor by Default) Measures the time that the processor spends responding to system requests. If this value is consistently above an average of 85 percent, you may have a processor bottleneck. Ideally, you want this value to be less than 75 percent on average.

Processor > Interrupts/Sec Shows the average number of hardware interrupts the processor receives each second. If this value is more than 3,500 on a Pentium-class computer, you might have a problem with a program or hardware that is generating spurious interrupts. Sources of spurious interrupts include badly designed device drivers, such as beta video drivers. To isolate this possibility, test in normal and in VGA mode. If the value is much higher in normal mode, then replace the driver. Sometimes an old adapter can generate spurious results.

System > Processor Queue Length Used to determine whether a processor bottleneck is due to high levels of demand for processor time. If a queue of two or more items exists on average, a processor bottleneck is indicated.

If you suspect that a processor bottleneck is due to excessive hardware I/O requests or improperly configured IRQs, you should also monitor the System > File Control Bytes/Sec counter.

Optimizing the Processor Subsystem

If you suspect that you have a processor bottleneck, you can try the following solutions:

- Upgrade your processor. When upgrading the processor, consider that a bigger cache can be more advantageous than a faster clock speed.
- Use applications that are less processor intensive.
- If your computer supports multiple processors, add one. An additional processor will have a greater positive result on performance than a faster processor, even for single-threaded applications. You can also use processor affinity to help manage processor intensive applications.

Every edition in the Windows Server 2003 family supports multiple processors as follows:

- Windows Server 2003 Web Edition can support up to two processors.
- Windows Server 2003 Standard Edition can support up to four processors.
- Windows Server 2003 Enterprise Edition can support up to eight processors.
- Windows Server 2003 Datacenter Edition can support up to 32 processors on an *x*-86-based computer and up to 64 processors on an Itanium-based computer.

If your computer is capable of supporting multiple processors, you should follow the computer manufacturer's instructions for installing the additional processors. This usually involves updating the processor's driver or HAL driver to a driver that supports multiple processors through the Upgrade Device Driver Wizard.

Once you install your second processor, you can monitor the processors through the System Monitor utility, as previously described. You can verify that multiple processors are recognized by the operating system, as well as configure multiple processors, through the Task Manager utility. In Exercise 10.6, you will monitor your computer's processor.

EXERCISE 10.6

Monitoring the System Processor

1. Open System Monitor by launching Start ➢ Administrative Tools ➢ Performance.
2. In the System Monitor window, click the Add button on the toolbar.
3. In the Add Counters dialog box, select the following performance object and counter:

   Select Processor from the performance object drop-down list, select Interrupts/Sec in the counter list box, and click the Add button.

EXERCISE 10.6 *(continued)*

4. Click the Close button. You will see the counter added to your chart.
5. Note the Processor > % Processor Time counter (which is monitored by default). If this counter's average is below 80 percent, you do not have a processor bottleneck.
6. Note the Processor > Interrupts/Sec counter. If this counter is below 3,500 on a Pentium computer, you do not have any processes or hardware that are generating excessive interrupts.

Leave System Monitor open, because you will use this utility again in Exercise 10.7.

To configure multiple processors, you can associate each processor with specific processes that are running on the computer. This is called *processor affinity*. Once you have two or more processors installed on your computer, you can set processor affinity. We will do this in Exercise 10.7.

EXERCISE 10.7

Configuring Multiple Processors

1. Press Ctrl+Alt+Delete to access the Windows Security dialog box. Click the Task Manager button.
2. The Task Manager dialog box will open. Click the Processes tab to see a list of all the processes that are currently running on your computer.

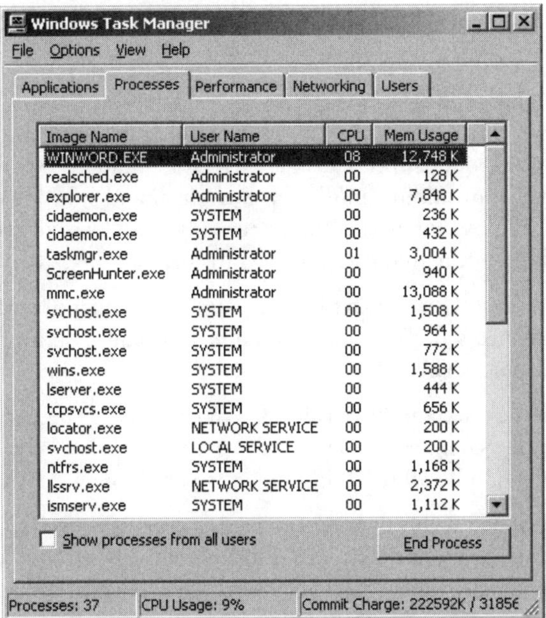

EXERCISE 10.7 *(continued)*

3. Right-click the process you want to associate with a specific processor, and select Processor Affinity from the pop-up menu. This option will appear only if your server has two or more processors installed.

4. The Processor Affinity dialog box appears. Specify the specific processor that the process will use, and click the OK button.

5. Close the Task Manager utility.

Monitoring the Disk Subsystem

Disk access is the amount of time it takes your disk subsystem to retrieve data that is requested by the operating system. The two factors that determine how quickly your disk subsystem will respond to system requests are the average disk access time on your hard drive and the speed of your disk controller.

During a disk write operation, the OS only writes to the controller. (The controller then writes to the actual disk.) Therefore, high-speed writes mandate a very fast controller. During a disk read operation, the data is accessed from the disk to the controller. Therefore, the disk access speed is critical to performance for disk read operations. Using high-speed disk controllers and drives in a stripe set, you can attain a disk access time of approximately 5.1 to 6.4 milliseconds.

Tracking Key Counters for the Disk Subsystem Object

You can monitor the PhysicalDisk object, which is the sum of all logical drives on a single physical drive, or you can monitor the LogicalDisk object, which represents a specific logical disk. The following are the most important counters for monitoring the disk subsystem:

PhysicalDisk > % Disk Time Shows the amount of time the physical disk is busy because it is servicing read or write requests. If the disk is busy more than 90 percent of the time, you will improve performance by adding another disk channel and splitting the disk I/O requests between the channels. High values in this counter can also indicate excessive disk thrashing due to paging to disk and, therefore, indicate the need for increased RAM.

PhysicalDisk > Current Disk Queue Length Indicates the number of outstanding disk requests that are waiting to be processed. This value should be less than 2 on average. A value greater than 2 indicates a disk bottleneck.

PhysicalDisk > Disk Reads/sec and PhysicalDisk > Writes/Sec These values are dependent on the specified transfer rate as defined by the hard drive manufacturer. As an example, Ultra Wide SCSI disks can typically handle 50 to 70 I/O requests per second.

LogicalDisk > % Free Space This counter tracks the amount of free space available on the hard drive. It can be used to track disk space usage proactively so users do not experience out-of-disk-space errors. This value should be above 15 percent at all times.

These counters can be tracked for both the PhysicalDisk object and the LogicalDisk object with the exception of LogicalDisk % Free Space.

Optimizing the Disk Subsystem

If you suspect that you have a disk subsystem bottleneck, the first thing you should check is your memory subsystem. Not having enough physical memory can cause excessive paging, which in turn affects the disk subsystem. If you do not have a memory problem, you can try the following solutions to improve disk performance:

- Use hardware RAID instead of software RAID. Software RAID has a high performance overhead that negates the advantages in read performance.
- Use faster disks and controllers.
- Use disk striping to take advantage of multiple I/O channels.
- Balance heavily used files on multiple I/O channels.
- Add another disk controller for load balancing.
- Use Disk Defragmenter to consolidate the files on the disk and optimize disk access.

In Exercise 10.8, you will monitor your disk subsystem.

EXERCISE 10.8

Monitoring the Disk Subsystem

1. Open System Monitor by launching Start ➢ Administrative Tools ➢ Performance.
2. In the System Monitor window, click the Add button on the toolbar.
3. In the Add Counters dialog box, select the following performance objects and counters:

   Select PhysicalDisk from the performance object drop-down list, select % Disk Time from the counter list box, and click the Add button.

   Select PhysicalDisk from the performance object drop-down list, select Current Disk Queue Length from the counter list box, and click the Add button.

   Select LogicalDisk from the performance object drop-down list, select % Idle Time from the counter list box, and click the Add button.

4. Click the Close button. You will see these counters added to your chart.
5. To generate some activity, open and close some applications and copy some files between your domain controller and the member server.
6. Note the PhysicalDisk > % Disk Time counter. If this counter's average is below 90 percent, you are not generating excessive requests to this disk.
7. Note the PhysicalDisk > Current Disk Queue Length counter. If this counter's average is below 2 on average, you are not generating excessive requests to this disk.

Monitoring the Network Subsystem

Windows Server 2003 does not have a built-in mechanism for monitoring the entire network. However, you can monitor and optimize the traffic that is generated on a specific Windows Server 2003 computer. You can monitor the network interface and the network protocols that have been installed on your computer.

Normally, you monitor and optimize the network subsystem from a network perspective rather than from a single computer. For example, you can use a network protocol analyzer to monitor all of the traffic on the network to determine if the network bandwidth is acceptable for your requirements or if the network bandwidth is saturated.

Tracking Key Counters for the Network Subsystem Object

The following are two of the counters that are useful for monitoring the network subsystem:

Network Interface > Bytes Total/Sec Measures the total number of bytes that are sent or received from the network interface and includes all network protocols. This counter can isolate problems with a NIC.

TCPv4 > Segments/Sec Measures the number of bytes that are sent or received from the network interface and includes only the TCPv4 protocol. (The TCPv6 protocol has a separate performance object.)

Optimizing the Network Subsystem

The following suggestions can help to optimize and minimize network traffic:

- Assign network adapters to IRQ10. By default, network adapters are usually assigned to IRQ5. IRQ10 has a higher priority.
- Eliminate extraneous protocols by unbinding them from a network interface. Where possible, use TCP/IP only and don't use NWLink and NetBEUI.
- If multiple network protocols are required, place the most commonly used protocols higher in the binding order.
- Use network cards that take full advantage of the bus width. This entails using 32-bit PCI cards instead of 16-bit and ISA cards.
- Use the fastest, affordable network cards in network servers. Use multiple NICs in servers to balance the load of network requests. Where possible, use multiple 100Mbps Ethernet NICs instead of 10Mbps Ethernet NICs. Use intelligent NICs (processor-based) with larger buffers. Also note that dedicated speed cards are faster than auto-sensing (i.e., 10/100) cards.

In Exercise 10.9, you will monitor your network subsystem.

EXERCISE 10.9

Monitoring the Network Subsystem

1. Open System Monitor by launching Start > Administrative Tools > Performance.
2. In the System Monitor window, click the Add button on the toolbar.

EXERCISE 10.9 *(continued)*

3. In the Add Counters dialog box, select the following performance objects and counters:

   Select Network Interface from the performance object drop-down list, select Bytes Total/Sec in the counter list box, and click the Add button.

   Select TCPv4 from the performance object drop-down list, select Segments/Sec from the counter list box, and click the Add button.

4. Click the Close button. You should see these counters added to your chart.

5. To generate some activity, copy some files between your domain controller and the member server.

6. Note the Network Interface > Bytes Total/Sec and TCPv4 > Segments/Sec counters. These numbers are cumulative. Use them in your baselines to determine network activity.

Monitoring Network Services

So far, you've learned how to optimize performance based on general system resources. However, not all servers are created equal, and different servers have different needs. Servers that provide network infrastructure services need to be optimized according to the specialized functions they perform. This section will introduce performance tuning for servers that perform various functions on the network.

Tracking Key Counters for Various Network Services

Most of the services that provide the underpinnings of a network infrastructure have one or more performance objects that can be used to capture data related to the service, and each performance object often has a myriad of performance counters associated with the object. For example, the Windows Internet Name Service (WINS) has a WINS Server performance object with many individual counters, while the Internet Authentication Service (IAS) has a total of eight separate performance objects, each with many individual counters.

Table 10.2 shows several network infrastructure services and the related performance objects that are available for tracking.

TABLE 10.2 Network Infrastructure Services and Performance Objects

Service	Performance Objects
TCP/IP	ICMP, IP, NBT, TCP, and UDP objects
Browser, Workstation, and Server services	Browser, Redirector, and Server objects
Windows Internet Name Service (WINS)	WINS Server object

TABLE 10.2 Network Infrastructure Services and Performance Objects *(continued)*

Service	Performance Objects
Connection Point Services	PBServer Monitor object
Directory service	NTDS object
Print server	Print Queue object
Indexing Service	Indexing Service, Indexing Service Filter, and HTTP Indexing Service objects
Web server	Web Service object, Web Service cache
DNS server	DNS object
DHCP server	DHCP Server object

The following performance objects and performance counters are the most useful for monitoring network servers and services:

Server > Bytes Total/Sec Measures the total number of bytes that the server has sent to and received from the network. This value provides an overall indication of how busy the server is.

Server > Server Sessions Measures the number of sessions currently active on the server. This value indicates current server activity.

Server > Sessions Errored Out Measures the total number of sessions that have been closed due to unexpected error conditions or sessions that have reached the autodisconnect time-out and have been disconnected normally.

WINS Server > Total Number of Registrations/sec Measures the sum of the Unique and Group registrations per second. This is the total rate at which registrations are received by the WINS server.

DNS > Total Query Received/sec Measures the average number of queries received by a DNS server every second.

Optimal values for these settings will differ depending on server configurations and network load. Create baseline reports using the important counters for a given service and compare the reports to periodic snapshots of activity in order to determine whether further performance tuning or an upgrade is necessary for a server performing a network infrastructure function.

You can identify security breaches by logging the Server > Errors Logon counter, which can indicate the use of a password guessing program, and the Server > Errors Access Permissions counter, which can indicate efforts to randomly access files in hopes of getting at something that was not properly protected.

Optimizing Network Services

The following suggestions can help to optimize network services and servers:

- Segment the network to reduce local traffic.
- Remove extraneous protocols.
- Use the most current drivers available, especially for network adapters.
- Use multiple fast Network Interface Cards (NICs) on all network servers. Ideally, you should use 100Mbps NICs on all servers. General file and print servers can use 10/100 Mbps NICs. Mission-critical applications and network infrastructure functions should be housed on servers with multiple 100Mbps NICs, ideally on a Gigabit Ethernet backbone. Most medium-sized to large networks today use Gigabit backbones and switches to down-speed the rest of the network. The best-case scenario would be to Gig the entire network infrastructure. However, this is slightly impractical at this time due to the significant cost of Gig switches.
- Monitor double-duty servers closely for overload.
- When isolating performance problems, always check for known bugs or viruses. This can save you hours of troubleshooting effort.
- Optimize the system resources for servers depending on the role they play.
- For print servers, take actions to optimize the disk subsystem, including ensuring adequate space for very large spool files and using fast disks and controllers. Printing is a very disk-intensive activity.
- For file servers, make sure that plenty of available disk space is available and that the disk subsystem is optimized for speed. File servers also consume RAM for caching data requests. File servers use approximately 25 percent of available RAM for caching.
- For application servers, make sure that there is plenty of RAM and use fast processors and/or multiprocessor systems. Application servers are processor-intensive and memory-intensive. If you notice heavy disk thrashing on an application server, insufficient memory is probably the culprit and the cause of excessive paging to disk.
- For database servers, ensure that the disk, processor, and memory subsystems are all optimized. Database servers voraciously consume all of these resources. Database servers house applications including Oracle, SQL Server, and MySQL; Enterprise Resource Planning (ERP) applications; Customer Relationship Management (CRM) applications; specialized financial applications such as the Great Plains suite of accounting software; and e-mail servers such as Microsoft Exchange Server. Servers that participate in Active Directory, WINS, DNS, and DHCP are also database servers, although they have fewer resource requirements than a true database server. Services such as DNS, WINS and DHCP account for approximately 1 to 3 percent of total traffic. They must have high performance when they are used but a true database server requires high performance for the majority (or better) of the day.
- For Web servers, make sure that sufficient memory is available. Web servers need lots of RAM in order to cache pages for rapid access. Make sure the NIC card is a high-performance adapter. The better the NIC, the more concurrent connections that can be handled.

- For network infrastructure servers including domain controllers, WINS servers, DNS servers, and DHCP servers, use the fastest possible hardware for all subsystems. These services are intensive consumers of resources on all the critical subsystems. Network throughput, fast disk access, ample RAM, and fast processing abilities are all critical requirements of these servers.

In Exercise 10.10, you will monitor network infrastructure services on your network.

EXERCISE 10.10

Monitoring Network Services

Monitoring Network Server Activity on a File and Print Server

1. Open System Monitor by launching Start ➤ Administrative Tools ➤ Performance.
2. Click the Add button on the toolbar.
3. In the Add Counters dialog box, specify a file and print server other than the local computer and select the following performance objects and counters:

   Select Server from the performance object drop-down list, select Bytes Total/Sec in the counter list box, and click the Add button.

   Select Server from the performance object drop-down list, select Server Sessions from the counter list box, and click the Add button.

   Select Server from the performance object drop-down list, select Sessions Errored Out from the counter list box, and click the Add button.

   Select Print Queue from the performance object drop-down list, select Jobs from the counter list box, and click the Add button.

   Select Print Queue from the performance object drop-down list, select Bytes Printed/sec from the counter list box, and click the Add button.

   Select Print Queue from the performance object drop-down list, select Out of Paper Errors from the counter list box, and click the Add button.
4. Click the Close button. You will see these counters added to your chart.
5. Change to the Histogram view by clicking the Histogram button on the toolbar.
6. From a client computer, generate activity to be measured by copying several files from the file server. Remove the paper from the printer and send three one-page print jobs to the printer.
7. Note the change in counters for the Server and Print Queue performance objects. These numbers are cumulative for the session. You can use them in your baselines to estimate the load on a file and print server.

EXERCISE 10.10 *(continued)*

8. Go to Start ➢ Control Panel ➢ Printers and Faxes, and open the print queue for the printer to which you sent the jobs. Clear the print queue by choosing Printer ➢ Cancel All Documents, and choose Yes when prompted.

Monitoring Network Server Activity on a Web Server

9. Launch System Monitor on a computer that is configured as a Web server.

10. Remove the default counters by highlighting each counter and clicking the Delete button on the toolbar.

11. Click the Add button on the toolbar.

12. In the Add Counters dialog box, specify a Web server other than the local computer and select the following performance objects and counters:

    Select Web Service from the performance object drop-down list, select Bytes Total/Sec in the counter list box, choose the appropriate instance, and click the Add button.

    Select Web Service from the performance object drop-down list, select Get Requests/Sec from the counter list box, choose the appropriate instance, and click the Add button.

    Select Web Service from the performance object drop-down list, select Total Not Found Errors from the counter list box, choose the appropriate instance, and click the Add button.

    Select Web Service from the performance object drop-down list, select Service Uptime from the counter list box, choose the appropriate instance, and click the Add button.

    Select Web Service Cache from the performance object drop-down list, select File Cache Hits % from the counter list box, choose the appropriate instance, and click the Add button.

13. Click the Close button. You will see these counters added to your chart.

14. Change to the Histogram view by clicking the Histogram button on the toolbar.

15. From a client computer, generate activity to be measured by accessing every page in the Web site through Internet Explorer.

16. Note the change in counters for the Web Service and Web Service Cache performance objects. These numbers are cumulative. You can use them in your baselines to estimate load on a Web server.

Optimizing Performance for Mission-Critical Network Infrastructure Functions

As the senior systems engineer for a small co-location facility in Silicon Valley, you are charged with evaluating Windows Server 2003 for a possible migration away from the current Unix environment, which is a mixture of Sun Solaris and Linux. You are skeptical about the ability of the new Windows OS to handle the intensive load you need with the availability your customers require. However, the CTO attended the Windows Server 2003 launch event, heard that the new version is significantly more robust and scalable, and asked you to design a test lab to evaluate the performance of Windows Server 2003 network infrastructure services and Active Directory as an LDAP directory services provider.

You design and deploy the test environment. Once all of the servers are in place, you are ready to begin capacity testing. You start with Performance Logs and Alerts, which you use to create a baseline of performance for each of the Active Directory and DNS servers. Using System Monitor, you define a custom console for each different server role, measuring and comparing the performance of all the servers in that role. You also acquire an evaluation copy of SMS. Using the version of Network Monitor that comes with SMS, you can capture and analyze network traffic for throughput and capacity testing.

During the testing phase, you subject your test network to a variety of different conditions and traffic loads. Once testing is complete, the monitoring tools in Windows Server 2003 provide you with all of the essential data you need to share with the CTO. You can use highlights from this data to justify your recommendations.

Using Additional Tools to Monitor Performance

The performance of network servers in Windows Server 2003 can also be monitored using the System applet in the Control panel, using Task Manager, and using Event Viewer, which are discussed in the following sections.

Managing Performance-Related Options in the System Applet in the Control Panel

The System Tool in Control Panel can be used to manage performance-related options including processor scheduling, memory usage, and page file configuration.

These options are located on the Advanced tab of the System applet in the Control Panel. Click the Settings button under the Performance section to open the Performance Options dialog box, and then click the Advanced tab. The dialog box is shown in Figure 10.11. From the Advanced tab, you can configure the following sets of options:

- Processor Scheduling, which enables you to optimize processor time for running programs or background services

- Memory Usage, which enables you to optimize memory for programs or system cache
- Virtual Memory, which enables you to configure the paging file

FIGURE 10.11 The Advanced Tab of the System Tool, Performance Options

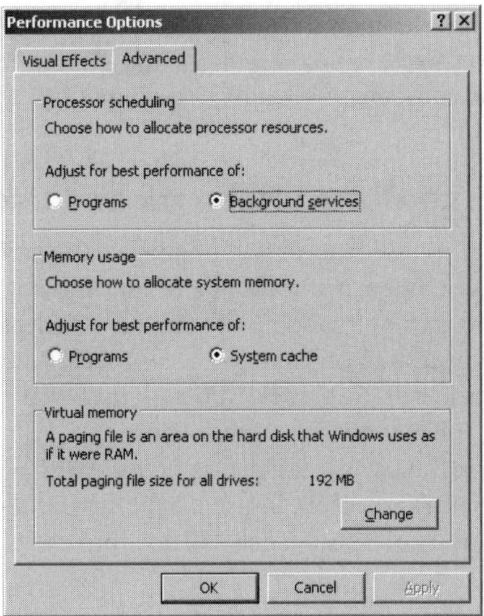

You manage the page file by clicking on the Change button within the Virtual Memory section of the Advanced tab. This will bring up the Virtual Memory dialog box, as shown in Figure 10.12.

FIGURE 10.12 Virtual Memory dialog box

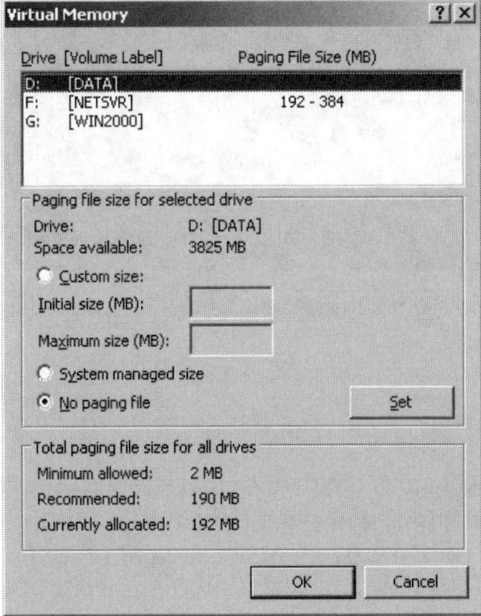

The page file is automatically set to 1.5 times the amount of physical memory. You can optimize the page file by moving it to a separate physical drive from the drive that contains the system partition and by locating it on a RAID-5 array, thereby splitting it over multiple disk I/O channels.

Before you can make any changes in the System Tool, you must be logged on to the local computer with administrative rights.

Using Task Manager to Obtain Network and User Statistics

The *Task Manager* utility can be used not only to manage applications, processes, and general system performance, but also to view networking and user statistics.

You can access Task Manager by engaging the Ctrl+Alt+Delete keystroke sequence and clicking the Task Manager button. You can also access Task Manager by right-clicking an empty area of the Taskbar and selecting Task Manager from the pop-up menu, or you can launch it by choosing Start ➢ Run and typing **taskmgr**.

The Networking tab of the Task Manager dialog box, shown in Figure 10.13, provides you with an overview of the network adapters in use on the server, the percentage of network utilization for each adapter, the link speed (such as 100Mbps Ethernet), and the current status of the adapter.

FIGURE 10.13 The Networking tab of the Task Manager dialog box

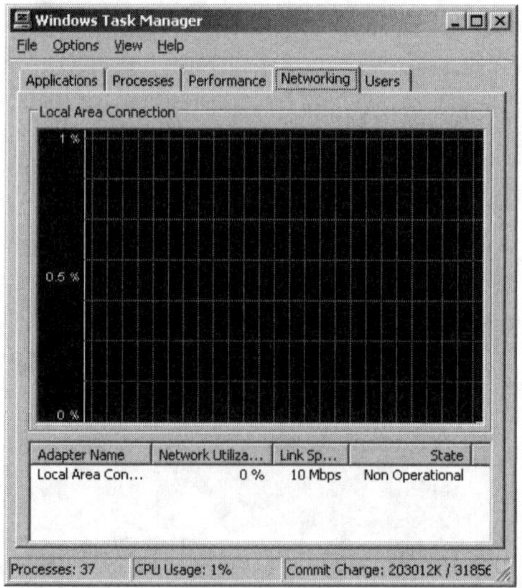

A graph displays the percentage of bandwidth that is being used by each adapter. If the server has two or more network adapters, you can see the traffic being generated on each adapter. If the network utilization is consistently high, you should tune your network subsystem, as described earlier in this chapter.

The Users tab of the Task Manager dialog box, as shown in Figure 10.14, provides you with a list of all the users who are currently connected to the server. For each user, you can see:

- The name of the user who is currently logged on
- The numeric ID that is used to uniquely identify the session number of the computer
- The current status of the session, either Active or Disconnected
- The name of the client computer that the user is using if applicable

FIGURE 10.14 The Users tab of the Task Manager dialog box

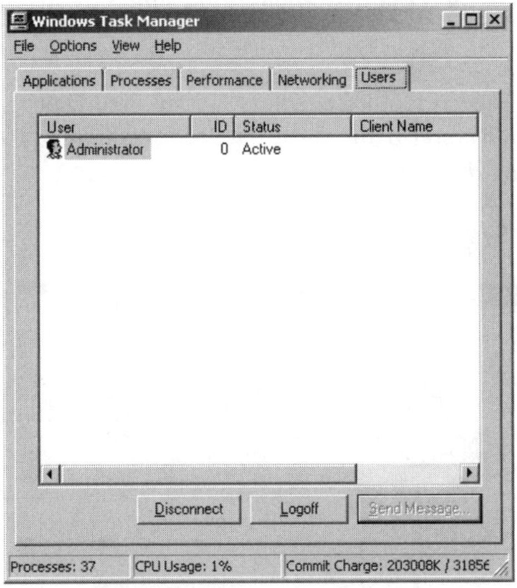

If you click on a specific user, you can disconnect the user, log the user off, or send the user a message using the associated buttons at the bottom of the Users tab.

Monitoring Server Logs with Event Viewer

When certain events occur on a Windows Server 2003 computer, the Event Log Service logs the event in a binary log file. The *Event Viewer* is the utility that is used to view the binary log files. Monitoring server event log files is a great place to start when performing preventative maintenance and troubleshooting existing problems. Thousands of event IDs are possible. Fortunately, events usually include a Web link for targeted information about the error. The Help and Support Center also provides a section on Error and Event Log Messages, which you can use to search the Internet for information about an error.

The information that is tracked is stored in three types of log files:

- The *System log* tracks operating system events, including hardware and service activity, as well as rejected connections due to insufficient licensing.
- The *Security log* tracks auditing events.
- The *Application log* tracks application events.

On Windows Server 2003 domain controllers, Event Viewer also includes Directory Service, DNS Server, and File Replication Service logs. Depending on how your server is configured, you may also have other Event Viewer logs.

Monitoring the DNS Server log is covered in Chapter 4, "Planning a DNS Strategy." Monitoring the directory service and file replication service logs is covered in *MCSE: Windows 2003 Active Directory Planning, Implementation, and Maintenance Study Guide* by Anil Desai with James Chellis (Sybex, 2003).

You can launch Event Viewer from the Administrative Tools program group. As an alternative, you can launch Event Viewer using the `eventvwr` command. Figure 10.15 shows Event Viewer with the System log displayed.

FIGURE 10.15 A System log in Event Viewer

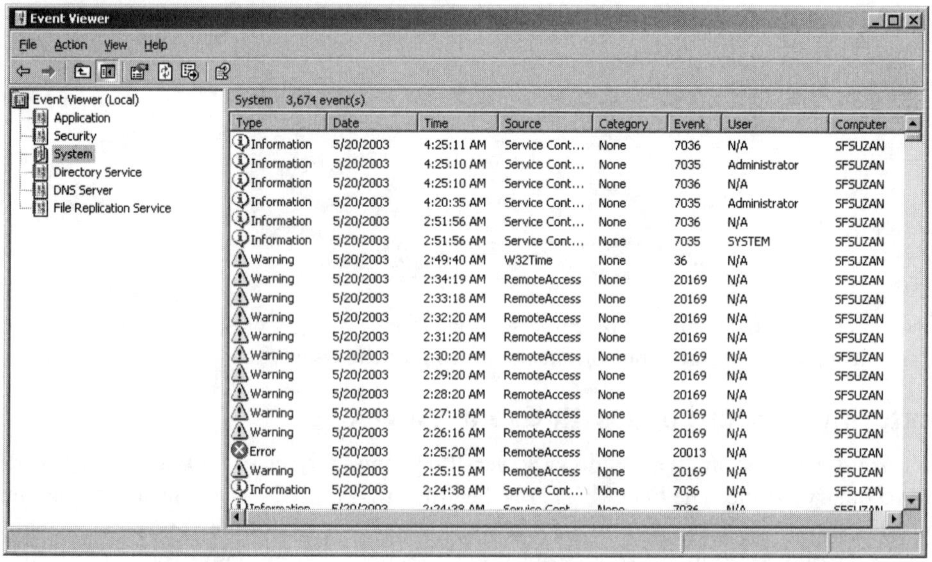

Event Viewer

File Action View Help

Event Viewer (Local)
- Application
- Security
- System
- Directory Service
- DNS Server
- File Replication Service

System 3,674 event(s)

Type	Date	Time	Source	Category	Event	User	Computer
Information	5/20/2003	4:25:11 AM	Service Cont...	None	7036	N/A	SFSUZAN
Information	5/20/2003	4:25:10 AM	Service Cont...	None	7035	Administrator	SFSUZAN
Information	5/20/2003	4:25:10 AM	Service Cont...	None	7036	N/A	SFSUZAN
Information	5/20/2003	4:20:35 AM	Service Cont...	None	7035	Administrator	SFSUZAN
Information	5/20/2003	2:51:56 AM	Service Cont...	None	7036	N/A	SFSUZAN
Information	5/20/2003	2:51:56 AM	Service Cont...	None	7035	SYSTEM	SFSUZAN
Warning	5/20/2003	2:49:40 AM	W32Time	None	36	N/A	SFSUZAN
Warning	5/20/2003	2:34:19 AM	RemoteAccess	None	20169	N/A	SFSUZAN
Warning	5/20/2003	2:33:18 AM	RemoteAccess	None	20169	N/A	SFSUZAN
Warning	5/20/2003	2:32:20 AM	RemoteAccess	None	20169	N/A	SFSUZAN
Warning	5/20/2003	2:31:20 AM	RemoteAccess	None	20169	N/A	SFSUZAN
Warning	5/20/2003	2:30:20 AM	RemoteAccess	None	20169	N/A	SFSUZAN
Warning	5/20/2003	2:29:20 AM	RemoteAccess	None	20169	N/A	SFSUZAN
Warning	5/20/2003	2:28:20 AM	RemoteAccess	None	20169	N/A	SFSUZAN
Warning	5/20/2003	2:27:18 AM	RemoteAccess	None	20169	N/A	SFSUZAN
Warning	5/20/2003	2:26:16 AM	RemoteAccess	None	20169	N/A	SFSUZAN
Error	5/20/2003	2:25:20 AM	RemoteAccess	None	20013	N/A	SFSUZAN
Warning	5/20/2003	2:25:15 AM	RemoteAccess	None	20169	N/A	SFSUZAN
Information	5/20/2003	2:24:38 AM	Service Cont...	None	7036	N/A	SFSUZAN

The default listing order displays events from the newest to the oldest. To change the view, select View ➢ Oldest First.

In the following sections, you'll learn how to review event types and get details about events.

Reviewing Event Types

The Event Viewer logs display five event types, denoted by their icons. Table 10.3 describes each event type.

TABLE 10.3 Event Viewer Log Events

Event Type	Icon	Description
Information		Informs you of the occurrence of a specific action, such as a system shutting down or starting. *Information events* are logged for informative purposes.
Warning		Indicates that you should be concerned with the event. *Warning events* may not be critical in nature, but they may be indicative of future errors.
Error		Indicates the occurrence of an error, such as a driver failing to load. You should be very concerned with *Error events*.
Success Audit		Indicates the occurrence of an event that has been audited for success. For example, a *Success Audit event* is a successful logon when system logons are being audited.
Failure Audit		Indicates the occurrence of an event that has been audited for failure. For example, a *Failure Audit event* is a failed logon due to an invalid user name and/or password when system logons are being audited.

Getting Event Details

Double-clicking an event in an Event Viewer log file brings up the Event Properties dialog box, which shows details about the event. An example of the Event Properties dialog box for an Error event is shown in Figure 10.16. Table 10.4 describes the information that appears in this dialog box.

FIGURE 10.16 The Event Properties dialog box

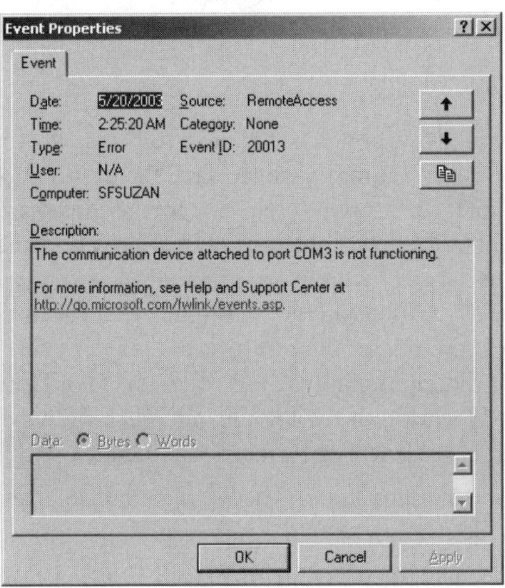

TABLE 10.4 Event Properties Dialog Box Items

Item	Description
Date	The date that the event was generated
Time	The time that the event was generated
Type	The type of event that was generated: Information, Warning, Error, Success Audit, or Failure Audit
User	The name of the user to whom the event is attributed, if applicable (not all events are attributed to a user)
Computer	The name of the computer on which the event occurred
Source	The software that generated the event (e.g., operating system components or drivers)
Category	The source that logged the event (this field will say None until this feature has been fully implemented in Windows Server 2003)
Event ID	The event number specific to the type of event that was generated (e.g., a print error event has the event ID 45)
Description	A detailed description of the event
Data	The binary data generated by the event (if any; some events do not generate binary data) in hexadecimal bytes or Words format (programmers can use this information to interpret the event)

Managing Log Files

Over time, your log files will grow, and you will need to decide how to manage them. You can clear a log file for a fresh start. You may want to save the existing log file before you clear it, to keep that log file available for future reference or further analysis.

To clear all log file events, right-click the log you want to clear and choose Clear All Events from the pop-up menu. Then specify whether or not you want to save the log before it is cleared.

If you just want to save as existing log file, right-click that log and choose Save Log File As. Then specify the location and name of the file.

To open an existing log file, right-click the log you want to open and choose Open Log File. Then specify the name and location of the log file, and click the Open button.

Each Event Viewer log has two sets of properties associated with it:

- General properties control items such as the log filename, its maximum size, and the action to take when the log file reaches its maximum size.
- Filter properties specify which events are displayed.

To access the log Properties dialog box, right-click the log you want to manage and select Properties from the pop-up menu.

The General tab of the log Properties dialog box, as shown in Figure 10.17, displays information about the log file and includes options to control its size.

FIGURE 10.17 The General tab of the log Properties dialog box

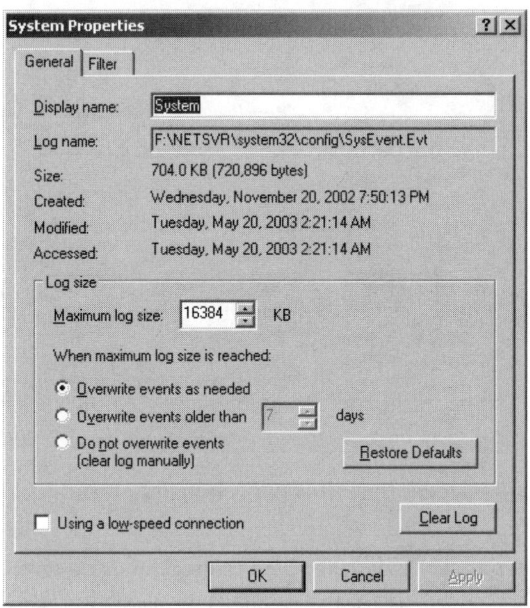

If you are monitoring the log file of a remote computer and you connect to that computer through a low-speed connection, then use the Using A Low-Speed Connection option on the General tab of the log Properties dialog box to optimize the access.

The Filter tab of the log Properties dialog box, as shown in Figure 10.18, allows you to control which events are listed in the log. For example, if your system generates a large number of log events, you might want to set the filter properties so that you can track specific events. You can filter log events based on the event type, source, category, ID, users, computer, or specific time period.

Assuming that a server is connected to the Internet, you can get online information about error messages from the Windows Help and Support Center. To do so, launch Help and Support from the Start menu. In the Support Tasks section, click Error and Event Log Messages to search for details on error messages and event logs.

FIGURE 10.18 The Filter tab of the log Properties dialog box

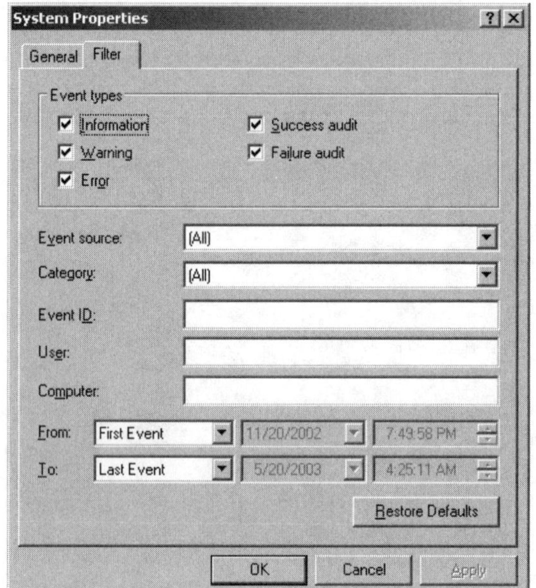

Windows Server 2003 includes the following command-line utilities that can be used to manage event logs:

`Eventcreate` The `Eventcreate` utility is used to create a customized application or system event log. For example, you can create a customized event log for error events.

`Eventquery` The `Eventquery` utility is used to query event logs. Filters are defined to include or exclude records based on information such as the event category or the user who generated the event.

`Eventtriggers` The `Eventtriggers` utility is used to create event triggers. For example, you could create an event trigger that automatically executes the Disk Cleanup utility when the percentage of free disk space falls below 13 percent.

Planning Secure Remote Administration Methods

Remote administration is an invaluable functionality that reduces administrative effort, empowers IT staff to accomplish more in less time, and increases the efficiency of help desk operations. Windows Server 2003 supports two new remote administration methods: Remote Desktop for Administration and Remote Assistance.

Remote Desktop for Administration allows you to remotely administer a Windows Server 2003 server from virtually any computer in the organization. For example, a network administrator at corporate headquarters could access and administer a server located in a remote field office.

Remote Assistance is a tool that enables users to request assistance from a technical expert. For example, a junior administrator troubleshooting a Windows Server 2003 Web server in the Network Operations Center (NOC) could ask a more seasoned administrator to remotely walk him through the process. An end user with questions about a feature in the new Microsoft Office suite could ask a help desk specialist to demonstrate the feature for her on her PC.

The following sections will cover what you need to know in order to plan a strategy for secure remote administration using Remote Desktop for Administration and Remote Assistance.

Planning to Remotely Administer Computers with Remote Desktop for Administration

Remote Desktop for Administration (formerly known as Terminal Services in Remote Administration mode) provides remote access to the desktop of any Microsoft Windows Server 2003 computer, allowing you to administer servers on your network from virtually any computer in the world. The Remote Desktop for Administration tool in Windows Server 2003 uses Terminal Services technology and is more powerful than the simplified Remote Desktop version found in Windows XP.

Remote Desktop for Administration can be used to troubleshoot organizational computers using a direct network connection, a secure Virtual Private Network (VPN) connection, or a secure remote access connection. Remote Desktop for Administration is used to control a remote computer's keyboard and mouse input and display the video output on the controlling computer's monitor. You can create up to two simultaneous remote connections. Each session is independent of other client sessions and the server console session.

No additional Terminal Services license is required to run Remote Desktop for Administration. However, computers using Remote Desktop for Administration must meet the following requirements:

- The controlled computer (the computer that will be accessed remotely) must be running Windows XP Professional or Windows Server 2003.
- The controlling computer (the computer that will access the remote computer) must be running Windows 95 or higher (with Remote Desktop client software) and use Remote Desktop Connection to establish a session with the controlled computer.
- An IP connection must be established between the two computers in order to establish a remote control session.

The following sections will cover the security considerations for using Remote Desktop for Administration, components of Remote Desktop for Administration, how to configure both the controlled computer (the remote computer) and the controlling computer (the computer that will be used to access the remote computer), and how to work with Remote Desktop sessions.

Security Considerations for Remote Desktop for Administration

Security requirements for Remote Desktop for Administration are increased beyond the inherent security in Windows Server 2003 as follows:

- Remote Desktop for Administration is disabled by default in Windows Server 2003 and must be enabled on any controlled computers.

- The Remote Desktop Users group is empty by default and must be populated. By default, only members of the Administrators group have remote access privileges. The Remote Desktop Users group allows the same access as the Users group, with the additional ability to connect remotely.
- Remote Desktop users should be required to use strong passwords.
- To maintain security, servers that will be administered with Remote Desktop for Administration should be located within the corporate firewall. To administer a computer outside of the firewall, you must go through a proxy server.
- Remote Desktop for Administration cannot be used to create a connection between two computers that are directly connected to the Internet. You must first establish a secure VPN connection to the internal network before you can establish a remote session via the Internet.

Remote Desktop for Administration provides remote access to the server desktop by using the Terminal Services Remote Desktop Protocol (RDP) on port 3389.

Components of Remote Desktop for Administration

Remote Desktop for Administration works with the following components:

Remote Desktop Connection or Terminal Services Client The Remote Desktop Connection or Terminal Services client is used to establish sessions with a remote computer. (Remote Desktop Connection is strongly preferred as the client of choice.) Remote Desktop Connection is included with Window XP and Windows Server 2003.

Remote Desktops Snap-in The Remote Desktops MMC snap-in is used to manage multiple Remote Desktop connections to terminal servers or to computers running Windows 2000 or Windows Server 2003.

Remote Desktop Web Connection The Remote Desktop Web Connection can be deployed on a Web server to provide client connectivity to terminal servers and other computers via Internet Explorer and TCP/IP.

Terminal Services Manager The Terminal Services Manager is used to manage and monitor users, sessions, and processes on any terminal server on the network.

Terminal Services Configuration The Terminal Services Configuration is used manage properties for the connections that are configured for the Remote Desktop Protocol (RDP). The connections provide the link clients use to log on to a session on the server for either Remote Desktop for Administration or Terminal Server connections.

Terminal Services Group Policies The Terminal Services Group Policies are used to configure individual computers or groups of computers, or to assign policies for Remote Desktop for Administration to users or user groups.

Active Directory Users and Computers and Local Users and Groups The Active Directory Users and Computers and Local Users and Groups extensions are used to control Terminal Services features for each user.

Terminal Services Manager, Terminal Services Configuration, Active Directory Users and Computers, and Local Users and Groups are covered in detail in *MCSA/MCSE: Windows Server 2003 Environment Management and Maintenance Study Guide.* Group Policy was introduced in Chapter 6, "Planning Secure Network Access," and Chapter 7, "Planning Server-Level Security." Group Policy is covered in greater detail in *MCSE: Windows 2003 Active Directory Planning, Implementation, and Maintenance Study Guide.*

The Remote Desktop Connection client can be installed on 32-bit Windows operating systems by connecting to a Terminal Services server and running the client setup program (`\\servername\Tsclient\Win32\Setup.exe`). The Tsclient folder should first be shared. To use Microsoft IntelliMirror to deploy Remote Desktop Connection, use the `Msrdpcli.msi` file in the *systemroot*`\system32\clients\Tsclient\Win32` folder. To install Remote Desktop Connection on Windows CE, see the Microsoft Web site for instructions.

Enabling Remote Access to a Computer for Administration

In order for a Windows Server 2003 computer to be accessed remotely, you must enable access through the System applet of the Control Panel. To enable remote access, select Start ➢ Control Panel ➢ System. On the System Properties dialog bog, click the Remote tab (see Figure 10.19). Within the Remote tab of the System Properties dialog box, check the option to Allow Users To Connect Remotely To This Computer. To enable remote access to a server, you must be logged on to the server as a member of the Administrators group.

FIGURE 10.19 The Remote tab of the System Properties dialog box

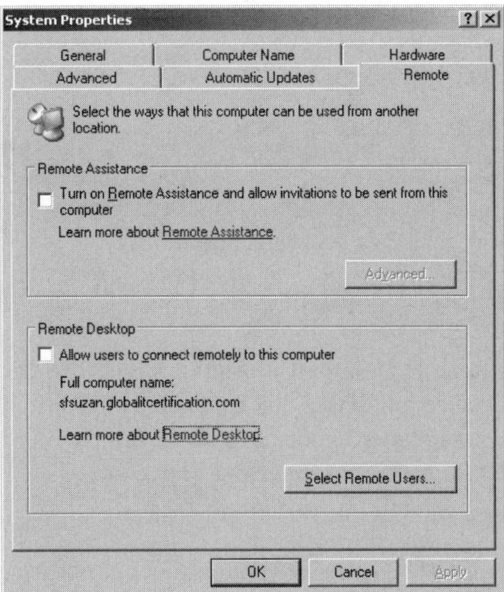

To enable nonadministrative users to access a server remotely, choose the Select Remote Users button. This calls up the Remote Desktop Users dialog box, as shown in Figure 10.20, where you can specify additional users. Members of the Administrators group can forcefully end a local user's session without the user's consent.

FIGURE 10.20 The Remote Desktop Users dialog box

Configuring the Remote Desktop Connection

Remote Desktop Connection is the client software component that is used from the controlling computer to initiate a remote control session with a Windows Server 2003 computer. This software is installed by default on computers running Windows XP and Windows Server 2003. The Remote Desktop Connection console (see Figure 10.21) is launched by choosing Start ➢ All Programs ➢ Accessories ➢ Communications ➢ Remote Desktop Connection. As an alternative, **you could use the command-line utility `mstsc`** to launch the Remote Desktop Connection. Simply open Start ➢ Run and type **mstsc.**

FIGURE 10.21 The Remote Desktop Connection dialog box

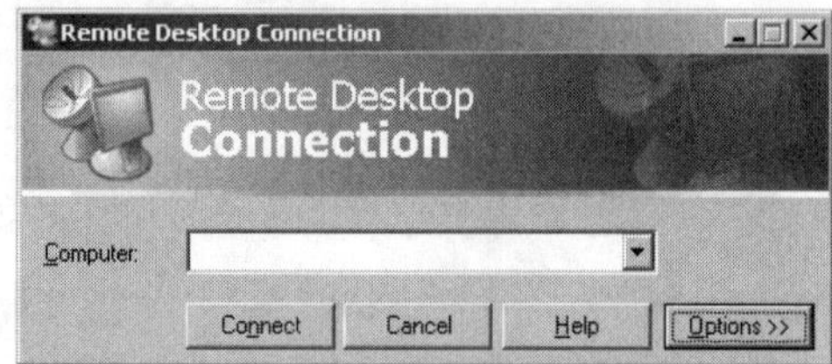

You can configure the Remote Desktop Connection options by clicking the Options button in the Remote Desktop Connection dialog box to display the configurable options.

The configurable options for the Remote Desktop Connection are grouped in five tabs: General, Display, Local Resources, Programs, and Experience.

The General Tab

The General tab (see Figure 10.22) is used to configure Logon Settings, such as the computer to which you will connect and the user name, password, and domain for the user who will remotely connect to the server, and Connection Settings, which include saving the current settings or opening a saved connection.

FIGURE 10.22 The General Tab of Remote Desktop Connection dialog box

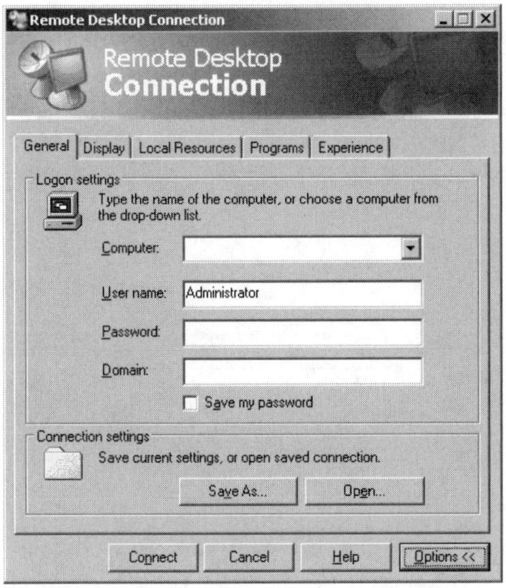

The Display Tab

The Display tab (see Figure 10.23) contains display-related options, including desktop size and number of colors.

FIGURE 10.23 The Display tab of the Remote Desktop Connection dialog box

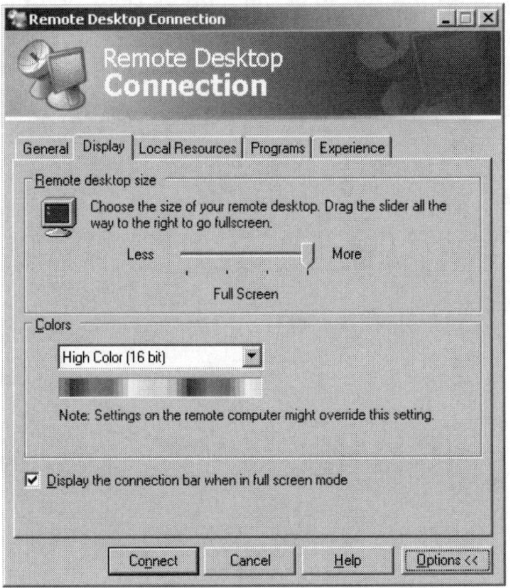

The Local Resources Tab

The Local Resources tab (see Figure 10.24) includes options to configure the remote computer sound, keyboard, and local devices to be connected, including disk drives, printers, and serial ports.

FIGURE 10.24 The Local Resources tab of the Remote Desktop Connection dialog box

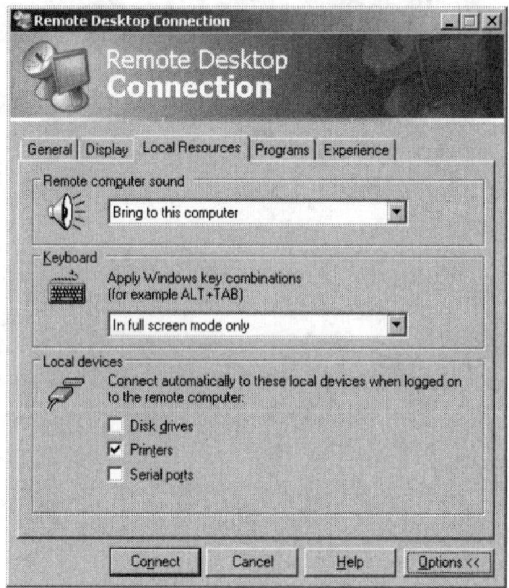

The Programs Tab

The Programs tab (see Figure 10.25) can be used to start a program after the remote session is established.

FIGURE 10.25 The Programs tab of the Remote Desktop Connection dialog box

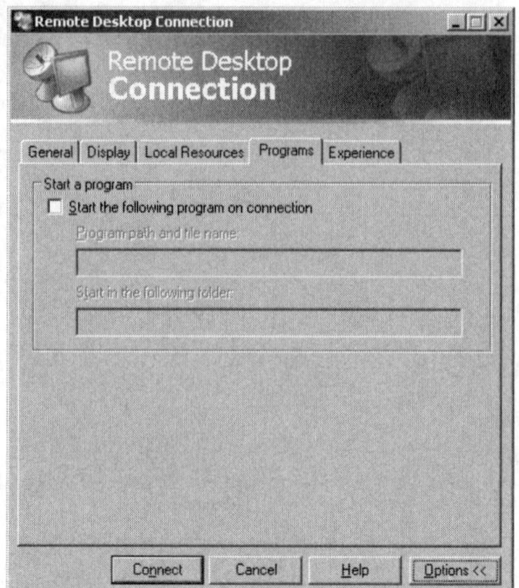

The Experience Tab

The Experience tab (see Figure 10.26) is used to optimize performance for the connection speed. Performance can be increased when connecting over a modem by disabling graphical options such as Desktop Background and Menu and Window Animation.

FIGURE 10.26 The Experience tab of the Remote Desktop Connection dialog box

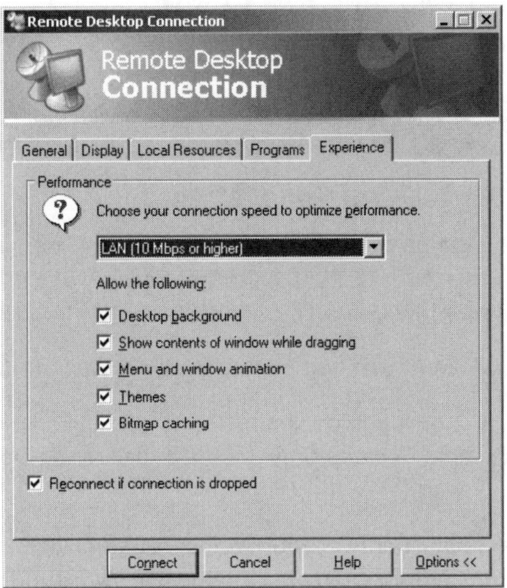

Working with Remote Desktop Connection Sessions

After enabling remote control access on the controlled computer and configuring a Remote Desktop Connection on the controlling computer, you can now establish a Remote Desktop Connection session. You can establish a session by following these steps:

1. Launch Remote Desktop Connection by choosing Start ➢ All Programs ➢ Accessories ➢ Communications ➢ Remote Desktop Connection.
2. On the General tab, in the Computer field, enter the name of the remote computer. Remote Desktop must be enabled on this computer and you must have remote access permissions on that computer.
3. Configure any desired settings or open saved connection settings if desired.
4. Choose Connect.
5. The Log On To Windows dialog box will appear. Type in your user name, password, and domain name, and click OK.
6. The Remote Desktop Connection window will open, and you will now have remote access.

Once a remote session has been established, the Remote Desktop Connection window appears. This window has a modified taskbar that displays the name of the server to which you are connected.

The Remote Desktop Connection can be closed using two different methods. In the Remote Desktop Connection window, choose Start ➤ Shutdown. The Shut Down Windows dialog box appears. In the drop-down menu, select Log Off and choose OK. As an alternative, you can simply click the X button of the Remote Desktop Connection window to close the session.

In Exercise 10.11, you will use a Windows XP Professional client computer to access a Windows Server 2003 domain controller.

EXERCISE 10.11

Establishing a Remote Desktop Connection

1. Enable remote administration of your Windows Server 2003 domain controller within the System applet. To do this, choose Start ➤ Control Panel ➤ System and click the Remote tab. Check the option to Allow Users To Connect Remotely To This Computer.
2. From your Windows XP computer, log on to the domain as Administrator.
3. Open Remote Desktop Connection by choosing Start ➤ All Programs ➤ Accessories ➤ Communications ➤ Remote Desktop Connection, and click the Options button to expand the window.
4. On the General tab, enter the name of your Windows Server 2003 domain controller in the Computer field. Enter the Administrator user name, password and domain name (NetBIOS domain name will work if connecting via an intranet) in the appropriate fields.
5. Click the Connect button.
6. The Log On To Windows dialog box appears, and the Administrator name and password are displayed. Click the OK button.
7. The remote session is initiated in a new window. Experiment with different administrative tasks on the remote computer. When you are finished, close the session by clicking the X at the top of the window.

Planning to Offer Remote Assistance to Client Computers

Sometimes the best way to help someone fix a problem is to demonstrate a solution. Likewise, sometimes the easiest way for a user to explain a problem or error is to step you through the actions she took and dialog boxes and other messages she encountered when the problem occurred.

Remote Assistance enables a trusted individual (who could be a friend, a support person, or an IT administrator) to remotely and interactively assist someone with a computer problem. The helper (also known as the expert) can view the user's screen remotely and offer advice based on what she sees. With the user's permission, the helper can even take control of the user's computer and perform tasks remotely.

Remote Assistance can be helpful for answering questions and resolving problems that are difficult for a user to explain, as well as for demonstrating the functionality of an application. Remote Assistance is also helpful when you need to perform a complicated set of instructions on an inexperienced user's computer. For instance, the local system configuration might need to be investigated.

Users can request help, and conversely, experts can initiate an offer to help by sending invitations either through e-mail or Windows Messenger. Users and experts can also send invitations by saving them to a file and transmitting them through other means such as across a network share or through a Yahoo! Mail account. Invitations can be password-protected, and they can be set to expire on a given date.

Unlike Remote Desktop for Administration, Remote Assistance establishes a concurrent session with the user at the remote computer, the user must authorize access, and both computers have to be running Windows XP or Windows Server 2003.

Remote Assistance can be used in the following situations:

- Within a local area network (LAN).
- Over the Internet.
- Over the Internet with one or both parties behind a firewall on a LAN. Connections through a firewall require that TCP port 3389 be open.

In the following sections, we'll explore how remote assistance works and identify methods for securing remote assistance.

How Remote Assistance Works

Remote Assistance must first be enabled. You can enable Remote Assistance in the System applet of the Control Panel by clicking the Remote tab and selecting the Turn On Remote Assistance And allow Invitations To Be Sent From This Computer checkbox (refer back to Figure 10.19).

If you click the Advanced button from the Remote tab, you can set configuration options for the maximum number of hours that invitations will remain open, as shown in Figure 10.27.

FIGURE 10.27 The Remote Assistance Settings dialog box

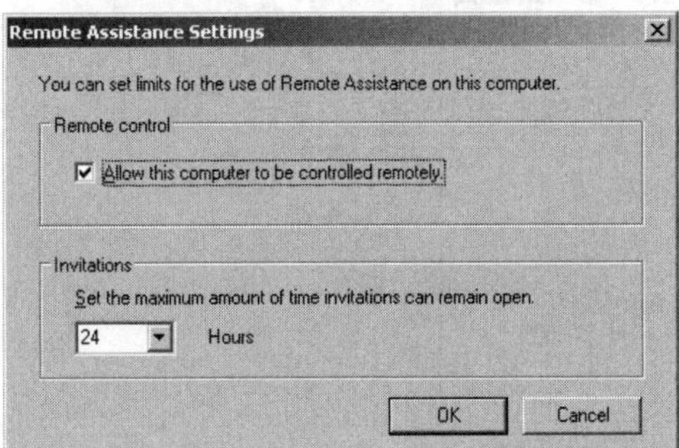

Invitations can be managed through the Windows Help and Support Center, which can be launched from the Start menu. The main window for the Help and Support Center is shown in Figure 10.28.

FIGURE 10.28 Help and Support Center window

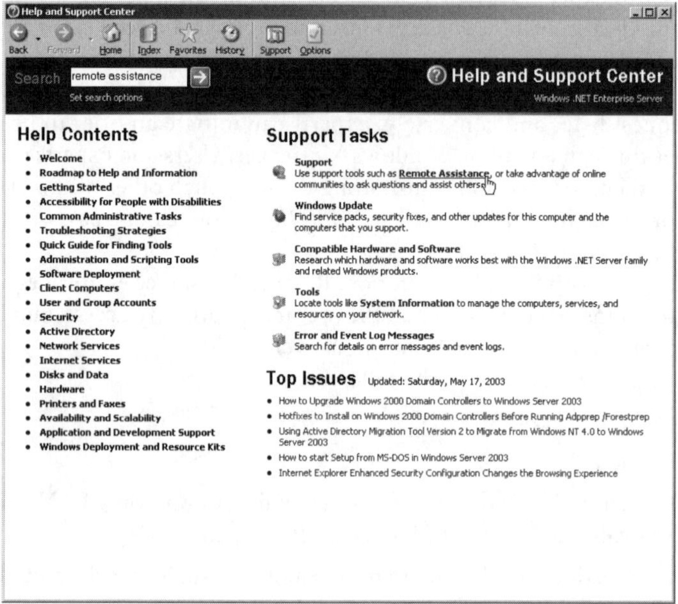

You open the Remote Assistance window of the Help and Support Center, shown in Figure 10.29, by clicking Remote Assistance. Here the user can send an invitation to request assistance or view the status of existing invitations.

FIGURE 10.29 Remote Assistance window

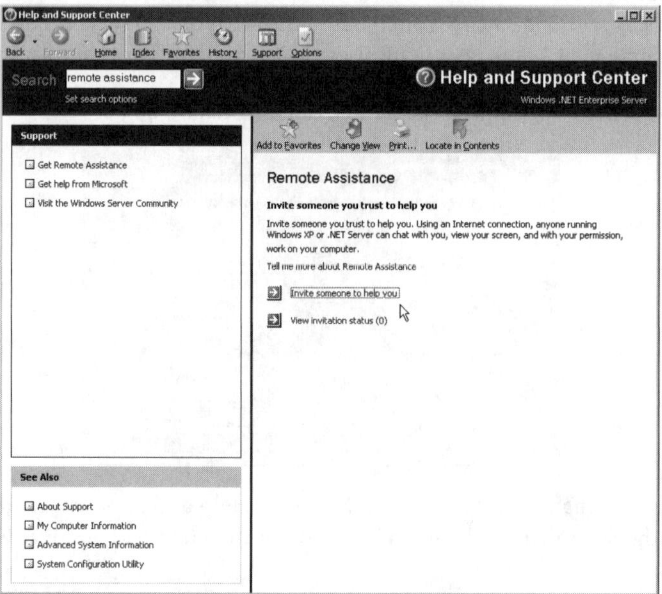

Help desk staff and administrators can also initiate a remote assistance session through the Offer Remote Assistance feature.

A sample Remote Assistance invitation sent by email is shown here:

```
Subject: YOU HAVE RECEIVED A REMOTE ASSISTANCE INVITATION
Hello Suzan:

I would like you to connect to my computer with Microsoft Remote
Assistance, in order to provide some assistance to me. Once connected,
you will be able to view my screen and chat online with me in real time.

To start a Remote Assistance session, you should select the following
link at URL
https://www.microsoft.com/remoteassistance/s.asp#1AjcAMOTD,xMCTeKNJW/KMU
W6Pu/mxoYDG1GW/11sboTa5JAnxA=,0zu2kNPe0cKnaiH1xDSlyK4Wcac=Z

****************************************************
Suzan, I'm getting a message that the .pst file couldn't be found when I
try to open Outlook. Please help!

****************************************************
```

Methods for Securing Remote Assistance

If a user accepts assistance, and if remote control is allowed by Group Policy, a helper can control the user's computer and perform any task that the user can perform, including accessing the network with that user's credentials. The following methods can be used to address the security concerns that such access introduces.

Firewall Configuration

To control whether a person within the organization can request help outside of the organization, configure the firewall to prohibit or permit inbound and outbound traffic through port 3389.

Group Policy

You can set Group Policy to permit or prohibit users from requesting help using Remote Assistance. You can also determine whether users can allow someone to remotely control their computers or just view them. In addition, you can set Group Policy to permit or prohibit a helper from offering Remote Assistance without a specific request from the user.

Two Remote Assistance policies can be configured in Group Policy: Offer Remote Assistance policy and Solicited Remote Assistance policy. Figure 10.30 displays these two policies.

The Offer Remote Assistance policy specifies whether an expert can offer unsolicited help via remote assistance to the computers for which the Group Policy Object (GPO) is applied. The Properties dialog box for this policy is shown in Figure 10.31.

FIGURE 10.30 Remote Assistance policies

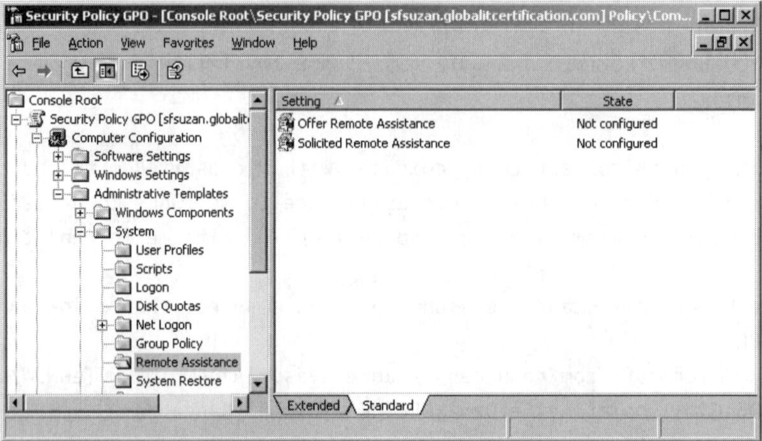

FIGURE 10.31 The Offer Remote Assistance Policy Properties dialog box

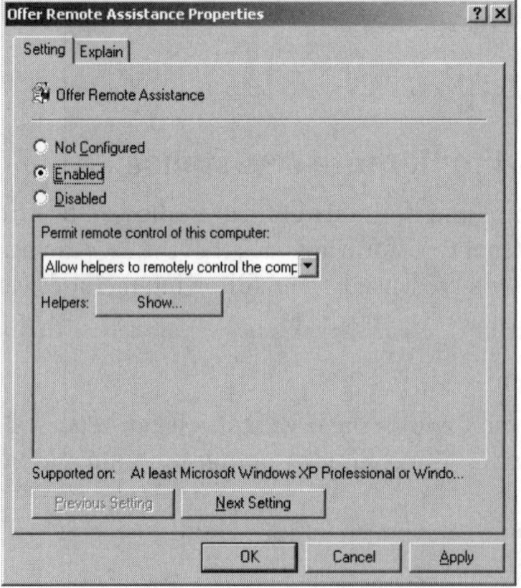

If enabled, this policy can be further configured to allow helpers to remotely control the computer (the default) or only to view the computer. A list of approved helpers can also be defined in the policy.

The Solicited Remote Assistance policy, shown in Figure 10.32, specifies whether users can solicit another user's assistance, in other words ask for help, via Remote Assistance.

Again, the policy can be further configured to allow helpers to remotely control the computer (the default) or only to view the computer. Tickets can be set to expire by configuring the Maximum Ticket Time (Hours) setting, which is 24 hours by default. This setting sets a limit on the amount of time that a Remote Assistance invitation can remain open.

FIGURE 10.32 The Solicited Remote Assistance Policy Properties dialog box

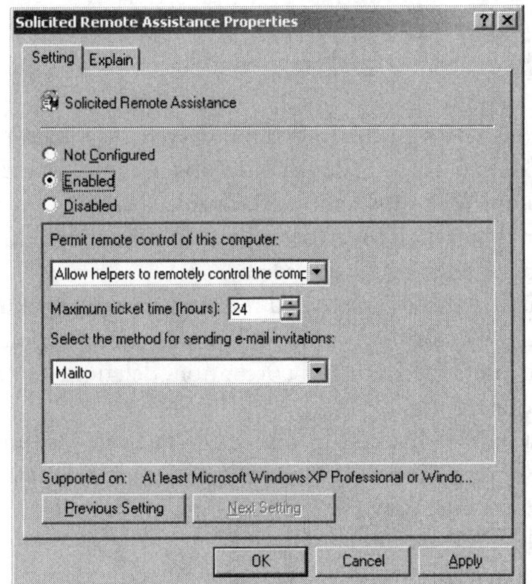

The Select The Method For Sending E-Mail Invitations setting specifies which e-mail standard to use to send Remote Assistance invitations. Depending on the format supported by your e-mail program, you can use either the Mailto (the invitation recipient connects through an Internet link) or SMAPI (Simple MAPI) standard (the invitation is attached to your e-mail message).

If Remote Assistance is disabled in this setting or set to Not Configured and disabled in Control Panel, the Offer Remote Assistance policy will also be disabled. If the status is set to Not Configured, users can enable or disable and configure Remote Assistance themselves in System properties in Control Panel.

Configuring either policy doesn't mean that an expert can connect to the computer unannounced or control it without permission from the user. When the expert tries to connect, the user is still given a chance to accept or deny the connection. If the user accepts, the expert is granted view-only privileges to the user's desktop. Thereafter, the user must explicitly click a button to give the expert the ability to remotely control the desktop assuming that remote control is enabled. The user can stop remote control at any time.

The Remote Tab of System Properties

Remote Assistance is disabled by default on a local computer. This prevents anyone using the computer from sending a Remote Assistance invitation.

You can enable Remote Assistance in the System applet of the Control Panel by clicking the Remote tab of the System Properties dialog box and selecting the Turn On Remote Assistance And Allow Invitations To Be Sent From This Computer checkbox.

Group Policy settings will override this setting.

Planning a Backup and Recovery Strategy

Backups are the best protection you can have against system failure. You can create backups through the Windows Backup utility. The Windows Backup utility offers options to run the Backup Wizard and Restore Wizard. Windows Backup also allows you to create an Automated System Recovery backup that is used to restore critical Windows operating system files. You can schedule the backup jobs as an automated process.

Windows Backup enables you to create and restore backups. Backups protect your data in the event of system failure by storing the data on another medium, such as another hard disk or a tape. If your original data is lost due to corruption, deletion, or media failure, you can restore the data using your backup.

The types of data that can be backed up with the Windows Backup utility include System State data and user data and applications. System State data is data related to the configuration of the Windows Server 2003 operating system. User data and applications are the data that have been created and stored on the computer.

By default users can back up their own data and any data to which they have Read permission. Users can restore their own data to any folder to which they have Write permission. Users who are members of the Administrators, Server Operators, or Backup Operators group can back up or restore any files on the server, regardless of file and folder permissions because these groups have the Backup Files and Directories and Restore Files and Directories user rights.

In the following sections, you will learn how to use Windows Backup as part of a strategy to back up and restore critical data such as network configuration and network volumes. You'll also learn how to use the new features Windows Server 2003 offers to make server recovery easy: Automated System Recovery and Volume Shadow Copy.

Using Windows Backup

Windows Backup is the backup utility included in Windows operating systems since NT. It is a simple tool and not robust enough for enterprise deployments, so it is likely that you will be using a third-party backup solution in all but the smallest network environments. However, Windows Backup in Windows Server 2003 has introduced two very useful features: Automated System Recovery and volume shadow copy.

In the next few sections, we'll jump in with a step-by-step description of using the Backup or Restore Wizard. Next, we'll consider how to schedule backup jobs and how to back up System State data. After that, you will learn how to select a backup type.

Using the Backup or Restore Wizard

The Windows Backup utility allows you to manually configure backup and restore sessions or to automate the process through the use of wizards. The *Backup Wizard* takes you through all of the steps that are required for a successful backup. Before you start the Backup Wizard, you should be logged on as a member of the Administrators, Server Operators, or Backup Operators groups.

To use the Backup Wizard, take the following steps:

1. Select Start ➢ All Programs ➢ Accessories ➢ System Tools ➢ Backup.
2. The Welcome To The Backup Or Restore Wizard page appears, as shown in Figure 10.33. Notice that the option to Always Start In Wizard Mode is checked by default. In this example, the backup is performed using the Backup Wizard; however, you can select the Advanced Mode link if you want to manually configure the backup. Click the Next button.

FIGURE 10.33 The Welcome To The Backup Or Restore Wizard page

3. The Backup Or Restore page appears, as shown in Figure 10.34. Ensure that the Backup Files And Settings option is selected and click the Next button.

FIGURE 10.34 The Backup Or Restore page

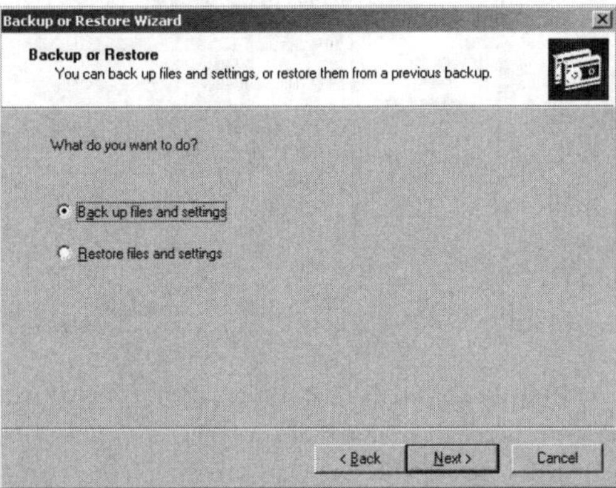

4. The What To Back Up page appears, as shown in Figure 10.35. This dialog box allows you to select what you will back up. You can choose two backup options: All Information On This Computer or Let Me Choose What To Back Up. If you choose what will be backed up,

you can choose to back up just selected files, drives, or network data; or back up only the System State data. System State data includes system configuration information, as explained in the next section. For this example, select Let Me Choose What To Back Up, and click the Next button.

FIGURE 10.35 The What To Back Up page

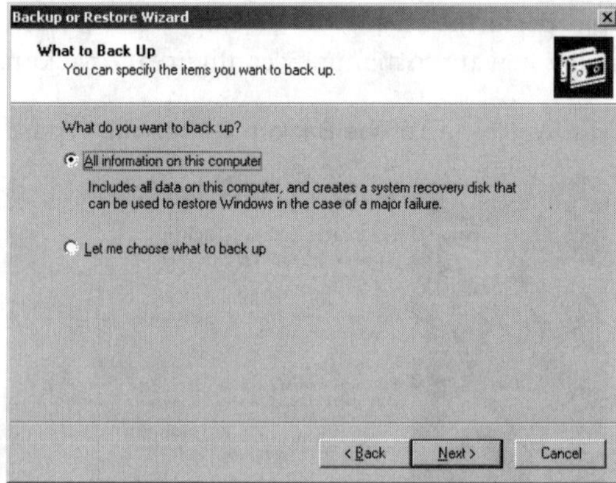

5. The Items To Back Up page appears, as shown in Figure 10.36. Check the items that you want to back up, and click the Next button.

FIGURE 10.36 The Items to Back Up page

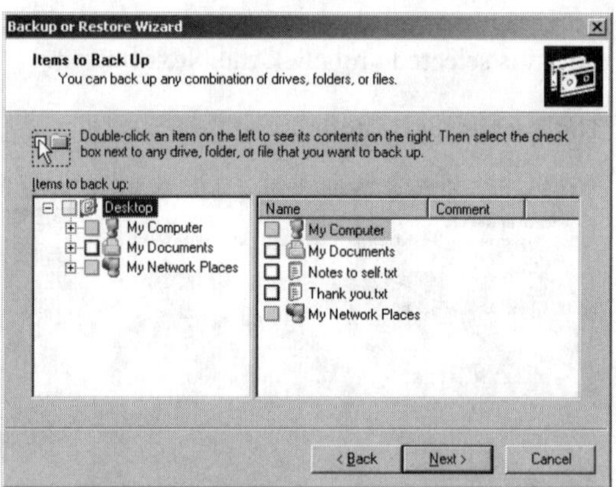

6. The Backup Type, Destination, And Name dialog box appears, as shown in Figure 10.37. You can enter the backup media or filename, or you can click the Browse button to locate the backup destination. Clicking the Browse button brings up the Open dialog box. Select the drive, give your backup a filename (for example, you might use the date as the filename), and click the Save button. You return to the Backup Type, Destination, And Name page. When your backup media or filename path is correct, click the Next button.

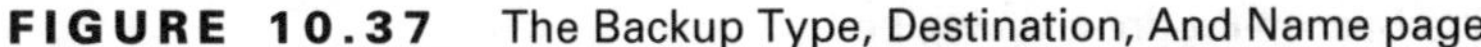

FIGURE 10.37 The Backup Type, Destination, And Name page

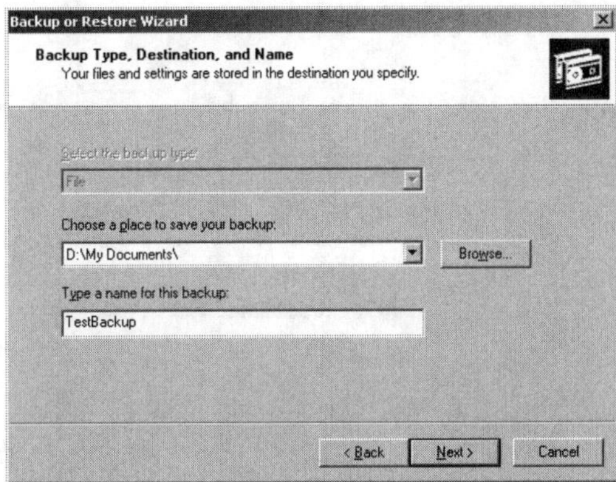

7. The Completing The Backup Or Restore Wizard page appears, as shown in Figure 10.38. Click the Finish button to start the backup.

FIGURE 10.38 The Completing the Backup Or Restore Wizard page

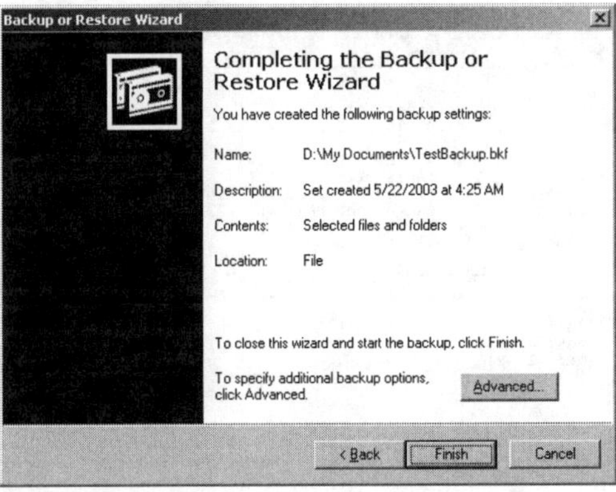

Clicking the Advanced button in the Completing The Backup Or Restore Wizard page brings up a dialog box that allows you to specify advanced options including the type of backup: Normal, Copy, Incremental, Differential, or Daily. These backup types are discussed later in this chapter in "Selecting a Backup Type."

8. During the backup process, the wizard displays the Backup Progress dialog box, as shown in Figure 10.39. Once the backup process is complete, you can click the Report button in this dialog box to see details of the backup session. Figure 10.40 shows an example of a backup report.

FIGURE 10.39 The Backup Progress dialog box

Backup Progress

Cancel

Drive: D: DATA

Label: TestBackup.bkf created 5/22/2003 at 4:32 AM

Status: Backing up files from your computer...

Progress:

Time: Elapsed: Estimated remaining:

Processing:

	Processed:	Estimated:
Files:	0	0
Bytes:	44	44

FIGURE 10.40 An example of a backup report

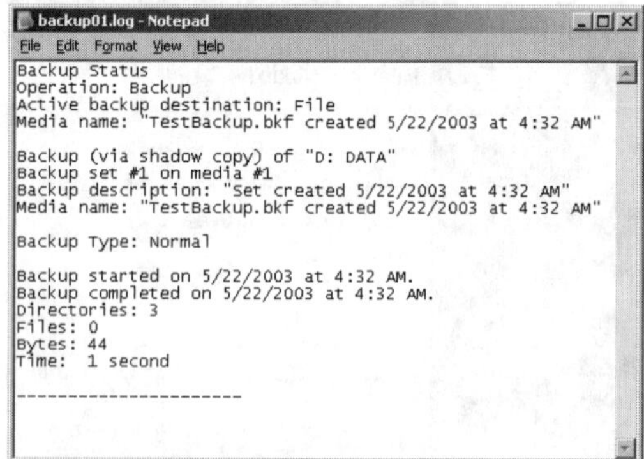

backup01.log - Notepad

File Edit Format View Help

```
Backup Status
Operation: Backup
Active backup destination: File
Media name: "TestBackup.bkf created 5/22/2003 at 4:32 AM"

Backup (via shadow copy) of "D: DATA"
Backup set #1 on media #1
Backup description: "Set created 5/22/2003 at 4:32 AM"
Media name: "TestBackup.bkf created 5/22/2003 at 4:32 AM"

Backup Type: Normal

Backup started on 5/22/2003 at 4:32 AM.
Backup completed on 5/22/2003 at 4:32 AM.
Directories: 3
Files: 0
Bytes: 44
Time:  1 second

----------------------
```

In Exercise 10.12, you will use the Backup Wizard. You will need a blank, formatted, high-density disk for this exercise.

EXERCISE 10.12

Using the Backup Wizard

1. Create a folder on your D: drive called **DATA**. Create some small text files in this folder. The size of all of the files combined should not exceed 1MB.

2. Select Start ➢ All Programs ➢ Accessories ➢ System Tools ➢ Backup.

EXERCISE 10.12 *(continued)*

3. The Welcome To The Backup Or Restore Wizard page appears. Click the Next button.

4. The Backup Or Restore page appears. Ensure that the Backup Files and Settings option is selected and click the Next button.

5. The What To Back Up page appears. Select Let Me Choose What To Back Up, and click the Next button.

6. On the Items To Back Up page, select My Computer, expand D:, and check the DATA folder. Click the Next button.

7. On the Backup Type, Destination, And Name page, click the Browse button. In the Open dialog box, select Floppy (A:). For the filename, enter the date (in the *mmddyy* format). Then click the Open button.

8. On the Where To Store the Backup page, click the Next button.

9. The Completing The Backup or Restore Wizard page appears. If all of the information is correct, click the Finish button.

10. When the Backup and Restore Wizard completes, click the Report button in the Backup Progress dialog box. This will show the backup log in a Notepad window. Close this window when you are finished viewing the report.

11. Close all of the Backup and Restore Wizard dialog boxes.

Having a complete backup won't help you if your system fails—unless you can successfully restore that backup. To be sure that you can restore your data, you should test the restoration process before anything goes wrong. You can use the *Restore Wizard* for testing purposes, as well as when you actually need to restore your backup.

To use the Restore Wizard, take the following steps:

1. Select Start ➢ All Programs ➢ Accessories ➢ System Tools ➢ Backup.
2. The Welcome To The Backup Or Restore Wizard page appears. Click the Next button.
3. The Backup Or Restore page appears. Select the Restore Files And Settings option, and click the Next button.
4. The What To Restore page appears. This page allows you to select which backup session you will restore, as shown in Figure 10.41. Select the backup session you want to restore by selecting the appropriate backup identification label, and then select the directories and files you want to restore. Click the Next button.

FIGURE 10.41 The What To Restore Page

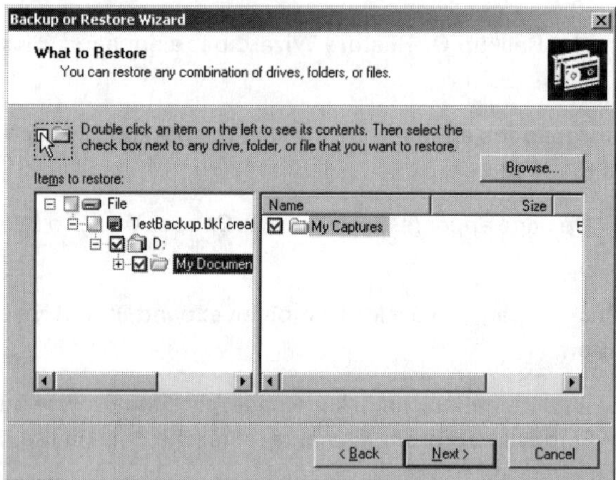

5. The Completing The Backup Or Restore Wizard page appears. If all of the information is correct, click the Finish button.
6. During the restore process, the wizard displays the Restore Progress dialog. Once the restore process is complete, you can click the Report button to verify that all the files were successfully restored.

In Exercise 10.13, you will use the Restore Wizard. You will need the disk that you created in Exercise 10.12 for this exercise.

EXERCISE 10.13

Using the Restore Wizard

1. Select Start ➢ All Programs ➢ Accessories ➢ System Tools ➢ Backup.
2. The Welcome To The Backup Or Restore Wizard page appears. Click the Next button.
3. The Backup Or Restore page appears. Select the Restore Files And Settings option and click the Next button.
4. The What To Restore page appears. Select the session you created in Exercise 10.12, and specify the files you want to restore. Click the Next button.
5. The Completing The Backup Or Restore Wizard page appears. If all of the information is correct, click the Finish button.
6. During the restore process, the Wizard displays the Restore Progress dialog. Once the restore process is complete, click the Report button to verify that all the files were successfully restored.

Scheduling Backup Jobs

The Backup utility allows you to schedule backup jobs on a specified schedule. You can choose from the following options:

- Once, which means the backup job will be run only one time based on the specified date and time.
- Daily, which allows you to schedule a backup job to run at the specified time on a recurring daily basis.
- Weekly, which is used to schedule a backup job to run on the specified day(s) at the specified time on a recurring weekly basis.
- Monthly, which is used to schedule a backup job to run on the specified day of the month at the specified time on a recurring monthly basis.
- At System Startup, which schedules a backup job to run each time the system is started.
- At Logon, which schedules a backup job to run each time the jobs owner logs on locally at the computer.
- When Idle, which will trigger a backup job to be run when the server has been idle for the specified number of minutes.

You can schedule backup jobs when the backup job is initially created or through the Scheduled Jobs tab of the Backup Utility.

Backing Up System State Data

System State data refers to a collection of system-specific configuration information.

On a Windows Server 2003 member server, System State data consists of the Registry, the COM+ Class Registration database, and the system boot files. On Windows Server 2003 domain controller computers, System State data also includes the Active Directory services database and the SYSVOL directory, which is a shared directory that stores the server copy of the domain's public files. If the server is configured as a certificate server, System State data will also include the Certificate Services database.

To back up System State data, take the following steps:

1. Select Start ➢ All Programs ➢ Accessories ➢ System Tools ➢ Backup.
2. From the Welcome To The Backup or Restore Wizard page, click the Advanced Mode option. You will see the dialog box shown in Figure 10.42.
3. Click the button for Backup Wizard (Advanced). The Welcome To The Backup Wizard page will appear. Click the Next button to continue.
4. On the What To Backup page (see Figure 10.43) select the Only Back Up the System State Data option and click the Next button.
5. On the Backup Type, Destination, And Name page, select the location of your backup media, and click the Next button.
6. The Completing The Backup Wizard page will appear. If all of the information is correct, click the Finish button.

FIGURE 10.42 The Welcome to the Backup Utility Advanced Mode dialog box

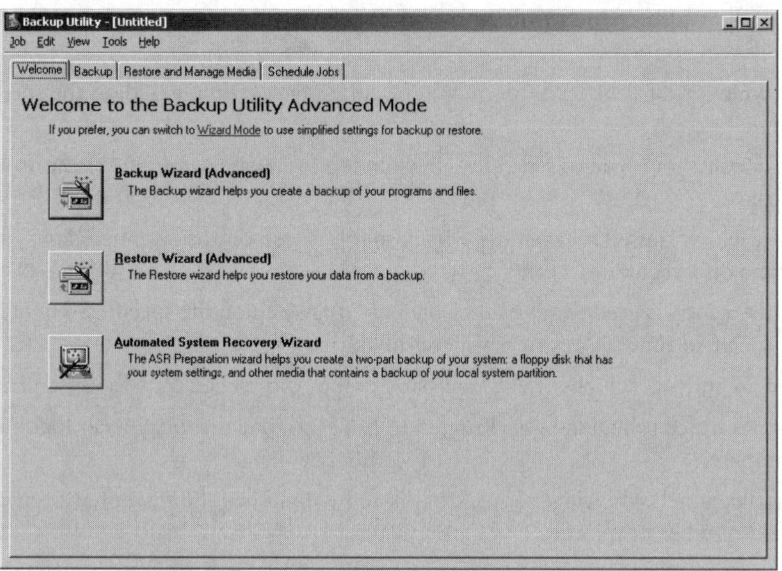

FIGURE 10.43 The What To Back Up page

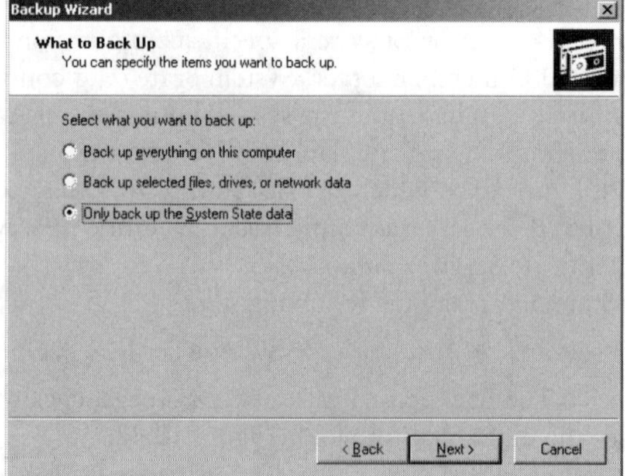

If you need to restore System State data on a domain controller, you should restart your computer with the Windows Advanced Options Menu option Directory Services Restore Mode. This allows the Active Directory service database and the SYSVOL directory to be restored. If the System State data is restored on a domain controller that is a part of a domain where data is replicated to other domain controllers, you must perform an authoritative restore. For an authoritative restore, use the `Ntdsutil.exe` command, and then restart the computer.

If you have a backup device attached to your computer, you can follow the steps in Exercise 10.14 to back up your System State data. This information will not fit on a single disk.

EXERCISE 10.14

Backing Up System State Data

1. Select Start ➢ All Programs ➢ Accessories ➢ System Tools ➢ Backup.
2. From the Welcome to the Backup Or Restore Wizard page, click the Advanced Mode option.
3. Click the button for Backup Wizard (Advanced). The Welcome To The Backup Wizard page will appear. Click the Next button to continue.
4. On the What To Back Up page, select the Only Back Up the System State Data option, and click the Next button.
5. On the Backup Type, Destination, And Name page, select the location of your backup media (for example `D:\Backup`), and click the Next button.
6. The Completing The Backup Wizard page will appear. If all of the information is correct, click the Finish button.
7. When the backup is complete, click the Report button in the Backup Progress dialog box.
8. The backup log appears in a Notepad window. Close this window when you are finished viewing the report.
9. Close all of the Backup dialog boxes.

Selecting a Backup Type

You can configure more specific backup configurations by selecting backup options. To access the backup options, start the Windows Backup tool in Advanced mode and select Tools ➢ Options. This brings up the Options dialog box. This dialog box has five tabs with options for controlling the backup and restore processes: General, Restore, Backup Type, Backup Log, and Exclude Files. For the exam, you should understand the options on the Backup Type tab. The Backup Type tab, as shown in Figure 10.44, allows you to specify the default backup type that will be used. You should select the type of backup based on the following:

- How much data you are backing up
- How quickly you want to be able to perform the backup
- The number of tapes you are willing to use in the event that you need to perform a restore operation

Table 10.5 describes the backup type options.

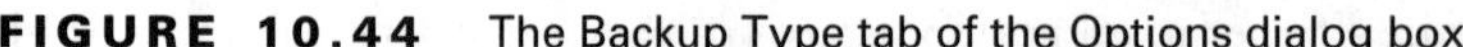

FIGURE 10.44 The Backup Type tab of the Options dialog box

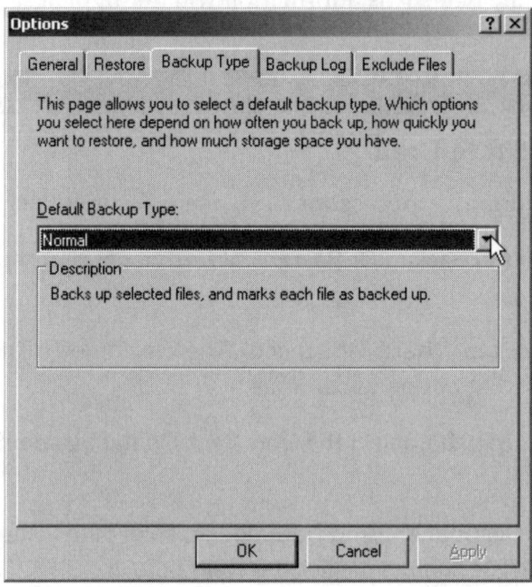

TABLE 10.5 Backup Type Options

Option	Description
Normal	Backs up all files and sets the archive bit as marked for each file that is backed up. Requires only one tape set for the restore process.
Copy	Backs up all files and does not set the archive bit as marked for each file that is backed up. Requires only one tape for the restore process.
Differential	Backs up only the files that have not been marked as archived and does not set the archive bit for each file that is backed up. Requires the last normal backup and the last differential tape set for the restore process.
Incremental	Backs up only the files that have not been marked as archived, and sets the archive bit for each file that is backed up. Requires the last normal backup and all of the incremental tape sets that have been created since the last normal backup for the restore process.
Daily	Backs up only the files that have been changed today and does not set the archive bit for each file that is backed up. Requires each daily backup and the last normal backup for the restore process.

The Ntbackup command-line utility can be used to back up and restore Windows Server 2003 data. Ntbackup supports backing up of only folders unless you create a backup selection file. Ntbackup does not allow you to back up data based on wildcards (for example *.doc). You can use Ntbackup to schedule backup jobs.

Using Volume Shadow Copy

A *volume shadow copy* is a point-in-time copy of an entire volume on a Windows Server 2003 server. Volume shadow copies are created through the advanced options of Windows Backup. This new functionality enables you to copy open files, a substantial improvement over the old Windows Backup. The ability to copy open files results in the following advantages:

- Applications can continue to write data to the volume during a backup.
- Files that are open are no longer omitted during a backup.
- Files that have changed during the backup process are copied correctly.
- Backups can be performed at any time, without locking out users.

Scheduling backups during times of low activity (usually at night) is still important because performing backups is a resource-intensive activity. The fact that some applications manage storage consistency differently while files are open is also important to note. This is especially true of database applications, and it can affect the internal consistency of the data in the files being backed up. Therefore, you should check with an application's documentation when in doubt in order to ensure that you are following the correct backup procedures.

Volume shadow copy is enabled by default and can be disabled in the Advanced options for a particular backup job. To disable volume shadow copy, follow these steps:

1. Launch the Windows Backup utility in Advanced mode.
2. Navigate to the Backup tab, choose the backup source and destination, and click the Start Backup button.
3. The Backup Job Information dialog box (see Figure 10.45) will appear.

FIGURE 10.45 The Backup Job Information dialog box

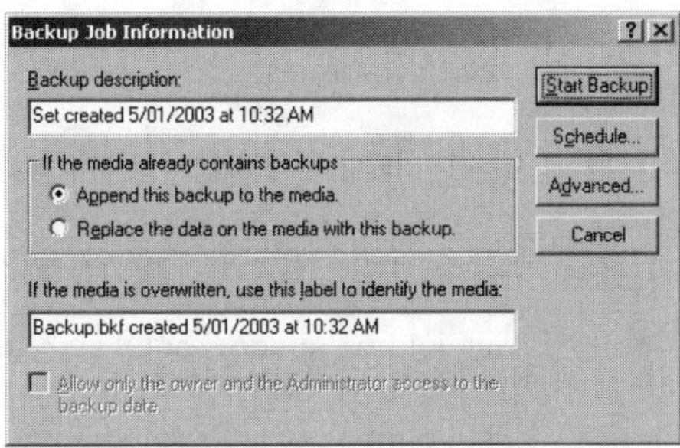

4. Click the Advanced button and the Advanced Backup Options dialog box is displayed, as shown in Figure 10.46.
5. Check the box labeled Disable volume shadow copy.

FIGURE 10.46 The Advanced Backup Options dialog box

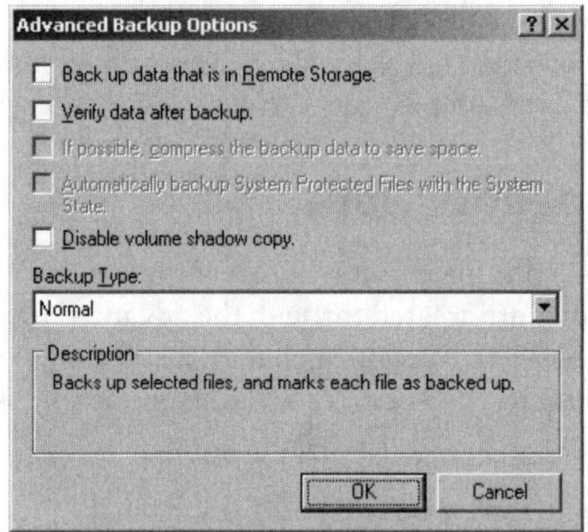

For details on how to use volume shadow copy, see *MCSA/MCSE: Windows Server 2003 Environment Management and Maintenance Study Guide.*

The `Vssadmin` command-line utility displays the current volume shadow copy backups and other shadow copy information from a command-line interface. Table 10.6 lists the available `Vssadmin` commands.

TABLE 10.6 `Vssadmin` Commands

Command	Description
`Add ShadowStorage`	Add a new volume shadow copy storage association
`Create Shadow`	Create a new volume shadow copy
`Delete Shadows`	Delete volume shadow copies
`Delete ShadowStorage`	Delete volume shadow copy storage associations
`List Providers`	List registered volume shadow copy providers
`List Shadows`	List existing volume shadow copies
`List ShadowStorage`	List volume shadow copy storage associations
`List Volumes`	List volumes eligible for shadow copies
`List Writers`	List subscribed volume shadow copy writers
`Resize ShadowStorage`	Resize a volume shadow copy storage association

Using Automated System Recovery

In Windows Server 2003, the Windows Backup utility includes a new feature called Automated System Recovery. *Automated System Recovery (ASR)* is used in conjunction with a full system backup for total system recovery in the event of failure.

ASR backs up the following system information:

- System State data
- System services
- Disk configuration information, which includes configuration information about basic and dynamic disks along with the file signatures associated with each disk

ASR does not back up folders and files. However, used together with a full system backup, ASR can be an invaluable part of a strategy to quickly restore a downed server to a fully functional state.

ASR backups and restores are performed using the Automated System Recovery Preparation Wizard, which is located in the Tools menu of Windows Backup utility (via the Advanced Mode option).

Do not use the Automated System Recovery Wizard for system recovery until you have tried less invasive methods of recovery, such as booting the computer to Safe mode and using the Last Known Good Configuration option. The ASR feature becomes mandatory when, on power up, you cannot access the Boot Menu or the Windows Advanced Options Menu screen.

In Exercise 10.15, you will perform an Automated System Recovery backup and restore. You will need a full system backup of all files and folders on the server, backup media, a 1.44MB disk to create the ASR recovery disk, and a Windows Server 2003 distribution CD.

Be sure to read Exercise 10.15 all the way through and have a full system backup handy prior to starting the exercise. This exercise walks you through a system restore. If you prefer, you can perform the first half of the exercise to create an ASR backup, and simply read the second section to learn how to perform an ASR restore.

EXERCISE 10.15

Performing ASR Backups and Restores with the Automated System Recovery Wizard

Perform an ASR Backup

1. Launch Windows Backup by choosing Start ➢ All Programs ➢ Accessories ➢ System Tools ➢ Backup. Choose the Advanced Mode option when prompted to open the main Windows Backup utility screen rather than the Backup Wizard.
2. Choose Tools ➢ ASR Wizard.
3. The Automated System Recovery Preparation Wizard starts. Choose Next.

EXERCISE 10.15 *(continued)*

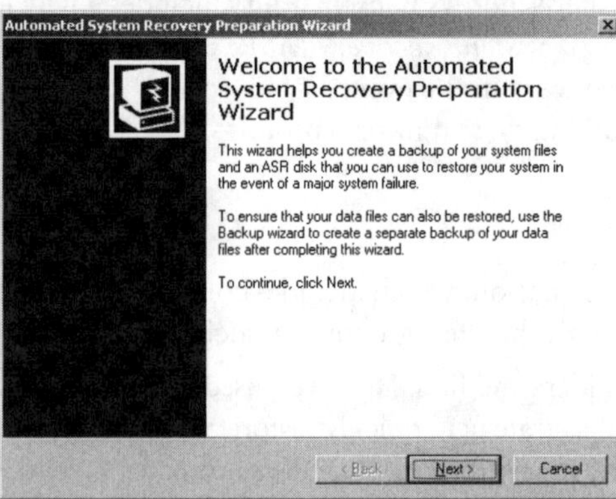

4. The Backup Destination dialog page appears. Specify the location of your backup media, and click the Next button.

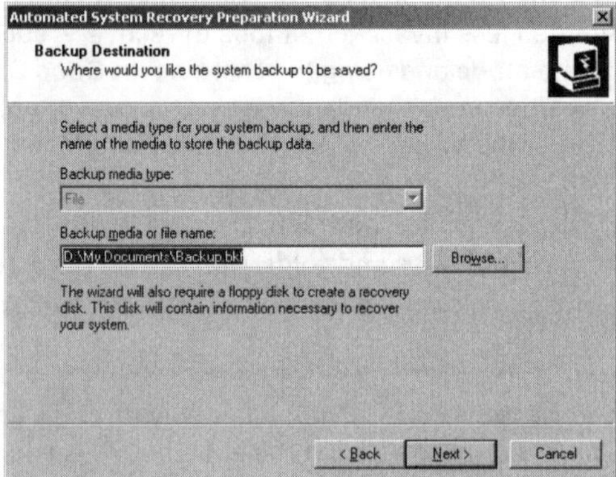

5. The Completing The Automated System Recovery Preparation Wizard page is displayed. Choose Finish to close the window and begin the backup.

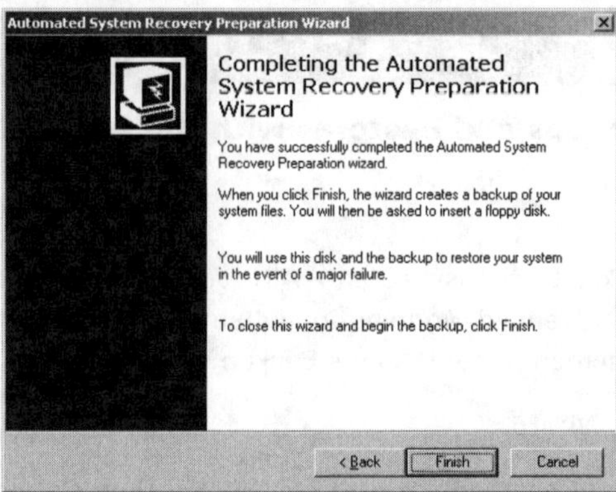

EXERCISE 10.15 *(continued)*

6. After the system files have been backed up, insert a disk when prompted.

Perform an ASR Restore

7. Boot to the Windows Server 2003 CD. Depending on how the BIOS is configured, you might need to press a certain key during the boot process to boot from CD.
8. Hit F2 when prompted during the text-mode portion of the Windows Server 2003 setup process. This will initiate the recovery process. You will then be prompted to insert the ASR disk. Insert the disk, and then press any key to continue.
9. If you desire, you can cancel the recovery process within the first few seconds by hitting the Esc key. Otherwise, the C: drive will be reformatted, and the Automated System Recover Preparation Wizard will begin the Windows Server 2003 installation process. The Windows Server 2003 files will be copied to the hard drive, after which the system will reboot.
10. After the system reboots, the Windows Server 2003 setup procedure will continue. The Automated System Recovery Preparation Wizard will prompt you during this process for the location of the full backup. When the Automated System Recovery process is completed, Windows Backup will automatically launch and restore the system.

Planning a Recovery Strategy for Domain Controllers

As the systems engineer in a large Windows Server 2003 enterprise internetwork with multiple domains, you want to ensure that servers performing domain controller and domain name services functions can be quickly recovered in the event of a failure.

If you need to restore System State data on a domain controller, you should restart your computer with the advanced startup option Directory Services Restore Mode. This allows the Active Directory service database and the SYSVOL directory to be restored. If the System State data is restored on a domain controller that is a part of a domain where data is replicated to other domain controllers, you must perform an authoritative restore. For an authoritative restore, you use the `Ntdsutil.exe` command, and then restart the computer.

Knowing the proper steps to recover a downed server before that server is downed will help ensure the prompt restoration of servers and seamless continuation of network infrastructure services for clients on your network.

Summary

In this chapter, you learned how to monitor and optimize network performance, how to plan for remote administration, and how to plan for recoverability. We covered the following topics:

- How to use Network Monitor to capture and analyze network traffic. The version of Network Monitor that is included with SMS is capable of capturing all network traffic. The standard version included with Windows Server 2003 can only capture traffic going to and from the Windows Server 2003 server.
- How to use System Monitor to monitor the performance of server resources and network services. First, create a baseline using Performance Logs and Alerts. Next, monitor performance objects and performance counters to isolate bottlenecks. Finally, take effective action based on the results of the data analysis.
- How to use the Event Viewer to get details about events and manage log files. You can also search for online information about error messages from the Windows Help and Support Center. The Support Tasks section has a section called "Error and Event Log Messages."
- How to plan for remote administration. Servers and clients are remotely administered using Remote Desktop for Administration. Remote Assistance is used to offer remote help for users from an expert.
- How to plan a recovery strategy using the Windows Backup utility. Windows Backup includes a Backup Wizard and Restore Wizard, and the option to schedule backups as well. You can plan a recovery strategy incorporating the new Automated System Recovery and volume shadow copy features of Windows Backup.

Exam Essentials

Know how to capture and analyze network traffic between two nodes using Network Monitor. Network Monitor is a network sniffer that can be used to capture traffic between two computers on a network. Know how to set up capture and display filters to capture data and filter the display of data.

Know how to conduct performance tuning for networks using System Monitor. Be able to create baseline reports using Performance Logs and Alerts to capture baseline data and create snapshots of system performance. Be able to use System Monitor to isolate bottlenecks related to system resources and network performance. Be able to recommend action based on the results of data analysis.

Understand the purpose of Event Viewer in troubleshooting. Know how to access the Event Viewer and understand which events are stored in each of the Event Viewer logs.

Know how to create a plan for remote administration using Remote Desktop for Administration and Remote Assistance. Be able to troubleshoot Windows Server 2003 computers remotely through the use of Remote Control and Remote Desktop. Know the requirements for configuring these options and how they are used.

Be able to create a strategy to ensure recoverability of network servers and services using Windows Backup. Be able to use the Windows Backup utility to perform backups and restores of System State data and network data. Understand the backup types and the amount of data backed up by each type and the number of tape sets that are required to restore a server based on the backup type used. Know how to schedule backups to run on a specified schedule. Understand what information is backed up through the System State Data option of backup. Be able to restore a Windows Server 2003 computer using Automated System Recovery. Understand the purpose of volume shadow copy.

Key Terms

Before you take the exam, be certain you are familiar with the following terms:

Application log

Automated System Recovery (ASR)

Backup Wizard

baseline

bottleneck

capture buffer

capture filters

error events

Event Viewer

Failure Audit event

Information events

page file

performance counter

performance objects

processor affinity

promiscuous mode

Remote Assistance

Remote Desktop for Administration

Restore Wizard

Security log

Success Audit event

System log

System Monitor

Task Manager

volume shadow copy

Warning events

Windows Backup

Review Questions

1. You are the system administrator of a technology startup company that provides hosted applications for Human Resources departments of companies with 50 to 500 employees. The applications run on IIS 6. You notice that, although they share identical hardware and software configurations, one of the IIS servers is significantly slower than the other servers when it responds to HTTP GET requests. Your personal observations are confirmed by user feedback. You want to run System Monitor on the server in an attempt to locate the bottleneck. However, because this is a production server that is already suffering a performance hit, you cannot accept any further degradation in performance. Which of the following options will enable you to launch System Monitor so that it does not significantly impact performance on the production IIS server?

    A. Launch System Monitor by choosing Start ➤ Run, and then enter **`start /low perfmon`**.

    B. Launch System Monitor by choosing Start ➤ Run, and then enter **`perfmon /low`**.

    C. Launch System Monitor by opening a command prompt and entering **`start /low perfmon`**.

    D. Launch System Monitor by opening the Performance tool in the Administrative Tools group. Then, use Task Manager to change the priority of the `perfmon.exe` process to low.

    E. Launch System Monitor by opening the Performance tool in the Administrative Tools group. Then, use Task Manager to change the priority of the `mmc.exe` process to low.

    F. C and E

    G. B and D

2. You are running a resource-intensive application on a Windows Server 2003 computer. This computer has a single processor, and you want to find out if it would be useful to move the application to a dual-processor server. You want to compare the resources this application is using against resources the other applications are using by viewing real-time statistics. You launch Task Manager and go to the Processes tab, and then you choose View ➤ Select Columns to change the data that is being displayed. The following exhibit shows the Select Columns dialog box. Which two columns should be displayed in order for you to get the performance data you need?

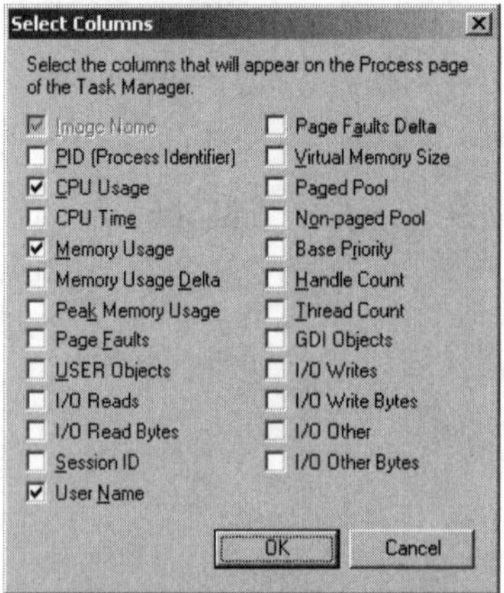

A. PID and Paged Pool

B. CPU Usage and Thread Count

C. Thread Count and CPU Time

D. CPU Time and CPU Usage

E. CPU Usage and Handle Count

3. You are the Director of Technical Services for a software company in the Midwest. Your system administrators are busily engaged in projects to optimize the network, and you want to offload some of the more routine tasks of data collection and performance monitoring onto the help desk staff. You recognize that this is also a great opportunity for help desk staff to gain experience and education that will help them in their current and future roles with the company. Therefore, you want to grant permission to the help desk staff so that they can create logs and alerts to analyze performance data and make recommendations about server upgrades. You want to assign the least amount of permission that enables them to accomplish this task. To which of the following groups should you add the help desk staff?

   A. Administrators

   B. Server Operators

   C. Power Users

   D. Performance Monitor Users

   E. Performance Log Operators

4. You are a system administrator analyzing the performance of various computers to determine whether or not a hardware upgrade or other optimization efforts are needed. You want to get a performance baseline for Wednesday's activity, because Wednesday represents a typical business day. You will collect performance information between 8:00 A.M. and 5:00 P.M. Counter readings should be taken every 5 minutes, so you can get a true average. Which of the following methods should you use to obtain the information with the least administrative effort?

   A. Create a trace log to take readings every 5 minutes throughout the business day.

   B. Create a counter log to take readings every 5 minutes throughout the business day.

   C. Create an alert to trigger every 5 minutes throughout the business day.

   D. Configure System Monitor to collect readings every 5 minutes throughout the business day and display current activity.

5. One of the single-processor servers in your company is running a mission-critical application. Other applications and processes are currently running on this server. You want to determine how much of the CPU this application is using, relative to the other applications running on the server. Which of the following methods will enable you to locate the information you desire in the most expedient way possible?

   A. Use the Task Manager, Applications tab.

   B. Use the Task Manager, Processes tab.

   C. Use the Task Manager, Performance tab.

   D. Use the % Processor Time counter with the Processor object in System Monitor.

   E. Use the % Processor Time counter with the Application object in System Monitor.

6. One of the Windows Server 2003 servers in your network has suddenly become very slow. You suspect that a rogue application is consuming system resources. You want to quickly identify and terminate the offending application. Which of the following methods should you use to accomplish this objective?

   A. Use the Services tool to stop an associated service.

   B. Restart the server.

   C. Use the System Monitor tool.

   D. Use the Task Manager tool.

7. You are a database administrator working with SQL Server and Windows Server 2003. You administer three database servers that are configured with dual processors and RAID-5 disk arrays. One of the database servers in your network has run out of physical memory. You ordered more RAM from your vendor and will install it as soon as it arrives. However, you need a temporary solution to help the server perform better until the memory arrives. Which of the following options will enable you to improve the server's performance until you can install more RAM?

   A. Launch the SQL Server application with a low process priority.

   B. Launch the SQL Server application with a real-time process priority.

   C. Create multiple page files.

   D. Stop all noncritical services related to the SQL Server service.

8. You are running a mission-critical, resource-intensive application on one of your Windows Server 2003 servers. You are looking for a way to improve the performance of the application. Because you suspect a memory bottleneck, you use System Monitor to analyze counters related to the memory object. The Paging File > % Usage counter averages 94 percent. You also analyze counters related to the processor object. The System > Processor Queue Length counter averages 2. The Processor > % Processor Time counter averages 87 percent. Which of the following actions will best enable you to improve the performance of the application?

   A. Upgrade the server by adding a processor.

   B. Upgrade the server by adding 25 percent more RAM.

   C. Increase the size of the page file.

   D. Spread the page file across multiple disks.

9. You are the network administrator for the XYZ Corporation and are located at the corporate headquarters in New York. Your network is configured behind a firewall that is configured for maximum security. You have a remote user who works out of his home in London and who accesses your network through the Internet. He is having problems with his Windows XP Professional configuration. Within your corporate network, you use Remote Assistance to help local users with problems. Users within the network can use Remote Assistance successfully. However, when your remote user requests Remote Assistance, it does not work at all. What is the most likely problem?

   A. The firewall is blocking the request, and you need to open TCP port 9833

   B. The firewall is blocking the request, and you need to open TCP port 8976

   C. The firewall is blocking the request, and you need to open TCP port 3389

   D. The firewall is blocking the request, and you need to open TCP port 7760

10. In your company, users access an ERP (Enterprise Resource Planning) program to handle business functionality from inventory and procurement to forecasting and business intelligence. The ERP application is very resource-intensive, so you want to optimize the server on which the application runs. The server runs Windows Server 2003 Standard Edition and has dual Athlon 1GHz processors with 2GB of RAM, and it has eight 100GB hard drives in a mirrored configuration. Using System Monitor, you analyze the counters related to memory, processor, and disk usage. The results are as follows. The LogicalDisk > % Free Space counter averages 35 percent. The PhysicalDisk > % Disk Time counter averages 70 percent. The Processor > % Processor Time counter averages 85 percent. The System > Processor Queue Length counter occasionally hits 2 or more. The Memory > Pages/Sec counter averages 3. The Paging File > % Usage averages 20. Based on these results, which of the following options represents the best way to optimize the server for this application?

    A. Upgrade to 8-way SMP.

    B. Upgrade to a RAID-5 disk array.

    C. Upgrade to 4-way SMP.

    D. Upgrade to 2-way SMP.

11. A Windows Server 2003 server on your network is functioning as a print server. You have noticed that as more users join the network, the time it takes to process print jobs increases. The last time you were in the server room, you noticed the disk light was on almost constantly, and you could hear the disk thrashing as you checked the print queue for jobs. You want to use System Monitor to analyze performance-related counters on the print server. With which of the following objects should you start when attempting to locate the bottleneck on the print server?

    A. The Print Redirector object

    B. The Processor object

    C. The Disk Subsystem object

    D. The Disk object

    E. The Memory object

12. You are the IT manager for a division of a regional insurance company. This division handles call center and customer service functions. Recently all client computers were upgraded from Windows 2000 Professional to Windows XP Professional. You want to establish a more proactive approach to ensuring that users get the help they need to understand how to use the new operating system. You decide to use the Offer Remote Assistance feature to invite users to get live assistance from your help desk staff. Which of the following actions must you take in order to use the Offer Remote Assistance feature?

    A. Enable the GPO for Remote Assistance, and add users who can offer Remote Assistance.

    B. Designate Windows XP Professional computers that can be used by the help desk staff to initiate Remote Assistance sessions.

    C. Open TCP port 3389 on the network firewall.

    D. Specify Windows Messenger or e-mail as the means of providing assistance.

13. You are a technical support engineer working in the corporate headquarters of a company with 500 sales and customer care associates, many of whom work from remote offices and from home. A user calls experiencing a problem with her Windows XP computer after installing a new sound card. You learn that the card was not supported on the HCL. She is logged on to the network through a VPN connection. Because this user is not very technically savvy, you know that you can fix her computer much faster by doing it yourself rather than by trying to walk her through the troubleshooting steps from a distance. You attempt to establish a Remote Desktop connection to her computer, but you are unable to do so. What is the most likely reason you cannot establish a Remote Desktop connection to the user's computer?

    A. Remote Desktop is supported only in Windows Server 2003.

    B. Remote Desktop is not enabled in Control Panel > System > Remote.

    C. The RDP protocol must be configured on the client computer before a Remote Desktop connection can be established.

    D. Remote Desktop cannot be used over a VPN connection.

14. You are the network administrator for a large network. You are responsible for all of the servers in the IT department. One of the servers has extremely large disk drives, and your tape backup system will not accommodate backing up all of the data at once. You want to back up any data that has changed each day. Which of the following backup options backs up only the files that have not been marked as archived and sets the archive bit for each file that is backed up?

    A. Copy

    B. Differential

    C. Incremental

    D. Normal

15. You are planning the disaster recovery strategy for your company. You want to ensure that the COM+ Class Registration database is included with backups of system information. Which of the following options will enable you to include the COM+ Class Registration database in your backup strategy?

    A. Include System State data with your backup.

    B. Include the folder `\`*`systemroot`*`\SYSVOL\sysvol` with your backup.

    C. Include the folder `\`*`systemroot`*`\SYSVOL\domain` with your backup.

    D. Configure the Directory Services Restore Mode console to back up the COM+ Class Registration database.

Answers to Review Questions

1. F. There are two ways to launch System Monitor with a low process priority so that it does not significantly impact performance on the production IIS server. You could launch System Monitor by opening a command prompt and typing **`start /low perfmon`**. You could also launch System Monitor by opening the Performance tool in the Administrative Tools group. You could then use Task Manager to change the priority of the process to low. System Monitor runs as an MMC snap-in, so the process is `mmc.exe`, not `perfmon.exe`. You cannot launch System Monitor with a low process priority directly from the Run dialog box by default.

2. D. The two columns that should be displayed are CPU Time and CPU Usage. These columns give you the most direct information about the application's processor usage. The other combinations are not relevant to the task of determining the resources this application is using in order to decide whether or not you should move the application to a dual-processor server.

3. D. Members of the Administrators and Server Operators security groups have permission to manage and view performance data on local and remote servers. In Windows Server 2003, two new groups have been created to allow staff who aren't members of the Administrators or Server Operators group to access performance-related counters through System Monitor or logs and alerts through Performance Logs and Alerts on a local server or on a remote computer. These two groups are Performance Monitor Users and Performance Log Users. Performance Log Users have access to schedule logging, while Performance Monitor Users have broader access to monitor performance on the target computer.

4. B. Baseline readings should be collected in a log so that the data can be analyzed for performance. Counter logs measure data through periodic samples and are ideal for recording data about hardware usage and the activity of system services. Trace logs measure data continuously (as opposed to measuring data through periodic samples), and they are used to track data that is collected by the operating system or programs. For example, you could specify that you want to trace the creation or deletion of processes or threads. Alerts are created to trigger an event when a counter surpasses a threshold, and they are not used when determining baseline performance. System Monitor is used to display real-time information, not to compare past to present performance information.

5. B. The most expedient way to find out how much of the CPU this application is using, relative to the other applications running on the server, is to use the Processes tab in Task Manager. The Applications tab lists currently running programs. The Performance tab shows a graphical view of overall resource usage for all the processes on the computer. The % Processor Time counter with the Processor object in System Monitor shows the percentage of time the processor is in use on the computer. The Application object is a made-up option.

6. D. The Task Manager tool is the best way to quickly identify and terminate the offending application. Restarting the server enables you to terminate, but not to identify the offending application. The System Monitor tool enables you to identify, but not to terminate the offending application. The Services tool does not enable you to identify or terminate the offending application.

7. C. The best solution is to create multiple page files. Memory is the most common bottleneck in a system. If you suspect a memory bottleneck, you can take several steps to improve performance: add more memory, optimize the size of the page file(s), create multiple page files, spread page files across multiple disk channels, locate page files on a separate partition from the system

files, increase disk space (to help optimize page file usage), and run fewer memory-intensive applications. Launching SQL Server with a low process priority will have the opposite effect than is desired, and launching SQL Server with a real-time process priority will severely compromise the stability of the system. If you stop all noncritical services related to the SQL Server service, SQL Server may not run as intended and other problems may result.

8. A. The processor is probably the bottleneck, so the best option for improving the application's performance is to upgrade the server by adding a quad processor. If the Paging File > % Usage counter consistently averaged 99 percent or more, you should take actions to optimize paging, which could include increasing the size of the page file or spreading the page file across multiple disks. The need for an increase in physical RAM is not indicated by the information provided.

9. C. If the Remote Assistance connections are made through a firewall, the firewall will have to be configured to open TCP port 3389 in both directions.

10. C. The statistics indicate a processor bottleneck; therefore, the best option is to upgrade to 4-way SMP. Windows Server 2003 Standard Edition does not support 8-way SMP, and you are already running 2-way SMP; therefore, options A and D are incorrect. There is no indicated need to upgrade to a RAID-5 disk array, so option B is incorrect.

11. D. Print server activities tend to be disk-intensive, so the place to start when attempting to locate a performance bottleneck on the print server is the disk subsystem. You would analyze this by measuring counters related to the Disk object in System Monitor. Options A and C are not valid options. Options B and E are far less likely as culprits for the bottleneck on this server—especially since you noticed almost constant disk activity and heavy disk thrashing.

12. A. The Offer Remote Assistance feature is enabled in Group Policy. When you enable the GPO for Remote Assistance, you add users who are permitted to offer Remote Assistance to other users. The other options either don't apply or don't need to be configured in order to use the Offer Remote Assistance feature. The Offer Remote Assistance feature can be used on any computer that supports Remote Assistance (Windows XP Professional or Windows Server 2003). If you are connecting across a firewall, you will need to open TCP port 3389 on the firewall. Remote Assistance can be provided through Windows Messenger or e-mail.

13. B. Remote Desktop is supported in Windows XP Professional and Windows Server 2003, and it is used to remotely administer desktops connected via a direct network connection, a VPN connection, or a remote access connection. No additional protocols need to be configured to establish a Remote Desktop connection.

14. C. Incremental backups are used to back up only the files that have not been marked as archived, and they set the archive bit for each file that is backed up. This option requires the last normal backup and all of the incremental tapes that have been created since the last normal backup for the restore process.

15. A. On a Windows Server 2003 member server, System State data consists of the Registry, the COM+ Class Registration database, and the system boot files. If the server is configured as a certificate server, System State data will also include the Certificate Services database. On Windows Server 2003 domain controller, System State data also includes the Active Directory services database and the SYSVOL directory, which is a shared directory that stores the server copy of the domain's public files. Directory Services Restore Mode is a special option on the Windows Advanced Options boot menu that is used to restore Active Directory and System State information on Windows Server 2003 domain controllers.

Glossary

A

Account Lockout policies Specify how invalid logon attempts will be tolerated.

Account policies Specify the user account properties that relate to the logon process. They allow you to configure computer security settings for passwords, account lockout specifications, and Kerberos authentication within a domain.

accounting provider The server that will provide accounting services for remote access or demand-dial connections. Options include Windows accounting, RADIUS accounting, or no accounting provider.

Active Directory Microsoft's hierarchical directory service, a centralized and standardized system designed especially for distributed networking environments. Active Directory stores information about objects on a network and enables single logon access to network resources for users and a single point of administration for network administrators.

Active Directory replication The process of synchronizing the data in the Active Directory database across all Active Directory servers. Uses a multimaster replication model. Only relevant changes are propagated. See also *multimaster replication model, full zone transfers, incremental zone transfers.*

Active Directory-Integrated (ADI) zone A form of DNS zone in which Active Directory stores all of the DNS zone data in AD, so it gains all of the benefits of AD—especially improved security and seamless replication.

adjacency A term that describes a group of neighboring routers that synchronize any changes to the network (routing) topology.

affinity See *group affinity.*

algorithm A small procedure, in a finite number of steps, that solves a recurrent mathematical problem.

anycast address In IPv6, used to identify a group of computers. Unlike the multicast address, which identifies a group of computers in order to send a broadcast to all computers in the group, the anycast address only sends the packet to the nearest member in the group and is used to locate the closest server for a resource such as DNS.

AppleTalk A network protocol used for communications and compatibility with Macintosh computers.

application log Log file that tracks application events. Viewed by using the Event Viewer.

area border router (ABR) A router that is attached to multiple areas and maintains separate topological databases for each area.

asymmetric encryption Uses one key to encrypt data and a different key to decrypt data. Asymmetric encryption is used in public key systems.

Asynchronous replication A method of replication used in multisite clusters in which a write operation is performed at Site 1 and is considered to be complete before the change is also written to the disk at Site 2. The I/O operation is complete the moment the write to the local disk is completed. Data can therefore be out of sync between the sites at any given moment in time.

Audit policies Specify whether to audit the success or failure of specific events.

authentication The process of establishing identity for the purpose of granting access to resources. It is required to log on to a computer locally. Authentication requires a valid username and a password that exists in the local accounts database or domain. An access token will be created if the information presented matches the account in the database. In a PKI, authentication is used to validate the entity and the origin of data.

authentication header (AH) The header of an IP packet used to digitally sign the entire contents of each packet.

Autoconfiguration An IPv6 feature used in stateless configuration and by which a computer can build its own address in the absence of a DHCP server. A node transmits a Neighbor Solicitation (NS) query to its desired address. If it receives a Neighbor Advertisement (NA) response from another node, then the address is already in use. Individual nodes listen to all NA confirmations and other traffic to keep tabs on who is still alive at a particular IP address. This information is cached and periodically verified by individual nodes by retransmitting NS queries. In the absence of a response, the query is deleted from the local cache. NS, NA, and DAD replace the ARP protocol.

autodiscovery An IPv6 feature. Also known as Neighbor Discovery, autodiscovery is a means for nodes to discover information about the local network and available routers. Autodiscovery uses the link-local address along with the Neighbor Discovery Protocol (NDP) to send ICMPv6 discovery messages. Routers use Router Advertisement (RA) multicast packets to advertise their existence, announce the on-link prefix, and signal stateless or stateful configuration.

Automated System Recovery (ASR) A new feature of the Windows Backup utility that is used in conjunction with a full system backup for total system recovery in the event of a disaster. Backs up system state data, system services, and disk configuration details.

autoregistration IPv6 features automatic registration in DNS for servers and clients.

auto-static update mode One of the two operational modes for a RIP router in which the router only broadcasts the contents of its routing table when requested by a remote router. Routes that the RRAS router learns from its RIP neighbors are marked as static routes in the routing table, and they persist until they are manually deleted. Auto-static mode is the default for demand-dial interfaces, because a table update will cause a dial-up. See also *periodic update mode*.

availability The ability to provide end users with access to a service for a high percentage of time while reducing unscheduled outages. Availability can be expressed numerically as the percentage of the time that a service is available for use, using this formula:

Percentage of availability = (total time – downtime)/total time * 100

B

backbone links Links that join border areas together. Backbone links interconnect networks through a central network (the backbone). With the OSPF protocol, the backbone connects all OSPF areas, allowing any router in the AS (the area) to connect to any other AS via tunnels.

Backup and Restore Wizard See *Windows Backup*.

baseline A moment-in-time snapshot of a system's performance.

Berkeley Internet Name Daemon (BIND) The Unix standard for DNS. Windows Server 2003 Server is compliant with several versions of BIND (specifically, BIND 4.9.7, 8.1.2, 8.2, and 9.1.0). Active Directory requires DNS and BIND version 8.1.2. BIND versions prior to 4.9.4 don't support compression, and they can receive only one Resource Record at a time. If your secondary servers are running older versions of BIND, then you will need to disable these features.

b-node Computer that uses broadcast for NetBIOS name queries and responses.

border routing The routing of packets between internetworks. Border routing is what happens when packets leave one internetwork and go to another internetwork, such as from a corporate network to the Internet.

bottleneck The least efficient point in a system. A server can perform only to the limits of its weakest link.

broadcast router A router that can talk to any number of other routers. An example is a typical LAN router, which can see any number of other routers on the LAN.

C

caching-only servers A type of DNS server that resolves names on behalf of clients and caches the results to speed up subsequent queries. Caching-only servers are not authoritative for a zone. They do not store standard primary or standard secondary zones. They do, however, help to reduce WAN traffic because they do not generate zone transfer traffic, and because cached queries reduce the amount of name resolution traffic that needs to cross the WAN.

capture buffer Used by the Network Monitor utility to capture network traffic data for analysis. A resizable storage area in memory to copy frames that are captured.

capture filters Used by the Network Monitor utility to screen out unwanted packets before they're recorded to the capture buffer.

certificate hierarchy Also known as a certification chain, can contain a series of certification authorities (CAs) from inside and outside a single organization, organized in a hierarchical trust model.

certificate policy and practice statements Outline how the CA and its certificates are to be used, the degree of trust that can be placed in these certificates, legal liabilities if the trust is broken, and so on.

Certificate Revocation List (CRL) A list of certificates that have been revoked before reaching the scheduled expiration date. The CAs build and maintain this list.

Certificate Services An integral component of a Public Key Infrastructure (PKI). Microsoft Certificate Services is a software service that issues and manages certificates for an enterprise using a certification authority (CA). MCS provides authentication support for secure e-mail, Web-based authentication, and smart-card authentication.

certificate store A database of certificates that contains end user and server certificates and the CRL. The certificates themselves may be stored in the local computer's Registry, in Active Directory, or in a database file, but they all appear as a single, seamless store.

Certificate Trust List (CTL) A list of trusted CAs that resides in Active Directory and is used to establish a trust for certificates issued by a given CA.

certification practices statements (CPSs) Statements that set forth the terms and conditions under which the CA will issue certificates. Most large commercial CAs (like VeriSign and GTE) include CPSs in their certificates.

Challenge Handshake Authentication Protocol (CHAP) A challenge-response authentication protocol used by non-Windows clients to provide challenge-response authentication using the RSA Message Digest 5 (MD5) hashing scheme to encrypt the response that is sent from the RAS client to the RAS server.

CIDR notation Classless Inter-domain Routing (CIDR) notation, also known as network prefix length notation, is a shorthand method of indicating the subnet scheme on an internetwork. A CIDR address is displayed as `<IP address>/<# of bits>`, where # of bits indicates the network or subnet portion (1s) and the remaining bits (0s) represent the host part of the IP address. Here's an example:

```
129.54.12.35/24
```

The 24 refers to the number of bits used in the network address. This is the same as the number of ones in a subnet mask shown in binary notation.

cipher A method of concealing the true meaning of data by disguising it in a new form. See also *ciphertext*.

ciphertext A disguised form of data. See also *cipher*.

classful IP addressing Classful IP addressing includes only the standard Class A, B, and C addresses and does not support VLSM or CIDR.

classful routing protocols Classful routing protocols can only recognize IP addresses that are based on the standard IP addresses such as Class A, B, or C. When classful routing protocols, such as RIP v1, are used, IP hosts and routers are unable to recognize subnets.

Classless Inter-domain Routing (CIDR) CIDR provides a method of overcoming the limitations of an IPv4 address space by fusing a range of network IDs of a given class into a larger network. CIDR can provide route summarization for the Internet. For example, in an organization with multiple Class C network IDs, CIDR can collapse the multiple network ID entries in a routing table into a single entry that encompasses all of an organization's Class C network IDs.

classless IP addressing Classless IP addressing allows you to use subnet addressing to better use the address space. This method lets you 'borrow' extra bits from the host portion of the address to divide the network into subnets.

classless routing protocols Classless routing protocols were created to enable subnetting. They transmit variable prefixes representing the network ID that go beyond the one, two, or three octets of the standard address classes. The advantage of prefix flexibility is that you can combine several networks as one routing table entry and thereby greatly reduce routing overhead. Examples of classless routing protocols are RIP v2, OSPF, and Border Gateway Routing Protocol (BGP).

cloned applications A multiple-instance application running in NLB clusters of stateful applications, and that runs against the same, relatively static dataset. An example is a Web server.

cluster See *server clusters.*

cluster host An individual computer, or node, that is a member of a server cluster.

Cluster Service The Windows service that runs server clusters. Applications and services must be compatible with the Cluster Service in order to respond appropriately to a failure.

cluster-aware A description of an application that can communicate with the Cluster API to receive status and notification information from the cluster.

clustering Combining two or more computers in a group that work together to provide higher availability, reliability, and scalability than could be obtained by using a single independent system. Application software and data are available on several servers linked together in a cluster configuration.

CNAME records DNS alias records (also known as canonical name, or CNAME, records) allow you to use more than one name to point to a single host. Entries follow the format:

```
mail        IN  CNAME  servername
ftp         IN  CNAME  servername
servername  IN  A      172.30.1.14
```

conditional forwarder A type of DNS server that will forward DNS queries for external DNS names to DNS servers outside of its own network based on the domain name in the query. Use when DNS clients in separate networks resolve each others' names without having to query a DNS server on the Internet.

confidentiality Ensures that data is secret to all except the authorized parties to a data transaction.

connectionless protocols Connectionless protocols are analogous to radio or television transmissions. These protocols optimistically assume that all data will get through in the correct order, so the protocol doesn't guarantee delivery or provide packet sequencing. No protocol overhead is spent on these activities, so connectionless protocols tend to be fast. The Internet Protocol (IP) and User Datagram Protocol (UDP) are examples of connectionless Internet transport protocols. IP provides logical addressing and provides a best-effort delivery of packets (datagrams). IP's role in transmitting datagrams is analogous to writing an address on an envelope and dropping it in a mailbox, with faith that the postal service will do the rest.

connection-oriented protocols Connection-oriented protocols are analogous to a telephone call, because they rely on a connection between the two parties to a data communication. They pessimistically assume that some data will be lost or disordered in most transmissions, and so they provide guaranteed delivery and packet sequencing. Transmission Control Protocol (TCP) is an example of a connection-oriented Internet protocol.

connection type A component of an IPSec policy that specifies whether the rule applies to LAN connections, dial-up connections, or both.

convergence time In a network with more than one WINS server, the convergence time for that network is the time it takes a change from any server to propagate to all other servers on that network.

cryptography The process of securing and maintaining the secrecy of data communications through encryption/decryption systems.

D

decryption The conversion of encrypted data back into its original form.

default route The route where packets go when there is no explicit route defined for them. This is similar to the default gateway for TCP/IP clients. When a router encounters a packet bound for some remote network and cannot find a network or host route by searching the routing table, it will use the default route instead.

delegated namespace Using a delegated namespace resembles creating separate public and private namespaces. However, in this case you are creating a single subdomain within the namespace in which the DNS servers for the namespace will reside, rather than dividing the namespace into public and private portions. For instance, for the `contoso.com` domain, the delegated namespace may be `corp.contoso.com`. In this model, you would enable internal clients to resolve both internal and external DNS namespaces, but deny access to the internal namespace to external clients. A separate DNS server or servers is required for the delegated internal domain.

delegation resource record Used to locate the authoritative DNS servers for a delegated zone. These records "glue" zones together and provide an effective path for delegation and referral that other DNS servers can follow in the process of resolving a name. Commonly used with stub zones.

demand-dial routing A feature of RRAS in which connections to specific networks can be launched when the router receives packets addressed to those networks. This allows you to use on-demand links instead of permanent connections.

Denial of Service (DoS) A type of attack in which an attacker seeks to overload a service in order to render it unavailable to other users. A DoS attack is commonly launched against Web and file servers.

DHCP allocator The component of Internet Connection Sharing (ICS) that acts as a simplified DHCP server by giving out IP addresses, in the range 192.168.0.2 through 192.168.0.254 using the standard 255.255.255.0 subnet mask.

DHCP relay agent For subnets without a DHCP server, the DHCP relay agent can be configured to listen for DHCP traffic, intercept requests, and forward them to a DHCP server on a remote subnet.

dial-up networking A method of providing remote access to network clients in which a remote access client makes a direct, physical, temporary connection to a physical port on a remote access server or connected device using the service of a telecommunications provider such as analog phone service or ISDN.

digest A unique mathematical value calculated by a special type of algorithm called a *hashing algorithm* or a *message authentication algorithm* from the actual message contents. The digest is then encrypted using the private key and either added to the end of the message or sent as a separate file attachment.

digital certificates The passports of the electronic world. Like your passport booklet, which contains the unique passport ID number, a digital certificate serves as a carrying case for a public key. A certificate contains the public key and a set of attributes, such as the key holder's name and e-mail address.

digital signatures An electronic signature used to authenticate the sender's identity as well as to ensure that the message was not altered in transit.

disaster recovery The method of recovering from a failure, such as power outages and server failures. A disaster recovery plan (DRP), also known as a business continuity plan (BCP) or business process contingency plan (BPCP) details how an organization will avoid and recover from potential disasters.

Discretionary Access Control List (DACL) Part of an object's security descriptor that grants or denies permission for access of an object to specific users and groups. Only an object's owner can change permissions in the object's DACL.

Disk Quota policies Specifies how the computer system will use disk quotas.

distance vector routing protocol Broadcasts the distance and the vector of a route to a network destination. The distance is the number of hop counts to a network destination, and the vector is the direction in which a network destination can be reached. A router sends updates to its immediate neighbors at regularly scheduled intervals, and each neighbor then adds its own distance value to the table and forwards it on to its immediate neighbors. This eventually results in a cumulative table with the distances to each network destination. RIP is the most common example of a distance vector routing protocol.

DNS client Any network node that issues queries to a DNS server to resolve a hostname to an IP address. The client host name may or may not be registered in a name server (DNS) database. This is also commonly referred to as the resolver. See also *resolvers*.

DNS namespace A naming convention for network resources. DNS uses a hierarchical naming structure in which names identify both the network resource and its place in the namespace hierarchy. In WINS, the namespace is a flat naming structure that uses a single, unique name to identify each unique network resource.

DNS server A server that maintains information about a part of the DNS database and that responds to and resolves DNS queries from DNS clients, or resolvers.

DNS zone A contiguous portion of the DNS tree in a DNS database. Administered as a single, separate entity by a DNS server. The zone contains resource records for all the names within the zone.

Domain Name System (DNS) A hierarchical, distributed database that contains mappings of DNS domain names to IP addresses and other data. DNS enables the location of computers and services by user-friendly names, and it also enables the discovery of additional information stored in the database.

Domain Security Policy Policies that control security at the domain level.

Dynamic DNS (DDNS) standard Allows DNS clients to update information in the DNS database files. For example, a Windows 2000 Server or Windows Server 2003 DHCP server can automatically tell a DDNS server which IP addresses it has assigned, and to what machines. Windows 2000 and XP Professional DHCP clients can do this, too, but for security reasons it's better to let the DHCP server do it on behalf of clients, or to use secure only updates, which are integrated within Active Directory security.

dynamic routing Unlike static routing, which uses manual configuration of routing tables, dynamic routing uses specialized routing protocols to communicate route information dynamically as well as to build the routing table on a given router, share information with other routers, and calculate the best path to a given destination on the fly. The types of dynamic routing protocols include distance vector and link link-state routing protocols.

E

EAP type An authentication method supported in EAP. EAP allows the use of almost any authentication method, including secure access tokens like SecurID, one-time password systems like S/Key, or ordinary username/password systems.

Encapsulating Security Payload (ESP) Security protocol used to encrypt the entire payload of an IPSec packet, rendering it undecipherable by anyone other than the intended recipient. ESP only provides confidentiality, but it can be combined with AH to gain maximum security.

encapsulation The process of wrapping other types of network traffic inside an IP datagram.

Encrypting File System (EFS) A PKI-aware Windows-based file system that can automatically encrypt and decrypt files.

encryption The conversion of data into a disguised form, called a *ciphertext*, for the purpose of protecting communications from unauthorized parties. Once data has been encrypted, a user must have a password or key to decrypt it.

entities In a PKI, parties to a transaction are known as entities, and they can be users, organizations, computers, or devices.

Error events Type of logged event that indicates the occurrence of a serious error, such as a driver failing to load.

Event Viewer The utility that is used to view the binary log files, which store certain events logged by the Event Log Service.

exit modules In Microsoft Certificate Services, predefined sets of instructions that tell the CA how to proceed after a request is approved. Contain rules that specify where and how a newly issued certificate is published.

Extensible Authentication Protocol (EAP) Protocol used to enable a client-server pair to negotiate an authentication method. EAP extends the authentication methods available for PPP connections. This allows the use of almost any authentication method, including secure access tokens like SecurID, one-time password systems like S/Key, or ordinary username/password systems.

external namespace The DNS namespace used to access a corporate network from outside the network (for example, `microsoft.com`).

F

failback The process of moving resources, either individually or in a group, back to their original node after a failed node rejoins a cluster and comes back online.

failover The process of taking resource groups offline on one node, such as a failed node, and bringing them back online on another node.

failover pairs configuration A common N+I variation. Failover pairs are often used in clusters with four or more nodes, and they are ideal for ensuring performance consistency after failover. Failover policies can be defined so that each application can fail over between two nodes.

Failure Audit event Type of logged event that indicates the occurrence of an event that has been audited for failure. For example, a Failure Audit event is a failed logon due to an invalid user name and/or password when system logons are being audited.

fault tolerance Describes the ability of a system to continue functioning when a component in the system fails.

filter action Specifies how traffic matching a filter will be handled (i.e., dropped, encrypted, etc.).

filter lists Groups of filters used to build rules that enforce complicated behavior to secure remote network connections. For each rule, a single filter list is selected that contains one or more predefined packet filters that describe the type of traffic to which the configured filter action for the rule is applied.

flat routing In a flat routing infrastructure, each network segment gets its own entry in every router's routing table. The network IDs have no network/subnet structure and cannot be summarized.

forward-only server A DNS server that is configured to use forwarders and that does not use recursion when forwarders fail, but instead fails the query.

full zone transfers A type of zone transfer in which the entire zone is propagated. Used in DNS under Windows NT 4 and higher.

full-mesh WINS replication design in which push/pull partnerships are configured between all WINS servers. Not a recommended configuration.

G

glue address (glue A) resource record A type of DNS record that provides the address of the host specified in the NS record.

group affinity An attribute of a dependency between groups that determines the groups' relative location in the server cluster. Used to configure the relative location of clustered applications in the event of failure.

Group Policy Object (GPO) An object that holds group policy settings and can be applied to OUs, domains, and sites within Active Directory.

Group Policy policies Specify how group policies will be applied to the computer.

H

hashing algorithm A special type of algorithm, also known as a message authentication algorithm, used to create a digital signature. It calculates a unique mathematical value, known as a digest, from the actual message contents.

high-level security A type of DNS security that uses all of the DNS security features of medium-level security, and adds the advanced security that is available when you run DNS servers on domain controllers and use Active Directory–integrated zones. In this configuration, there is no DNS communication at all with the Internet.

h-node Computer that uses first p-node (directed) then b-node (broadcast) methods in order to resolve NetBIOS names.

host record Also called an *address* or an *A record*. Used to statically associate a host's name to its IP addresses. The format is given here:

```
server1       IN  A  192.168.0.204
server2       IN  A  192.168.3.144
```

host routes Function like shortcuts to provide a route to a single system. They provide a slightly more efficient way for a router to "know" how to get traffic to a remote machine, and are normally used when you want to direct traffic to remote networks through a particular computer.

I

inbound port mappings In ICS, static mappings of a public address and port number to a private address and port number.

incremental zone transfers (IXFRs) Supported in Windows 2000 Server and higher and under BIND version 8.2.1 and higher. Just like an incremental backup, an incremental transfer enables the secondary server to pull only the changes it needs in order to synchronize its copy of the zone data with its configured source. Zone transfers are completed much more quickly and with far less network traffic generated.

Information events Type of logged event that informs you of the occurrence of a specific action, such as a system shutting down or starting up. Information events are logged for informative purposes.

inheritance Describes how policies are applied within the hierarchical structure of Active Directory.

integrity Provides the means of verifying that data was not altered in transit. Data integrity is provided by using a digital signature.

iterative query A type of DNS query in which a DNS server returns the best answer it can provide to a name resolution request without seeking help from other DNS servers as is performed in a recursive query. Also called a nonrecursive query.

internal namespace The DNS namespace used to access a corporate network internally. May be the same as or different from the existing external DNS namespace. For instance, you might use `contoso.com` as the external namespace, and `corp.contoso.com` or `contoso.net` as the internal DNS namespace. See also *external namespace*.

internal routing The process of routing packets within an internetwork.

Internet Key Exchange (IKE) Security protocol that provides services to dynamically exchange and manage keys between computers. IKE also dynamically negotiates a common set of security settings, so it is not necessary for both parties to have identical IPSec policies defined. Dynamic rekeying during exchanges over unsecured session pipes blocks most impersonation and interception attacks.

Internet Protocol Security Extensions (IPSec) A framework of open standards for ensuring private, secure communications over IP networks, through the use of cryptographic security services. These services allow for authentication, integrity, access control, and confidentiality. Implemented as a set of security extensions to the IP protocol.

Internet Security Agreement/Key Management Protocol (ISAKMP) Security protocol that provides a way for two computers to agree on security settings and exchange a security key that they will use to communicate securely. Information is secured with a combination of an algorithm and a key.

internetwork A network of networks. Examples include the Internet and large, multisite corporate networks such as an organization with sites in New York City, San Francisco, and Hong Kong.

IP datagram The structure that enables a client and server to transfer other types of data by wrapping the data within an IP packet. A unit of data communication and transmission in IP which contains all of the necessary addressing information to be delivered by IP.

IP spoofing IP spoofing is a method of attack that involves the impersonation of a computer using a stolen IP address in order to obtain passwords and other data or to conceal the true identity of a computer.

ipconfig A command line utility that lists the IP address, subnet mask, and default gateway. You can also see more advanced TCP/IP parameters, such as WINS server and primary DNS suffix when you employ the /all switch.

IPSec client A computer that attempts to establish a connection to an IPSec server. Any Windows 2000, XP, or Windows Server 2003 computer may be an IPSec client or server.

IPSec Policy Agent A service running on a Windows 2003 machine that connects to an Active Directory server and fetches the IPSec policy and then passes it to the IPSec code.

IPSec server The server that services security requests (for a security key and to initiate a secure communications channel) from IPSec clients.

IPv4 The most widely used version of the TCP/IP protocol suite, which is based on a 32-bit address structure.

IPv4-compatible IPv6 address An IPv4 address embedded within an IPv6 address. It is created by simply inserting leading zeros to create a 128-bit address. For example, the IPv4 address `209.64.12.10` in decimal would be represented as follows:

`0000:0000:0000:0000:0000:0000: 209.64.12.10`

or

`:: 209.64.12.10` in shorthand.

IPv4-mapped IPv6 address Addresses for IPv4-only nodes that do not support IPv6. They are represented as follows:

`0000:0000:0000:0000:0000:FFFF:209.64.12.10`

or

`::FFFF: 209.64.12.10` in shorthand.

IPv6 Version 6 of the IP protocol (IPv6) was designed to resolve the problems of addressing, scalability, security, and performance inherent in IPv4. IPv6, previously known as IPng (for Next Generation), is a new suite of protocols and standards that features a radically more scalable 128-bit address space, built-in security, a streamlined packet, and self-configuration intelligence. IPv6 is a rapidly evolving standard that is supported on only the newest operating systems, including Windows Server 2003, Windows XP, Linux kernel version 2.4.18, and Mac OS 10.2.

K

Kerberos v5 The default authentication method used by Windows 2000, XP, and Server 2003 clients and servers to authenticate users and network services. Also the default authentication method for Active Directory. This is called *dual verification*, or *mutual authentication.*

key An algorithm that "undoes" the work of the encryption algorithm. Used in cryptographic systems such as Microsoft Certificate Services.

Key Distribution Center (KDC) Server that is responsible for holding all of the client passwords and account information for Kerberos authentication. When a Windows Server 2003 is installed as a domain controller, it automatically becomes a KDC server.

key escrow Method employed by some cryptographic systems in which a third party holds a copy of an organization's encryption keys.

L

Layer 2 Tunneling Protocol (L2TP) A generic tunneling protocol that allows encapsulation of one network protocol's data within another protocol. Used in conjunction with IPSec to enable secure virtual private network (VPN) access to Windows 2003 networks.

limited replication partnerships Describes pull-only or push-only unidirectional partnerships for WINS replication. In enterprise internetworks, limited replication partnerships are the most effective choice for supporting replication over slow WAN links.

link state map A routing table that contains the current links or paths that are available for routers to use and determines what router should service a route request. OSPF is an example of a routing protocol that uses a link state map.

link state routing protocols Unlike the chatty distance vector protocols that broadcast updates to every router in the group at regular intervals, link state protocols send updates only when a network link changes state. Link state routing protocols offer faster convergence and are more scalable, more reliable, and require less bandwidth than distance vector protocols but are more resource-intensive. OSPF is the most widely used link state routing protocol.

link-local address An IPv6 address that leads with FE80: and is analogous to the `169.254` network address in APIPA. It is used for a single, nonrouted network segment and can autoconfigure an IP based on the MAC address.

LMHOSTS Stands for "Lan Manager hosts," and the LMHOSTS file is the static alternative to WINS—just as the HOSTS file is the static alternative to DNS.

Local policies Control what a user can do after logging on. Local policies include the following subsets: auditing, user rights assignment, and security options.

local quorum cluster A cluster model that consists of a single node. This type of cluster is commonly used for testing, development, as well as to create dynamic file shares, often for home directories.

Local Security policies Policies that control security at the local computer level.

logon policies Specify the behavior of logon events, such as logon scripts.

low-level security Describes a standard DNS deployment with no configured security precautions. Should be used only in cases in which there is absolutely no reason to be concerned for the security of the DNS information. For instance, you may choose this level of security (or nonsecurity) in a private network that has no connection to the Internet and where there is no threat of someone compromising the DNS data.

M

machine accounts Special accounts that computers use to transparently log on to a domain during network initialization and before user logon. They do not have to be on the same domain as the user accounts for users logging on to a particular machine.

machine certificates Digital certificates issued to machines.

mail exchange (MX) record Defines servers that can accept e-mail bound for this domain. Each MX record contains two parameters—a preference and a mail server—as shown in the following format example:

```
<domain> IN MX <preference> <mailserver host>
```

majority node set cluster A cluster model in which each node maintains its own copy of the cluster configuration data. The quorum resource ensures consistency of the cluster configuration data across the nodes. Frequently used for geographically dispersed clusters. Unlike single quorum device clusters, which can still survive with only one node, majority node set clusters require a majority of the cluster nodes surviving after a failure for the server cluster to continue operating.

mapped address See *IPv4-mapped IPv6 address.*

masked bits In a subnet mask, refers to the bit positions of 1, which identify the network portion of the IP address.

medium-level security Uses DNS security features, but not the advanced security that is available when you run DNS servers on domain controllers and use Active Directory–integrated zones.

metric Cost information used by routing protocols to calculate the most efficient route for packets to take to reach a destination.

Microsoft Baseline Security Analyzer (MBSA) A tool that can be used to perform local or remote scans of servers and workstations. It's commonly used to check for security updates, verify service pack status, and identify common security misconfigurations.

Microsoft Certificate Services (MCS) Microsoft's service that uses certificates and certification authorities (CAs) to provide authentication support, including secure e-mail, Web-based authentication, and smart-card authentication.

mirrored IPSec filter A mirrored IPSec filter automatically filters its opposite—if you set up a filter from your IP address to a remote address and configure it to allow only port 80, with mirroring you'll also get a filter that allows traffic from the remote end back to you on port 80.

m-node Computer that first uses b-node (broadcast) then p-node (directed) methods in order to resolve NetBIOS names.

MS-CHAP A remote access authentication protocol and Microsoft's extension to the CHAP protocol. It is designed to work with computers and networks that are using Windows 98, Windows Me, Windows NT 4 (all versions), Windows 2000 (all versions), Windows XP (all versions), and Windows Server 2003.

multicast address An IPv6 address that leads with FF and is used to identify a group of computers that will receive a broadcast to this address.

multicast routing A special type of routing in which a packet is sent to multiple host computers based on a special Class D IP address.

multimaster replication model Used in Active Directory replication and in Active Directory Integrated zone transfers. Enables multiple masters to update the zone. A master is any domain controller running Active Directory–Integrated DNS. Any of the domain controllers for the domain can modify the zone and replicate changes to the other domain controllers. This is better than standard DNS replication, in which only the primary server for a zone can modify the zone.

multiple host filtering NLB configuration that specifies that multiple hosts in the cluster handle network traffic for the port rule. This filter mode provides scalable performance in addition to fault tolerance, because you can distribute the network load among the hosts. You can do this equally, or indicate that each host should handle a specific load weight.

multiple-instance application Clustered application in which nodes run either multiple instances of the same code, or different pieces of code that provide a service. The client sees the application as though only a single instance were running on a single server. Multiple instances of an application are created by either cloning or partitioning the application.

mutual authentication The type of authentication used with Kerberos version 5. With mutual authentication (also called *dual verification*), the user is authenticated to the service and the service is authenticated to the user.

N

N+I configuration The most common clustered server configuration used for failover policies. In this model, N nodes will host applications and I (for idle) nodes will stand by as spares.

name registration The process of a computer registering its name and IP address with its designated DNS and/or WINS server.

name release A WINS client can relinquish ownership of its name at any time by sending a name release message, which contains its IP address and name. However, this is most often done when the client machine is cleanly shut down.

name renewal WINS clients must renew their names with the server at periodic intervals. With WINS, the client must notify the server that it wants to continue using its registered name so that the server will reset the TTL.

name resolution Name resolution services resolve computer host names and NetBIOS computer names to IP addresses. Examples are DNS and WINS.

name resolution component A NAT service that acts like a proxy for DNS. When a client resolver makes a DNS query, it goes to the name resolution component on the NAT server, which forwards it to the DNS server defined on the Internet-connected adapter and returns the reply.

name server A server that can give an authoritative answer to queries about a domain registered in the DNS.

name server (NS) records List of the name servers for a domain; this allows other name servers to look up names in your domain. A zone file may contain more than one name server record. The format of these records is given here:

```
<domain> @ IN NS <nameserver host>
```

NAT address pool A range or collection of individual addresses defined to inform NAT of the IP addresses from which it should expect traffic.

NAT addressing component A stripped-down DHCP server within NAT that assigns an IP address, a subnet mask, a default gateway, and the IP address of a DNS server. The latter two options will be assigned only if a DHCP relay agent is configured.

NAT editor A special NAT component that is responsible for changing data in protocols that embed addressing information in the packet payload. Windows Server 2003 includes NAT editors for FTP, PPTP, NBT, and the Internet Control Message Protocol (ICMP).

NAT interface An interface created in the RRAS console to provide NAT services.

nbtstat The command-line utility used to test, verify, and troubleshoot NetBIOS name resolution.

NetBIOS naming A naming protocol for Windows networks in which NetBIOS names are used as the means of identifying computers and other resources on the network. NetBIOS names are "friendly" computer names such as SalesSrv1. Works by broadcasting information about network resources, such as which shares a server offers.

NetBIOS The Network Basic Input/Output System (NetBIOS) provides a method by which Windows-based computers can locate network resources and computers. In Windows Server 2003, NetBIOS uses a WINS server to resolve NetBIOS names to IP addresses on behalf of clients.

NetBIOS name server (NBNS) A server such as a WINS server that resolves NetBIOS names on behalf of network clients.

NetBIOS over TCP/IP (NBT) Protocol that enables nonroutable NetBIOS traffic to be transmitted over IP networks and is used in conjunction with WINS servers.

Network Access Server (NAS) Server that provides authentication and connectivity services to provide remote clients access to a network.

Network Address Translation (NAT) A service defined in RFC 3022. Uses an IP router that can translate IP addresses from private or unauthorized public network addresses used internally within a company to public addresses used externally, for instance on the Internet. NAT is most often used to protect internal systems on the private network from outsider attack.

network infrastructure The collection of hardware and software components that together support the flow and processing of digital information.

Network Load Balancing (NLB) A special type of clustering used to provide scalability. NLB is most commonly used to distribute incoming Web requests among a cluster of Internet server applications (IIS applications, for instance).

Network Load Balancing (NLB) clusters A special type of server cluster that uses groups of identical computers that can operate independently. All of the nodes in an NLB cluster are active, and they are often cloned. NLB is best suited for applications that are stateless or can otherwise be cloned with no decline in performance. NLB is designed for stateless applications, such as front-end Web servers, FTP servers, and VPNs. Stateless applications treat each client request as an independent operation and have read-only data or data that changes infrequently.

network routes TCP/IP network segments are interconnected by IP routers, which pass IP datagrams from one network segment to another. Network routes are the paths that are stored in the routing table of the routers.

network topology The physical and logical structure of a network.

node See *cluster host.*

non-broadcast multiple access (NBMA) A type of router that can talk to multiple peers without using a broadcast.

noncontiguous subnets Subnets of a class-based network ID that do not share a neighboring router.

nonrecursive DNS server Unlike a forward-only DNS server, the nonrecursive server will neither build up a cache, nor perform recursion if the query fails. You can disable recursion on the entire DNS server, which will prevent you from using forwarders on that server, or you can disable recursion on a per–domain name basis.

nonrepudiation A benefit of digital signatures that can provide the same assurance and even legal binding for electronic transmissions as currently exists for paper documents with handwritten signatures. Protects against a party to a transaction later claiming that he/she/it didn't agree to the terms of the contract.

nslookup The command-line utility used to test, verify, and troubleshoot a DNS configuration.

NWLink Microsoft's implementation of Novell's IPX/SPX protocol stack, which is used in Novell NetWare. Think of NWLink as IPX for Windows, where NWLink is the networking component that implements the network protocol IPX.

O

offline compaction Refers to manually compacting the WINS database using the `jetpack.exe` utility while the WINS service is stopped, a more efficient means of reclaiming unused space in your WINS database. Monthly offline compaction is recommended for large, busy networks of more than 1,000 WINS clients. Less frequent offline compaction will be suitable for smaller networks.

online compaction Refers to the dynamic and automatic process of compacting the WINS database while the WINS service is running. Not as efficient a means of reclaiming unused space as offline compaction.

on-link prefix In IPv6, describes the network portion of the address. In stateless configuration, the computer builds its own address by starting with the on-link prefix and appending its own MAC address.

Open Shortest Path First (OSPF) OSPF is the most popular link-state routing protocol. OSPF compiles a complete topological database of the internetwork. OSPF uses the shortest path first (SPF), or Djikstra algorithm, to calculate the least-cost path, enabling it to base its decision on a calculation of several metrics such as link speed and reliability in addition to hop count. OSPF is more complex, but also faster and more reliable than RIP. Advantages of OSPF over RIP include no limit on hop counts, reduced processor demand in LAN environments due to multicast frames, and the ability to hierarchically structure the router network into subdivisions (areas), thereby reducing memory and CPU overhead on a router. It also supports VLSMs and noncontiguous subnets.

organizational units (OUs) A unit of organization within Active Directory. Functions as a container that holds other objects, including users, groups, computers, and other OUs.

owner-version mapping table Used in WINS replication. Each WINS server maintains this table, which keeps track of which WINS server owns (or holds) a particular registration, along with the highest version ID received from that server. When one server sends another a replication trigger, the sending server includes a copy of its owner-version mapping table; this allows the receiving server to determine what the sending server "knows" about the state of the WINS databases.

P

packet authentication Verifies that a packet is actually from the sender. Packet authentication is a built-in security feature of IPv6.

packet confidentiality Verifies that the payload of a data packet cannot be read by an unauthorized third party. Packet confidentiality is a built-in security feature of IPv6.

packet filtering A technology that filters the type of inbound and/or outbound traffic that is allowed to cross the router.

packet integrity Verifies that a data packet was not altered in transit. Packet integrity is a built-in security feature of IPv6.

packet payload The actual data contents of a packet. Consists of the data to be transmitted to the remote computer minus any header and trailer information.

packets Collections of information to be transmitted between computers. Packets may include source and destination addresses, routing information, reassembly information, the actual data (or payload), and error-checking information. Network protocols at various levels of the OSI model construct, modify, and disassemble packets as they move data down the sending stack, across the network, and back up the OSI stack of the receiving computer.

page file Logical or virtual memory that physically exists on the hard drive and is used to extend the physical memory space.

partitioned applications Multiple-instance applications designed for server clusters of stateless applications that have frequent updates to memory. An example is a database, where records A through M can reside on one partition, and N through Z can reside on another partition. Other types of applications can partition the functionality rather than the actual data. For instance, billing inquiries could be directed to a separate billing node, which has sole access to the billing database. Catalog inquiries could be directed to a separate catalog node, which has sole access to the catalog database. This example would provide scalability, but not availability because there is no option for failover.

passthrough action In IPSec filters, the Permit action. Tells the IPSec filter to take no action and allows traffic to pass through without modification.

Password Authentication Protocol (PAP) The simplest and least secure authentication protocol. It transmits all authentication information as clear text, making it completely vulnerable to snooping.

Password policies Specify the password security requirements that are enforced on the computer. Note that the Password policy applies to computers only, and it cannot be configured for specific users.

pathping A utility that provides statistical analysis of network traffic. Pathping is essentially a hybrid of the ping and tracert tools, and provides even more useful information to enable an administrator to isolate the cause of a network problem. In addition to returning the computer name and IP address for each hop, pathping computes the percentage of lost/sent packets to each router or link.

peer filters A technology used by routers that specifies the neighboring routers to which a local router will listen.

performance counter A data item that is associated with a performance object and that carries a value corresponding to a particular aspect of performance for its object. Counters are used to track specific information regarding the performance object. For example, the Pages/sec counter provided by the Memory object tracks the rate of memory paging.

performance objects Categories within the System Monitor utility that organize all of the system resources that can affect performance. A system is essentially the sum of all of its performance objects.

periodic update mode RIP update mode in which routing table updates are automatically and periodically sent to all other RIP routers on the internetwork. See also *auto-static update mode*.

ping The command-line utility used to test basic IP-level connectivity. Ping sends Internet Control Message Protocol (ICMP) echo requests to the destination host and analyzes ICMP echo replies.

p-node Computer that uses direct queries to an NBNS to resolve NetBIOS names.

pointer (PTR) record Maps an IP address to a host name, so it does the opposite job of the A record. Used to perform reverse lookups.

Point-to-Point Protocol (PPP) Remote access protocol that enables any two computers to establish a peer-to-peer connection. This could be a dial-up modem connection, but it could just as easily be a direct serial cable connection, an infrared connection, or any other type of serial connection.

point-to-point router A router with only one peer. For example, a typical DSL installation will have a point-to-point configuration featuring one router on your end and one on the ISP end.

Point-to-Point Tunneling Protocol (PPTP) A Microsoft-specific VPN protocol that encapsulates IP, IPX, or NetBEUI information inside IP packets, hiding data from onlookers.

policy modules Predefined sets of instructions that contain the rules that govern how the CA handles an incoming request.

port mappings Used to specify to which ports inbound traffic should be mapped. This allows you to take traffic coming to any port on any of your public IP addresses and direct it to the port you want on any machine on your private network. For example, you could channel any incoming Web requests to a single machine by mapping port 80 on the public interface to port 80 on your internal Web server.

pre-shared keys A shared, secret key that is previously agreed upon by two users. It is quick to use and does not require the client to run the Kerberos protocol or to have a public-key certificate. Most commonly used for testing in a PKI.

primary DNS server The "owner" of the zone files defined in the DNS database. The primary DNS server has authority to make changes to the zone files it owns.

primary WINS server The server configured as the first server a WINS client will attempt to reach to register, release, or resolve a NetBIOS name.

primary zones With a primary zone, the default for a newly created zone, the server has a read/write copy of the zone information and acts as the point of update for the zone. The server periodically replicates its zone file to the secondary zone server to ensure that the secondary zone server's copy of the file is current. At first the server transfers a complete copy of the zone file. Later transfers consist of changes only. The primary zone server can administer zone information separately.

private addresses A predefined set of IP addresses for workstations and servers within a company that do not need to be directly connected to the Internet. Private addresses are not reachable from the Internet. They are used to increase security and provide more addressing flexibility than can be obtained by using public addresses. The following private address blocks are defined in RFC 1918: `10.0.0.0/8`, `172.16.0.0/12`, and `192.168.0.0/16`.

private key Also called a *secret key*. A key that is known only to its owner and should never be revealed to any other party. Used in asymmetric encryption systems along with the public key. Can be used to encrypt data that then can be decrypted only with the public key. Can be used to decrypt data that has been encrypted with the public key.

processor affinity For a computer that has multiple processors, describes the process of associating each processor with specific processes that are running on the computer.

promiscuous mode A mode in which a network card will accept packets not addressed to it. Used by Network Monitor and other packet analyzers to capture network traffic.

protocol binding Links the protocol stack to the network device driver for the network interface adapter. Multiple protocols can be bound to the same card. For best performance, you should unbind unused protocols from an adapter or change the binding order so that the most commonly used protocols are listed first.

public addresses Public addresses are assigned by an Internet name registrar such as the Internet Assigned Numbers Authority (IANA) and guaranteed to be globally unique on the Internet. When public addresses are assigned, the routers of the Internet have those routes programmed in so that the public addresses will be reachable on the Internet.

public key A key that is designed to be freely distributed. Used in asymmetric encryption systems along with the private key. Can be used to encrypt data that then can only be decrypted with the private key. Can be used to decrypt data that has been encrypted with the private key.

public key certificates A form of digital passport used to verify the identities of non-Windows computers, standalone computers, computers that do not belong to a trusted domain, and computers that do not support Kerberos v5.

public key cryptography A cryptographic system that employs a pair of keys: a public key, which is designed to be freely distributed, and a private key (also called a *secret key*).

Public Key Infrastructure (PKI) A system of cryptographic security services that enables users of a basically unsecure public network, such as the Internet, to securely and privately exchange data and even money through the use of a public and private cryptographic key pair that is obtained and shared through a trusted authority. The PKI uses digital certificates to identify an individual or organization and directory services to store, manage, and revoke the certificates. This approach resolves many security problems by presenting security credentials without compromising them in the process. PKI involves emerging standards and approaches. A PKI is used to provide several security benefits, including certificate-based authentication, data integrity, confidentiality, and nonrepudiation.

pull partners In WINS replication, a pull partner pulls, or fetches, the database entries from its replication partner. This is accomplished by sending a request for entries with a version number higher than that of the last entry it received during the last replication with that partner.

pull replication trigger In WINS replication, the message that is sent by a pull replication partner to request entries with a version number higher than that of the last entry it received during the last replication with that partner.

push partners In WINS replication, a push replication partner pushes, or sends, update notification messages to its partners when the database changes.

push replication trigger In WINS replication, the message that is sent by a push replication partner to announce changes to the WINS database and signal the receiving server to request the changed data.

push/pull partnerships In WINS replication, partnerships in which both servers are pull and push partners of each other.

Q

quorum resource A disk that maintains configuration data that would enable recovery of the cluster. This data includes all changes that have been applied to the cluster database. By default there is only one quorum resource per cluster, and each cluster node has access to it.

R

recovery agents Users who have recovery authority and can use special certificates and keys to enable recovery of lost keys. The Administrator account is automatically set up as the default recovery agent, and additional recovery agents can also be named through Microsoft Certificate Services.

recovery keys The idea behind recovery keys is that if the key used to encrypt a piece of data (on an EFS volume, e-mail message, or wherever else) is lost, the recovery key can be used to decrypt the data.

reliability Describes the time between failures. You can calculate the mean time between failures using this formula:

Mean time between failures = (total elapsed time – sum of downtime)/number of failures

remote access policy An ordered set of rules that defines how connections are either authorized or rejected.

Remote Assistance A tool that enables users to request assistance from a technical expert, referred to as the *Helper*.

Remote Authentication Dial-In User Service (RADIUS) Used in RADIUS Authentication to authenticate remote access requests. Used in networks with multiple RRAS servers. Stores a central authentication database and allows you to manage the RRAS servers from a single location. RADIUS offers a hybrid of hardware and software authentication. The Windows implementation of RADIUS is known as the Internet Authentication Service (IAS).

Remote Desktop for Administration A tool that allows you to remotely administer a Windows 2003 Server from virtually any computer in the organization.

renew interval In WINS, the amount of time that elapses between a client's initial registration and subsequent renewal of that registration.

replication partners In WINS, the configuration of two servers that replicate data with each other.

resolvers DNS clients, meaning any network node that issues queries to a DNS server to resolve a hostname to an IP address.

resource A physical or logical "entity" that is managed by a cluster. Resources can be brought online, taken offline, and moved between nodes. Only one node at a time can own a resource.

resource groups In server clusters, resources that are treated as a single, indivisible unit and hosted on one node at any point in time. Resource groups can be started and stopped as a unit.

resource records In DNS, each resource record, or RR, contains information about some resource on the network, such as the IP address of the resource. DNS zone files consist of resource records that function to provide information about resources within the zone.

reverse lookup file A type of DNS file that holds information on a single reverse lookup zone. These zones are usually named after the IP address range they cover. For example, 1.30.172.in-addr.arpa.

root certificate authority A top-level CA. Because there is no authority above the root CA in the hierarchy, there's no higher authority to vouch for its certificate. Instead, the root CA signs its own certificate, asserting that it is the root.

root server The server responsible for returning an authoritative answer for a particular domain or a referral to a server that can provide an authoritative answer. Because each DNS server is supposed to have a full set of root hints (which point to root servers for various top-level domains), your DNS server can refer queries recursively to other servers with the assistance of the root servers. You can also configure a DNS server to contain its own root zone; you might want to do so if you don't want your servers to be able to answer queries for names outside of your network.

route filters Filters that can be configured by routers to identify networks from which network traffic will be accepted.

route summarization In a hierarchical routing infrastructure, route summarization (also called *aggregation*) describes one route in a routing table that represents many routes. Therefore, a routing table entry for the highest level in the hierarchy, the entire network, is also the route used for subnets. This means that packets designated for a subnet of a network will be sent to the subnetwork by way of a router with the main network's address. For instance, packets intended for the `130.57.40` network, a subnet of the `130.57` network would be sent through a router in the `130.57` network.

router discovery messages Messages that allow clients to automatically locate neighboring routers.

routing The process of forwarding a packet from a source host to a destination host through an internetwork.

Routing and Remote Access Service (RRAS) The Windows service that provides routing and remote access functionality.

Routing Information Protocol (RIP) The most widely used of the distance vector protocols. RIP version 1 (RIP v1) was the first routing protocol used with TCP/IP. RIP version 2 (RIP v2) provides new features including authentication support, multicast announcing, and better support for classless networks. A RIP router sends updates to its immediate neighbors at regularly scheduled intervals, at which each neighbor then adds its own distance value to the table and forwards it on to its immediate neighbors. This eventually results in a cumulative table with the distances to each network destination.

routing table A local database that stores route information. Think of it as a road map for the internetwork—the routing table lists which routes exist between networks, so the router or host can look up the necessary information when it encounters a packet bound for a foreign network. Each entry in the routing table contains the following four pieces of information: the network address of the remote host or network, the forwarding address to which traffic for the remote network should be sent, the network interface that should be used to send to the forwarding address, and a cost, or metric, that indicates what relative priority should be assigned to this route. Routing tables typically contain network routes, host routes, and the default route.

S

scaling out Adding servers to meet demand. In a server cluster, this means adding nodes to the cluster. Scaling out also helps you to improve application and server response time.

scaling up Increasing system resources (such as processors, memory, disks, and network adapters) to your existing hardware or replacing existing hardware with greater system resources. Scaling up helps you to improve application and server response time, such as by adding RAM or CPUs.

secondary DNS server Server that pulls DNS information from the specified master server. Secondary DNS servers pull a read-only copy of zone files from one (or more) of the specified master servers. The secondary DNS server is authoritative and can resolve queries from this read-only copy but cannot make changes or updates.

secondary WINS server A server configured as the server a WINS client will attempt to reach to register, release, or resolve a NetBIOS name if the primary WINS server cannot be reached.

secondary zones Store a complete, local, read-only copy of the zone information. They are used to improve availability and performance at local and remote locations.

secret key cryptography A cryptography system in which two parties to a communication transaction use a single shared key that must be kept secret. This is the equivalent of a secret password on which both parties agree. The same key is used to encrypt and decrypt data, so if the secret key is compromised through loss or theft, then the data encrypted with that key becomes vulnerable. Secret key systems tend to be fast and flexible, but their dependence on a single key makes them better suited for applications like IPSec where you can change the key frequently. In addition, secret-key systems can only be used for encryption, not authentication.

secured dynamic updates A feature of Active Directory– Integrated zones, which can use the Active Directory security features to provide secured dynamic updates. Dynamic updates enable DNS records to be updated on the fly.

security association (SA) Used in IPSec to enable two computers to communicate securely. The SA contains a policy agreement that controls which algorithms and key lengths the two machines will use (for instance, it can use 128-bit RC5 and SHA-1), plus the actual security keys used to securely exchange information. Think of this agreement like a contract: It specifies what each party is and is not willing to do as part of the agreement.

Security Configuration and Analysis utility A utility used to analyze and configure a computer's security settings. This utility works by comparing the actual security configuration to a security template configured with the desired settings.

security database Used with the Security Configuration and Analysis utility to store the results of a security analysis.

security infrastructure The combination of services and tools that provide a framework for security in the network. In Windows Server 2003, this includes such things as certificate services, policy-based security, and security update tools such as MBSA and SUS.

Security log Log file that tracks auditing events. Viewed by using the Event Viewer.

security method A prespecified encryption algorithm with a negotiated key length and key lifetime that is used in IPSec communications.

Security options Options that configure security for the computer. Unlike User Rights policies, which are applied to a user or group, Security Option policies apply to the computer.

Security Policy A subset of Group Policy settings that define security configurations for computers.

security template A tool that works with the Security Configuration and Analysis utility and is where you organize all of your security attributes in a single location.

server cluster Two or more computers working together to provide higher availability, reliability, and scalability than can be obtained by using a single system.

server role Describes the functional purpose of a network server. There are roles for application servers, such as e-mail, Web, database, and media servers. There are roles for servers that host network resources, such as file and print servers. There are also roles for servers that provide network infrastructure services, such as name resolution and connectivity.

service (SRV) record SRV records tie together the location of a service (like a domain controller) with information about how to contact the service. They have the format:

```
ldap.tcp.chellis.net  SRV  10  100  389  hsv.chellis.net
```

Shiva Password Authentication Protocol (SPAP) A slightly more secure version of PAP that is intended for communication with remote-access hardware devices made by Shiva (which is now owned by Intel). It is included for backward-compatibility, though it is not in wide use.

signing Uses encryption to prove the origin and authenticity of a data transaction.

single host filtering NLB configuration that specifies that network traffic for the rule will be handled by a single cluster host according to the specified handling priority. This mode provides port-specific fault tolerance but not scalable performance.

single quorum device cluster The most widely used cluster model, also known as the standard quorum model, which uses a single cluster storage device connected to all nodes to store the cluster configuration data.

single-instance applications Method of clustered application deployment in which only one application instance is running on the cluster at any time, and the application typically has data sets that cannot be partitioned across multiple nodes. The Dynamic Host Configuration Protocol (DHCP) service is an example of a single-instance application. The set of leased IP addresses that the application provides is small, but would be complicated to replicate across a cluster. Therefore, the DHCP instance exists as a single instance, and high availability is provided by failing over the instance to another node in the cluster.

site-local address In IPv6, represents the local site and uses FEC0: as the leading block. This is similar to the leading bits used to represent address classes in IPv4.

sniffing The process of capturing network traffic using a device or application that monitors and analyzes network traffic. Sniffers are not intended to be used maliciously. They are intended to optimize network throughput, but they can be used maliciously to intercept and read data packets on a network.

Software Update Services (SUS) A simplified solution targeted for medium-sized enterprises as a means to manage and distribute critical Windows patches. You can think of SUS as an intranet-hosted version of the Windows Update service.

split-brain A failure scenario that happens when some of the nodes fail and the cluster loses quorum. In this instance, you can force the remaining nodes to form a quorum and restart the cluster.

spoofing A form of attack in which an attacker assumes the identity of another computer.

standard zone files Also called *traditional DNS zone files*. Stored as text files on the server's hard drive. To use standard zone files, you create a zone on a DNS server which then becomes the primary zone server where all updates occur. These updates may include things like resource record additions or deletions. You can use secondary zone servers to provide load balancing and a certain degree of fault tolerance by pointing them to the primary zone server to get a copy of the zone file.

standby server configuration A variation of N+I, which uses idle nodes as standbys that are capable of taking on the workload of one or more of the currently active nodes. Standby servers are used to maintain a performance level after failover that is the same as performance before the failover.

start of authority (SOA) record The first record in any database file is the start of authority (SOA) record, which follows this format:

```
@ IN SOA <source host> <contact e-mail> <ser. no.> <refresh time> <retry time>
   <expiration time> <TTL>
```

stateful applications Applications and services such as SQL Server or Exchange Server, which have a long-running in-memory state, or large frequently updated datasets. These types of applications and services should be hosted on a server cluster.

stateful configuration In IPv6, stateful configuration uses a DHCPv6 server to handle IP address allocation and configuration.

stateless applications Applications and services applications, such as front-end Web servers, FTP servers, and VPNs, that treat each client request as an independent operation and, therefore, do not have a long-running in-memory state and that have either read-only data or data that changes infrequently. This type of application can independently load-balance each client request. These types of applications and services should be hosted on an NLB cluster.

stateless configuration In IPv6, stateless configuration is used in the absence of a DHCP server. The computer builds its own address starting with the on-link prefix (the network part of the address) and appending its own MAC address. This process uses Duplicate Address Detection (DAD) to check for duplicate addresses on the network.

static mapping In WINS, static mapping enables you to manually enter IP addresses and NetBIOS names, just as you would manually create host records in DNS.

static routing Uses the `route add` command to manually enter route information on a given computer. Unlike dynamic routing, static routing doesn't scale well. As a manual process, it is prone to simple human errors that can lead to huge problems on the network. It cannot adapt to topology changes. Therefore, when you add or remove routers, you must visit every routing device to make changes to the local routing table.

Storage Area Network (SAN) A set of interconnected servers and storage devices such as disks and tape drives that are connected to a common data transfer infrastructure to provide a pool of storage with multiple server access.

stub zone Functions like dynamic delegation. The stub zone server will periodically query the target name servers for updates. This is used to keep the DNS server that hosts the parent zone aware of its child zone for more efficient name resolution. The DNS server that hosts both the parent zone and the stub zone maintains a current list of authoritative DNS servers for the child zone by regularly updating the stub zone. Stub zones keep delegated zone information current, as well as simplify DNS administration.

subnet address Describes a logical IP subnetwork created by subdividing the host portion of a classful IP address.

subnet mask A screen of numbers used as a "lens" that tells a router which numbers in an IP address represent the network portion of the address. In a subnet mask, the network portion of the address is represented by binary "1"s and the host portion is represented by binary "0"s. An example of a decimal equivalent of a subnet mask is `255.255.255.0`, the default subnet mask for Class C addresses.

subnets A subnetwork that exists as an identifiably separate part of an organization's network.

subnetting The process of subdividing a single IP network into smaller logical subnetworks, called *subnets*, each with its own unique network ID.

Success Audit event Type of logged event that indicates the occurrence of an event that has been audited for success. For example, a Success Audit event is a successful logon when system logons are being audited.

supernetting Supernetting works in the opposite direction from subnetting in that it allows you to fuse contiguous subnets into larger supernets by "borrowing" bits from the network part of the address. See also *Classless Inter-Domain Routing (CIDR)*.

symmetric encryption Uses the same key to encrypt and decrypt data. Symmetric encryption is used in preshared secret key systems. The main problem with symmetric encryption is key distribution.

Synchronous replication A method of replication used in multisite clusters in which a write operation is performed at Site 1 and is not considered to be complete until the change is also written to the disk at Site 2. Application performance can be much slower for synchronous replication than for asynchronous replication because of the latency between the time an operation is executed and the time when the I/O operation is completed.

System log Log file that tracks operating system events, including hardware and service activity, as well as rejected connections due to insufficient licensing. Viewed by using the Event Viewer.

System Monitor A component of the Performance utility used for performance monitoring of system services and hardware resources.

system policy Under NT, system configuration management was accomplished by creating System Policy files. System Policy was limited in the scope of settings that could be controlled. In addition, settings could not be easily backed out because they were written to various locations in the local Registry.

T

tampering A form of attack in which an attacker intercepts and alters data in transit, often by assuming the identity of another computer.

Task Manager Utility that can be used not only to manage applications, processes, and general system performance, but also to view networking and user statistics. Launched by accessing the security menu with the Ctrl+Alt+Del keystroke combination.

TCP/IP An industry standard suite of networking protocols that enables communications across heterogeneous, interconnected networks. The TCP/IP protocol suite defines standards for communication, connectivity, and routing.

ticket-granting service (TGS) The Kerberos service that allows the user to authenticate to services within the domain.

ticket-granting ticket (TGT) In Kerberos v5 authentication, issued by the KDC to an authenticated client. The client uses the TGT to access the ticket-granting service (TGS).

tombstone In WINS, a tombstone flags a record as deleted so that replication partners will flag the record as deleted and the record will be permanently deleted from the WINS database after the appropriate time interval has expired.

top-level domains Internet DNS depends on a set of top-level domains that serve as the level below the root of the DNS hierarchy. These domains include `.com`, `.net`, `.org`, and `.uk`, among many others.

tracert A utility used to isolate problems related to an improper router configuration or link failure. Traces the route to a destination network and tells you exactly where a packet stopped on the journey.

traditional DNS zone files See *standard zone files*.

traditional DNS zones Store the zone information in a file, use a single master model, replicate through full and incremental zone transfers, and are used for compatibility with NT 4 DNS infrastructures and BIND-based DNS infrastructures hosted on Unix servers.

transport mode The default mode for IPSec communications, which uses IPSec for end-to-end communications to encrypt or authenticate a direct connection between two computers.

tunnel A secure connection between two nodes over an inherently unsecure network. This technology is associated with VPNs and is most commonly used to establish a secure channel for communications over the Internet.

tunnel endpoint The systems at the end of a two-way IPSec tunnel. Indicated by the IP address of one of the destination nodes in an IPSec communication taking place through tunnel mode.

tunnel mode Encrypts traffic that passes through a tunnel established by L2TP and secured by IPSec. Tunnel mode encrypts the entire IP packet (both the header and the payload). IPSec communications can take place through either transport mode (the default) or tunnel mode.

U

unauthorized addresses Public addresses that have not been assigned to an organization and cannot be used to connect to the Internet. Also known as *illegal addresses*. They are sometimes used by organizations when there is no current or future intent to connect directly to the Internet, which would require a complete change of the current addressing scheme.

unicast routing Routing in which one machine sends data directly to one destination address.

unmasked bits In a subnet mask, refers to the bit positions of 0, which identify the node or host portion of the IP address.

unspecified address An IPv6 address that consists of all zeros and is used to send a broadcast or DHCP client request from a computer that does not yet have a configured address.

User Profile policies Control the behavior of network connections and roaming profiles.

User Rights Assignment Determine what rights a user or group has on the computer. User rights apply to the system. They are not the same as permissions, which apply to a specific object. An example of a user right is the Back Up Files And Directories right.

V

Variable Length Subnet Masks (VLSMs) Enables the use of different-sized subnets in the same network. You can create subnets of different sizes by applying different masks to the address space. Requires a dynamic routing protocol.

version ID In WINS, an internal record that is incremented with each change to a record held by a server.

virtual link A logical point-to-point connection between a backbone area border router (ABR) and a non-backbone area border router. The first area is known as the transit area, the area across which the virtual link is created in order to logically connect the second area to the backbone. Once the link is created, the two routers can share routing information just as though they were connected to the same physical network. To create a virtual link, both routers, called *virtual link neighbors*, are configured with the transit area, the router ID of the virtual link neighbor, matching hello and dead intervals, and a matching password.

virtual link neighbors The routers in a virtual link.

Virtual Private Network (VPN) A secure, point-to-point connection across either a private network or a public network such as the Internet.

virtual server A collection of services (usually a resource group) that may be hosted on multiple servers in a server cluster. Clients can access the virtual server as though it were a single physical server.

volume shadow copy A point-in-time copy (snapshot) of an entire volume on a Windows Server 2003 server. Volume shadow copies are created through the advanced options of Windows Backup. This new functionality enables you to copy open files.

W

Warning events Type of logged event that indicates that you should be concerned with the event. Warning events may not be critical in nature, but they may be indicative of downward trends or problems that could result in future errors.

Windows Backup Utility that enables you to create and restore backups.

Windows File Protection policies Specify how Windows file protection will be configured.

Windows Internet Name Service (WINS) A name resolution service that resolves Network Basic Input Output System (NetBIOS) computer names to IP addresses in Windows networks. WINS is an advanced method of NetBIOS name resolution using specialized NBNS servers.

WINS database The database that holds the WINS records.

WINS forward lookup resource record Lists WINS servers to which a name query can be sent in the event that the query cannot be resolved in DNS. The WINS record only applies to the topmost level of a zone, and does not apply to subdomains within the zone. The WINS resource record follows a specific syntax as follows:

```
owner class WINS [LOCAL] [Lookup_timeout] [Cache_timeout] wins_server_ip
```

WINS proxy agent A WINS client computer can be configured to run the WINS proxy agent, which listens for NetBIOS broadcast queries and attempts to register and resolve names on behalf of b-node (broadcast) network clients.

WINS-R resource record Used in a reverse lookup zone for reverse queries that were not found in the DNS zone. Performs the opposite task of the WINS resource record in the same way that the PTR record performs the opposite task of the A record in DNS.

Z

zone delegation Involves assigning authority over portions of a DNS namespace to other zones. The NS record is used to specify a delegated zone and the DNS name of the server that is authoritative for that zone. Used to assign responsibility for a part of a DNS namespace to another organization, workgroup or department.

zone transfers Action in which information is copied from a master DNS server to a secondary DNS server.

Index

Note to the Reader: Throughout this index **boldfaced** page numbers indicate primary discussions of a topic. *Italicized* page numbers indicate illustrations.

A

A (Address) records, **183**
ABRs (area border routers)
  defined, 660
  in OSPF, 98, *98*, 127
Accept All Routes setting, 113
Accept Routes From All Route Sources Except Those Selected option, 128
Accept Unsecured action, 333
Accept Unsecured Communication, But Always Respond Using IPSec option, 338, 360
access
  network. *See* network access
  to RRAS servers, **311–312**, *312*
access control lists (ACLs), 199
Access Method page, 321, *322*
Access This Computer From The Network right, 423
Account Lockout policies
  defined, 660
  for server-level security, **417–419**, *419*
Account Lockout Duration policy, 418–419
Account Lockout Threshold policy, 418–419, *419*
account logon events, auditing, 421
account management, auditing, 421
Account policies
  defined, 660
  for security templates, 436
  for server-level security, **414–415**
    Account Lockout, **417–419**, *419*
    Kerberos, **419–420**
    Password, **415–417**, *416–417*
Account Provider setting, 308
accounting providers, **308**, 660
Accounts security category, 427
ACLs (access control lists), 199
Act As Part Of The Operating System right, 423
Action list in RIP, 113
actions
  for certificate requests, 496–497
  defined, 669
  for IP filters, **332–333**
  for IPSec rules
    adding, **358–361**, *359–360*
    managing, 356
    settings for, 354, *354*
Activate Authentication option, 113
Active Directory
  defined, 660
  with DNS, **180**
  and Group Policy, **402–414**, *403*, *405*, *407–414*
  for IPSec deployment policies, **340**
  for PKI deployment, **498**
  replication, **206**, 660
  secured dynamic updates in, 199
Active Directory-Integrated (ADI) zones
  defined, 660
  with DNS, 180, **198**
Active Directory Users, 622
Add Counters dialog box, 592, *592*
Add/Edit Port Rule dialog box, 558–559, *559*
Add IP Filter dialog box, 134, *134*
Add/Remove Snap-In dialog box, 342, *342*
Add Reservations dialog box, 155, *155*
Add Standalone Snap-In dialog box, 343, *343*
Add Workstations To Domain right, 424
Added Cost For Routes setting, 113
Adding a New Filter Action, 358
Address Assignment settings, **158**, *159*
Address Pool settings, **153–154**, *154*
Address (A) records, **183**
address space, IPv6, **65–67**
addresses
  IP. *See* IP addresses
  for IPSec filters, **357–358**, *358*
  in NAT. *See* NAT (Network Address Translation)
Addresses settings, **357–358**, *358*
ADI (Active Directory-Integrated) zones
  defined, 660
  with DNS, 180, **198**
adjacency
  defined, 660
  in OSPF, 98
Adjust Memory Quotas For A Process right, 424
administration, remote, **16–17**
  enabling, **623–624**, *623–624*
  Remote Assistance, **628–633**, *629–630*, *632–633*
  Remote Desktop Connection, **624–628**, *624–628*
  Remote Desktop for Administration, **620–623**
Administrative templates, **405–406**
Administrator template, 475
administrators, zone permissions for, 201
Advanced Backup Options dialog box, 645, *646*
Advanced settings
  for ICS, 147, *147*
  for OSPF, **119–120**, *120*
  for performance, 612–613, *613*
  for remote access policies, 315, 320, *320*
  for RIP, **115–117**, *116*
  for WINS, **269–270**, *270*
  for WINS replication partners, **273–274**, *274*, **276**, *276*
Advanced TCP/IP Settings dialog box, 246–247, *247*

Advertisement Lifetime (Minutes) setting, 106
Affinity options for NLB, **559–560**
AHs (Authentication Headers)
  defined, 661
  in IPSec, 326, **330**, *589*
algorithms
  defined, 660
  encryption, 464
  hashing, 465, 481, 669
alias records, **184**
All Information On This Computer option, 635
Allow Certificates To Be Published To The File System option, 490
Allow Log On Locally right, 424
Allow Log On Through Terminal Services right, 424
Allow Other Network Users to Connect Through This Computer's Internet Connection option, 147
Allow Unsecured action, 333
Allow Unsecured Communication With Non IPSec-Aware Computer option, 360
Allow Users To Connect Remotely To This Computer option, 623
Always Start In Wizard Mode option, 635
Always use classic logon policy, 430
Always wait for the network at computer startup and logon policy, 431
ANDing operations, **44–45**
Announce All Routes setting, 113
Announce All Routes In The Ranges Listed setting, 113
anycast addresses
  defined, 660
  purpose of, 67
AppleTalk protocol
  defined, 660
  installing, 31
application deployment for server clusters, **539–547**, *539–541*
Application log
  defined, 660
  purpose of, 615
application protocols, 27, *27*
applications
  failures in, 534
  multiple-instance, 539
  PKI-aware, **467–468**
  stateful and stateless, 532–533
Apply policy to removable media policy, 431
area border routers (ABRs)
  defined, 660
  in OSPF, 98, *98*, 127
Area ID list, 118
Areas settings
  for OSPF, 127, *127*
  for RIP, 127
ASR (Automated System Recovery), 7
  defined, 661
  working with, **647–649**, *648*
asymmetric encryption
  defined, 660
  in PKI, 464
asynchronous replication
  defined, 661
  vs. synchronous, **551–552**
At Logon backup option, 641
At System Startup backup option, 641
attributes for certificates, **474–475**
au domain, 179
Audit policies
  defined, 661
  options for, **421**
  setting, **422–423**, *422–423*
Audit security category, 427
Authenticated Session template, 475
Authenticated Users, permissions for, 201
authentication, **11–12**
  certificate services for, **15**
  defined, 661
  in IPSec, **325–327**, *367*, 376
    for default response rule, 346, *346*
    methods for, **333–335**
    settings for, 354, *355*
  in IPv6, 64
  Kerberos
    defined, 672
    process, **333–334**
    for server-level security, **419–420**
  in PKI, 463
  in remote access security, **305–309**, *306–307*, *309*, 319–320, *319*
Authentication Headers (AHs)
  defined, 661
  in IPSec, 326, **330**, *589*
Authentication Method page, 367, *367*
Authentication Methods dialog box, **306–309**, *307*
Authentication Methods page, 323, *323*
Authentication Methods settings, 354, *355*
Authentication settings, 315, 319, *319*
Authentication-Type option, 320
auto-static update mode
  defined, 661
  in RIP, 97
Autoconfiguration
  defined, 661
  in IPv6, 67–68
autodiscovery
  defined, 661
  in IPv6, 67
Automated System Recovery (ASR), 7
  defined, 661
  working with, **647–649**, *648*
Automated System Recovery Preparation Wizard, 647–649, *648*
automatic certificate enrollment, 6, **494–496**, *495–496*
Automatic Certificate Request Setup Wizard, 495–496, *496*
automatic IP configuration, **62–63**, **67–68**

automatic partner configuration, **256**, 274–275
Automatic Updates, 14
Automatically Assign IP Addresses By Using The DHCP Allocator option, 158
Automatically Select The Certificate Store Based On The Type Of Certificate option, 518
Automatically Update Statistics Every setting, 265–266
autoregistration, 64, 68, 661
availability
  defined, 534, 661
  high availability services. *See* high availability services
  in WINS, **253**
Available Bytes counter, 599
Available Mbytes counter, 598
Average field for counters, 593
Avg. Disk Queue Length counter, 591
AXFRs (full zone transfers)
  contents of, 191
  defined, 669

B

b-node
  defined, 662
  in WINS, 240
Back Up Database During Server Shutdown option, 266
Back Up Files And Directories right, 424
Back Up To This Location setting, 486
backbone links
  in border routing, 100, *100*
  defined, 662
Backup Destination dialog box, 648, *648*
Backup Job Information dialog box, 645, *645*
Backup Or Restore page, 635, *635*
Backup or Restore Wizard, **634–640**, *635–638*, *640*
Backup Progress dialog box, 637, *638*
Backup Type, Destination, And Name page, 636, *637*
Backup Type settings, 643–644, *644*
backups and recovery, **634**
  automated system recovery, **647–649**, *648*
  CA data, **485–486**, *485*
  domain controller recovery, **649**
  server clusters, **560–561**
  volume shadow copy, **645–646**, *645–646*
  with Windows Backup. *See* Windows Backup
baselines
  defined, 662
  for performance, 589
  System Monitor reports for, **595–598**, *597*
Basic constraints attribute, 474
Basic EFS template, 475
Basic Firewall Only option, 152
BCPs (business continuity plans), 17
#BEGIN_ ALTERNATE statement, 247–248
Begin verifying At setting, 268
BIND (Berkeley Internet Name Daemon), 187
  defined, 662
  in DNS, **190**
  in upgrades, 192
binding, **29**
Block action, 333
Block Inheritance option, 404–405
boolean calculations, 44
boot files, **187**
border routing
  defined, 662
  operation of, **99–100**, *100*
bottlenecks
  defined, 662
  in performance, 590
  server cluster, 543
  System Monitor for, **601**
BPCPs (business process contingency plans), 17
branch offices, WINS deployment for, **262–263**, *262*
bridging, 4
broadcast routers
  defined, 662
  in OSPF, 118
Browse For A Group Policy Object dialog box, 347, *347*, 412, *412*
browser services, performance objects for, 607
burst mode in WINS, 270
business continuity plans (BCPs), 17
business process contingency plans (BPCPs), 17
Bypass Traverse Checking right, 424
Bytes Total/Sec counter, 606, 608

C

ca domain, 179
CA Identifying Information page, 481, *481*
CA Properties dialog box, 488–493, *489–492*
CA Type page, 479, *480*
cache command, 187
caching in DNS, **186–187**, **189**
  caching-only servers, **209–210**, 662
  and forwarding, **209**
  stub zones, **210–212**
caching-only servers, **209–210**, 662
Callback Control Protocol (CBCP), 302
Called-Station-ID option, 320
Calling-Station-ID option, 320
canonical name (CNAME) records
  defined, 664
  purpose of, **184**
capacity
  DNS servers, **213–214**
  server clusters, **542–544**, *543–544*
capture buffers, 577, 582–588, 662
capture filters
  defined, 662
  in Network Monitor, **584–587**, *585–586*
Capture Filters dialog box, 584–585, *585*

capturing Network Monitor data, **582–589**, *583*, *585–586*
CAs (certificate authorities), 467
  controlling, **484–487**, *485*, *487–488*
  data flow with, **472**, *472*
  installing, **479–483**, *480–482*
  in PKI, **468–471**
  planning, **504–505**
  for renewing certificates, **487**, *488*
  roles of, **471**
  trusts for, **497–501**, *499–500*
  types of, **470–471**
categories
  Event Viewer, 618
  security, 427
CBCP (Callback Control Protocol), 302
CCP (Compression Control Protocol), 302
certificate authorities (CAs). *See* CAs (certificate authorities)
Certificate Database Settings page, 482, *482*
Certificate Export Wizard, 515–517, *516*
Certificate Friendly Name And Description page, 512, *512*
Certificate Import Wizard, 517–519, *518–519*
Certificate Information page, 507, *507*
certificate publishers, 467
Certificate Renewal Wizard, 514–515
Certificate Request Wizard, 510–513, *511–512*
certificate revocation lists (CRLs), 467, 497, **501–502**
  defined, 663
  distribution points for, 504
  publishing, **502–504**, *502–503*
Certificate Server, **478**
  for CA configuration, **488–492**, *489–492*, **496–497**
  for certificate templates, **492–496**, *493–496*
  for controlling CA services, **484–487**, *485*, *487–488*
  installing, **478–484**, *480–482*
  for revocation, *502–503*
  for revoking certificates, **501–504**
  for trusts, **497–501**, *499–500*
Certificate Services
  authentication through, **15**
  defined, 663
Certificate Store page, 518, *519*
certificate stores, 498
  contents of, 505–506
  defined, 663
  selecting, 518, *519*
certificate templates
  configuring, **492–496**, *493–496*
  in PKI, **475–476**
Certificate Templates folder, 484
certificate-to-account mapping in IPSec, **328–329**
Certificate Trust List Purpose page, 499, *499*
Certificate Trust List Wizard, 499–501, *499–500*
Certificate Trust Lists (CTLs)
  defined, 663
  designating, 497
  managing, **499–501**, *499–500*
  purpose of, 474
Certificate Types page, 510–511, *511*
certificates, **462–463**
  attributes for, **474–475**
  certificate authorities for. *See* CAs (certificate authorities)
  Certificate Server for. *See* Certificate Server
  Certificates snap-in for, **505–506**, *506*
    for certificate properties, **506–510**, *507–509*
    installing, **483–484**, *483*
  defined, 666
  exam essentials, **520–521**
  exporting, **515–517**, *516*
  hierarchies in, 468–469, *469*, 662
  importing, 498, **517–519**, *518–519*
  improvements in, 6
  issuing, **513–514**, *513–514*
  key terms, **522**
  PKI, **466–467**
    attributes for, **474–475**
    CAs, **468–471**, *469*
    services, **472**, *472*
    templates, **475–476**
  policy and practice statements for, 468, 663
  purposes for, **509**, *510*
  rekeying, **514**
  renewing, **487**, *488*, **514–515**
  requesting, **510–514**, *511–514*
  review questions, **523–527**
  review questions, answers to, **528–529**
  revoking, 467, **501–504**, *502–503*
  summary, **519**
Certificates In The CTL page, 500, *500*
Certificates snap-in, **505–506**, *506*
  for certificate properties, **506–510**, *507–509*
  installing, **483–484**, *483*
Certification Authority Backup Wizard, 485–486, *485*
Certification Authority Restore Wizard, 486–487, *487*
Certification Authority snap-in, **483–484**, *483*
Certification Path settings, 508–509, *509*
certification practices statements (CPSs)
  defined, 663
  purpose of, 507–508
Change The System Time right, 424
CHAP (Challenge Handshake Authentication Protocol), **308**
  defined, 663
  for dial-up services, 302
Check For Policy Changes Every: X Minutes setting, 351
CIDR (Classless Inter-Domain Routing)
  defined, 664
  and supernetting, 58–59
CIDR (Classless Inter-Domain Routing) notation
  defined, 663
  for subnets, 55–56

ciphers
  defined, 663
  purpose of, 462
ciphertext
  defined, 663
  in PKI, 464
Class-C affinity option, 560
classes, network address, **37–38**
  Class A networks, subnetting, **55**
  Class B networks, subnetting, **52–54**
  Class C networks, subnetting, **49–52**
  Class D address space, 100
classful IP addressing
  vs. classless, **56**
  defined, 663
classful routing protocols
  vs. classless, **57**
  defined, 663
Classless Inter-Domain Routing (CIDR)
  defined, 664
  and supernetting, 58–59
Classless Inter-Domain Routing (CIDR) notation
  defined, 663
  for subnets, 55–56
classless IP addressing
  vs. classful, **56**
  defined, 664
classless routing protocols
  vs. classful, **57**
  defined, 664
CLB (Component Load Balancing), 534
Client-Friendly-Name option, 320
Client-IP-Address option, 321
Client (Respond Only) policy, **336–337**
client traffic in WINS, **254–255**
Client-Vendor option, 321
clients
  DHCP, **76–77**
  DNS, 180–181, 200, 667
  IPSec, 325
  SUS, **445**
Clients Using Domain Name System (DNS) option, 160
cloned applications
  defined, 664
  in multiple-instance applications, 539, *539*
cluster-aware applications, 538, 664
Cluster Disk Signatures and Partitions data, 560
cluster hosts
  defined, 664
  in server clusters, 537
Cluster IP Addresses settings, 558, *558*
cluster node failures, **560**
Cluster Parameters settings, 557, *557*
Cluster Quorum Data, 561
Cluster Service, 535
  defined, 664
  for failures, 547, 551, 561–563
  for networks, 552–554
  support for, 537
clustering. *See also* server clusters
  defined, 664
  for high server availability, **16**
  in Windows Server 2003, 398
CNAME (canonical name) records
  defined, 664
  purpose of, **184**
Code Signing template, 475
colon-hexadecimal format, 65–66
com domain, 178
comments in LMHOSTS, 248–249
Committed Bytes counter, 599
Common.adm template, 406
compacting WINS database, **281**
compatibility for Group Policy, **405–406**
Compatible (Compatws.inf) template, 435
Completing The Automated System Recovery Preparation Wizard page, 648, *648*
Completing The Backup Or Restore Wizard page, 637, *637*
Completing the New Remote Access Policy Wizard page, 323
Completing the Security Rule Wizard page, 368, *368*
Component Load Balancing (CLB), 534
Compression Control Protocol (CCP), 302
Computer template, 475
computers
  counters for, 592
  in Event Viewer, 618
conditional forwarders
  defined, 664
  operation of, **211–212**
confdisk utility, 562
confidentiality
  defined, 664
  in IPv6, 64
  in PKI, 463
configuration improvements, **4**
Configure Your Server Wizard, **391–393**, *392–393*
Connect To The Public Network When A Name Needs To Be Resolved option, 160
connection-oriented protocols
  vs. connectionless, **29–30**
  defined, 665
connection point services, performance objects for, 608
Connection Type page, 109, *109*
Connection Type settings, 355–356, *355*
connection types
  defined, 665
  in IP routing, 109, *109*
  in IPSec, 335, 355–356, *355*
connectionless protocols
  vs. connection-oriented protocols, **29–30**
  defined, 665
connectivity. *See* network connectivity

convergence time
  defined, *665*
  in WINS replication, 249
Copy backup type, 644
Cost setting, 118
costs
  in IP routing, 91
  in OSPF, 118
counters, performance, **591–593**
  defined, 679
  for disk objects, **604–605**
  for memory objects, **598–599**
  for network services, **607–608**
  for network subsystem, **606–607**
  for processor objects, **601–602**
CPSs (certification practices statements)
  defined, 663
  purpose of, 507–508
CPU speed requirements, 396
Create A Pagefile right, 424
Create A Token Object right, 424
Create Permanent Shared Objects right, 424
Creator Owners, permissions for, 201
credentials for demand-dial connections, **108**
CRL Publishing Parameters settings, 502, *503*
CRLs (certificate revocation lists), 467, 497, **501–502**
  defined, 663
  distribution points for, 504
  publishing, **502–504**, *502–503*
Cryptographic Service Provider page, 511, *511*
cryptography. *See also* encryption
  defined, 665
  history of, 462
CSPs (cryptographic service providers), **473**
CTLs (Certificate Trust Lists)
  defined, 663
  designating, 497
  managing, **499–501**, *499–500*
  purpose of, 474
Current Disk Queue Length counter, 604
custom MMC consoles, **411–414**, *411–414*
Custom Security Method Settings dialog box, 361, *362*
customized failover policies, 547

D

DACLs (discretionary access control lists)
  defined, 666
  purpose of, 200
Daily backup type, 641, 644
data
  encrypting. *See* encryption
  in Event Viewer, 618
  in network packets, 28, *29*
Database Backup group, 266
Database Path setting, 270
Database Verification settings for WINS, **268–269**, *268*
databases
  DNS
    contents of, **181–186**
    location of, **186–187**
    migrating, **192**
  Security Configuration and Analysis tool, **434**, *434*, 439
  WINS
    compacting, **281**
    defined, 690
    in NetBIOS name resolution, **243**
Datacenter Edition, 396–399
dates in Event Viewer, 618
Day-and-Time-Restrictions option, 321
DC Security.inf (Dedicated domain controller) template, 436
DDNS (Dynamic DNS) standard
  defined, 667
  purpose of, **180**
  updates, **199–200**
Dead Interval (Seconds) setting, 119
Debug Programs right, 424
decryption
  defined, 665
  in PKI, 464
Dedicated domain controller (DC Security.inf) template, 436
Default CSP list attribute, 474
Default Domain Controller Policy, 406–408, *407–408*
Default Domain Policy console window, 408
Default quota limit and warning level policy, 431
Default Response Rule Authentication Method page, 346, *346*
Default security (Setup security.inf) template, 435
defaults
  certificate request actions, 496–497
  IPSec policies, **336–338**
  IPSec response rules, **345–346**, *345–346*
  remote access policies, **313–320**, *314–320*
  routes, 94, 665
  zone permissions, **200–201**
delegated namespaces, 194
  characteristics of, 195
  defined, 665
delegating zones, **208–209**, 691
delegation resource records
  defined, 665
  purpose of, 210
Delete cached copies of roaming profiles policy, 429
Delete The Private Key If The Export Is Successful option, 516
deleting WINS records, **281–282**
delta CRLs, 502, 504
Demand-Dial Interface Wizard, 108–111, *109–111*
demand-dial routing
  defined, 666
  interfaces for, **106–111**, *107–111*
  in RRAS, 102
Denial of Service (DoS) attacks, 65

defined, 666
IPSec for, 338
Deny Access To This Computer From The Network right, 424
Deny Log On Through Terminal Services right, 425
Deny Logon As A Batch Job right, 424
Deny Logon As A Service right, 424
Deny Logon Locally right, 424
deploying
IPSec, **339–341**
IPSec policies, **346–350**, *347–348*
server-level security policies, **441–443**
WINS, **261–263**, *261–262*, *264*
Description Of Service setting, 156
Description settings, 357
descriptions
in Event Viewer, 618
for IPSec filters, 357
destination addresses for IPSec filters, 357
Destination Network option, 134
details
for certificates, 508
in Event Viewer, **617–618**, *617*
Details settings, 508
Devices security category, 427
DHCP
dynamic DNS updates from, **200**
for IP configuration, **62–63**
troubleshooting, **76–77**
DHCP allocators
defined, 666
in ICS, 146
in NAT, 148
DHCP relay agents
defined, 666
for subnets, 63
DHCP servers, **77**
performance objects for, 608
working with, **389**
Dial-In Constraints settings, 315, 317
dial-in credentials, **108**
Dial-In settings, 312, *312*
dial-out credentials, **108**
Dial Out Credentials page, 111, *111*
dial-up networking
defined, 666
operation of, **301–303**, *303*
Differential backup type, 644
digests
defined, 666
in PKI, 465
digital certificates. *See* certificates
digital signatures
defined, 666
in PKI, **465–466**
directory command in DNS, 187
directory services
auditing access to, 421
performance objects for, 608
in Windows Server 2003, 398
Disable All Purposes For This Certificate option, 509
Disable Event Logging option, 121
Disable Subnet Summarization option, 117
Disabled option for GPOs, 404
disaster recovery
ASR for, **647–649**, *648*
defined, 666
domain controller, **649**
high server availability, **17–18**
server cluster failures, **561–563**
disaster recovery plans (DRPs), 17
discretionary access control lists (DACLs)
defined, 666
purpose of, 200
disk corruption and failure in server clusters, **561–562**
Disk Quota policies
defined, 666
list of, **431**
Disk Quota policy processing policy, 432
Disk Reads/sec counter, 604
disk subsystem, monitoring, **604–605**
% Disk Time counter, 604
display
Network Monitor filters for, **584–587**, *586*
Remote Desktop Connection, *625*, *625*
System Monitor, **593–595**, *594*
Display Filter dialog box, *585–587*, *586*
Display name attribute, 474
Display Records dialog box, **279–280**, *279–280*
Display settings, *625*, *625*
distance vector routing protocols
defined, 666–667
working with, **34**
distribution points for CRLs, 504
DNS (Domain Name System), **9–10**, **176–177**
caching and forwarding in, **209**
caching-only servers, **209–210**, 662
conditional forwarders, **211–212**
forward-only servers, **212**
stub zones, **210–212**
clients for, 180–181, 200, 667
databases for
contents of, **181–186**
location of, **186–187**
migrating, **192**
defined, 667
domain naming in, **177–178**, *178*
exam essentials, **224–225**
and Internet, **178–179**
key terms, **225–226**
name resolution in, **187–191**, *188*
namespaces for, **192–193**
defined, 667
domain names in, **193–194**
options for, **194–195**
for Windows NT Server migration, **195–196**
review questions, **227–233**
review questions, answers to, **234–236**
secure dynamic updates for, **199–200**
servers for, **180–181**, **212–213**, **388**

    caching-only, **209–210**
    capacity of, **213–214**
    defined, 667
    forward-only, **212**
    performance objects for, 608
    requirements, **213**
    securing, **214–216**
  summary, **224**
  terminology, **180–181**
  troubleshooting, **216–219**
    DNS monitoring, **217–218**, *217–218*
    ipconfig for, **222–223**
    log files for, **223–224**
    nslookup for, **219–222**
  in Windows Server 2003, **179–180**
  WINS integration with, **202–204**
  zones in. *See* zones
DnsAdmins, permissions for, 201
Do Not Announce All Routes In The Ranges Listed setting, 114
Do not detect slow network connections policy, 429
Do not process the Legacy Run list policy, 431
Do not process the Run Once list policy, 430
#DOM statement, 248
Domain Admins, permissions for, 201
Domain Controller security category, 427
Domain Controller template, 476
domain controllers, **387–388**
  recovery strategy for, **649**
  server clusters for access to, **553–554**
Domain Member security category, 427
domain name files, **186**
domain name records, 180
Domain Name System. *See* DNS (Domain Name System)
Domain Security policies, 401
Domain Security Policy, 401
  console window, 408, *408*
  defined, 667
domains, 177
  IPSec policies for, **347–349**, *347–348*
  names and namespace for, **177–178**, *178*, **193–194**
  top-level, **178–179**, 688
  untrusted, in WINS replication, 260
  Windows NT vs. Windows 2003, **402**
Domains/OU settings, 412
Don't display the Getting Started welcome screen at logon policy, 430
DoS (Denial of Service) attacks, 65
  defined, 666
  IPSec for, 338
Download A CA Certificate, Certificate Chain, Or CRL task, 513
Drop All Packets Except Those That Meet The Criteria Below option, 133, 135
DRPs (disaster recovery plans), 17
dual verification in Kerberos, 419
Duration field for counters, 593
Dynamic DNS (DDNS) standard
  defined, 667
  purpose of, **180**
  updates, **199–200**
dynamic routing, **33–35**, **95–96**, *96*
  defined, 667
  OSPF, **98–99**, *98*
  RIP, **96–97**

E

E-mail name attribute, 475
EAP (Extensible Authentication Protocol)
  characteristics of, **307**
  defined, 668
  purpose of, **304**
EAP types
  defined, 667
  purpose of, 307
Edit Dial-In Profile dialog box, 314–315, *315*, 317–320, *318–320*
Edit Rule Properties dialog box, 353–356, *353–355*, 363–364, *364*
Edit Services dialog box, 156, *156*
editors, NAT, **145**, 675
edu domain, 179
EFS (Encrypting File System), 429
  defined, 668
  in PKI, **467–468**
EFS Recovery Agent template, 476
EFS Recovery policy processing policy, 432
Enable All Purposes For This Certificate option, 509
Enable Automatic Partner Configuration option, 274
Enable Autonomous System Boundary Router option, 127, 129
Enable Burst Handling option, 270
Enable Computer And User Accounts To Be Trusted For Delegation right, 425
Enable disk quotas policy, 431
Enable Fragmentation Checking option, 106
Enable IP Router Manager option, 105
Enable On-Demand Dialing option, 147
Enable Only The Following Purposes option, 509
Enable OSPF For This Address option, 118
Enable Poison-Reverse Processing option, 116
Enable Router Discovery Advertisements option, 106
Enable Split-Horizon Processing option, 116
Enable Strong Protection option, 516
Enable Triggered Updates option, 116
Encapsulating Security Payload (ESP), 327
  defined, 668
  packets for, **331**, *331*
encapsulation
  defined, 668
  for dial-up services, 303
  in protocol security, **309–310**, *310*

Encrypting File System (EFS), 429
  defined, 668
  in PKI, **467–468**
encryption, 11
  defined, 668
  in IPSec, 325, 327
  in PKI, 464
  for remote access policies, 315, 319, *319*
Encryption settings, 315, 319, *319*
#END_ALTERNATE statement, 247–248
Enforce disk quota limit policy, 431
Enforce Password History policy, 415–416
Enforce User Logon Restrictions policy, 420
Enrollment Agent template, 476
enrollment agents, **512–514**, *513–514*
Enterprise Admins, permissions for, 201
enterprise CAs, **470–471**
Enterprise Domain Controllers, permissions for, 201
Enterprise Edition, 396–399
Enterprise Trust Folder, 506
entities, 668
Error events
  defined, 668
  in Event Viewer, 617
ESP (Encapsulating Security Payload), 327
  defined, 668
  packets for, **331**, *331*
event IDs in Event Viewer, 618
Event log option, 436
Event Logging settings, 217, *217*
event logs
  for DNS monitoring, 217, *217*
  for IPSec, **372–374**, *374*
  for security templates, 436
Event Properties dialog box, 617–618, *617*
Event Viewer utility, **615–616**, *616*
  defined, 668
  details in, **617–618**, *617*
  event types in, **616–617**
  for IPSec, 369
  for log files, **618–620**, *619–620*
Eventcreate utility, 620
Eventquery utility, 620
Eventtriggers utility, 620
Everyone, permissions for, 201
exam essentials
  certificates, **520–521**
  DNS, **224–225**
  high availability services, **564**
  network access, **376**
  network connectivity strategy, **162–163**
  network infrastructure, **19**
  network monitoring, remote administration, and backups, **650–651**
  server-level security, **450–451**
  TCP/IP network infrastructure, **78–79**
  WINS, **286–287**
Exchange Enrollment Agent (Offline request) template, 476
Exchange Signature Only template, 476
Exchange User template, 476
Exclude Reserved Addresses dialog box, 158, *159*
Exit Module settings, 490–491, *490*
exit modules
  CA settings for, 490–491, *490*
  defined, 668
  in PKI, **473–474**
Experience settings, 627, *627*
experts, **140–141**
Export File Format page, 515–516, *516*
exporting
  certificates, **515–517**, *516*
  IPSec policies, 350
Extended key usage attribute, 475
Extensible Authentication Protocol (EAP)
  characteristics of, **307**
  defined, 668
  purpose of, **304**
extensions for certificates, 474
external namespaces
  defined, 668
  in DNS, 193–196
External Routing settings, **128–129**, *129*
Extinction Interval setting, 267
Extinction Timeout setting, 267

F

failback
  defined, 668
  in server clusters, 537
Failed Requests folder, 484
failover pairs
  configuration, **546–547**, *546*
  defined, 668
failover process and policies, 16
  defined, 668
  in server clusters, 537, **544–547**, *545–547*
Failure Audit events
  defined, 668
  in Event Viewer, 617
fault tolerance, 534
  defined, 669
  in WINS, **253**
file servers
  performance objects for, 610
  purpose of, **387**
File system option, 436
file systems and services
  for security templates, 436
  in Windows Server 2003, 399
File To Import page, 517, *518*
Filter Action page, 367, *367*

Filter Action settings, 354, *354*
Filter settings, 618–620, *620*
filters
  actions for. *See* actions
  defined, 669
  for Event Viewer, 618–620, *620*
  in IPSec, **332–333**, **356–358**, *356–358*
    adding, **358–361**, *359–360*
    managing, 356
    for rules, **353**, *353*, **356**
    settings for, 354, *354*
  for LANs, 106
  for Network Monitor, **584–587**, *584–586*
  for NLB, *559*
  for TCP/IP packets, **132–133**
    creating, **133–135**, *133–134*
    VPN, **135–137**, *136*
Firewall settings, **152**, *153*
firewalls
  for NAT, **152**, *153*
  for Remote Assistance, 631
/fixquorum parameter, 562
flat routing
  defined, 669
  vs. route summarization, 57
Folder Redirection policy processing policy, 432
Force Shutdown From A Remote System right, 425
forcing
  IPSec policy updates, **349–350**
  WINS replication, 260
forward-only servers
  defined, 669
  working with, **212**
forwarding DNS
  conditional forwarders for, **211–212**
  forward-only servers for, **212**
Frame Viewer window, 583, *584*
Framed-Protocol option, 321
% Free Space counter, 604
full-mesh design
  defined, 669
  WINS deployment in, 263, *264*
full zone transfers (AXFRs)
  contents of, 191
  defined, 669

G

General settings
  for CAs, 488, *489*
  for certificates, 507–508, *507*
  for Event Viewer, 618–619, *619*
  for IPSec policies, **351–352**, *351–352*
  for LANs, 105, *105*
  for NAT, **157**, *157*
  for OSPF, **117–118**, *117*, **125–127**, *126*
  for Remote Desktop Connection, 624–625, *625*
  for RIP, **112–113**, *112*, 124, *125*
  for System Monitor, 596, *597*
  for WINS replication partners, **271**, *271*
  for WINS servers, **265–266**, *266*
Generate Security Audits right, 425
geographical region, address assignments by, 60
glue A (glue address) resource records
  defined, 669
  purpose of, 210
gov domain, 179
GPMC (Group Policy Management Console)
  for IPSec, 369
  working with, 410, *410*
GPT (GUID partition table) disks, 537
Graph Pane in Network Monitor, 582
graph View in System Monitor, 593
group affinity attribute
  defined, 669
  purpose of, 547
group permissions in DNS, **200–201**
Group Policy and Group Policy Objects (GPOs)
  and Active Directory, **402–414**, *403*, *405*, *407–414*
  defined, 669
  improvements in, 4
  for IPSec, 325, **327–328**, 340
  legacy compatibility for, **405–406**
  for Remote Assistance, **631–633**, *632–633*
Group Policy Management Console (GPMC)
  for IPSec, 369
  working with, 410, *410*
Group Policy Object Editor
  console for, **408–410**, *409–410*
  for IPSec, 369
Group Policy policies
  defined, 669
  list of, **432**
Group Policy refresh intervals for computers policy, 432
Group Policy refresh intervals for domain controllers policy, 432
Group Policy settings, 403, *403*, 409–410, *409*
Group Policy slow link detection policy, 432
Group Policy Wizard, 411, *412*
Groups dialog box, 316, *317*
GUID partition table (GPT) disks, 537

H

h-node
  defined, 670
  in WINS, 240
Handle Count counter, 599
hardware failures, 534–535
hardware requirements
  DNS servers, **213**
  Windows Server 2003, **396–397**

hardware routers, **99**
hardware routing, **32–33**
hardware support, 397–398
Hash Algorithms setting, 481
hashing algorithms
  defined, 669
  in PKI, 465
  selecting, 481
HBAs (host bus adapters), *542*
headers
  in IPSec, 326, **330**, *589*, *661*
  in network packets, 28, *29*
Hello Interval (Seconds) setting, 119
help
  from experts, **140–141**
  Remote Assistance, **628–633**, *629–630*, *632–633*
Help and Support Center, 629–630, *630*
Hide the File Scan Progress window policy, 433
hierarchies
  certificate, 468–469, *469*, 662
  IP addressing schemes, **36**
high availability services, **532**
  disaster recovery strategy, **17–18**
  evaluating, **532–534**
  exam essentials, **564**
  improvements in, **6–7**
  key terms, **565**
  network load balancing in, **16**
    monitoring, **556–560**, *556–559*
    planning, **554–556**
  network performance monitoring, **17**
  remote administration security, **16–17**
  review questions, **566–572**
  review questions, answers to, **573–574**
  scalability methods, **535**
  server clusters for. *See* server clusters
  summary, **563–564**
  threats to, **534–535**
high-level security
  defined, 669
  for DNS servers, **215–216**
Highly secure (Hisec*.inf) template, 435
histogram View in System Monitor, 593, *594*
host addresses, **41–45**, *41*
host bus adapters (HBAs), 542
host name resolution, troubleshooting, **216–219**
  DNS monitoring for, **217–218**, *217–218*
  ipconfig for, **222–223**
  log files for, **223–224**
  nslookup for, **219–222**
host records
  defined, 670
  purpose of, **183**
host routes
  defined, 670
  in IP routing, 94
hub-and-spoke design, **263**, *264*

I

ICS (Internet Connection Sharing), 90
  installing, **145–147**, *147*
  vs. NAT, **145**
IGMP (Internet Group Management Protocol), 101
IGMP proxy mode, 101
IGMP router mode, 101
Ignore All Routes In The Ranges Listed setting, 114
Ignore Routes From All Route Sources Except Those Selected option, 128
IIS (Web Application) Servers, **389–390**
IKE (Internet Key Exchange)
  defined, 670–671
  for IPSec, 329
Import Template dialog box, 434, 440, *440*
importing
  certificates, 498, **517–519**, *518–519*
  IPSec Policies, 350
  security templates, **434–437**, **440**, *440*
inbound filters
  in L2TP, 137
  for LANs, 106
Inbound Filters dialog box, 133, *133*, 136, *136*
inbound packets in NAT, **144–145**, *144*
inbound port mappings, 670
Include All Certificates In The Certification Path If Possible option, 516
Include Default Routes In Sent Announcements option, 117
Include Host Routes In Sent Announcements option, 117
#INCLUDE statement, 247–249
Incoming Packet Protocol list, 113
Increase Scheduling Priority right, 425
Incremental backup type, 644
incremental zone transfers (IXFRs)
  defined, 670
  purpose of, 191
Indexing service, performance objects for, 608
Information events
  defined, 670
  in Event Viewer, 617
information hiding, **39–40**
inheritance
  defined, 670
  in GPOs, 403–405
installing
  AppleTalk, 31
  CAs, **479–483**, *480–482*
  Certificate Server, **478–484**, *480–482*
  Certificates and Certification Authority, **483–484**, *483*
  ICS, **145–147**, *147*
  NAT, **148–151**, *150–151*
  Network Monitor, **578–580**, *578–580*

RIP, **123–124**, *123–124*
WINS, **264–265**
instances of performance objects, 593
int domain, 179
integrity
defined, 670
in IPv6, 64
in PKI, 463
inter-forest replication, **282–283**
Interactive Logon security category, 427
interfaces
for IP routing, **103–104**
demand-dial, **106–111**, *107–111*
LAN, **104–106**, *105–106*
OSPF, **117–120**, **125–129**, *126–129*
RIP, **111–117**, *112*, *114–117*, **123–125**, *123–126*
for NAT, **151–156**, *153–156*, 676
intermediate CAs, 470
Intermediate Certification Authorities folder, 506
internal namespaces, 670
internal routing
defined, 670
in internetworks, 93
Internet
connectivity strategy, **9**
and DNS, **178–179**
Internet Connection Sharing (ICS), 90
installing, **145–147**, *147*
vs. NAT, **145**
Internet Explorer Maintenance policy processing policy, 432
Internet Group Management Protocol (IGMP), 101
Internet Key Exchange (IKE)
defined, 670–671
for IPSec, 329
Internet Protocol (IP)
for dial-up services, 303
testing, **71–76**
Internet Protocol Security Extensions. *See* IPSec (IP Security)
Internet Security Agreement/Key Management Protocol (ISAKMP)
defined, 671
working with, 329–330
internetworks
defined, 671
in IP routing, **93**, *93*
Interrupts/Sec counter, 601
Intervals settings, **266–267**, *267*
Intres.adm template, 406
inverse queries, 189
IP (Internet Protocol)
for dial-up services, 303
testing, **71–76**
IP addresses, **35**
classes of, **37–38**
hierarchical scheme, **36**
incorrect, 71
requirements of, **55**
address assignment model, **56–59**
automatic IP configuration, **62–63**
public and private addresses, **60–62**
subnet structure, **59–60**
schemes for, **8**
translating. *See* NAT (Network Address Translation)
IP Control Protocol (IPCP), 302
IP datagrams
defined, 671
encapsulation in, 310
IP Filter List dialog box, 357, *357*
IP Filter List page, 367, *367*
IP Filter List settings, **353**, *353*
IP Filter Properties dialog box, *357–359*, *358–359*
IP filters. *See* filters
IP masquerading. *See* NAT (Network Address Translation)
IP routing, **32**, **91**
border routing, **99–100**, *100*
dynamic, **33–35**, **95–99**, *96*, *98*
hardware vs. software, **32–33**
interfaces for, **103–104**
demand-dial, **106–111**, *107–111*
LAN, **104–106**, *105–106*
OSPF, **117–120**, **125–129**, *126–129*
RIP, **111–117**, *112*, *114–117*, **123–125**, *123–126*
internetworks in, **93**, *93*
Logging settings for, **121**, *121*
managing, **103**, *103*
multicast routing, **100–102**
operation of, **91–94**, *92*
Preference Levels settings for, **122**, *122*
routing tables in, **94**
static, **33–35**, **94–95**, **129–132**, *130–132*
subnets in. *See* subnetting networks
troubleshooting, **137–141**, *138–139*
Windows Server 2003, **102**
IP security. *See* IPSec (IP Security)
IP Security Filter Action Wizard, 359
IP Security Monitor
description, 369
working with, **371–372**, *372*
IP Security Policy Management, 369
IP Security policy processing policy, 432
IP Security Policy Wizard, 345–346, *345–346*, 365, *365*
IP settings for remote access policies, 315, 318, *318*
IP spoofing
defined, 671
description, 65
IP version 4 (IPv4), 32, 671
IP version 6 (IPv6), *5*, **63–64**
address space in, **65–67**
automatic configuration in, **67–68**

benefits of, **64–65**
defined, 672
ipconfig utility
defined, 671
for DNS, **222–223**
for TCP/IP, **69–70**
IPCP (IP Control Protocol), 302
IPSec (IP Security), 5, **12–13**, 324
authentication in, **325–327**, *367*, 376
for default response rule, 346, *346*
methods for, **333–335**
settings for, 354, *355*
clients, 325, 671
defined, 671
deploying, **339–341**
evaluating, **324–326**
example, **338–339**
filters and filter actions in, **332–333**, **356–358**, *356–358*
adding, **358–361**, *359–360*
managing, 356
for rules, **353**, *353*, **356**
settings for, 354, *354*
IP Security Policy Management console for, **341–344**, *342–344*
monitoring
IP Security Monitor for, **371–372**, *372*
Network Monitor for, **588–589**
with NLB, 6
policies in, **13**, **331–338**, **344**
actions for, **358–361**, *359–360*
creating, **345–346**, *345–346*
deploying, **346–350**, *347–348*
filters for, **356–358**, *356–358*
General settings for, **351–352**, *351–352*
Rules settings for, **352–356**, *352–355*
testing, **374–375**
in Transport Mode, **361–363**, *361–362*
protocols for, **329–331**, *330–331*
security in, **326–338**
servers, 671
troubleshooting
best practices, **374–375**
data transmission security, **368–370**
event logs for, **372–374**, *374*
IP Security Monitor for, **371–372**, *372*
RSoP for, **370–371**, *370–371*
in Tunnel mode, **362–368**, *363–368*
in Windows Server 2003, **327–329**
IPSec Policy Agents, 671
IPv4 (IP version 4), 32, 671
IPv4-compatible IPv6 addresses, 671
IPv4-mapped IPv6 addresses, 672
IPv6 (IP version 6), 5, **63–64**
address space in, **65–67**
automatic configuration in, **67–68**
benefits of, **64–65**
defined, 672
IRQ10, 606
ISAKMP (Internet Security Agreement/Key Management Protocol)
defined, 671
working with, 329–330
ISAKMP master keys, 330
ISAKMP SAs, 330
Issue and Manage Certificates permission, 492
Issued Certificates folder, 484
issuing certificates, **513–514**, *513–514*
Items To Back Up page, 485–486, *485*, 636, *636*
Items To Restore page, 487, *487*
iterative queries, 181
defined, 670
vs. recursive, 188
IXFRs (incremental zone transfers)
defined, 670
purpose of, 191

J

jetpack.exe utility, 281
jp domain, 179

K

KDCs (Key Distribution Centers)
defined, 672
functions of, 334, 420
Kerberos authentication
defined, 672
process, **333–334**
for server-level security, **419–420**
Key Distribution Centers (KDCs)
defined, 672
functions of, 334, 420
key escrow method
defined, 672
in PKI, 477
Key Exchange Settings dialog box, 351, *352*
Key Length setting, 481
key terms
certificates, **522**
DNS, **225–226**
high availability services, **565**
network access, **377**
network connectivity strategy, **163–164**
network infrastructure, **19**
network monitoring, remote administration, and backups, **651**
server-level security, **451**
TCP/IP network infrastructure, **79–80**
WINS, **287–288**
Key usage attribute, 475
keys
defined, 672
ISAKMP, 330

in PKI, 465, **477**
preshared, **335**

L

L2TP (Layer 2 Tunneling Protocol)
defined, 672
packet filters in, **137**
L2TP/IPSec (Layer 2 Tunneling Protocol over IPSec), 5, 311, **328**
LANs
managing, **104–106**, *105–106*
for WINS replication, **257–258**, *258*
Last field for counters, 593
Layer 2 Tunneling Protocol (L2TP)
defined, 672
packet filters in, **137**
Layer 2 Tunneling Protocol over IPSec (L2TP/IPSec), 5, 311, **328**
LCP (Link Control Protocol), 302
legacy compatibility for Group Policy, **405–406**
Let Me Choose What To Back Up option, 635–636
Level of Preference setting, 106
Limit Windows file protection cache size policy, 433
limited replication partnerships
defined, 672
in WINS, 256–257
Link Control Protocol (LCP), 302
link-local addresses
defined, 673
purpose of, 67
link state maps
defined, 672
in OSPF, 98
link state protocols
characteristics of, **34–35**
defined, 672–673
linking WINS replication partners, 275
LMHOSTS file
defined, 673
for NetBIOS name resolution, **246–249**, *247*
Load And Unload Device Drivers right, 425
load balancing
in DNS, **189–190**
network. *See* NLB (Network Load Balancing)
Local Area Connection Properties page, 578–579, *578–579*
Local Computer Policy, 401
for IPSec deployment, **340**
working with, 406–407, *407*
Local policies, 420
creating, 401
defined, 673
for server-level security, **420–421**
Audit, **421–423**, *422–423*
Security options, **426–428**, *428*
for security templates, 436
User Rights Assignment, **423–426**
Local policies option, 436
local quorum clusters
defined, 673
purpose of, 548
Local Resources settings, 626, *626*
Local Security policies
defined, 673
purpose of, 401
Local Users and Groups, 622
Lock Pages in Memory right, 425
lockout policies, **417–419**, *419*
Log Detailed Events To Windows Event Log option, 269–270
Log Errors And Warnings option, 121
Log Errors Only option, 121
Log event when quota limit exceeded policy, 431
Log event when quota warning level exceeded policy, 431
log files
CA, 486
for DNS, **223–224**
for events
for DNS monitoring, 217, *217*
for IPSec, **372–374**, *374*
for security templates, 436
in IP routing, **121**, *121*
server, monitoring, **615–620**, *616–617*, *619–620*
in System Monitor, 597, *597*
Log Files settings, 597, *597*
Log On As A Batch Job right, 425
Log On As A Service right, 425
Log The Maximum Amount Of Information option, 121
Log users off when roaming profile fails policy, 430
logging mode in RSoP, 370
Logging settings, **121**, *121*
LogicalDisk object, 604–605
logon events, auditing, 421
Logon policies
defined, 673
list of, **430–431**
low-level security
defined, 673
for DNS servers, **214–215**
ls command in nslookup, 221
LUN masking, 540–541, *541*

M

m-node
defined, 674
in WINS, 240
machine accounts, 673
Machine certificate template attribute, 475
machine certificates
defined, 673
issuing, 334

mail exchange (MX) records
  defined, 673
  purpose of, **184–185**
Mail (POP3) Servers, **390**
majority node set clusters, 537
  defined, 673
  purpose of, *549–550*, *549*
  recovering from failures in, **562–563**
majority node set quorums, **552**
Manage Auditing And Security Log right, 425
Manage CA permission, 492
Manage Filter Actions settings, 358, *359*
Manage IP Filter Lists And Filter Actions dialog box, 356, *356*
Manage IP Filter Lists settings, 356, *356*
Manage Your Server tool, **393–395**, *394*
Management and Monitoring Tools dialog box, 580, *580*
management consoles, 327
management services, 399
manual WINS replication, 276
mapping
  in IPSec, **328–329**
  in NAT, 155
  in NetBIOS name resolution, **243–244**, *244*
  in OSPF, 98
  in WINS replication, 251
masked bits
  defined, 674
  in subnets, 45
master keys in ISAKMP, 330
Maximum field for counters, 593
Maximum Lifetime for Service Ticket policy, 420
Maximum Lifetime for User Ticket policy, 420
Maximum Lifetime for User Ticket Renewal policy, 420
Maximum Number Of Records Verified Each Period setting, 268–269
Maximum Password Age policy, 415–416
Maximum retries to unload and update user profile policy, 430
Maximum Tolerance for Computer Clock Synchronization policy, 420
Maximum Transmission Unit (MTU) Size (Bytes) setting, 120
MBSA (Microsoft Baseline Security Analyzer), 14
  defined, 674
  operation of, **447–448**
  troubleshooting, **449**
MCS (Microsoft Certificate Services)
  defined, 674
  history of, 462
mean time between failures (MTBF), 534
medium-level security
  defined, 674
  for DNS servers, **215**
Memory object, 591, **598–599**
memory subsystem, System Monitor for, **598–600**
Memory Usage option, 613
metrics
  defined, 674
  in distance vector protocols, 34
  in IP routing, 91
#MH statement, 248
Microsoft Baseline Security Analyzer (MBSA), 14
  defined, 674
  operation of, **447–448**
  troubleshooting, **449**
Microsoft Certificate Services (MCS)
  defined, 674
  history of, 462
Microsoft CHAP (MS-CHAP)
  defined, 674
  description of, **307–308**
Microsoft Network Client security category, 427
Microsoft Network Server security category, 427
Microsoft Software Update Services, 14
  defined, 686
  working with, **444–447**
migrating
  DNS, **192**, **195–196**
  WINS services, **277**
mil domain, 179
minimum and maximum time intervals setting, 106
Minimum field for counters, 593
Minimum Password Age policy, 415–416
Minimum Password Length policy, 415–416
mirrored filters
  benefits of, 358
  characteristics of, 357
  defined, 674
mismatches, policy, **375**
mission-critical functions, optimizing, **612**
MMC consoles
  creating, **411–414**, *411–414*
  for Security Policy, **406–408**, *407–408*
mobile users in WINS networks, **255**
Modify Firmware Environment Variables right, 425
monitoring
  DNS, **217–218**, *217–218*
  IPSec
    with IP Security Monitor, **371–372**, *372*
    with Network Monitor, **588–589**
  network traffic. *See* network monitoring
  routing status, **138–140**, *138–139*
  system performance, **589–590**
    with Event Viewer, **615–620**, *616–617*, *619–620*
    with System applet, **612–614**
    with System Monitor. *See* System Monitor
    with Task Manager, **614–615**, *614–615*
  WINS, **278**
    client traffic, **254–255**
    records, **279–280**, *279–280*
    statistics, **278–279**, *278*
Monitoring settings, 217, *218*
Monthly backup option, 641
Mountvol utility, 540
MS-CHAP (Microsoft CHAP)

defined, 674
description of, **307–308**
MS-RAS-Vendor option, 321
_msdcs domain, 191
MTBF (mean time between failures), 534
multicast addresses
defined, 674
purpose of, 67
multicast routing
defined, 674
operation of, **100–102**
Multilink settings, 315, 318, *318*
multimaster replication model
for Active Directory, 206
defined, 674
multimedia services, 399
multiple host filtering
defined, 674
options for, **559–560**
multiple-instance applications
characteristics of, 539
defined, 674–675
multiple processor configuration, **603–604**, *603*
multiple sites
server clusters in, **550–552**, *550*
WINS deployment for, **261–263**, *261–262*
multipurpose servers, security templates for, **441**
mutual authentication
defined, 675
in Kerberos, **333–334**, 419
MX (mail exchange) records
defined, 673
purpose of, **184–185**

N

name registration
defined, 675
in NetBIOS name resolution, **241–242**
name releases
defined, 675
in NetBIOS name resolution, **242**
name renewals
defined, 675
in NetBIOS name resolution, **242**
name resolution
defined, 675
in DNS, **187–191**, *188*
in NAT, 148, **160**, *160*
in WINS. *See* NetBIOS (Network Basic Input/Output System)
name resolution components, 675
Name Resolution settings, **160**, *160*
Name Server (NS) records
defined, 675
purpose of, **183**
name servers
defined, 675
in DNS, 177
namespaces in DNS, **192–193**
defined, 667
domain, **177–178**, *178*, **193–194**
options for, **194–195**
for Windows NT Server migration, **195–196**
NAS-Identifier option, 321
NAS-IP-Address option, 321
NAS-Port-Type option, 321
NASs (Network Access Servers)
defined, 676
RRAS servers as, 301
NAT (Network Address Translation), **62**, 90, **141–142**, *141*
addressing components in, 675
defined, 676
editors for, **145**, 675
in ICS, **145–147**, *147*
inbound packets in, **144–145**, *144*
installing, **148–151**, *150–151*
interfaces for, **151–156**, *153–156*, 676
for IPSec, **328**
need for, **160–161**
outbound packets in, **143–144**, *143*
in RRAS, 102, **149–150**, *150–151*
settings for
Address Assignment, **158**, *159*
Address Pool, **153–154**, *154*
Firewall, **152**, *153*
General, **157**, *157*
Name Resolution, **160**, *160*
Services And Ports, **154–156**, *155*
Translation, **157–158**, *158*
in Windows Server 2003, **142–143**
NAT address pools, 675
NBMA (non-broadcast multiple access) routers
defined, 676
in OSPF, **118**, *119*
NBMA Neighbors settings, **118**, *119*
NBNS (NetBIOS name server)
defined, 676
in WINS, 239
NBT (NetBIOS over TCP/IP)
defined, 676
limitations of, 239
nbtstat utility
defined, 676
for name registrations, 255
for WINS troubleshooting, **284–286**
Neighbor Discovery, 67
Neighbors settings, **114–115**, *115*
.NET application services, 399
net domain, 178
NetBEUI protocol, **31**
NetBIOS (Network Basic Input/Output System), 31
defined, 676

name resolution in, **238–239**
LMHOSTS for, **246–249**, *247*
name registration in, **241–242**
name releases in, **242**
name renewals in, **242**
for non-WINS clients, **243–245**, *244*
operation of, **239–240**
resolution in, **242–243**
in Windows Server 2003, **240**
WINS database in, **243**
WINS proxy agents for, **245**
WINS replication in, **249–251**
NetBIOS name server (NBNS)
defined, 676
in WINS, 239
NetBIOS naming protocol
defined, 676
purpose of, 238
NetBIOS over TCP/IP (NBT)
defined, 676
limitations of, 239
netmask ordering for load balancing, **189–190**
netsh command, **329**
network access, **300**
exam essentials, **376**
IP security for. *See* IPSec (IP Security)
key terms, **377**
remote access. *See* remote access
review questions, **378–382**
review questions, answers to, **383–384**
summary, **375**
Network Access security category, 427
Network Access Servers (NASs)
defined, 676
RRAS servers as, 301
Network Address Translation. *See* NAT (Network Address Translation)
network analyzers, 577
Network Basic Input/Output System. *See* NetBIOS (Network Basic Input/Output System)
network connectivity, **90**
exam essentials, **162–163**
failures in, *535*
filtering in. *See* filters
improvements in, **4**
Internet, **9**
IP routing in. *See* IP routing
key terms, **163–164**
NAT in. *See* NAT (Network Address Translation)
private addressing, **142**
review questions, **165–170**
review questions, answers to, **171–173**
summary, **161**
Network Interface object, 606
Network Load Balancing. *See* NLB (Network Load Balancing)
Network Load Balancing Manager, 6, 556, *556*, 560
Network Monitor tool, 577, **581–582**, *581*
capturing data in, **582–583**, *583*, **588–589**
from command line, **587–588**
installing, **578–580**, *578–580*
viewing data in, **583–587**, *584–586*
network monitoring, **17**, **576–577**
exam essentials, **650–651**
key terms, **651**
network load balancing, **556–560**, *556–559*
with Network Monitor. *See* Network Monitor tool
review questions, **652–656**
review questions, answers to, **657–658**
summary, **650**
system performance, **17**, **589–590**
with Event Viewer, **615–620**, *616–617*, *619–620*
with System applet, **612–614**
with System Monitor. *See* System Monitor
with Task Manager, **614–615**, *614–615*
network packets, **28**, *29*
network protocols, **27**, *27*
binding, **29**, 680
connectionless versus connection-oriented, **29–30**
for IPSec, **329–331**, *330–331*
network packets in, **28**, *29*
operation of, **28**
in Windows Server 2003, **30–32**
network routes
defined, 676
in IP routing, 94
Network Security security category, 427
Network Type page, 366, *366*
Network Type settings, 118
Networking settings, 614, *614*
networks, **2**
access to. *See* network access
addresses in. **37–38**, **40–45**, *41*. *See also* IP addresses
bridging, **4**
connectivity. *See* network connectivity
defined, 676
defining, **2–3**
exam essentials, **19**
high server availability. *See* high availability services
key terms, **19**
monitoring. *See* network monitoring
protocols for. *See* network protocols
review questions, **20–22**
review questions, answers to, **23–24**
routing strategies **9**
secure data flow, **10–11**
remote access strategy, **11–12**
security, **12–13**
security infrastructure, **13**
authentication through certificate services, **15**
policy-based security for server roles, **14**
security update infrastructure, **14–15**
summary, **18**
TCP. *See* TCP/IP protocol

topologies
address assignments by, 60
defined, *676*
designing, **8**
TCP/IP in, **7–8**
in Windows Server 2003, **3–4**
configuration and connectivity improvements, **4**
data security improvements, **4–5**
high availability improvements, **6–7**
security infrastructure improvements, **6**
services, 398–399
New Remote Access Policy Wizard, 321–324, *322–324*
New Routing Protocol dialog box
for NAT, 150, *150*
for RIP and OSPF, 123–124, *123*
New Security Method dialog box, 361, *361*
next hops, 33
N+I configuration
defined, 675
description, **545**, *545*
NLB (Network Load Balancing), 6
defined, 676
for high server availability, **16**
monitoring, **556–560**, *556–559*
planning, **554–556**
remote administration of, **560**
and round robin DNS, **555**
NLB (Network Load Balancing) clusters
defined, 676
working with, **533–534**
No Override option, 404–405
nodes in server clusters, 533, 537
non-broadcast multiple access (NBMA) routers
defined, 676
in OSPF, 118
non-WINS clients, NetBIOS name resolution for, **243–245**, *244*
noncontiguous subnets
defined, 677
planning, 57
None affinity option, *559*
nonrecursive DNS servers
defined, 677
vs. forward-only, 212
nonrepudiation
defined, 677
in PKI, 463
Normal backup type, 644
NS (Name Server) records
defined, 675
purpose of, **183**
nslookup tool, 217
defined, 677
for DNS, **219–222**
NT Server migration
DNS namespaces for, **195–196**
WINS services, **277**
ntbackup utility, 645
Number Of Changes In Version ID Before Replication setting, 272
Number of Retries setting, 273
number of servers needed
for DNS, **214**
for WINS, **252–253**
NWLink protocol
defined, 677
purpose of, **31**

O

Oakley protocol, 330
object access, auditing, 421
octets in IP addressing, 36
Offer Remote Assistance Policy Properties dialog box, 631, *632*
offline compaction
defined, 677
WINS database, 281
on-link prefixes, 677
Once backup option, 641
online compaction
defined, 677
WINS database, 281
Open Database dialog box, 434
Open Shortest Path First protocol. *See* OSPF (Open Shortest Path First) protocol
Open Systems Interconnect (OSI) model, 27, *27*
opening security templates, **437**
Operation Mode list, 112
optimizing
monitoring for. *See* monitoring
system performance, **589–590**
with Event Viewer, **615–620**, *616–617*, *619–620*
with System applet, **612–614**
with System Monitor. *See* System Monitor
with Task Manager, **614–615**, *614–615*
Options dialog box
for backups, 643–644, *644*
for GPOs, 404, *405*
order of IPSec policy application, **349**
org domain, 179
organization charts, address assignments by, 60
organizational units (OUs), 677
OSI (Open Systems Interconnect) model, 27, *27*
OSPF (Open Shortest Path First) protocol, 35, **98–99**, *98*
Advanced settings for, **119–120**, *120*
Areas settings for, 127, *127*
defined, 677
External Routing settings for, **128–129**, *129*
General settings for, **117–118**, *117*, **125–127**, *126*
interfaces, **117**
NBMA Neighbors settings for, **118**, *119*
Virtual Interfaces settings for, **127–128**, *128*
OUs (organizational units), 677

outbound filters
  in L2TP, 137
  for LANs, 106
outbound packets
  in NAT, **143–144**, *143*
  in RIP, 112–113
Outgoing Packet Protocol list, 112–113
Outgoing Port setting, 156
Overwrite Unique Static Mappings At This Server (Migrate On) option, 271
owner-version mapping tables
  defined, 677–678
  in WINS replication, 251

P

p-node
  defined, 679
  in WINS, 240
packets, **28**, *29*
  authenticating
    defined, 678
    in IPv6, 64
  confidentiality in, 678
  defined, 678
  filters for, **132–133**
    creating, **133–135**, *133–134*
    defined, 678
    in RRAS, 102
    VPN, **135–137**, *136*
  integrity of, 678
  payloads in, 28, 678
page files
  defined, 678
  performance of, 598
Pages/Sec counter, 591, 598–599
paging, 598
Paging File object, 598–599
PAP (Password Authentication Protocol)
  defined, 678
  description of, 308
partitioned applications
  defined, 678
  for server clusters, *539*, *540*
partners in WINS replication, **250–251**
  adding, **275**
  controlling, **270**, **275–276**, *276*
  defined, 682
  in manual replication, 276
  planning, **255–261**, *258–259*
  settings for
    Advanced, **273–274**, *274*, **276**, *276*
    General, **271**, *271*
    Pull Replication, **273**, *273*
    Push Replication, **272**, *272*
passthrough actions
  defined, 678
  for IP filters, 332–333
Password Authentication Protocol (PAP)
  defined, 678
  description of, 308
Password policies
  defined, 678
  for server-level security, **415–417**, *416–417*
Password setting
  in OSPF, 118
  in RIP, 113
passwords for certificates, 518
Passwords Must Meet Complexity Requirements policy, 415–416
PAT (Port Address Translation), **62**
pathping utility
  defined, 679
  for IP communications, **75–76**
peer filters, 97, 679
Pending Requests folder, 484, 497
Perform Analysis dialog box, 440, *440*
Perform Automatic Testing At The Following Interval option, 217
Perform Volume Maintenance Tasks right, 425
performance, **65**
  monitoring for. *See* monitoring
  optimizing, **589–590**
    with Event Viewer, **615–620**, *616–617*, *619–620*
    with System applet, **612–614**
    with System Monitor. *See* System Monitor
    with Task Manager, **614–615**, *614–615*
  of replication, **206–207**
  of WINS servers, **252–253**
performance counters, **591–593**
  defined, 679
  for disk objects, **604–605**
  for memory objects, **598–599**
  for network services, **607–608**
  for network subsystem, **606–607**
  for processor objects, **601–602**
Performance Options dialog box, 612–613, *613*
Performance utility, 591
Periodic Announcement Interval (Seconds) setting, 115
periodic update mode
  defined, 679
  in RIP, 97
permissions
  for CAs, 491–492, *492*
  for templates, **493–494**, *493–494*
  for zones, **200–201**
Permit action, 332–333
Personal Folder, 506
Phone Number page, 110
PhysicalDisk object, 591, 604–605
ping utility
  defined, 679
  for IP communications, **71–73**
PKI (Public Key Infrastructure), 334, **463**
  certificates in, **466–467**
    attributes for, **474–475**

CAs, **468–471**, *469*
services, **472**, *472*
templates, **475–476**
concepts in, **464**
CSPs in, **473**
CTLs in, 474
defined, 681
digital signatures in, **465–466**
elements of, **467–468**
policy and exit modules in, **473–474**
public key cryptography in, **465**
recovery keys in, **477**
secret key cryptography in, **464**
SGC in, **477**
smart cards in, **477–478**
PKI-aware applications, **467–468**
Place All Certificates In The Following Store option, 518
placement of DNS servers, **214**
planning mode in RSoP, 370
Point-to-Point Protocol (PPP)
defined, 679
for dial-up services, **302–303**, *303*
Point-to-Point Protocol over Ethernet (PPPoE), 4
point-to-point routers
defined, 679
in OSPF, 118
Point-to-Point Tunneling Protocol (PPTP)
defined, 679
operation of, 311
packet filters for, **135–137**, *136*
pointer (PTR) records
defined, 679
purpose of, **184**
policies
auditing changes to, 421
group. *See* Group Policy and Group Policy Objects (GPOs)
IPSec, **13**, **331–338**, **344**
actions for, **358–361**, *359–360*
creating, **345–346**, *345–346*
deploying, **346–350**, *347–348*
filters for, **356–358**, *356–358*
General settings for, **351–352**, *351–352*
Rules settings for, **352–356**, *352–355*
testing, **374–375**
in Transport Mode, **361–363**, *361–362*
remote access, **313**
creating, **320–324**, *322–324*
default, modifying, **313–320**, *314–320*
defined, 682
for Remote Assistance, **631–633**, *632–633*
server-level security
Account, **414–420**, *416–417*, *419*
deploying, **441–443**
Local, **420–428**, *422–423*, *428*
Public Key, **428–429**
Security. *See* Security Policy
policy-based security for server roles, **14**
Policy Configuration Method page, 321, *322*
Policy Encryption Level page, 323, *324*
Policy Module settings, 488, *489*
policy modules
for CAs, 488, *489*
defined, 679
in PKI, **473–474**
Poll Interval (Seconds) setting, 120
Pool Nonpaged Allocs counter, 599
Pool Nonpaged Bytes counter, 599
POP3 (Mail) Servers, **390**
Port Address Translation (PAT), **62**
port mappings
defined, 679
for NAT, 155
port number setting for NAT, 156
Port Rules settings, *558*, *558*
Post Office Protocol, version 3 (POP3), 390
PPP (Point-to-Point Protocol)
defined, 679
for dial-up services, **302–303**, *303*
PPP frames, 310
PPPoE (Point-to-Point Protocol over Ethernet), 4
PPTP (Point-to-Point Tunneling Protocol)
defined, 679
operation of, 311
packet filters for, **135–137**, *136*
pre-shared keys, 680
#PRE statement, 247–249
Preference Levels setting, **122**, *122*
Preserve Existing Certificate Database option, 482
preshared keys, **335**
primary command in DNS, 187
primary DNS servers
characteristics of, 180–181
defined, 680
primary WINS servers
addresses for, 241
defined, 680
primary zones
characteristics of, 197
defined, 680
print servers
performance objects for, 608, 610
purpose of, **387**
Private Address setting, 156
private addresses, **142**
defined, 680
vs. public, **60–62**
Private Bytes counter, 599
Private Interface Connected To Private Network option, 152
Private Key And CA Certificate setting, 486
private keys
defined, 680
in PKI, 465
private namespaces, 195

privilege use, auditing, 421
Process Default Routes In Received Announcements option, 117
Process Host Routes In Received Announcements option, 116
Process objects, *599*
process tracking, auditing, 421
processor affinity
  defined, 680
  for optimizing, 602–604
Processor object, *591*, **601–602**
Processor Queue Length counter, 601
Processor Scheduling option, 612
processor subsystem, System Monitor for, **601–604**, *603*
% Processor Time counter, *591*, 601
Profile Single Process right, 425
Profile System Performance right, 425
Programs settings, *626*, *626*
promiscuous mode
  defined, 680
  drivers for, 577
Prompt user when slow link is detected policy, 430
protocol security, **11**
  planning, **12–13**
  in remote access security, **309–312**, *310*, *312*
Protocol settings
  for IPSec filters, 358, *359*
  for NAT, 156
protocol stacks, 27
protocol suites, 27
protocols, network, **27**, *27*
  binding, **29**, 680
  connectionless versus connection-oriented, **29–30**
  for IPSec, **329–331**, *330–331*
  network packets in, **28**, *29*
  operation of, **28**
  in Windows Server 2003, **30–32**
Protocols And Security page, 110, *110*
providers, authentication, **306–309**
proxy agents, **245**, 690
PTR (pointer) records
  defined, 679
  purpose of, **184**
Public Address group, 156
public addresses
  defined, 680
  vs. private, **60–62**
Public and Private Key Pair Selection page, 480, *480*
Public Interface Connected To The Internet option, 152
public key certificates
  defined, 681
  working with, **334–335**
public key cryptography
  defined, 681
  in PKI, **465**
Public Key Infrastructure. *See* PKI (Public Key Infrastructure)
Public Key Policies, **428–429**
public keys
  defined, 680
  in PKI, 465
public namespaces, 195
publishing CRLs, **502–504**, *502–503*
pull partners
  defined, 681
  in WINS replication, **250–251**, **256–257**
Pull Replication settings, **273**, *273*
pull replication triggers
  defined, 681
  description, 250
  in WAN replication, 260
purposes for certificates, **509**, *510*
push partners
  defined, 681
  in WINS replication, **250–251**, **256–257**
push-pull partners
  defined, 681
  in WINS replication, **256–257**
Push Replication settings, **272**, *272*
push replication triggers
  defined, 681
  description, 250
  in LAN replication, 257
  in WAN replication, 260

Q

quads in IP addressing, 36
queries
  DNS, 181, **188–189**, *188*
  for services, **190–191**
quorum resources, **548–550**, *549*, **552**
  corruption of, 561
  defined, 681
  in server clusters, 537

R

RADIUS (Remote Authentication Dial-In User Service)
  defined, 682
  with RRAS, 306
RAM requirements, 397
random address allocation, 59
random failover policies, 547
Read permission for CAs, 492
Receive All Packets Except Those That Meet The Criteria Below option, 133
Record Mapping settings, **279**, *279*
Record Owners settings, 279, *280*
Record Types settings, 280

records, WINS
  deleting and tombstoning, **281–282**
  monitoring, **279–280**, *279–280*
  resource, 182, **202–204**, 682
recovery
  ASR for, **647–649**, *648*
  domain controller, **649**
  high server availability, **17–18**
  server cluster failures, **561–563**
recovery agents
  defined, 681–682
  in PKI, 477
Recovery Console security category, 427
recovery keys
  defined, 682
  in PKI, **477**
recursive queries, 181, 188
Recursive To Other DNS Servers option, 217
reduced network traffic, subnetting for, 38
Registry option, 436
Registry policy processing policy, 432
rekeying certificates, **514**
relay agents, 63, 666
releases, name, **242**, 675
reliability
  in availability, *534*
  defined, 682
remote access
  policies for, **313**
    creating, **320–324**, *322–324*
    default, modifying, **313–320**, *314–320*
    defined, 682
  security for
    evaluating, **300–301**
    protocol security in, **309–312**, *310*, *312*
    remote access services, **301–305**, *303–304*
    user authentication in, **305–309**, *306–307*, *309*
  services for, **301**
    dial-up, **301–303**, *303*
    VPNs, **303–305**, *304*
  strategy for, **11–12**
remote administration
  of network load balancing, **560**
  secure, **16–17**
    enabling, **623–624**, *623–624*
    Remote Assistance, **628–633**, *629–630*, *632–633*
    Remote Desktop Connection, **624–628**, *624–628*
    Remote Desktop for Administration, **620–623**
Remote Assistance Settings dialog box, 629, *629*
Remote Assistance tool, 621, **628–629**
  defined, 682
  operation of, **629–631**, *629–631*
  securing, **631–633**, *632–633*
Remote Assistance window, 630–631, *630*
Remote Authentication Dial-In User Service (RADIUS)
  defined, 682
  with RRAS, 306
remote computers for identifying system bottlenecks, **601**
Remote Desktop Connection, 622, **624**, *624*
  Display settings for, 625, *625*
  Experience settings for, 627, *627*
  General settings for, 624–625, *625*
  Local Resources settings for, 626, *626*
  Programs settings for, 626, *626*
  working with, **627–628**
Remote Desktop for Administration, 6, **620–621**
  components of, **622–623**
  defined, 682
  security for, **621–622**
Remote Desktop Users dialog box, 624, *624*
Remote Desktop Users group, 622
Remote Desktop Web Connection, 622
Remote settings
  for remote administration, 623, *623*
  for Remote Assistance, 633
Remove Computer From Docking Station right, 425
Remove TCP Mapping After (Minutes) setting, 157
Remove UDP Mapping After (Minutes) setting, 157
Renew CA Certificate dialog box, 487, *488*
renew intervals
  defined, 682
  for WINS servers, 252, 266
renewing
  certificates, **487**, *488*, **514–515**
  names, **242**
Replace a Process Level Token right, 426
replay attacks, IPSec for, 326
Replicate Only With Partners option, 271
replication
  Active Directory, **206**, 660
  performance for, **206–207**
  synchronous vs. asynchronous, **551–552**
  WINS, **249–251**
    inter-forest, **282–283**
    partners in. *See* partners in WINS replication
  zones, **205–209**
Replication Interval setting, 273
report view in System Monitor, 594, *594*
reports in System Monitor, **594–598**, *594*, *597*
Request A Certificate task, 513
Request certificates permission, 492
requesting certificates, **510–514**, *511–514*
Requests For Secure Communication page, 345, *345*
Reset Account Lockout Counter After policy, 418
resolvers
  defined, 682
  DNS, 181, 188
resource groups
  defined, 682
  in server clusters, 537
resource records (RRs)
  defined, 682
  in DNS, **182–186**
  in WINS, **202–204**
resources
  defined, 682
  in server clusters, 537
Restore Defaults option, 267

Restore Files And Directories right, 426
Restore Wizard, 639–640, *640*
restoring CA data, **485–487**, *487*
Resultant Set of Policy (RSoP) tool, *5*, **13**, **328**, **370–371**, *370–371*
Retransmit Interval (Seconds) setting, 119
reverse lookup
  files for, **186**, 682
  resource records for, 184
review questions
  certificates, **523–527**
  DNS, **227–233**
  high availability services, **566–572**
  network access, **378–382**
  network connectivity strategy, **165–170**
  network infrastructure, **20–22**
  network monitoring, remote administration, and backups, **652–656**
  server-level security, **452–457**
  TCP/IP network infrastructure, **81–85**
  WINS, **289–295**
review questions, answers to
  certificates, **528–529**
  DNS, **234–236**
  high availability services, **573–574**
  network access, **383–384**
  network connectivity strategy, **171–173**
  network infrastructure, **23–24**
  network monitoring, remote administration, and backups, **657–658**
  server-level security, **458–460**
  TCP/IP network infrastructure, **86–87**
  WINS, **296–298**
Revoked Certificates folder, 484
revoking certificates, 467, **501–504**, *502–503*
RIP (Routing Information Protocol), 34, **96–97**
  defined, 683
  installing, **123–124**, *123–124*
  interfaces, **111–112**
  settings for
    Advanced, **115–117**, *116*
    General, **112–113**, *112*, 124, *125*
    Neighbors, **114–115**, *115*
    Security, **113–114**, *114*, 125, *126*
Role Removal Confirmation page, 393, *394*
roles
  CA, **471**
  server, **386–391**
    Configure Your Server Wizard for, **391–393**, *392–393*
    Manage Your Server tool for, **393–395**, *394*
    security for, **14**
root CA certificates, importing, 498
root certificate authorities
  defined, 683
  description, **469–470**, *469*
  role of, 471
root servers
  defined, 683
  purpose of, 181
rootsec.inf (System root security) template, 436
round robin ordering, **189–190**, 555
route add command, 130, 139
route filters
  defined, 683
  in OSPF, 98
Route Filters option, 129
route print command, 139
route summarization
  defined, 683
  vs. flat routing, **57**
routed networks, mobile users in, **255**
router discovery, *95*
router discovery messages
  defined, 683
  enabling, 106
Router Identification setting, 127
Router Priority setting, 118
routers
  in OSPF, 118
  software and hardware, **99**
routing, 90
  defined, 683
  IP. *See* IP routing
  monitoring, **138–140**, *138–139*
  planning, **9**
Routing and Remote Access Service (RRAS)
  defined, 683
  features of, 102–103, *103*
  for NAT, **149–150**, *150–151*
  for static routes, **130–131**, *130*
Routing and Remote Access Service (RRAS) servers, 301
  access control for, **311–312**, *312*
  purpose of, **390**
Routing Information Protocol (RIP). *See* RIP (Routing Information Protocol)
routing metrics
  defined, 674
  in distance vector protocols, 34
  in IP routing, 91
routing tables
  defined, 683
  in IP routing, **94**
RRAS (Routing and Remote Access Service)
  defined, 683
  features of, 102–103, *103*
  for NAT, **149–150**, *150–151*
  for static routes, **130–131**, *130*
RRAS (Routing and Remote Access Service) servers, 301
  access control for, **311–312**, *312*
  purpose of, **390**
RRs (resource records)
  defined, 682
  in DNS, **182–186**
  in WINS, **202–204**
RSoP (Resultant Set of Policy) tool, *5*, **13**, **328**, **370–371**, *370–371*
RSoP Wizard, 371
Rules settings, **352–356**, *352–355*, 365, *365*
Run these programs at user logon policy, 430

S

SANs (Storage Area Networks), *538*
- defined, 687
- working with, **540–542**, *541*

SAs (security associations)
- defined, 684
- for IPSec, **330**

scalability, **532–534**
- in IPv6, **64**
- methods for, **535**

scaling out, *535*, 684
scaling up, *535*, 684
scheduling backup jobs, **641**
scope of IP addresses, 62
Scripts policy processing policy, 432
secondary command in DNS, 187
secondary DNS servers
- characteristics of, 181
- defined, 684

secondary WINS servers
- addresses for, 241
- defined, 684

secondary zones
- characteristics of, 197
- creating, **205**
- defined, 684

secret key cryptography
- defined, 684
- in PKI, 464–465

Secure (Secure*.inf) template, 435
Secure Server (Require Security) policy, **336–338**
security, **13**
- authentication for. *See* authentication
- for data flow, **10–13**
- defined, 684
- for demand-dial connections, 107
- for DNS servers, **214–216**
- for dynamic updates, 199, 684
- improvements in, **4–6**
- in IPSec, **326–338**
- in IPv6, **64–65**
- network access. *See* network access
- protocol, **11–13**, **309–312**, *310*, *312*
- for remote administration, **16–17**
  - enabling, **623–624**, *623–624*
  - Remote Assistance, **628–633**, *629–630*, *632–633*
  - Remote Desktop Connection, **624–628**, *624–628*
  - Remote Desktop for Administration, **620–623**
- server-level. *See* server-level security
- for server roles, **14**
- services for, 398
- updates for, **14–15**
- in WINS, **253–254**
- for zones, **199–202**, **207**

security associations (SAs)
- defined, 684
- for IPSec, **330**

Security Configuration and Analysis tool, **433**
- database for, **434**, *434*, 439
- defined, 684
- for importing security templates, **434–437**
- for IPSec, 369
- review and discrepancies with, **437–441**, *438–440*
- security analysis with, **437**

security databases
- defined, 684
- for Security Configuration and Analysis tool, 434, *434*, 439

Security log
- defined, 685
- purpose of, 615

security methods
- defined, 685
- in IPSec, **331**, 360, *360*

Security Methods settings, 360, *360*
Security options
- defined, 685
- for server-level security, **426–428**, *428*

Security permissions attribute, 475
Security Policy, **401–402**
- Account policies for, **414–420**, *416–417*, *419*
- defined, 685
- Group Policy and Active Directory, **402–414**, *403*, *405*, *407–414*
- Local policies for, **420–428**, *428*
- MMC consoles for, **406–408**, *407–408*
- Public Key Policies, **428–429**
- system options, **429–433**

Security Policy Management console, **341–344**, *342–344*
Security policy processing policy, 432
Security Rule Wizard, 366–368, *366–368*
Security settings
- for CAs, **491–492**, *492*
- for RIP, **113–114**, *114*, 125, *126*
- for user authentication, 305, *306*

security templates
- creating, **439**, **441**
- defined, 685
- importing, **434–437**, **440**, *440*
- opening, **437**

Segment/Sec counter, 606
Select A Device page, 109, *109*
Select Attribute dialog box, 316, *316*
Select Computer dialog box
- for GPOs, 413, *413*
- for IPSec, 343, *343*

Select Groups dialog box, 317, *317*
Select Network Component Type dialog box, 578, *579*
Select Network Protocol dialog box, 579, *579*
Select The Method For Sending E-Mail Invitations setting, 633

Send Clean-Up Updates When Stopping option, 116
server clusters, **532–534**, **536–537**
  application deployment for, **539–547**, *539–541*, *543–546*
  backing up, **560–561**
  business and application requirements, **538–539**
  capacity of, **542–544**, *543–544*
  cluster models for, **547–550**, *549*
  cluster node failure in, **560**
  defined, 685
  failover policies for, **544–547**, *545–547*
  multisite, **550–552**, *550*
  networking, **552–554**
  in NLB, **554–560**, *556–559*
  recovering from failures, **561–563**
  storage methods for, **540–542**, *541*
  terminology for, **537–538**
Server Gated Cryptography (SGC), **477**
server-level security, **386**
  exam essentials, **450–451**
  key terms, **451**
  policies
    Account, **414–420**, *416–417*, *419*
    deploying, **441–443**
    Local, **420–428**, *422–423*, *428*
    Public Key, **428–429**
    Security. *See* Security Policy
  review questions, **452–457**
  review questions, answers to, **458–460**
  roles in, **386–391**
    Configure Your Server Wizard for, **391–393**, *392–393*
    Manage Your Server tool for, **393–395**, *394*
  Security Configuration and Analysis tool. *See* Security Configuration and Analysis tool
  summary, **449–450**
  system options, **429–433**
  updates for, **443–444**
    Microsoft Baseline Security Analyzer for, **447–449**
    Microsoft Software Update Services for, **444–447**
  Windows Server 2003 editions, **395–401**
Server object, 608
Server (Request Security) policy, **336–337**
Server Role page, 393, *393*
server roles
  defined, 685
  managing, 393, *393*
  policy-based security for, **14**
Server Sessions counter, 608
servers
  clusters. *See* server clusters
  DHCP, 77, **389**, 608
  DNS, **180–181**, **212–213**, **388**
    caching-only, **209–210**
    capacity of, **213–214**
    defined, 667
    forward-only, **212**
    performance objects for, 608
    requirements, **213**
    securing, **214–216**
  IPSec, 325
  monitoring logs of, **615–620**, *616–617*, *619–620*
  performance objects for, 607–608
  security for. *See* server-level security
  SUS, **445**
  WINS
    configuring, **389**
    General settings for, **265–266**, *266*
service (SRV) records
  defined, 685
  purpose of, **185–186**
Service-Type option, 321
services
  failures in, 534
  queries for, **190–191**
  for remote access policies, 321
Services And Ports settings, **154–156**, *155*
Session Stats Pane in Network Monitor, 582
Sessions Errored Out counter, 608
set command in nslookup, 220
Set Windows File Protection scanning policy, 433
Settings tab for remote access policies, 314, *314*, 316
Setup security.inf (Default security) template, 435
#SG statement, 248
SGC (Server Gated Cryptography), **477**
Shiva Password Authentication Protocol (SPAP)
  defined, 685
  description of, 308
Show Areas command, 137
Show IP Routing Table command, 137
Show Link-State Database command, 137
Show Neighbors command, 137–138
Show TCP/IP Information command, 137
Show Virtual Interfaces command, 138
Shut Down The System right, 426
Shutdown security category, 427
Signature Certificate page, 500, *500*
signatures in PKI, **465–466**
signing
  defined, 685
  in PKI, 465
Simple Mail Transfer Protocol (SMTP) service, 390
Simple Query Against This DNS Server option, 217
simplified management, subnetting for, 38
Single affinity option, 559
single cluster node corruption and failure, **562**
single host filtering
  defined, 685
  selecting, 559
Single Host Filtering option, 559
single-instance applications
  characteristics of, 539
  defined, 685
single quorum clusters, 552
  defined, 685
  purpose of, 548, *549*

site failures, *535*
site-local addresses
  defined, 685
  purpose of, 67
_sites domain, 191
Slow network connection timeout for user profiles policy, 429
smart cards, **477–478**
Smartcard Logon template, 476
Smartcard User template, 476
SMP (Symmetric Multi-Processor) support requirements, 397
SMS (Systems Management Server), 444
SMTP (Simple Mail Transfer Protocol) service, 390
sniffers, *577*
sniffing
  defined, 686
  in IPv6, *65*
SOA (start of authority) records
  defined, 686
  purpose of, **182–183**
Software Installation policy processing policy, 432
software routers, **32–33, 99**
Software Update Services (SUS), 14
  defined, 686
  working with, **444–447**
Solicited Remote Assistance policy, 632–633, *633*
source addresses for IPSec filters, 357
source in Event Viewer, 618
Source Network option, 134
SPAP (Shiva Password Authentication Protocol)
  defined, 685
  description of, 308
Specify Windows file protection cache location policy, 433
split-brains
  defined, 686
  in server clusters, *563*
spoofing, *65*
  defined, 686
  IPSec for, 327
SRV (service) records
  defined, 685
  purpose of, **185–186**
Stand-alone CAs, **470–471**
  configuring, **496–497**
  root, 471
  subordinate, 471
Standard Edition, 395, 397–399
standard zone files
  defined, 686
  working with, 196
standby server configuration
  characteristics of, **545–546**, *546*
  defined, 686
start netmon command, 587–588
start of authority (SOA) records
  defined, 686
  purpose of, **182–183**
start of day, WINS client traffic at, **254–255**
Start Pull Replication At Service Startup option, 273
Start Push Replication group, 272
Start Time setting, 273
starting CA Services, 485
Starting Version ID (Hexadecimal) setting, 270
stateful applications
  defined, 686
  server clusters for, 532
stateful configuration
  defined, 686
  in IPv6, 67
stateless applications
  defined, 686
  NLB for, 533
stateless configuration
  defined, 686
  in IPv6, 67
static IP routing, **94–95**
static mapping
  defined, 687
  in NetBIOS name resolution, **243–244**, *244*
Static Route dialog box, 130–131, *130*
static routes, **129–132**, *130–132*
Static Routes For Remote Networks page, 110, *110*
static routing
  defined, 687
  vs. dynamic, **33–35**
Station Stats Pane in Network Monitor, 582
statistics, WINS, **278–279**, *278*
stopping CA Services, 485
Storage Area Networks (SANs), 538
  defined, 687
  working with, **540–542**, *541*
storage methods for server clusters, **540–542**, *541*
Storage settings for CAs, 491, *491*
Store Password Using Reversible Encryption for All Users in the Domain policy, 415–416
streaming media servers, **391**
stub zones, 197
  defined, 687
  working with, **210–212**
subnet masks, 39
  defined, 687
  incorrect, 71
  representing, **42–45**, *42–44*
subnets
  defined, 687
  noncontiguous, *57*, 677
  systems for, **59–60**
subnetting networks, **38–40**
  Class A, **55**
  Class B, **52–54**
  Class C, **49–52**
  concepts in, **39–40**
  defined, 687
  for information hiding, **39–40**
  number of subnets in, **45–47**, *46*
  shortcuts for, **47–48**

strategy for, 8
TCP/IP networks, **39–44**, *41–44*
and WAN links, **54**
subordinate CAs, 470–471
Subordinate Certification Authority template, 476
Success Audit events
defined, 687
in Event Viewer, 617
Suggested Value Changes dialog box, 419, *419*
supernetting
and CIDR, 58–59
defined, 687
SUS (Software Update Services), 14
defined, 686
working with, **444–447**
switching CAs, **484–485**
symmetric encryption
defined, 687
in PKI, 464
Symmetric Multi-Processor (SMP) support requirements, 397
Synchronize Directory Service Data right, 426
synchronous replication
vs. asynchronous, **551–552**
defined, 687–688
System, permissions for, 201
System.adm template, 406
System Applet, **612–614**
system bottlenecks, **601**
System Cryptography security category, 427
system events policy, 421
system failures, *534–535*
System log
contents of, 615–616, *616*
defined, 688
System Monitor, **590–593**, *591–592*
baseline reports in, **595–598**, *597*
defined, 688
for disk subsystem, **604–605**
display format for, **593–595**, *594*
for memory subsystem, **598–600**
for network services, **607–611**
for network subsystem, **606–607**
for processor subsystem, **601–604**, *603*
for system bottlenecks, **601**
System object, 601
System Objects security category, 427
system options, **429**
Disk Quota policies, **431**
Group Policy policies, **432**
Logon policies, **430–431**
User Profile policies, **429–430**
Windows File Protection policies, **433**
system performance, monitoring, **589–590**
with Event Viewer, **615–620**, *616–617*, *619–620*
with System applet, **612–614**
with System Monitor. *See* System Monitor
with Task Manager, **614–615**, *614–615*
System Policy files
defined, 688
limitations of, 405
System Properties dialog box, 623, *623*
System root security (rootsec.inf) template, 436
System services option, 436
System Settings security category, 427
system state data, backing up, **641–643**, *642*
Systems Management Server (SMS), 444

T

Tag For Announced Routes setting, 113
Take Ownership Of Files Or Other Objects right, 426
tampering
defined, 688
IPSec for, 327
Task Manager
defined, 688
for multiple processors, 603–604, *603*
for performance, **614–615**, *614–615*
_tcp domain, 191
TCP/IP protocol, **26–27**, **31–32**
defined, 688
exam essentials, **78–79**
filters for, **132–133**
creating, **133–135**, *133–134*
VPN, **135–137**, *136*
IP addresses. *See* IP addresses
IP routing. *See* IP routing
IPv6, *5*, **63–64**
address space in, **65–67**
automatic configuration in, **67–68**
benefits of, **64–65**
defined, 672
key terms, **79–80**
network protocols, **27**, *27*
binding, **29**
connectionless versus connection-oriented, **29–30**
network packets in, **28**, *29*
operation of, **28**
in Windows Server 2003, **30–32**
in network topology strategy, **7–8**
performance objects for, 607
review questions, **81–85**
review questions, answers to, **86–87**
subnetting networks in. *See* subnetting networks
summary, **77–78**
troubleshooting TCP/IP addressing, **68**
DHCP, **76–77**
identifying TCP/IP configuration, **69–71**
IP communications, **71–76**
TCPv4 object, 606
templates
certificate
configuring, **492–496**, *493–496*

in PKI, **475–476**
security
creating, **439**, **441**
defined, 685
importing, **434–437**, 440, *440*
opening, **437**
terminal services, 398
Terminal Services Client, 622
Terminal Services Configuration, 622
Terminal Services Group Policies, 622
Terminal Services Manager, 622
Terminal Services servers, **391**
testing
IP communications, **71–76**
IPSec policies, **374–375**
TGSs (ticket-granting-services)
accessing, 334, 420
defined, 688
TGTs (ticket-granting tickets)
defined, 688
issuing, 334, 420
Time Before Route Is Removed (Seconds) setting, 115
Time Before Routes Expire (Seconds) setting, 115
time to live (TTL) in DNS, **189**
Timeout for dialog boxes policy, 430
timeout settings for WINS, 267
times in Event Viewer, 618
tombstoning
defined, 688
WINS records, **281–282**
top-level domains
defined, 688
list of, **178–179**
topologies
address assignments by, 60
defined, 676
designing, **8**
TCP/IP in, **7–8**
Total Number of Registrations/sec counter, 608
Total Query Received/sec counter, 608
Total Stats Pane in Network Monitor, 582
tracert utility
defined, 688
for IP communications, **73–75**
traditional DNS zones
defined, 689
storing, 196, **198**
traffic exemptions in IPSec, 329
trailers in network packets, 28, *29*
transfers, zone, 181, **191–192**, **205–207**, 691
Transit Delay (Seconds) setting, 119
translation component in NAT, 148, **157–158**, *158*
Translation settings, **157–158**, *158*
transport mode
defined, 689
in IPSec, 326, **361–363**, *361–362*
transport protocols, 27, *27*
triggers in WINS replication, 250
troubleshooting
host name resolution, **216–219**
DNS monitoring, **217–218**, *217–218*
ipconfig for, **222–223**
log files for, **223–224**
nslookup for, **219–222**
IP routing, **137–141**, *138–139*
IPSec
best practices, **374–375**
data transmission security, **368–370**
event logs for, **372–374**, *374*
IP Security Monitor for, **371–372**, *372*
RSoP for, **370–371**, *370–371*
MBSA scans, 449
TCP/IP addressing, **68**
DHCP, **76–77**
identifying TCP/IP configuration, **69–71**
IP communications, **71–76**
WINS, **283**
general considerations, **283–284**
nbtstat for, **284–286**
Trust List Signing template, 476
Trusted Root Certification Authorities folder, 497–498, 506
trusts for CAs, **497–501**, *499–500*
TTL (time to live) in DNS, **189**
Tunnel Endpoint page, 366, *366*
tunnel endpoints
defined, 689
in IPSec, 335
tunnel mode
defined, 689
in IPSec, 326, 354, **362–368**, *363–368*
Tunnel Setting settings, 354, 363–364, *364*
Tunnel-Type option for remote access policies, 321
tunnels
defined, 689
in VPNs, 303–304, *304*
Turn off background refresh of Group Policy policy, 432
types, event, in Event Viewer, 618

U

_udp domain, 191
uk domain, 179
unauthenticated access option, 308
unauthorized addresses
defined, 689
working with, **61–62**
unicast routing
defined, 689
in RRAS, 102
unique names in name resolution, **241**

unmasked bits
  defined, 689
  in subnets, 45
unreachable interfaces, 104
unspecific addresses
  defined, 689
  purpose of, 67
untrusted domains, 260
updates
  DNS, **199–200**
  RIP, 97
  for security infrastructure, **14–15**
  for server-level security, **443–444**
    Microsoft Baseline Security Analyzer for, **447–449**
    Microsoft Software Update Services for, **444–447**
upgrading, DNS in, 192
us domain, 179
% Usage counter, 599
% Usage Peak counter, 599
Use Add Wizard option, 353, 359
Use An Existing Key option, 481
Use Broadcast Or Multicast Only option, 114
Use Computer Names That Are Compatible With LAN Manager option, 270
Use Neighbors In Addition To Broadcast Or Multicast option, 114
Use Neighbors Instead Of Broadcast Or Multicast option, 114
Use Persistent Connections For Pull Replication Partners option, 273
Use Persistent Connections For Push Replication Partners option, 272
Use Session Key Perfect Forward Secrecy option, 360
Use The Certificate Associated With This Key option, 481
Use These Security Settings option, 333
Use This Route To Initiate Demand-Dial Connections, 130
user authentication, **305–309**, *306–307*, *309*
User Group Policy Loopback processing mode policy, 432
User or Group Access page, 323, *323*
user permissions for DNS zones, **200–201**
User Profile policies
  defined, 689
  list of, **429–430**
user properties for RRAS server access control, 312, *312*
User Rights Assignments
  defined, 689
  policies for, **423–426**
User Signature Only template, 476
user statistics, Task Manager for, **614–615**, *614–615*
User template, 476
users in Event Viewer, 618
Users settings for performance, 615, *615*

valid names in name resolution, **241–242**
Variable Length Subnet Masks (VLSMs)
  defined, 689
  OSPF support for, 54
  purpose of, 58
vectors in distance vector protocols, 34
Verification Interval setting, 267
Verify Against setting, 269
Verify Database Consistency Every setting, 268
version IDs
  defined, 689
  in WINS replication, 251
View CRLs settings, 502, *503*
View The Status Of A Pending Certificate Request task, 513
Virtual Interfaces settings, **127–128**, *128*
virtual link neighbors
  defined, 690
  in OSPF, 128
virtual links
  defined, 690
  in OSPF, 127
Virtual Memory dialog box, 613–614, *613*
Virtual Memory option, 613
Virtual Private Networks (VPNs)
  defined, 690
  for demand-dial connections, 107
  for remote access services, **303–305**, *304*
virtual servers
  defined, 690
  in server clusters, 537
VLSMs (Variable Length Subnet Masks)
  defined, 689
  OSPF support for, 54
  purpose of, 58
volume shadow copy, 6
  defined, 690
  working with, **645–646**, *645–646*
VPNs (Virtual Private Networks)
  defined, 690
  for demand-dial connections, 107
  for remote access services, **303–305**, *304*
Vssadmin command-line utility, **646**

W

Wait for remote user profile policy, 430
WANs
  and subnetting, **54**
  for WINS replication, **258–260**, *259*
Warning events
  defined, 690
  in Event Viewer, 617

Web Application (IIS) Servers, **389–390**
Web Edition, 396–399
Web enrollment agents, **512–514**, *513–514*
Web servers, performance objects for, 608, **611**
Web services, **400–401**
Weekly backup option, 641
Welcome To The Backup Or Restore Wizard page, 635, *635*, 641
Welcome To The Backup Utility Advanced Mode dialog box, *642*
Welcome to the Create IP Security Rule Wizard page, 366, *366*
What To Back Up page, 635–636, *636*, 641, *642*
What To Restore page, 639–640, *640*
When Idle backup option, 641
Windows.adm template, 406
Windows Authentication, 306
Windows Backup, **634**
  Backup or Restore Wizard, **634–640**, *635–638*, *640*
  backup types with, **643–645**, *644*
  defined, 690
  scheduling backup jobs, **641**
  system state data, **641–643**, *642*
Windows Components Wizard, 479–483, *480–482*
Windows File Protection policies
  defined, 690
  list of, **433**
Windows-Groups option, 321
Windows NT Server migration
  DNS namespaces for, **195–196**
  WINS services, **277**
Winnt.adm template, 406
WINS (Windows Internet Naming Service), **9–10**, **238**
  availability and fault tolerance in, **253**
  database for
    compacting, **281**
    defined, 690
    in NetBIOS name resolution, **243**
  defined, 690
  deleting and tombstoning records in, **281–282**
  deployment scenarios, **261–263**, *261–262*, *264*
  designing, **251**
  exam essentials, **286–287**
  installing, **264–265**
  integrating with DNs, **202–204**
  key terms, **287–288**
  monitoring, **278**
    client traffic, **254–255**
    records, **279–280**, *279–280*
    statistics, **278–279**, *278*
  NetBIOS name resolution. *See* NetBIOS (Network Basic Input/Output System)
  number of servers, **252–253**
  performance objects for, 607
  proxy agents for, **245**, 690
  replication, **249–251**
    inter-forest, **282–283**
    partners in. *See* partners in WINS replication
  resource records in, **202–204**, 690
  review questions, **289–295**
  review questions, answers to, **296–298**
  securing, **253–254**
  settings for
    Advanced, **269–270**, *270*
    Database Verification, **268–269**, *268*
    Intervals, **266–267**, *267*
  summary, **286**
  troubleshooting, **283**
    general considerations, **283–284**
    nbtstat for, **284–286**
  WINS snap-in, **265–270**, *266–269*
WINS console, 244, *244*
WINS-R resource records, **203–204**, 691
    WINS servers
  configuring, **389**
  General settings for, **265–266**, *266*
WINS services, migrating, **277**
WINS settings, 246–247, *247*
wireless connections, security for, 6
Working Set counter, 599
workstation services, performance objects for, 607
Writes/Sec counter, 604

Z

zones, 182, **196**
  Active Directory-Integrated, **198**
  combination, **198–199**
  data location for, **197–199**
  database location for, **186–187**
  default permissions for, **200–201**
  defined, 667
  delegating, **208–209**, 691
  integrating DNS and WINs, **202–204**
  replication, **205–209**
  for SANs, 540–542, *541*
  secondary, **205**
  securing, **199–202**, **207**
  strategies for, **201–202**
  traditional, **198**
  transfers, 181, **191–192**, **205–207**, 691
  types of, **196–197**